PERSONAL MEMOIRS OF
P. H. SHERIDAN

PERSONAL MEMOIRS OF

P. H. SHERIDAN

P. H. SHERIDAN

Borgo Military Reference • MMIII

PERSONAL MEMOIRS OF P. H. SHERIDAN

New elements copyright © 2003 by **Wildside Press**. All rights reserved.
Cover design copyright © 2003 by **JT Lindroos**
Series Editor: **Sean Wallace**

Wildside Press, LLC
PO Box 301, Holicong, PA 18928-0301
www.wildsidepress.com

ISBN : 0-8095-4450-4 (casebound)
ISBN: 0-8095-4451-2 (paperback)

PREFACE

When, yielding to the solicitations of my friends, I finally decided to write these Memoirs, the greatest difficulty which confronted me was that of recounting my share in the many notable events of the last three decades, in which I played a part, without entering too fully into the history of these years, and at the same time without giving to my own acts an unmerited prominence. To what extent I have overcome this difficulty I must leave the reader to judge.

In offering this record, penned by my own hand, of the events of my life, and of my participation in our great struggle for national existence, human liberty, and political equality, I make no pretension to literary merit; the importance of the subject-matter of my narrative is my only claim on the reader's attention.

Respectfully dedicating this work to my comrades in arms during the War of the Rebellion, I leave it as a heritage to my children, and as a source of information for the future historian.

P. H. SHERIDAN.
Nonguitt, Mass., August 2, 1888

VOLUME I

CHAPTER I.

ANCESTRY—BIRTH—EARLY EDUCATION—A CLERK IN A GROCERY STORE—APPOINTMENT—MONROE SHOES—JOURNEY TO WEST POINT—HAZING—A FISTICUFF BATTLE—SUSPENDED—RETURNS TO CLERKSHIP—GRADUATION.

My parents, John and Mary Sheridan, came to America in 1830, having been induced by the representations of my father's uncle, Thomas Gainor, then living in Albany, N. Y., to try their fortunes in the New World. They were born and reared in the County Cavan, Ireland, where from early manhood my father had tilled a leasehold on the estate of Cherrymoult; and the sale of this leasehold provided him with means to seek a new home across the sea. My parents were blood relations—cousins in the second degree—my mother, whose maiden name was Minor, having descended from a collateral branch of my father's family. Before leaving Ireland they had two children, and on the 6th of March, 1831, the year after their arrival in this country, I was born, in Albany, N. Y., the third child in a family which eventually increased to six—four boys and two girls.

The prospects for gaining a livelihood in Albany did not meet the expectations which my parents had been led to entertain, so in 1832 they removed to the West, to establish themselves in the village of Somerset, in Perry County, Ohio, which section, in the earliest days of the State, had been colonized from Pennsylvania and Maryland. At this period the great public works of the Northwest—the canals and macadamized roads, a result of clamor for internal improvements—were in course of construction, and my father turned his attention to them, believing that they offered opportunities for a successful occupation. Encouraged by a civil engineer named Bassett, who had taken a fancy to him, he put in bids for a small contract on the Cumberland Road, known as the "National Road," which was then being extended west from the Ohio River. A little success in this first enterprise led him to take up contracting as a business, which he followed on various canals and macadamized roads then building in different parts of the State of Ohio, with some good fortune for awhile, but in 1853 what little means he had saved were swallowed up—in bankruptcy, caused by the failure of the Sciota and Hocking Valley Railroad Company, for which he was fulfilling a contract at the time, and this disaster left him finally only a small farm, just outside the village of Somerset, where he dwelt until his death in 1875.

My father's occupation kept him away from home much of the time during my boyhood, and as a consequence I grew up under the sole guidance and training of my mother, whose excellent common sense and clear discernment in every way fitted her for such maternal duties. When old enough I was sent to the village school, which was taught by an old-time Irish "master"—one of those itinerant dominies of the early frontier—who, holding that to spare the rod was to spoil the child, if unable to detect the real culprit when any offense had been committed, would consistently apply the switch to the whole school without discrimination. It must be conceded that by this means he never failed to catch the guilty mischief-maker. The school-year was divided into terms of three months, the teacher being paid in each term a certain sum—three dollars, I think, for each pupil—and having an additional perquisite in the privilege of boarding around at his option in the different families to which his scholars belonged. This feature was more than acceptable to the parents at times, for how else could they so thoroughly learn all the neighborhood gossip? But the pupils were in almost unanimous opposition, because Mr. McNanly's unheralded advent at any one's house resulted frequently in the discovery that some favorite child had been playing "hookey," which means (I will say to the uninitiated, if any such there be) absenting one's self from school without permission, to go on a fishing or a swimming frolic. Such at least was my experience more than once, for Mr. McNanly particularly favored my mother's house, because of a former acquaintanceship in Ireland, and many a time a comparison of notes proved that I had been in the woods with two playfellows, named Binckly and Greiner, when the master thought I was home, ill, and my mother, that I was at school, deeply immersed in study. However, with these and other delinquencies not uncommon among boys, I learned at McNanly's school, and a little later, under a pedagogue named Thorn, a smattering of geography and history, and explored the mysteries of Pike's Arithmetic and Bullions' English Grammar, about as far as I could be carried up to the age of fourteen. This was all the education then bestowed upon me, and this—with the exception of progressing in some of these branches by voluntary study, and by practical application in others, supplemented by a few months of preparation after receiving my appointment as a cadet—was the extent of my learning on entering the Military Academy.

When about fourteen years old I began to do something for myself: Mr. John Talbot, who kept a country store in the village, employing me to deal out sugar, coffee, and calico to his customers at the munificent salary of twenty-four dollars a year. After I had gained a twelve-months' experience with Mr. Talbot my services began to be sought by others, and a Mr. David Whitehead secured them by the offer of sixty dollars a year—Talbot refusing to increase my pay, but not objecting to my advancement. A few months later, before my year was up, another chance to increase my salary came about; Mr. Henry Dittoe, the enterprising man of the village, offering me one hundred and twenty dollars a year to take a position in the dry-goods store of Fink & Dittoe. I laid the matter before Mr. Whitehead, and he frankly advised me to accept, though he cautioned me that I might regret it, adding that he was afraid Henry (referring to Mr. Dittoe) "had too many irons in the fire." His warning in regard to the enterprising merchant proved a prophecy, for "too many irons in the fire" brought about Mr. Dittoe's bankruptcy, although this misfortune did not befall him till long after I had left his service. I am glad to say, however, that his failure was an exceptionally honest one, and due more to the fact that he was in advance of his surroundings than to any other cause.

I remained with Fink & Dittoe until I entered the Military Academy, principally in charge of the book-keeping, which was no small work for one of my years, considering that in those days the entire business of country stores in the West was conducted on the credit system; the customers, being mostly farmers, never expecting to pay till the product of their farms could be brought to market; and even then usually squared the book-accounts by notes of hand, that were often slow of collection.

From the time I ceased to attend school my employment had

necessitated, to a certain degree, the application of what I had learned there, and this practical instruction I reinforced somewhat by doing considerable reading in a general way, until ultimately I became quite a local authority in history, being frequently chosen as arbiter in discussions and disputes that arose in the store. The Mexican War, then going on, furnished, of course, a never-ending theme for controversy, and although I was too young to enter the military service when volunteers were mustering in our section, yet the stirring events of the times so much impressed and absorbed me that my sole wish was to become a soldier, and my highest aspiration to go to West Point as a Cadet from my Congressional district. My chances for this seemed very remote, however, till one day an opportunity was thrown in my way by the boy who then held the place failing to pass his examination. When I learned that by this occurrence a vacancy existed, I wrote to our representative in Congress, the Hon. Thomas Ritchey, and asked him for the appointment, reminding him that we had often met in Fink & Dittoe's store, and that therefore he must know something of my qualifications. He responded promptly by enclosing my warrant for the class of 1848; so, notwithstanding the many romances that have been published about the matter, to Mr. Ritchey, and to him alone, is due all the credit—if my career justifies that term—of putting me in the United States Army.

At once I set about preparing for the examination which precedes admission to the Military Academy, studying zealously under the direction of Mr. William Clark; my old teachers, McNanly and Thorn, having disappeared from Somerset and sought new fields of usefulness. The intervening months passed rapidly away, and I fear that I did not make much progress, yet I thought I should be able to pass the preliminary examination. That which was to follow worried me more and gave me many sleepless nights; but these would have been less in number, I fully believe, had it not been for one specification of my outfit which the circular that accompanied my appointment demanded. This requirement was a pair of "Monroe shoes." Now, out in Ohio, what "Monroe shoes" were was a mystery—not a shoemaker in my section having so much as an inkling of the construction of the perplexing things, until finally my eldest brother brought an idea of them from Baltimore, when it was found that they were a familiar pattern under another name.

At length the time for my departure came, and I set out for West Point, going by way of Cleveland and across Lake Erie to Buffalo. On the steamer

I fell in with another appointee en route to the academy, David S. Stanley, also from Ohio; and when our acquaintanceship had ripened somewhat, and we had begun to repose confidence in each other, I found out that he had no "Monroe shoes," so I deemed myself just that much ahead of my companion, although my shoes might not conform exactly to the regulations in Eastern style and finish. At Buffalo, Stanley and I separated, he going by the Erie Canal and I by the railroad, since I wanted to gain time on account of commands to stop in Albany to see my father's uncle. Here I spent a few days, till Stanley reached Albany, when we journeyed together down the river to West Point. The examination began a few days after our arrival, and I soon found myself admitted to the Corps of Cadets, to date from July 1, 1848, in a class composed of sixty-three members, many of whom—for example, Stanley, Slocum, Woods, Kautz, and Crook—became prominent generals in later years, and commanded divisions, corps, and armies in the war of the rebellion.

Quickly following my admission I was broken in by a course of hazing, with many of the approved methods that the Cadets had handed down from year to year since the Academy was founded; still, I escaped excessive persecution, although there were in my day many occurrences so extreme as to call forth condemnation and an endeavor to suppress the senseless custom, which an improved civilization has now about eradicated, not only at West Point, but at other colleges.

Although I had met the Academic board and come off with fair success, yet I knew so little of Algebra or any of the higher branches of mathematics that during my first six months at the Academy I was discouraged by many misgivings as to the future, for I speedily learned that at the January examination the class would have to stand a test much severer than that which had been applied to it on entering. I resolved to try hard, however, and, besides, good fortune gave me for a room-mate a Cadet whose education was more advanced than mine, and whose studious habits and willingness to aid others benefited me immensely. This room-mate was Henry W. Slocum, since so signally distinguished in both military and civil capacities as to win for his name a proud place in the annals of his country. After taps—that is, when by the regulations of the Academy all the lights were supposed to be extinguished, and everybody in bed—Slocum and I would hang a blanket over the one window of our room and continue our studies—he guiding me around scores of stumbling-blocks in Algebra and elucidating many knotty points in other branches of the course with which

I was unfamiliar. On account of this association I went up before the Board in January with less uneasiness than otherwise would have been the case, and passed the examination fairly well. When it was over, a self-confidence in my capacity was established that had not existed hitherto, and at each succeeding examination I gained a little in order of merit till my furlough summer came round—that is, when I was half through the four-year course.

My furlough in July and August, 1850, was spent at my home in Ohio, with the exception of a visit or two to other Cadets on furlough in the State, and at the close of my leave I returned to the Academy in the full expectation of graduating with my class in 1852.

A quarrel of a belligerent character in September, 1851, with Cadet William R. Terrill, put an end to this anticipation, however, and threw me back into the class which graduated in 1853. Terrill was a Cadet Sergeant, and, while my company was forming for parade, having given me an order, in what I considered an improper tone, to "dress" in a certain direction, when I believed I was accurately dressed, I fancied I had a grievance, and made toward him with a lowered bayonet, but my better judgment recalled me before actual contact could take place. Of course Terrill reported me for this, and my ire was so inflamed by his action that when we next met I attacked him, and a fisticuff engagement in front of barracks followed, which was stopped by an officer appearing on the scene. Each of us handed in an explanation, but mine was unsatisfactory to the authorities, for I had to admit that I was the assaulting party, and the result was that I was suspended by the Secretary of War, Mr. Conrad, till August 28, 1852—the Superintendent of the Academy, Captain Brewerton, being induced to recommend this milder course, he said, by my previous good conduct. At the time I thought, of course, my suspension a very unfair punishment, that my conduct was justifiable and the authorities of the Academy all wrong, but riper experience has led me to a different conclusion, and as I look back, though the mortification I then endured was deep and trying, I am convinced that it was hardly as much as I deserved for such an outrageous breach of discipline.

There was no question as to Terrill's irritating tone, but in giving me the order he was prompted by the duty of his position as a file closer, and I was not the one to remedy the wrong which I conceived had been done me, and clearly not justifiable in assuming to correct him with my own hands. In 1862, when General Buell's army was assembling at Louisville, Terrill was with it as a brigadier-general (for, although a Virginian, he had remained loyal), and I then took the initiative toward a renewal of our acquaintance. Our renewed friendship was not destined to be of long duration, I am sorry to say, for a few days later, in the battle of Perryville, while gallantly fighting for his country, poor Terrill was killed.

My suspension necessitated my leaving the Academy, and I returned home in the fall of 1851, much crestfallen. Fortunately, my good friend Henry Dittoe again gave me employment in keeping the books of his establishment, and this occupation of my time made the nine months which were to elapse before I could go back to West Point pass much more agreeably than they would have done had I been idle. In August, 1852, I joined the first class at the Academy in accordance with the order of the War Department, taking my place at the foot of the class and graduating with it the succeeding June, number thirty-four in a membership of fifty-two. At the head of this class graduated James B. McPherson, who was killed in the Atlanta campaign while commanding the Army of the Tennessee. It also contained such men as John M. Schofield, who commanded the Army of the Ohio; Joshua W. Sill, killed as a brigadier in the battle of Stone River; and many others who, in the war of the rebellion, on one side or the other, rose to prominence, General John B. Hood being the most distinguished member of the class among the Confederates.

At the close of the final examination I made no formal application for assignment to any particular arm of the service, for I knew that my standing would not entitle me to one of the existing vacancies, and that I should be obliged to take a place among the brevet second lieutenants. When the appointments were made I therefore found myself attached to the First Infantry, well pleased that I had surmounted all the difficulties that confront the student at our national school, and looking forward with pleasant anticipation to the life before me.

CHAPTER II.

ORDERED TO FORT DUNCAN, TEXAS—"NORTHERS"—SCOUTING DUTY—HUNTING— NEARLY CAUGHT BY THE INDIANS—A PRIMITIVE HABITATION—A BRAVE DRUMMERBOYS DEATH—A MEXICAN BALL.

On the 1st day of July, 1853, I was commissioned a brevet second lieutenant in the First Regiment of United States Infantry, then stationed in Texas. The company to which I was attached was quartered at Fort Duncan, a military post on the Rio Grande opposite the little town of Piedras Negras, on the boundary line between the United States and the Republic of Mexico.

After the usual leave of three months following graduation from the Military Academy I was assigned to temporary duty at Newport Barracks, a recruiting station and rendezvous for the assignment of young officers preparatory to joining their regiments. Here I remained from September, 1853, to March, 1854, when I was ordered to join my company at Fort Duncan. To comply with this order I proceeded by steamboat down the Ohio and Mississippi rivers to New Orleans, thence by steamer across the Gulf of Mexico to Indianola, Tex., and after landing at that place, continued in a small schooner through what is called the inside channel on the Gulf coast to Corpus Christi, the headquarters of Brigadier-General Persifer F. Smith, who was commanding the Department of Texas. Here I met some of my old friends from the Military Academy, among them Lieutenant Alfred Gibbs, who in the last year of the rebellion commanded under me a brigade of cavalry, and Lieutenant Jerome Napoleon Bonaparte, of the Mounted Rifles, who resigned in 1854 to accept service in the French Imperial army, but to most of those about headquarters I was an entire stranger. Among the latter was Captain Stewart Van Vliet, of the Quartermaster's Department, now on the retired list. With him I soon came in frequent contact, and, by reason of his connection with the Quartermaster's Department, the kindly interest he took in forwarding my business inaugurated between us—a lasting friendship.

A day or two after my arrival at Corpus Christi a train of Government wagons, loaded with subsistence stores and quartermaster's supplies, started for Laredo, a small town on the Rio Grande below Fort Duncan. There being no other means of reaching my station I put my small personal possessions, consisting of a trunk, mattress, two blankets, and a pillow into one of the heavily loaded wagons and proceeded to join it, sitting on the boxes or bags of coffee and sugar, as I might choose. The movement of the train was very slow, as the soil was soft on the newly made and sandy roads. We progressed but a few miles on our first day's journey, and in the evening parked our train at a point where there was no wood, a scant supply of water—and that of bad quality—but an abundance of grass. There being no comfortable place to sleep in any of the wagons, filled as they were to the bows with army supplies, I spread my blankets on the ground between the wheels of one of them, and awoke in the morning feeling as fresh and bright as would have been possible if all the comforts of civilization had been at my command.

It took our lumbering train many days to reach Laredo, a distance of about one hundred and sixty miles from Corpus Christi. Each march was but a repetition of the first day's journey, its monotony occasionally relieved, though, by the passage of immense flocks of ducks and geese, and the appearance at intervals of herds of deer, and sometimes droves of wild cattle, wild horses and mules. The bands of wild horses I noticed were sometimes led by mules, but generally by stallions with long wavy manes, and flowing tails which almost touched the ground.

We arrived at Laredo during one of those severe storms incident to that section, which are termed "Northers" from the fact that the north winds culminate occasionally in cold windstorms, frequently preceded by heavy rains. Generally the blow lasts for three days, and the cold becomes intense and piercing. While the sudden depression of the temperature is most disagreeable, and often causes great suffering, it is claimed that these "Northers" make the climate more healthy and endurable. They occur from October to May, and in addition to the destruction which, through the sudden depression of the temperature, they bring on the herds in the interior, they are often of sufficient violence to greatly injure the harbors on the coast.

The post near Laredo was called Fort McIntosh, and at this period the troops stationed there consisted of eight companies of the Fifth Infantry and two of the First, one of the First Artillery, and three of the Mounted Rifles. Just before the "Norther" began these troops had completed a redoubt for the defense of the post, with the exception of the ditches, but as the parapet was built of sand—the only material about Laredo which could be obtained for its construction—the severity of the winds was too much for such a shifting substance, and the work was entirely blown away early in the storm.

I was pleasantly and hospitably welcomed by the officers at the post, all of whom were living in tents, with no furniture except a cot and trunk, and an improvised bed for a stranger, when one happened to come along. After I had been kindly taken in by one of the younger officers, I reported to the commanding officer, and was informed by him that he would direct the quartermaster to furnish me, as soon as convenient, with transportation to Fort Duncan, the station of my company.

In the course of a day or two, the quartermaster notified me that a Government six-mule wagon would be placed at my disposal to proceed to my destination. No better means offering, I concluded to set out in this conveyance, and, since it was also to carry a quantity of quartermaster's property for Fort Duncan, I managed to obtain room enough for my bed in the limited space between the bows and load, where I could rest tolerably well, and under cover at night, instead of sleeping on the ground under the wagon, as I had done on the road from Corpus Christi to Laredo.

I reached Fort Duncan in March, 1854, and was kindly received by the commanding officer of the regiment, Lieutenant-Colonel Thompson Morris, and by the captain of my company ("D"), Eugene E. McLean, and his charming wife the only daughter of General E. V. Sumner, who was already distinguished in our service, but much better known in after years in the operations of the Army of the Potomac, during its early campaigns in Virginia. Shortly after joining company "D" I was sent out on scouting duty with another company of the regiment to Camp La Pena, about sixty or seventy miles east of Fort Duncan, in a section of country that had for some time past been subjected to raids by the Lipan and Comanche Indians. Our outpost at La Pena was intended as a protection against the predatory incursions of these savages, so almost constant scouting became a daily occupation. This enabled me soon to become familiar with and make maps of the surrounding country, and, through constant association with our Mexican guide, to pick up in a short time quite a smattering of the Spanish language, which was very useful to one serving on that frontier.

At that early day western Texas was literally filled with game, and the region in the immediate vicinity of La Pena contained its full proportion of deer, antelope, and wild turkeys. The temptation to hunt was therefore constantly before me, and a desire to indulge in this pastime, whenever free from the legitimate duty of the camp, soon took complete possession of me, so expeditions in pursuit of game were of frequent occurrence. In these expeditions I was always accompanied by a soldier named Frankman, belonging to "D" company, who was a fine sportsman, and a butcher by trade. In a short period I learned from Frankman how to approach and secure the different species of game, and also how to dress and care for it when killed. Almost every expedition we made was rewarded with a good supply of deer, antelope, and wild turkeys, and we furnished the command in camp with such abundance that it was relieved from the necessity of drawing its beef ration, much to the discomfiture of the disgruntled beef contractor.

The camp at La Pena was on sandy ground, unpleasant for men and animals, and by my advice it was moved to La Pendencia, not far from Lake Espantosa. Before removal from our old location, however, early one bright morning Frankman and I started on one of our customary expeditions, going down La Pena Creek to a small creek, at the head of which we had established a hunting rendezvous. After proceeding along the stream for three or four miles we saw a column of smoke on the prairie, and supposing it arose from a camp of Mexican rancheros catching wild horses or wild cattle, and even wild mules, which were very numerous in that section of country along the Nueces River, we thought we would join the party and see how much success they were having, and observe the methods employed in this laborious and sometimes dangerous vocation. With this object in view, we continued on until we found it necessary to cross to the other side of the creek to reach the point indicated by the smoke. Just before reaching the crossing I discovered moccasin tracks near the water's edge, and realizing in an instant that the camp we were approaching might possibly be one of hostile Indians—all Indians in that country at that time were hostile—Frankman and I backed out silently, and made eager strides for La Pena, where we had scarcely arrived when

Captain M. E. Van Buren, of the Mounted Rifle regiment, came in with a small command, and reported that he was out in pursuit of a band of Comanche Indians, which had been committing depredations up about Fort Clark, but that he had lost the trail. I immediately informed him of what had occurred to me during the morning, and that I could put him on the trail of the Indians he was desirous of punishing.

We hurriedly supplied with rations his small command of thirteen men, and I then conducted him to the point where I had seen the smoke, and there we found signs indicating it to be the recently abandoned camp of the Indians he was pursuing, and we also noticed that prairie rats had formed the principal article of diet at the meal they had just completed. As they had gone, I could do no more than put him on the trail made in their departure, which was well marked; for Indians, when in small parties, and unless pressed, usually follow each other in single file. Captain Van Buren followed the trail by Fort Ewell, and well down toward Corpus Christi, day and night, until the Indians, exhausted and used up, halted, on an open plain, unsaddled their horses, mounted bareback, and offered battle. Their number was double that of Van Buren's detachment, but he attacked them fearlessly, and in the fight was mortally wounded by an arrow which entered his body in front, just above the sword belt, and came through the belt behind. The principal chief of the Indians was killed, and the rest fled. Captain Van Buren's men carried him to Corpus Christi, where in a few days he died.

After our removal to La Pendencia a similar pursuit of savages occurred, but with more fortunate results. Colonel John H. King, now on the retired list, then a captain in the First Infantry, came to our camp in pursuit of a marauding band of hostile Indians, and I was enabled to put him also on the trail. He soon overtook them, and killing two without loss to himself, the band dispersed like a flock of quail and left him nothing to follow. He returned to our camp shortly after, and the few friendly Indian scouts he had with him held a grand pow-wow and dance over the scalps of the fallen braves.

Around La Pendencia, as at La Pena, the country abounded in deer, antelope, wild turkeys, and quail, and we killed enough to supply abundantly the whole command with the meat portion of the ration. Some mornings Frankman and I would bring in as many as seven deer, and our hunting expeditions made me so familiar with the region between our camp and Fort Duncan, the headquarters of the regiment, that I was soon enabled to suggest a more direct route of communication than the circuitous one then traversed, and in a short time it was established.

Up to this time I had been on detached duty, but soon my own company was ordered into the field to occupy a position on Turkey Creek, about ten or twelve miles west of the Nueces River, on the road from San Antonio to Fort Duncan, and I was required to join the company. Here constant work and scouting were necessary, as our camp was specially located with reference to protecting from Indian raids the road running from San Antonio to Fort Duncan, and on to the interior of Mexico. In those days this road was the great line of travel, and Mexican caravans were frequently passing over it, to and fro, in such a disorganized condition as often to invite attack from marauding Comanches and Lipans. Our time, therefore, was incessantly occupied in scouting, but our labors were much lightened because they were directed with intelligence and justice by Captain McLean, whose agreeable manners and upright methods are still so impressed on my memory that to this day I look back upon my service with "D" Company of the First Infantry as among those events which I remember with most pleasure.

In this manner my first summer of active field duty passed rapidly away, and in the fall my company returned to Fort Duncan to go into winter quarters. These quarters, when constructed, consisted of "A" tents pitched under a shed improvised by the company. With only these accommodations I at first lived around as best I could until the command was quartered, and then, requesting a detail of wagons from the quartermaster, I went out some thirty miles to get poles to build a more comfortable habitation for myself. In a few days enough poles for the construction of a modest residence were secured and brought in, and then the building of my house began. First, the poles were cut the proper length, planted in a trench around four sides of a square of very small proportions, and secured at the top by string-pieces stretched from one angle to another, in which half-notches hack been made at proper intervals to receive the uprights. The poles were then made rigid by strips nailed on half-way to the ground, giving the sides of the structure firmness, but the interstices were large and frequent; still, with the aid of some old condemned paulins obtained from the quartermaster, the walls were covered and the necessity for chinking obviated. This method of covering the holes in the side walls also possessed the advantage of permitting some little light to penetrate to the interior of the house, and avoided the necessity of constructing a window, for which, by the way, no glass could have been obtained. Next a good large fire-place and chimney were built in one corner by means of stones and mud, and then the roof was put on—a thatched one of prairie grass. The floor was dirt compactly tamped.

My furniture was very primitive: a chair or two, with about the same number of camp stools, a cot, and a rickety old bureau that I obtained in some way not now remembered. My washstand consisted of a board about three feet long, resting on legs formed by driving sticks into the ground until they held it at about the proper height from the floor. This washstand was the most expensive piece of furniture I owned, the board having cost me three dollars, and even then I obtained it as a favor, for lumber on the Rio Grande was so scarce in those days that to possess even the smallest quantity was to indulge in great luxury. Indeed, about all that reached the post was what came in the shape of bacon boxes, and the boards from these were reserved for coffins in which to bury our dead.

In this rude habitation I spent a happy winter, and was more comfortably off than many of the officers, who had built none, but lived in tents and took the chances of "Northers." During this period our food was principally the soldier's ration: flour, pickled pork, nasty bacon—cured in the dust of ground charcoal—and fresh beef, of which we had a plentiful supply, supplemented with game of various kinds. The sugar, coffee, and smaller parts of the ration were good, but we had no vegetables, and the few jars of preserves and some few vegetables kept by the sutler were too expensive to be indulged in. So during all the period I lived at Fort Duncan and its sub-camps, nearly sixteen months, fresh vegetables were practically unobtainable. To prevent scurvy we used the juice of the maguey plant, called pulque, and to obtain a supply of this anti-scorbutic I was often detailed to march the company out about forty miles, cut the plant, load up two or three wagons with the stalks, and carry them to camp. Here the juice was extracted by a rude press, and put in bottles until it fermented and became worse in odor than sulphureted hydrogen. At reveille roll-call every morning this fermented liquor was dealt out to the company, and as it was my duty, in my capacity of subaltern, to attend these roll-calls and see that the men took their ration of pulque, I always began the duty by drinking a cup of the repulsive stuff myself. Though hard to swallow, its well-known specific qualities in the prevention and cure of scurvy were familiar to all, so every man in the command gulped down his share notwithstanding its vile taste and odor.

Considering our isolation, the winter passed very pleasantly to us all. The post was a large one, its officers congenial, and we had many enjoyable occasions. Dances, races, and horseback riding filled in much of the time, and occasional raids from Indians furnished more serious occupation in the way of a scout now and then. The proximity of the Indians at times rendered the surrounding country somewhat dangerous for individuals or small parties at a distance from the fort; but few thought the savages would come near, so many risks were doubtless run by various officers, who carried the familiar six-shooter as their only weapon while out horseback riding, until suddenly we were awakened to the dangers we had been incurring.

About mid-winter a party of hostile Lipans made a swoop around and skirting the garrison, killing a herder—a discharged drummer-boy—in sight of the flag-staff. Of course great excitement followed. Captain J. G. Walker, of the Mounted Rifles, immediately started with his company in pursuit of the Indians, and I was directed to accompany the command. Not far away we found the body of the boy filled with arrows, and near him the body of a fine looking young Indian, whom the lad had undoubtedly killed before he was himself overpowered. We were not a great distance behind the Indians when the boy's body was discovered, and having good trailers we gained on them rapidly, with the prospect of overhauling them, but as soon as they found we were getting near they headed for the Rio Grande, made the crossing to the opposite bank, and were in Mexico before we could overtake them. When on the other side of the boundary they grew very brave, daring us to come over to fight them, well aware all the time that the international line prevented us from continuing the pursuit. So we had to return to the post without reward for our exertion except the consciousness of having made the best effort we could to catch the murderers. That night, in company with Lieutenant Thomas G. Williams, I crossed over the river to the Mexican village of Piedras Negras, and on going to a house where a large baille, or dance, was going on we found among those present two of the Indians we had been chasing. As soon as they saw us they strung their bows for a fight, and we drew our sixshooters, but the Mexicans quickly closed in around the Indians and forced them out of the house—or rude jackal—where the "ball" was being held, and they escaped. We learned later something about the nature of the fight the drummer had made, and that his death had cost them dear, for, in addition to the Indian killed and lying by his side, he had mortally wounded another and seriously wounded a third, with the three shots that he had fired.

At this period I took up the notion of making a study of ornithology, incited to it possibly by the great number of bright-colored birds that made their winter homes along the Rio Grande, and I spent many a leisure hour in catching specimens by means of stick traps, with which I found little difficulty in securing almost every variety of the feathered tribes. I made my traps by placing four sticks of a length suited to the size desired so as to form a square, and building up on them in log-cabin fashion until the structure came almost to a point by contraction of the corners. Then the sticks were made secure, the trap placed at some secluded spot, and from the centre to the outside a trench was dug in the ground, and thinly covered when a depth had been obtained that would leave an aperture sufficiently large to admit the class of birds desired. Along this trench seeds and other food were scattered, which the birds soon discovered, and of course began to eat, unsuspectingly following the tempting bait through the gallery till they emerged from its farther end in the centre of the trap, where they contentedly fed till the food was all gone. Then the fact of imprisonment first presented itself, and they vainly endeavored to escape through the interstices of the cage, never once guided by their instinct to return to liberty through the route by which they had entered.

Among the different kinds of birds captured in this way, mocking-birds, blue-birds, robins, meadow larks, quail, and plover were the most numerous. They seemed to have more voracious appetites than other varieties, or else they were more unwary, and consequently more easily caught. A change of station, however, put an end to my ornithological plans, and activities of other kinds prevented me from resuming them in after life.

There were quite a number of young officers at the post during the winter, and as our relations with the Mexican commandant at Piedras Negras were most amicable, we were often invited to dances at his house. He and his hospitable wife and daughter drummed up the female portion of the elite of Piedras Negras and provided the house, which was the official as well as the personal residence of the commandant, while we—the young officers—furnished the music and such sweetmeats, candies, &c., for the baille as the country would afford.

We generally danced in a long hall on a hard dirt floor. The girls sat on one side of the hall, chaperoned by their mothers or some old duennas, and the men on the other. When the music struck up each man asked the lady whom his eyes had already selected to dance with him, and it was not etiquette for her to refuse—no engagements being allowed before the music began. When the dance, which was generally a long waltz, was over, he seated his partner, and then went to a little counter at the end of the room and bought his dulcinea a plate of the candies and sweetmeats provided. Sometimes she accepted them, but most generally pointed to her duenna or chaperon behind, who held up her apron and caught the refreshments as they were slid into it from the plate. The greatest decorum was maintained at these dances, primitively as they were conducted; and in a region so completely cut off from the world, their influence was undoubtedly beneficial to a considerable degree in softening the rough edges in a half-breed population.

The inhabitants of this frontier of Mexico were strongly marked with Indian characteristics, particularly with those of the Comanche type, and as the wild Indian blood predominated, few of the physical traits of the Spaniard remained among them, and outlawry was common. The Spanish conquerors had left on the northern border only their graceful manners and their humility before the cross. The sign of Christianity was prominently placed at all important points on roads or trails, and especially where any one had been killed; and as the Comanche Indians, strong and warlike, had devastated northeastern Mexico in past years, all along the border, on both sides of the Rio Grande, the murderous effects of their raids were evidenced by numberless crosses. For more than a century forays had been made on the settlements and towns by these bloodthirsty savages, and, the Mexican Government being too weak to afford protection, property was destroyed, the women and children carried off or ravished, and the men compelled to look on in an agony of helplessness till relieved by death. During all this time, however, the forms and ceremonials of religion, and the polite manners received from the Spaniards, were retained, and reverence for the emblems of Christianity was always uppermost in the mind of even the most ignorant.

CHAPTER III.

ORDERED TO FORT READING, CAL.—A DANGEROUS UNDERTAKING—A RESCUED SOLDIER—DISCOVERING INDIANS—PRIMITIVE FISHING—A DESERTED VILLAGE—CAMPING OPPOSITE FORT VANCOUVER.

In November, 1854, I received my promotion to a second lieutenancy in the Fourth Infantry, which was stationed in California and Oregon. In order to join my company at Fort Reading, California, I had to go to New York as a starting point, and on arrival there, was placed on duty, in May, 1855, in command of a detachment of recruits at Bedloe's Island, intended for assignment to the regiments on the Pacific coast. I think there were on the island (now occupied by the statue of Liberty Enlightening the World) about three hundred recruits. For a time I was the only officer with them, but shortly before we started for California, Lieutenant Francis H. Bates, of the Fourth Infantry, was placed in command. We embarked for the Pacific coast in July, 1855, and made the journey without incident via the Isthmus of Panama, in due time landing our men at Benecia Barracks, above San Francisco.

From this point I proceeded to join my company at Fort Reading, and on reaching that post, found orders directing me to relieve Lieutenant John B. Hood—afterward well known as a distinguished general in the Confederate service. Lieutenant Hood was in command of the personal mounted escort of Lieutenant R. S. Williamson, who was charged with the duty of making such explorations and surveys as would determine the practicability of connecting, by railroad, the Sacramento Valley in California with the Columbia River in Oregon Territory, either through the

Willamette Valley, or (if this route should prove to be impracticable) by the valley of the Des Chutes River near the foot-slopes of the Cascade chain. The survey was being made in accordance with an act of Congress, which provided both for ascertaining the must practicable and economical route for a railroad between the Mississippi River and the Pacific Ocean, and for military and geographical surveys west of the Mississippi River.

Fort Reading was the starting-point for this exploring expedition, and there I arrived some four or five days after the party under Lieutenant Williamson had begun its march. His personal escort numbered about sixty mounted men, made up of detachments from companies of the First Dragoons, under command of Lieutenant Hood, together with about one hundred men belonging to the Fourth Infantry arid Third Artillery, commanded by Lieutenant Horatio Gates Gibson, the present colonel of the Third United States Artillery. Lieutenant George Crook—now major-general—was the quartermaster and commissary of subsistence of the expedition.

The commanding officer at Fort Reading seemed reluctant to let me go on to relieve Lieutenant Hood, as the country to be passed over was infested by the Pit River Indians, known to be hostile to white people and especially to small parties. I was very anxious to proceed, however, and willing to take the chances; so, consent being finally obtained, I started with a corporal and two mounted men, through a wild and uninhabited region, to overtake if possible Lieutenant Williamson. Being on horseback, and unencumbered by luggage of any kind except blankets and a little hard bread, coffee and smoking-tobacco, which were all carried on our riding animals, we were sanguine of succeeding, for we traversed in one day fully the distance made in three by Lieutenant Williamson's party on foot.

The first day we reached the base of Lassan's Butte, where I determined to spend the night near an isolated cabin, or dugout, that had been recently constructed by a hardy pioneer. The wind was blowing a disagreeable gale, which had begun early in the day. This made it desirable to locate our camp under the best cover we could find, and I spent some little time in looking about for a satisfactory place, but nothing better offered than a large fallen tree, which lay in such a direction that by encamping on its lee side we would be protected from the fury of the storm. This spot was therefore fixed upon, and preparation made for spending the night as comfortably as the circumstances would permit.

After we had unsaddled I visited the cabin to inquire in regard to the country ahead, and there found at first only a soldier of Williamson's party; later the proprietor of the ranch appeared. The soldier had been left behind by the surveying party on account of illness, with instructions to make his way back to Fort Reading as best he could when he recovered. His condition having greatly improved, however, since he had been left, he now begged me in beseeching terms to take him along with my party, which I finally consented to do, provided that if he became unable to keep up with me, and I should be obliged to abandon him, the responsibility would be his, not mine. This increased my number to five, and was quite a reinforcement should we run across any hostile Indians; but it was also certain to prove an embarrassment should the man again fall ill.

During the night, notwithstanding the continuance of the storm, I had a very sound and refreshing sleep behind the protecting log where we made our camp, and at daylight next morning we resumed our journey, fortified by a breakfast of coffee and hard bread. I skirted around the base of Lassan's Butte, thence down Hat Creek, all the time following the trail made by Lieutenant Williamson's party. About noon the soldier I had picked up at my first camp gave out, and could go no farther. As stipulated when I consented to take him along, I had the right to abandon him, but when it came to the test I could not make up my mind to do it. Finding a good place not far off the trail, one of my men volunteered to remain with him until he died; and we left them there, with a liberal supply of hard bread and coffee, believing that we would never again see the invalid. My reinforcement was already gone, and another man with it.

With my diminished party I resumed the trail and followed it until about 4 o'clock in the afternoon, when we heard the sound of voices, and the corporal, thinking we were approaching Lieutenant Williamson's party, was so overjoyed in anticipation of the junction, that he wanted to fire his musket as an expression of his delight. This I prevented his doing, however, and we continued cautiously and slowly on to develop the source of the sounds in front. We had not gone far before I discovered that the noise came from a band of Pit River Indians, who had struck the trail of the surveying expedition, and were following it up, doubtless with evil intent. Dismounting from my horse I counted the moccasin tracks to ascertain the number of Indians, discovered it to be about thirty, and then followed on behind them cautiously, but with little difficulty, as appearances of speed on their part indicated that they wished to overtake

Lieutenant Williamson's party, which made them less on the lookout than usual for any possible pursuers. After following the trail until nearly sundown, I considered it prudent to stop for the night, and drew off some little distance, where, concealed in a dense growth of timber, we made our camp.

As I had with me now only two men, I felt somewhat nervous, so I allowed no fires to be built, and in consequence our supper consisted of hard bread only. I passed an anxious night, but beyond our own solicitude there was nothing to disturb us, the Indians being too much interested in overtaking the party in front to seek for victims in the rear, After a hard-bread breakfast we started again on the trail, and had proceeded but a short distance when, hearing the voices of the Indians, we at once slackened our speed so as not to overtake them.

Most of the trail on which we traveled during the morning ran over an exceedingly rough lava formation—a spur of the lava beds often described during the Modoc war of 1873 so hard and flinty that Williamson's large command made little impression on its surface, leaving in fact, only indistinct traces of its line of march. By care and frequent examinations we managed to follow his route through without much delay, or discovery by the Indians, and about noon, owing to the termination of the lava formation, we descended into the valley of Hat Greek, a little below where it emerges from the second canon and above its confluence with Pit River. As soon as we reached the fertile soil of the valley, we found Williamson's trail well defined, deeply impressed in the soft loam, and coursing through wild-flowers and luxuriant grass which carpeted the ground on every hand.

When we struck this delightful locality we traveled with considerable speed, and after passing over hill and vale for some distance, the trail becoming more and more distinct all the time, I suddenly saw in front of me the Pit River Indians.

This caused a halt, and having hurriedly re-capped our guns and six-shooters, thus preparing for the worst, I took a look at the band through my field-glass. They were a half-mile or more in our front and numbered about thirty individuals, armed with bows and arrows only. Observing us they made friendly demonstrations, but I had not implicit faith in a Pit River Indian at that period of the settlement of our country, and especially in that wild locality, so after a "council of war" with the corporal and man, I concluded to advance to a point about two hundred yards distant from the party, when, relying on the speed of our horses rather than on the peaceable intentions of the savages, I hoped to succeed in cutting around them and take the trail beyond. Being on foot they could not readily catch us, and inasmuch as their arrows were good for a range of only about sixty yards, I had no fear of any material damage on that score.

On reaching the place selected for our flank movement we made a dash to the left of the trail, through the widest part of the valley, and ran our horses swiftly by, but I noticed that the Indians did not seem to be disturbed by the manoeuvre and soon realized that this indifference was occasioned by the knowledge that we could not cross Hat Creek, a deep stream with vertical banks, too broad to be leaped by our horses. We were obliged, therefore, to halt, and the Indians again made demonstrations of friendship, some of them even getting into the stream to show that they were at the ford. Thus reassured, we regained our confidence and boldly crossed the river in the midst of them. After we had gained the bluff on the other side of the creek, I looked down into the valley of Pit River, and could plainly see the camp of the surveying party. Its proximity was the influence which had doubtless caused the peaceable conduct of the Indians. Probably the only thing that saved us was their ignorance of our being in their rear, until we stumbled on them almost within sight of the large party under Williamson.

The Pit River Indians were very hostile at that time, and for many succeeding years their treachery and cruelty brought misfortune and misery to the white settlers who ventured their lives in search of home and fortune in the wild and isolated section over which these savages roamed. Not long after Williamson's party passed through their country, the Government was compelled to send into it a considerable force for the purpose of keeping them under control. The outcome of this was a severe fight—resulting in the loss of a good many lives—between the hostiles and a party of our troops under Lieutenant George Crook. It finally ended in the establishment of a military post in the vicinity of the battle-ground, for the permanent occupation of the country.

A great load was lifted from my heart when I found myself so near Williamson's camp, which I joined August 4, 1855, receiving a warm welcome from the officers. During the afternoon I relieved Lieutenant Hood of the command of the personal escort, and he was ordered to return, with twelve of the mounted men, over the trail I had followed. I pointed out to him on the map the spot where he would find the two men left on the roadside, and he was directed to take them into Fort Reading. They were found without difficulty, and carried in to the post. The sick man—Duryea—whom I had expected never to see again, afterward became the hospital steward at Fort Yamhill, Oregon, when I was stationed there.

The Indians that I had passed at the ford came to the bluff above the camp, and arranging themselves in a squatting posture, looked down upon Williamson's party with longing eyes, in expectation of a feast. They were a pitiable lot, almost naked, hungry and cadaverous. Indians are always hungry, but these poor creatures were particularly so, as their usual supply of food had grown very scarce from one cause and another.

In prosperity they mainly subsisted on fish, or game killed with the bow and arrow. When these sources failed they lived on grasshoppers, and at this season the grasshopper was their principal food. In former years salmon were very abundant in the streams of the Sacramento Valley, and every fall they took great quantities of these fish and dried them for winter use, but alluvial mining had of late years defiled the water of the different streams and driven the fish out. On this account the usual supply of salmon was very limited. They got some trout high up on the rivers, above the sluices and rockers of the miners, but this was a precarious source from which to derive food, as their means of taking the trout were very primitive. They had neither hooks nor lines, but depended entirely on a contrivance made from long, slender branches of willow, which grew on the banks of most of the streams. One of these branches would be cut, and after sharpening the butt-end to a point, split a certain distance, and by a wedge the prongs divided sufficiently to admit a fish between. The Indian fisherman would then slyly put the forked end in the water over his intended victim, and with a quick dart firmly wedge him between the prongs. When secured there, the work of landing him took but a moment. When trout were plentiful this primitive mode of taking them was quite successful, and I have often known hundreds of pounds to be caught in this way, but when they were scarce and suspicious the rude method was not rewarded with good results.

The band looking down on us evidently had not had much fish or game to eat for some time, so when they had made Williamson understand that they were suffering for food he permitted them to come into camp, and furnished them with a supply, which they greedily swallowed as fast as it was placed at their service, regardless of possible indigestion. When they had eaten all they could hold, their enjoyment was made complete by the soldiers, who gave them a quantity of strong plug tobacco. This they smoked incessantly, inhaling all the smoke, so that none of the effect should be lost. When we abandoned this camp the next day, the miserable wretches remained in it and collected the offal about the cooks' fires to feast still more, piecing out the meal, no doubt, with their staple article of food—grasshoppers.

On the morning of August 5 Lieutenant Hood started back to Fort Reading, and Lieutenant Williamson resumed his march for the Columbia River. Our course was up Pit River, by the lower and upper canons, then across to the Klamath Lakes, then east, along their edge to the upper lake. At the middle Klamath Lake, just after crossing Lost River and the Natural Bridge, we met a small party of citizens from Jacksonville, Oregon, looking for hostile Indians who had committed some depredations in their neighborhood. From them we learned that the Rogue River Indians in southern Oregon were on the war-path, and that as the "regular troops up there were of no account, the citizens had taken matters in hand, and intended cleaning up the hostiles." They swaggered about our camp, bragged a good deal, cursed the Indians loudly, and soundly abused the Government for not giving them better protection. It struck me, however, that they had not worked very hard to find the hostiles; indeed, it could plainly be seen that their expedition was a town-meeting sort of affair, and that anxiety to get safe home was uppermost in their thoughts. The enthusiasm with which they started had all oozed out, and that night they marched back to Jacksonville. The next day, at the head of the lake, we came across an Indian village, and I have often wondered since what would have been the course pursued by these valiant warriors from Jacksonville had they gone far enough to get into its vicinity.

When we reached the village the tepees—made of grass—were all standing, the fires burning and pots boiling—the pots filled with camas and tula roots—but not an Indian was to be seen. Williamson directed that nothing in the village should be disturbed; so guards were placed over it to carry out his instructions and we went into camp just a little beyond. We had scarcely established ourselves when a very old Indian rose up from the high grass some distance off, and with peaceable signs approached our camp, evidently for the purpose of learning whether or not our intentions were hostile. Williamson told him we were friendly; that we had passed through his village without molesting it, that we had put a guard there to secure the property his people had abandoned in their fright, and that they might come back in safety. The old man searchingly eyed everything around for some little time, and gaining confidence from the peaceable appearance of the men, who were engaged in putting up the tents and preparing their evening meal, he concluded to accept our professions of friendship, and bring his people in. Going out about half a mile from the village he gave a peculiar yell, at which between three and four hundred Indians arose simultaneously from the ground, and in answer to his signal came out of the tall grass like a swarm of locusts and soon overran our camp in search of food, for like all Indians they were hungry. They too, proved to be Pit Rivers, and were not less repulsive than those of their tribe we had met before. They were aware of the hostilities going on between the Rogue Rivers and the whites, but claimed that they had not taken any part in them. I question if they had, but had our party been small, I fear we should have been received at their village in a very different manner.

From the upper Klamath Lake we marched over the divide and down the valley of the Des Chutes River to a point opposite the mountains called the Three Sisters. Here, on September 23, the party divided, Williamson and I crossing through the crater of the Three Sisters and along the western slope of the Cascade Range, until we struck the trail on McKenzie River, which led us into the Willamette Valley not far from Eugene City. We then marched down the Willamette Valley to Portland, Oregon, where we arrived October 9, 1855.

The infantry portion of the command, escorting Lieutenant Henry L. Abbot, followed farther down the Des Chutes River, to a point opposite Mount Hood, from which it came into the Willamette Valley and then marched to Portland. At Portland we all united, and moving across the point between the Willamette and Columbia rivers, encamped opposite Fort Vancouver, on the south bank of the latter stream, on the farm of an old settler named Switzler, who had located there many years before.

CHAPTER IV.

"OLD RED"—SKILLFUL SHOOTING—YAKIMA—WAR—A LUDICROUS MISTAKE— "CUT-MOUTH JOHN'S" ENCOUNTER—FATHER PANDOZA'S MISSION—A SNOW-STORM—FAILURE OF THE EXPEDITION.

Our camp on the Columbia, near Fort Vancouver, was beautifully situated on a grassy sward close to the great river; and—as little duty was required of us after so long a journey, amusement of one kind or another, and an interchange of visits with the officers at the post, filled in the time acceptably. We had in camp an old mountaineer guide who had accompanied us on the recent march, and who had received the sobriquet of "Old Red," on account of the shocky and tangled mass of red hair and beard, which covered his head and face so completely that only his eyes could be seen. His eccentricities constantly supplied us with a variety of amusements. Among the pastimes he indulged in was one which exhibited his skill with the rifle, and at the same time protected the camp from the intrusions and ravages of a drove of razor-backed hogs which belonged to Mr. Switzler. These hogs were frequent visitors, and very destructive to our grassy sward, rooting it up in front of our tents and all about us; in pursuit of bulbous roots and offal from the camp. Old Red conceived the idea that it would be well to disable the pigs by shooting off the tips of their snouts, and he proceeded to put his conception into execution, and continued it daily whenever the hogs made their appearance. Of course their owner made a row about it; but when Old Red daily settled for his fun by paying liberally with gold-dust from some small bottles of the precious metal in his possession, Switzler readily became contented, and I think even encouraged the exhibitions—of skill.

It was at this period (October, 1855) that the Yakima Indian war broke out, and I was detached from duty with the exploring party and required by Major Gabriel J. Rains, then commanding the district, to join an expedition against the Yakimas. They had some time before killed their agent, and in consequence a force under Major Granville O. Haller had been sent out from the Dalles of the Columbia to chastise them; but the expedition had not been successful; in fact, it had been driven back, losing a number of men and two mountain howitzers.

The object of the second expedition was to retrieve this disaster. The force was composed of a small body of regular troops, and a regiment of Oregon mounted volunteers under command of Colonel James W. Nesmith—subsequently for several years United States Senator from Oregon. The whole force was under the command of Major Rains, Fourth Infantry, who, in order that he might rank Nesmith, by some hocus-pocus had been made a brigadier-general, under an appointment from the Governor of Washington Territory.

We started from the Dalles October 30, under conditions that were not conducive to success. The season was late for operations; and worse still, the command was not in accord with the commanding officer, because of general belief in his incompetency, and on account of the fictitious rank he assumed. On the second day out I struck a small body of Indians with my detachment of dragoons, but was unable to do them any particular injury beyond getting possession of a large quantity of their winter food, which their hurried departure compelled them to abandon. This food consisted principally of dried salmon-pulverized and packed in sacks made of grass-dried huckleberries, and dried camas; the latter a bulbous root about the size of a small onion, which, when roasted and ground, is made into bread by the Indians and has a taste somewhat like cooked chestnuts.

Our objective point was Father Pandoza's Mission, in the Yakima Valley, which could be reached by two different routes, and though celerity of movement was essential, our commanding officer "strategically" adopted the longer route, and thus the Indians had ample opportunity to get away with their horses, cattle, women and children, and camp property.

After the encounter which I just now referred to, the command, which had halted to learn the results of my chase, resumed its march to and through the Klikitat canon, and into the lower Yakima Valley, in the direction of the Yakima River. I had charge at the head of the column as it passed through the canon, and on entering the valley beyond, saw in the distance five or six Indian scouts, whom I pressed very closely, until after a run of several miles they escaped across the Yakima River.

The soil in the valley was light and dry, and the movement of animals over it raised great clouds of dust, that rendered it very difficult to distinguish friend from foe; and as I was now separated from the main column a considerable distance, I deemed it prudent to call a halt until we could discover the direction taken by the principal body of the Indians. We soon learned that they had gone up the valley, and looking that way, we discovered a column of alkali dust approaching us, about a mile distant, interposing between my little detachment and the point where I knew General Rains intended to encamp for the night. After hastily consulting with Lieutenant Edward H. Day, of the Third United States Artillery, who was with me, we both concluded that the dust was caused by a body of the enemy which had slipped in between us and our main force. There seemed no alternative left us but to get back to our friends by charging through these Indians; and as their cloud of dust was much larger than ours, this appeared a desperate chance. Preparations to charge were begun, however, but, much to our surprise, before they were completed the approaching party halted for a moment and then commenced to retreat. This calmed the throbbing of our hearts, and with a wild cheer we started in a hot pursuit, that continued for about two miles, when to our great relief we discovered that we were driving into Rains's camp a squadron of Nesmith's battalion of Oregon volunteers that we had mistaken for Indians, and who in turn believed us to be the enemy. When camp was reached, we all indulged in a hearty laugh over the affair, and at the fright each party had given the other. The explanations which ensued proved that the squadron of volunteers had separated from the column at the same time that I had when we debouched from the canon, and had pursued an intermediate trail through the hills, which brought it into the valley of the Yakima at a point higher up the river than where I had struck it.

Next day we resumed our march up the valley, parallel to the Yakima. About 1 o'clock we saw a large body of Indians on the opposite side of the river, and the general commanding made up his mind to cross and attack them. The stream was cold, deep, and swift, still I succeeded in passing my dragoons over safely, but had hardly got them well on the opposite bank when the Indians swooped down upon us. Dismounting my men, we received the savages with a heavy fire, which brought them to a halt with some damage and more or less confusion.

General Rains now became very much excited and alarmed about me, and endeavored to ford the swift river with his infantry and artillery, but soon had to abandon the attempt, as three or four of the poor fellows were swept off their feet and drowned. Meantime Nesmith came up with his mounted force, crossed over, and joined me.

The Indians now fell back to a high ridge, on the crest of which they marched and countermarched, threatening to charge down its face. Most of them were naked, and as their persons were painted in gaudy colors and decorated with strips of red flannel, red blankets and gay war-bonnets, their appearance presented a scene of picturesque barbarism, fascinating but repulsive. As they numbered about six hundred, the chances of whipping them did not seem overwhelmingly in our favor, yet Nesmith and I concluded we would give them a little fight, provided we could engage them without going beyond the ridge. But all our efforts were in vain, for as we advanced they retreated, and as we drew back they reappeared and renewed their parade and noisy demonstrations, all the time beating their drums and yelling lustily. They could not be tempted into a fight where we desired it, however, and as we felt unequal to any pursuit beyond the ridge without the assistance of the infantry and artillery, we re-crossed the river and encamped with Rains. It soon became apparent that the noisy demonstrations of the Indians were intended only as a blind to cover the escape of their women and children to a place of safety in the mountains.

Next morning we took up our march without crossing the river; and as our route would lead us by the point on the opposite bank where the Indians had made their picturesque display the day before, they at an early hour came over to our side, and rapidly moved ahead of us to some distant hills, leaving in our pathway some of the more venturesome young braves, who attempted, to retard our advance by opening fire at long range from favorable places where they lay concealed. This fire did us little harm, but it had the effect of making our progress so slow that the patience of every one but General Rains was well-nigh exhausted.

About 2 o'clock in the afternoon we arrived well up near the base of the range of hills, and though it was growing late we still had time to accomplish something, but our commanding officer decided that it was best to go into camp, and make a systematic attack next morning. I proposed that he let me charge with my dragoons through the narrow canon where the river broke through the range, while the infantry should charge up the hill and drive the enemy from the top down on the other side. In this way I thought we might possibly catch some of the fugitives, but his extreme caution led him to refuse the suggestion, so we pitched our tents out of range of their desultory fire, but near enough to observe plainly their menacing and tantalizing exhibitions of contempt.

In addition to firing occasionally, they called us all sorts of bad names, made indecent gestures, and aggravated us, so that between 3 and 4 o'clock in the afternoon, by an inexplicable concert of action, and with a serious breach of discipline, a large number of the men and many of the officers broke en masse from the camp with loud yells and charged the offending savages. As soon as this mob got within musket-shot they opened fire on the Indians, who ran down the other face of the ridge without making the slightest resistance. The hill was readily taken by this unmilitary proceeding, and no one was hurt on either side, but as Rains would not permit it to be held, a large bonfire was lighted on the crest in celebration of the victory, and then all hands marched back to camp, where they had no sooner arrived and got settled down than the Indians returned to the summit of the ridge, seemingly to enjoy the fire that had been so generously built for their benefit, and with renewed taunts and gestures continued to insult us.

Our camp that night was strongly picketed, and when we awoke in the morning the Indians still occupied their position on the hill. At daylight we advanced against them, two or three companies of infantry moving forward to drive them from the summit, while our main column passed through the canon into the upper Yakima Valley led by my dragoons, who were not allowed to charge into the gorge, as the celerity of such a movement might cause the tactical combination to fail.

As we passed slowly and cautiously through the canon the Indians ran rapidly away, and when we reached the farther end they had entirely disappeared from our front, except one old fellow, whose lame horse prevented him keeping up with the main body. This presented an opportunity for gaining results which all thought should not be lost, so our guide, an Indian named "Cut-mouth John," seized upon it, and giving hot chase, soon, overtook the poor creature, whom he speedily killed without much danger to himself, for the fugitive was armed with only an old Hudson's Bay flint-lock horse-pistol which could not be discharged.

"Cut-mouth John's" engagement began and ended all the fighting that took place on this occasion, and much disappointment and discontent followed, Nesmith's mounted force and my dragoons being particularly disgusted because they had not been "given a chance." During the remainder of the day we cautiously followed the retreating foe, and late in the evening went into camp a short distance from Father Pandoza's Mission; where we were to await a small column of troops under command of Captain Maurice Maloney, of the Fourth Infantry, that was to join us from Steilicom by way of the Natchez Pass, and from which no tidings had as yet been received.

Next morning the first thing I saw when I put my head out from my blankets was "Cut-mouth John," already mounted and parading himself through the camp. The scalp of the Indian he had despatched the day before was tied to the cross-bar of his bridle bit, the hair dangling almost to the ground, and John was decked out in the sacred vestments of Father Pandoza, having, long before any one was stiring in camp, ransacked the log-cabin at the Mission in which the good man had lived. John was at all times a most repulsive looking individual, a part of his mouth having been shot away in a fight with Indians near Walla Walla some years before, in which a Methodist missionary had been killed; but his revolting personal appearance was now worse than ever, and the sacrilegious use of Father Pandoza's vestments, coupled with the ghastly scalp that hung from his bridle, so turned opinion against him that he was soon captured, dismounted, and his parade brought to an abrupt close, and I doubt whether he ever after quite reinstated himself in the good graces of the command.

In the course of the day nearly all the men visited the Mission, but as it had been plundered by the Indians at the outbreak of hostilities, when Father Pandoza was carried off, little of value was left about it except a considerable herd of pigs, which the father with great difficulty had succeeded in accumulating from a very small beginning. The pigs had not been disturbed by the Indians, but the straggling troops soon disposed of them, and then turned their attention to the cabbages and potatoes in the garden, with the intention, no doubt, of dining that day on fresh pork and fresh vegetables instead of on salt junk and hard bread, which formed their regular diet on the march. In digging up the potatoes some one discovered half a keg of powder, which had been buried in the garden by the good father to prevent the hostile Indians from getting it to use against the whites. As soon as this was unearthed wild excitement ensued, and a cry arose that Father Pandoza was the person who furnished powder to the Indians; that here was the proof; that at last the mysterious means by which the Indians obtained ammunition was explained—and a rush was made for the mission building. This was a comfortable log-house of good size, built by the Indians for a school and church, and attached to one end was the log-cabin residence of the priest. Its destruction was a matter of but a few moments. A large heap of dry wood was quickly collected and piled in the building, matches applied, and the whole Mission, including the priest's house, was soon enveloped in flames, and burned to the ground before the officers in camp became aware of the disgraceful plundering in which their men were engaged.

The commanding officer having received no news from Captain Maloney during the day, Colonel Nesmith and I were ordered to go to his rescue, as it was concluded that he had been surrounded by Indians in the Natchez Pass. We started early the next morning, the snow falling slightly as we set out, and soon arrived at the eastern mouth of the Natchez Pass. On the way we noticed an abandoned Indian village, which had evidently not been occupied for some time. As we proceeded the storm increased, and the snow-fall became deeper and deeper, until finally our horses could not travel through it. In consequence we were compelled to give up further efforts to advance, and obliged to turn back to the abandoned village, where we encamped for the night. Near night-fall the storm greatly increased, and our bivouac became most uncomfortable; but spreading my blankets on the snow and covering them with Indian matting, I turned in and slept with that soundness and refreshment accorded by nature to one exhausted by fatigue. When I awoke in the morning I found myself under about two feet of snow, from which I arose with difficulty, yet grateful that it had kept me warm during the night.

After a cup of coffee and a little hard bread, it was decided we should return to the main camp near the Mission, for we were now confident that Maloney was delayed by the snow, and safe enough on the other side of the mountains. At all events he was beyond aid from us, for the impassable snowdrifts could not be overcome with the means in our possession. It turned out that our suppositions as to the cause of his delay were correct. He had met with the same difficulties that confronted us, and had been compelled to go into camp.

Meanwhile valuable time had been lost, and the Indians, with their families and stock, were well on their way to the Okenagan country, a region into which we could not penetrate in the winter season. No other course was therefore left but to complete the dismal failure of the expedition by returning home, and our commander readily gave the order to march back to the Dalles by the "short" route over the Yakima Mountains.

As the storm was still unabated, it was evident our march home would be a most difficult one, and it was deemed advisable to start back at once, lest we should be blocked up in the mountains by the snows for a period beyond which our provisions would not last. Relying on the fact that the short route to the Dalles would lead us over the range at its most depressed point, where it was hoped the depth of snow was not yet so great as to make the route impassable, we started with Colonel Nesmith's battalion in advance to break the road, followed by my dragoons. In the valley we made rapid progress, but when we reached the mountain every step we took up its side showed the snow to be growing deeper and deeper. At last Nesmith reached the summit, and there found a depth of about six feet of snow covering the plateau in every direction, concealing all signs of the trail so thoroughly that his guides became bewildered and took the wrong divide. The moment I arrived at the top my guide—Donald Mc Kay—who knew perfectly the whole Yakima range, discovered Nesmith's mistake. Word was sent to bring him back, but as he had already nearly crossed the plateau, considerable delay occurred before he returned. When he arrived we began anew the work of breaking a road for the foot troops behind us, my detachment now in advance. The deep snow made our work extremely laborious, exhausting men and horses almost to the point of relinquishing the struggle, but our desperate situation required that we should get down into the valley beyond, or run the chance of perishing on the mountain in a storm which seemed unending. About midnight the column reached the valley, very tired and hungry, but much elated over its escape. We had spent a day of the most intense anxiety, especially those who had had the responsibility of keeping to the right trail, and been charged with the hard work of breaking the road for the infantry and artillery through such a depth of snow.

Our main difficulties were now over, and in due time we reached the Dalles, where almost everyone connected with the expedition voted it a wretched failure; indeed, General Rains himself could not think otherwise, but he scattered far and wide blame for the failure of his combinations. This, of course, led to criminations and recriminations, which eventuated in charges of incompetency preferred against him by Captain Edward O. C. Ord, of the Third Artillery. Rains met the charges with counter-charges against Ord, whom he accused of purloining Father Pandoza's shoes, when the soldiers in their fury about the ammunition destroyed the Mission. At the time of its destruction a rumor of this nature was circulated through camp, started by some wag, no doubt in jest; for Ord, who was somewhat eccentric in his habits, and had started on the expedition rather indifferently shod in carpet-slippers, here came out in a brand-new pair of shoes. Of course there was no real foundation for such a report, but Rains was not above small things, as the bringing of this petty accusation attests. Neither party was ever tried, for General John E. Wool the department commander, had not at command a sufficient number of officers of appropriate rank to constitute a court in the case of Rains, and the charges against Ord were very properly ignored on account of their trifling character.

Shortly after the expedition returned to the Dalles, my detachment was sent down to Fort Vancouver, and I remained at that post during the winter of 1855-'56, till late in March.

CHAPTER V.
AN INDIAN CONFEDERATION—MASSACRE AT THE CASCADES OF THE COLUMBIA—PLAN TO RELIEVE THE BLOCKHOUSE—A HAZARDOUS FLANK MOVEMENT—A NEW METHOD OF ESTABLISHING GUILT—EXECUTION OF THE INDIAN MURDERERS.

The failure of the Haller expedition from lack of a sufficient force, and of the Rains expedition from the incompetency of its commander, was a great mortification to the officers and men connected with them, and, taken together, had a marked effect upon the Indian situation in Oregon and Washington Territories at that particular era. Besides, it led to further complications and troubles, for it had begun to dawn upon the Indians that the whites wanted to come in and dispossess them of their lands and homes, and the failures of Haller and Rains fostered the belief with the Indians that they could successfully resist the pressure of civilization.

Acting under these influences, the Spokanes, Walla Wallas, Umatillas, and Nez Perces cast their lot with the hostiles, and all the savage inhabitants of the region east of the Cascade Range became involved in a dispute as to whether the Indians or the Government should possess certain sections of the country, which finally culminated in the war of 1856.

Partly to meet the situation that was approaching, the Ninth Infantry had been sent out from the Atlantic coast to Washington Territory, and upon its arrival at Fort Vancouver encamped in front of the officers' quarters, on the beautiful parade-ground of that post, and set about preparing for the coming campaign. The commander, Colonel George Wright, who had been promoted to the colonelcy of the regiment upon its organization the previous year, had seen much active duty since his graduation over thirty years before, serving with credit in the Florida and Mexican wars. For the three years previous to his assignment to the Ninth Infantry he had been stationed on the Pacific coast, and the experience he had there acquired, added to his excellent soldierly qualities, was of much benefit in the active campaigns in which, during the following years, he was to participate. Subsequently his career was brought to an untimely close when, nine years after this period, as he was returning to the scene of his successes, he, in common with many others was drowned by the wreck of the ill-fated steamer Brother Jonathan. Colonel Wright took command of the district in place of Rains, and had been at Vancouver but a short time before he realized that it would be necessary to fight the confederated tribes east of the Cascade Range of mountains, in order to disabuse them of the idea that they were sufficiently strong to cope with the power of the Government. He therefore at once set about the work of organizing and equipping his troops for a start in the early spring against the hostile Indians, intending to make the objective point of his expedition the heart of the Spokane country on the Upper Columbia River, as the head and front of the confederation was represented in the person of old Cammiackan, chief of the Spokanes.

The regiment moved from Fort Vancouver by boat, March 25, 1856, and landed at the small town called the Dalles, below the mouth of the Des Chutes River at the eastern base of the Cascade Range, and just above where the Columbia River enters those mountains. This rendezvous was to be the immediate point of departure, and all the troops composing the expedition were concentrated there.

On the morning of March 26 the movement began, but the column had only reached Five Mile Creek when the Yakimas, joined by many young warriors-free lances from other tribes, made a sudden and unexpected attack at the Cascades of the Columbia, midway between Vancouver and the Dalles, killed several citizens, women and children, and took possession of the Portage by besieging the settlers in their cabins at the Upper Cascades, and those who sought shelter at the Middle Cascades in the old military block-house, which had been built some years before as a place of refuge under just such circumstances. These points held out, and were not captured, but the landing at the Lower Cascades fell completely into the hands of the savages. Straggling settlers from the Lower Cascades made their way down to Fort Vancouver, distant about thirty-six miles, which they reached that night; and communicated the condition of affairs. As the necessity for early relief to the settlers and the re-establishment of communication with the Dalles were apparent, all the force that could be spared was ordered out, and in consequence I immediately received directions to go with my detachment of dragoons, numbering about forty effective men, to the relief of the middle blockhouse, which really meant to retake the Cascades. I got ready at once, and believing that a piece of artillery would be of service to me, asked for one, but as there proved to be no guns at the post, I should have been obliged to proceed without one had it not been that the regular steamer from San Francisco to Portland was lying at the Vancouver dock unloading military supplies, and the commander, Captain Dall, supplied me with the steamer's small iron cannon, mounted on a wooden platform, which he used in firing salutes at different ports on the arrival and departure of the vessel. Finding at the arsenal a supply of solid shot that would fit the gun, I had it put upon the steamboat Belle, employed to carry my command to the scene of operations, and started up the Columbia River at 2 A.M. on the morning of the 27th. We reached the Lower Cascades early in the day, where, selecting a favorable place for the purpose, I disembarked my men and gun on the north bank of the river, so that I could send back the steamboat to bring up any volunteer assistance that in the mean time might have been collected at Vancouver.

The Columbia River was very high at the time, and the water had backed up into the slough about the foot of the Lower Cascades to such a degree that it left me only a narrow neck of firm ground to advance over toward the point occupied by the Indians. On this neck of land the hostiles had taken position, as I soon learned by frequent shots, loud shouting, and much blustering; they, by the most exasperating yells and indecent exhibitions, daring me to the contest.

After getting well in hand everything connected with my little command, I advanced with five or six men to the edge of a growth of underbrush to make a reconnoissance. We stole along under cover of this underbrush until we reached the open ground leading over the causeway or narrow neck before mentioned, when the enemy opened fire and killed a soldier near my side by a shot which, just grazing the bridge of my nose, struck him in the neck, opening an artery and breaking the spinal cord. He died instantly. The Indians at once made a rush for the body, but my men in the rear, coming quickly to the rescue, drove them back; and Captain Doll's gun being now brought into play, many solid shot were thrown into the jungle where they lay concealed, with the effect of considerably moderating their impetuosity. Further skirmishing at long range took place at intervals during the day, with little gain or loss, however, to either side, for both parties held positions which could not be assailed in flank, and only the extreme of rashness in either could prompt a front attack. My left was protected by the back water driven into the slough by the high stage of the river, and my right rested secure on the main stream. Between us was only the narrow neck of land, to cross which would be certain death. The position of the Indians was almost the exact counterpart of ours.

In the evening I sent a report of the situation back to Vancouver by the steamboat, retaining a large Hudson's Bay bateau which I had brought up with me. Examining this I found it would carry about twenty men, and made up my mind that early next morning I would cross the command to the opposite or south side of the Columbia River, and make my way up along the mountain base until I arrived abreast the middle blockhouse, which was still closely besieged, and then at some favorable point recross to the north bank to its relief, endeavoring in this manner to pass around and to the rear of the Indians, whose position confronting me was too strong for a direct attack. This plan was hazardous, but I believed it could be successfully carried out if the boat could be taken with me; but should I not be able to do this I felt that the object contemplated in sending me out would miserably fail, and the small band cooped up at the block-house would soon starve or fall a prey to the Indians, so I concluded to risk all the chances the plan involved.

On the morning of March 28 the savages were still in my front, and after giving them some solid shot from Captain Dall's gun we slipped down to the river-bank, and the detachment crossed by means of the Hudson's Bay boat, making a landing on the opposite shore at a point where the south channel of the river, after flowing around Bradford's Island, joins the main stream. It was then about 9 o'clock, and everything had thus far proceeded favorably, but examination of the channel showed that it would be impossible to get the boat up the rapids along the mainland, and that success could only be assured by crossing the south channel just below the rapids to the island, along the shore of which there was every probability we could pull the boat through the rocks and swift water until the head of the rapids was reached, from which point to the block-house there was smooth water. Telling the men of the embarrassment in which I found myself, and that if I could get enough of them to man the boat and pull it up the stream by a rope to the shore we would cross to the island and make the attempt, all volunteered to go, but as ten men seemed sufficient I selected that number to accompany me. Before starting, however, I deemed it prudent to find out if possible what was engaging the attention of the Indians, who had not yet discovered that we had left their front. I therefore climbed up the side of the abrupt mountain which skirted the water's edge until I could see across the island. From this point I observed the Indians running horse-races and otherwise enjoying themselves behind the line they had held against me the day before. The squaws decked out in gay colors, and the men gaudily dressed in war bonnets, made the scene most attractive, but as everything looked propitious for the dangerous enterprise in hand I spent little time watching them. Quickly returning to the boat, I crossed to the island with my ten men, threw ashore the rope attached to the bow, and commenced the difficult task of pulling her up the rapids. We got along slowly at first, but soon striking a camp of old squaws who had been left on the island for safety, and had not gone over to the mainland to see the races, we utilized them to our advantage. With unmistakable threats and signs we made them not only keep quiet, but also give us much needed assistance in pulling vigorously on the towrope of our boat.

I was laboring under a dreadful strain of mental anxiety during all this time, for had the Indians discovered what we were about, they could easily have come over to the island in their canoes, and, by forcing us to take up our arms to repel their attack, doubtless would have obliged the abandonment of the boat, and that essential adjunct to the final success of my plan would have gone down the rapids. Indeed, under such circumstances, it would have been impossible for ten men to hold out against the two or three hundred Indians; but the island forming an excellent screen to our movements, we were not discovered, and when we reached the smooth water at the upper end of the rapids we quickly crossed over and joined the rest of the men, who in the meantime had worked their way along the south bank of the river parallel with us. I felt very grateful to the old squaws for the assistance they rendered. They worked well under compulsion, and manifested no disposition to strike for higher wages. Indeed, I was so much relieved when we had crossed over from the island and joined the rest of the party, that I mentally thanked the squaws one and all. I had much difficulty in keeping the men on the main shore from cheering at our success, but hurriedly taking into the bateau all of them it could carry, I sent the balance along the southern bank, where the railroad is now built, until both detachments arrived at a point opposite the block-house, when, crossing to the north bank, I landed below the blockhouse some little distance, and returned the boat for the balance of the men, who joined me in a few minutes.

When the Indians attacked the people at the Cascades on the 26th, word was sent to Colonel Wright, who had already got out from the Dalles a few miles on his expedition to the Spokane country. He immediately turned his column back, and soon after I had landed and communicated with the beleaguered block-house the advance of his command arrived under Lieutenant-Colonel Edward J. Steptoe. I reported to Steptoe, and related what had occurred during the past thirty-six hours, gave him a description of the festivities that were going on at the lower Cascades, and also communicated the intelligence that the Yakimas had been joined by the Cascade Indians when the place was first attacked. I also told him it was my belief that when he pushed down the main shore the latter tribe without doubt would cross over to the island we had just left, while the former would take to the mountains. Steptoe coincided with me in this opinion, and informing me that Lieutenant Alexander Piper would join my detachment with a mountain' howitzer, directed me to convey the command to the island and gobble up all who came over to it.

Lieutenant Piper and I landed on the island with the first boatload, and after disembarking the howitzer we fired two or three shots to let the Indians know we had artillery with us, then advanced down the island with the whole of my command, which had arrived in the mean time; all of the men were deployed as skirmishers except a small detachment to operate the howitzer. Near the lower end of the island we met, as I had anticipated, the entire body of Cascade Indian men, women, and children—whose homes were in the vicinity of the Cascades. They were very much frightened and demoralized at the turn events had taken, for the Yakimas at the approach of Steptoe had abandoned them, as predicted, and fled to the mountains. The chief and head-men said they had had nothing to do with the capture of the Cascades, with the murder of men at the upper landing, nor with the massacre of men, women, and children near the block-house, and put all the blame on the Yakimas and their allies. I did not believe this, however, and to test the truth of their statement formed them all in line with their muskets in hand. Going up to the first man on the right I accused him of having engaged in the massacre, but was met by a vigorous denial. Putting my forefinger into the muzzle of his gun, I found unmistakable signs of its having been recently discharged. My finger was black with the stains of burnt powder, and holding it up to the Indian, he had nothing more to say in the face of such positive evidence of his guilt. A further examination proved that all the guns were in the same condition. Their arms were at once taken possession of, and leaving a small, force to look after the women and children and the very old men, so that there could be no possibility of escape, I arrested thirteen of the principal miscreants, crossed the river to the lower landing, and placed them in charge of a strong guard.

Late in the evening the steamboat, which I had sent back to Vancouver, returned, bringing to my assistance from Vancouver, Captain Henry D. Wallen's company of the Fourth Infantry and a company of volunteers hastily organized at Portland, but as the Cascades had already been retaken, this reinforcement was too late to participate in the affair. The volunteers from Portland, however, were spoiling for a fight, and in the absence of other opportunity desired to shoot the prisoners I held (who, they alleged, had killed a man named Seymour), and proceeded to make their arrangements to do so, only desisting on being informed that the Indians were my prisoners, subject to the orders of Colonel Wright, and would be protected to the last by my detachment. Not long afterward Seymour turned up safe and sound, having fled at the beginning of the attack on the Cascades, and hid somewhere in the thick underbrush until the trouble was over, and then made his way back to the settlement. The next day I turned my prisoners over to Colonel Wright, who had them marched to the upper landing of the Cascades, where, after a trial by a military commission, nine of them were sentenced to death and duly hanged. I did not see them executed, but was afterward informed that, in the absence of the usual mechanical apparatus used on such occasions, a tree with a convenient limb under which two empty barrels were placed, one on top of the other, furnished a rude but certain substitute. In executing the sentence each Indian in turn was made to stand on the top barrel, and after the noose was adjusted the lower barrel was knocked away, and the necessary drop thus obtained. In this way the whole nine were punished. Just before death they all acknowledged their guilt by confessing their participation in the massacre at the block-house, and met their doom with the usual stoicism of their race.

CHAPTER VI.
MISDIRECTED VENGEANCE—HONORABLE MENTION—CHANGE OF COMMAND—EDUCATED OXEN—FEEDING THE INDIANS—PURCHASING A BURYING-GROUND—KNOWING RATS.

While still encamped at the lower landing, some three or four days after the events last recounted, Mr. Joseph Meek, an old frontiersman and guide for emigrant trains through the mountains, came down from the Dalles, on his way to Vancouver, and stopped at my camp to inquire if an Indian named Spencer and his family had passed down to Vancouver since my arrival at the Cascades. Spencer, the head of the family, was a very influential, peaceable Chinook chief, whom Colonel Wright had taken with him from Fort Vancouver as an interpreter and mediator with the Spokanes and other hostile tribes, against which his campaign was directed. He was a good, reliable Indian, and on leaving Vancouver to join Colonel Wright, took his family along, to remain with relatives and friends at Fort Dalles until the return of the expedition. When Wright was compelled to retrace his steps on account of the capture of the Cascades, this family for some reason known only to Spencer, was started by him down the river to their home at Vancouver.

Meek, on seeing the family leave the Dalles, had some misgivings as to their safe arrival at their destination, because of the excited condition of the people about the Cascades; but Spencer seemed to think that his own peaceable and friendly reputation, which was widespread, would protect them; so he parted from his wife and children with little apprehension as to their safety. In reply to Meek's question, I stated that I had not seen

Spencer's family, when he remarked, "Well, I fear that they are gone up," a phrase used in that country in early days to mean that they had been killed. I questioned him closely, to elicit further information, but no more could be obtained; for Meek, either through ignorance or the usual taciturnity of his class, did not explain more fully, and when the steamer that had brought the reinforcement started down the river, he took passage for Vancouver, to learn definitely if the Indian family had reached that point. I at once sent to the upper landing, distant about six miles, to make inquiry in regard to the matter, and in a, little time my messenger returned with the information that the family had reached that place the day before, and finding that we had driven the hostiles off, continued their journey on foot toward my camp, from which point they expected to go by steamer down the river to Vancouver.

Their non-arrival aroused in me suspicions of foul play, so with all the men I could spare, and accompanied by Lieutenant William T. Welcker, of the Ordnance Corps—a warm and intimate friend—I went in search of the family, deploying the men as skirmishers across the valley, and marching them through the heavy forest where the ground was covered with fallen timber and dense underbrush, in order that no point might escape our attention. The search was continued between the base of the mountain and the river without finding any sign of Spencer's family, until about 3 o'clock in the afternoon, when we discovered them between the upper and lower landing, in a small open space about a mile from the road, all dead—strangled to death with bits of rope. The party consisted of the mother, two youths, three girls, and a baby. They had all been killed by white men, who had probably met the innocent creatures somewhere near the blockhouse, driven them from the road into the timber, where the cruel murders were committed without provocation, and for no other purpose than the gratification of the inordinate hatred of the Indian that has often existed on the frontier, and which on more than one occasion has failed to distinguish friend from foe. The bodies lay in a semicircle, and the bits of rope with which the poor wretches had been strangled to death were still around their necks. Each piece of rope—the unwound strand of a heavier piece—was about two feet long, and encircled the neck of its victim with a single knot, that must have been drawn tight by the murderers pulling at the ends. As there had not been quite enough rope to answer for all, the babe was strangled by means of a red silk handkerchief, taken, doubtless, from the neck of its mother. It was a distressing sight. A most cruel outrage had been committed upon unarmed people—our friends and allies—in a spirit of aimless revenge. The perpetrators were citizens living near the middle block-house, whose wives and children had been killed a few days before by the hostiles, but who well knew that these unoffending creatures had had nothing to do with those murders.

In my experience I have been obliged to look upon many cruel scenes in connection with Indian warfare on the Plains since that day, but the effect of this dastardly and revolting crime has never been effaced from my memory. Greater and more atrocious massacres have been committed often by Indians; their savage nature modifies one's ideas, however, as to the inhumanity of their acts, but when such wholesale murder as this is done by whites, and the victims not only innocent, but helpless, no defense can be made for those who perpetrated the crime, if they claim to be civilized beings. It is true the people at the Cascades had suffered much, and that their wives and children had been murdered before their eyes, but to wreak vengeance on Spencer's unoffending family, who had walked into their settlement under the protection of a friendly alliance, was an unparalleled outrage which nothing can justify or extenuate. With as little delay as possible after the horrible discovery, I returned to camp, had boxes made, and next day buried the bodies of these hapless victims of misdirected vengeance.

The summary punishment inflicted on the nine Indians, in their trial and execution, had a most salutary effect on the confederation, and was the entering wedge to its disintegration; and though Colonel Wright's campaign continued during the summer and into the early winter, the subjugation of the allied bands became a comparatively easy matter after the lesson taught the renegades who were captured at the Cascades. My detachment did not accompany Colonel Wright, but remained for some time at the Cascades, and while still there General Wool came up from San Francisco to take a look into the condition of things. From his conversation with me in reference to the affair at the Cascades, I gathered that he was greatly pleased at the service I had performed, and I afterward found that his report of my conduct had so favorably impressed General Scott that that distinguished officer complimented me from the headquarters of the army in general orders.

General Wool, while personally supervising matters on the Columbia River, directed a redistribution to some extent of the troops in the district, and shortly before his return to San Francisco I was ordered with my detachment of dragoons to take station on the Grande Ronde Indian Reservation in Yamhill County, Oregon, about twenty-five miles southwest of Dayton, and to relieve from duty at that point Lieutenant William B. Hazen—late brigadier-general and chief signal officer—who had established a camp there some time before. I started for my new station on April 21, and marching by way of Portland and Oregon City, arrived at Hazen's camp April 25. The camp was located in the Coast range of mountains, on the northeast part of the reservation, to which last had been added a section of country that was afterward known as the Siletz reservation. The whole body of land set aside went under the general name of the "Coast reservation," from its skirting the Pacific Ocean for some distance north of Yaquina Bay, and the intention was to establish within its bounds permanent homes for such Indians as might be removed to it. In furtherance of this idea, and to relieve northern California and southwestern Oregon from the roaming, restless bands that kept the people of those sections in a state of constant turmoil, many of the different tribes, still under control but liable to take part in warfare, were removed to the reservation, so that they might be away from the theatre of hostilities.

When I arrived I found that the Rogue River Indians had just been placed upon the reservation, and subsequently the Coquille, Klamath, Modocs, and remnants of the Chinooks were collected there also, the home of the latter being in the Willamette Valley. The number all told amounted to some thousands, scattered over the entire Coast reservation, but about fifteen hundred were located at the Grande Ronde under charge of an agent, Mr. John F. Miller, a sensible, practical man, who left the entire police control to the military, and attended faithfully to the duty of settling the Indians in the work of cultivating the soil.

As the place was to be occupied permanently, Lieutenant Hazen had begun, before my arrival, the erection of buildings for the shelter of his command, and I continued the work of constructing the post as laid out by him. In those days the Government did not provide very liberally for sheltering its soldiers; and officers and men were frequently forced to eke out parsimonious appropriations by toilsome work or go without shelter in most inhospitable regions. Of course this post was no exception to the general rule, and as all hands were occupied in its construction, and I the only officer present, I was kept busily employed in supervising matters, both as commandant and quartermaster, until July, when Captain D. A.

Russell, of the Fourth Infantry, was ordered to take command, and I was relieved from the first part of my duties.

About this time my little detachment parted from me, being ordered to join a company of the First Dragoons, commanded by Captain Robert Williams, as it passed up the country from California by way of Yamhill. I regretted exceedingly to see them go, for their faithful work and gallant service had endeared every man to me by the strongest ties. Since I relieved Lieutenant Hood on Pit River, nearly a twelvemonth before, they had been my constant companions, and the zeal with which they had responded to every call I made on them had inspired in my heart a deep affection that years have not removed. When I relieved Hood—a dragoon officer of their own regiment—they did not like the change, and I understood that they somewhat contemptuously expressed this in more ways than one, in order to try the temper of the new "Leftenant," but appreciative and unremitting care, together with firm and just discipline, soon quieted all symptoms of dissatisfaction and overcame all prejudice. The detachment had been made up of details from the different companies of the regiment in order to give Williamson a mounted force, and as it was usual, under such circumstances, for every company commander to shove into the detail he was called upon to furnish the most troublesome and insubordinate individuals of his company, I had some difficulty, when first taking command, in controlling such a medley of recalcitrants; but by forethought for them and their wants, and a strict watchfulness for their rights and comfort, I was able in a short time to make them obedient and the detachment cohesive. In the past year they had made long and tiresome marches, forded swift mountain streams, constructed rafts of logs or bundles of dry reeds to ferry our baggage, swum deep rivers, marched on foot to save their worn-out and exhausted animals, climbed mountains, fought Indians, and in all and everything had done the best they could for the service and their commander. The disaffected feeling they entertained when I first assumed command soon wore away, and in its place came a confidence and respect which it gives me the greatest pleasure to remember, for small though it was, this was my first cavalry command. They little thought, when we were in the mountains of California and Oregon—nor did I myself then dream—that but a few years were to elapse before it would be my lot again to command dragoons, this time in numbers so vast as of themselves to compose almost an army.

Shortly after the arrival of Captain Russell a portion of the Indians at the

Grande Ronde reservation were taken down the coast to the Siletz reservation, and I was transferred temporarily to Fort Haskins, on the latter reserve, and assigned to the duty of completing it and building a blockhouse for the police control of the Indians placed there.

While directing this work, I undertook to make a road across the coast mountains from King's Valley to the Siletz, to shorten the haul between the two points by a route I had explored. I knew there were many obstacles in the way, but the gain would be great if we could overcome them, so I set to work with the enthusiasm of a young path-finder. The point at which the road was to cross the range was rough and precipitous, but the principal difficulty in making it would be from heavy timber on the mountains that had been burned over years and years before, until nothing was left but limbless trunks of dead trees—firs and pines—that had fallen from time to time until the ground was matted with huge logs from five to eight feet in diameter. These could not be chopped with axes nor sawed by any ordinary means, therefore we had to burn them into suitable lengths, and drag the sections to either side of the roadway with from four to six yoke of oxen.

The work was both tedious and laborious, but in time perseverance surmounted all obstacles and the road was finished, though its grades were very steep. As soon as it was completed, I wished to demonstrate its value practically, so I started a Government wagon over it loaded with about fifteen hundred pounds of freight drawn by six yoke of oxen, and escorted by a small detachment of soldiers. When it had gone about seven miles the sergeant in charge came back to the post and reported his inability to get any further. Going out to the scene of difficulty I found the wagon at the base of a steep hill, stalled. Taking up a whip myself, I directed the men to lay on their gads, for each man had supplied himself with a flexible hickory withe in the early stages of the trip, to start the team, but this course did not move the wagon nor have much effect on the demoralized oxen; but following as a last resort an example I heard of on a former occasion, that brought into use the rough language of the country, I induced the oxen to move with alacrity, and the wagon and contents were speedily carried to the summit. The whole trouble was at once revealed: the oxen had been broken and trained by a man who, when they were in a pinch, had encouraged them by his frontier vocabulary, and they could not realize what was expected of them under extraordinary conditions until they heard familiar and possibly profanely urgent phrases. I took the wagon to its destination, but as it was not brought back, even in all the time I was stationed in that country, I think comment on the success of my road is unnecessary.

I spent many happy months at Fort Haskins, remaining there until the post was nearly completed and its garrison increased by the arrival of Captain F. T. Dent—a brother-in-law of Captain Ulysses S. Grant—with his company of the Fourth Infantry, in April, 1857. In the summer of 1856, and while I was still on duty there, the Coquille Indians on the Siletz, and down near the Yaquina Bay, became, on account of hunger and prospective starvation, very much excited and exasperated, getting beyond the control of their agent, and even threatening his life, so a detachment of troops was sent out to set things to rights, and I took command of it. I took with me most of the company, and arrived at Yaquina Bay in time to succor the agent, who for some days had been besieged in a log hut by the Indians and had almost abandoned hope of rescue.

Having brought with me over the mountains a few head of beef cattle for the hungry Indians, without thinking of running any great personal risk I had six beeves killed some little distance from my camp, guarding the meat with four Soldiers, whom I was obliged to post as sentinels around the small area on which the carcasses lay. The Indians soon formed a circle about the sentinels, and impelled by starvation, attempted to take the beef before it could be equally divided. This was of course resisted, when they drew their knives— their guns having been previously taken away from them—and some of the inferior chiefs gave the signal to attack. The principal chief, Tetootney John, and two other Indians joined me in the centre of the circle, and protesting that they would die rather than that the frenzied onslaught should succeed, harangued the Indians until the rest of the company hastened up from camp and put an end to the disturbance. I always felt grateful to Tetootney John for his loyalty on this occasion, and many times afterward aided his family with a little coffee and sugar, but necessarily surreptitiously, so as not to heighten the prejudices that his friendly act had aroused among his Indian comrades.

The situation at Yaquina Bay did not seem very safe, notwithstanding the supply of beef we brought; and the possibility that the starving Indians might break out was ever present, so to anticipate any further revolt, I called for more troops. The request was complied with by sending to my assistance the greater part of my own company ("K") from Fort Yamhill. The men, inspired by the urgency of our situation, marched more than forty miles a day, accomplishing the whole distance in so short a period, that I doubt if the record has ever been beaten. When this reinforcement arrived, the Indians saw the futility of further demonstrations against their agent, who they seemed to think was responsible for the insufficiency of food, and managed to exist with the slender rations we could spare and such indifferent food as they could pick up, until the Indian Department succeeded in getting up its regular supplies. In the past the poor things had often been pinched by hunger and neglect, and at times their only food was rock oysters, clams and crabs. Great quantities of these shell-fish could be gathered in the bay near at hand, but the mountain Indians, who had heretofore lived on the flesh of mammal, did not take kindly to mollusks, and, indeed, ate the shell-fish only as a last resort.

Crab catching at night on the Yaquina Bay by the coast Indians was a very picturesque scene. It was mostly done by the squaws and children, each equipped with a torch in one hand, and a sharp-pointed stick in the other to take and lift the fish into baskets slung on the back to receive them. I have seen at times hundreds of squaws and children wading about in Yaquina Bay taking crabs in this manner, and the reflection by the water of the light from the many torches, with the movements of the Indians while at work, formed a weird and diverting picture of which we were never tired.

Not long after the arrival of the additional troops from Yamhill, it became apparent that the number of men at Yaquina Bay would have to be reduced, so in view of this necessity, it was deemed advisable to build a block-house for the better protection of the agents and I looked about for suitable ground on which to erect it. Nearly all around the bay the land rose up from the beach very abruptly, and the only good site that could be found was some level ground used as the burial-place of the Yaquina Bay Indians—a small band of fish-eating people who had lived near this point on the coast for ages. They were a robust lot, of tall and well-shaped figures, and were called in the Chinook tongue "salt chuck," which means fish-eaters, or eaters of food from the salt water. Many of the young men and women were handsome in feature below the forehead, having fine eyes, aquiline noses and good mouths, but, in conformity with a long-standing custom, all had flat heads, which gave them a distorted and hideous appearance, particularly some of the women, who went to the extreme of fashion and flattened the head to the rear in a sharp horizontal ridge by confining it between two boards, one running back from the forehead at an angle of about forty degrees, and the other up perpendicularly from the back of the neck. When a head had been shaped artistically the dusky maiden owner was marked as a belle, and one could become reconciled to it after a time, but when carelessness and neglect had governed in the adjustment of the boards, there probably was nothing in the form of a human being on the face of the earth that appeared so ugly.

It was the mortuary ground of these Indians that occupied the only level spot we could get for the block-house. Their dead were buried in canoes, which rested in the crotches of forked sticks a few feet above-ground. The graveyard was not large, containing probably from forty to fifty canoes in a fair state of preservation. According to the custom of all Indian tribes on the Pacific coast, when one of their number died all his worldly effects were buried with him, so that the canoes were filled with old clothes, blankets, pieces of calico and the like, intended for the use of the departed in the happy hunting grounds.

I made known to the Indians that we would have to take this piece of ground for the blockhouse. They demurred at first, for there is nothing more painful to an Indian than disturbing his dead, but they finally consented to hold a council next day on the beach, and thus come to some definite conclusion. Next morning they all assembled, and we talked in the Chinook language all day long, until at last they gave in, consenting, probably, as much because they could not help themselves, as for any other reason. It was agreed that on the following day at 12 o'clock, when the tide was going out, I should take my men and place the canoes in the bay, and let them float out on the tide across the ocean to the happy hunting-grounds.

At that day there existed in Oregon in vast numbers a species of wood-rat, and our inspection of the graveyard showed that the canoes were thickly infested with them. They were a light gray animal, larger than the common gray squirrel, with beautiful bushy tails, which made them strikingly resemble the squirrel, but in cunning and deviltry they were much ahead of that quick-witted rodent. I have known them to empty in one night a keg of spikes in the storehouse in Yamhill, distributing them along the stringers of the building, with apparently no other purpose than amusement. We anticipated great fun watching the efforts of these rats to escape the next day when the canoes should be launched on the ocean, and I therefore forbade any of the command to visit the graveyard in the interim, lest the rats should be alarmed. I well knew that they would not be disturbed by the Indians, who held the sacred spot in awe. When the work of taking down the canoes and carrying them to the water began, expectation was on tiptoe, but, strange as it may seem, not a rat was to be seen. This unexpected development was mystifying. They had all disappeared; there was not one in any of the canoes, as investigation proved, for disappointment instigated a most thorough search. The Indians said the rats understood Chinook, and that as they had no wish to accompany the dead across the ocean to the happy hunting-grounds, they took to the woods for safety. However that may be, I have no doubt that the preceding visits to the burial-ground, and our long talk of the day before, with the unusual stir and bustle, had so alarmed the rats that, impelled, by their suspicious instincts, they fled a danger, the nature of which they could not anticipate, but which they felt to be none the less real and impending.

CHAPTER VII.
LEARNING THE CHINOOK LANGUAGE—STRANGE INDIAN CUSTOMS—THEIR DOCTORS—SAM PATCH—THE MURDER OF A WOMAN—IN A TIGHT PLACE—SURPRISING THE INDIANS—CONFLICTING REPORTS OF THE BATTLE OF BULL RUN—SECESSION QUESTION IN CALIFORNIA—APPOINTED A CAPTAIN—TRANSFERRED TO THE EAST.

The troubles at the Siletz and Yaquina Bay were settled without further excitement by the arrival in due time of plenty of food, and as the buildings, at Fort Haskins were so near completion that my services as quartermaster were no longer needed, I was ordered to join my own company at Fort Yamhill, where Captain Russell was still in command. I returned to that place in May, 1857, and at a period a little later, in consequence of the close of hostilities in southern Oregon, the Klamaths and Modocs were sent back to their own country, to that section in which occurred, in 1873, the disastrous war with the latter tribe. This reduced considerably the number of Indians at the Grande Ronde, but as those remaining were still somewhat unruly, from the fact that many questions requiring adjustment were constantly arising between the different bands, the agent and the officers at the post were kept pretty well occupied. Captain Russell assigned to me the special work of keeping up the police control, and as I had learned at an early day to speak Chinook (the "court language" among the coast tribes) almost as well as the Indians themselves, I was thereby enabled to steer my way successfully on many critical occasions.

For some time the most disturbing and most troublesome element we had was the Rogue River band. For three or four years they had fought our troops obstinately, and surrendered at the bitter end in the belief that they were merely overpowered, not conquered. They openly boasted to the other Indians that they could whip the soldiers, and that they did not wish to follow the white man's ways, continuing consistently their wild habits, unmindful of all admonitions. Indeed, they often destroyed their household utensils, tepees and clothing, and killed their horses on the graves of the dead, in the fulfillment of a superstitious custom, which demanded that they should undergo, while mourning for their kindred, the deepest privation in a property sense. Everything the loss of which would make them poor was sacrificed on the graves of their relatives or distinguished warriors, and as melancholy because of removal from their old homes caused frequent deaths, there was no lack of occasion for the sacrifices. The widows and orphans of the dead warriors were of course the chief mourners, and exhibited their grief in many peculiar ways. I remember one in particular which was universally practiced by the near kinsfolk. They would crop their hair very close, and then cover the head with a sort of hood or plaster of black pitch, the composition being clay, pulverized charcoal, and the resinous gum which exudes from the pine-tree. The hood, nearly an inch in thickness, was worn during a period of mourning that lasted through the time it would take nature, by the growth of the hair, actually to lift from the head the heavy covering of pitch after it had become solidified and hard as stone. It must be admitted that they underwent considerable discomfort in memory of their relatives. It took all the influence we could bring to bear to break up these absurdly superstitious practices, and it looked as if no permanent improvement could be effected, for as soon as we got them to discard one, another would be invented. When not allowed to burn down their tepees or houses, those poor souls who were in a dying condition would be carried out to the neighboring hillsides just before dissolution, and there abandoned to their sufferings, with little or no attention, unless the placing under their heads of a small stick of wood—with possibly some laudable object, but doubtless great discomfort to their victim—might be considered such.

To uproot these senseless and monstrous practices was indeed most difficult. The most pernicious of all was one which was likely to bring about tragic results. They believed firmly in a class of doctors among their people who professed that they could procure the illness of an individual at will, and that by certain incantations they could kill or cure the sick person. Their faith in this superstition was so steadfast that there was no doubting its sincerity, many indulging at times in the most trying privations, that their relatives might be saved from death at the hands of the doctors. I often talked with them on the subject, and tried to reason them out of the superstitious belief, defying the doctors to kill me, or even make me ill; but my talks were unavailing, and they always met my arguments with the remark that I was a white man, of a race wholly different from the red man, and that that was the reason the medicine of the doctors would not affect me. These villainous doctors might be either men or women, and any one of them finding an Indian ill, at once averred that his influence was the cause, offering at the same time to cure the invalid for a fee, which generally amounted to about all the ponies his family possessed. If the proposition was accepted and the fee paid over, the family, in case the man died, was to have indemnity through the death of the doctor, who freely promised that they might take his life in such event, relying on his chances of getting protection from the furious relatives by fleeing to the military post till time had so assuaged their grief that matters could be compromised or settled by a restoration of a part of the property, when the rascally leeches could again resume their practice. Of course the services of a doctor were always accepted when an Indian fell ill; otherwise the invalid's death would surely ensue, brought about by the evil influence that was unpropitiated. Latterly it had become quite the thing, when a patient died, for the doctor to flee to our camp—it was so convenient and so much safer than elsewhere—and my cellar was a favorite place of refuge from the infuriated friends of the deceased.

Among the most notable of these doctors was an Indian named Sam Patch, who several times sought asylum in any cellar, and being a most profound diplomat, managed on each occasion and with little delay to negotiate a peaceful settlement and go forth in safety to resume the practice of his nefarious profession. I often hoped he would be caught before reaching the post, but he seemed to know intuitively when the time had come to take leg-bail, for his advent at the garrison generally preceded by but a few hours the death of some poor dupe.

Finally these peculiar customs brought about the punishment of a noted doctress of the Rogue River tribe, a woman who was constantly working in this professional way, and who had found a victim of such prominence among the Rogue Rivers that his unlooked for death brought down on her the wrath of all. She had made him so ill, they believed, as to bring him to death's door notwithstanding the many ponies that had been given her to cease the incantations, and it was the conviction of all that she had finally caused the man's death from some ulterior and indiscernible motive. His relatives and friends then immediately set about requiting her with the just penalties of a perfidious breach of contract. Their threats induced her instant flight toward my house for the usual protection, but the enraged friends of the dead man gave hot chase, and overtook the witch just inside the limits of the garrison, where, on the parade-ground, in sight of the officers' quarters, and before any one could interfere, they killed her. There were sixteen men in pursuit of the doctress, and sixteen gun-shot wounds were found in her body when examined by the surgeon of the post. The killing of the woman was a flagrant and defiant outrage committed in the teeth of the military authority, yet done so quickly that we could not prevent it. This necessitated severe measures, both to allay the prevailing excitement and to preclude the recurrence of such acts. The body was cared for, and delivered to the relatives the next day for burial, after which Captain Russell directed me to take such steps as would put a stop to the fanatical usages that had brought about this murderous occurrence, for it was now seen that if timely measures were not taken to repress them, similar tragedies would surely follow.

Knowing all the men of the Rogue River tribe, and speaking fluently the Chinook tongue, which they all understood, I went down to their village the following day, after having sent word to the tribe that I wished to have a council with them. The Indians all met me in council, as I had desired, and I then told them that the men who had taken part in shooting the woman would have to be delivered up for punishment. They were very stiff with me at the interview, and with all that talent for circumlocution and diplomacy with which the Indian is lifted, endeavored to evade my demands and delay any conclusion. But I was very positive, would hear of no compromise whatever, and demanded that my terms be at once complied with. No one was with me but a sergeant of my company, named Miller, who held my horse, and as the chances of an agreement began to grow remote, I became anxious for our safety. The conversation waxing hot and the Indians gathering close in around me, I unbuttoned the flap of my pistol holster, to be ready for any emergency. When the altercation became most bitter I put my hand to my hip to draw my pistol, but discovered it was gone—stolen by one of the rascals surrounding me. Finding myself unarmed, I modified my tone and manner to correspond with my helpless condition, thus myself assuming the diplomatic side in the parley, in order to gain time. As soon as an opportunity offered, and I could, without too much loss of self-respect, and without damaging my reputation among the Indians, I moved out to where the sergeant held my horse, mounted, and crossing the Yamhill River close by, called back in Chinook from the farther bank that "the sixteen men who killed the woman must be delivered up, and my six-shooter also." This was responded to by contemptuous laughter, so I went back to the military post somewhat crestfallen, and made my report of the turn affairs had taken, inwardly longing for another chance to bring the rascally Rogue Rivers to terms.

When I had explained the situation to Captain Russell, he thought that we could not, under any circumstances, overlook this defiant conduct of the Indians, since, unless summarily punished, it would lead to even more serious trouble in the future. I heartily seconded this proposition, and gladly embracing the opportunity it offered, suggested that if he would give me another chance, and let me have the effective force of the garrison, consisting of about fifty men, I would chastise the Rogue Rivers without fail, and that the next day was all the time I required to complete arrangements. He gave me the necessary authority, and I at once set to work to bring about a better state of discipline on the reservation, and to put an end to the practices of the medicine men (having also in view the recovery of my sixshooter and self-respect), by marching to the village and taking the rebellious Indians by force.

In the tribe there was an excellent woman called Tighee Mary (Tighee in Chinook means chief), who by right of inheritance was a kind of queen of the Rogue Rivers. Fearing that the insubordinate conduct of the Indians would precipitate further trouble, she came early the following morning to see me and tell me of the situation Mary informed me that she had done all in her power to bring the Indians to reason, but without avail, and that they were determined to fight rather than deliver up the sixteen men who had engaged in the shooting. She also apprised me of the fact that they had taken up a position on the Yamhill River, on the direct road between the post and village, where, painted and armed for war, they were awaiting attack.

On this information I concluded it would be best to march to the village by a circuitous route instead of directly, as at first intended, so I had the ferry-boat belonging to the post floated about a mile and a half down the

Yamhill River and there anchored. At 11 o'clock that night I marched my fifty men, out of the garrison, in a direction opposite to that of the point held by the Indians, and soon reached the river at the ferryboat. Here I ferried the party over with little delay, and marched them along the side of the mountain, through underbrush and fallen timber, until, just before daylight, I found that we were immediately in rear of the village, and thence in rear, also, of the line occupied by the refractory Indians, who were expecting to meet me on the direct road from the post. Just at break of day we made a sudden descent upon the village and took its occupants completely by surprise, even capturing the chief of the tribe, "Sam," who was dressed in all his war toggery, fully armed and equipped, in anticipation of a fight on the road where his comrades were in position. I at once put Sam under guard, giving orders to kill him instantly if the Indians fired a shot; then forming my line on the road beyond the edge of the village, in rear of the force lying in wait for a front attack, we moved forward. When the hostile party realized that they were completely cut off from the village, they came out from their stronghold on the river and took up a line in my front, distant about sixty yards with the apparent intention of resisting to the last.

As is usual with Indians when expecting a fight, they were nearly naked, fantastically painted with blue clay, and hideously arrayed in war bonnets. They seemed very belligerent, brandishing their muskets in the air, dancing on one foot, calling us ugly names, and making such other demonstrations of hostility, that it seemed at first that nothing short of the total destruction of the party could bring about the definite settlement that we were bent on. Still, as it was my desire to bring them under subjection without loss of life, if possible, I determined to see what result would follow when they learned that their chief was at our mercy. So, sending Sam under guard to the front, where he could be seen, informing them that he would be immediately shot if they fired upon us, and aided by the cries and lamentations of the women of the village, who deprecated any hostile action by either party, I soon procured a parley.

The insubordinate Indians were under command of "Joe," Sam's brother, who at last sent me word that he wanted to see me, and we met between our, respective lines. I talked kindly to him, but was firm in my demand that the men who killed the woman must be given up and my six-shooter returned. His reply was he did not think it could be done, but he would consult his people. After the consultation, he returned and notified me that fifteen would surrender and the six-shooter would be restored, and further, that we could kill the sixteenth man, since the tribe wished to get rid of him anyhow, adding that he was a bad Indian, whose bullet no doubt had given the woman her death wound. He said that if I assented to this arrangement, he would require all of his people except the objectionable man to run to the right of his line at a preconcerted signal. The bad Indian would be ordered to stand fast on the extreme left, and we could open fire on him as his comrades fell away to the right. I agreed to the proposition, and gave Joe fifteen minutes to execute his part of it. We then returned to our respective forces, and a few minutes later the fifteen ran to the right flank as agreed upon, and we opened fire on the one Indian left standing alone, bringing him down in his tracks severely wounded by a shot through the shoulder.

While all this was going on, the other bands of the reservation, several thousand strong, had occupied the surrounding hills for the purpose of witnessing the fight, for as the Rogue Rivers had been bragging for some time that they could whip the soldiers, these other Indians had come out to see it done. The result, however, disappointed the spectators, and the Rogue Rivers naturally lost caste. The fifteen men now came in and laid down their arms (including my six-shooter) in front of us as agreed, but I compelled them to take the surrendered guns up again and carry them to the post, where they were deposited in the block-house for future security. The prisoners were ironed with ball and chain, and made to work at the post until their rebellious spirit was broken; and the wounded man was correspondingly punished after he had fully recovered. An investigation as to why this man had been selected as the offering by which Joe and his companions expected to gain immunity, showed that the fellow was really a most worthless character, whose death even would have been a benefit to the tribe. Thus it seemed that they had two purposes in view—the one to propitiate me and get good terms, the other to rid themselves of a vagabond member of the tribe.

The punishment of these sixteen Indians by ball and chain ended all trouble with the Rogue River tribe. The disturbances arising from the incantations of the doctors and doctresses, and the practice of killing horses and burning all worldly property on the graves of those who died, were completely suppressed, and we made with little effort a great stride toward the civilization of these crude and superstitious people, for they now began to recognize the power of the Government. In their management afterward a course of justice and mild force was adopted, and unvaryingly applied. They were compelled to cultivate their land, to attend church, and to send their children to school. When I saw them, fifteen years later, transformed into industrious and substantial farmers, with neat houses, fine cattle, wagons and horses, carrying their grain, eggs, and butter to market and bringing home flour, coffee, sugar, and calico in return, I found abundant confirmation of my early opinion that the most effectual measures for lifting them from a state of barbarism would be a practical supervision at the outset, coupled with a firm control and mild discipline.

In all that was done for these Indians Captain Russell's judgment and sound, practical ideas were the inspiration. His true manliness, honest and just methods, together with the warm-hearted interest he took in all that pertained to matters of duty to his Government, could not have produced other than the best results, in what position soever he might have been placed. As all the lovable traits of his character were constantly manifested, I became most deeply attached to him, and until the day of his death in 1864, on the battle-field of Opequan, in front of Winchester, while gallantly leading his division under my command, my esteem and affection were sustained and intensified by the same strong bonds that drew me to him in these early days in Oregon.

After the events just narrated I continued on duty at the post of Yamhill, experiencing the usual routine of garrison life without any incidents of much interest, down to the breaking out of the war of the rebellion in April, 1861. The news of the firing on Fort Sumter brought us an excitement which overshadowed all else, and though we had no officers at the post who sympathized with the rebellion, there were several in our regiment—the Fourth Infantry—who did, and we were considerably exercised as to the course they might pursue, but naturally far more so concerning the disposition that would be made of the regiment during the conflict.

In due time orders came for the regiment to go East, and my company went off, leaving me, however—a second lieutenant—in command of the post until I should be relieved by Captain James J. Archer, of the Ninth Infantry, whose company was to take the place of the old garrison. Captain Archer, with his company of the Ninth, arrived shortly after, but I had been notified that he intended to go South, and his conduct was such after reaching the post that I would not turn over the command to him for fear he might commit some rebellious act. Thus a more prolonged detention occurred than I had at first anticipated. Finally the news came that he had tendered his resignation and been granted a leave of absence for sixty days. On July 17 he took his departure, but I continued in command till September 1, when Captain Philip A. Owen, of the Ninth Infantry, arrived and, taking charge, gave me my release.

From the day we received the news of the firing on Sumter until I started East, about the first of September, 1861, I was deeply solicitous as to the course of events, and though I felt confident that in the end the just cause of the Government must triumph, yet the thoroughly crystallized organization which the Southern Confederacy quickly exhibited disquieted me very much, for it alone was evidence that the Southern leaders had long anticipated the struggle and prepared for it. It was very difficult to obtain direct intelligence of the progress of the war. Most of the time we were in the depths of ignorance as to the true condition of affairs, and this tended to increase our anxiety. Then, too, the accounts of the conflicts that had taken place were greatly exaggerated by the Eastern papers, and lost nothing in transition. The news came by the pony express across the Plains to San Francisco, where it was still further magnified in republishing, and gained somewhat in Southern bias. I remember well that when the first reports reached us of, the battle of Bull Run—that sanguinary engagement—it was stated that each side had lost forty thousand men in killed and wounded, and none were reported missing nor as having run away. Week by week these losses grew less, until they finally shrunk into the hundreds, but the vivid descriptions of the gory conflict were not toned down during the whole summer.

We received our mail at Yamhill only once a week, and then had to bring it from Portland, Oregon, by express. On the day of the week that our courier, or messenger, was expected back from Portland, I would go out early in the morning to a commanding point above the post, from which I could see a long distance down the road as it ran through the valley of the Yamhill, and there I would watch with anxiety for his coming, longing for good news; for, isolated as I had been through years spent in the wilderness, my patriotism was untainted by politics, nor had it been disturbed by any discussion of the questions out of which the war grew, and I hoped for the success of the Government above all other considerations. I believe I was also uninfluenced by any thoughts of the promotion that might result to me from the conflict, but, out of a sincere desire to contribute as much as I could to the preservation of the Union, I earnestly wished to be at the seat of war, and feared it might end before I could get East. In no sense did I anticipate what was to happen to me afterward, nor that I was to gain any distinction from it. I was ready to do my duty to the best of my ability wherever I might be called, and I was young, healthy, insensible to fatigue, and desired opportunity, but high rank was so distant in our service that not a dream of its attainment had flitted through my brain.

During the period running from January to September, 1861, in consequence of resignations and the addition of some new regiments to the regular army, I had passed through the grade of first lieutenant and reached that of captain in the Thirteenth United States Infantry, of which General W. T. Sherman had recently been made the colonel. When relieved from further duty at Yamhill by Captain Owen, I left for the Atlantic coast to join my new regiment. A two days' ride brought me down to Portland, whence I sailed to San Francisco, and at that city took passage by steamer for New York via the Isthmus of Panama, in company with a number of officers who were coming East under circumstances like my own.

At this time California was much agitated—on the question of secession, and the secession element was so strong that considerable apprehension was felt by the Union people lest the State might be carried into the Confederacy. As a consequence great distrust existed in all quarters, and the loyal passengers on the steamer, not knowing what might occur during our voyage, prepared to meet emergencies by thoroughly organizing to frustrate any attempt that might possibly be made to carry us into some Southern port after we should leave Aspinwall. However, our fears proved groundless; at all events, no such attempt was made, and we reached New York in safety in November, 1861. A day or two in New York sufficed to replenish a most meagre wardrobe, and I then started West to join my new regiment, stopping a day and a night at the home of my parents in Ohio, where I had not been since I journeyed from Texas for the Pacific coast. The headquarters of my regiment were at Jefferson Barracks, Missouri, to which point I proceeded with no further delay except a stay in the city of St. Louis long enough to pay my respects to General H. W. Halleck.

CHAPTER VIII.
AUDITING ACCOUNTS—CHIEF QUARTERMASTER AND COMMISSARY OF THE ARMY OF SOUTHWEST MISSOURI—PREPARING FOR THE PEA RIDGE CAMPAIGN—A DIFFERENCE WITH GENERAL CURTIS—ORDERED TO THE FRONT—APPOINTED A COLONEL.

Some days after I had reached the headquarters of my regiment near St. Louis, General Halleck sent for me, and when I reported he informed me that there existed a great deal of confusion regarding the accounts of some of the disbursing officers in his department, whose management of its fiscal affairs under his predecessor, General John C. Fremont, had been very loose; and as the chaotic condition of things could be relieved only by auditing these accounts, he therefore had determined to create a board of officers for the purpose, and intended to make me president of it. The various transactions in question covered a wide field, for the department embraced the States of Missouri, Iowa, Minnesota, Illinois, Arkansas, and all of Kentucky west of the Cumberland River.

The duty was not distasteful, and I felt that I was qualified to undertake it, for the accounts to be audited belonged exclusively to the Quartermaster and Subsistence departments, and by recent experience I had become familiar with the class of papers that pertained to those branches of the army. Indeed, it was my familiarity with such transactions, returns, etc., that probably caused my selection as president of the board.

I entered upon the work forthwith, and continued at it until the 26th of December, 1861. At that date I was relieved from the auditing board and assigned to duty as Chief Commissary of the Army of Southwest Missouri, commanded by General Samuel R. Curtis. This army was then organizing at Rolla, Missouri, for the Pea Ridge campaign, its strength throughout the campaign being in the aggregate about fifteen thousand men.

As soon as I received information of my selection for this position, I went to General Halleck and requested him to assign me as Chief Quartermaster also. He was reluctant to do so, saying that I could not perform both duties, but I soon convinced him that I could do both better than the one, for I reminded him that as Chief Quartermaster I should control the transportation, and thus obviate all possible chances of discord between the two staff departments; a condition which I deemed essential to success, especially as it was intended that Curtis's army should mainly subsist on the country. This argument impressed Halleck, and becoming convinced, he promptly issued the order making me Chief Quartermaster and Chief Commissary of Subsistence of the Army of Southwest Missouri, and I started for Rolla to enter upon the work assigned me.

Having reported to General Curtis, I quickly learned that his system of supply was very defective, and the transportation without proper organization, some of the regiments having forty to fifty wagon each, and others only three or four. I labored day and night to remedy these and other defects, and with the help of Captain Michael P. Small, of the Subsistence Department, who was an invaluable assistant, soon brought things into shape, putting the transportation in good working order, giving each regiment its proper quota of wagons, and turning the surplus into the general supply trains of the army. In accomplishing this I was several times on the verge of personal conflict with irate regimental commanders, but Colonel G. M. Dodge so greatly sustained me with General Curtis by strong moral support, and by such efficient details from his regiment—the Fourth Iowa Volunteer Infantry—that I still bear him and it great affection and lasting gratitude.

On January 26, 1862, General Curtis's army began its march from Rolla to Springfield, Missouri, by way of Lebanon. The roads were deep with mud, and so badly cut up that the supply trains in moving labored under the most serious difficulties, and were greatly embarrassed by swollen streams. Under these circumstances many delays occurred, and when we arrived at Lebanon nearly all the supplies with which we had started had been consumed, and the work of feeding the troops off the country had to begin at that point. To get flour, wheat had to be taken from the stacks, threshed, and sent to the mills to be ground. Wheat being scarce in this region, corn as a substitute had to be converted into meal by the same laborious process. In addition, beef cattle had to be secured for the meat ration.

By hard work we soon accumulated a sufficient quantity of flour and corn meal to justify the resumption of our march on Springfield; at or near which point the enemy was believed to be awaiting us, and the order was given to move forward, the commanding general cautioning me, in the event of disaster, to let no salt fall into General Price's hands. General Curtis made a hobby of this matter of salt, believing the enemy was sadly in need of that article, and he impressed me deeply with his conviction that our cause would be seriously injured by a loss which would inure so greatly and peculiarly to the enemy's benefit; but we afterward discovered, when Price abandoned his position, that about all he left behind was salt.

When we were within about eight miles of Springfield, General Curtis decided to put his troops in line of battle for the advance on the town, and directed me to stretch out my supply trains in a long line of battle, so that in falling back, in case the troops were repulsed, he could rally the men on the wagons. I did not like the tactics, but of course obeyed the order. The line moved on Springfield, and took the town without resistance, the enemy having fled southward, in the direction of Pea Ridge, the preceding day. Of course our success relieved my anxiety about the wagons; but fancy has often pictured since, the stampede of six mule teams that, had we met with any reverse, would have taken place over the prairies of southwest Missouri.

The army set out in pursuit of Price, but I was left at Springfield to gather supplies from the surrounding country, by the same means that had been used at Lebanon, and send them forward. To succeed in this useful and necessary duty required much hard work. To procure the grain and to run the mills in the country, replacing the machinery where parts had been carried away, or changing the principle and running the mills on some different plan when necessary, and finally forward the product to the army, made a task that taxed the energy of all engaged in it. Yet, having at command a very skillful corps of millwrights, machinists, and millers, detailed principally from the Fourth Iowa and Thirty-sixth Illinois volunteer regiments, we soon got matters in shape, and were able to send such large quantities of flour and meal to the front, that only the bacon and small parts of the ration had to be brought forward from our depot at Rolla. When things were well systematized, I went forward myself to expedite the delivery of supplies, and joined the army at Cross Hollows, just south of Pea Ridge.

Finding everything working well at Cross Hollows, I returned to Springfield in a few days to continue the labor of collecting supplies. On my way back I put the mills at Cassville in good order to grind the grain in that vicinity, and perfected there a plan for the general supply from the neighboring district of both the men and animals of the army, so that there should, be no chance of a failure of the campaign from bad roads or disaster to my trains. Springfield thus became the centre of the entire supply section.

Just after my return to Springfield the battle of Pea Ridge was fought. The success of the Union troops in this battle was considerable, and while not of sufficient magnitude to affect the general cause materially, it was decisive as to that particular campaign, and resulted in driving all organized Confederate forces out of the State of Missouri. After Pea Ridge was won, certain efforts were made to deprive Curtis of the credit due him for the victory; but, no matter what merit belonged to individual commanders, I was always convinced that Curtis was deserving of the highest commendation, not only for the skill displayed on the field, but for a zeal and daring in campaign which was not often exhibited at that early period of the war. Especially should this credit be awarded him, when we consider the difficulties under which he labored, how he was hampered in having to depend on a sparsely settled country for the subsistence of his troops. In the reports of the battle that came to Springfield, much glory was claimed for some other general officers, but as I had control of the telegraph line from Springfield east, I detained all despatches until General Curtis had sent in his official report. He thus had the opportunity of communicating with his superior in advance of some of his vain subordinates, who would have laid claim to the credit of the battle had I not thwarted them by this summary means.

Not long afterward came the culmination of a little difference that had arisen between General Curtis and me, brought about, I have since sometimes thought, by an assistant quartermaster from Iowa, whom I had on duty with me at Springfield. He coveted my place, and finally succeeded in getting it. He had been an unsuccessful banker in Iowa, and early in the war obtained an appointment as assistant quartermaster of volunteers with the rank of captain. As chief quartermaster of the army in Missouri, there would be opportunities for the recuperation of his fortunes which would not offer to one in a subordinate place; so to gain this position he doubtless intrigued for it while under my eye, and Curtis was induced to give it to him as soon as I was relieved. His career as my successor, as well as in other capacities in which he was permitted to act during the war, was to say the least not savory. The war over he turned up in Chicago as president of a bank, which he wrecked; and he finally landed in the penitentiary for stealing a large sum of money from the United States Treasury at Washington while employed there as a clerk. The chances that this man's rascality would be discovered were much less when chief of the departments of transportation and supply of an army than they afterward proved to be in the Treasury. I had in my possession at all times large sums of money for the needs of the army, and among other purposes for which these funds were to be disbursed was the purchase of horses and mules. Certain officers and men more devoted to gain than to the performance of duty (a few such are always to be found in armies) quickly learned this, and determined to profit by it. Consequently they began a regular system of stealing horses from the people of the country and proffering them to me for purchase. It took but a little time to discover this roguery, and when I became satisfied of their knavery I brought it to a sudden close by seizing the horses as captured property, branding them U.S., and refusing to pay for them. General Curtis, misled by the misrepresentations that had been made, and without fully knowing the circumstances, or realizing to what a base and demoralizing state of things this course was inevitably tending, practically ordered me to make the Payments, and I refused. The immediate result of this disobedience was a court-martial to try me; and knowing that my usefulness in that army was gone, no matter what the outcome of the trial might be, I asked General Halleck to relieve me from duty with General Curtis and order me to St. Louis. This was promptly done, and as my connection with the Army of Southwest Missouri was thus severed before the court could be convened, my case never came to trial. The man referred to as being the cause of this condition of affairs was appointed by General Curtis to succeed me. I turned over to the former all the funds and property for which I was responsible, also the branded horses and mules stolen from the people of the country, requiring receipts for everything. I heard afterward that some of the blooded stock of southwest Missouri made its way to Iowa in an unaccountable manner, but whether the administration of my successor was responsible for it or not I am unable to say.

On my arrival at St. Louis I felt somewhat forlorn and disheartened at the turn affairs had taken. I did not know where I should be assigned, nor what I should be required to do, but these uncertainties were dispelled in a few days by General Halleck, who, being much pressed by the Governors of some of the Western States to disburse money in their sections, sent me out into the Northwest with a sort of roving commission to purchase horses for the use of the army. I went to Madison and Racine, Wis., at which places I bought two hundred horses, which were shipped to St. Louis. At Chicago I bought two hundred more, and as the prices paid at the latter point showed that Illinois was the cheapest market—it at that time producing a surplus over home demands—I determined to make Chicago the centre of my operations.

While occupied in this way at Chicago the battle of Shiloh took place, and the desire for active service with troops became uppermost in my thoughts, so I returned to St. Louis to see if I could not get into the field. General Halleck having gone down to the Shiloh battle-field, I reported to his Assistant Adjutant-General, Colonel John C. Kelton, and told him of my anxiety to take a hand in active field-service, adding that I did not wish to join my regiment, which was still organizing and recruiting at Jefferson Barracks, for I felt confident I could be more useful elsewhere. Kelton knew that the purchasing duty was but temporary, and that on its completion, probably at no distant date, I should have to join my company at the barracks; so, realizing the inactivity to which that situation of affairs would subject me, he decided to assume the responsibility of sending me to report to General Halleck at Shiloh, and gave me an order to that effect.

This I consider the turning-point in my military career, and shall always feel grateful to Colonel Kelton for his kindly act which so greatly influenced my future. My desire to join the army at Shiloh had now taken possession of me, and I was bent on getting there by the first means available. Learning that a hospital-boat under charge of Dr. Hough was preparing to start for Pittsburg Landing, I obtained the Doctor's consent to take passage on it, and on the evening of April 15, I left St. Louis for the scene of military operations in northeastern Mississippi.

At Pittsburg Landing I reported to General Halleck, who, after some slight delay, assigned me to duty as an assistant to Colonel George Thom, of the topographical engineers. Colonel Thom put me at the work of getting the trains up from the landing, which involved the repair of roads for that purpose by corduroying the marshy places. This was rough, hard work, without much chance of reward, but it, was near the field of active operations, and I determined to do the best I could at it till opportunity for something better might arise.

General Halleck did not know much about taking care of himself in the field. His camp arrangements were wholly inadequate, and in consequence he and all the officers about him were subjected to much unnecessary discomfort and annoyance. Someone suggested to him to appoint me quartermaster for his headquarters, with a view to systematizing the establishment and remedying the defects complained of, and I was consequently assigned to this duty. Shortly after this assignment I had the satisfaction of knowing that General Halleck was delighted with the improvements made at headquarters, both in camp outfit and transportation, and in administration generally. My popularity grew as the improvements increased, but one trifling incident came near marring it. There was some hitch about getting fresh beef for General Halleck's mess, and as by this time everybody had come to look to me for anything and everything in the way of comfort, Colonel Joe McKibben brought an order from the General for me to get fresh beef for the headquarters mess. I was not caterer for this mess, nor did I belong to it even, so I refused point-blank. McKibben, disliking to report my disobedience, undertook persuasion, and brought Colonel Thom to see me to aid in his negotiations, but I would not give in, so McKibben in the kindness of his heart rode several miles in order to procure the beef himself, and thus save me from the dire results which be thought would follow should Halleck get wind of such downright insubordination. The next day I was made Commissary of Subsistence for the headquarters in addition to my other duties, and as this brought me into the line of fresh beef, General Halleck had no cause thereafter to complain of a scarcity of that article in his mess.

My stay at General Halleck's headquarters was exceedingly agreeable, and my personal intercourse with officers on duty there was not only pleasant and instructive, but offered opportunities for improvement and advancement for which hardly any other post could have afforded like chances. My special duties did not occupy all my time, and whenever possible I used to go over to General Sherman's division, which held the extreme right of our line in the advance on Corinth, to witness the little engagements occurring there continuously during the slow progress which the army was then making, the enemy being forced back but a short distance each day. I knew General Sherman very well. We came from near the same section of country in Ohio, and his wife and her family had known me from childhood. I was always kindly received by the General, and one day he asked me if I would be willing to accept the colonelcy of a certain Ohio regiment if he secured the appointment. I gladly told him yes, if General Halleck would let me go; but I was doomed to disappointment, for in about a week or so afterward General Sherman informed me that the Governor of Ohio would not consent, having already decided to appoint some one else.

A little later Governor Blair, of Michigan, who was with the army temporarily in the interest of the troops from his State, and who just at this time was looking around for a colonel for the Second Michigan Cavalry, and very anxious to get a regular officer, fixed upon me as the man. The regiment was then somewhat run down by losses from sickness, and considerably split into factions growing out of jealousies engendered by local differences previous to organization, and the Governor desired to bridge over all these troubles by giving the regiment a commander who knew nothing about them. I presume that some one said to the Governor about this time, "Why don't you get Sheridan?" This, however, is only conjecture. I really do not know how my name was proposed to him, but I have often been told since that General Gordon Granger, whom I knew slightly then, and who had been the former colonel of the regiment, first suggested the appointment. At all events, on the morning of May 27, 1862, Captain Russell A. Alger—recently Governor of Michigan— accompanied by the quartermaster of the regiment, Lieutenant Frank Walbridge, arrived at General Halleck's headquarters and delivered to me this telegram:

(By Telegraph.)
"MILITARY DEPT OF MICHIGAN,
"ADJUTANT-GENERAL'S OFFICE,
"DETROIT, May 25, 1862.
GENERAL ORDERS NO. 148.

"Captain Philip H. Sheridan, U. S. Army, is hereby appointed Colonel of the Second Regiment Michigan Cavalry, to rank from this date.

"Captain Sheridan will immediately assume command of the regiment.

"By order of the Commander-in-Chief,
"JNO. ROBERTSON,
"Adjutant-General."

I took the order to General Halleck, and said that I would like to accept, but he was not willing I should do so until the consent of the War Department could be obtained. I returned to my tent much disappointed, for in those days, for some unaccountable reason, the War Department did not favor the appointment of regular officers to volunteer regiments, and I feared a disapproval at Washington. After a further consultation with Captain Alger and Lieutenant Walbridge, I determined to go to the General again and further present the case. Enlarging on my desire for active service with troops, and urging the utter lack of such opportunity where I was, I pleaded my cause until General Halleck finally resolved to take the responsibility of letting me go without consulting the War Department. When I had thanked him for the kindness, he said that inasmuch as I was to leave him, he would inform me that the regiment to which I had just been appointed was ordered out as part of a column directed to make a raid to the south of the enemy, then occupying Corinth, and that if I could turn over my property, it would probably be well for me to join my command immediately, so that I could go with the expedition. I returned to my tent, where Alger and Walbridge were still waiting, and told them of the success of my interview, at the same time notifying them that I would join the regiment in season to accompany the expedition of which Halleck had spoken.

In the course of the afternoon I turned over all my property to my successor, and about 8 o'clock that evening made my appearance at the camp of the Second Michigan Cavalry, near Farmington, Mississippi. The regiment was in a hubbub of excitement making preparations for the raid, and I had barely time to meet the officers of my command, and no opportunity at all to see the men, when the trumpet sounded to horse. Dressed in a coat and trousers of a captain of infantry, but recast as a colonel of cavalry by a pair of well-worn eagles that General Granger had kindly given me, I hurriedly placed on my saddle a haversack, containing some coffee, sugar, bacon, and hard bread, which had been prepared, and mounting my horse, I reported my regiment to the brigade commander as ready for duty.

CHAPTER IX.
EXPEDITION TO BOONEVILLE—DESTROYING SUPPLIES—CONFEDERATE STRAGGLERS—SUCCESS OF THE EXPEDITION—A RECONNOISSANCE—THE IMPORTANCE OF BODILY SUSTENANCE—THE BATTLE OF BOONEVILLE—RECOMMENDED FOR APPOINTMENT AS A BRIGADIER-GENERAL.

The expedition referred to by General Halleck in his parting conversation was composed of the Second Michigan and Second Iowa regiments of cavalry, formed into a brigade under command of Colonel Washington L. Elliott, of the Second Iowa. It was to start on the night of the 27th of May at 12 o'clock, and proceed by a circuitous route through Iuka, Miss., to Booneville, a station on the Mobile and Ohio Railroad, about twenty-two miles below Corinth, and accomplish all it could in the way of destroying the enemy's supplies and cutting his railroad communications.

The weather in that climate was already warm, guides unobtainable, and both men and horses suffered much discomfort from the heat, and fatigue from the many delays growing out of the fact that we were in almost total ignorance of the roads leading to the point that we desired to reach. In order that we might go light we carried only sugar, coffee, and salt, depending on the country for meat and bread. Both these articles were scarce, but I think we got all there was, for our advent was so unexpected by the people of the region through which we passed that, supposing us to be Confederate cavalry, they often gave us all they had, the women and servants contributing most freely from their, reserve stores.

Before reaching Booneville I had the advance, but just as we arrived on the outskirts of the town the brigade was formed with the Second Iowa on my right, and the whole force moved forward, right in front, preceded by skirmishers. Here we encountered the enemy, but forced him back with little resistance. When we had gained possession of the station, Colonel Elliott directed me to take the left wing of my regiment, pass to the south, and destroy a bridge or culvert supposed to be at a little distance below the town on the Mobile and Ohio Railroad. The right wing, or other half of the regiment, was to be held in reserve for my support if necessary. I moved rapidly in the designated direction till I reached the railroad, and then rode down it for a mile and a half, but found neither bridge nor culvert. I then learned that there was no bridge of any importance except the one at Baldwin, nine miles farther down, but as I was aware, from information recently received, that it was defended by three regiments and a battery, I concluded that I could best accomplish the purpose for which I had been detached—crippling the road—by tearing up the track, bending the rails, and burning the cross-ties. This was begun with alacrity at four different points, officers and men vieing with one another in the laborious work of destruction. We had but few tools, and as the difficulties to overcome were serious, our progress was slow, until some genius conceived the idea that the track, rails and ties, might be lifted from its bed bodily, turned over, and subjected to a high heat; a convenient supply of dry fence-rails would furnish ample fuel to render the rails useless. In this way a good deal of the track was effectively broken up, and communication by rail from Corinth to the south entirely cut off. While we were still busy in wrecking the road, a dash was made at my right and rear by a squadron of Confederate cavalry. This was handsomely met by the reserve under Captain Archibald P. Campbell, of the Second Michigan, who, dismounting a portion of his command, received the enemy with such a volley from his Colt's repeating rifles that the squadron broke and fled in all directions. We were not molested further, and resumed our work, intending to extend the break toward Baldwin, but receiving orders from Elliott to return to Booneville immediately, the men were recalled, and we started to rejoin the main command.

In returning to Booneville, I found the railroad track above where I had struck it blocked by trains that we had thus cut off, and the woods and fields around the town covered with several thousand Confederate soldiers. These were mostly convalescents and disheartened stragglers belonging to General Beauregard's army, and from them we learned that Corinth was being evacuated. I spent some little time in an endeavor to get these demoralized men into an open field, with a view to some future disposition of them; but in the midst of the undertaking I received another order from Colonel Elliott to join him at once. The news of the evacuation had also reached Elliott, and had disclosed a phase of the situation so different from that under which he had viewed it when we arrived at Booneville, that he had grown anxious to withdraw, lest we should be suddenly pounced upon by an overwhelming force from some one of the columns in retreat. Under such circumstances my prisoners would prove a decided embarrassment, so I abandoned further attempts to get them together—not even paroling them, which I thought might have been done with but little risk.

In the meantime the captured cars had been fired, and as their complete destruction was assured by explosions from those containing ammunition, they needed no further attention, so I withdrew my men and hastened to join Elliott, taking along some Confederate officers whom I had retained from among four or five hundred prisoners captured when making the original dash below the town.

The losses in my regiment, and, in fact, those of the entire command, were insignificant. The results of the expedition were important; the railroad being broken so thoroughly as to cut off all rolling stock north of Booneville, and to place at the service of General Halleck's army the cars and locomotives of which the retreating Confederates were now so much in need. In addition, we burned twenty-six cars containing ten thousand stand of small arms, three pieces of artillery, a great quantity of clothing, a heavy supply of ammunition, and the personal baggage of General Leonidas Polk. A large number of prisoners, mostly sick and convalescent, also fell into our hands; but as we could not carry them with us such a hurried departure was an immediate necessity, by reason of our critical situation—the process of paroling them was not completed, and they doubtless passed back to active service in the Confederacy, properly enough unrecognized as prisoners of war by their superiors.

In returning, the column marched back by another indirect route to its old camp near Farmington, where we learned that the whole army had moved into and beyond Corinth, in pursuit of Beauregard, on the 13th of May, the very day we had captured Booneville. Although we had marched about one hundred and eighty miles in four days, we were required to take part, of course, in the pursuit of the Confederate army. So, resting but one night in our old camp, we were early in the saddle again on the morning of the 2d of June. Marching south through Corinth, we passed on the 4th of June the scene of our late raid, viewing with much satisfaction, as we took the road toward Blackland, the still smoldering embers of the burned trains.

On the 4th of June I was ordered to proceed with my regiment along the Blackland road to determine the strength of the enemy in that direction, as it was thought possible we might capture, by a concerted movement which General John Pope had suggested to General Halleck, a portion of Beauregard's rear guard. Pushing the Confederate scouts rapidly in with a running fire for a mile or more, while we were approaching a little stream, I hoped to gobble the main body of the enemy's pickets. I therefore directed the sabre battalion of the regiment, followed by that portion of it armed with revolving rifles, to dash forward in column, cut off these videttes before they could cross the stream, and then gather them in. The pickets fled hastily, however, and a pell-mell pursuit carried us over the stream at their heels by a little bridge, with no thought of halting till we gained a hill on the other side, and suddenly found ourselves almost in the camp of a strong body of artillery and infantry. Captain Campbell being in advance, hurriedly dismounted his battalion for a further forward movement on foot, but it was readily seen that the enemy was present in such heavy force as almost to ensure our destruction, and I gave orders for a hasty withdrawal. We withdrew without loss under cover of thick woods, aided much, however, by the consternation of the Confederates, who had hardly recovered from their surprise at our sudden appearance in their camp before we had again placed the stream between them and us by recrossing the bridge. The reconnoissance was a success in one way— that is, in finding out that the enemy was at the point supposed by, General Pope; but it also had a tendency to accelerate Beauregard's retreat, for in a day or two his whole line fell back as far south as Guntown, thus rendering abortive the plans for bagging a large portion of his army.

General Beauregard's evacuation of Corinth and retreat southward were accomplished in the face of a largely superior force of Union troops, and he reached the point where he intended to halt for reorganization without other loss than that sustained in the destruction of the cars and supplies at Booneville, and the capture of some stragglers and deserters that fell into our hands while we were pressing his rear from General Pope's flank. The number of these was quite large, and indicated that the enemy was considerably demoralized. Under such circumstances, an energetic and skillfully directed pursuit might not have made certain the enemy's destruction, but it would largely have aided in disintegrating his forces, and I never could quite understand why it was not ordered. The desultory affairs between rear and advance guards seemed as a general, thing to have no particular purpose in view beyond finding out where the enemy was, and when he was found, since no supporting columns were at hand and no one in supreme control was present to give directions, our skirmishing was of little avail and brought but small reward.

A short time subsequent to these occurrences, Colonel Elliott was made a brigadier-general, and as General Pope appointed him his Chief-of-Staff, I, on the 11th of June, 1862, fell in command of the brigade by seniority. For the rest of the month but little of moment occurred, and we settled down into camp at Booneville on the 26th of June, in a position which my brigade had been ordered to take up some twenty miles, in advance of the main army for the purpose of covering its front. Although but a few days had elapsed from the date of my appointment as colonel of the Second Michigan to that of my succeeding to the command of the brigade, I believe I can say with propriety that I had firmly established myself in the confidence of the officers and men of the regiment, and won their regard by thoughtful care. I had striven unceasingly to have them well fed and well clothed, had personally looked after the selection of their camps, and had maintained such a discipline as to allay former irritation.

Men who march, scout, and fight, and suffer all the hardships that fall to the lot of soldiers in the field, in order to do vigorous work must have the best bodily sustenance, and every comfort that can be provided. I knew from practical experience on the frontier that my efforts in this direction would not only be appreciated, but requited by personal affection and gratitude; and, further, that such exertions would bring the best results to me. Whenever my authority would permit I saved my command from needless sacrifices and unnecessary toil; therefore, when hard or daring work was to be done I expected the heartiest response, and always got it. Soldiers are averse to seeing their comrades killed without compensating results, and none realize more quickly than they the blundering that often takes place on the field of battle. They want some tangible indemnity for the loss of life, and as victory is an offset the value of which is manifest, it not only makes them content to shed their blood, but also furnishes evidence of capacity in those who command them. My regiment had lost very few men since coming under my command, but it seemed, in the eyes of all who belonged to it, that casualties to the enemy and some slight successes for us had repaid every sacrifice, and in consequence I had gained not only their confidence as soldiers, but also their esteem and love as men, and to a degree far beyond what I then realized.

As soon as the camp of my brigade was pitched at Booneville, I began to scout in every direction, to obtain a knowledge of the enemy's whereabouts and learn the ground about me. My standing in drawing at the Military Academy had never been so high as to warrant the belief that I could ever prove myself an expert, but a few practical lessons in that line were impressed on me there, and I had retained enough to enable me to make rough maps that could be readily understood, and which would be suitable to replace the erroneous skeleton outlines of northern Mississippi, with which at this time we were scantily furnished; so as soon as possible I compiled for the use of myself and my regimental commanders an information map of the surrounding country. This map exhibited such details as country roads, streams, farmhouses, fields, woods, and swamps, and such other topographical features as would be useful. I must confess that my crude sketch did not evidence much artistic merit, but it was an improvement on what we already possessed in the way of details to guide the command, and this was what I most needed; for it was of the first importance that in our exposed condition we should be equipped with a thorough knowledge of the section in which we were operating, so as to be prepared to encounter an enemy already indicating recovery from the disorganizing effects of his recent retreat.

In the immediate vicinity of Booneville the country was covered with heavy forests, with here and there clearings or intervening fields that had been devoted to the cultivation of cotton and corn. The ground was of a low character, typical of northeastern Mississippi, and abounded in small creeks that went almost totally dry even in short periods of drought, but became flooded with muddy water under the outpouring of rain peculiar to a semi-tropical climate. In such a region there were many chances of our being surprised, especially by an enemy who knew the country well, and whose ranks were filled with local guides; and great precautions as well as the fullest information were necessary to prevent disaster. I therefore endeavored to familiarize all with our surroundings, but scarcely had matters begun to shape themselves as I desired when our annihilation was attempted by a large force of Confederate cavalry.

On the morning of July 1, 1862, a cavalry command of between five and six thousand men, under the Confederate General James R. Chalmers, advanced on two roads converging near Booneville. The head of the enemy's column on the Blackland and Booneville road came in contact with my pickets three miles and a half west of Booneville. These pickets, under Lieutenant Leonidas S. Scranton, of the Second Michigan Cavalry, fell back slowly, taking advantage of every tree or other cover to fire from till they arrived at the point where the converging roads joined. At this junction there was a strong position in the protecting timber, and here Scranton made a firm stand, being reinforced presently by the few men he had out as pickets on the road to his left, a second company I had sent him from camp, and subsequently by three companies more, all now commanded by Captain Campbell. This force was dismounted and formed in line, and soon developed that the enemy was present in large numbers. Up to this time Chalmers had shown only the heads of his columns, and we had doubts as to his purpose, but now that our resistance forced him to deploy two regiments on the right and left of the road, it became apparent that he meant business, and that there was no time to lose in preparing to repel his attack.

Full information of the situation was immediately sent me, and I directed Campbell to hold fast, if possible, till I could support him, but if compelled to retire he was authorized to do so slowly, taking advantage of every means that fell in his way to prolong the fighting. Before this I had stationed one battalion of the Second Iowa in Booneville, but Colonel Edward Hatch, commanding that regiment, was now directed to leave one company for the protection of our camp a little to the north of the station, and take the balance of the Second Iowa, with the battalion in Booneville except two sabre companies, and form the whole in rear of Captain Campbell, to protect his flanks and support him by a charge should the enemy break his dismounted line.

While these preparations were being made, the Confederates attempted to drive Campbell from his position by a direct attack through an open field. In this they failed, however, for our men, reserving their fire until the enemy came within about thirty yards, then opened on him with such a shower of bullets from our Colt's rifles that it soon became too hot for him, and he was repulsed with considerable loss. Foiled in this move, Chalmers hesitated to attack again in front, but began overlapping both flanks of Campbell's line by force of numbers, compelling Campbell to retire toward a strong position I had selected in his rear for a line on which to make our main resistance. As soon as the enemy saw this withdrawing he again charged in front, but was again as gallantly repelled as in the first assault, although the encounter was for a short time so desperate as to have the character of a hand-to-hand conflict, several groups of friend and foe using on each other the butts of their guns. At this juncture the timely arrival of Colonel Hatch with the Second Iowa gave a breathing-spell to Campbell, and made the Confederates so chary of further direct attacks that he was enabled to retire; and at the same time I found opportunity to make disposition of the reinforcement to the best advantage possible, placing the Second Iowa on the left of the new line and strengthening Campbell on its right with all the men available.

In view of his numbers, the enemy soon regained confidence in his ability to overcome us, and in a little while again began his flanking movements, his right passing around my left flank some distance, and approaching our camp and transportation, which I had forbidden to be moved out to the rear. Fearing that he would envelop us and capture the camp and transportation, I determined to take the offensive. Remembering a circuitous wood road that I had become familiar with while making the map heretofore mentioned, I concluded that the most effective plan would be to pass a small column around the enemy's left, by way of this road, and strike his rear by a mounted charge simultaneously with an advance of our main line on his front. I knew that the attack in rear would be a most hazardous undertaking, but in the face of such odds as the enemy had the condition of affairs was most critical, and could be relieved, only by a bold and radical change in our tactics; so I at once selected four sabre companies, two from the Second Michigan and two from the Second Iowa, and placing Captain Alger, of the former regiment, in command of them, I informed him that I expected of them the quick and desperate work that is usually imposed on a forlorn hope.

To carry out the purpose now in view, I instructed Captain Alger to follow the wood road as it led around the left of the enemy's advancing forces, to a point where 'it joined the Blackland road, about three miles from Booneville, and directed him, upon reaching the Blackland road, to turn up it immediately, and charge the rear of the enemy's line. Under no circumstances was he to deploy the battalion, but charge in column right through whatever he came upon, and report to me in front of Booneville, if at all possible for him to get there. If he failed to break through the enemy's line, he was to go ahead as far as he could, and then if any of his men were left, and he was able to retreat, he was to do so by the same route he had taken on his way out. To conduct him on this perilous service I sent along a thin, sallow, tawny-haired Mississippian named Beene, whom I had employed as a guide and scout a few days before, on account of his intimate knowledge of the roads, from the public thoroughfares down to the insignificant by-paths of the neighboring swamps. With such guidance I felt sure that the column would get to the desired point without delay, for there was no danger of its being lost or misled by taking any of the many by-roads which traversed the dense forests through which it would be obliged to pass. I also informed Alger that I should take the reserve and join the main line in front of Booneville for the purpose of making an advance of my whole force, and that as a signal he must have his men cheer loudly when he struck the enemy's rear, in order that my attack might be simultaneous with his.

I gave him one hour to go around and come back through the enemy, and when he started I moved to the front with the balance of the reserve, to put everything I had into the fight. This meant an inestimable advantage to the enemy in case of our defeat, but our own safety demanded the hazard. All along our attenuated line the fighting was now sharp, and the enemy's firing indicated such numerical strength that fear of disaster to Alger increased my anxiety terribly as the time set for his cheering arrived and no sound of it was heard.

Relying, however, on the fact that Beene's knowledge of the roads would prevent his being led astray, and confident of Alger's determination to accomplish the purpose for which he set out, as soon as the hour was up I ordered my whole line forward. Fortunately, just as this moment a locomotive and two cars loaded with grain for my horses ran into Booneville from Corinth. I say fortunately, because it was well known throughout the command that in the morning, when I first discovered the large numbers of the enemy, I had called for assistance; and my troops, now thinking that reinforcements had arrived by rail from Rienzi, where a division of infantry was encamped, and inspired by this belief, advanced with renewed confidence and wild cheering. Meantime I had the engineer of the locomotive blow his whistle loudly, so that the enemy might also learn that a train had come; and from the fact that in a few moments he began to give way before our small force, I thought that this strategem had some effect. Soon his men broke, and ran in the utmost disorder over the country in every direction. I found later, however, that his precipitous retreat was due to the pressure on his left from the Second

Iowa, in concert with the front attack of the Second Michigan, and the demoralization wrought in his rear by Alger, who had almost entirely accomplished the purpose of his expedition, though he had failed to come through, or so near that I could hear the signal agreed upon before leaving Booneville.

After Alger had reached and turned up the Blackland road, the first thing he came across was the Confederate headquarters; the officers and orderlies about which he captured and sent back some distance to a farm-house. Continuing on a gallop, he soon struck the rear of the enemy's line, but was unable to get through; nor did he get near enough for me to hear his cheering; but as he had made the distance he was to travel in the time allotted, his attack and mine were almost coincident, and the enemy, stampeded by the charges in front and rear, fled toward Blackland, with little or no attempt to capture Alger's command, which might readily have been done. Alger's troopers soon rejoined me at Booneville, minus many hats, having returned by their original route. They had sustained little loss except a few men wounded and a few temporarily missing. Among these was Alger himself, who was dragged from his saddle by the limb of a tree that, in the excitement of the charge, he was unable to flank. The missing had been dismounted in one way or another, and run over by the enemy in his flight; but they all turned up later, none the worse except for a few scratches and bruises.

My effective strength in this fight was 827 all told, and Alger's command comprised ninety officers and men. Chalmers's force was composed of six regiments and two battalions, and though I have been unable to find any returns from which to verify his actual numbers, yet, from the statements of prisoners and from information obtained from citizens along his line of march, it is safe to say that he had in the action not less than five-thousand men. Our casualties were not many—forty-one in all. His loss in killed and wounded was considerable, his most severely wounded—forty men—falling into our hands, having been left at farm-houses in the vicinity of the battlefield.

The victory in the face of such odds was most gratifying, and as it justified my disinclination—in fact, refusal—to retire from Booneville without fighting (for the purpose of saving my transportation, as directed by superior authority when I applied in the morning for reinforcements), it was to me particularly grateful. It was also very valuable in, view of the fact that it increased the confidence between the officers and men of my brigade and me, and gave us for the balance of the month not only comparative rest, but entire immunity from the dangers of a renewed effort to gobble my isolated outpost. In addition to all this, commendation from my immediate superiors was promptly tendered through oral and written congratulations; and their satisfaction at the result of the battle took definite form a few days later, in the following application for my promotion, when, by an expedition to Ripley, Miss., most valuable information as to the enemy's location and plans was captured:

"HEADQUARTERS ARMY OF THE MISSISSIPPI,
"JULY 30, 1862.—3.05 P. M.
"MAJOR-GENERAL HALLECK,
"Washington, D. C.

"Brigadiers scarce; good ones scarce. Asboth goes on the month's leave you gave him ten months since; Granger has temporary command. The undersigned respectfully beg that you will obtain the promotion of Sheridan. He is worth his weight in gold. His Ripley expedition has brought us captured letters of immense value, as well as prisoners, showing the rebel plans and dispositions, as you will learn from District Commander.

"W. S. ROSECRANS, Brigadier-General.
"C. C. SULLIVAN,   "   "
"G. GRANGER,   "   "
"W. L. ELLIOTT,   "   "
"A. ASBOTH,   "   "   "

CHAPTER X.

IN CAMP NEAR RIENZI—GENERAL GRANGER—A VALUABLE CAPTURE AT RIPLEY— RAIDING A CORNFIELD—REPULSING AN ATTACK—PRESENTED WITH THE BLACK HORSE "RIENZI"—MEETING GENERAL GRANT—APPOINTED A BRIGADIER-GENERAL.

After the battle of Booneville, it was decided by General Rosecrans, on the advice of General Granger, that my position at Booneville was too much exposed, despite the fact that late on the evening of the fight my force had been increased by the addition of, a battery of four guns and two companies of infantry, and by the Third Michigan Cavalry, commanded by Colonel John K. Mizner; so I was directed to withdraw from my post and go into camp near Rienzi, Mississippi, where I could equally well cover the roads in front of the army, and also be near General Asboth's division of infantry, which occupied a line in rear of the town. This section of country, being higher and more rolling than that in the neighborhood of Booneville, had many advantages in the way of better camping-grounds, better grazing and the like, but I moved with reluctance, because I feared that my proximity to Asboth would diminish to a certain extent my independence of command.

General Asboth was a tall, spare, handsome man, with gray mustache and a fierce look. He was an educated soldier, of unquestioned courage, but the responsibilities of outpost duty bore rather heavily on him, and he kept all hands in a state of constant worry in anticipation of imaginary attacks. His ideas of discipline were not very rigid either, and as by this time there had been introduced into my brigade some better methods than those obtaining when it first fell to my command, I feared the effect should he, have any control over it, or meddle with its internal affairs. However, there was nothing to do but to move to the place designated, but General Granger, who still commanded the cavalry division to which the brigade belonged, so arranged matters with General Rosecrans, who had succeeded to the command of the Army of the Mississippi, that my independence was to be undisturbed, except in case of a general attack by the enemy.

We went into camp near Rienzi, July 22, sending back to the general field-hospital at Tuscumbia Springs all our sick—a considerable number—stricken down by the malarial influences around Booneville. In a few days the fine grazing arid abundance of grain for our exhausted horses brought about their recuperation; and the many large open fields in the vicinity gave opportunity for drills and parades, which were much needed. I turned my attention to those disciplinary measures which, on account of active work in the field, had been necessarily neglected since the brigade had arrived at Pittsburg Landing, in April; and besides, we had been busy in collecting information by scouting parties and otherwise, in prosecution of the purpose for which we were covering the main army.

I kept up an almost daily correspondence with General Granger, concerning the, information obtained by scouts and reconnoitring parties, and he came often to Rienzi to see me in relation to this and other matters. Previously I had not had much personal association with Granger. While I was at Halleck's headquarters we met on one or two occasions, and the day I joined the Second Michigan at Farmington I saw him for a few moments, but, with such slight exception, our intercourse had been almost exclusively official. He had suggested my name, I was told, to Governor Blair, when the Governor was in search of an officer of the regular army to appoint to the colonelcy of the Second Michigan Cavalry, but his recommendation must have been mainly based on the favorable opinions he had heard expressed by General Halleck and by some of the officers of his staff, rather than from any personal knowledge of my capacity. Of course I was very grateful for this, but some of his characteristics did not impress me favorably, and I sometimes wished the distance between our camps greater. His most serious failing was an uncontrollable propensity to interfere with and direct the minor matters relating to the command, the details for which those under him were alone responsible. Ill-judged meddling in this respect often led to differences between us, only temporary it is true, but most harassing to the subordinate, since I was compelled by the circumstances of the situation not only invariably to yield my own judgment, but many a time had to play peacemaker—smoothing down ruffled feelings, that I knew had been excited by Granger's freaky and spasmodic efforts to correct personally some trifling fault that ought to have been left to a regimental or company commander to remedy. Yet with all these small blemishes Granger had many good qualities, and his big heart was so full of generous impulses and good motives as to far outbalance his short-comings; and not-withstanding the friction and occasional acerbity of our official intercourse, we maintained friendly relations till his death.

In pursuance of the fatal mistake made by dispersing Halleck's forces after the fall of Corinth, General Don Carlos Buell's Army of the Ohio had been started some time before on its march eastward toward Chattanooga; and as this movement would be followed of course by a manoeuvre on the part of the enemy, now at Tupelo under General Braxton Bragg, either to meet Buell or frustrate his designs by some counter-operation, I was expected to furnish, by scouting and all other means available, information as to what was going on within the Confederate lines. To do the work required, necessitated an increase of my command, and the Seventh Kansas Cavalry was therefore added to it, and my picket-line extended so as to cover from Jacinto southwesterly to a point midway between Rienzi and Booneville, and then northwesterly to the Hatchie River. Skirmishes between outposts on this line were of frequent occurrence, with small results to either side, but they were somewhat annoying, particularly in the direction of Ripley, where the enemy maintained a considerable outpost. Deciding to cripple if not capture this outpost, on the evening of July 27, I sent out an expedition under Colonel Hatch, which drove the enemy from the town of Ripley and took a few prisoners, but the most valuable prize was in the shape of a package of thirty-two private letters, the partial reading of which disclosed to me the positive transfer from Mississippi of most of Bragg's army, for the purpose of counteracting Buell's operations in northern Alabama and East Tennessee. This decisive evidence was of the utmost importance, and without taking time to read all the letters, I forwarded them to General Granger July 28, in a despatch which stated: "I deem it necessary to send them at once; the enemy is moving in large force on Chattanooga." Other than this the results of the expedition were few; and the enemy, having fled from Ripley with but slight resistance, accompanied by almost all the inhabitants, re-occupied the place next day after our people had quitted it, and resumed in due time his annoying attacks on our outposts, both sides trying to achieve something whenever occasion offered.

The prevalence of a severe drought had resulted in drying up many of the streams within the enemy's lines, and, in consequence, he was obliged to shift his camps often, and send his beef-cattle and mules near his outposts for water. My scouts kept me well posted in regard to the movements of both camps and herds; and a favorable opportunity presenting itself, I sent an expedition on August 14 to gather in some animals located on Twenty-Mile Creek, a stream always supplied with water from a source of never-failing, springs. Our side met with complete success in this instance, and when the expedition returned, we were all made happy by an abundance of fresh beef, and by some two hundred captured mules, that we thus added to our trains at a time when draft animals were much needed.

Rations for the men were now supplied in fair quantities, and the only thing required to make us wholly contented was plenty of grain for our animals. Because of the large number of troops then in West Tennessee and about Corinth, the indifferent railroad leading down from Columbus, Ky., was taxed to its utmost capacity to transport supplies. The quantity of grain received at Corinth from the north was therefore limited, and before reaching the different outposts, by passing through intermediate depots of supply, it had dwindled to insignificance. I had hopes, however, that this condition of things might be ameliorated before long by gathering a good supply of corn that was ripening in the neighborhood, and would soon, I thought, be sufficiently hard to feed to my animals. Not far from my headquarters there was a particularly fine field, which, with this end in view, I had carefully protected through the milky stage, to the evident disappointment of both Asboth's men and mine. They bore the prohibition well while it affected only themselves, but the trial was too great when it came to denying their horses; and men whose discipline kept faith with my guards during the roasting-ear period now fell from grace. Their horses were growing thin, and few could withstand the mute appeals of their suffering pets; so at night the corn, because of individual foraging, kept stealthily and steadily vanishing, until the field was soon fringed with only earless stalks. The disappearance was noticed, and the guard increased, but still the quantity of corn continued to grow less, the more honest troopers bemoaning the loss, and questioning the honor of those to whose safekeeping it had been entrusted. Finally, doubtless under the apprehension that through their irregularities the corn would all disappear and find its way to the horses in accordance with the stealthy enterprise of their owners, a general raid was made on the field in broad daylight, and though the guard drove off the marauders, I must admit that its efforts to keep them back were so unsuccessful that my hopes for an equal distribution of the crop were quickly blasted. One look at the field told that it had been swept clean of its grain. Of course a great row occurred as to who was to blame, and many arrests and trials took place, but there had been such an interchanging of cap numbers and other insignia that it was next to impossible to identify the guilty, and so much crimination and acrimony grew out of the affair that it was deemed best to drop the whole matter.

On August 27 about half of the command was absent reconnoitring, I having sent it south toward Tupelo, in the hope of obtaining some definite information regarding a movement to Holly Springs of the remainder of the Confederate army, under General Price, when about mid-day I was suddenly aroused by excited cries and sounds of firing, and I saw in a moment that the enemy was in my camp. He had come in on my right flank from the direction of the Hatchie River, pell-mell with our picket-post stationed about three miles out on the Ripley road. The whole force of the enemy comprised about eight hundred, but only his advance entered with my pickets, whom he had charged and badly stampeded, without, on their part, the pretense of a fight in behalf of those whom it was their duty to protect until proper dispositions for defense could be made. The day was excessively hot, one of those sultry debilitating days that had caused the suspending of all military exercises; and as most of the men were lounging or sleeping in their tents, we were literally caught napping. The alarm spread instantly through the camp, and in a moment the command turned out for action, somewhat in deshabille it is true, but none the less effective, for every man had grabbed his rifle and cartridge-box at the first alarm. Aided by a few shots from Captain Henry Hescock's battery, we soon drove the intruders from our camp in about the same disorder in which they had broken in on us. By this time Colonel Hatch and Colonel Albert L. Lee had mounted two battalions each, and I moved them out at a lively pace in pursuit, followed by a section of the battery. No halt was called till we came upon the enemy's main body, under Colonel Faulkner, drawn up in line of battle near Newland's store. Opening on him with the two pieces of artillery, I hurriedly formed line confronting him, and quickly and with but little resistance drove him in confusion from the field. The sudden turning of the tables dismayed Faulkner's men, and panic seizing them, they threw away every loose article of arms or clothing of which they could dismember themselves, and ran in the wildest disorder in a mad effort to escape. As the chase went on the panic increased, the clouds of dust from the road causing an intermingling of friend and foe. In a little while the affair grew most ludicrous, Faulkner's hatless and coatless men taking to the woods in such dispersed order and so demoralized that a good many prisoners were secured, and those of the enemy who escaped were hunted until dark. When the recall was sounded, our men came in loaded down with plunder in the shape of hats, haversacks, blankets, pistols, and shotguns, in a quantity which amply repaid for the surprise of the morning, but did not excuse the delinquent commander of our picket-guard, who a few days later was brought to a realizing sense of his duty by a court-martial.

Shortly after this affair Captain Archibald P. Campbell, of the Second Michigan Cavalry, presented me with the black horse called Rienzi, since made historical from having been ridden by me in many battles, conspicuously in the ride from Winchester to Cedar Creek, which has been celebrated in the poem by T. Buchanan Read. This horse was of Morgan stock, and then about three years old. He was jet black, excepting three white feet, sixteen hands high, and strongly built, with great powers of endurance. He was so active that he could cover with ease five miles an hour at his natural walking gait. The gelding had been ridden very seldom; in fact, Campbell had been unaccustomed to riding till the war broke out, and, I think, felt some disinclination to mount the fiery colt. Campbell had an affection for him, however, that never waned, and would often come to my headquarters to see his favorite, the colt being cared for there by the regimental farrier, an old man named John Ashley, who had taken him in charge when leaving Michigan, and had been his groom ever since. Seeing that I liked the horse—I had ridden him on several occasions—Campbell presented him to me on one of these visits, and from that time till the close of the war I rode him almost continuously, in every campaign and battle in which I took part, without once finding him overcome by fatigue, though on many occasions his strength was severely tested by long marches and short rations. I never observed in him any vicious habit; a nervousness and restlessness and switch of the tail, when everything about him was in repose, being the only indication that he might be untrustworthy. No one but a novice could be deceived by this, however, for the intelligence evinced in every feature, and his thoroughbred appearance, were so striking that any person accustomed to horses could not misunderstand such a noble animal. But Campbell thought otherwise, at least when the horse was to a certain degree yet untrained, and could not be persuaded to ride him; indeed, for more than a year after he was given to me, Campbell still retained suspicions of his viciousness, though, along with this mistrust, an undiminished affection. Although he was several times wounded, this horse escaped death in action; and living to a ripe old age, died in 1878, attended to the last with all the care and surrounded with every comfort due the faithful service he had rendered.

In moving from Corinth east toward Chattanooga, General Buell's army was much delayed by the requirement that he should repair the Memphis and Charleston railroad as he progressed. The work of repair obliged him to march very slowly, and was of but little use when done, for guerrillas and other bands of Confederates destroyed the road again as soon as he had passed on. But worst of all, the time thus consumed gave General Bragg the opportunity to reorganize and increase his army to such an extent that he was able to contest the possession of Middle Tennessee and Kentucky. Consequently, the movement of this army through Tennessee and Kentucky toward the Ohio River—its objective points being Louisville and Cincinnati—was now well defined, and had already rendered abortive General Buell's designs on Chattanooga and East Tennessee. Therefore extraordinary efforts on the part of the Government became necessary, and the concentration of National troops at Louisville and Cincinnati to meet the contingency of Bragg's reaching those points was an obvious requirement. These troops were drawn from all sections in the West where it was thought they could be spared, and among others I was ordered to conduct thither—to Louisville or Cincinnati, as subsequent developments might demand—my regiment, Hescock's battery, the Second and Fifteenth Missouri, and the Thirty-sixth and Forty-fourth Illinois regiments of infantry, known as the "Pea Ridge Brigade." With this column I marched back to Corinth on the 6th of September, 1862, for the purpose of getting railroad transportation to Columbus, Kentucky.

At Corinth I met General Grant, who by this time had been reestablished in favor and command somewhat, General Halleck having departed for Washington to assume command of the army as General-in-Chief. Before and during the activity which followed his reinstatement, General Grant had become familiar with my services through the transmission to Washington of information I had furnished concerning the enemy's movements, and by reading reports of my fights and skirmishes in front, and he was loth to let me go. Indeed, he expressed surprise at seeing me in

Corinth, and said he had not expected me to go; he also plainly showed that he was much hurt at the inconsiderate way in which his command was being depleted. Since I was of the opinion that the chief field of usefulness and opportunity was opening up in Kentucky, I did not wish him to retain me, which he might have done, and I impressed him with my conviction, somewhat emphatically, I fear. Our conversation ended with my wish gratified. I afterward learned that General Granger, whom General Grant did not fancy, had suggested that I should take to Cincinnati the main portion of Granger's command—the Pea Ridge Brigade—as well as the Second Michigan Cavalry, of which I was still colonel. We started that night, going by rail over the Mobile and Ohio road to Columbus, Ky., where we embarked on steamboats awaiting us. These boats were five in number, and making one of them my flag-ship, expecting that we might come upon certain batteries reported to be located upon the Kentucky shore of the Ohio, I directed the rest to follow my lead. Just before reaching Caseyville, the captain of a tin-clad gunboat that was patrolling the river brought me the information that the enemy was in strong force at Caseyville, and expressed a fear that my fleet could not pass his batteries. Accepting the information as correct, I concluded to capture the place before trying to pass up the river. Pushing in to the bank as we neared the town, I got the troops ashore and moved on Caseyville, in the expectation of a bloody fight, but was agreeably surprised upon reaching the outskirts of the village by an outpouring of its inhabitants—men, women, and children—carrying the Stars and Stripes, and making the most loyal professions. Similar demonstrations of loyalty had been made to the panic-stricken captain of the gunboat when he passed down the river, but he did not stay to ascertain their character, neither by landing nor by inquiry, for he assumed that on the Kentucky bank of the river there could be no loyalty. The result mortified the captain intensely; and deeming his convoy of little further use, he steamed toward Cairo in quest of other imaginary batteries, while I re-embarked at Caseyville, and continued up the Ohio undisturbed. About three miles below Cincinnati I received instructions to halt, and next day I was ordered by Major-General H. G. Wright to take my troops back to Louisville, and there assume command of the Pea Ridge Brigade, composed of the Second and Fifteenth Missouri, Thirty-sixth and Forty-fourth Illinois infantry, and of such other regiments as might be sent me in advance of the arrival of General Buell's army. When I reached Louisville I reported to Major-General William Nelson, who was sick, and who received me as he lay in bed. He asked me why I did not wear the shoulder-straps of my rank. I answered that I was the colonel of the Second Michigan cavalry, and had on my appropriate shoulder-straps. He replied that I was a brigadier-general for the Booneville fight, July 1, and that I should wear the shoulder-straps of that grade. I returned to my command and put it in camp; and as I had no reluctance to wearing the shoulder-straps of a brigadier-general, I was not long in procuring a pair, particularly as I was fortified next day by receiving from Washington official information of my appointment as a brigadier-general, to date from July 1, 1862, the day of the battle of Booneville

CHAPTER XI.
GOOD ADVICE FROM GENERAL NELSON—HIS TRAGIC DEATH—PUTTING LOUISVILLE IN A STATE OF DEFENSE—ASSIGNED TO THE COMMAND OF THE ELEVENTH DIVISION—CAPTURE OF CHAPLIN HEIGHTS—BATTLE OF PERRYVILLE—REPORTED AMONG THE KILLED—A THRILLING INCIDENT—GENERAL BUELL RELIEVED BY GENERAL ROSECRANS.

I reported to Major-General Nelson at the Galt House in Louisville, September 14, 1862, who greeted me in the bluff and hearty fashion of a sailor—for he had been in the navy till the breaking out of the war. The new responsibilities that were now to fall upon me by virtue of increased rank caused in my mind an uneasiness which, I think, Nelson observed at the interview, and he allayed it by giving me much good advice, and most valuable information in regard to affairs in Kentucky, telling me also that he intended I should retain in my command the Pea Ridge Brigade and Hescock's battery. This latter assurance relieved me greatly, for I feared the loss of these troops in the general redistribution which I knew must soon take place; and being familiar with their valuable service in Missouri, and having brought them up from Mississippi, I hoped they would continue with me. He directed me to take position just below the city with the Pea Ridge Brigade, Hescock's battery, and the Second Michigan Cavalry, informing me, at the same time, that some of the new regiments, then arriving under a recent call of the President for volunteers, would also be assigned to my command. Shortly after the interview eight new regiments and an additional battery joined me, thus making good his promise of more troops.

A few days later came Nelson's tragic end, shocking the whole country. Those of us in camp outside of the city were startled on the morning of September 29 by the news that General Jefferson C. Davis, of the Union Army, had shot General Nelson at the Galt House, and the wildest rumors in regard to the occurrence came thick and fast; one to the effect that Nelson was dead, another having it that he was living and had killed Davis, and still others reflecting on the loyalty of both, it being supposed by the general public at first that the difficulty between the two men had grown out of some political rather than official or personal differences. When the news came, I rode into the city to the Galt House to learn the particulars, reaching there about 10 o'clock in the forenoon. Here I learned that Nelson had been shot by Davis about two hours before, at the foot of the main stairway leading from the corridor just beyond the office to the second floor, and that Nelson was already dead. It was almost as difficult to get reliable particulars of the matter at the hotel as it had been in my camp, but I gathered that the two men had met first at an early hour near the counter of the hotel office, and that an altercation which had begun several days before in relation to something official was renewed by Davis, who, attempting to speak to Nelson in regard to the subject-matter of their previous dispute, was met by an insulting refusal to listen. It now appears that when Nelson made this offensive remark, Davis threw a small paper ball that he was nervously rolling between his fingers into Nelson's face, and that this insult was returned by Nelson slapping Davis (Killed by a Brother Soldier.—Gen. J. B. Fry.) in the face. But at the time, exactly what had taken place just before the shooting was shrouded in mystery by a hundred conflicting stories, the principal and most credited of which was that Davis had demanded from Nelson an apology for language used in the original altercation, and that Nelson's refusal was accompanied by a slap in the face, at the same moment denouncing Davis as a coward. However this may be, Nelson, after slapping Davis, moved toward the corridor, from which a stairway led to the second floor, and just as he was about to ascend, Davis fired with a pistol that he had obtained from some one near by after the blow had been struck. The ball entered Nelson's breast just above the heart, but his great strength enabled him to ascend the stairway notwithstanding the mortal character of the wound, and he did not fall till he reached the corridor on the second floor. He died about half an hour later. The tragedy cast a deep gloom over all who knew the men, for they both had many warm personal friends; and affairs at

Louisville had hardly recovered as yet from the confused and discouraging condition which preceded the arrival of General Buell's army. General Buell reported the killing of Nelson to the authorities at Washington, and recommended the trial of Davis by court-martial, but no proceedings were ever instituted against him in either a civil or military court, so to this day it has not been determined judicially who was the aggressor. Some months later Davis was assigned to the command of a division in Buell's army after that officer had been relieved from its command.

Two Confederate armies, under General Kirby Smith and General Braxton Bragg, had penetrated into Kentucky, the one under Smith by the way of Cumberland Gap, the other and main army under Bragg by way of the Sequatche Valley, Glasgow, and Mumfordsville. Glasgow was captured by the enemy on the 17th of September, and as the expectation was that Buell would reach the place in time to save the town, its loss created considerable alarm in the North, for fears were now entertained that Bragg would strike Louisville and capture the city before Buell could arrive on the ground. It became necessary therefore to put Louisville in a state of defense, and after the cordon of principal works had been indicated, my troops threw up in one night a heavy line of rifle-pits south of the city, from the Bardstown pike to the river. The apprehended attack by Bragg never came, however, for in the race that was then going on between him and Buell on parallel roads, the Army of the Ohio outmarched the Confederates, its advance arriving at Louisville September 25.

General Buell immediately set about reorganizing the whole force, and on September 29 issued an order designating the troops under my command as the Eleventh Division, Army of the Ohio, and assigning Brigadier-General J. T. Boyle to command the division, and me to command one of its brigades. To this I could not object, of course, for I was a brigadier-general of very recent date, and could hardly expect more than a brigade. I had learned, however, that at least one officer to whom a high command had been given—a corps—had not yet been appointed a general officer by the President, and I considered it somewhat unfair that I should be relegated to a brigade, while men who held no commissions at all were being made chiefs of corps and divisions; so I sought an interview with General Buell's chief-of-staff, Colonel Fry, and, while not questioning Buell's good intentions nor his pure motives, insisted that my rights in the matter should be recognized. That same evening I was assigned to the command of the Eleventh Division, and began preparing it at once for a forward movement, which I knew must soon take place in the resumption of offensive operations by the Army of the Ohio.

During the interval from September 25 till October 1 there was among the officers much criticism of General Buell's management of the recent campaign, which had resulted in his retirement to Louisville; and he was particularly censured by many for not offering battle to General Bragg while the two armies were marching parallel to each other, and so near that an engagement could have been brought on at any one of several points—notably so at Glasgow, Kentucky, if there had been a desire to join issue. It was asserted, and by many conceded, that General Buell had a sufficient force to risk a fight. He was much blamed for the loss of Mumfordsville also. The capture of this point, with its garrison, gave Bragg an advantage in the race toward the Ohio River, which odds would most likely have ensured the fall of Louisville had they been used with the same energy and skill that the Confederate commander displayed from Chattanooga to Glasgow; but something always diverted General Bragg at the supreme moment, and he failed to utilize the chances falling to him at this time, for, deflecting his march to the north toward Bardstown, he left open to Buell the direct road to Louisville by way of Elizabethtown.

At Bardstown Bragg's army was halted while he endeavored to establish a Confederate government in Kentucky by arranging for the installation of a provisional governor at Lexington. Bragg had been assured that the presence of a Confederate army in Kentucky would so encourage the secession element that the whole State could be forced into the rebellion and his army thereby largely increased; but he had been considerably misled, for he now found that though much latent sympathy existed for his cause, yet as far as giving active aid was concerned, the enthusiasm exhibited by the secessionists of Kentucky in the first year of the war was now replaced by apathy, or at best by lukewarmness. So the time thus spent in political machinations was wholly lost to Bragg; and so little reinforcement was added to his army that it may be said that the recruits gained were not enough to supply the deficiencies resulting from the recent toilsome marches of the campaign.

In the meanwhile Buell had arrived at Louisville, system had been substituted for the chaos which had previously obtained there, and orders were issued for an advance upon the enemy with the purpose of attacking and the hope of destroying him within the limits of the "blue grass" region, and, failing in that, to drive him from Kentucky. The army moved October 1, 1862, and my division, now a part of the Third Corps, commanded by General C. C. Gilbert, marched directly on Bardstown, where it was thought the enemy would make a stand, but Bragg's troops retreated toward Perryville, only resisting sufficiently to enable the forces of General Kirby Smith to be drawn in closer—they having begun a concentration at Frankfort—so they could be used in a combined attack on Louisville as soon as the Confederate commander's political projects were perfected.

Much time was consumed by Buell's army in its march on Perryville, but we finally neared it on the evening of October 7. During the day, Brigadier-General Robert B. Mitchell's division of Gilbert's corps was in the advance on the Springfield pike, but as the enemy developed that he was in strong force on the opposite side of a small stream called Doctor's Creek, a tributary of Chaplin River, my division was brought up and passed to the front. It was very difficult to obtain water in this section of Kentucky, as a drought had prevailed for many weeks, and the troops were suffering so for water that it became absolutely necessary that we should gain possession of Doctor's Creek in order to relieve their distress. Consequently General Gilbert, during the night, directed me to push beyond Doctor's Creek early the next morning. At daylight on the 8th I moved out Colonel Dan McCook's brigade and Barnett's battery for the purpose, but after we had crossed the creek with some slight skirmishing, I found that we could not hold the ground unless we carried and occupied a range of hills, called Chaplin Heights, in front of Chaplin River. As this would project my command in the direction of Perryville considerably beyond the troops that were on either flank, I brought up Laiboldt's brigade and Hescock's battery to strengthen Colonel McCook. Putting both brigades into line we quickly carried the Heights, much to the surprise of the enemy, I think, for he did not hold on to the valuable ground as strongly as he should have done. This success not only ensured us a good supply of water, but also, later in the day, had an important bearing in the battle of Perryville. After taking the Heights, I brought up the rest of my division and intrenched, without much difficulty, by throwing up a strong line of rifle-pits, although the enemy's sharpshooters annoyed us enough to make me order Laiboldt's brigade to drive them in on the main body. This was successfully done in a few minutes, but in pushing them back to Chaplin River, we discovered the Confederates forming a line of battle on the opposite bank, with the apparent purpose of an attack in force, so I withdrew the brigade to our intrenchments on the crest and there awaited the assault.

While this skirmishing was going on, General Gilbert—the corps commander—whose headquarters were located on a hill about a mile distant to the rear, kept sending me messages by signal not to bring on an engagement. I replied to each message that I was not bringing on an engagement, but that the enemy evidently intended to do so, and that I believed I should shortly be attacked. Soon after returning to the crest and getting snugly fixed in the rifle-pits, my attention was called to our left, the high ground we occupied affording me in that direction an unobstructed view. I then saw General A. McD. McCook's corps—the First-advancing toward Chaplin River by the Mackville road, apparently unconscious that the Confederates were present in force behind the stream. I tried by the use of signal flags to get information of the situation to these troops, but my efforts failed, and the leading regiments seemed to approach the river indifferently prepared to meet the sudden attack that speedily followed, delivered as it was from the chosen position of the enemy. The fury of the Confederate assault soon halted this advance force, and in a short time threw it into confusion, pushed it back a considerable distance, and ultimately inflicted upon it such loss of men and guns as to seriously cripple McCook's corps, and prevent for the whole day further offensive movement on his part, though he stoutly resisted the enemy's assaults until 4 o'clock in the afternoon.

Seeing McCook so fiercely attacked, in order to aid him I advanced Hescock's battery, supported by six regiments, to a very good position in front of a belt of timber on my extreme left, where an enfilading fire could be opened on that portion of the enemy attacking the right of the First Corps, and also on his batteries across Chaplin River. But at this juncture he placed two batteries on my right and began to mass troops behind them, and General Gilbert, fearing that my intrenched position on the heights might be carried, directed me to withdraw Hescock and his supports and return them to the pits. My recall was opportune, for I had no sooner got back to my original line than the Confederates attacked me furiously, advancing almost to my intrenchments, notwithstanding that a large part of the ground over which they had to move was swept by a heavy fire of canister from both my batteries. Before they had quite reached us, however, our telling fire made them recoil, and as they fell back, I directed an advance of my whole division, bringing up my reserve regiments to occupy the crest of the hills; Colonel William P. Carlin's brigade of Mitchell's division meanwhile moving forward on my right to cover that flank. This advance pressed the enemy to Perryville, but he retired in such good order that we gained nothing but some favorable ground that enabled me to establish my batteries in positions where they could again turn their attention to the Confederates in front of McCook, whose critical condition was shortly after relieved, however, by a united pressure of Gilbert's corps against the flank of McCook's assailants, compelling them to retire behind Chaplin River.

The battle virtually ended about 4 o'clock in the afternoon, though more or less desultory firing continued until dark. Considering the severity of the engagement on McCook's front, and the reverses that had befallen him, I question if, from that part of the line, much could have been done toward retrieving the blunders of the day, but it did seem to me that, had the commander of the army been able to be present on the field, he could have taken advantage of Bragg's final repulse, and there would have remained in our hands more than the barren field. But no attempt was made to do anything more till next morning, and then we secured little except the enemy's killed and most severely wounded.

The operations of my division during the engagement pleased. General Gilbert very much, and he informed me that he would relax a rigidly enforced order which General Buell had issued some days before, sufficiently to permit my trains to come to the front and supply my almost starving troops with rations. The order in question was one of those issued, doubtless with a good intent, to secure generally the safety of our trains, but General Gilbert was not elastic, and on the march he had construed the order so illiberally that it was next to impossible to supply the men with food, and they were particularly short in this respect on the eve of the battle. I had then endeavored to persuade him to modify his iron-clad interpretation of the order, but without effect, and the only wagons we could bring up from the general parks in rear were ambulances and those containing ammunition. So to gain access to our trains was a great boon, and at that moment a more welcome result than would have been a complete victory minus this concession.

When the battle ceased General Gilbert asked me to join him at Buell's headquarters, which were a considerable distance to the rear, so after making some dispositions for the evening I proceeded there as requested. I arrived just as Buell was about to sit down to his supper, and noticing that he was lame, then learned that he had been severely injured by a recent fall from his horse. He kindly invited me to join him at the table, an invitation which I accepted with alacrity, enjoying the meal with a relish known only to a very-hungry man, for I had eaten nothing since morning. Of course the events of the day were the chief topic of discussion—as they were during my stay at headquarters—but the conversation indicated that what had occurred was not fully realized, and I returned to my troops impressed with the belief that General Buell and his staff-officers were unconscious of the magnitude of the battle that had just been fought.

It had been expected by Buell that he would fight the enemy on the 9th of October, but the Confederates disposed of that proposition by attacking us on the 8th, thus disarranging a tactical conception which, with our superior numbers, would doubtless have proved successful had it not been anticipated by an enterprising foe. During the battle on the 8th the Second Corps, under General Thomas L. Crittenden, accompanied by General George H. Thomas, lay idle the whole day for want of orders, although it was near enough to the field to take an active part in the fight; and, moreover, a large part of Gilbert's corps was unengaged during the pressure on McCook. Had these troops been put in on the enemy's left at any time after he assaulted McCook, success would have been beyond question; but there was no one on the ground authorized to take advantage of the situation, and the battle of Perryville remains in history an example of lost opportunities. This was due in some measure probably to General Buell's accident, but is mainly attributable to the fact that he did not clearly apprehend Bragg's aim, which was to gain time to withdraw behind Dick's River all the troops he had in Kentucky, for the Confederate general had no idea of risking the fate of his army on one general battle at a place or on a day to be chosen by the Union commander.

Considering the number of troops actually engaged, the losses to Buell were severe, amounting to something over five thousand in killed, wounded, and missing. Among the killed were two brigade commanders of much promise—General James S. Jackson and General William R. Terrill. McCook's corps lost twelve guns, some of which were recovered next day. The enemy's loss in killed and wounded we never learned, but it must have equalled ours; and about four thousand prisoners, consisting principally of sick and wounded, fell into our hands. In the first report of the battle sent North to the newspapers I was reported among the killed; but I was pleased to notice, when the papers reached us a few days later, that the error had been corrected before my obituary could be written.

The enemy retired from our front the night of the 8th, falling back on Harrodsburg to form a junction with Kirby Smith, and by taking this line of retreat opened to us the road to Danville and the chance for a direct march against his depot of supplies at Bryantsville. We did not take advantage of this opening, however, and late in the day—on the 9th—my division marched in pursuit, in the direction of Harrodsburg, which was the apex of a triangle having for its base a line from Perryville to Danville. The pursuit was slow, very slow, consuming the evening of the 9th and all of the 10th and 11th. By cutting across the triangle spoken of above, just south of the apex, I struck the Harrodsburg-Danville road, near Cave Springs, joining there Gilbert's left division, which had preceded me and marched through Harrodsburg. Here we again rested until the intention of the enemy could be divined, and we could learn on which side of Dick's River he would give us battle. A reconnoissance sent toward the Dickville crossing developed to a certainty that we should not have another engagement, however; for it disclosed the fact that Bragg's army had disappeared toward Camp Dick Robinson, leaving only a small rear-guard at Danville, which in turn quickly fled in the direction of Lancaster, after exchanging a few shots with Hescock's battery.

While this parting salute of deadly projectiles was going on, a little, daughter of Colonel William J. Landram, whose home was in Danville, came running out from his house and planted a small national flag on one of Hescock's guns. The patriotic act was so brave and touching that it thrilled all who witnessed the scene; and until the close of the war, when peace separated the surviving officers and men of the battery, that little flag was protected and cherished as a memento of the Perryville campaign.

Pursuit of the enemy was not continued in force beyond Crab Orchard, but some portions of the army kept at Bragg's heels until he crossed the Cumberland River, a part of his troops retiring to Tennessee by way of Cumberland Gap, but the major portion through Somerset. As the retreat of Bragg transferred the theatre of operations back to Tennessee, orders were now issued for a concentration of Buell's army at Bowling Green, with a view to marching it to Nashville, and my division moved to that point without noteworthy incident. I reached Bowling Green with a force much reduced by the losses sustained in the battle of Perryville and by sickness. I had started from Louisville on October 1 with twelve regiments of infantry—four old and eight new ones—and two batteries, but many poor fellows, overcome by fatigue, and diseases induced by the heat, dust, and drought of the season, had to be left at roadside hospitals. This was particularly the case with the new regiments, the men of which, much depressed by homesickness, and not yet inured to campaigning, fell easy victims to the hardships of war.

At Bowling Green General Buell was relieved, General W. S. Rosecrans succeeding him. The army as a whole did not manifest much regret at the change of commanders, for the campaign from Louisville on was looked upon generally as a lamentable failure, yet there were many who still had the utmost confidence in General Buell, and they repelled with some asperity the reflections cast upon him by his critics. These admirers held him blameless throughout for the blunders of the campaign, but the greater number laid every error at his door, and even went to the absurdity of challenging his loyalty in a mild way, but they particularly charged incompetency at Perryville, where McCook's corps was so badly crippled while nearly 30,000 Union troops were idle on the field, or within striking distance. With these it was no use to argue that Buell's accident stood in the way of his activity, nor that he did not know that the action had assumed the proportions of a battle. The physical disability was denied or contested, but even granting this, his detractors claimed that it did not excuse his ignorance of the true condition of the fight, and finally worsted his champions by pointing out that Bragg's retreat by way of Harrodsburg beyond Dick's River so jeopardized the Confederate army, that had a skillful and energetic advance of the Union troops been made, instead of wasting precious time in slow and unnecessary tactical manoeuvres, the enemy could have been destroyed before he could quit the State of Kentucky.

CHAPTER XII.
MOVING TO BOWLING GREEN—JAMES CARD, THE SCOUT AND GUIDE—GENERAL SILL—COLONEL SCHAEFER—COLONEL G. W. ROBERTS—MOVEMENT ON MURFREESBORO'—OPENING OF THE BATTLE OF STONE RIVER.

My division had moved from Crab Orchard to Bowling Green by easy marches, reaching this place November 1. General Rosecrans assumed command of the department October 30, at Louisville, and joined the army November 2. There had been much pressure brought to bear on General Buell to induce him to take measures looking to the occupancy of East Tennessee, and the clamor to this end from Washington still continued; but now that Bragg was south of the Cumberland River, in a position threatening Nashville, which was garrisoned by but a small force, it was apparent to every one at all conversant with the situation that a battle would have to be fought somewhere in Middle Tennessee. So, notwithstanding the pressure from Washington, the army was soon put in motion for Nashville, and when we arrived there my division went into camp north of the river, on a plateau just outside the little town of Edgefield, until the movements of the enemy should be further developed.

While in this camp, on the plantation of Mr. Hobson, there came to my headquarters one morning an East Tennessean named James Card, who offered to the Union cause his services in any capacity in which they might be made useful. This offer, and the relation of his personal history, were given with such sincerity of speech and manner that in a short time I became convinced of his honesty of purpose. He was a small, active, busy man, with a determined way about him, and his countenance indicated great intelligence. He gave minute information that was of inestimable value to me regarding East and Middle Tennessee and northern Georgia, for, with a view to the army's future movements, I was then making a study of the topography of this region, and posting myself as to Middle Tennessee, for all knew this would be the scene of active operations whenever the campaign was resumed. This man, like most of the East Tennesseans whom I had met, was intensely loyal and patriotic, and the interview led in a few days to his employment as a scout and guide, and subsequently to the engaging in the same capacity of two of his brothers, who were good men; but not quite as active nor so intelligent as he was. Card had been a colporter, having pedled books, especially religious tracts, over all Middle and East Tennessee and Georgia, assisted by his brothers at times, and was therefore thoroughly familiar with these regions, their roads and inhabitants. He also preached to country congregations occasionally, when ministers were scarce, and I have no doubt often performed the functions of family physician in the mountain district. Thus his opportunities were great; and the loyal people in every section of the country being well known to him and his brothers, the three began, at this time, a system of scouting and investigation which bore its first-fruits in specifically locating the different divisions of Bragg's army, with statements of their strength and condition, and all with so much accuracy that I thereafter felt reasonably sure that I could at all times procure such knowledge of the enemy's operations as would well equip me for any contingency that might arise.

By the middle of November the enemy, having assembled his forces in Middle Tennessee, showed considerable boldness, and it became necessary to rearrange the Union lines; so my troops were moved to the south side of the river, out on the Murfreesboro' pike, to Mill Creek, distant from Nashville about seven miles. While we were in camp on Mill Creek the army was reorganized, and General Joshua W. Sill, at his own request, was assigned to my division, and took command of Colonel Nicholas Greusel's brigade. My division became at the same time the Third Division, Right Wing, Fourteenth Army Corps, its three brigades of four regiments each being respectively commanded by General Sill, Colonel Frederick Schaefer and Colonel Dan McCook; but a few days later Colonel George W. Roberts's brigade, from the garrison at Nashville, was substituted for McCook's.

General Sill was a classmate of mine at the Military Academy, having graduated in 1853. On graduating he was appointed to the Ordnance Corps, and served in that department at various arsenals and ordnance depots throughout the country till early in 1861, when he resigned to accept a professorship of mathematics and civil engineering at the Brooklyn Collegiate and Polytechnic Institute. At the breaking out of the war he immediately tendered his services to the Government, and soon rose to the colonelcy of the Thirty-Third Ohio Volunteers, and afterward to the rank of brigadier-general. I knew him well, and was glad that he came to my division, though I was very loth to relieve Colonel Greusel, of the Thirty-Sixth Illinois, who had already indicated much military skill and bravery, and at the battle of Perryville had handled his men with the experience of a veteran. Sill's modesty and courage were exceeded only by a capacity that had already been demonstrated in many practical ways, and his untimely death, almost within a month of his joining me, abruptly closed a career which, had it been prolonged a little more, not only would have shed additional lustre on his name, but would have been of marked benefit to his country.

Colonel Schaefer, of the Second Missouri Infantry, had been absent on sick-leave during the Kentucky campaign, but about this date he returned to duty, and by seniority fell in command of the second brigade. He was of German birth, having come from Baden, where, prior to 1848, he had been a non-commissioned officer in the service of his State. He took part as an insurgent in the so-called revolution which occurred at Baden in that year, and, compelled to emigrate on the suppression of the insurrection, made his way to this country and settled in St. Louis. Here the breaking out of the war found him, and through the personal interest which General Sigel took in him he was commissioned a colonel of volunteers. He had had a pretty fair education, a taste for the military profession, and was of tall and slender build, all of which gave him a student-like appearance. He was extremely excitable and nervous when anticipating a crisis, but always calmed down to cool deliberation when the critical moment came. With such a man I could not be less than well satisfied, although the officer whom he replaced—Colonel Laiboldt— had performed efficient service and shown much capacity in the recent campaign.

Colonel G. W. Roberts, of the Forty-Second Illinois Infantry, also came to me in the reorganization. He was an ideal soldier both in mind and body. He was young, tall, handsome, brave, and dashing, and possessed a balance-wheel of such good judgment that in his sphere of action no occasion could arise from which he would not reap the best results. But he too was destined to lay, down his life within a few days, and on the same fatal field. His brigade had been performing garrison duty in Nashville during the siege of that city while Buell's army was in Kentucky, but disliking the prospect of inactivity pending the operations opening before us, Roberts had requested and obtained a transfer to the army in the field. His brigade relieved Colonel Dan McCook's, the latter reluctantly joining the garrison at Nashville, every one in it disappointed and disgusted that the circumstances existing at this time should necessitate their relegation to the harassing and tantalizing duty of protecting our depots and line of supply.

I was fortunate in having such brigade commanders, and no less favored in the regimental and battery commanders. They all were not only patriots, but soldiers, and knowing that discipline must be one of the most potent factors in bringing to a successful termination, the mighty contest in which our nation was struggling for existence, they studied and practiced its methods ceaselessly, inspiring with the same spirit that pervaded themselves the loyal hearts of their subordinate officers and men. All worked unremittingly in the camp at Mill Creek in preparing for the storm, which now plainly indicated its speedy coming. Drills, parades, scouts, foraging expeditions, picket and guard duty, made up the course in this school of instruction, supplemented by frequent changes in the locations of the different brigades, so that the division could have opportunity to learn to break camp quickly and to move out promptly on the march. Foraging expeditions were particularly beneficial in this respect, and when sent out, though absent sometimes for days, the men went without tents or knapsacks, equipped with only one blanket and their arms, ammunition, and rations, to teach them to shift for themselves with slender means in the event of necessity. The number of regimental and headquarters wagons was cut down to the lowest possible figure, and everything made compact by turning into the supply and ammunition trains of the division all surplus transportation, and restricting the personal baggage of officers to the fewest effects possible.

My own staff also was somewhat reorganized and increased at Mill Creek, and though it had been perfectly satisfactory before, yet, on account of the changes of troops that had occurred in the command, I found it necessary to replace valuable officers in some instances, and secure additional ones in others. The gathering of information about the enemy was also industriously pursued, and Card and his brothers were used constantly on expeditions within the Confederate lines, frequently visiting Murfreesboro', Sparta, Tullahoma, Shelbyville, and other points. What they learned was reported to army headquarters, often orally through me or personally communicated by Card himself, but much was forwarded in official letters, beginning with November 24, when I transmitted accurate information of the concentration of Bragg's main force at Tullahoma. Indeed, Card kept me so well posted as to every movement of the enemy, not only with reference to the troops in my immediate front, but also throughout his whole army, that General Rosecrans placed the most unreserved reliance on all his statements, and many times used them to check and correct the reports brought in by his own scouts.

Slight skirmishes took place frequently during this period, and now and then heavy demonstrations were made in the neighborhood of Nolensville by reconnoitring parties from both armies, but none of these ever grew into a battle. These affairs sprung from the desire of each side to feel his antagonist, and had little result beyond emphasizing the fact that behind each line of pickets lay a massed and powerful army busily preparing for the inevitable conflict and eager for its opening. So it wore on till the evening of December 25, 1862; then came the order to move forward.

General Rosecrans, in the reorganization of the army, had assigned Major-General A. McD. McCook to command the right wing, Major-General George H. Thomas the centre, and Major-General T. L. Crittenden the left wing. McCook's wing was made up of three divisions, commanded in order of rank by Brigadier-General Jeff. C. Davis; Brigadier-General R. W. Johnson, and Brigadier-General P. H. Sheridan. Although the corps nomenclature established by General Buell was dropped, the grand divisions into which he had organized the army at Louisville were maintained, and, in fact, the conditions established then remained practically unaltered, with the exception of the interchange of some brigades, the transfer of a few general officers from one wing or division to another, and the substitution of General Thomas for Gilbert as a corps commander. The army was thus compact and cohesive, undisturbed by discord and unembarrassed by jealousies of any moment; and it may be said that under a commander who, we believed, had the energy and skill necessary to direct us to success, a national confidence in our invincibility made us all keen for a test of strength with the Confederates. We had not long to wait.

Early on the morning of December 26, 1862, in a heavy rain, the army marched, the movement being directed on Murfreesboro', where the enemy had made some preparation to go into winter-quarters, and to hold which town it was hoped he would accept battle. General Thomas moved by the Franklin and Wilson pikes, General Crittenden by the Murfreesboro' pike, through Lavergne, and General McCook by the Nolensville pike—Davis's division in advance. As McCook's command neared Nolensville, I received a message from Davis informing me that the Confederates were in considerable force, posted on a range of hills in his front, and requesting me to support him in an attack he was about to make. When the head of my column arrived at Nolensville I began massing my troops on the right of the road, and by the time this formation was nearly completed Davis advanced, but not meeting with sufficient resistance to demand active assistance from me, he with his own command carried the hills, capturing one piece of artillery. This position of the Confederates was a strong one, defending Knob's Gap, through which the Nolensville and Triune pike passed. On the 27th Johnson's division, followed by mine, advanced to Triune, and engaged in a severe skirmish near that place, but my troops were not called into action, the stand made by the enemy being only for the purpose of gaining time to draw in his outlying troops, which done, he retired toward Murfreesboro'. I remained inactive at Triune during the 28th, but early on the 29th moved out by the Bole Jack road to the support of, Davis in his advance to Stewart's Creek, and encamped at Wilkinson's crossroads, from which point to Murfreesboro', distant about six miles, there was a good turnpike. The enemy had sullenly resisted the progress of Crittenden and McCook throughout the preceding three days, and as it was thought probable that he might offer battle at Stewart's Creek, Thomas, in pursuance of his original instructions looking to just such a contingency, had now fallen into the centre by way of the Nolensville crossroads.

On the morning of the 3oth I had the advance of McCook's corps on the Wilkinson pike, Roberts's brigade leading. At first only slight skirmishing took place, but when we came within about three miles of Murfreesboro' the resistance of the enemy's pickets grew serious, and a little further on so strong that I had to put in two regiments to push them back. I succeeded in driving them about half a mile, when I was directed by McCook to form line of battle and place my artillery in position so that I could act in concert with Davis's division, which he wished to post on my right in the general line he desired to take up. In obedience to these directions I deployed on the right of, and oblique to the Wilkinson pike, with a front of four regiments, a second line of four regiments within short supporting distance, and a reserve of one brigade in column of regiments to the rear of my centre. All this time the enemy kept up a heavy artillery and musketry fire on my skirmishers, he occupying, with his sharpshooters, beyond some open fields, a heavy belt of timber to my front and right, where it was intended the left of Davis should finally rest. To gain this point Davis was ordered to swing his division into it in conjunction with a wheeling movement of my right brigade, until our continuous line should face nearly due east. This would give us possession of the timber referred to, and not only rid us of the annoying fire from the skirmishers screened by it, but also place us close in to what was now developing as Bragg's line of battle. The movement was begun about half-past 2, and was successfully executed, after a stubborn resistance. In this preliminary affair the enemy had put in one battery of artillery, which was silenced in a little while, however, by Bush's and Hescock's guns. By sundown I had taken up my prescribed position, facing almost east, my left (Roberts's brigade) resting on the Wilkinson pike, the right (Sill's brigade) in the timber we had just gained, and the reserve brigade (Schaefer's) to the rear of my centre, on some rising ground in the edge of a strip of woods behind Houghtaling's and Hescock's batteries. Davis's division was placed in position on my right, his troops thrown somewhat to the rear, so that his line formed nearly a right angle with mine, while Johnson's division formed in a very exposed position on the right of Davis, prolonging the general line just across the Franklin pike.

The centre, under Thomas, had already formed to my left, the right of Negley's division joining my left in a cedar thicket near the Wilkinson pike, while Crittenden's corps was posted on the left of Thomas, his left resting on Stone River, at a point about two miles and a half from Murfreesboro'.

The precision that had characterized every manoeuvre of the past three days, and the exactness with which each corps and division fell into its allotted place on the evening of the 30th, indicated that at the outset of the campaign a well-digested plan of operations had been prepared for us; and although the scheme of the expected battle was not known to subordinates of my grade, yet all the movements up to this time had been so successfully and accurately made as to give much promise for the morrow, and when night fell there was general anticipation of the best results to the Union army.

CHAPTER XIII.

ASSAULT ON OUR RIGHT FLANK—OCCUPYING A NEW POSITION—THE ENEMY CHECKED—TERRIBLE LOSS OF OFFICERS—AMMUNITION GIVES OUT— RECONSTRUCTING THE LINE—COLLECTING THE WOUNDED AND BURYING THE DEAD—DEALING WITH COWARDS—RESULTS OF THE VICTORY.

The enemy under Bragg lay between us and stone River in order of battle, his general line conforming to the course of that stream. In my immediate front he appeared to be established in strong force in a dense cedar wood, just beyond an open valley, which varied from two hundred to four hundred yards in width, the cedars extending the entire length of the valley. From the events of the day and evening of the 3oth, it was apparent that the two armies were in close proximity, and orders received during the night revealed the fact that Rosecrans intended to attack by throwing his left on the enemy's right, with the expectation of driving it in toward Murfreesboro', so that the right of Crittenden's corps could attack Bragg's centre in reverse, while Thomas supported Crittenden by a simultaneous front assault; and from the movements of the enemy at daylight next morning, it was plainly indicated that Bragg had planned to swing his left on our right by an exactly similar manoeuvre, get possession of the railroad and the Nashville pike, and if possible cut us off from our base at Nashville. The conceptions in the minds of the two generals were almost identical; but Bragg took the initiative, beginning his movement about an hour earlier than the time set by Rosecrans, which gained him an immense advantage in execution in the earlier stages of the action.

During the evening, feeling keenly all the solicitude which attends one in anticipation of a battle, I examined my position with great care, inspecting its whole length several times to remedy any defects that might exist, and to let the men see that I was alive to their interests and advantages. After dark, I went back to the rear of my reserve brigade, and establishing my headquarters behind the trunk of a large fallen tree, which would shelter me somewhat from the cold December wind, lay down beside a small camp-fire to get some rest.

At 2 o'clock on the morning of the 31st General Sill came back to me to report that on his front a continuous movement of infantry and artillery had been going on all night within the Confederate lines, and that he was convinced that Bragg was massing on our right with the purpose of making an attack from that direction early in the morning. After discussing for a few minutes the probabilities of such a course on the part of the enemy, I thought McCook should be made acquainted with what was going on, so Sill and I went back to see him at his headquarters, not far from the Griscom House, where we found him sleeping on some straw in the angle of a worm-fence. I waked him up and communicated the intelligence, and our consequent impressions. He talked the matter over with us for some little time, but in view of the offensive-defensive part he was to play in the coming battle, did not seem to think that there was a necessity for any further dispositions than had already been taken. He said that he thought Johnson's division would be able to take care of the right, and seemed confident that the early assault which was to be made from Rosecrans's left would anticipate and check the designs which we presaged. We two then returned to my little camp-fire behind the log, and as we continued talking of what might be expected from the indications on the right, and Sill becoming more anxious, I directed two regiments from the reserve to report to him, that they might be placed within very short supporting distance of his line. He then rejoined his brigade, better satisfied, but still adhering to the belief he had expressed when first making his report.

Long before dawn my division breakfasted, and was assembled under arms, the infantry in line, the cannoneers at their pieces, but while we were thus preparing, all the recent signs of activity in the enemy's camp were hushed, a death-like stillness prevailing in the cedars to our front. Shortly after daylight General Hardee opened the engagement, just as Sill had predicted, by a fierce attack on Johnson's division, the extreme right of the Union line. Immediate success attending this assault, Hardee extended the attack gradually along in front of Davis, hip movement taking the form of a wheel to the right, the pivot being nearly opposite the left of my division. Johnson's division soon gave way, and two of Davis's brigades were forced to fall back with it, though stubbornly resisting the determined and sweeping onset.

In the meantime the enemy had also attacked me, advancing across an old cotton-field in Sill's front in heavy masses, which were furiously opened upon by Bush's battery from Sill's line, and by Hescock's and Houghtaling's batteries, which had an oblique fire on the field from a commanding position in rear of my centre. The effect of this fire on the advancing column was terrible, but it continued on till it reached the edge of the timber where Sill's right lay, when my infantry opened at a range of not over fifty yards. For a short time the Confederates withstood the fire, but then wavered, broke, and fell back toward their original line. As they retired, Sill's brigade followed in a spirited charge, driving them back across the open ground and behind their intrenchments. In this charge the gallant Sill was killed; a rifle ball passing through his upper lip and penetrating the brain. Although this was a heavy loss, yet the enemy's discomfiture was such as to give us an hour's time, and as Colonel Greusel, Thirty-sixth Illinois, succeeded to Sill's command, I directed him, as he took charge, to recall the brigade to its original position, for the turning-column on my extreme right was now assuming the most menacing attitude, and it was urgently necessary to prepare for it.

When that portion of the enemy driven back by Sill recovered from its repulse it again advanced to the attack, this time directing its efforts chiefly upon my extreme right, and the front of Woodruff's brigade of Davis's division, which brigade still held on in its first position. In front of my centre the Confederates were again driven back, but as the assault on Woodruff was in conjunction with an advance of the column that had forced Johnson to retire, Woodruff was compelled unfortunately to give way, and two regiments on the right of my line went with him, till they rallied on the two reserve regiments which, in anticipation of the enemy's initiatory attack I had sent to Sill's rear before daylight.

Both Johnson's and Davis's divisions were now practically gone from our line, having retired with a loss of all formation, and they were being closely pursued by the enemy, whose columns were following the arc of a circle that would ultimately carry him in on my rear. In consequence of the fact that this state of things would soon subject me to a fire in reverse, I hastily withdrew Sill's brigade and the reserve regiments supporting it, and ordered Roberts's brigade, which at the close of the enemy's second repulse had changed front toward the south and formed in column of regiments, to cover the withdrawal by a charge on the Confederates as they came into the timber where my right had originally rested. Roberts made the charge at the proper time, and was successful in checking the enemy's advance, thus giving us a breathing-spell, during which I was able to take up a new position with Schaefer's and Sill's brigades on the commanding ground to the rear, where Hescock's and Houghtaling's batteries had been posted all the morning.

The general course of this new position was at right angles with my original line, and it took the shape of an obtuse angle, with my three batteries at the apex. Davis, and Carlin of his division, endeavored to rally their men here on my right, but their efforts were practically unavailing,—though the calm and cool appearance of Carlin, who at the time was smoking a stumpy pipe, had some effect, and was in strong contrast to the excited manner of Davis, who seemed overpowered by the disaster that had befallen his command. But few could be rallied, however, as the men were badly demoralized, and most of them fell back beyond the Wilkinson pike, where they reorganized behind the troops of General Thomas.

At this juncture the enemy's turning-column began advancing again in concert with Cheatham's division, and as the extreme left of the Confederates was directed on Griscom's house, and their right on the Blanton house, my new position was in danger of envelopment. No hope of stemming the tide at this point seemed probable, but to gain time I retained my ground as long as possible, and until, under directions from General McCook, I moved to the front from my left flank and attached myself to the right of Negley's division, which up to this hour had been left almost undisturbed by the enemy in the line it had taken up the night before. Under a heavy fire we succeeded in this manoeuvre, Schaefer's brigade marching first, then the batteries, and Roberts's and Sill's brigades following. When my division arrived on this new ground, I posted Roberts on Negley's right, with Hescock's and Bush's guns, the brigade and guns occupying a low rocky ridge of limestone, which faced them toward Murfreesboro', nearly south. The rest of my division was aligned facing west, along the edge of a cedar thicket, the rear rank backed up on the right flank of Roberts, with Houghtaling's battery in the angle. This presented

Sill's and Schaefer's brigades in an almost opposite direction to the line we had so confidently taken up the night before, and covered Negley's rear. The enemy, in the meantime, had continued his wheeling movement till he occupied the ground that my batteries and reserve brigade had held in the morning, and I had now so changed my position that the left brigade of my division approached his intrenchments in front of Stone River, while Sill's and Schaeffer's brigades, by facing nearly west, confronted the successful troops that had smashed in our extreme right.

I had hardly got straightened out in this last place when I was attacked by Cheatham's division, which, notwithstanding the staggering blows it had previously received from Sill and Roberts, now again moved forward in conjunction with the wheeling movement under the immediate command of Hardee. One of the most sanguinary contests of the day now took place. In fulfillment of Bragg's original design no doubt, Cheatham's division attacked on my left, while heavy masses under Hardee, covered by batteries posted on the high ground formerly occupied by my guns, assaulted my right, the whole force advancing simultaneously. At the same time the enemy opened an artillery fire from his intrenchments in front of Murfreesboro', and it seemed that he was present on every side. My position was strong, however, located in the edge of a dense cedar thicket and commanding a slight depression of open ground that lay in my front. My men were in good spirits too, notwithstanding they had been a good deal hustled around since daylight, with losses that had told considerably on their numbers. Only a short distance now separated the contending lines, and as the batteries on each side were not much more than two hundred yards apart when the enemy made his assault, the artillery fire was fearful in its effect on the ranks of both contestants, the enemy's heavy masses staggering under the torrent of shell and canister from our batteries, while our lines were thinned by his ricochetting projectiles, that rebounded again and again over the thinly covered limestone formation and sped on to the rear of Negley. But all his efforts to dislodge or destroy us were futile, and for the first time since daylight General Hardee was seriously checked in the turning movement he had begun for the purpose of getting possession of the Nashville pike, and though reinforced until two-fifths of Bragg's army was now at his command, yet he met with repulse after repulse, which created great gaps in his lines and taught him that to overwhelm us was hopeless.

As the enemy was recoiling from his first attack, I received a message from Rosecrans telling me that he was making new dispositions, and directing me to hold on where I was until they were completed. From this I judged that the existing conditions of the battle would probably require a sacrifice of my command, so I informed Roberts and Schaefer that we must be prepared to meet the demand on us by withstanding the assault of the enemy, no matter what the outcome. Every energy was therefore bent to the simple holding of our ground, and as ammunition was getting scarce, instructions were given throughout the command to have it reserve its fire till the most effective moment. In a little while came a second and a third assault, and although they were as daring and furious as the first, yet in each case the Confederates were repulsed, driven back in confusion, but not without deadly loss to us, for the noble Roberts was killed, and Colonel Harrington, of the Twenty-Seventh Illinois, who succeeded to his brigade, was mortally wounded a few minutes later. I had now on the death-roll three brigade commanders, and the loss of subordinate officers and men was appalling, but their sacrifice had accomplished the desired result; they had not fallen in vain. Indeed, the bravery and tenacity of my division gave to Rosecrans the time required to make new dispositions, and exacted from our foes the highest commendations.

A lull followed the third fierce assault, and an investigation showed that, with the exception of a few rounds in my brigade, our ammunition was entirely exhausted; and while it was apparent that the enemy was reluctant to renew the conflict in my front, yet I was satisfied I could not hold on much longer without the danger of ultimate capture, so I prepared to withdraw as soon as the troops of Rousseau's division, which had been ordered to take up a line on my right, came into position. Schaefer's and Sill's brigades being without a cartridge, I directed them to fix bayonets for a charge, and await any attempt of the enemy to embarrass my retreat, while Roberts's brigade, offering such resistance as its small quantity of ammunition would permit, was pulled slowly in toward the Nashville pike. Eighty of the horses of Houghtaling's battery having been killed, an attempt was made to bring his guns back by hand over the rocky ground, but it could not be done, and we had to abandon them. Hescock also had lost most of his horses, but all his guns were saved. Bush's battery lost two pieces, the tangled underbrush in the dense cedars proving an obstacle to getting them away which his almost superhuman exertions could not surmount. Thus far the bloody duel had cost me heavily, one-third of my division being killed or wounded. I had already three brigade commanders killed; a little later I lost my fourth—Colonel Schaefer.

The difficulties of withdrawing were very great, as the ground was exceptionally rocky, and the growth of cedars almost impenetrable for wheeled carriages. Retiring sullenly under a heavy fire, while the general line was reformed to my right and rear, my division was at length drawn through the cedars and debouched into an open space near the Murfreesboro' pike, behind the right of Palmer's division. Two regiments of Sill's brigade, however, on account of the conformation of the ground, were obliged to fall back from the point where Woodruff's brigade of Davis's division had rallied after the disaster of the early morning. The division came out of the cedars with unbroken ranks, thinned by only its killed and wounded—but few missing. When we came into the open ground, McCook directed Roberts's brigade—now commanded by Colonel Luther P. Bradley—to proceed a short distance to the rear on the Nashville pike, to repel the enemy's threatening attempt at our communications. Willingly and cheerfully the brigade again entered the fight under these new conditions, and although it was supplied with but three or four cartridges to the man now, it charged gallantly and recaptured two pieces of artillery which the Union troops had had to abandon at that point.

Shortly after we debouched from the cedars I was directed by Rosecrans to send some aid to the right of General Palmer's division; and two of Schaefer's regiments, having obtained ammunition, were pushed up on Palmer's right, accompanied by four of Hescock's guns; but the advance of the enemy here had already been checked by Palmer, and only a desultory contest ensued. Rosecrans, whom I now met in the open ground west of the railroad, behind Palmer, directed that my command should relieve Wood's division, which was required to fall back and take up the new line that had been marked out while I was holding on in the cedars. His usually florid face had lost its ruddy color, and his anxious eyes told that the disasters of the morning were testing his powers to the very verge of endurance, but he seemed fully to comprehend what had befallen us. His firmly set lips and, the calmness with which his instructions were delivered inspired confidence in all around him; and expressing approbation of what my division had done, while deliberately directing it to a new point, he renewed in us all the hope of final victory, though it must be admitted that at this phase of the battle the chances lay largely with the enemy.

Withdrawing the two regiments and Hescock's battery, that I had posted on the right of Palmer, I moved as directed by Rosecrans into the position to the east of the railroad, and formed immediately to the right of Wood, who was now being attacked all along his front, but more particularly where his right rested near the railroad. Under a storm of shot and shell that came in torrents my troops took up the new ground, advancing through a clump of open timber to Wood's assistance. Forming in line in front of the timber we poured a telling fire into the enemy's ranks, which were then attacking across some cleared fields; but when he discovered additional troops confronting him, he gave up the attempt to carry Wood's position. It was here that I lost Schaefer, who was killed instantly, making my fourth brigade commander dead that day. The enemy in front of Wood having been checked, our whole line east of the railroad executed undisturbed its retrograde movement to a position about three hundred yards to its rear. When I fell back to the edge of the clump of timber, where when first coming on the ground I had formed to help Wood, I was ordered by Rosecrans to prepare to make a charge should the enemy again assault us. In anticipation of this work I massed my troops in close column. The expected attack never came, however, but the shot and shell of a furious cannonade told with fatal effect upon men and officers as they lay on their faces hugging the ground. The torments of this trying situation were almost unbearable, but it was obvious to all that it was necessary to have at hand a compact body of troops to repel any assault the enemy might make pending the reconstruction of the extreme right of our line, and a silent determination to stay seemed to take hold of each individual soldier; nor was this grim silence interrupted throughout the cannonade, except in one instance, when one of the regiments broke out in a lusty cheer as a startled rabbit in search of a new hiding-place safely ran the whole length of the line on the backs of the men.

While my troops were still lying here, General Rosecrans, with a part of his staff and a few orderlies, rode out on the rearranged line to supervise its formation and encourage the men, and in prosecution of these objects moved around the front of my column of attack, within range of the batteries that were shelling us so viciously. As he passed to the open ground on my left, I joined him. The enemy seeing this mounted party, turned his guns upon it, and his accurate aim was soon rewarded, for a solid shot carried away the head of Colonel Garesche, the chief-of-staff, and killed or wounded two or three orderlies. Garesche's appalling death stunned us all, and a momentary expression of horror spread over Rosecrans's face; but at such a time the importance of self-control was vital, and he pursued his course with an appearance of indifference, which, however, those immediately about him saw was assumed, for undoubtedly he felt most deeply the death of his friend and trusted staff-officer.

No other attacks were made on us to the east of the railroad for the rest of the afternoon, and just before dark I was directed to withdraw and take up a position along the west side of the Nashville pike, on the extreme right of our new line, where Roberts's brigade and the Seventy-third and Eighty-eighth Illinois had already been placed by McCook. The day had cost me much anxiety and sadness, and I was sorely disappointed at the general result, though I could not be other than pleased at the part taken by my command. The loss of my brigade commanders—Sill, Roberts, Schaefer, and Harrington-and a large number of regimental and battery officers, with so many of their men, struck deep into my heart: My thinned ranks told the woeful tale of the fierce struggles, indescribable by words, through which my division had passed since 7 o'clock in the morning; and this, added to our hungry and exhausted condition, was naturally disheartening. The men had been made veterans, however, by the fortunes and misfortunes of the day, and as they went into their new places still confident of final success, it was plain to see that they felt a self-confidence inspired by the part they had already played.

My headquarters were now established on the Nashville pike, about three miles and a half from Murfreesboro'; my division being aligned to the west of the pike, bowed out and facing almost west, Cleburn's division of the Confederates confronting it. Davis's division was posted on my right, and Walker's brigade of Thomas's corps, which had reported to me, took up a line that connected my left with Johnson's division.

Late in the evening General Rosecrans, accompanied by General McCook, and several other officers whose names I am now unable to recall, rode by my headquarters on their way to the rear to look for a new line of battle—on Overall's creek it was said—that would preserve our communications with Nashville and offer better facilities for resistance than the one we were now holding. Considerable time had elapsed when they returned from this exploration and proceeded to their respective commands, without intimating to me that anything had been determined upon by the reconnoissance, but a little later it was rumored through the different headquarters that while the party was looking for a new position it discovered the enemy's troops moving toward our right and rear, the head of his columns being conducted in the darkness by the aid of torches, and that no alternative was left us but to hold the lines we then occupied. The torches had been seen unquestionably, and possibly created some alarm at first in the minds of the reconnoitring party, but it was soon ascertained that the lights came from a battalion of the Fourth regular cavalry that was picketing our flank and happened to be starting its bivouac fires at the moment. The fires and the supposed movements had no weight, therefore, in deciding the proposition to take up a line at Overall's creek, but General Rosecrans, fortunately for the army, decided to remain where he was. Doubtless reflections during his ride caused him to realize that the enemy must be quite as much crippled as himself. If it had been decided to fall back to Overall's creek, we could have withdrawn without much difficulty very likely, but such a retrograde movement would have left to the enemy the entire battle-field of Stone River and ultimately compelled our retreat to Nashville.

In the night of December 3rd several slight demonstrations were made on my front, but from the darkness neither party felt the effect of the other's fire, and when daylight came again the skirmishers and lines of battle were in about the same position they had taken up the evening before. Soon after daybreak it became evident that the conflict was to be renewed, and a little later the enemy resumed the offensive by an attack along my left front, especially on Walker's brigade. His attempt was ineffectual, however, and so easily repulsed as to demonstrate that the desperate character of his assaults the day before had nearly exhausted his strength. About 3 o'clock in the afternoon he made another feeble charge on my front, but our fire from the barricades and rifle-pits soon demoralized his advancing lines, which fell back in some confusion, thus enabling us to pick up about a hundred prisoners. From this time till the evening of January 3 Bragg's left remained in our front, and continued to show itself at intervals by weak demonstrations, which we afterward ascertained were directly intended to cover the desperate assault he made with Breckenridge on the left of Rosecrans, an assault that really had in view only a defensive purpose, for unless Bragg dislodged the troops which were now massing in front of his right he would be obliged to withdraw General Polk's corps behind Stone River and finally abandon Murfreesboro'. The sequel proved this to be the case; and the ill-judged assault led by Breckenridge ending in entire defeat, Bragg retired from Murfreesboro' the night of January 3.

General Rosecrans occupied Murfreesboro' on the 4th and 5th, having gained a costly victory, which was not decisive enough in its character to greatly affect the general course of the war, though it somewhat strengthened and increased our hold on Middle Tennessee. The enemy in retiring did not fall back very far—only behind Duck River to Shelbyville and Tullahoma—and but little endeavor was made to follow him. Indeed, we were not in condition to pursue, even if it had been the intention at the outset of the campaign.

As soon as possible after the Confederate retreat I went over the battle-field to collect such of my wounded as had not been carried off to the South and to bury my dead. In the cedars and on the ground where I had been so fiercely assaulted when the battle opened, on the morning of the 31st, evidences of the bloody struggle appeared on every hand in the form of broken fire-arms, fragments of accoutrements, and splintered trees. The dead had nearly all been left unburied, but as there was likelihood of their mutilation by roving swine, the bodies had mostly been collected in piles at different points and inclosed by rail fences. The sad duties of interment and of caring for the wounded were completed by the 5th, and on the 6th I moved my division three miles, south of Murfreesboro' on the Shelbyville pike, going into camp on the banks of Stone River. Here the condition of my command was thoroughly looked into, and an endeavor made to correct such defects as had been disclosed by the recent battle.

During the engagement there had been little straggling, and my list of missing was small and legitimate; still, it was known that a very few had shirked their duty, and an example was necessary. Among this small number were four officers who, it was charged, had abandoned their colors and regiments. When their guilt was clearly established, and as soon as an opportunity occurred, I caused the whole division to be formed in a hollow square, closed in mass, and had the four officers marched to the centre, where, telling them that I would not humiliate any officer or soldier by requiring him to touch their disgraced swords, I compelled them to deliver theirs up to my colored servant, who also cut from their coats every insignia of rank. Then, after there had been read to the command an order from army headquarters dismissing the four from the service, the scene was brought to a close by drumming the cowards out of camp. It was a mortifying spectacle, but from that day no officer in that division ever abandoned his colors.

My effective force in the battle of Stone River was 4,154 officers and men. Of this number I lost 1,633 killed, wounded, and missing, or nearly 40 per cent. In the remaining years of the war, though often engaged in most severe contests, I never experienced in any of my commands so high a rate of casualties. The ratio of loss in the whole of Rosecrans's army was also high, and Bragg's losses were almost equally great. Rosecrans carried into the action about 42,000 officers and men. He lost 13,230, or 31 per cent. Bragg's effective force was 37,800 officers and men; he lost 10,306, or nearly 28 per cent.

Though our victory was dearly bought, yet the importance of gaining the day at any price was very great, particularly when we consider what might have been the result had not the gallantry of the army and the manoeuvring during the early disaster saved us from ultimate defeat. We had started out from Nashville on an offensive campaign, probably with no intention of going beyond Murfreesboro', in midwinter, but still with the expectation of delivering a crushing blow should the enemy accept our challenge to battle. He met us with a plan of attack almost the counterpart of our own. In the execution of his plan he had many advantages, not the least of which was his intimate knowledge of the ground, and he came near destroying us. Had he done so, Nashville would probably have fallen; at all events, Kentucky would have been opened again to his incursions, and the theatre of war very likely transferred once more to the Ohio River. As the case now stood, however, Nashville was firmly established as a base for future operations, Kentucky was safe from the possibility of being again overrun, and Bragg, thrown on the defensive, was compelled to give his thoughts to the protection of the interior of the Confederacy and the security of Chattanooga, rather than indulge in schemes of conquest north of the Cumberland River. While he still held on in Middle Tennessee his grasp was so much loosened that only slight effort would be necessary to push him back into Georgia, and thus give to the mountain region of East Tennessee an opportunity to prove its loyalty to the, Union.

The victory quieted the fears of the West and Northwest, destroyed the hopes of the secession element in Kentucky, renewed the drooping spirits of the East Tennesseans, and demoralized the disunionists in Middle Tennessee; yet it was a negative victory so far as concerned the result on the battle-field. Rosecrans seems to have planned the battle with the idea that the enemy would continue passive, remain entirely on the defensive, and that it was necessary only to push forward our left in order to force the evacuation of Murfreesboro'; and notwithstanding the fact that on the afternoon of December 30 McCook received information that the right of Johnson's division. resting near the Franklin pike, extended only to about the centre of the Confederate army, it does not appear that attack from that quarter was at all apprehended by the Union commanders.

The natural line of retreat of the Confederates was not threatened by the design of Rosecrans; and Bragg, without risk to his communications, anticipated it by a counter-attack of like character from his own left, and demolished his adversary's plan the moment we were thrown on the defensive. Had Bragg followed up with the spirit which characterized its beginning the successful attack by Hardee on our right wing—and there seems no reason why he should not have done so—the army of Rosecrans still might have got back to Nashville, but it would have been depleted and demoralized to such a degree as to unfit it for offensive operations for a long time afterward. Bragg's intrenchments in front of Stone River were very strong, and there seems no reason why he should not have used his plain advantage as explained, but instead he allowed us to gain time, intrench, and recover a confidence that at first was badly shaken. Finally, to cap the climax of his errors, he directed Breckenridge to make the assault from his right flank on January 2, with small chance for anything but disaster, when the real purpose in view could have been accomplished without the necessity of any offensive manoeuvre whatever.

CHAPTER XIV.
APPOINTED A MAJOR-GENERAL—THE SECRET EXPEDITION UNDER CARD THE SCOUT—HIS CAPTURE BY GUERRILLAS—ESCAPE—A REVENGE PARTY—WOMEN SOLDIERS—A FIGHT WITH SABRES—TULLAHOMA CAMPAIGN—A FOOLISH ADVENTURE.

On the 6th of January, 1863, my division settled quietly down in its camp south of Murfreesboro'. Its exhausted condition after the terrible experiences of the preceding week required attention. It needed recuperation, reinforcement, and reorganization, and I set about these matters without delay, in anticipation of active operations early in the spring. No forward movement was made for nearly six months, however, and throughout this period drills, parades, reconnoissances, and foraging expeditions filled in the time profitably. In addition to these exercises the construction of permanent fortifications for the security of Murfreesboro' was undertaken by General Rosecrans, and large details from my troops were furnished daily for the work. Much attention was also given to creating a more perfect system of guard and picket duty-a matter that had hitherto been somewhat neglected in the army, as its constant activity had permitted scant opportunity for the development of such a system. It was at this time that I received my appointment as a major-general of Volunteers. My promotion had been recommended by General Rosecrans immediately after the battle of Stone River, but for some reason it was delayed until April, and though a long time elapsed between the promise and the performance, my gratification was extreme.

My scout, Card, was exceedingly useful while encamped near

Murfreesboro, making several trips to East Tennessee within the enemy's lines to collect information as to the condition of the loyal people there, and to encourage them with the hope of early liberation. He also brought back from each trip very accurate statements as to the strength and doings of the Confederate army, fixing almost with certainty its numbers and the locations of its different divisions, and enabling my engineer-officer—Major Morhardt—to construct good maps of the country in our front. On these dangerous excursions Card was always accompanied by one of his brothers, the other remaining with me to be ready for duty if any accident occurred to those who had gone out, or in case I wanted to communicate with them. In this way we kept well posted, although the intelligence these men brought was almost always secured at the risk of their lives.

Early in the spring, before the Tullahoma campaign began, I thought it would be practicable, by sending out a small secret expedition of but three or four men, to break the Nashville and Chattanooga railroad between Chattanooga and the enemy's position at Tullahoma by burning the bridges in Crow Creek valley from its head to Stevenson, Alabama, and then the great bridge across the Tennessee River at Bridgeport. Feeling confident that I could persuade Card to undertake the perilous duty, I broached the contemplated project to him, and he at once jumped at the opportunity of thus distinguishing himself, saying that with one of his brothers and three other loyal East Tennesseeans, whose services he knew could be enlisted, he felt sure of carrying out the idea, so I gave him authority to choose his own assistants. In a few days his men appeared at my headquarters, and when supplied with money in notes of the State Bank of Tennessee, current everywhere as gold in those days, the party, composed of Card, the second brother, and the three East Tennesseeans, started on their precarious enterprise, their course being directed first toward the Cumberland Mountains, intending to strike the Nashville and Chattanooga railroad somewhere above Anderson's station. They expected to get back in about fifteen days, but I looked for some knowledge of the progress of their adventure before the expiration of that period, hoping to hear through Confederate sources prisoners and the like-of the destruction of the bridges. I waited in patience for such news, but none came, and as the time Card had allotted himself passed by, I watched anxiously for his return, for, as there was scarcely a doubt that the expedition had proved a failure, the fate of the party became a matter of deep concern to Card's remaining brother and to me. Finally this brother volunteered to go to his father's house in East Tennessee to get tidings of the party, and I consented, for the probabilities were that some of them had made their way to that point, or at least that some information had reached there about them. As day after day went by, the time fixed for this brother's return came round, yet he also remained out; but some days after the lad was due Card himself turned up accompanied by the brother he had taken with him, soon explained his delay in getting back, and gave me the story of his adventures while absent.

After leaving my camp, his party had followed various byways across the Cumberland Mountains to Crow Creek Valley, as instructed; but when nearing the railroad above Anderson's Station, they were captured by some guerrillas prowling about that vicinity, and being suspected of disloyalty to the Confederacy, were carried to Chattanooga and imprisoned as Yankee spies. Their prospects now were decidedly discouraging, for death stared them in the face. Fortunately, however, some delays occurred relative to the disposition that should be made of them, and they, meanwhile, effected their escape from their jailors by way of one of the prison windows, from which they managed to displace a bar, and by a skiff, in the darkness of night, crossed the Tennessee River a little below Chattanooga. From this point the party made their way back to my camp, traveling only at night, hiding in the woods by day, and for food depending on loyal citizens that Card had become acquainted with when preaching and pedling.

Card's first inquiry after relating his story was for the youngest brother, whom he had left with me. I told him what I had done, in my anxiety about himself, and that more than sufficient time had elapsed for his brother's return. His reply was: "They have caught him. The poor fellow is dead." His surmise proved correct; for news soon came that the poor boy had been captured at his father's house, and hanged. The blow to Card was a severe one, and so hardened his heart against the guerrillas in the neighborhood of his father's home—for he knew they were guilty of his brother's murder—that it was with difficulty I could persuade him to continue in the employment of the Government, so determined was he to avenge his brother's death at the first opportunity. Finally, however, I succeeded in quieting the almost uncontrollable rage that seemed to possess him, and he remained with me during the Tullahoma and Chickamauga campaigns; but when we reached Knoxville the next winter, he took his departure, informing me that he was going for the bushwhackers who had killed his brother. A short time after he left me, I saw him at the head of about thirty well-armed East Tennesseeans—refugees. They were determined-looking men, seeking revenge for the wrongs and sufferings that had been put upon them in the last two years, and no doubt wreaked their vengeance right and left on all who had been in any way instrumental in persecuting them.

The feeding of our army from the base at Louisville was attended with a great many difficulties, as the enemy's cavalry was constantly breaking the railroad and intercepting our communications on the Cumberland River at different points that were easily accessible to his then superior force of troopers. The accumulation of reserve stores was therefore not an easy task, and to get forage ahead a few days was well-nigh impossible, unless that brought from the North was supplemented by what we could gather from the country. Corn was abundant in the region to the south and southwest of Murfreesboro', so to make good our deficiencies in this respect, I employed a brigade about once a week in the duty of collecting and bringing in forage, sending out sometimes as many as a hundred and fifty wagons to haul the grain which my scouts had previously located. In nearly every one of these expeditions the enemy was encountered, and the wagons were usually loaded while the skirmishers kept up a running fire, Often there would occur a respectable brush, with the loss on each side of a number of killed and wounded. The officer in direct command always reported to me personally whatever had happened during the time he was out—the result of his reconnoissance, so to speak, for that war the real nature of these excursions—and on one occasion the colonel in command, Colonel Conrad, of the Fifteenth Missouri, informed me that he got through without much difficulty; in fact, that everything had gone all right and been eminently satisfactory, except that in returning he had been mortified greatly by the conduct of the two females belonging to the detachment and division train at my headquarters. These women, he said, had given much annoyance by getting drunk, and to some extent demoralizing his men. To say that I was astonished at his statement would be a mild way of putting it, and had I not known him to be a most upright man and of sound sense, I should have doubted not only his veracity, but his sanity. Inquiring who they were and for further details, I was informed that there certainly were in the command two females, that in some mysterious manner had attached themselves to the service as soldiers; that one, an East Tennessee woman, was a teamster in the division wagon-train and the other a private soldier in a cavalry company temporarily attached to my headquarters for escort duty. While out on the foraging expedition these Amazons had secured a supply of "apple-jack" by some means, got very drunk, and on the return had fallen into Stone River and been nearly drowned. After they had been fished from, the water, in the process of resuscitation their sex was disclosed, though up to this time it appeared to be known only to each other. The story was straight and the circumstance clear, so, convinced of Conrad's continued sanity, I directed the provost-marshal to bring in arrest to my headquarters the two disturbers of Conrad's peace of mind. After some little search the East Tennessee woman was found in camp, somewhat the worse for the experiences of the day before, but awaiting her fate content idly smoking a cob-pipe. She was brought to me, and put in duress under charge of the division surgeon until her companion could be secured. To the doctor she related that the year before she had "refugeed" from East Tennessee, and on arriving in Louisville assumed men's apparel and sought and obtained employment as a teamster in the quartermaster's department. Her features were very large, and so coarse and masculine was her general appearance that she would readily have passed as a man, and in her case the deception was no doubt easily practiced. Next day the "she dragoon" was caught, and proved to be a rather prepossessing young woman, and though necessarily bronzed and hardened by exposure, I doubt if, even with these marks of campaigning, she could have deceived as readily as did her companion. How the two got acquainted, I never learned, and though they had joined the army independently of each other, yet an intimacy had sprung up between them long before the mishaps of the foraging expedition. They both were forwarded to army headquarters, and, when provided with clothing suited to their sex, sent back to Nashville, and thence beyond our lines to Louisville.

On January 9, by an order from the War Department, the Army of the Cumberland had been divided into three corps, designated the Fourteenth, Twentieth, and Twenty-first. This order did not alter the composition of the former grand divisions, nor change the commanders, but the new nomenclature was a decided improvement over the clumsy designations Right Wing, Centre, and Left Wing, which were well calculated to lead to confusion sometimes. McCook's wing became the Twentieth Corps, and my division continued of the same organization, and held the same number as formerly-the Third Division, Twentieth Corps. My first brigade was now commanded by Brigadier-General William H. Lytle, the second by Colonel Bernard Laiboldt, and the third by Colonel Luther P. Bradley.

On the 4th of March I was directed to move in light marching order toward Franklin and join General Gordon Granger, to take part in some operations which he was projecting against General Earl Van Dorn, then at Spring Hill. Knowing that my line of march would carry me through a region where forage was plentiful, I took along a large train of empty wagons, which I determined to fill with corn and send back to Murfreesboro', believing that I could successfully cover the train by Minty's brigade of cavalry, which had joined me for the purpose of aiding in a reconnoissance toward Shelbyville. In marching the column I placed a regiment of infantry at its head, then the wagon-train, then a brigade of infantry—masking the cavalry behind this brigade. The enemy, discovering that the train was with us, and thinking he could capture it, came boldly out with his, cavalry to attack. The head of his column came up to the crossroads at Versailles, but holding him there, I passed the train and infantry brigade beyond toward Eagleville, and when my cavalry had been thus unmasked, Minty, followed by the balance of my division, which vas still behind, charged him with the sabre. Success was immediate and complete, and pursuit of the routed forces continued through Unionville, until we fell upon and drove in the Confederate outposts at Shelbyville. Here the enemy was taken by surprise evidently, which was most fortunate for us, otherwise the consequences might have been disastrous. Minty captured in the charge about fifty prisoners and a few wagons and mules, and thus enabled me to load my train with corn, and send it back to Murfreesboro' unmolested. In this little fight the sabre was freely used by both sides, and I do not believe that during the whole war I again knew of so large a percentage of wounds by that arm in proportion to the numbers engaged.

That night I encamped at Eagleville, and next day reported to Granger at Franklin, arriving in the midst of much excitement prevailing on account of the loss of Coburn's brigade, which had been captured the day before a little distance south of that point, while marching to form a junction with a column that had been directed on Columbia from Murfreesboro'. Shortly after Coburn's capture General Granger had come upon the scene, and the next day he advanced my division and Minty's troops directly on Spring Hill, with a view to making some reprisal; but Van Dorn had no intention of accommodating us, and retired from Spring Hill, offering but little resistance. He continued to fall back, till finally he got behind Duck River, where operations against him ceased; for, in consequence of the incessant rains of the season, the streams had become almost impassable. Later, I returned by way of Franklin to my old camp at Murfreesboro', passing over on this march the ground on which the Confederate General Hood met with such disaster the following year in his attack on Stanley's corps.

My command had all returned from the Franklin expedition to Murfreesboro' and gone into camp on the Salem pike by the latter part of March, from which time till June it took part in only the little affairs of out-posts occurring every now and then on my own front. In the meanwhile General Rosecrans had been materially reinforced by the return of sick and wounded men; his army had become well disciplined, and was tolerably supplied; and he was repeatedly pressed by the authorities at Washington to undertake offensive operations.

During the spring and early summer Rosecrans resisted, with a great deal of spirit and on various grounds, these frequent urgings, and out of this grew up an acrimonious correspondence and strained feeling between him and General Halleck. Early in June, however, stores had been accumulated and other preparations made for a move forward, Resecrans seeming to have decided that he could safely risk an advance, with the prospect of good results. Before finally deciding, he called upon most of his corps and division commanders for their opinions on certain propositions which he presented, and most of them still opposed the projected movement, I among the number, reasoning that while General Grant was operating against Vicksburg, it was better to hold Bragg in Middle Tennessee than to push him so far back into Georgia that interior means of communication would give the Confederate Government the opportunity of quickly joining a part of his force to that of General Johnson in Mississippi.

At this stage, and in fact prior to it, Rosecrans seemed to manifest special confidence in me, often discussing his plans with me independent of the occasions on which he formally referred them for my views. I recollect that on two different occasions about this time he unfolded his designs to me in this informal way, outlining generally how he expected ultimately to force Bragg south of the Tennessee River, and going into the details of the contemplated move on Tullahoma. His schemes, to my mind, were not only comprehensive, but exact, and showed conclusively, what no one doubted then, that they were original with him. I found in them very little to criticise unfavorably, if we were to move at all, and Rosecrans certainly impressed me that he favored an advance at an early day, though many of his generals were against it until the operations on the Mississippi River should culminate in something definite. There was much, fully apparent in the circumstances about his headquarters, leading to the conviction that Rosecrans originated the Tullahoma campaign, and the record of his prior performances collaterally sustains the visible evidence then existing. In my opinion, then, based on a clear recollection of various occurrences growing out of our intimacy, he conceived the plan of the Tullahoma campaign and the one succeeding it; and is therefore entitled to every credit that attended their execution, no matter what may be claimed for others.

On the 23d of June Bragg was covering his position north of Duck River with a front extending from McMinnville, where his cavalry rested, through Wartrace and Shelbyville to Columbia, his depot being at Tullahoma. Rosecrans, thinking that Bragg would offer strong resistance at Shelbyville—which was somewhat protected by a spur of low mountains or hills, offshoots of the Cumberland Mountains— decided to turn that place; consequently, he directed the mass of the Union army on the enemy's right flank, about Manchester.

On the 26th of June McCook's corps advanced toward Liberty Gap, my divisions marching on the Shelbyville pike. I had proceeded but a few miles when I encountered the enemy's pickets, who fell back to Christiana, about nine miles from Murfreesboro'. Here I was assailed pretty wickedly by the enemy's sharpshooters and a section of artillery, but as I was instructed to do nothing more than cover the road from Eagleville, over which Brannan's division was to approach Christiana, I made little reply to this severe annoyance, wishing to conceal the strength of my force. As soon as the head of Brannan's column arrived I marched across-country to the left, and encamped that night at the little town of Millersburg, in the vicinity of Liberty Gap. I was directed to move from Millersburg, on Hoover's Gap—a pass in the range of hills already referred to, through which ran the turnpike from Murfreesboro' to Manchester—but heavy rains had made the country roads almost impassable, and the last of my division did not reach Hoover's Gap till the morning of June 27, after its abandonment by the enemy. Continuing on to Fairfield, the head of my column met, south of that place, a small force of Confederate infantry and cavalry, which after a slight skirmish Laiboldt's brigade drove back toward Wartrace. The next morning I arrived at Manchester, where I remained quiet for the day. Early on the 29th I marched by the Lynchburg road for Tullahoma, where the enemy was believed to be in force, and came into position about six miles from the town.

By the 31st the whole army had been concentrated, in spite of many difficulties, and though, on account of the heavy rains that had fallen almost incessantly since we left Murfreesboro', its movements had been slow and somewhat inaccurate, yet the precision with which it took up a line of battle for an attack on Tullahoma showed that forethought and study had been given to every detail. The enemy had determined to fall back from Tullahoma at the beginning of the campaign, however, and as we advanced, his evacuation had so far progressed that when, on July 1. We reached the earthworks thrown. up early in the year for the defense of the place, he had almost wholly disappeared, carrying off all his stores and munitions of war except some little subsistence and eleven pieces of artillery. A strong rearguard remained to cover the retreat, and on my front the usual encounters between advancing and retreating forces took place. Just before reaching the intrenchments on the Lynchburg road, I came upon an open space that was covered by a network of fallen trees and underbrush, which had been slashed all along in front of the enemy's earthworks. This made our progress very difficult, but I shortly became satisfied that there were only a few of the enemy within the works, so moving a battalion of cavalry that had joined me the day before down the road as rapidly as the obstructions would permit, the Confederate pickets quickly departed, and we gained possession of the town. Three siege guns, four caissons, a few stores, and a small number of prisoners fell into my hands.

That same evening orders were issued to the army to push on from Tullahoma in pursuit, for, as it was thought that we might not be able to cross Elk River on account of its swollen condition, we could do the enemy some damage by keeping close as possible at his heels. I marched on the Winchester road at 3 o'clock on the 2d of July and about 8 o'clock reached Elk River ford. The stream was for the time truly an impassable torrent, and all hope of crossing by the Winchester ford had to be abandoned. Deeming that further effort should be made, however, under guidance of

Card, I turned the head of my column in the direction of Alisona, marching up the river and nearly parallel with it till I came to Rock Creek. With a little delay we got across Rock Creek, which was also much swollen, and finding a short distance above its mouth a ford on Elk River that Card said was practicable, I determined to attempt it: Some of the enemy's cavalry were guarding this ford, but after a sharp little skirmish my battalion of cavalry crossed and took up a strong position on the other bank. The stream was very high and the current very swift, the water, tumbling along over its rocky bed in an immense volume, but still it was fordable for infantry if means could be devised by which the men could keep their feet. A cable was stretched across just below the ford as a lifeline for the weaker ones, and then the men of the entire division having secured their ammunition by placing the cartridge-boxes on their shoulders, the column pushed cheerfully into the rushing current. The men as they entered the water joined each other in sets of four in a close embrace, which enabled them to retain a foothold and successfully resist the force of the flood. When they were across I turned the column down the left bank of Elk River, and driving the enemy from some slight works near Estelle Springs, regained the Winchester road.

By this time it was clear that Bragg intended to fall back behind the Tennessee River, and our only chance of accomplishing anything of importance was to smash up his rear-guard before it crossed the Cumberland Mountains, and in pursuance of this idea I was directed to attack such of his force as was holding on to Winchester. At 4 o'clock on the morning of July 2 I moved on that town, and when we got close to it directed my mounted troops to charge a small force of Confederate cavalry that was picketing their front. The Confederates resisted but little, and our men went with them in a disorderly chase through the village to Boiling Fork, a small stream about half a mile beyond. Here the fleeing pickets, rallying behind a stronger force, made a stand, and I was directed by McCook to delay till I ascertained if Davis's division, which was to support me, had made the crossing of Elk River, and until I could open up communication with Brannan's division, which was to come in on my left at Decherd. As soon as I learned that Davis was across I pushed on, but the delay had permitted the enemy to pull his rear-guard up on the mountain, and rendered nugatory all further efforts to hurt him materially, our only returns consisting in forcing him to relinquish a small amount of transportation and forage at the mouth of the pass just beyond Cowan, a station on the line of the Nashville and Chattanooga railroad.

At Cowan, Colonel Watkins, of the Sixth Kentucky Cavalry, reported to me with twelve hundred mounted men. Having heard during the night that the enemy had halted on the mountain near the University—an educational establishment on the summit—I directed Watkins to make a reconnoissance and find out the value of the information. He learned that Wharton's brigade of cavalry was halted at the University to cover a moderately large force of the enemy's infantry which had not yet got down the mountain on the other side, so I pushed Watkins out again on the 5th, supporting him by a brigade of infantry, which I accompanied myself. We were too late, however, for when we arrived at the top of the mountain Wharton had disappeared, and though Watkins pursued to Bridgeport, he was able to do nothing more, and on his return reported that the last of the enemy had crossed the Tennessee River and burned the railroad bridge.

Nothing further could now be done, so I instructed Watkins to rejoin the division at Cowan, and being greatly fatigued by the hard campaigning of the previous ten days, I concluded to go back to my camp in a more comfortable way than on the back of my tired horse. In his retreat the enemy had not disturbed the railway track at all, and as we had captured a hand-car at Cowan, I thought I would have it brought up to the station near the University to carry me down the mountain to my camp, and, desiring company, I persuasively invited Colonel Frank T. Sherman to ride with me. I sent for the car by a courier, and for a long time patiently awaited its arrival, in fact, until all the returning troops had passed us, but still it did not come. Thinking it somewhat risky to remain at the station without protection, Sherman and myself started our horses to Cowan by our orderlies, and set out on foot to meet the car, trudging along down the track in momentary expectation of falling in with our private conveyance. We had not gone very far before night overtook us, and we then began to realize the dangers surrounding us, for there we were alone and helpless, tramping on in the darkness over an unknown railroad track in the enemy's country, liable on the one hand to go tumbling through some bridge or trestle, and on the other, to possible capture or death at the hands of the guerrillas then infesting these mountains. Just after dark we came to a little cabin near the track, where we made bold to ask for water, notwithstanding the fact that to disclose ourselves to the inmates might lead to fatal consequences. The water was kindly given, but the owner and his family were very much exercised lest some misfortune might befall us near their house, and be charged to them, so they encouraged us to move on with a frankness inspired by fear of future trouble to themselves.

At every turn we eagerly hoped to meet the hand-car, but it never came, and we jolted on from tie to tie for eleven weary miles, reaching Cowan after midnight, exhausted and sore in every muscle from frequent falls on the rough, unballasted road-bed. Inquiry. developed that the car had been well manned, and started to us as ordered, and nobody could account for its non-arrival. Further investigation next day showed, however, that when it reached the foot of the mountain, where the railroad formed a junction, the improvised crew, in the belief no doubt that the University was on the main line instead of near the branch to Tracy City, followed the main stem until it carried them clear across the range down the Crow Creek Valley, where the party was captured.

I had reason to remember for many a day this foolish adventure, for my sore bones and bruised muscles, caused me physical suffering until I left the Army of the Cumberland the next spring; but I had still more reason to feel for my captured men, and on this account I have never ceased to regret that I so thoughtlessly undertook to rejoin my troops by rail, instead of sticking to my faithful horse.

CHAPTER XV.
ORDERED TO OCCUPY BRIDGEPORT—A SPY—THE BATTLE OF CHICKAMAUGA— GENERAL THOMAS—TREATED TO COFFEE—RESULTS OF THE BATTLE.

The Tullahoma campaign was practically closed by the disappearance of the enemy from the country north of the Tennessee River. Middle Tennessee was once more in the possession of the National troops, and Rosecrans though strongly urged from Washington to continue on, resisted the pressure until he could repair the Nashville and Chattanooga railroad, which was of vital importance in supplying his army from its secondary base at Nashville. As he desired to hold this road to where it crossed the Tennessee, it was necessary to push a force beyond the mountains, and after a few days of rest at Cowan my division was ordered to take station at Stevenson, Alabama, the junction of the Memphis and Charleston road with the Nashville and Chattanooga, with instructions to occupy Bridgeport also.

The enemy had meanwhile concentrated most of his forces at Chattanooga for the twofold purpose of holding this gateway of the Cumberland Mountains, and to assume a defensive attitude which would enable him to take advantage of such circumstances as might arise in the development of the offensive campaign he knew we must make. The peculiar topography of the country was much to his advantage, and while we had a broad river and numerous spurs and ridges of the Cumberland Mountains to cross at a long distance from our base, he was backed up on his depots of supply, and connected by interior lines of railway with the different armies of the Confederacy, so that he could be speedily reinforced.

Bridgeport was to be ultimately a sub-depot for storing subsistence supplies, and one of the points at which our army would cross the Tennessee, so I occupied it on July 29 with two brigades, retaining one at Stevenson, however, to protect that railway junction from raids by way of Caperton's ferry. By the 29th of August a considerable quantity of supplies had been accumulated, and then began a general movement of our troops for crossing the river. As there were not with the army enough pontoons to complete the two bridges required, I was expected to build one of them of trestles; and a battalion of the First Michigan Engineers under Colonel Innis was sent me to help construct the bridge. Early on the 3ist I sent into the neighboring woods about fifteen hundred men with axes and teams, and by nightfall they had delivered on the riverbank fifteen hundred logs suitable for a trestle bridge. Flooring had been shipped to me in advance by rail, but the quantity was insufficient, and the lack had to be supplied by utilizing planking and weather-boarding taken from barns and houses in the surrounding country. The next day Innis's engineers, with the assistance of the detail that had felled the timber, cut and half-notched the logs, and put the bridge across; spanning the main channel, which was swimming deep, with four or five pontoons that had been sent me for this purpose. On the 2d and 3d of September my division crossed on the bridge in safety, though we were delayed somewhat because of its giving way once where the pontoons joined the trestles. We were followed by a few detachments from other commands, and by nearly all the transportation of McCook's corps.

After getting to the south side of the Tennessee River I was ordered to Valley Head, where McCook's corps was to concentrate. On the 4th of September I ascended Sand Mountain, but had got only half way across the plateau, on top, when night came, the march having been a most toilsome one. The next day we descended to the base, and encamped near Trenton. On the 10th I arrived at Valley Head, and climbing Lookout Mountain, encamped on the plateau at Indian Falls. The following day I went down into Broomtown Valley to Alpine. The march of McCook's corps from Valley Head to Alpine was in pursuance of orders directing it to advance on Summerville, the possession of which place would further threaten the enemy's communications, it being assumed that Bragg was in full retreat south, as he had abandoned Chattanooga on the 8th. This assumption soon proved erroneous, however, and as we, while in Broomtown Valley, could not communicate directly with Thomas's corps, the scattered condition of the army began to alarm us all, and McCook abandoned the advance to Summerville, ordering back to the summit of Lookout Mountain such of the corps trains as had got down into Broomtown Valley.

But before this I had grown uneasy in regard to the disjointed situation of our army, and, to inform myself of what was going on, determined to send a spy into the enemy's lines. In passing Valley Head on the 10th my scout Card, who had been on the lookout for some one capable to undertake the task, brought me a Union man with whom he was acquainted, who lived on Sand Mountain, and had been much persecuted by guerrillas on account of his loyal sentiments. He knew the country well, and as his loyalty was vouched for I asked him to go into the enemy's camp, which I believed to be near Lafayette, and, bring me such information as he could gather. He said such a journey would be at the risk of his life, and that at best he could not expect to remain in that section of country if he undertook it, but that he would run all the chances if I would enable him to emigrate to the West at the end c f the "job," which I could do by purchasing the small "bunch" of stock he owned on the mountain. To this I readily assented, and he started on the delicate undertaking. He penetrated the enemy's lines with little difficulty, but while prosecuting his search for information was suspected, and at once arrested and placed under guard. From this critical situation he escaped; however, making his way through the enemy's picket-line in the darkness by crawling on his belly and deceiving the sentinels by imitating the grunts of the half-wild, sand-colored hogs with which the country abounded. He succeeded in reaching Rosecrans's headquarters finally, and there gave the definite information that Bragg intended to fight, and that he expected to be reinforced by Longstreet.

By this time it was clear that Bragg had abandoned Chattanooga with the sole design of striking us in detail as we followed in pursuit; and to prevent his achieving this purpose orders came at 12 o'clock, midnight, for McCook to draw in toward Chattanooga. This could be done only by recrossing Lookout Mountain, the enemy's army at Lafayette now interposing between us and Thomas's corps. The retrograde march began at once. I moved back over the mountain on the 13th and 14th to Stevens's Mills, and on the 15th and 16th recrossed through Stevens's Gap, in the Lookout range, and encamped at its base in McLamore's cove. The march was made with all possible celerity, for the situation was critical and demanded every exertion. The ascent and descent of the mountains was extremely exhausting, the steep grades often rendering it necessary to drag up and let down by hand both the transportation and artillery. But at last we were in conjunction with the main army, and my division breathed easier.

On the 17th I remained in line of battle all day and night in front of McLamore's cove, the enemy making slight demonstrations against me from the direction of Lafayette. The main body of the army having bodily moved to the left meanwhile, I followed it on the 18th, encamping at Pond Spring. On the 19th I resumed the march to the left and went into line of battle at Crawfish Springs to cover our right and rear. Immediately after forming this line, I again became isolated by the general movement to the left, and in consequence was directed to advance and hold the ford of Chickamauga Creek at Lee and Gordon's Mills, thus coming into close communication with the balance of our forces. I moved into this position rapidly, being compelled, though, first to drive back the enemy's cavalry skirmishers, who, having crossed to the west side of the creek, annoyed the right flank of my column a good deal while en route.

Upon arrival at Lee and Gordon's Mills I found the ford over Chickamauga Creek temporarily uncovered, through the hurried movement of Wood to the assistance of Davis's division. The enemy was already present in small force, with the evident intention of taking permanent possession, but my troops at once actively engaged him and recovered the ford with some slight losses. Scarcely had this been done when I was directed to assist Crittenden. Leaving Lytle's brigade at the ford, I proceeded with Bradley's and Laiboldt's to help Crittenden, whose main line was formed to the east of the Chattanooga and Lafayette road, its right trending toward a point on Chickamauga Creek about a mile and a half north of Lee and Gordon's Mills. By the time I had joined Crittenden with my two brigades, Davis had been worsted in an attack Rosecrans had ordered him to make on the left of that portion of the enemy's line which was located along the west bank of the Chickamauga, the repulse being so severe that one of Davis's batteries had to be abandoned. Bradley's brigade arrived on the ground first and was hastily formed and thrown into the fight, which up to this moment had been very doubtful, fortune inclining first to one side, then to the other. Bradley's brigade went in with steadiness, and charging across an open corn-field that lay in front of the Lafayette road, recovered Davis's guns and forced the enemy to retire. Meanwhile Laiboldt's brigade had come on the scene, and forming it on Bradley's right, I found myself at the end of the contest holding the ground which was Davis's original position. It was an ugly fight and my loss was heavy, including Bradley wounded. The temporary success was cheering, and when Lytle's brigade joined me a little later I suggested to Crittenden that we attack, but investigation showed that his troops, having been engaged all day, were not in condition, so the suggestion could not be carried out.

The events of the day had indicated that Bragg's main object was to turn Rosecrans's left; it was therefore still deemed necessary that the army should continue its flank movement to the left, so orders came to draw my troops in toward the widow Glenn's house. By strengthening the skirmish line and shifting my brigades in succession from right to left until the point designated was reached, I was able to effect the withdrawal without much difficulty, calling in my skirmish line after the main force had retired.

My command having settled down for the night in this new line I rode to army headquarters, to learn if possible the expectations for the morrow and hear the result of the battle in General Thomas's front. Nearly all the superior officers of the army were at headquarters, and it struck me that much depression prevailed, notwithstanding the fact that the enemy's attempts during the day to turn our left flank and also envelop our right had been unsuccessful. It was now positively known, through prisoners and otherwise, that Bragg had been reinforced to such an extent as to make him materially outnumber us, consequently there was much apprehension for the future.

The necessity of protecting our left was most apparent, and the next day the drifting in that direction was to be continued. This movement in the presence of the enemy, who at all points was actively seeking an opportunity to penetrate our line and interpose a column between its right and left, was most dangerous. But the necessity for shifting the army to the left was obvious, hence only the method by which it was undertaken is open to question. The move was made by the flank in the face of an exultant foe superior in numbers, and was a violation of a simple and fundamental military principle. Under such circumstances columns naturally stretch out into attenuated lines, organizations become separated, and intervals occur, all of which we experienced; and had the orders for the movement been construed properly I doubt if it could have been executed without serious danger. Necessity knows no law, however, and when all the circumstances of this battle are fully considered it is possible that justification may be found for the manoeuvres by which the army was thus drifted to the left. We were in a bad strait unquestionably, and under such conditions possibly the exception had to be applied rather than the rule.

At daylight on the morning of the 20th a dense fog obscured everything; consequently both armies were passive so far as fighting was concerned. Rosecrans took advantage of the inaction to rearrange his right, and I was pulled back closer to the widow Glenn's house to a strong position, where I threw together some rails and logs as barricades, but I was disconnected from the troops on my left by a considerable interval. Here I awaited the approach of the enemy, but he did not disturb me, although about 9 o'clock in the forenoon he had opened on our extreme left with musketry fire and a heavy cannonade. Two hours later it was discovered by McCook that the interval between the main army and me was widening, and he ordered me to send Laiboldt's brigade to occupy a portion of the front that had been covered by Negley's division. Before getting this brigade into place, however, two small brigades of Davis's division occupied the ground, and I directed Laiboldt to form in column of regiments on the crest of a low ridge in rear of Carlin's brigade, so as to prevent Davis's right flank from being turned. The enemy was now feeling Davis strongly, and I was about sending for Lytle's and Bradley's brigades when I received an order to move these rapidly to the, extreme left of the army to the assistance of General Thomas. I rode hastily back toward their position, but in the meanwhile, they had been notified by direct orders from McCook, and were moving out at a double-quick toward the Lafayette road. By this time the enemy had assaulted Davis furiously in front and flank, and driven him from his line, and as the confused mass came back, McCook ordered Laiboldt to charge by deploying to the front. This he did through Davis's broken ranks, but failed to check the enemy's heavy lines, and finally Laiboldt's brigade broke also and fell to the rear. My remaining troops, headed by Lytle, were now passing along the rear of the ground where this disaster took place—in column on the road—en route to Thomas, and as the hundreds of fugitives rushed back, McCook directed me to throw in Lytle's and Bradley's brigades. This was hastily done, they being formed to the front under a terrible fire. Scarcely were they aligned when the same horde of Confederates that had overwhelmed Davis and Laiboldt poured in upon them a deadly fire and shivered the two brigades to pieces. We succeeded in rallying them, however, and by a counter attack regained the ridge that Laiboldt had been driven from, where we captured the colors of the Twenty-fourth Alabama. We could not hold the ridge, though, and my troops were driven back with heavy loss, including General Lytle killed, past the widow Glenn's house, and till I managed to establish them in line of battle on a range of low hills behind the Dry Valley road.

During these occurrences General Rosecrans passed down the road behind my line, and sent word that he wished to see me, but affairs were too critical to admit of my going to him at once, and he rode on to Chattanooga. It is to be regretted that he did not wait till I could join him, for the delay would have permitted him to see that matters were not in quite such bad shape as he supposed; still, there is no disguising the fact that at this juncture his army was badly crippled.

Shortly after my division had rallied on the low hills already described, I discovered that the enemy, instead of attacking me in front, was wedging in between my division and the balance of the army; in short, endeavoring to cut me off from Chattanooga. This necessitated another retrograde movement, which brought me back to the southern face of Missionary Ridge, where I was joined by Carlin's brigade of Davis's division. Still thinking I could join General Thomas, I rode some distance to the left of my line to look for a way out, but found that the enemy had intervened so far as to isolate me effectually. I then determined to march directly to Rossville, and from there effect a junction with Thomas by the Lafayette road. I reached Rossville about o'clock in the afternoon, bringing with me eight guns, forty-six caissons, and a long ammunition train, the latter having been found in a state of confusion behind the widow Glenn's when I was being driven back behind the Dry Valley road.

The head of my column passed through Rossville, appearing upon Thomas's left about 6 o'clock in the evening, penetrated without any opposition the right of the enemy's line, and captured several of his field-hospitals. As soon as I got on the field I informed Thomas of the presence of my command, and asked for orders. He replied that his lines were disorganized, and that it would be futile to attack; that all I could do was to hold on, and aid in covering his withdrawal to Rossville.

I accompanied him back to Rossville, and when we reached the skirt of the little hamlet General Thomas halted and we dismounted. Going into one of the angles of a worm fence near by I took a rail from the top and put it through the lower rails at a proper height from the ground to make a seat, and General Thomas and I sat down while, my troops were moving by. The General appeared very much exhausted, seemed to forget what he had stopped for, and said little or nothing of the incidents of the day. This was the second occasion on which I had met him in the midst of misfortune, for during the fight in the cedars at Stone River, when our prospects were most disheartening, we held a brief conversation respecting the line he was then taking up for the purpose of helping me. At other times, in periods of inactivity, I saw but little of him. He impressed me, now as he did in the cedars, his quiet, unobtrusive: demeanor communicating a gloomy rather than a hopeful view of the situation. This apparent depression was due no doubt to the severe trial through which he had gone in the last forty-eight hours, which, strain had exhausted him very much both physically and mentally. His success in maintaining his ground was undoubtedly largely influenced by the fact that two-thirds of the National forces had been sent to his succor, but his firm purpose to save the army was the mainstay on which all relied after Rosecrans left the field. As the command was getting pretty well past, I rose to go in order to put my troops into camp. This aroused the General, when, remarking that he had a little flask of brandy in his saddle-holster, he added that he had just stopped for the purpose of offering me a drink, as he knew I must be very tired. He requested one of his staff-officers to get the flask, and after taking a sip himself, passed it to me. Refreshed by the brandy, I mounted and rode off to supervise the encamping of my division, by no means an easy task considering the darkness, and the confusion that existed among the troops that had preceded us into Rossville.

This done, I lay down at the foot of a tree, with my saddle for a pillow, and saddle-blanket for a cover. Some soldiers near me having built a fire, were making coffee, and I guess I must have been looking on wistfully, for in a little while they brought me a tin-cupful of the coffee and a small piece of hard bread, which I relished keenly, it being the first food that had passed my lips since the night before. I was very tired, very hungry, and much discouraged by what had taken place since morning. I had been obliged to fight my command under the most disadvantageous circumstances, disconnected, without supports, without even opportunity to form in line of battle, and at one time contending against four divisions of the enemy. In this battle of Chickamauga, out of an effective strength of 4,000 bayonets, I had lost 1,517 officers and men, including two brigade commanders. This was not satisfactory indeed, it was most depressing—and then there was much confusion prevailing around Rossville; and, this condition of things doubtless increasing my gloomy reflections, it did not seem to me that the outlook for the next day was at all auspicious, unless the enemy was slow to improve his present advantage. Exhaustion soon quieted all forebodings, though, and I fell into a sound sleep, from which I was not aroused till daylight.

On the morning of the 21st the enemy failed to advance, and his inaction gave us the opportunity for getting the broken and disorganized army into shape. It took a large part of the day to accomplish this, and the chances of complete victory would have been greatly in Bragg's favor if he could have attacked us vigorously at this time. But he had been badly hurt in the two days' conflict, and his inactivity on the 21st showed that he too had to go through the process of reorganization. Indeed, his crippled condition began to show itself the preceding evening, and I have always thought that, had General Thomas held on and attacked the Confederate right and rear from where I made the junction with him on the Lafayette road, the field of Chickamauga would have been relinquished to us; but it was fated to be otherwise.

Rosecrans, McCook, and Crittenden passed out of the battle when they went back to Chattanooga, and their absence was discouraging to all aware of it. Doubtless this had much to do with Thomas's final withdrawal, thus leaving the field to the enemy, though at an immense cost in killed and wounded. The night of the 21st the army moved back from Rossville, and my division, as the rearguard of the Twentieth Corps, got within our lines at Chattanooga about 8 o'clock the morning of the 22d. Our unmolested retirement from Rossville lent additional force to the belief that the enemy had been badly injured, and further impressed me with the conviction that we might have held on. Indeed, the battle of Chickamauga was somewhat like that of Stone River, victory resting with the side that had the grit to defer longest its relinquishment of the field.

The manoeuvres by which Rosecrans had carried his army over the Cumberland Mountains, crossed the Tennessee River, and possessed himself of Chattanooga, merit the highest commendation up to the abandonment of this town by Bragg on the 8th of September; but I have always fancied that that evacuation made Rosecrans over-confident, and led him to think that he could force Bragg south as far as Rome. After the Union army passed the river and Chattanooga fell into our hands; we still kept pressing the enemy's communications, and the configuration of the country necessitated more or less isolation of the different corps. McCook's corps of three divisions had crossed two difficult ridges—Sand and Lookout mountains—to Alpine in Broomtown Valley with intentions against Summerville. Thomas's corps had marched by the way of Stevens's Gap toward Lafayette, which he expected to occupy. Crittenden had passed through Chattanooga, at first directing his march an Ringgold. Thus the corps of the army were not in conjunction, and between McCook and Thomas there intervened a positive and aggressive obstacle in the shape of Bragg's army concentrating and awaiting reinforcement at Lafayette. Under these circumstances Bragg could have taken the different corps in detail, and it is strange that he did not, even before receiving his reinforcements, turn on McCook in Broomtown Valley and destroy him.

Intelligence that Bragg would give battle began to come to us from various sources as early as the 10th of September, and on the 11th McCook found that he could not communicate with Thomas by the direct road through Broomtown Valley; but we did not begin closing in toward Chattanooga till the 13th, and even then the Twentieth Corps had before it the certainty of many delays that must necessarily result from the circuitous and difficult mountain roads which we would be obliged to follow. Had the different corps, beginning with McCook's, been drawn in toward Chattanooga between the 8th and 12th of September, the objective point of the campaign would have remained in our hands without the battle of Chickamauga, but, as has been seen, this was not done. McCook was almost constantly on the march day and night between the 13th and the 19th, ascending and descending mountains, his men worried and wearied, so that when they appeared on the battle-field, their fatigued condition operated greatly against their efficiency. This delay in concentration was also the original cause of the continuous shifting toward our left to the support of Thomas, by which manoeuvre Rosecrans endeavored to protect his communications with Chattanooga, and out of which grew the intervals that offered such tempting opportunities to Bragg. In addition to all this, much transpired on the field of battle tending to bring about disaster. There did not seem to be any well-defined plan of action in the fighting; and this led to much independence of judgment in construing orders among some of the subordinate generals. It also gave rise to much license in issuing orders: too many people were giving important directions, affecting the whole army, without authority from its head. In view, therefore, of all the errors that were committed from the time Chattanooga fell into our hands after our first crossing the Tennessee, it was fortunate that the Union defeat was not more complete, that it left in the enemy's possession not much more than the barren results arising from the simple holding of the ground on which the engagement was fought.

CHAPTER XVI.
AT CHATTANOOGA—THE ENEMY FORTIFIES LOOKOUT MOUNTAIN AND MISSIONARY RIDGE—REORGANIZING THE ARMY—REMOVAL OF GENERAL ROSECRANS— PUNISHMENT OF DESERTERS—GRANT AT CHATTANOOGA—THE FIGHT ON LOOKOUT MOUNTAIN—A BRAVE COLOR-BEARER—BATTLE OF MISSIONARY RIDGE.

By 9 o'clock on the morning of September 22 my command took up a position within the heavy line of intrenchments at Chattanooga, the greater part of which defenses had been thrown up since the army commenced arriving there the day before. The enemy, having now somewhat recovered from the shock of the recent battle, followed carefully, and soon invested us close into our lines with a parallel system of rifle-pits. He also began at once to erect permanent lines of earthworks on Missionary Ridge and to establish himself strongly on Lookout Mountain. He then sent Wheeler's cavalry north of the Tennessee, and, aided greatly by the configuration of the ground, held us in a state of partial siege, which serious rains might convert into a complete investment. The occupation of Lookout Mountain broke our direct communication with Bridgeport-our sub-depot—and forced us to bring supplies by way of the Sequatchie Valley and Waldron's Ridge of the Cumberland Mountains, over a road most difficult even in the summer season, but now liable to be rendered impassable by autumn rains. The distance to Bridgeport by this circuitous route was sixty miles, and the numerous passes, coves, and small valleys through which the road ran offered tempting opportunities, for the destruction of trains, and the enemy was not slow to take advantage of them. Indeed, the situation was not promising, and General Rosecrans himself, in communicating with the President the day succeeding the battle of Chickamauga, expressed doubts of his ability to hold the gateway of the Cumberland Mountains.

The position taken up by my troops inside the lines of Chattanooga was near the old iron-works, under the shadow of Lookout Mountain. Here we were exposed to a continual fire from the enemy's batteries for many days, but as the men were well covered by secure though simple intrenchments, but little damage was done. My own headquarters were established on the grounds of Mr. William Crutchfield, a resident of the place, whose devotion to the Union cause knew no bounds, and who rendered me—and, in fact, at one time or another, nearly every general officer in the Army of the Cumberland—invaluable service in the way of information about the Confederate army. My headquarters camp frequently received shots from the point of Lookout Mountain also, but fortunately no casualties resulted from this plunging fire, though, I am free to confess, at first our nerves were often upset by the whirring of twenty-pounder shells dropped inconsiderately into our camp at untimely hours of the night.

In a few days rain began to fall, and the mountain roads by which our supplies came were fast growing impracticable. Each succeeding train of wagons took longer to make the trip from Bridgeport, and the draft mules were dying by the hundreds. The artillery horses would soon go too, and there was every prospect that later the troops would starve unless something could be done. Luckily for my division, a company of the Second Kentucky Cavalry had attached itself to my headquarters, and, though there without authority, had been left undisturbed in view of a coming reorganization of the army incidental to the removal of McCook and Crittenden from the command of their respective corps, a measure that had been determined upon immediately after the battle of Chickamauga. Desiring to remain with me, Captain Lowell H. Thickstun, commanding this company, was ready for any duty I might find, for him, so I ordered him into the Sequatchie Valley for the purpose of collecting supplies for my troops, and sent my scout, Card along to guide him to the best locations. The company hid itself away in a deep cove in the upper end of the valley, and by keeping very quiet and paying for everything it took from the people, in a few days was enabled to send me large quantities of corn for my animals and food for the officers and men, which greatly supplemented the scanty supplies we were getting from the sub-depot at Bridgeport. In this way I carried men and animals through our beleaguerment in pretty fair condition, and of the turkeys, chickens, ducks, and eggs sent in for the messes of my officers we often had enough to divide liberally among those at different headquarters. Wheeler's cavalry never discovered my detached company, yet the chances of its capture were not small, sometimes giving much uneasiness; still, I concluded it was better to run all risks than to let the horses die of starvation in Chattanooga. Later, after the battle of Missionary Ridge, when I started to Knoxville, the company joined me in excellent shape, bringing with it an abundance of food, including a small herd of beef cattle.

The whole time my line remained near the iron-mills the shelling from Lookout was kept up, the screeching shots inquisitively asking in their well-known way, "Where are you? Where are you?" but it is strange to see how readily, soldiers can become accustomed to the sound of dangerous missiles under circumstances of familiarity, and this case was no exception to the rule. Few casualties occurred, and soon contempt took the place of nervousness, and as we could not reply in kind on account of the elevation required for our guns, the men responded by jeers and imprecations whenever a shell fell into their camp.

Meantime, orders having been issued for the organization of the army, additional troops were attached to my command, and it became the Second Division of the Fourth Army Corps, to which Major-General Gordon Granger was assigned as commander. This necessitated a change of position of the division, and I moved to ground behind our works, with my right resting on Fort Negley and my left extending well over toward Fort Wood, my front being parallel to Missionary Ridge. My division was now composed of twenty-five regiments, classified into brigades and demi-brigades, the former commanded by Brigadier-General G. D. Wagner, Colonel C. G. Harker, and Colonel F. T. Sherman; the latter, by Colonels Laiboldt, Miller, Wood, Walworth, and Opdyke. The demi-brigade was an awkward invention of Granger's; but at this time it was necessitated—perhaps by the depleted condition of our regiments, which compelled the massing of a great number of regimental organizations into a division to give it weight and force.

On October 16, 1863, General Grant had been assigned to the command of the "Military Division of the Mississippi," a geographical area which embraced the Departments of the Ohio, the Cumberland, and the Tennessee, thus effecting a consolidation of divided commands which might have been introduced most profitably at an earlier date. The same order that assigned General Grant relieved General Rosecrans, and placed

General Thomas in command of the Army of the Cumberland. At the time of the reception of the order, Rosecrans was busy with preparations for a movement to open the direct road to Bridgeport— having received in the interval, since we came back to Chattanooga, considerable reinforcement by the arrival in his department of the Eleventh and Twelfth corps, under General Hooker, from the Army of the Potomac. With this force Rosecrans had already strengthened certain important points on the railroad between Nashville and Stevenson, and given orders to Hooker to concentrate at Bridgeport such portions of his command as were available, and to hold them in readiness to advance toward Chattanooga.

On the 19th of October, after turning the command over to Thomas, General Rosecrans quietly slipped away from the army. He submitted uncomplainingly to his removal, and modestly left us without fuss or demonstration; ever maintaining, though, that the battle of Chickamauga was in effect a victory, as it had ensured us, he said, the retention of Chattanooga. When his departure became known deep and almost universal regret was expressed, for he was enthusiastically esteemed and loved by the Army of the Cumberland, from the day he assumed command of it until he left it, notwithstanding the censure poured upon him after the battle of Chickamauga.

The new position to which my division had been moved, in consequence of the reorganization, required little additional labor to strengthen it, and the routine of fatigue duty and drills was continued as before, its monotony occasionally broken by the excitement of an expected attack, or by amusements of various kinds that were calculated to keep the men in good spirits. Toward this result much was contributed by Mr. James E. Murdock, the actor, who came down from the North to recover the body of his son, killed at Chickamauga, and was quartered with me for the greater part of the time he was obliged to await the successful conclusion of his sad mission. He spent days, and even weeks, going about through the division giving recitations before the camp-fires, and in improvised chapels, which the men had constructed from refuse lumber and canvas. Suiting his selections to the occasion, he never failed to excite intense interest in the breasts of all present, and when circumstances finally separated him from us, all felt that a debt of gratitude was due him that could never be paid. The pleasure he gave, and the confident feeling that was now arising from expected reinforcements, was darkened, however, by one sad incident. Three men of my division had deserted their colors at the beginning of the siege and made their way north. They were soon arrested, and were brought back to stand trial for the worst offense that can be committed by a soldier, convicted of the crime, and ordered to be shot. To make the example effective I paraded the whole division for the execution, and on the 13th of November, in the presence of their former comrades, the culprits were sent, in accordance with the terms of their sentence, to render their account to the Almighty. It was the saddest spectacle I ever witnessed, but there could be no evasion, no mitigation of the full letter of the law; its timely enforcement was but justice to the brave spirits who had yet to fight the rebellion to the end.

General Grant arrived at Chattanooga on October 23, and began at once to carry out the plans that had been formed for opening the shorter or river road to Bridgeport. This object was successfully accomplished by the moving of Hooker's command to Rankin's and Brown's ferries in concert with a force from the Army of the Cumberland which was directed on the same points, so by the 27th of October direct communication with our depots was established. The four weeks which followed this cheering result were busy with the work of refitting and preparing for offensive operations as soon as General Sherman should reach us with his troops from West Tennessee. During this period of activity the enemy committed the serious fault of detaching Longstreet's corps—sending it to aid in the siege of Knoxville in East Tennessee—an error which has no justification whatever, unless it be based on the presumption that it was absolutely necessary that Longstreet should ultimately rejoin Lee's army in Virginia by way of Knoxville and Lynchburg, with a chance of picking up Burnside en route. Thus depleted, Bragg still held Missionary Ridge in strong force, but that part of his line which extended across the intervening valley to the northerly point of Lookout Mountain was much attenuated.

By the 18th of November General Grant had issued instructions covering his intended operations. They contemplated that Sherman's column, which was arriving by the north bank of the Tennessee, should cross the river on a pontoon bridge just below the mouth of Chickamauga Creek and carry the northern extremity of Missionary Ridge as far as the railroad tunnel; that the Army of the Cumberland—the centre—should co-operate with Sherman; and that Hooker with a mixed command should continue to hold Lookout Valley and operate on our extreme right as circumstances might warrant. Sherman crossed on the 24th to perform his alloted part of the programme, but in the meantime Grant becoming impressed with the idea that Bragg was endeavoring to get away, ordered Thomas to make a strong demonstration in his front, to determine the truth or falsity of the information that had been received. This task fell to the Fourth Corps, and at 12 o'clock on the 23d I was notified that Wood's division would make a reconnoissance to an elevated point in its front called Orchard Knob, and that I was to support it with my division and prevent Wood's right flank from being turned by an advance of the enemy on Moore's road or from the direction of Rossville. For this duty I marched my division out of the works about 2 p.m., and took up a position on Bushy Knob. Shortly after we reached this point Wood's division passed my left flank on its reconnoissance, and my command, moving in support of it, drove in the enemy's picket-line. Wood's took possession of Orchard Knob easily, and mine was halted on a low ridge to the right of the Knob, where I was directed by General Thomas to cover my front by a strong line of rifle-pits, and to put in position two batteries of the Fourth regular artillery that had joined me from the Eleventh Corps. After dark Wood began to feel uneasy about his right flank, for a gap existed between it and my left, so I moved in closer to him, taking up a line where I remained inactive till the 25th, but suffering some inconvenience from the enemy's shells.

On the 24th General Sherman made an attack for the purpose of carrying the north end of Missionary Ridge. His success was not complete, although at the time it was reported throughout the army to be so. It had the effect of disconcerting Bragg, however, and caused him to strengthen his right by withdrawing troops from his left, which circumstance led Hooker to advance on the northerly face of Lookout Mountain. At first, with good glasses, we could plainly see Hooker's troops driving the Confederates up the face of the mountain. All were soon lost to view in the dense timber, but emerged again on the open ground, across which the Confederates retreated at a lively pace, followed by the pursuing line, which was led by a color-bearer, who, far in advance, was bravely waving on his comrades. The gallantry of this man elicited much enthusiasm among us all, but as he was a considerable distance ahead of his comrades I expected to see his rashness punished at any moment by death or capture. He finally got quite near the retreating Confederates, when suddenly they made a dash at him, but he was fully alive to such a move, and ran back, apparently uninjured, to his friends. About this time a small squad of men reached the top of Lookout and planted the Stars and Stripes on its very crest. Just then a cloud settled down on the mountain, and a heavy bank of fog obscured its whole face.

After the view was lost the sharp rattle of musketry continued some time, but practically the fight had been already won by Hooker's men, the enemy only holding on with a rear-guard to assure his retreat across Chattanooga Valley to Missionary Ridge. Later we heard very heavy cannonading, and fearing that Hooker was in trouble I sent a staff-officer to find out whether he needed assistance, which I thought could be given by a demonstration toward Rossville. The officer soon returned with the report that Hooker was all right, that the cannonading was only a part of a little rear-guard fight, two sections of artillery making all the noise, the reverberations from point to point in the adjacent mountains echoing and reechoing till it seemed that at least fifty guns were engaged.

On the morning of the 25th of November Bragg's entire army was holding only the line of Missionary Ridge, and our troops, being now practically connected from Sherman to Hooker, confronted it with the Army of the Cumberland in the centre—bowed out along the front of Wood's division and mine. Early in the day Sherman, with great determination and persistence, made an attempt to carry the high ground near the tunnel, first gaining and then losing advantage, but his attack was not crowned with the success anticipated. Meanwhile Hooker and Palmer were swinging across Chattanooga Valley, using me as a pivot for the purpose of crossing Missionary Ridge in the neighborhood of Rossville. In the early part of the day I had driven in the Confederate pickets in my front, so as to prolong my line of battle on that of Wood, the necessity of continuing to refuse my right having been obviated by the capture of Lookout Mountain and the advance of Palmer.

About 2 o'clock orders came to carry the line at the foot of the ridge, attacking at a signal of six guns. I had few changes or new dispositions to make. Wagner's brigade, which was next to Wood's division, was formed in double lines, and Harker's brigade took the same formation on Wagner's right. Colonel F. T. Sherman's brigade came on Harker's right, formed in a column of attack, with a front of three regiments, he having nine. My whole front was covered with a heavy line of skirmishers. These dispositions made, my right rested a little distance south of Moore's road, my left joined Wood over toward Orchard Knob, while my centre was opposite Thurman's house—the headquarters of General Bragg—on Missionary Ridge. A small stream of water ran parallel to my front, as far as which the ground was covered by a thin patch of timber, and beyond the edge of the timber was an open plain to the foot of Missionary Ridge, varying in width from four to nine hundred yards. At the foot of the ridge was the enemy's first line of rifle-pits; at a point midway up its face, another line, incomplete; and on the crest was a third line, in which Bragg had massed his artillery.

The enemy saw we were making dispositions for an attack, and in plain view of my whole division he prepared himself for resistance, marching regiments from his left flank with flying colors; and filling up the spaces not already occupied in his intrenchments. Seeing the enemy thus strengthening himself, it was plain that we would have to act quickly if we expected to accomplish much, and I already began to doubt the feasibility of our remaining in the first line of rifle-pits when we should have carried them. I discussed the order with Wagner, Harker, and Sherman, and they were similarly impressed, so while anxiously awaiting the signal I sent Captain Ransom of my staff to Granger, who was at Fort Wood, to ascertain if we were to carry the first line or the ridge beyond. Shortly after Ransom started the signal guns were fired, and I told my brigade commanders to go for the ridge.

Placing myself in front of Harker's brigade, between the line of battle and the skirmishers, accompanied by only an orderly so as not to attract the enemy's fire, we moved out. Under a terrible storm of shot and shell the line pressed forward steadily through the timber, and as it emerged on the plain took the double-quick and with fixed bayonets rushed at the enemy's first line. Not a shot was fired from our line of battle, and as it gained on my skirmishers they melted into and became one with it, and all three of my brigades went over the rifle-pits simultaneously. They then lay down on the face of the ridge, for a breathing-spell and for protection' from the terrible fire, of canister and musketry pouring over us from the guns on the crest. At the rifle-pits there had been little use for the bayonet, for most of the Confederate troops, disconcerted by the sudden rush, lay close in the ditch and surrendered, though some few fled up the slope to the next line. The prisoners were directed to move out to our rear, and as their intrenchments had now come under fire from the crest, they went with alacrity, and without guard or escort, toward Chattanooga.

After a short pause to get breath the ascent of the ridge began, and I rode, into the ditch of the intrenchments to drive out a few skulkers who were hiding there. Just at this time I was joined by Captain Ransom, who, having returned from Granger, told me that we were to carry only the line at the base, and that in coming back, when he struck the left of the division, knowing this interpretation of the order, he in his capacity as an aide-de-camp had directed Wagner, who was up on the face of the ridge, to return, and that in consequence Wagner was recalling his men to the base. I could not bear to order the recall of troops now so gallantly climbing the hill step by step, and believing we could take it, I immediately rode to Wagner's brigade and directed it to resume the attack. In the meantime Harker's and F. T. Sherman's troops were approaching the partial line of works midway of the ridge, and as I returned to the centre of their rear, they were being led by many stands of regimental colors. There seemed to be a rivalry as to which color should be farthest to the front; first one would go forward a few feet, then another would come up to it, the color-bearers vying with one another as to who should be foremost, until finally every standard was planted on the intermediate works. The enemy's fire from the crest during the ascent was terrific in the noise made, but as it was plunging, it over-shot and had little effect on those above the second line of pits, but was very uncomfortable for those below, so I deemed it advisable to seek another place, and Wagner's brigade having reassembled and again pressed up the ridge, I rode up the face to join my troops.

As soon as the men saw me, they surged forward and went over the works on the crest. The parapet of the intrenchment was too high for my horse to jump, so, riding a short distance to the left, I entered through a low place in the line. A few Confederates were found inside, but they turned the butts of their muskets toward me in token of surrender, for our men were now passing beyond them on both their flanks.

The right and right centre of my division gained the summit first, they being partially sheltered by a depression in the face of the ridge, the Confederates in their immediate front fleeing down the southern face. When I crossed the rifle-pits on the top the Confederates were still holding fast at Bragg's headquarters, and a battery located there opened fire along the crest; making things most uncomfortably hot. Seeing the danger to which I was exposed, for I was mounted, Colonel Joseph Conrad, of the Fifteenth Missouri, ran up and begged me to dismount. I accepted his excellent advice, and it probably saved my life; but poor Conrad was punished for his solicitude by being seriously wounded in the thigh at the moment he was thus contributing to my safety.

Wildly cheering, the men advanced along the ridge toward Bragg's headquarters, and soon drove the Confederates from this last position, capturing a number of prisoners, among them Breckenridge's and Bates's adjutant-generals, and the battery that had made such stout resistance on the crest-two guns which were named "Lady Breckenridge" and "Lady Buckner" General Bragg himself having barely time to escape before his headquarters were taken.

My whole division had now reached the summit, and Wagner and

Harker— the latter slightly wounded—joined me as I was standing in the battery just secured. The enemy was rapidly retiring, and though many of his troops, with disorganized wagon-trains and several pieces of artillery, could be distinctly seen in much confusion about half a mile distant in the valley below, yet he was covering them with a pretty well organized line that continued to give us a desultory fire. Seeing this, I at once directed Wagner and Harker to take up the pursuit along Moore's road, which led to Chickamauga Station— Bragg's depot of supply—and as they progressed, I pushed Sherman's brigade along the road behind them. Wagner and Harker soon overtook the rearguard, and a slight skirmish caused it to break, permitting nine guns and a large number of wagons which were endeavoring to get away in the stampede to fall into our hands.

About a mile and a half beyond Missionary Ridge, Moore's road passed over a second ridge or high range of hills, and here the enemy had determined to make a stand for that purpose, posting eight pieces of artillery with such supporting force as he could rally. He was immediately attacked by Harker and Wagner, but the position was strong, the ridge being rugged and difficult of ascent, and after the first onset our men recoiled. A staff-officer from Colonel Wood's demi-brigade informing me at this juncture that that command was too weak to carry the position in its front, I ordered the Fifteenth Indiana and the Twenty-Sixth Ohio to advance to Wood's aid, and then hastening to the front I found his men clinging to the face of the ridge, contending stubbornly with the rear-guard of the enemy. Directing Harker to put Opdyke's demi-brigade in on the right, I informed Wagner that it was necessary to flank the enemy by carrying the high bluff on our left where the ridge terminated, that I had designated the Twenty-Sixth Ohio and Fifteenth Indiana for the work, and that I wished him to join them.

It was now dusk, but the two regiments engaged in the flanking movement pushed on to gain the bluff. Just as they reached the crest of the ridge the moon rose from behind, enlarged by the refraction of the atmosphere, and as the attacking column passed along the summit it crossed the moon's disk and disclosed to us below a most interesting panorama, every figure nearly being thrown out in full relief. The enemy, now outflanked on left and right, abandoned his ground, leaving us two pieces of artillery and a number of wagons. After this ridge was captured I found that no other troops than mine were pursuing the enemy, so I called a halt lest I might become too much isolated. Having previously studied the topography of the country thoroughly, I knew that if I pressed on my line of march would carry me back to Chickamauga station, where we would be in rear of the Confederates that had been fighting General Sherman, and that there was a possibility of capturing them by such action; but I did not feel warranted in marching there alone, so I rode back to Missionary Ridge to ask for more troops, and upon arriving there I found Granger in command, General Thomas having gone back to Chattanooga.

Granger was at Braggy's late headquarters in bed. I informed him of my situation and implored him to follow me up with the Army of the Cumberland, but he declined, saying that he thought we had done well enough. I still insisting, he told me finally to push on to the crossing of Chickamauga Creek, and if I, encountered the enemy he would order troops to my support. I returned to my division about 12 o'clock at night, got it under way, and reached the crossing, about half a mile from the station, at 2 o'clock on the morning of the 26th, and there found the bridge destroyed, but that the creek was fordable. I did not encounter the enemy in any force, but feared to go farther without assistance. This I thought I might bring up by practicing a little deception, so I caused two regiments to simulate an engagement by opening fire, hoping that this would alarm Granger and oblige him to respond with troops, but my scheme failed. General Granger afterward told me that he had heard the volleys, but suspected their purpose, knowing that they were not occasioned by a fight, since they were too regular in their delivery.

I was much disappointed that my pursuit had not been supported, for I felt that great results were in store for us should the enemy be vigorously followed. Had the troops under Granger's command been pushed out with mine when Missionary Ridge was gained, we could have reached Chickamauga Station by 12 o'clock the night of the 25th; or had they been sent even later, when I called for them, we could have got there by daylight and worked incalculable danger to the Confederates, for the force that had confronted Sherman did not pass Chickamauga Station in their retreat till after daylight on the morning of the 26th.

My course in following so close was dictated by a thorough knowledge of the topography of the country and a familiarity with its roads, bypaths, and farm-houses, gained with the assistance of Mr. Crutchfield; and sure my column was heading in the right direction, though night had fallen I thought that an active pursuit would almost certainly complete the destruction of Bragg's army. When General Grant came by my bivouac at the crossing of Chickamauga Creek on the 26th, he realized what might have been accomplished had the successful assault on Missionary Ridge been supplemented by vigorous efforts on the part of some high officers, who were more interested in gleaning that portion of the battle-field over which my command had passed than in destroying a panic-stricken enemy.

Although it cannot be said that the result of the two days' operations was reached by the methods which General Grant had indicated in his instructions preceding the battle, yet the general outcome was unquestionably due to his genius, for the manoeuvring of Sherman's and Hooker's commands created the opportunity for Thomas's corps of the Army of the Cumberland to carry the ridge at the centre. In directing Sherman to attack the north end of the ridge, Grant disconcerted Bragg—who was thus made to fear the loss of his depot of supplies at Chickamauga Station—and compelled him to resist stoutly; and stout resistance to Sherman meant the withdrawal of the Confederates from Lookout Mountain. While this attack was in process of execution advantage was taken of it by Hooker in a well-planned and well-fought battle, but to my mind an unnecessary one, for our possession of Lookout was the inevitable result that must follow from Sherman's threatening attitude. The assault on Missionary Ridge by Granger's and Palmer's corps was not premeditated by Grant, he directing only the line at its base to be carried, but when this fell into our hands the situation demanded our getting the one at the top also.

I took into the action an effective force of 6,000, and lost 123 officers and 1,181 men killed and wounded. These casualties speak louder than words of the character of the fight, and plainly tell where the enemy struggled most stubbornly for these figures comprise one-third the casualties of the entire body of Union troops— Sherman's and all included. My division captured 1,762 prisoners and, in all, seventeen pieces of artillery. Six of these guns I turned over with caissons complete; eleven were hauled off the field and appropriated by an officer of high rank—General Hazen. I have no disposition to renew the controversy which grew out of this matter. At the time the occurrence took place I made the charge in a plain official report, which was accepted as correct by the corps and army commanders, from General Granger up to General Grant. General Hazen took no notice of this report then, though well aware of its existence. Nearly a quarter of a century later, however, he endeavored to justify his retention of the guns by trying to show that his brigade was the first to reach the crest of Missionary Ridge, and that he was therefore entitled to them. This claim of being the first to mount the ridge is made by other brigades than Hazen's, with equal if not greater force, so the absurdity of his deduction is apparent:

NOTE: In a book published by General Hazen in 1885, he endeavored to show, by a number of letters from subordinate officers of his command, written at his solicitation from fifteen to twenty years after the occurrence, that his brigade was the first to mount Missionary Ridge, and that it was entitled to possess these guns. The doubtful character of testimony dimmed by the lapse of many years has long been conceded, and I am content to let the controversy stand the test of history, based on the conclusions of General Grant, as he drew them from official reports made when the circumstances were fresh in the minds of all.

General Grant says: "To Sheridan's prompt movement, the Army of the Cumberland and the nation are indebted for the bulk of the capture of prisoners, artillery, and small-arms that day. Except for his prompt pursuit, so much in this way would not have been accomplished."

General Thomas says: "We captured all their cannon and ammunition before they could be removed or destroyed. After halting a few moments to reorganize the troops, who had become somewhat scattered in the assault of the hill, General Sheridan pushed forward in pursuit, and drove those in his front who had escaped capture across Chickamauga Creek."

REPORT OF COLONEL FRANCIS T. SHERMAN, COMMANDING FIRST BRIGADE: "When within ten yards of the crest, our men seemed to be thrown forward as if by some powerful engine, and the old flag was planted firmly and surely on the last line of works of the enemy, followed by the men, taking one battery of artillery."

REPORT OF COLONEL MICHAEL GOODING, TWENTY-SECOND INDIANA: . . . "I pushed men up to the second line of works as fast as possible; on and on, clear to the top, and over the ridge they went, to the hollow beyond, killing and wounding numbers of the enemy as we advanced, and leaving the rebel battery in our rear. We captured great numbers of prisoners, and sent them to the rear without guards, as we deemed the pursuit of the enemy of greater importance . . . 'I cannot give too much praise to Captain Powers, Company "H," Lieutenant Smith, Company "K," Lieutenant Gooding, Company "A," and Second Lieutenant Moser, Company "G," for their assistance, and for the gallant manner in which they encouraged their men up the side of the mountain, and charging the enemy's works right up to the muzzles of their guns.'"

REPORT OF COLONEL JASON MARSH, SEVENTY-FOURTH ILLINOIS: . . . "The first on the enemy's works, and almost simultaneously, were Lieutenant Clement, Company "A," Captain Stegner, Company "I,"

Captain Bacon, Company "G," and Captain Leffingwell, with some of their men. The enemy was still in considerable force behind their works; but, for some unaccountable reason, they either fled or surrendered instantly upon the first few of our men reaching them— not even trying to defend their battery, which was immediately captured by Captain Stegner."

REPORT OF LIEUTENANT-COLONEL PORTER C. OLSON, THIRTY-SIXTH ILLINOIS: . . . In connection with other regiments of this brigade, we assisted in capturing several pieces of artillery, a number of caissons, and a great quantity of small-arms."

REPORT OF COLONEL JOHN Q. LANE: . . . "At the house known as Bragg's headquarters, the enemy were driven from three guns, which fell into our hands."

REPORT OF BRIGADIER-GENERAL G. D. WAGNER, SECOND BRIGADE: . . . "I ordered the command to storm the ridge, bringing up the Fifteenth Indiana and Ninety-seventh Ohio, which had not yet been engaged, although suffering from the enemy's artillery. The result is a matter of history, as we gained the ridge, capturing artillery, prisoners, and small-arms; to what amount, however, I do not know, as we pushed on after the enemy as soon as I had re-formed the command. . . . Captain Tinney, with his usual gallantry, dashed up the line with the first troops, and with the aid of an orderly (George Dusenbury, Fifteenth Indiana), turned the loaded gun of the enemy on his retreating ranks."

REPORT OF CAPTAIN BENJAMIN F. HEGLER, FIFTEENTH INDIANA: . . . "Our captures amounted to prisoners not counted, representing many different regiments; several pieces of artillery, and some wagons."

REPORT OF LIEUTENANT-COLONEL ELIAS NEFF, FORTIETH INDIANA: . . . "As the regiment reached the top of the ridge and swept forward, the right passed through, without stopping to take possession, the battery at General Bragg's headquarters that had fired so venomously during the whole contest."

REPORT OF LIEUTENANT-COLONEL J. MOORE, FIFTY-EIGHTH INDIANA: . . . "In passing to the front from Missionary Ridge, we saw several pieces of artillery which had been abandoned by the enemy, though I did not leave any one in charge of them."

REPORT OF MAJOR C, M. HAMMOND, ONE HUNDREDTH ILLINOIS: . . . "I immediately organized my regiment, and while so doing discovered a number of pieces of artillery in a ravine on my left. I sent Lieutenant Stewart, of Company A, to see if these guns which the enemy had abandoned could not be turned upon them. He returned and reported them to be four ten-pound Parrotts and two brass Napoleons; also that it would require a number of men to place them in position. I ordered him to report the same to General Wagner, and ask permission, but before receiving a reply was ordered by you to move forward my regiment on the left of the Fifty-Eighth Indiana Volunteers."

REPORT OF COLONEL CHARLES G. HARKER, THIRD BRIGADE: . . . "My right and Colonel Sherman's left interlocked, so to speak, as we approached the summit, and it was near this point that I saw the first part of my line gain the crest. This was done by a few brave men of my own and Colonel Sherman's command driving the enemy from his intrenchments. The gap thus opened, our men rushed rapidly in, and the enemy, loth to give up their position, still remained, firing at my command toward the left, and the battery in front of the house known as General Bragg's headquarters was still firing at the troops, and was captured by our men while the gunners were still at their posts . . . . . . "We captured and sent to division and corps headquarters 503 prisoners and a large number of small-arms. In regard to the number of pieces of artillery, it will probably be difficult to reconcile the reports of my regimental commanders with the reports of other regiments and brigades who fought so nobly with my own command, and who alike are entitled to share the honors and glories of the day. More anxious to follow the enemy than to appropriate trophies already secured, we pushed to the front, while the place we occupied on ascending the hill was soon occupied by other troops, who, I have learned, claim the artillery as having fallen into their own hands. It must therefore remain with the division and corps commanders, who knew the relative position of each brigade and division, to accord to each the trophies to which they are due. . . . "From my personal observation I can claim a battery of six guns captured by a portion of my brigade."

REPORT OF COLONEL EMERSON OPDYKE, FIRST DEMI-BRIGADE: . . . "My command captured Bragg's headquarters, house, and the six guns which were near there; one of these I ordered turned upon the enemy, which was done with effect."

REPORT OF COLONEL H. C. DUNLAP, THIRD KENTUCKY: . . . "The point at which the centre of my regiment reached the crest was at the stable to the left of the house said to be Bragg's headquarters, and immediately in front of the road which leads down the southern slope of the ridge. One piece of the abandoned battery, was to the left of this point, the remainder to the right, near by."

REPORT OF LIEUTENANT-COLONEL W. A. BULLITT, SIXTY-FIFTH OHIO: . . . "The position in which my regiment found itself was immediately in front of a battery, which belched forth a stream of canister upon us with terrible rapidity. In addition to this, the enemy, whenever driven from other points, rallied around this battery, and defended it with desperation. It cost a struggle to take it; but we finally succeeded, and the colors of the Sixty-fifth Ohio were the first planted upon the yet smoking guns. Captain Smith, of my regiment, was placed in charge of the captured battery, which consisted of 5 guns, 3 caissons, and 17 horses."

REPORT OF CAPTAIN E. P. BATES, ONE HUNDRED AND TWENTY-FIFTH OHIO: . . . "Perceiving that the ridge across which my regiment extended was commanded to the very crest by a battery in front, also by those to right and left, I directed the men to pass up the gorges on either side. About forty men, with Captain Parks and Lieutenant Stinger, passed to the left, the balance to the right, and boldly charged on, till, foremost with those of other regiments, they stood on the strongest point of the enemy's works, masters alike of his guns and position. . . . Captain Parks reports his skirmish-line to have charged upon and captured one gun, that otherwise would have been hauled off."

REPORT OF COLONEL ALLEN BUCKNER, SEVENTY-NINTH ILLINOIS: . . . "The right of the regiment rested on the left of the road, where it crossed the rebel fortification, leading up the hill toward Bragg's headquarters. We took a right oblique direction through a peach orchard until arriving at the woods and logs on the side of the ridge, when I ordered the men to commence firing, which they did with good effect, and continued it all the way up until the heights were gained. At this point the left of the regiment was near the right of the house, and I claim that my officers and men captured two large brass pieces, literally punching the cannoniers from their guns. Privates John Fregan and Jasper Patterson, from Company "A," rushed down the hill, captured one caisson, with a cannonier and six horses, and brought them back."

REPORT OF COLONEL J. R. MILES, TWENTY-SEVENTH ILLINOIS: . . . "The regiment, without faltering, finally, at about 4.30 P.M., gained the enemy's works in conjunction with a party of the Thirty-sixth Illinois, who were immediately on our right. The regiment, or a portion of it, proceeded to the left, down the ridge, for nearly or quite a quarter of a mile capturing three or four pieces of cannon, driving the gunners from them."

CHAPTER XVII.
ORDERED TO RETURN TO CHATTANOOGA—MARCH TO KNOXVILLE—COLLECTING SUBSISTENCE STORES—A CLEVER STRATAGEM—A BRIDGE OF WAGONS—LOOKING OUT FOR THE PERSONAL COMFORT OF THE SOLDIERS-A LEAVE OF ABSENCE— ORDERED TO WASHINGTON—PARTING WITH SHERIDAN'S DIVISION.

The day after the battle of Missionary Ridge I was ordered in the evening to return to Chattanooga, and from the limited supply of stores to be had there outfit my command to march to the relief of Knoxville, where General Burnside was still holding out against the besieging forces of General Longstreet. When we left Murfreesboro' in the preceding June, the men's knapsacks and extra clothing, as well as all our camp equipage, had been left behind, and these articles had not yet reached us, so we were poorly prepared for a winter campaign in the mountains of East Tennessee. There was but little clothing to be obtained in Chattanooga, and my command received only a few overcoats and a small supply of India-rubber ponchos. We could get no shoes, although we stood in great need of them, for the extra pair with which each man had started out from Murfreesboro' was now much the worse for wear. The necessity for succoring Knoxville was urgent, however, so we speedily refitted as thoroughly as was possible with the limited means at hand. My division teams were in very fair condition in consequence of the forage we had procured in the Sequatchie Valley, so I left the train behind to bring up clothing when any should arrive in Chattanooga.

Under these circumstances, on the 29th of November the Fourth Corps

(Granger's) took up the line of march for Knoxville, my men carrying in their haversacks four days' rations, depending for a further supply of food on a small steamboat loaded with subsistence stores, which was to proceed up the Tennessee River and keep abreast of the column.

Not far from Philadelphia, Tennessee, the columns of General Sherman's army, which had kept a greater distance from the river than Granger's corps, so as to be able to subsist on the country, came in toward our right and the whole relieving force was directed on Marysville, about fifteen miles southwest of Knoxville. We got to Marysville December 5, and learned the same day that Longstreet had shortly before attempted to take Knoxville by a desperate assault, but signally failing, had raised the siege and retired toward Bean's Station on the Rutledge, Rogersville, and Bristol road, leading to Virginia. From Marysville General Sherman's troops returned to Chattanooga, while Granger's corps continued on toward Knoxville, to take part in the pursuit of Longstreet.

Burnside's army was deficient in subsistence, though not to the extent that we had supposed before leaving Chattanooga. It had eaten out the country in the immediate vicinity of Knoxville, however; therefore my division did not cross the Holstein River, but was required, in order to maintain itself, to proceed to the region of the French Broad River. To this end I moved to Sevierville, and making this village my headquarters, the division was spread out over the French Broad country, between Big Pigeon and Little Pigeon rivers, where we soon had all the mills in operation, grinding out plenty of flour and meal. The whole region was rich in provender of all kinds, and as the people with rare exceptions were enthusiastically loyal, we in a little while got more than enough food for ourselves, and by means of flatboats began sending the surplus down the river to the troops at Knoxville.

The intense loyalty of this part of Tennessee exceeded that of any other section I was in during the war. The people could not do too much to aid the Union cause, and brought us an abundance of everything needful. The women were especially loyal, and as many of their sons and husbands, who had been compelled to "refugee" on account of their loyal sentiments, returned with us, numbers of the women went into ecstasies of joy when this part of the Union army appeared among them. So long as we remained in the French Broad region, we lived on the fat of the land, but unluckily our stay was to be of short duration, for Longstreet's activity kept the department commander in a state of constant alarm.

Soon after getting the mills well running, and when the shipment of their surplus product down the river by flatboats had begun, I was ordered to move to Knoxville, on account of demonstrations by Longstreet from the direction of Blain's crossroads. On arriving at Knoxville, an inspection of my command, showed that the shoes of many of the men were entirely worn out, the poor fellows having been obliged to protect their feet with a sort of moccasin, made from their blankets or from such other material as they could procure. About six hundred of the command were in this condition, plainly not suitably shod to withstand the frequent storms of sleet and snow. These men I left in Knoxville to await the arrival of my train, which I now learned was en route from Chattanooga with shoes, overcoats, and other clothing, and with the rest of the division proceeded to Strawberry Plains, which we reached the latter part of December.

Mid-winter was now upon us, and the weather in this mountain region of East Tennessee was very cold, snow often falling to the depth of several inches. The thin and scanty clothing of the men afforded little protection, and while in bivouac their only shelter was the ponchos with which they had been provided before leaving Chattanooga; there was not a tent in the command. Hence great suffering resulted, which I anxiously hoped would be relieved shortly by the arrival of my train with supplies. In the course of time the wagons reached Knoxville, but my troops derived little comfort from this fact, for the train was stopped by General Foster, who had succeeded Burnside in command of the department, its contents distributed pro rata to the different organizations of the entire army, and I received but a small share. This was very disappointing, not to say exasperating, but I could not complain of unfairness, for every command in the army was suffering to the same extent as mine, and yet it did seem that a little forethought and exertion on the part of some of the other superior officers, whose transportation was in tolerable condition, might have ameliorated the situation considerably. I sent the train back at once for more clothing, and on its return, just before reaching Knoxville, the quartermaster in charge, Captain Philip Smith, filled the open spaces in the wagons between the bows and load with fodder and hay, and by this clever stratagem passed it through the town safe and undisturbed as a forage train. On Smith's arrival we lost no time in issuing the clothing, and when it had passed into the hands of the individual soldiers the danger of its appropriation for general distribution, like the preceding invoice, was very remote.

General Foster had decided by this time to move his troops to Dandridge for the twofold purpose of threatening the enemy's left and of getting into a locality where we could again gather subsistence from the French Broad region. Accordingly we began an advance on the 15th of January, the cavalry having preceded us some time before. The Twenty-third Corps and Wood's division of the Fourth Corps crossed the Holstein River by a bridge that had been constructed at Strawberry Plains. My division being higher up the stream, forded it, the water very deep and bitter cold, being filled with slushy ice. Marching by way of New Market, I reached Dandridge on the 17th, and here on my arrival met General Sturgis, then commanding our cavalry. He was on the eve of setting out to, "whip the enemy's cavalry," as he said, and wanted me to go along and see him do it. I declined, however, for being now the senior officer present, Foster, Parke, and Granger having remained at Knoxville and Strawberry Plains, their absence left me in command, and it was necessary that I should make disposition of the infantry when it arrived. As there were indications of a considerable force of the enemy on the Russellville road I decided to place the troops in line of battle, so as to be prepared for any emergency that might arise in the absence of the senior officers, and I deemed it prudent to supervise personally the encamping of the men. This disposition necessarily required that some of the organizations should occupy very disagreeable ground, but I soon got all satisfactorily posted with the exception of General Willich, who expressed some discontent at being placed beyond the shelter of the timber, but accepted the situation cheerfully when its obvious necessity was pointed out to him.

Feeling that all was secure, I returned to my headquarters in the village with the idea that we were safely established in ease of attack, and that the men would now have a good rest if left undisturbed; and plenty to eat, but hardly had I reached my own camp when a staff-officer came post-haste from Sturgis with the information that he was being driven back to my lines, despite the confident invitation to me (in the morning) to go out and witness the whipping which was to be given to the enemy's cavalry. Riding to the front, I readily perceived that the information was correct, and I had to send a brigade of infantry out to help Sturgis, thus relieving him from a rather serious predicament. Indeed, the enemy was present in pretty strong force, both cavalry and infantry, and from his vicious attack on Sturgis it looked very much as though he intended to bring on a general engagement.

Under such circumstances I deemed it advisable that the responsible commanders of the army should be present, and so informed them. My communication brought Parke and Granger to the front without delay, but Foster could not come, since the hardships of the winter had reopened an old wound received during the Mexican War, and brought on much suffering. By the time Parke and Granger arrived, however, the enemy, who it turned out was only making a strong demonstration to learn the object of our movement on Dandridge, seemed satisfied with the results of his reconnoissance, and began falling back toward Bull's Gap. Meanwhile Parke and Granger concluded that Dandridge was an untenable point, and hence decided to withdraw a part of the army to Strawberry Plains; and the question of supplies again coming up, it was determined to send the Fourth Corps to the south side of the French Broad to obtain subsistence, provided we could bridge the river so that men could get across the deep and icy stream without suffering.

I agreed to undertake the construction of a bridge on condition that each division should send to the ford twenty-five wagons with which to make it. This being acceded to, Harker's brigade began the work next morning at a favorable point a few miles down the river. As my quota of wagons arrived, they were drawn into the stream one after another by the wheel team, six men in each wagon, and as they successively reached the other side of the channel the mules were unhitched, the pole of each wagon run under the hind axle of the one just in front, and the tailboards used so as to span the slight space between them. The plan worked well as long as the material lasted, but no other wagons than my twenty-five coming on the ground, the work stopped when the bridge was only half constructed. Informed of the delay and its cause, in sheer desperation I finished the bridge by taking from my own division all the wagons needed to make up the deficiency.

It was late in the afternoon when the work was finished, and I began putting over one of my brigades; but in the midst of its crossing word came that Longstreet's army was moving to attack us, which caused an abandonment of the foraging project, and orders quickly followed to retire to Strawberry Plains, the retrograde movement to begin forthwith. I sent to headquarters information of the plight I was in—baggage and supplies on the bank and wagons in the stream— begged to know what was to become of them if we were to hurry off at a moment's notice, and suggested that the movement be delayed until I could recover my transportation. Receiving in reply no assurances that I should be relieved from my dilemma—and, in fact, nothing satisfactory—I determined to take upon myself the responsibility of remaining on the ground long enough to get my wagons out of the river; so I sent out a heavy force to watch for the enemy, and with the remainder of the command went to work to break up the bridge. Before daylight next morning I had recovered everything without interference by Longstreet, who, it was afterward ascertained, was preparing to move east toward Lynchburg instead of marching to attack us; the small demonstration against Dandridge, being made simply to deceive us as to his ultimate object. I marched to Strawberry Plains unmolested, and by taking the route over Bay's Mountain, a shorter one than that followed by the main body of our troops, reached the point of rendezvous as soon as the most of the army, for the road it followed was not only longer, but badly cut up by trains that had recently passed over it.

Shortly after getting into camp, the beef contractor came in and reported that a detachment of the enemy's cavalry had captured my herd of beef cattle. This caused me much chagrin at first, but the commissary of my division soon put in an appearance, and assured me that the loss would not be very disastrous to us nor of much benefit to the enemy, since the cattle were so poor and weak that they could not be driven off. A reconnoissance in force verified the Commissary's statement. From its inability to travel, the herd, after all efforts to carry it off had proved ineffectual, had been abandoned by its captors.

After the troops from Chattanooga arrived in the vicinity of Knoxville and General Sherman had returned to Chattanooga, the operations in East Tennessee constituted a series of blunders, lasting through the entire winter; a state of affairs doubtless due, in the main, to the fact that the command of the troops was so frequently changed. Constant shifting of responsibility from one to another ensued from the date that General Sherman, after assuring himself that Knoxville was safe, devolved the command on Burnside. It had already been intimated to Burnside that he was to be relieved, and in consequence he was inactive and apathetic, confining his operations to an aimless expedition whose advance extended only as far as Blain's crossroads, whence it was soon withdrawn. Meanwhile General Foster had superseded Burnside, but physical disabilities rendered him incapable of remaining in the field, and then the chief authority devolved on Parke. By this time the transmission of power seemed almost a disease; at any rate it was catching, so, while we were en route to Dandridge, Parke transferred the command to Granger. The latter next unloaded it on me, and there is no telling what the final outcome would have been had I not entered a protest against a further continuance of the practice, which remonstrance brought Granger to the front at Dandridge.

While the events just narrated were taking place, General Grant had made a visit to Knoxville—about the last of December—and arranged to open the railroad between there and Chattanooga, with a view to supplying the troops in East Tennessee by rail in the future, instead of through Cumberland Gap by a tedious line of wagon-trains. In pursuance of his plan the railroad had already been opened to Loudon, but here much delay occurred on account of the long time it took to rebuild the bridge over the Tennessee. Therefore supplies were still very scarce, and as our animals were now dying in numbers from starvation, and the men were still on short allowance, it became necessary that some of the troops east of Knoxville should get nearer to their depot, and also be in a position to take part in the coming Georgia campaign, or render assistance to General Thomas, should General Johnston (who had succeeded in command of the Confederate army) make any demonstration against Chattanooga. Hence my division was ordered to take station at Loudon, Tennessee, and I must confess that we took the road for that point with few regrets, for a general disgust prevailed regarding our useless marches during the winter.

At this time my faithful scout Card and his younger brother left me, with the determination, as I have heretofore related, to avenge their brother's death. No persuasion could induce Card to remain longer, for knowing that my division's next operation would be toward Atlanta, and being ignorant of the country below Dalton, he recognized and insisted that his services would then become practically valueless.

At Loudon, where we arrived January 27, supplies were more plentiful, and as our tents and extra clothing reached us there in a few days, every one grew contented and happy. Here a number of my regiments, whose terms of service were about to expire, went through the process of "veteranizing," and, notwithstanding the trials and hardships of the preceding nine months, they re-enlisted almost to a man.

When everything was set in motion toward recuperating and refitting my troops, I availed myself of the opportunity during a lull that then existed to take a short leave of absence—a privilege I had not indulged in since entering the service in 1853. This leave I spent in the North with much benefit to my physical condition, for I was much run down by fatiguing service, and not a little troubled by intense pain which I at times still suffered from my experience in the unfortunate hand-car incident on the Cumberland Mountains the previous July. I returned from leave the latter part of March, rejoining my division with the expectation that the campaign in that section would begin as early as April.

On the 12th of March, 1864, General Grant was assigned to the command of the armies of the United States, as general-in-chief. He was already in Washington, whither he had gone to receive his commission as lieutenant-general. Shortly after his arrival there, he commenced to rearrange the different commands in the army to suit the plans which he intended to enter upon in the spring, and out of this grew a change in my career. Many jealousies and much ill-feeling, the outgrowth of former campaigns, existed among officers of high grade in the Army of the Potomac in the winter of 1864, and several general officers were to be sent elsewhere in consequence. Among these, General Alfred Pleasonton was to be relieved from the command of the cavalry, General Grant having expressed to the President dissatisfaction that so little had hitherto been accomplished by that arm of the service, and I was selected as chief of the cavalry corps of the Army of the Potomac, receiving on the night of the 23d of March from General Thomas at Chattanooga the following telegram:

"MARCH 23, 1864.
"MAJOR-GENERAL THOMAS, Chattanooga
 "Lieutenant-General Grant directs that Major-General Sheridan immediately repair to Washington and report to the Adjutant-General of the Army.
 " H. W. HALLECK, Major-General, Chief-of-Staff."

I was not informed of the purpose for which I was to proceed to Washington, but I conjectured that it meant a severing of my relations with the Second Division, Fourth Army Corps. I at once set about obeying the order, and as but little preparation was necessary, I started for Chattanooga the next day, without taking any formal leave of the troops I had so long commanded. I could not do it; the bond existing between them and me had grown to such depth of attachment that I feared to trust my emotions in any formal parting from a body of soldiers who, from our mutual devotion, had long before lost their official designation, and by general consent within and without the command were called "Sheridan's Division." When I took the train at the station the whole command was collected on the hill-sides around to see me off. They had assembled spontaneously, officers and men, and as the cars moved out for Chattanooga they waved me farewell with demonstrations of affection.

A parting from such friends was indeed to be regretted. They had never given me any trouble, nor done anything that could bring aught but honor to themselves. I had confidence in them, and I believe they had in me. They were ever steady, whether in victory or in misfortune, and as I tried always to be with them, to put them into the hottest fire if good could be gained, or save them from unnecessary loss, as occasion required, they amply repaid all my care and anxiety, courageously and readily meeting all demands in every emergency that arose.

In Kentucky, nearly two years before, my lot had been cast with about half of the twenty-five regiments of infantry that I was just leaving, the rest joining me after Chickamauga. It was practically a new arm of the service to me, for although I was an infantry officer, yet the only large command which up to that time I had controlled was composed of cavalry, and most of my experience had been gained in this arm of the service. I had to study hard to be able to master all the needs of such a force, to feed and clothe it and guard all its interests. When undertaking these responsibilities I felt that if I met them faithfully, recompense would surely come through the hearty response that soldiers always make to conscientious exertion on the part of their superiors, and not only that more could be gained in that way than from the use of any species of influence, but that the reward would be quicker. Therefore I always tried to look after their comfort personally; selected their camps, and provided abundantly for their subsistence, and the road they opened for me shows that my work was not in vain. I regretted deeply to have to leave such soldiers, and felt that they were sorry I was going, and even now I could not, if I would, retain other than the warmest sentiments of esteem and the tenderest affection for the officers and men of "Sheridan's Division," Army of the Cumberland.

On reaching Chattanooga I learned from General Thomas the purpose for which I had been ordered to Washington. I was to be assigned to the command of the Cavalry Corps of the Army of the Potomac. The information staggered me at first, for I knew well the great responsibilities of such a position; moreover, I was but slightly acquainted with military operations in Virginia, and then, too, the higher officers of the Army of the Potomac were little known to me, so at the moment I felt loth to undergo the trials of the new position. Indeed, I knew not a soul in Washington except General Grant and General Halleck, and them but slightly, and no one in General Meade's army, from the commanding general down, except a few officers in the lower grades, hardly any of whom I had seen since graduating at the Military Academy.

Thus it is not much to be wondered at that General Thomas's communication momentarily upset me. But there was no help for it, so after reflecting on the matter a little I concluded to make the best of the situation. As in Virginia I should be operating in a field with which I was wholly unfamiliar, and among so many who were strangers, it seemed to me that it would be advisable to have, as a chief staff-officer, one who had had service in the East, if an available man could be found. In weighing all these considerations in my mind, I fixed upon Captain James W. Forsyth, of the Eighteenth Infantry, then in the regular brigade at Chattanooga—a dear friend of mine, who had served in the Army of the Potomac, in the Peninsula and Antietam campaigns. He at once expressed a desire to accept a position on my staff, and having obtained by the next day the necessary authority, he and I started for Washington, accompanied by Lieutenant T. W. C. Moore, one of my aides, leaving behind Lieutenant M. V. Sheridan, my other aide, to forward our horses as soon as they should be sent down to Chattanooga from Loudon, after which he was to join me.

CHAPTER XVIII.

AT WASHINGTON—MEETING SECRETARY STANTON—INTERVIEW WITH PRESIDENT LINCOLN—MADE COMMANDER OF THE CAVALRY CORPS OF THE ARMY OF THE POTOMAC—ITS OFFICERS—GENERAL MEADE'S METHOD OF USING CAVALRY— OPENING OF THE CAMPAIGN—SPOTTSYLVANIA C. H.—A DIFFERENCE WITH GENERAL MEADE—PREPARING TO FIGHT STUART'S CAVALRY.

Accompanied by Captain Forsyth and Lieutenant Moore, I arrived in Washington on the morning of April, 4, 1864, and stopped at Willard's Hotel, where, staying temporarily, were many officers of the Army of the Potomac en route to their commands from leave at the North. Among all these, however, I was an entire stranger, and I cannot now recall that I met a single individual whom I had ever before known.

With very little delay after reaching my hotel I made my way to General Halleck's headquarters and reported to that officer, having learned in the meantime that General Grant was absent from the city. General Halleck talked to me for a few minutes, outlining briefly the nature and duties of my new command, and the general military situation in Virginia. When he had finished all he had to say about these matters, he took me to the office of the Secretary of War, to present me to Mr. Stanton. During the ceremony of introduction, I could feel that Mr. Stanton was eying me closely and searchingly, endeavoring to form some estimate of one about whom he knew absolutely nothing, and whose career probably had never been called to his attention until General Grant decided to order me East, after my name had been suggested by General Halleck in an interview the two generals had with Mr. Lincoln. I was rather young in appearance—looking even under than over thirty-three years—but five feet five inches in height, and thin almost to emaciation, weighing only one hundred and fifteen pounds. If I had ever possessed any self-assertion in manner or speech, it certainly vanished in the presence of the imperious Secretary, whose name at the time was the synonym of all that was cold and formal. I never learned what Mr. Stanton's first impressions of me were, and his guarded and rather calculating manner gave at this time no intimation that they were either favorable or unfavorable, but his frequent commendation in after years indicated that I gained his goodwill before the close of the war, if not when I first came to his notice; and a more intimate association convinced me that the cold and cruel characteristics popularly ascribed to him were more mythical than real.

When the interview with the Secretary was over, I proceeded with General Halleck to the White House to pay my respects to the President. Mr. Lincoln received me very cordially, offering both his hands, and saying that he hoped I would fulfill the expectations of General Grant in the new command I was about to undertake, adding that thus far the cavalry of the Army of the Potomac had not done all it might have done, and wound up our short conversation by quoting that stale interrogation so prevalent during the early years of the war, "Who ever saw a dead cavalryman?" His manner did not impress me, however, that in asking the question he had meant anything beyond a jest, and I parted from the President convinced that he did not believe all that the query implied.

After taking leave I separated from General Halleck, and on returning to my hotel found there an order from the War Department assigning me to the command of the Cavalry Corps, Army of the Potomac. The next morning, April 5, as I took the cars for the headquarters of the Army of the Potomac, General Grant, who had returned to Washington the previous night from a visit to his family, came aboard the train on his way to Culpeper Court House, and on the journey down I learned among other things that he had wisely determined to continue personally in the field, associating himself with General Meade's army; where he could supervise its movements directly, and at the same time escape the annoyances which, should he remain in Washington, would surely arise from solicitude for the safety of the Capital while the campaign was in progress. When we reached Brandy Station, I left the train and reported to General Meade, who told me that the headquarters of the Cavalry Corps were some distance back from the Station, and indicated the general locations of the different divisions of the corps, also giving me, in the short time I remained with him, much information regarding their composition.

I reached the Cavalry Corps headquarters on the evening of April 5, 1864, and the next morning issued orders assuming command. General Pleasonton had but recently been relieved, and many of his staff-officers were still on duty at the headquarters awaiting the arrival of the permanent commander. I resolved to retain the most of these officers on my staff, and although they were all unknown to me when I decided on this course, yet I never had reason to regret it, nor to question the selections made by my predecessor.

The corps consisted of three cavalry divisions and twelve batteries of horse artillery. Brigadier-General A. T. A. Torbert was in command of the First Division, which was composed of three brigades; Brigadier-General D. McM. Gregg, of the Second, consisting of two brigades; and Brigadier-General J. H. Wilson was afterward assigned to command the Third, also comprising two brigades: Captain Robinson, a veteran soldier of the Mexican war, was chief of artillery, and as such had a general supervision of that arm, though the batteries, either as units or in sections, were assigned to the different divisions in campaign.

Each one of my division commanders was a soldier by profession. Torbert graduated from the Military Academy in 1855, and was commissioned in the infantry, in which arm he saw much service on the frontier, in Florida, and on the Utah expedition. At the beginning of hostilities in April, 1861, he was made a colonel of New Jersey volunteers, and from that position was promoted in the fall of 1862 to be a brigadier-general, thereafter commanding a brigade of infantry in the Army of the Potomac till, in the redistribution of generals, after Grant came to the East, he was assigned to the First Cavalry Division.

Gregg graduated in 1855 also, and was appointed to the First Dragoons, with which regiment, up to the breaking out of the war, he saw frontier service extending from Fort Union, New Mexico, through to the Pacific coast, and up into Oregon and Washington Territories, where I knew him slightly. In the fall of 1861 he became colonel of the Eighth Pennsylvania Cavalry, and a year later was made a brigadier-general. He then succeeded to the command of a division of cavalry, and continued in that position till the close of his service, at times temporarily commanding the Cavalry Corps. He was the only division commander I had whose experience had been almost exclusively derived from the cavalry arm.

Wilson graduated in 1860 in the Topographical Engineers, and was first assigned to duty in Oregon, where he remained till July, 1861. In the fall of that year his active service in the war began, and he rose from one position to another, in the East and West, till, while on General Grant's staff, he was made a brigadier-general in the fall of 1863 in reward for services performed during the Vicksburg campaign and for engineer duty at Chattanooga preceding the battle of Missionary Ridge. At my request he was selected to command the Third Division. General Grant thought highly of him, and, expecting much from his active mental and physical ability, readily assented to assign him in place of General Kilpatrick. The only other general officers in the corps were Brigadier-General Wesley Merritt, Brigadier-General George A. Custer, and Brigadier-General Henry E. Davies, each commanding a brigade.

In a few days after my arrival at Brandy Station I reviewed my new command, which consisted of about twelve thousand officers and men, with the same number of horses in passable trim. Many of the general officers of the army were present at the review, among them Generals Meade, Hancock, and Sedgwick. Sedgwick being an old dragoon, came to renew his former associations with mounted troops, and to encourage me, as he jestingly said, because of the traditional prejudices the cavalrymen were supposed to hold against being commanded by an infantry officer. The corps presented a fine appearance at the review, and so far as the health and equipment of the men were concerned the showing was good and satisfactory; but the horses were thin and very much worn down by excessive and, it seemed to me, unnecessary picket duty, for the cavalry picket-line almost completely encircled the infantry and artillery camps of the army, covering a distance, on a continuous line, of nearly sixty miles, with hardly a mounted Confederate confronting it at any point. From the very beginning of the war the enemy had shown more wisdom respecting his cavalry than we. Instead of wasting its strength by a policy of disintegration he, at an early day, had organized his mounted force into compact masses, and plainly made it a favorite; and, as usual, he was now husbanding the strength of his horses by keeping them to the rear, so that in the spring he could bring them out in good condition for the impending campaign.

Before and at the review I took in this situation, and determined to remedy it if possible; so in due time I sought an interview with General

Meade and informed him that, as the effectiveness of my command rested mainly on the strength of its horses, I thought the duty it was then performing was both burdensome and wasteful. I also gave him my idea as to what the cavalry should do, the main purport of which was that it ought to be kept concentrated to fight the enemy's cavalry. Heretofore, the commander of the Cavalry Corps had been, virtually, but an adjunct at army headquarters—a sort of chief of cavalry—and my proposition seemed to stagger General Meade not a little. I knew that it would be difficult to overcome the recognized custom of using the cavalry for the protection of trains and the establishment of cordons around the infantry corps, and so far subordinating its operations to the movements of the main army that in name only was it a corps at all, but still I thought it my duty to try.

At first General Meade would hardly listen to my proposition, for he was filled with the prejudices that, from the beginning of the war, had pervaded the army regarding the importance and usefulness of cavalry, General Scott then predicting that the contest would be settled by artillery, and thereafter refusing the services of regiment after regiment of mounted troops. General Meade deemed cavalry fit for little more than guard and picket duty, and wanted to know what would protect the transportation trains and artillery reserve, cover the front of moving infantry columns, and secure his flanks from intrusion, if my policy were pursued. I told him that if he would let me use the cavalry as I contemplated, he need have little solicitude in these respects, for, with a mass of ten thousand mounted men, it was my belief that I could make it so lively for the enemy's cavalry that, so far as attacks from it were concerned, the flanks and rear of the Army of the Potomac would require little or no defense, and claimed, further, that moving columns of infantry should take care of their own fronts. I also told him that it was my object to defeat the enemy's cavalry in a general combat, if possible, and by such a result establish a feeling of confidence in my own troops that would enable us after awhile to march where we pleased, for the purpose of breaking General Lee's communications and destroying the resources from which his army was supplied.

The idea as here outlined was contrary to Meade's convictions, for though at different times since he commanded the Army of the Potomac considerable bodies of the cavalry had been massed for some special occasion, yet he had never agreed to the plan as a permanency, and could not be bent to it now. He gave little encouragement, therefore, to what I proposed, yet the conversation was immediately beneficial in one way, for when I laid before him the true condition of the cavalry, he promptly relieved it from much of the arduous and harassing picket service it was performing, thus giving me about two weeks in which to nurse the horses before the campaign opened.

The interview also disclosed the fact that the cavalry commander should be, according to General Meade's views, at his headquarters practically as one of his staff, through whom he would give detailed directions as, in his judgment, occasion required. Meade's ideas and mine being so widely divergent, disagreements arose between us later during the battles of the Wilderness, which lack of concord ended in some concessions on his part after the movement toward Spottsylvania Court House began, and although I doubt that his convictions were ever wholly changed, yet from that date on, in the organization of the Army of the Potomac, the cavalry corps became more of a compact body, with the same privileges and responsibilities that attached to the other corps—conditions that never actually existed before.

On the 4th of May the Army of the Potomac moved against Lee, who was occupying a defensive position on the south bank of the Rapidan. After detailing the various detachments which I was obliged to supply for escorts and other mounted duty, I crossed the river with an effective force of about 10,000 troopers. In the interval succeeding my assignment to the command of the cavalry, I had taken the pains to study carefully the topography of the country in eastern Virginia, and felt convinced that, under the policy Meade intended I should follow, there would be little opportunity for mounted troops to acquit themselves well in a region so thickly wooded, and traversed by so many almost parallel streams; but conscious that he would be compelled sooner or later either to change his mind or partially give way to the pressure of events, I entered on the campaign with the loyal determination to aid zealously in all its plans.

General Lee's army was located in its winter quarters behind intrenchments that lay along the Rapidan for a distance of about twenty miles; extending from Barnett's to Morton's ford. The fords below Morton's were watched by a few small detachments of Confederate cavalry, the main body of which, however, was encamped below Hamilton's crossing, where it could draw supplies from the rich country along the Rappahannock. Only a few brigades of Lee's infantry guarded the works along the river, the bulk of it being so situated that it could be thrown to either flank toward which the Union troops approached.

General Grant adopted the plan of moving by his left flank, with the purpose of compelling Lee to come out from behind his intrenchments along Mine Run and fight on equal terms. Grant knew well the character of country through which he would have to pass, but he was confident that the difficulties of operation in the thickly wooded region of the Wilderness would be counterbalanced by the facility with which his position would enable him to secure a new base; and by the fact that as he would thus cover Washington, there would be little or no necessity for the authorities there to detach from his force at some inopportune moment for the protection of that city.

In the move forward two divisions of my cavalry took the advance, Gregg crossing the Rapidan at Ely's ford and Wilson at Germania ford. Torbert's division remained in the rear to cover the trains and reserve artillery, holding from Rapidan Station to Culpeper, and thence through Stevensburg to the Rappahannock River. Gregg crossed the Rapidan before daylight, in advance of the Second Corps, and when the latter reached Ely's ford, he pushed on to Chancellorsville; Wilson preceded the Fifth Corps to Germania ford, and when it reached the river he made the crossing and moved rapidly by Wilderness Tavern, as far as Parker's Store, from which point he sent a heavy reconnoissance toward Mine Run, the rest of his division bivouacking in a strong position. I myself proceeded to Chancellorsville and fixed my headquarters at that place, whereon the 5th I was joined by Torbert's division.

Meanwhile, General Meade had crossed the Rapidan and established his headquarters not far from Germania ford. From that point he was in direct communication with Wilson, whose original instructions from me carried him only as far as Parker's Store, but it being found, during the night of the 4th, that the enemy was apparently unacquainted with the occurrences of the day, Meade directed Wilson to advance in the direction of Craig's Meeting House; leaving one regiment to hold Parker's Store. Wilson with the second brigade encountered Rosser's brigade of cavalry just beyond the Meeting House, and drove it back rapidly a distance of about two miles, holding it there till noon, while his first brigade was halted on the north side of Robinson's Run near the junction of the Catharpen and Parker's Store roads.

Up to this time Wilson had heard nothing of the approach of the Fifth Corps, and the situation becoming threatening, he withdrew the second brigade to the position occupied by the first, but scarcely had he done so when he learned that at an early hour in the forenoon the enemy's infantry had appeared in his rear at Parker's Store and cut off his communication with General Meade. Surprised at this, he determined to withdraw to Todd's Tavern, but before his resolution could be put into execution the Confederates attacked him with a heavy force, and at the same time began pushing troops down the Catharpen road. Wilson was now in a perplexing situation, sandwiched between the Confederates who had cut him off in the rear at Parker's store and those occupying the Catharpen road, but he extricated his command by passing it around the latter force, and reached Todd's Tavern by crossing the Po River at Corbin's bridge. General Meade discovering that the enemy had interposed at Parker's store between Wilson and the Fifth Corps, sent me word to go to Wilson's relief, and this was the first intimation I received that Wilson had been pushed out so far, but, surmising that he would retire in the direction of Todd's Tavern I immediately despatched Gregg's division there to his relief. Just beyond Todd's Tavern Gregg met Wilson, who was now being followed by the enemy's cavalry. The pursuing force was soon checked, and then driven back to Shady Grove Church, while Wilson's troops fell in behind Gregg's line, somewhat the worse for their morning's adventure.

When the Army of the Potomac commenced crossing the Rapidan on the 4th, General J. E. B. Stuart, commanding the Confederate cavalry, began concentrating his command on the right of Lee's infantry, bringing it from Hamilton's crossing and other points where it had been wintering. Stuart's force at this date was a little more than eight thousand men, organized in two divisions, commanded by Generals Wade Hampton and Fitzhugh Lee. Hampton's division was composed of three brigades, commanded by Generals Cordon, Young, and Rosser; Fitzhugh Lee's division comprised three brigades also, Generals W. H. F. Lee, Lomax, and Wickham commanding them.

Information of this concentration, and of the additional fact that the enemy's cavalry about Hamilton's crossing was all being drawn in, reached me on the 5th, which obviated all necessity for my moving on that point as I intended at the onset of the campaign. The responsibility for the safety of our trains and of the left flank of the army still continued, however, so I made such dispositions of my troops as to secure these objects by holding the line of the Brock road beyond the Furnaces, and thence around to Todd's Tavern and Piney Branch Church. On the 6th, through some false information, General Meade became alarmed about his left flank, and sent me the following note:

"HEADQUARTERS ARMY OF THE POTOMAC,
"May 6, 1864.—1 o'clock P. M.
"MAJOR-GENERAL SHERIDAN,
"Commanding Cavalry Corps

"Your despatch of 11.45 a.m., received. General Hancock has been heavily pressed, and his left turned. The major-general commanding thinks that you had better draw in your cavalry, so as to secure the protection of the trains. The order requiring an escort for the wagons to-night has been rescinded.
"A. A. HUMPHREYS,
"Major-General, Chief-of-Staff."

On the morning of the 6th Custer's and Devin's brigades had been severely engaged at the Furnaces before I received the above note. They had been most successful in repulsing the enemy's attacks, however, and I felt that the line taken up could be held; but the despatch from General Humphreys was alarming, so I drew all the cavalry close in toward Chancellorsville. It was found later that Hancock's left had not been turned, and the points thus abandoned had to be regained at a heavy cost in killed and wounded, to both the cavalry and the infantry.

On the 7th of May, under directions from headquarters, Army of the Potomac, the trains were put in motion to go into park at Piney Branch Church, in anticipation of the movement that was about to be made for the possession of Spottsylvania Court House. I felt confident that the order to move the trains there had been given without a full understanding of the situation, for Piney Branch Church was now held by the enemy, a condition which had resulted from the order withdrawing the cavalry on account of the supposed disaster to Hancock's left the day before; but I thought the best way to remedy matters was to hold the trains in the vicinity of Aldrich's till the ground on which it was intended to park them should be regained.

This led to the battle of Todd's Tavern, a spirited fight for the possession of the crossroads at that point, participated in by the enemy's cavalry and Gregg's division, and two brigades of Torbert's division, the latter commanded by Merritt, as Torbert became very ill on the 6th, and had to be sent to the rear. To gain the objective point—the crossroads—I directed

Gregg to assail the enemy on the Catharpen road with Irvin Gregg's brigade and drive him over Corbin's bridge, while Merritt attacked him with the Reserve brigade on the Spottsylvania road in conjunction with Davies's brigade of Gregg's division, which was to be put in on the Piney Branch Church road, and unite with Merritt's left. Davies's and Irvin Gregg's brigades on my right and left flanks met with some resistance, yet not enough to deter them from, executing their orders. In front of Merritt the enemy held on more stubbornly, however, and there ensued an exceedingly severe and, at times, fluctuating fight. Finally the Confederates gave way, and we pursued them almost to Spottsylvania Court House; but deeming it prudent to recall the pursuers about dark, I encamped Gregg's and Merritt's divisions in the open fields to the east of Todd's Tavern.

During the preceding three days the infantry corps of the army had been engaged in the various conflicts known as the battles of the Wilderness. The success of the Union troops in those battles had not been all that was desired, and General Grant now felt that it was necessary to throw himself on Lee's communications if possible, while preserving his own intact by prolonging the movement to the left. Therefore, on the evening of the 7th he determined to shift his whole army toward Spottsylvania Court House, and initiated the movement by a night march of the infantry to Todd's Tavern. In view of what was contemplated, I gave orders to Gregg and Merritt to move at daylight on the morning of the 8th, for the purpose of gaining possession of Snell's bridge over the Po River, the former by the crossing at Corbin's bridge and the latter by the Block House. I also directed Wilson, who was at Alsop's house, to take possession of Spottsylvania as early as possible on the morning of the 8th, and then move into position at Snell's bridge conjointly with the other two divisions. Wilson's orders remained as I had issued them, so he moved accordingly and got possession of Spottsylvania, driving the enemy's cavalry a mile beyond, as will be seen by the following despatch sent me at 9 A. M. of the 8th:

"HEADQUARTERS THIRD DIVISION, CAVALRY CORPS,
"ARMY OF THE POTOMAC.
"SPOTTSYLVANIA COURT HOUSE, May 8, 1864, 9 A. M.
"LIEUTENANT-COLONEL FORSYTH, CHIEF-OF-STAFF, C. C.

"Have run the enemy's cavalry a mile from Spottsylvania Court House; have charged them, and drove them through the village; am fighting now with a considerable force, supposed to be Lee's division. Everything all right.

"J. H. WILSON,
"Brigadier-General Commanding.

During the night of the 7th General Meade arrived at Todd's Tavern and modified the orders I had given Gregg and Merritt, directing Gregg simply to hold Corbin's bridge, and Merritt to move out in front of the infantry column marching on the Spottsylvania road. Merritt proceeded to obey, but in advancing, our cavalry and infantry became intermingled in the darkness, and much confusion and delay was the consequence. I had not been duly advised of these changes in Gregg's and Merritt's orders, and for a time I had fears for the safety of Wilson, but, while he was preparing to move on to form his junction with Gregg and Merritt at Snell's bridge, the advance of Anderson (who was now commanding Longstreet's corps) appeared on the scene and drove him from Spottsylvania.

Had Gregg and Merritt been permitted to proceed as they were originally instructed, it is doubtful whether the battles fought at Spottsylvania would have occurred, for these two divisions would have encountered the enemy at the Pa River, and so delayed his march as to enable our infantry to reach Spottsylvania first, and thus force Lee to take up a line behind the Po. I had directed Wilson to move from the left by "the Gate" through Spottsylvania to Snell's bridge, while Gregg and Merritt were to advance to the same point by Shady Grove and the Block House. There was nothing to prevent at least a partial success of these operations; that is to say, the concentration of the three divisions in front of Snell's bridge, even if we could not actually have gained it. But both that important point and the bridge on the Block House road were utterly ignored, and Lee's approach to Spottsylvania left entirely unobstructed, while three divisions of cavalry remained practically ineffective by reason of disjointed and irregular instructions.

On the morning of the 8th, when I found that such orders had been given, I made some strong remonstrances against the course that had been pursued, but it was then too late to carry out the combinations I had projected the night before, so I proceeded to join Merritt on the Spottsylvania road. On reaching Merritt I found General Warren making complaint that the cavalry were obstructing his infantry column, so I drew Merritt off the road, and the leading division of the Fifth Corps pushed up to the front. It got into line about 11 o'clock, and advanced to take the village, but it did not go very far before it struck Anderson's corps, and was hurled back with heavy loss. This ended all endeavor to take Spottsylvania that day.

A little before noon General Meade sent for me, and when I reached his headquarters I found that his peppery temper had got the better of his good judgment, he showing a disposition to be unjust, laying blame here and there for the blunders that had been committed. He was particularly severe on the cavalry, saying, among other things, that it had impeded the march of the Fifth Corps by occupying the Spottsylvania road. I replied that if this were true, he himself had ordered it there without my knowledge. I also told him that he had broken up my combinations, exposed Wilson's division to disaster, and kept Gregg unnecessarily idle, and further, repelled his insinuations by saying that such disjointed operations as he had been requiring of the cavalry for the last four days would render the corps inefficient and useless before long. Meade was very much irritated, and I was none the less so. One word brought on another, until, finally, I told him that I could whip Stuart if he (Meade) would only let me, but since he insisted on giving the cavalry directions without consulting or even notifying me, he could henceforth command the Cavalry Corps himself—that I would not give it another order.

The acrimonious interview ended with this remark, and after I left him he went to General Grant's headquarters and repeated the conversation to him, mentioning that I had said that I could whip Stuart. At this General Grant remarked: "Did he say so? Then let him go out and do it." This intimation was immediately acted upon by General Meade, and a little later the following order came to me:

"HEADQUARTERS ARMY OF THE POTOMAC
"May 8th, 1864 1 P. M.
"GENERAL SHERIDAN,
"Commanding Cavalry Corps.

"The major general commanding directs you to immediately concentrate your available mounted force, and with your ammunition trains and such supply trains as are filled (exclusive of ambulances) proceed against the enemy's cavalry, and when your supplies are exhausted, proceed via New Market and Green Bay to Haxall's Landing on the James River, there communicating with General Butler, procuring supplies and return to this army. Your dismounted men will be left with the train here.

"A. A. HUMPHREYS,

"Major-General, Chief-of-staff."

As soon as the above order was received I issued instructions for the concentration of the three divisions of cavalry at Aldrich's to prepare for the contemplated expedition. Three days' rations for the men were distributed, and half rations of grain for one day were doled out for the horses. I sent for Gregg, Merritt, and Wilson and communicated the order to them, saying at the same time, "We are going out to fight Stuart's cavalry in consequence of a suggestion from me; we will give him a fair, square fight; we are strong, and I know we can beat him, and in view of my recent representations to General Meade I shall expect nothing but success." I also indicated to my division commanders the line of march I should take—moving in one column around the right flank of Lee's army to get in its rear—and stated at the same time that it was my intention to fight Stuart wherever he presented himself, and if possible go through to Haxall's Landing; but that if Stuart should successfully interpose between us and that point we would swing back to the Army of the Potomac by passing around the enemy's left flank by way of Gordonsville. At first the proposition seemed to surprise the division commanders somewhat, for hitherto even the boldest, mounted expeditions had been confined to a hurried ride through the enemy's country, without purpose of fighting more than enough to escape in case of molestation, and here and there to destroy a bridge. Our move would be a challenge to Stuart for a cavalry duel behind Lee's lines, in his own country, but the advantages which it was reasonable to anticipate from the plan being quickly perceived, each division commander entered into its support unhesitatingly, and at once set about preparing for the march next day.

CHAPTER XIX.
THE EXPEDITION STARTS—DESTROYING SUPPLIES—OPENING OF THE FIGHT AT YELLOW TAVERN—GENERAL CUSTER'S BRILLIANT CHARGE—DEATH OF GENERAL STUART—REMOVING TORPEDOES—EXCITEMENT IN RICHMOND—A NIGHT MARCH— ENTERPRISING NEWSBOYS—THE EFFECTS OF STUART'S DEFEAT AND DEATH—END OF THE FIRST EXPEDITION—ITS GREAT SUCCESS AND BENEFICIAL RESULTS.

The expedition which resulted in the battle of Yellow Tavern and the death of General Stuart started from the vicinity of Aldrich's toward Fredericksburg early on the morning of May 9, 1864, marching on the plank-road, Merritt's division leading. When the column reached Tabernacle Church it headed almost due east to the telegraph road, and thence down that highway to Thornburg, and from that point through Childsburg to Anderson's crossing of the North Anna River, it being my desire to put my command south of that stream if possible, where it could procure forage before it should be compelled to fight. The corps moved at a walk, three divisions on the same road, making a column nearly thirteen miles in length, and marched around the right flank of the enemy unsuspected until my rear guard had passed Massaponax Church. Although the column was very long, I preferred to move it all on one road rather than to attempt combinations for carrying the divisions to any given point by different routes. Unless the separate commands in an expedition of this nature are very prompt in movement, and each fully equal to overcoming at once any obstacle it may meet, combinations rarely work out as expected; besides, an engagement was at all times imminent, hence it was specially necessary to keep the whole force well together.

As soon as the Ny, Po, and Ta rivers were crossed, each of which streams would have afforded an excellent defensive line to the enemy, all anxiety as to our passing around Lee's army was removed, and our ability to cross the North Anna placed beyond doubt. Meanwhile General Stuart had discovered what we were about, and he set his cavalry in motion, sending General Fitzhugh Lee to follow and attack my rear on the Childsburg road, Stuart himself marching by way of Davenport's bridge, on the North Anna, toward Beaver Dam Station, near which place his whole command was directed to unite the next day.

My column having passed the Ta River, Stuart attacked its rear with considerable vigor, in the hope that he could delay my whole force long enough to permit him to get at least a part of his command in my front; but this scheme was frustrated by Davies's brigade, which I directed to fight as a rear-guard, holding on at one position and then at another along the line of march just enough to deter the enemy from a too rapid advance. Davies performed this responsible and trying duty with tact and good judgment, following the main column steadily as it progressed to the south, and never once permitting Fitzhugh Lee's advance to encroach far enough to compel a halt of my main body. About dark Merritt's division crossed the North Anna at Anderson's ford, while Gregg and Wilson encamped on the north side, having engaged the enemy, who still hung on my rear up to a late hour at night.

After Merritt's division passed the river, Custer's brigade proceeded on to Beaver Dam Station to cut the Virginia Central railroad. Before reaching the station he met a small force of the enemy, but this he speedily drove off, recapturing from it about four hundred Union prisoners, who had been taken recently in the Wilderness and were being conducted to Richmond. Custer also destroyed the station, two locomotives, three trains of cars, ninety wagons, from eight to ten miles of railroad and telegraph lines, some two hundred thousand pounds of bacon and other supplies, amounting in all to about a million and a half of rations, and nearly all they medical stores of General Lee's army, which had been moved from Orange Court House either because Lee wished to have them directly in his rear or because he contemplated falling back to the North Anna.

On the morning of the 10th Gregg and Wilson, while crossing the North Anna, were again attacked, but were covered by the division on the south side of the stream; the passage was effected without much loss, notwithstanding the approach of Stuart on the south bank from the direction of Davenport's bridge. The possession of Beaver Dam gave us an important point, as it opened a way toward Richmond by the Negro-foot road. It also enabled us to obtain forage for our well-nigh famished animals, and to prepare for fighting the enemy, who, I felt sure, would endeavor to interpose between my column and Richmond.

Stuart had hardly united his troops near Beaver Dam when he realized that concentrating there was a mistake, so he began making dispositions for remedying his error, and while we leisurely took the Negro-foot toad toward Richmond, he changed his tactics and hauled off from my rear, urging his horses to the death in order to get in between Richmond and my column. This he effected about 10 o'clock on the morning of the 11th, concentrating at Yellow Tavern, six miles from the city, on the Brook turnpike. His change of tactics left my march on the 10th practically unmolested, and we quietly encamped that night on the south bank of the South Anna, near Ground Squirrel Bridge. Here we procured an abundance of forage, and as the distance traveled that day had been only fifteen to eighteen miles, men and horses were able to obtain a good rest during the night.

At 2 o'clock in the morning, May 11, Davies's brigade of Gregg's division marched for Ashland to cut the Fredericksburg railroad. Arriving there before the head of the enemy's column, which had to pass through this same place to reach Yellow Tavern, Davies drove out a small force occupying the town, burnt a train of cars and a locomotive, destroyed the railroad for some distance, and rejoined the main column at Allen's Station on the Fredericksburg and Richmond railroad. From Allen's Station the whole command moved on Yellow Tavern, Merritt in the lead, Wilson following, and Gregg in the rear.

The appearance of Davies's brigade at Ashland in the morning had had the effect of further mystifying the enemy as to my intentions; and while he held it incumbent to place himself between me and Richmond, yet he was still so uncertain of my movements that he committed the same fault that he did the first day, when he divided his force and sent a part to follow me on the Childsburg road. He now divided his command again, sending a portion to hang upon my rear, while he proceeded with the rest to Yellow Tavern. This separation not only materially weakened the force which might have been thrown across my line of march, but it also enabled me to attack with almost my entire corps, while occupying the pursuers with a small rearguard.

By forced marches General Stuart succeeded in reaching Yellow Tavern ahead of me on May 11; and the presence of, his troops, on the Ashland and Richmond road becoming known to Merritt as he was approaching the

Brook turnpike, this general pressed forward at once to the attack. Pushing his division to the front, he soon got possession of the turnpike and drove the enemy back several hundred yards to the east of it. This success had the effect of throwing the head of my column to the east of the pike, and I quickly brought up Wilson and one of Gregg's brigades to take advantage of the situation by forming a line of battle on that side or the road. Meanwhile the enemy, desperate but still confident, poured in a heavy fire from his line and from a battery which enfiladed the Brook road, and made Yellow Tavern an uncomfortably hot place. Gibbs's and Devin's brigades, however, held fast there, while Custer, supported by Chapman's brigade, attacked the enemy's left and battery in a mounted charge.

Custer's charge, with Chapman on his flank and the rest of Wilson's division sustaining him, was brilliantly executed. Beginning at a walk, he increased his gait to a trot, and then at full speed rushed at the enemy. At the same moment the dismounted troops along my whole front moved forward, and as Custer went through the battery, capturing two of the guns with their cannoneers and breaking up the enemy's left, Gibbs and Devin drove his centre and right from the field. Gregg meanwhile, with equal success, charged the force in his rear-Gordon's brigade and the engagement ended by giving us complete control of the road to Richmond. We captured a number of prisoners, and the casualties on both sides were quite severe, General Stuart himself falling mortally wounded, and General James B. Gordon, one of his brigade commanders, being killed.

After Custer's charge, the Confederate cavalry was badly broken up, the main portion of it being driven in a rout toward Ashland and a small part in the direction of Richmond, which latter force finally rejoined Fitzhugh Lee near Mechanicsville. A reconnoitring party being now sent up the Brook turnpike toward the city, dashed across the South Fork of the Chickahominy, drove a small force from the enemy's exterior intrenchments and went within them. I followed this party, and after a little exploration found between the two lines of works a country road that led across to the pike which runs from Mechanicsville to Richmond. I thought we could go around within the outer line of works by this country road across to the Mechanicsville pike on the south side of the Chickahominy, and encamp the next night at Fair Oaks; so I determined to make the movement after dark, being influenced in this to some extent by reports received during the afternoon from colored people, to the effect that General B. F. Butler's army had reached a small stream on the south side of the James, about four miles south of Richmond. If I could succeed in getting through by this road, not only would I have a shorter line of march to Haxall's landing, but there was also a possibility that I could help Butler somewhat by joining him so near Richmond. Therefore, after making the wounded as comfortable as possible, we commenced the march about 11 o'clock on the night of the 11th, and massed the command on the plateau south of the Meadow bridge near daylight on the 12th.

The enemy, anticipating that I would march by this route, had planted torpedoes along it, and many of these exploded as the column passed over them, killing several horses and wounding a few men, but beyond this we met with no molestation. The torpedoes were loaded shells planted on each side of the road, and so connected by wires attached to friction-tubes in the shells, that when a horse's hoof struck a wire the shell was exploded by the jerk on the improvised lanyard. After the loss of several horses and the wounding of some of the men by these torpedoes, I gave directions to have them removed, if practicable, so about twenty-five of the prisoners were brought up and made to get down on their knees, feel for the wires in the darkness, follow them up and unearth the shells. The prisoners reported the owner of one of the neighboring houses to be the principal person who had engaged in planting these shells, and I therefore directed that some of them be carried and placed in the cellar of his house, arranged to explode if the enemy's column came that way, while he and his family were brought off as prisoners and held till after daylight.

Meanwhile the most intense excitement prevailed in Richmond. The Confederates, supposing that their capital was my objective point, were straining every effort to put it in a state of defense, and had collected between four and five thousand irregular troops, under General Bragg, besides bringing up three brigades of infantry from the force confronting General Butler south of the James River, the alarm being intensified by the retreat, after the defeat at Yellow Tavern, of Stuart's cavalry, now under General Fitzhugh Lee, by way of Ashland to Mechanicsville, on the north side of the Chickahominy, for falling back in that direction, left me between them and Richmond.

Our march during the night of the 11th was very tedious, on account of the extreme darkness and frequent showers of rain; but at daylight on the 12th the head of my column, under Wilson, reached the Mechanicsville pike. Here Wilson, encountering the enemy's works and batteries manned by General Bragg's troops, endeavored to pass. In this he failed, and as soon as I was notified that it was impracticable to reach Fair Oaks by passing between the works and the Chickahominy, Custer's brigade was directed to make the crossing to the north side of the Chickahominy, at the Meadow bridge. Custer moved rapidly for the bridge, but found it destroyed, and that the enemy's cavalry was posted on the north side, in front of Mechanicsville. When this information came back, I ordered Merritt to take his whole division and repair the bridge, instructing him that the crossing must be made at all hazards; for, in view of an impending attack by the enemy's infantry in Richmond, it was necessary that I should have the bridge as a means of egress in case of serious disaster.

All the time that Merritt was occupied in this important duty, the enemy gave great annoyance to the working party by sweeping the bridge with a section of artillery and a fire from the supporting troops, so a small force was thrown across to drive them away. When Merritt had passed two regiments over, they attacked, but were repulsed. The work on the, bridge continued, however, not-withstanding this discomfiture; and when it was finished, Merritt crossed nearly all his division, dismounted, and again attacked the enemy, this time carrying the line, of temporary breastworks, built with logs and rails, and pursuing his broken troops toward Gaines's Mills.

While Merritt was engaged in this affair, the Confederates advanced from behind their works at Richmond, and attacked Wilson and Gregg. Wilson's troops were driven back in some confusion at first; but Gregg, in anticipation of attack, had hidden a heavy line of dismounted men in a bushy ravine on his front, and when the enemy marched upon it, with much display and under the eye of the President of the Confederacy, this concealed line opened a destructive fire with repeating carbines; and at the same time the batteries of horse-artillery, under Captain Robinson, joining in the contest, belched forth shot and shell with fatal effect. The galling fire caused the enemy to falter, and while still wavering Wilson rallied his men, and turning some of them against the right flank of the Confederates, broke their line, and compelled them to withdraw for security behind the heavy works thrown up for the defense of the city in 1862.

By destroying the Meadow bridge and impeding my column on the Mechanicsville, pike, the enemy thought to corner us completely, for he still maintained the force in Gregg's rear that had pressed it the day before; but the repulse of his infantry ended all his hopes of doing us any serious damage on the limited ground between the defenses of Richmond and the Chickahominy. He felt certain that on account of the recent heavy rains we could not cross the Chickahominy except by the Meadow bridge, and it also seemed clear to him that we could not pass between the river and his intrenchments;

therefore he hoped to ruin us, or at least compel us to return by the same route we had taken in coming, in which case we would run into Gordon's brigade, but the signal repulse of Bragg's infantry dispelled these illusions.

Even had it not been our good fortune to defeat him, we could have crossed the Chickahominy if necessary at several points that were discovered by scouting parties which, while the engagement was going on, I had sent out to look up fords. This means of getting out from the circumscribed plateau I did not wish to use, however, unless there was no alternative, for I wished to demonstrate to the Cavalry Corps the impossibility of the enemy's destroying or capturing so large a body of mounted troops.

The chances of seriously injuring, us were more favorable to the enemy this time than ever they were afterward, for with the troops from Richmond, comprising three brigades of veterans and about five thousand irregulars on my front and right flank, with Gordon's cavalry in the rear, and Fitzhugh Lee's cavalry on my left flank, holding the Chickahominy and Meadow bridge, I was apparently hemmed in on every side, but relying on the celerity with which mounted troops could be moved, I felt perfectly confident that the seemingly perilous situation could be relieved under circumstances even worse than those then surrounding us. Therefore, instead of endeavoring to get away without a fight, I concluded that there would be little difficulty in withdrawing, even should I be beaten, and none whatever if I defeated the enemy.

In accordance with this view I accepted battle; and the complete repulse of the enemy's infantry, which assailed us from his intrenchments, and of Gordon's cavalry, which pressed Gregg on the Brook road, ended the contest in our favor. The rest of the day we remained on the battle-field undisturbed, and our time was spent in collecting the wounded, burying the dead, grazing the horses, and reading the Richmond journals, two small newsboys with commendable enterprise having come within our lines from the Confederate capital to sell their papers. They were sharp youngsters, and having come well supplied, they did a thrifty business. When their stock in trade was all disposed of they wished to return, but they were so intelligent and observant that I thought their mission involved other purposes than the mere sale of newspapers, so they were held till we crossed the Chickahominy and then turned loose.

After Merritt had crossed the Chickahominy and reached Mechanicsville, I sent him orders to push on to Gaines's Mills. Near the latter place he fell in with the enemy's cavalry again, and sending me word, about 4 o'clock in the afternoon I crossed the Chickahominy with Wilson and Gregg, but when we overtook Merritt he had already brushed the Confederates away, and my whole command went into camp between Walnut Grove and Gaines's Mills.

The main purposes of the expedition had now been executed. They were "to break up General Lee's railroad communications, destroy such depots of supplies as could be found in his rear, and to defeat General Stuart's cavalry." Many miles of the Virginia Central and of the, Richmond and Fredericksburg railroads were broken up, and several of the bridges on each burnt. At Beaver Dam, Ashland, and other places, about two millions of rations had been captured and destroyed. The most important of all, however, was the defeat of Stuart. Since the beginning of the war this general had distinguished himself by his management of the Confederate mounted force. Under him the cavalry of Lee's army had been nurtured, and had acquired such prestige that it thought itself well-nigh invincible; indeed, in the early years of the war it had proved to be so. This was now dispelled by the successful march we had made in Lee's rear; and the discomfiture of Stuart at Yellow Tavern had inflicted a blow from which entire recovery was impossible.

In its effect on the Confederate cause the defeat of Stuart was most disheartening, but his death was even a greater calamity, as is evidenced by the words of a Confederate writer (Cooke), who says: "Stuart could be ill spared at this critical moment, and General Lee was plunged into the deepest melancholy at the intelligence of his death. When it reached him he retired from those around him, and remained for some time communing with his own heart and memory. When one of his staff entered and spoke of Stuart, General Lee said: 'I can scarcely think of him without weeping.'"

From the camp near Gaines's Mills I resumed the march to Haxall's Landing, the point on the James River contemplated in my instructions where I was to obtain supplies from General Butler. We got to the James on the 14th with all our wounded and a large number of prisoners, and camped between Haxall's and Shirley. The prisoners, as well as the captured guns, were turned over to General Butler's provost-marshal, and our wounded were quickly and kindly cared for by his surgeons. Ample supplies, also, in the way of forage and rations, were furnished us by General Butler, and the work of refitting for our return to the Army of the Potomac was vigorously pushed. By the 17th all was ready, and having learned by scouting parties sent in the direction of Richmond and as far as Newmarket that the enemy's cavalry was returning to Lee's army I started that evening on my return march, crossing the Chickahominy at Jones's bridge, and bivouacking on the 19th near Baltimore crossroads.

My uncertainty of what had happened to the Army of the Potomac in our absence, and as to where I should find it, made our getting back a problem somewhat difficult of solution, particularly as I knew that reinforcements for Lee had come up from the south to Richmond, and that most likely some of these troops were being held at different points on the route to intercept my column. Therefore I determined to pass the Pamunkey River at the White House, and sent to Fort Monroe for a pontoon-bridge on which to make the crossing. While waiting for the pontoons I ordered Custer to proceed with his brigade to Hanover Station, to destroy the railroad bridge over the South Anna, a little beyond that place; at the same time I sent Gregg and Wilson to Cold Harbor, to demonstrate in the direction of Richmond as far as Mechanicsville, so as to cover Custer's movements. Merritt, with the remaining brigades of his division, holding fast at Baltimore crossroads to await events.

After Gregg and Custer had gone, it was discovered that the railroad bridge over the Pamunkey, near the White House, had been destroyed but partially—the cross-ties and stringers being burned in places only—and that it was practicable to repair it sufficiently to carry us over. In view of this information General Merritt's two brigades were at once put on the duty of reconstructing the bridge. By sending mounted parties through the surrounding country, each man of which would bring in a board or a plank, Merritt soon accumulated enough lumber for the flooring, and in one day the bridge was made practicable. On the 22d Gregg, Wilson, and Custer returned. The latter had gone on his expedition as far as Hanover Station, destroyed some commissary stores there, and burned two trestle bridges over Hanover Creek. This done, he deemed it prudent to retire to Hanovertown. The next morning he again marched to Hanover Station, and there ascertained that a strong force of the enemy, consisting of infantry, cavalry, and artillery, was posted at the South Anna bridges. These troops had gone there from Richmond en route to reinforce Lee. In the face of this impediment Custer's mission could not be executed fully, so he returned to Baltimore crossroads.

The whole command was drawn in by noon of the 22d, and that day it crossed the Pamunkey by Merritt's reconstructed bridge, marching to Ayletts, on the Mattapony River, the same night. Here I learned from citizens, and from prisoners taken during the day by scouting parties sent toward Hanover Court House, that Lee had been, forced from his position near Spottsylvania Court House and compelled to retire to the line of the North Anna. I then determined to rejoin the Army of the Potomac at the earliest moment, which I did by making for Chesterfield Station, where I reported to General Meade on the 24th of May.

Our return to Chesterfield ended the first independent expedition the Cavalry Corps had undertaken since coming under my command, and our success was commended highly by Generals Grant and Meade, both realizing that our operations in the rear of Lee had disconcerted and alarmed that general so much as to aid materially in forcing his retrograde march, and both acknowledged that, by drawing off the enemy's cavalry during the past fortnight, we had enabled them to move the Army of the Potomac and its enormous trains without molestation in the manoeuvres that had carried it to the North Anna. Then, too, great quantities of provisions and munitions of war had been destroyed—stores that the enemy had accumulated at sub-depots from strained resources and by difficult means; the railroads that connected Lee with Richmond broken, the most successful cavalry leader of the South killed, and in addition to all this there had been inflicted on the Confederate mounted troops the most thorough defeat that had yet befallen them in Virginia.

When the expedition set out the Confederate authorities in Richmond were impressed, and indeed convinced, that my designs contemplated the capture of that city, and notwithstanding the loss they sustained in the defeat and death of Stuart, and their repulse the succeeding day, they drew much comfort from the fact that I had not entered their capital. Some Confederate writers have continued to hold this theory and conviction since the war. In this view they were and are in error. When Stuart was defeated the main purpose of my instructions had been carried out, and my thoughts then turned to joining General Butler to get supplies. I believed that I could do this by cutting across to the Mechanicsville pike and Fair Oaks on the south side of the Chickahominy, but the failure of Wilson's column to get possession of the outwork which commanded the pike necessitated my crossing at Meadow bridge, and then moving by Mechanicsville and Gaines's Mills instead of by the shorter route. Moreover, my information regarding General Butler's position was incorrect, so that even had I been successful in getting to Fair Oaks by the direct road I should still have gained nothing thereby, for I should still have been obliged to continue down the James River to Haxall's.

CHAPTER XX.
GENERAL WILSON'S ADVANCE TOWARD HANOVER COURT HOUSE—CROSSING THE PAMUNKEY—ENGAGEMENT OF HAWE'S SHOP—FIGHT AT MATADEQUIN CREEK— CAPTURE OF COLD HARBOR—THE FIGHT TO RETAIN THE PLACE—MOVEMENTS OF GENERAL WILSON.

When I rejoined the Army of the Potomac, near Chesterfield Station, the heavy battles around Spottsylvania had been fought, and the complicated manoeuvres by which the whole Union force was swung across the North Anna were in process of execution. In conjunction with these manoeuvres Wilson's division was sent to the right flank of the army, where he made a reconnoissance south of the North Anna as far as Little River, crossing the former stream near Jericho Mills. Wilson was to operate from day to day on that flank as it swung to the south, covering to New Castle ferry each advance of the infantry and the fords left behind on the march. From the 26th to the 30th these duties kept Wilson constantly occupied, and also necessitated a considerable dispersion of his force, but by the 31st he was enabled to get all his division together again, and crossing to the south side of the Pamunkey at New Castle ferry, he advanced toward Hanover Court House. Near Dr Pride's house he encountered a division of the enemy's cavalry under General W. H. F. Lee, and drove it back across Mcchamp's Creek, thus opening communication with the right of our infantry resting near Phillips's Mills. Just as this had been done, a little before dark, Wilson received an order from General Meade directing him to push on toward Richmond until he encountered the Confederates in such strength that he could no longer successfully contend against them, and in compliance with this order occupied Hanover Court House that same day. Resuming his march at daylight on June 1, he went ahead on the Ashland road while sending Chapman's brigade up the south bank of the South Anna to destroy the bridges on that stream. Chapman having succeeded in this work, Wilson re-united his whole command and endeavored to hold Ashland, but finding the Confederate cavalry and infantry there in strong force, he was obliged to withdraw to Dr. Price's house. Here he learned that the army had gone to the left toward Cold Harbor, so on the 2d of June he moved to Hawe's Shop.

While Wilson was operating thus on the right, I had to cover with Gregg's and Torbert's divisions the crossing of the army over the Pamunkey River at and near Hanovertown. Torbert having recovered from the illness which overtook him in the Wilderness, had now returned to duty. The march to turn the enemy's right began on the 26th. Torbert and Gregg in advance, to secure the crossings of the Pamunkey and demonstrate in such manner as to deceive the enemy as much as possible in the movement, the two cavalry divisions being supported by General D. A. Russell's division of the Sixth Corps.

To attain this end in the presence of an ever-watchful foe who had just recently been reinforced in considerable numbers from Richmond and further south—almost enough to make up the losses he had sustained in the Wilderness and at Spottsylvania—required the most vigorous and zealous work on the part of those to whom had been allotted the task of carrying out the initial manoeuvres. Torbert started for Taylor's ford on the Pamunkey with directions to demonstrate heavily at that point till after dark, as if the crossing was to be made there, and having thus impressed the enemy, he was to leave a small guard, withdraw quietly, and march to Hanovertown ford, where the real crossing was to be effected. Meanwhile Gregg marched to Littlepage's crossing of the Pamunkey, with instructions to make feints in the same manner as Torbert until after dark, when he was to retire discreetly, leaving a small force to keep up the demonstration, and then march rapidly to Hanovertown crossing, taking with him the pontoon-bridge.

At the proper hour Russell took up the march and followed the cavalry. The troops were in motion all night, undergoing the usual delays incident to night marches, and, early on the morning of the 27th the crossing was made, Custer's brigade of Torbert's division driving from the ford about one hundred of the enemy's cavalry, and capturing between thirty and forty prisoners. The remainder of Torbert's division followed this brigade and advanced to Hanovertown, where General Gordon's brigade of Confederate cavalry was met. Torbert attacked this force with Devin's brigade, while he sent Custer to Hawe's Shop, from which point a road leading to the right was taken that brought him in rear of the enemy's cavalry; when the Confederates discovered this manoeuvre, they retired in the direction of Hanover Court House. Pursuit continued as far as a little stream called Crump's Creek, and here Torbert was halted, Gregg moving up on his line meanwhile, and Russell encamping near the crossing of the river. This completed our task of gaining a foothold south of the Pamunkey, and on the 28th the main army crossed unharassed and took up a position behind my line, extending south from the river, with the Sixth Corps on the right across the Hanover Court House road at Crump's Creek, the Second Corps on the left of the Sixth, and the Fifth Corps about two miles in front of Hanovertown, its left extending to the Tolopotomy.

There was now much uncertainty in General Grant's mind as to the enemy's whereabouts, and there were received daily the most conflicting statements as to the nature of Lee's movements. It became necessary, therefore, to find out by an actual demonstration what Lee was doing, and I was required to reconnoitre in the direction of Mechanicsville. For this purpose I moved Gregg's division out toward this town by way of Hawe's Shop, and when it had gone about three-fourths of a mile beyond the Shop the enemy's cavalry was discovered dismounted and disposed behind a temporary breastwork of rails and logs.

This was the first occasion on which, since the battle of Yellow Tavern, the Confederate troopers had confronted us in large numbers, their mounted operations, like ours, having been dependent more or less on the conditions that grew out of the movements in which Lee's infantry had been engaged since the 14th of May.

On that date General Lee had foreshadowed his intention of using his cavalry in connection with the manoeuvres of his infantry by issuing an order himself, now that Stuart was dead, directing that the "three divisions of cavalry serving with the army [Lee's] will constitute separate commands, and will report directly to and receive orders from the headquarters of the army." The order indicates that since Stuart's death the Confederate cavalry had been re-organized into three divisions, that were commanded respectively by General Wade Hampton, General Fitzhugh Lee, and General W. H. F. Lee, the additional division organization undoubtedly growing out of the fact, that General M. C. Butler's brigade of about four thousand men had joined recently from South Carolina.

When this force developed in Gregg's front, he attacked the moment his troops could be dismounted; and the contest became one of exceeding stubborness, for he found confronting him Hampton's and Fitzhugh Lee's divisions, supported by what we then supposed to be a brigade of infantry, but which, it has since been ascertained, was Butler's brigade of mounted troops; part of them armed with long-range rifles. The contest between the opposing forces was of the severest character and continued till late in the evening. The varying phases of the fight prompted me to reinforce Gregg as much as possible, so I directed Custer's brigade to report to him, sending, meanwhile, for the other two brigades of Torbert, but these were not available at the time—on account of delays which occurred in relieving them from the line at Crump's Creek—and did not get up till the fight was over. As soon as Custer joined him, Gregg vigorously assaulted the Confederate position along his whole front; and notwithstanding the long-range rifles of the South Carolinians, who were engaging in their first severe combat it appears, and fought most desperately, he penetrated their barricades at several points.

The most determined and obstinate efforts for success were now made on both sides, as the position at Hawe's Shop had become of very great importance on account of the designs of both Lee and Grant. Lee wished to hold this ground while he manoeuvred his army to the line of the Tolopotomy, where he could cover the roads to Richmond, while Grant, though first sending me out merely to discover by a strong reconnoissance the movements of the enemy, saw the value of the place to cover his new base at the White House, and also to give us possession of a direct road to Cold Harbor. Hawe's Shop remained in our possession finally, for late in the evening Custer's brigade was dismounted and formed in close column in rear of Gregg, and while it assaulted through an opening near the centre of his line, the other two brigades advanced and carried the temporary works. The enemy's dead and many of his wounded fell into our hands; also a considerable number of prisoners, from whom we learned that Longstreet's and Ewell's corps were but four miles to the rear.

The battle was a decidedly severe one, the loss on each side being heavy in proportion to the number of troops engaged. This fight took place almost immediately in front of our infantry, which, during the latter part of the contest, was busily occupied in throwing up intrenchments. Late in the afternoon I reported to General Meade the presence of the enemy's infantry, and likewise that Hampton's and Fitzhugh Lee's divisions were in my front also, and asked, at the same time; that some of our infantry, which was near at hand, be sent to my assistance. I could not convince Meade that anything but the enemy's horse was fighting us, however, and he declined to push out the foot-troops, who were much wearied by night marches. It has been ascertained since that Meade's conclusions were correct in so far as they related to the enemy's infantry; but the five cavalry brigades far outnumbered my three, and it is to be regretted that so much was risked in holding a point that commanded the roads to Cold Harbor and Meadow bridge, when there was at hand a preponderating number of Union troops which might have been put into action. However, Gregg's division and Custer's brigade were equal to the situation, all unaided as they were till dark, when Torbert and Merritt came on the ground. The contest not only gave us the crossroads, but also removed our uncertainty regarding Lee's movements, clearly demonstrating that his army was retiring by its right flank, so that it might continue to interpose between Grant and the James River; as well as cover the direct route to Richmond.

General Lee reported this battle to his Government as a Confederate victory, but his despatch was sent early in the day, long before the fight ended, and evidently he could not have known the final result when he made the announcement, for the fight lasted until dark. After dark, our own and the Confederate dead having been buried, I withdrew, and moving to the rear of our infantry, marched all night and till I reached the vicinity of Old Church, where I had been instructed to keep a vigilant watch on the enemy with Gregg's and Torbert's divisions. As soon as I had taken position at Old Church my pickets were pushed out in the direction of Cold Harbor, and the fact that the enemy was holding that point in some force was clearly ascertained. But our occupation of Cold Harbor was of the utmost importance; indeed, it was absolutely necessary that we should possess it, to secure our communications with the White House, as well as to cover the extension of our line to the left toward the James River. Roads from Bethesda Church, Old Church, and the White House centred at Cold Harbor, and from there many roads diverged also toward different crossings of the Chickahominy, which were indispensable to us.

The enemy too realized the importance of the place, for as soon as he found himself compelled to take up the line of the Tolopotomy he threw a body of troops into Cold Harbor by forced marches, and followed it up by pushing a part of this force out on the Old Church road as far as Matadequin Creek, where he established a line of battle, arranging the front of it parallel to the road along the south bank of the Pamunkey; this for the purpose of endangering our trains as they moved back and forth between the army and the White House.

Meanwhile I had occupied Old Church and pushed pickets down toward Cold Harbor. The outposts struck each other just north of Matadequin Creek, and a spirited fight immediately took place. At first our pickets were sorely pressed, but Torbert, who was already preparing to make a reconnoissance, lost no time in reinforcing them on the north side of the creek with Devin's brigade. The fight then became general, both sides, dismounted, stubbornly contesting the ground. Of the Confederates, General Butler's South Carolinians bore the brunt of the fight, and, strongly posted as they were on the south bank of the creek, held their ground with the same obstinacy they had previously shown at Hawe's Shop. Finally, however, Torbert threw Merritt's and Custer's brigades into the action, and the enemy retired, we pursuing to within a mile and a half of Cold Harbor and capturing a number of prisoners. Gregg's division took no part in the actual fighting, but remained near Old Church observing the roads on Torbert's flanks, one leading toward Bethesda Church on his right, the other to his left in the direction of the White House. This latter road Gregg was particularly instructed to keep open, so as to communicate with General W. F. Smith, who was then debarking his corps at the White House, and on the morning of the 3ist this general's advance was covered by a brigade which Gregg had sent him for the purpose.

Torbert having pursued toward Cold Harbor the troops he fought at Matadequin Creek, had taken up a position about a mile and a half from that place, on the Old Church road. The morning of the 31st I visited him to arrange for his further advance, intending thus to anticipate an expected attack from Fitzhugh Lee, who was being reinforced by infantry. I met Torbert at Custer's headquarters, and found that the two had already been talking over a scheme to capture Cold Harbor, and when their plan was laid before me it appeared so plainly feasible that I fully endorsed it, at once giving directions for its immediate execution, and ordering Gregg to come forward to Torbert's support with such troops as he could spare from the duty with which he had been charged.

Torbert moved out promptly, Merritt's brigade first, followed by Custer's, on the direct road to Cold Harbor, while Devin's brigade was detached, and marched by a left-hand road that would bring him in on the right and rear of the enemy's line, which was posted in front of the crossroads. Devin was unable to carry his part of the programme farther than to reach the front of the Confederate right, and as Merritt came into position to the right of the Old Church road Torbert was obliged to place a part of Custer's brigade on Merritt's left so as to connect with Devin. The whole division was now in line, confronted by Fitzhugh Lee's cavalry, supported by Clingman's brigade from Hoke's division of infantry; and from the Confederate breastworks, hastily constructed out of logs, rails, and earth, a heavy fire was already being poured upon us that it seemed impossible to withstand. None of Gregg's division had yet arrived, and so stubborn was the enemy's resistance that I began to doubt our ability to carry the place before reinforcements came up, but just then Merritt reported that he could turn the enemy's left, and being directed to execute his proposition, he carried it to a most successful issue with the First and Second regular cavalry. Just as these two regiments passed around the enemy's left and attacked his rear, the remainder of the division assailed him in front. This manoeuvre of Merritt's stampeded the Confederates, and the defenses falling into our hands easily, we pushed ahead on the Bottom's bridge road three-fourths of a mile beyond Cold Harbor.

Cold Harbor was now mine, but I was about nine miles away from our nearest infantry, and had been able to bring up only Davies's brigade of cavalry, which arrived after the fight. My isolated position therefore made me a little uneasy. I felt convinced that the enemy would attempt to regain the place, for it was of as much importance to him as to us, and the presence of his infantry disclosed that he fully appreciated this. My uneasiness increased as the day grew late, for I had learned from prisoners that the balance of Hoke's division was en route to Cold Harbor, and Kershaw near at hand, interposing between the Union left near Bethesda Church and my position. In view of this state of affairs, I notified General Meade that I had taken Cold Harbor, but could not with safety to my command hold it, and forthwith gave directions to withdraw during the night. The last of my troops had scarcely pulled out, however, when I received a despatch from Meade directing me to hold Cold Harbor at every hazard. General Grant had expected that a severe battle would have to be fought before we could obtain possession of the place; and its capture by our cavalry not being anticipated, no preparation had been made for its permanent occupancy. No time was to be lost, therefore, if the advantages which possession of

Cold Harbor gave us were to be improved, so at the same hour that Meade ordered me to hold the place at all hazards the Sixth Corps was started on a forced march, by Grant's directions, to aid in that object, and on arrival to relieve my cavalry.

The moment Meade's order was received, I directed a reoccupation of Cold Harbor, and although a large portion of Torbert's command was already well on its way back to the line we held on the morning of the 31st, this force speedily retraced its steps, and re-entered the place before daylight; both our departure and return having been effected without the enemy being aware of our movements. We now found that the temporary breastworks of rails and logs which the Confederates had built were of incalculable benefit to us in furnishing material with which to establish a line of defense, they being made available by simply reversing them at some points, or at others wholly reconstructing them to suit the circumstances of the ground: The troops, without reserves, were then placed behind our cover dismounted, boxes of ammunition distributed along the line, and the order passed along that the place must be held. All this was done in the darkness, and while we were working away at our cover the enemy could be distinctly heard from our skirmish-line giving commands and making preparations to attack.

Just after daylight on the 1st of June the Confederate infantry under General Kershaw endeavored to drive us out, advancing against my right from the Bethesda Church road. In his assault he was permitted to come close up to our works, and when within short range such a fire was opened on him from our horse-artillery and repeating carbines that he recoiled in confusion after the first onset; still, he seemed determined to get the place, and after reorganizing, again attacked; but the lesson of the first repulse was not without effect, and his feeble effort proved wholly fruitless. After his second failure we were left undisturbed, and at 9 A.M. I sent the following despatch to army headquarters:

"HEADQUARTERS CAVALRY CORPS,
"ARMY OF THE POTOMAC.
"Cold Harbor, Va., June 1, 1864—9 A.M.
"MAJOR-GENERAL HUMPHREYS,
"Chief-of-Staff.

"GENERAL: In obedience to your instructions I am holding Cold Harbor. I have captured this morning more prisoners; they belong to three different infantry brigades. The enemy assaulted the right of my lines this morning, but were handsomely repulsed. I have been very apprehensive, but General Wright is now coming up. I built slight works for my men; the enemy came up to them, and were driven back. General Wright has just arrived.

"P. H. SHERIDAN, "Major-General Commanding."

About 10 o'clock in the morning the Sixth Corps relieved Torbert and Davies, having marched all night, and these two generals moving out toward the Chickahominy covered the left of the infantry line till Hancock's corps took their place in the afternoon. By this time Gregg had joined me with his two brigades, and both Torbert and Gregg were now marched to Prospect Church, from which point I moved them to a position on the north side of the Chickahominy at Bottom's bridge. Here the enemy's cavalry confronted us, occupying the south bank of the stream, with artillery in position at the fords prepared to dispute our passage; but it was not intended that we should cross; so Gregg and Torbert lay quiet in camp at Bottom's bridge and at Old Church without noteworthy event until the 6th of June.

As before related, Wilson's division struck the enemy's infantry as well as W. H. F. Lee's cavalry near Ashland on the 1st of June, and although Chapman destroyed the bridges over the South Anna, which was his part of the programme, Wilson found it necessary to return to Price's Store. From this point he continued to cover the right of the Army of the Potomac, on the 2d of June driving the rear-guard of the enemy from Hawe's Shop, the scene of the battle of May 28. The same day he crossed Tolopotomy Creek, and passed around the enemy's left flank so far that Lee thought his left was turned by a strong force, and under cover of darkness withdrew from a menacing position which he was holding in front of the Ninth Corps. This successful manoeuvre completed, Wilson returned to Hawe's Shop, and on the 4th went into camp at New Castle ferry, in anticipation of certain operations of the Cavalry Corps, which were to take place while the Army of the Potomac was crossing to the south side of the James.

CHAPTER XXI.

THE MOVEMENT TO THE JAMES—THE SECOND EXPEDITION—BATTLE OF TREVILLIAN STATION—DEFEAT OF GENERAL WADE HAMPTON—MALLORY'S CROSSROADS—SUFFERING OF THE WOUNDED—SECURING THE TRAINS—GENERAL GREGG'S STUBBORN FIGHT.

By the 6th of June General Grant again determined to continue the movement of the army by its left flank to the south bank of the James River, his unsuccessful attack on the enemy's works near Cold Harbor having demonstrated that Lee's position north of the Chickahominy could not be carried by assault with results that would compensate for the enormous loss of life which must follow; therefore a further attempt to fight a decisive battle north of Richmond was abandoned. In carrying the army to the James River the hazardous manoeuvres would be hampered by many obstacles, such as the thick timber, underbrush, and troublesome swamps to be met in crossing the Chickahominy. Besides, Lee held an interior line, from which all the direct roads to Richmond could be covered with his infantry, leaving his cavalry free to confront our advance on the south bank of the Chickahominy as far down as Jones's bridge, and thence around to Charles City Court House. In view of these difficulties it became necessary to draw off the bulk of the enemy's cavalry while the movement to the James was in process of execution, and General Meade determined to do this by requiring me to proceed with two divisions as far as Charlottesville to destroy the railroad bridge over the Rivanna River near that town, the railroad itself from the Rivanna to Gordonsville, and, if practicable, from Gordonsville back toward Hanover Junction also.

"HEADQUARTERS ARMY OF THE POTOMAC,
"June 5, 1864. 3.30 P. M.
"MAJOR-GENERAL SHERIDAN, Commanding Cavalry Corps.

"I am directed by the major-general commanding to furnish the following instructions for your guidance in the execution of the duty referred to in the order for movements and changes of position to-night, a copy of which order accompanies this communication.

"With two divisions of your corps you will move on the morning of the 7th instant to Charlottesville and destroy the railroad bridge over the Rivanna near that town; you will then thoroughly destroy the railroad from that point to Gordonsville, and from Gordonsville toward Hanover Junction, and to the latter point, if practicable. The chief engineer, Major Duane, will furnish you a canvas pontoon-train of eight boats. The chief quartermaster will supply you with such tools, implements, and materials as you may require for the destruction of the road. Upon the completion of this duty you will rejoin this army.

"A. HUMPHREYS,
"Major-General, Chief-of-Staff."

After Meade's instructions reached me they were somewhat modified by General Grant, who on the same evening had received information that General Hunter, commanding the troops in West Virginia, had reached Staunton and engaged with advantage the Confederate commander, General Jones, near that place. General Grant informed me orally that he had directed Hunter to advance as far as Charlottesville, that he expected me to unite with him there, and that the two commands, after destroying the James River canal and the Virginia Central road, were to join the Army of the Potomac in the manner contemplated in my instructions from General Meade; and that in view of what was anticipated, it would be well to break up as much of the railroad as possible on my way westward. A copy of his letter to Hunter comprised my written instructions. A junction with this general was not contemplated when the expedition was first conceived, but became an important though not the paramount object after the reception of the later information. The diversion of the enemy's cavalry from the south side of the Chickahominy was its main purpose, for in the presence of such a force as Lee's contracted lines would now permit him to concentrate behind the Chickahominy, the difficulties of crossing that stream would be largely increased if he also had at hand a strong body of horse, to gain the time necessary for him to oppose the movement at the different crossings with masses of his infantry.

The order calling for two divisions for the expedition, I decided to take Gregg's and Torbert's, leaving Wilson's behind to continue with the infantry in its march to the James and to receive instructions directly from, the headquarters of the army. All my dismounted men had been sent to the White House some days before, and they were directed to report to Wilson as they could be provided with mounts.

"COLD HARBOR, VA., June 6, 1964.
"MAJOR-GENERAL D. HUNTER, Commanding Dept West Virginia.

"General Sheridan leaves here to-morrow morning with instructions to proceed to Charlottesville, Va., and to commence there the destruction of the Virginia Central railroad, destroying this way as much as possible. The complete destruction of this road and of the canal on James River is of great importance to us. According to the instructions I sent to General Halleck for your guidance, you will proceed to Lynchburg and commence there. It would be of great value to us to get possession of Lynchburg for a single day. But that point is of so much importance to the enemy, that in attempting to get it such resistance may be met as to defeat your getting into the road or canal at all. I see, in looking over the letter to General Halleck on the subject of your instructions, that it rather indicates that your route should be from Staunton via Charlottesville. If you have so understood it, you will be doing just what I want. The direction I would now give is, that if this letter reaches you in the valley between Staunton and Lynchburg, you immediately turn east by the most practicable road until you strike the Lynchburg branch of the Virginia Central road. From there move eastward along the line of the road, destroying it completely and thoroughly, until you join General Sheridan. After the work laid out for General Sheridan and yourself is thoroughly done, proceed to join the Army of the Potomac by the route laid out in General Sheridan's instructions. If any portion of your force, especially your cavalry, is needed back in your department, you are authorized to send it back. If on receipt of this you should be near to Lynchburg and deem it practicable to reach that point, you will exercise your judgment about going there. If you should be on the railroad between Charlottesville and Lynchburg, it may be practicable to detach a cavalry force to destroy the canal. Lose no opportunity to destroy the canal.

"U. S. GRANT, Lieutenant-General."

Owing to the hard service of the preceding month we had lost many horses, so the number of dismounted men was large; and my strength had also been much reduced by killed and wounded during the same period of activity. The effective mounted force of my two divisions was therefore much diminished, they mustering only about six thousand officers and men when concentrated on June 6 at New Castle ferry. Here they were provided with three days' rations, intended to last five days, and with two days' grain for the horses. The rations and forty rounds of ammunition per man were to be carried on the persons of the troopers, the grain on the pommel of the saddle, and the reserve ammunition in wagons. One medical wagon and eight ambulances were also furnished, and one wagon was authorized for each division and brigade headquarters; enough canvas-covered boats for a small pontoon-bridge were also provided.

My instructions permitting latitude in the route I should take, I decided to march along the north bank of the North Anna River, cross that stream at Carpenter's ford, strike the Virginia Central railroad at Trevillian Station, destroy it toward Louisa Court House, march past Gordonsville, strike the railroad again at Cobham's Station, and destroy it thence to Charlottesville as we proceeded west. The success of the last part of this programme would of course depend on the location of General Hunter when I should arrive in the region where it would be practicable for us to communicate with each other.

From my camp at New Castle ferry we crossed the Pamunkey, marched between Aylett's and Dunkirk on the Mattapony River, and on the 8th of June encamped at Polecat Station. The next day we resumed the march along the North Anna—our advance guard skirmishing with a few mounted men of the enemy, who proved to be irregulars—and bivouacked on Northeast Creek, near Young's Mills. This day I learned from some of these irregulars whom we made prisoners that Breckenridge's division of infantry, en route to the Shenandoah Valley by way of Gordonsville, was passing slowly up the railroad parallel to me, and that the enemy's cavalry had left its position on the south side of the Chickahominy, and was marching on the old Richmond and Gordonsville road toward Gordonsville, under command of General Wade Hampton, the information being confirmed by a scouting party sent out to cut the telegraph wires along the railroad in the night. Breckenridge had been ordered back to the valley by General Lee as soon as he heard of Hunter's victory near Staunton, but now that my expedition had been discovered, the movement of Breckenridge's troops on the railroad was being timed to correspond with the marches of my command till Hampton could get more nearly parallel with me.

On the 10th we resumed the march, passing by Twyman's store, crossing the North Anna at Carpenter's ford and encamping on the road leading along the south fork of the North Anna to Trevillian Station. During the evening and night of the Loth the boldness of the enemy's scouting parties, with which we had been coming into collision more or less every day, perceptibly increased, thus indicating the presence of a large force, and evidencing that his shorter line of march had enabled him to bring to my front a strong body of cavalry, although it started from Lee's army nearly two days later than I did from Grant's. The arrival of this body also permitted Breckenridge to pass on to Gordonsville, and from there to interpose between General Hunter and me at either Charlottesville or Waynesboro' as circumstances might determine.

On the night of the Loth General Hampton's division camped about three miles northwest of Trevillian, at a place called Green Spring Valley and Fitzhugh Lee's division not far from Louisa Court House, some six miles east of Trevillian. Learning that I was at Carpenter's ford, Hampton marched his division by way of Trevillian Station toward Clayton's store, on the road from Trevillian to Carpenter's ford, intending to attack me at Clayton's. Fitzhugh Lee's division was to join Hampton at Clayton's store from Louisa Court House; but on the morning of the 11th the two generals were separated by several miles.

At daylight of the 11th my march, to Trevillian Station was resumed on the direct road to that point, and engaging the enemy's pickets and advanced parties soon after setting out, we began to drive them in. Torbert had the lead with Merritt's and Devin's brigades, and as he pressed back the pickets he came upon the enemy posted behind a line of barricades in dense timber about three miles from Trevillian. Meanwhile Custer's brigade had been sent from where we bivouacked, by a wood road found on our left, to destroy Trevillian Station. In following this road Custer got to the rear of Hampton's division, having passed between its right flank and Fitzhugh Lee's division, which was at the time marching on the road leading from Louisa Court House to Clayton's store to unite with Hampton.

Custer, the moment he found himself in Hampton's rear, charged the led horses, wagons, and caissons found there, getting hold of a vast number of each, and also of the station itself. The stampede and havoc wrought by Custer in Hampton's rear compelled him to turn Rosser's brigade in that direction, and while it attacked Custer on one side, Fitzhugh Lee's division, which had followed Custer toward Trevillian, attacked him on the other. There then ensued a desperate struggle for the possession of the captured property, resulting finally in its being retaken by the enemy. Indeed, the great number of horses and vehicles could not be kept on the limited space within Custer's line, which now formed almost a complete circle; and while he was endeavoring to remove them to a secure place they, together with Custer's headquarters wagon and four of his caissons, fell into the hands of their original owners.

As soon as the firing told that Custer had struck the enemy's rear, I directed Torbert to press the line in front of Merritt and Devin, aided by one brigade of Gregg's division on their left, Gregg's other brigade in the meantime attacking Fitzhugh Lee on the Louisa Court House road. The effect of this was to force Hampton back, and his division was so hard pushed that a portion of it was driven pell-mell into Custer's lines, leaving there about five hundred prisoners. The rest of Hampton's men did not rally till they got some distance west of Trevillian, while, in the meantime, Gregg had driven Fitzhugh Lee toward Louisa Court House so far that many miles now intervened between the two Confederate divisions, precluding their union until about noon the next day, when Fitzhugh Lee effected the junction after a circuitous march in the night. The defeat of Hampton at the point where he had determined to resist my further advance, and his retreat westward, gave me undisturbed possession of the station; and after destroying the railroad to some extent toward Gordonsville, I went into camp.

From prisoners taken during the day, I gathered that General Hunter, instead of coming toward Charlottesville, as I had reason to expect, both from the instructions given me and the directions sent him by General Grant, was in the neighborhood of Lexington—apparently moving on Lynchburg—and that Breckenridge was at Gordonsville and Charlottesville. I also heard, from the same source, that Ewell's corps was on its way to Lynchburg, but this intelligence proved afterward to be incorrect, for these troops, commanded by General Early, did not leave Richmond till two days later.

There was no doubt as to the information about Hunter's general location, however. He was marching toward Lynchburg, away from instead of toward me, thus making the junction of our commands beyond all reasonable probability. So in view of this, I made up my mind to abandon that part of the scheme, and to return by leisurely marches, which would keep Hampton's cavalry away from Lee while Grant was crossing the James River. I was still further influenced to this course by the burden which was thrown on me in the large number of wounded—there being about five hundred cases of my own—and the five hundred prisoners that I would probably be forced to abandon, should I proceed farther. Besides, the recent battle had reduced my supply of ammunition to a very small amount—not more than enough for one more respectable engagement; and as the chances were that I would have to fight a great deal before I could reach Hunter, now that the enemy's cavalry and Breckenridge's infantry were between us, the risks of the undertaking seemed too great to warrant it.

The morning of June 12 Gregg's division commenced destroying the railroad to Louisa Court House, and continued the work during the day, breaking it pretty effectually. While Gregg was thus occupied, I directed Torbert to make a reconnoissance up the Gordonsville road, to secure a by-road leading over Mallory's ford, on the North Anna, to the Catharpen road, as I purposed following that route to Spottsylvania Court House on my return, and thence via Bowling Green and Dunkirk to the White House. About a mile beyond Trevillian the Gordonsville road fork—the left fork leading to Charlottesville—and about a mile beyond the fork Hampton had taken up and strongly intrenched a line across both roads, being reinforced by Fitzhugh Lee, who, as before related, had joined him about noon by a roundabout march. Torbert soon hotly engaged this line, and by the impetuosity of his first attack, gained some advantage; but the appearance of Fitzhugh Lee's troops on the right, and Hampton's strong resistance in front, rendered futile all efforts to carry the position; and, although I brought up one of Gregg's brigades to Torbert's assistance, yet the by-road I coveted was still held by the enemy when night closed in.

This engagement, like that off the day before around Trevillian, was mostly fought dismounted by both sides, as had also been the earlier fights of the cavalry during the summer in the Wilderness, at Todd's Tavern, Hawe's Shop, and Matadequin Creek. Indeed, they could hardly have been fought otherwise than on foot, as there was little chance for mounted fighting in eastern Virginia, the dense woods, the armament of both parties, and the practice of barricading making it impracticable to use the sabre with anything like a large force; and so with the exception of Yellow Tavern the dismounted method prevailed in almost every engagement.

The losses at Mallory's Crossroads were very heavy on both sides. The character of the fighting, together with the day's results, demonstrated that it was impossible to make the passage of the North Anna at Mallory's ford without venturing another battle the next day. This would consume the little ammunition left, and though we might gain the road, yet the possibility of having no ammunition whatever to get back with was too great a hazard, so I gave orders to withdraw during the night of the 12th. We retired along the same road by which we had come, taking with us the prisoners, and all of our wounded who could be moved. Those who could not be transported, some ninety in number, and all the Confederate wounded in my hands, were left at Trevillian in hospitals, under charge of one of our surgeons, with plenty of medical and other stores.

We recrossed the North Anna at Carpenter's ford the following morning, and halting there, unsaddled and turned the horses out to graze, for they were nearly famished, having had neither food nor water during the preceding forty-eight hours. Late in the afternoon we saddled up and proceeded to Twyman's Store, while General Hampton's main body moved down the south bank of the North Anna, with the purpose of intervening between me and the Army of the Potomac, in the hope of preventing my return to it; but his movements took no definite shape beyond watching me, however, till several days later, near St. Mary's Church, when I was crossing the peninsula to the James River.

On the 14th the march was continued, and we reached the Catharpen road, upon which it was originally intended to move if we had been able to cross at Mallory's ford, and this conducted me to Shady Grove Church. The next day we passed over the battle-field of Spottsylvania Court House. The marks of the recent conflicts about there were visible on every hand, and in the neighboring houses were found many Union and Confederate wounded, who had been too severely hurt to be removed from the field-hospitals at the time of the battles. Such of our wounded as were able to travel were brought away.

On the 16th I marched from Edge Hill on the Ta River through Bowling Green to Dr. Butler's, on the north side of the Mattapony. When I arrived here I was unable to ascertain the position of the Army of the Potomac, and was uncertain whether or not the base at the White House had been discontinued. I had heard nothing from the army for nine days except rumors through Southern sources, and under these circumstances did not like to venture between the Mattapony and Pamunkey rivers, embarrassed as I was with some four hundred wounded, five hundred prisoners, and about two thousand negroes that had joined my column in the hope of obtaining their freedom. I therefore determined to push down the north bank of the Mattapony far enough to enable me to send these impediments directly to West Point, where I anticipated finding some of our gunboats and transports, that could carry all to the North. Following this plan, we proceeded through Walkerton to King and Queen Court House, and bivouacked in its vicinity the night of the 18th. Next day I learned that the depot at the White House had not yet been broken up entirely, and that supplies were in store for me there; so after sending the wounded, prisoners, and negroes to West Point under an escort of two regiments, I turned back to Dunkirk, on the Mattapony, and crossed to the south side at a place where the stream was narrow enough to bridge with my pontoon-boats.

In returning from Trevillian, as the most of our wounded were hauled in old buggies, carts, and such other vehicles as could be made available in the absence of a sufficient number of ambulances, the suffering was intense, the heat of the season and dusty roads adding much to the discomfort. Each day we halted many times to dress the wounds of the injured and to refresh them as much as possible, but our means for mitigating their distress were limited. The fortitude and cheerfulness of the poor fellows under such conditions were remarkable, for no word of complaint was heard. The Confederate prisoners and colored people being on foot, our marches were necessarily made short, and with frequent halts also, but they too suffered considerably from the heat and dust, though at times the prisoners were relieved by being mounted on the horses of some of our regiments, the owners meantime marching on foot. Where all the colored people came from and what started them was inexplicable, but they began joining us just before we reached Trevillian—men, women, and children with bundles of all sorts containing their few worldly goods, and the number increased from day to day until they arrived at West Point. Probably not one of the poor things had the remotest idea, when he set out, as to where he would finally land, but to a man they followed the Yankees in full faith that they would lead to freedom, no matter what road they took.

On the morning of the 20th, at an early hour, we resumed our march, and as the column proceeded sounds of artillery were heard in the direction of the White House, which fact caused us to quicken the pace. We had not gone far when despatches from General Abercrombie, commanding some fragmentary organizations at the White House, notified me that the place was about to be attacked. I had previously sent an advance party with orders to move swiftly toward the cannonading and report to me by couriers the actual condition of affairs. From this party I soon learned that there was no occasion to push our jaded animals, since the crisis, if there had been one, was over and the enemy repulsed, so the increased gait was reduced to a leisurely march that took us late in the afternoon to the north bank of the Pamunkey, opposite Abercrombie's camp. When I got to the river the enemy was holding the bluffs surrounding the White House farm, having made no effort to penetrate General Abercrombie's line or do him other hurt than to throw a few shells among the teamsters there congregated.

Next day Gregg's division crossed the Pamunkey dismounted, and Torbert's crossed mounted. As soon as the troops were over, Gregg, supported by Merritt's brigade, moved out on the road to Tunstall's Station to attack Hampton, posted an the west side of Black Creek, Custer's brigade meanwhile moving, mounted, on the road to Cumberland, and Devin's in like manner on the one to Baltimore crossroads. This offer of battle was not accepted, however, and Hampton withdrew from my front, retiring behind the Chickahominy, where his communications with Lee would be more secure.

While at the White House I received orders to break up that depot wholly, and also instructions to move the trains which the Army of the Potomac had left there across the peninsula to the pontoon-bridge at Deep Bottom on the James River. These trains amounted to hundreds of wagons and other vehicles, and knowing full well the dangers which would attend the difficult problem of getting them over to Petersburg, I decided to start them with as little delay as circumstances would permit, and the morning of the 22d sent Torbert's division ahead to secure Jones's bridge on the Chickahominy, so that the wagons could be crossed at that point. The trains followed Torbert, while Gregg's division marched by a road parallel to the one on which the wagons were moving, and on their right flank, as they needed to be covered and protected in that direction only.

The enemy made no effort to attack us while we were moving the trains that day, and the wagons were all safely parked for the night on the south side of the Chickahominy, guarded by General Getty, who had relieved Abercrombie from command of the infantry fragments before we started off from the White House.

To secure the crossing at Jones's bridge, Torbert had pushed Devin's brigade out on the Long Bridge road, on the side of the Chickahominy where, on the morning of the 23d, he was attacked by Chambliss's brigade of W. H. F. Lee's division. Devin was driven in some little distance, but being reinforced by Getty with six companies of colored troops, he quickly turned the tables on Chambliss and re-established his picketposts. From this affair I learned that Chambliss's brigade was the advance of the Confederate cavalry corps, while Hampton discovered from it that we were already in possession of the Jones's bridge crossing of the Chickahominy; and as he was too late to challenge our passage of the stream at this point he contented himself with taking up a position that night so as to cover the roads leading from Long Bridge to Westover, with the purpose of preventing the trains from following the river road to the pontoon-bridge at Deep Bottom.

My instructions required me to cross the trains over the James River on this pontoon-bridge if practicable, and to reach it I should be obliged to march through Charles City Court House, and then by Harrison's Landing and Malvern Hill, the latter point being held by the enemy. In fact, he held all the ground between Long Bridge on the Chickahominy and the pontoon-bridge except the Tete de pont at the crossing. Notwithstanding this I concluded to make the attempt, for all the delays of ferrying the command and trains would be avoided if we got through to the bridge; and with this object in view I moved Torbert's division out on the Charles City road to conduct the wagons. Just beyond Charles City Court House Torbert encountered Lomax's brigade, which he drove across Herring Creek on the road to Westover Church; and reporting the affair to me, I surmised, from the presence of this force in my front, that Hampton would endeavor to penetrate to the long column of wagons, so I ordered them to go into park near Wilcox's landing, and instructed Gregg, whose division had been marching in the morning along the road leading from Jones's bridge to St. Mary's Church for the purpose of covering the exposed flank of the train, to hold fast near the church without fail till all the transportation had passed Charles City Court House.

Meanwhile, General Hampton, who had conjectured that I would try to get the train across the James by the pontoonbridge at Deep Bottom, began concentrating all his troops except Lomax's brigade, which was to confront the head of my column on the river road, in the vicinity of Nance's

Shop. This was discovered by Gregg at an early hour, and divining this purpose he had prepared to meet it by constructing hasty cover for his men before receiving my instructions. About 4 o'clock in the afternoon Hampton got his force in hand, and with Fitzhugh Lee's division assailed the whole front of Gregg's line, and his left flank with Chambliss's and Geary's brigades. For two hours he continued to attack, but made little impression on Gregg—gain at one point being counterbalanced by failure at another. Because of the evident strength of Hampton, Gregg had placed all his troops in line of battle from the first, and on discovery of the enemy's superior numbers sent message after message to me concerning the situation, but the messengers never arrived, being either killed or captured, and I remained in total ignorance till dark of the strait his division was in.

Toward night it became clear to Gregg that he could maintain the unequal contest no longer, and he then decided to retreat, but not until convinced that the time won had enabled all the trains to pass Charles City Court House in safety. When he had got all his led horses fairly on the way, and such of the wounded as could be transported, he retired by his right flank—in some confusion, it is true, but stubbornly resisting to Hopewell Church, where Hampton ceased to press him.

Gregg's losses were heavy, and he was forced to abandon his dead and most seriously wounded, but the creditable stand made ensured the safety of the train, the last wagon of which was now parked at Wilcox's Landing. His steady, unflinching determination to gain time for the wagons to get beyond the point of danger was characteristic of the man, and this was the third occasion on which he had exhibited a high order of capacity and sound judgment since coming under my command. The firmness and coolness with which he always met the responsibilities of a dangerous place were particularly strong points in Gregg's make-up, and he possessed so much professional though unpretentious ability, that it is to be regretted he felt obliged a few months later to quit the service before the close of the war.

Gregg's fight fully satisfied me that we could not get the trains up to the pontoon-bridge, for of course Hampton would now throw all his cavalry in my front, on the river road, where it could be backed up by Lee's infantry. Meanwhile, General Meade had become assured of the same thing, and as he was now growing anxious about the fate of Wilson's division—which, during my absence, had been sent out to break the enemy's communications south of Petersburg, by destroying the Southside and Danville railroads—he sent ferryboats to cross me over the James. During the night of the 24th, and next morning, the immense train—which ought never to have been left for the cavalry to escort, after a fatiguing expedition of three weeks—was moved back through Charles City Court House to Douthard's landing, and there ferried over the river, followed by my troops in like manner. When General Hampton discovered this, he moved to Drury's Bluff, and there, on the morning of the 27th, crossed the James by the Confederate pontoon-bridge.

CHAPTER XXII.
GENERAL WILSON'S RAID—DESTROYING RAILROADS—HIS DISCOMFITURE— RESULTS OF HIS RAID—REMOUNTS— MOVEMENT TO THE NORTH SIDE OF THE JAMES—DECEIVING LEE—MY ISOLATED POSITION—ESTIMATE OF HANCOCK— SUCCESS OF THE CAVALRY—THEIR CONSTANT DUTIES.

While I was absent on the expedition to Trevillian, the movement of the Army of the Potomac across the James River was effected, and Wilson, whom I had left behind for the purpose, was engaged in the duty of covering its front and rear. Late on the night of June 12 he, with Chapman's brigade, crossed the Chickahominy at Long Bridge, in advance of the Fifth Corps, and by 7 o'clock next morning had driven the enemy's pickets up to White Oak bridge, where he waited for our infantry. When that came up, he pushed on as far as Riddle's Shop, but late that evening the Confederate infantry forced him to withdraw to St. Mary's Church; for early in the morning General Lee had discovered the movement of our army, and promptly threw this column of infantry south of the Chickahominy to White Oak Swamp, with the design of covering Richmond. From St. Mary's Church Wilson guarded all the roads toward White Oak Swamp and Riddle's Shop, McIntosh's brigade joining him on the 14th, by way of Long Bridge, as the rear of the Army of the Potomac passed the Chickahominy. In the performance of this duty Wilson did not have to fight any engagement of magnitude, for the bulk of the enemy's cavalry had followed me to Trevillian. During the 15th and 16th Wilson drew his troops in toward the James River, and next day crossed it on the pontoon-bridge and camped on the Blackwater, near Mt. Sinai Church. Here he remained till the 22d of June—the same day I reached the White House with Gregg and Torbert—when, under orders from General Meade, he set out to cut the enemy's communications to the south and southwest of Petersburg.

His instructions implied that the breaking up of the Petersburg and Lynchburg, and Richmond and Danville railroads at Burkeville was the most important part of his mission, and that when the work of destruction began, it should be continued till he was driven off by the enemy. Wilson's force consisted of about 5,500 men, General A. V. Kautz, with the cavalry of the Army of the James, having joined him for the expedition. In moving out Wilson crossed the Weldon road near Ream's Station, first destroying it effectually at that point. About fourteen miles west of Petersburg he struck the Southside railroad, and broke it up clear to Burkeville, a distance of thirty miles. Having destroyed everything at Burkeville Junction, he moved along the Danville road to Staunton River, completely wrecking about thirty miles of that line also. At Staunton River he found the railroad bridge strongly guarded, and seeing that he could not burn it, he began his return march that night, and reached Nottoway River, some thirty miles south of Petersburg, at noon of the next day—the 28th.

In this expedition Wilson was closely followed from the start by Barringer's brigade of W. H. F. Lee's cavalry, but the operations were not interfered with materially, his success being signal till he reached the vicinity of Stony Creek depot on his return. At this point General Hampton, with his own and Fitzhugh Lee's cavalry, got between Wilson and the Army of the Potomac, there being behind them at Ream's Station, at the same time, two brigades of infantry under General Mahone. A severe battle ensued, resulting in Wilson's defeat, with the loss of twelve guns and all his wagons. In consequence of this discomfiture he was obliged to fall back across the Nottoway River with his own division, and rejoined the army by way of Peter's bridge on that stream, while Kautz's division, unable to unite with Wilson after the two commands had become separated in the fight, made a circuit of the enemy's left, and reached the lines of our army in the night of the 28th.

Neither the presence of Hampton's cavalry at Stony Creek depot, nor the possession of Ream's Station by the Confederate infantry, seems to have been anticipated by Wilson, for in the report of the expedition he states:

"Foreseeing the probability of having to return northward, I wrote to General Meade the evening before starting that I anticipated no serious difficulty in executing his orders; but unless General Sheridan was required to keep Hampton's cavalry engaged, and our infantry to prevent Lee from making detachments, we should probably experience great difficulty in rejoining the army. In reply to this note, General Humphreys, chief-of-staff, informed me it was intended the Army of the Potomac should cover the Weldon road the next day, the Southside road the day after, and that Hampton having followed Sheridan toward Gordonsville, I need not fear any trouble from him."

I doubt that General Meade's letter of instructions and Wilson's note of the same evening, warrant what General Wilson here says. It is true that the Weldon railroad near Ream's Station was not covered by our infantry, as General Humphreys informed him it would be, but Wilson is in error when he intimates that he was assured that I would look after Hampton. I do not think General Meade's instructions are susceptible of this interpretation. I received no orders requiring me to detain Hampton. On the contrary, when I arrived at the White House my instructions required me to break up the depot there, and then bring the train across the Peninsula as soon as practicable, nor were these instructions ever modified. I began the duty imposed on me on the morning of the 23d, totally in the dark as to what was expected of Wilson, though it seems, from some correspondence between Generals Grant and Meade, which I never saw till after the war, that Grant thought Wilson could rely on Hampton's absence from his field of operations throughout the expedition.

"HEADQUARTERS ARMY OF THE POTOMAC,
"June 21, 1864. 9:20 A. M.
"BRIGADIER-GENERAL WILSON,
"Commanding Third Division Cavalry Corps.

"The major-general commanding directs that you move your command at 2 A. M. to-morrow, the 22d instant, in execution of the duty assigned you of destroying certain railroads. Despatches received from the White House state that Hampton's cavalry was before that place yesterday evening, and that General Sheridan had also reached there, hence it is desirable that you should march at the earliest moment. In passing Petersburg you will endeavor to avoid the observation of the enemy, and then move by the shortest routes to the intersection of the Petersburg and Lynchburg, and the Richmond and Danville railroads, and destroy both these roads to the greatest extent possible, continuing their destruction until driven from it by such attacks of the enemy as you can no longer resist. The destruction of those roads to such an extent that they cannot be used by the enemy in connection with Richmond during the remainder of the campaign is an important part of the plan of campaign. The latest information from Major-General Hunter represents him to be a few miles west of Lynchburg. He may endeavor to form a junction with this army; you will communicate with him if practicable, and have delivered to him verbally the contents of the following copy of a communication from Lieutenant-General Grant to the major-general commanding this army. Lieutenant Brooks, who will accompany your expedition part of the way, should be informed where General Hunter will probably be found.

"The success of your expedition will depend upon the secrecy with which it is commenced, and the celerity with which its movements are conducted; your command will, therefore, have with it the lightest supplies and smallest number of wheels consistent with the thorough execution of the duty, the supplies of the section of country you will operate in being taken into account. Upon the completion of the work assigned you, you will rejoin this army.

"The chief quartermaster was directed yesterday to supply you with the implements and material for the destruction of railroads obtained for General Sheridan.

"[Signed]

"A. A. HUMPHREYS,

"Major-General, Chief-of-Staff."

"HEADQUARTERS CAVALRY FORCES, Mount Sinai Church, June 21, 1864—6 P.M.
"MAJOR-GENERAL HUMPHREYS,"
"Chief-of-Staff.

"The instructions of the major-general commanding, of this date, are received. I shall march in obedience thereto at 2 A. M. to-morrow. Before starting I would like to know if our infantry forces cover the Weldon road.

"I propose striking the Southside road first at Sutherland Station, or some point in that vicinity, tearing up the track sufficiently to delay railroad communication ten or twelve hours. At this place I shall detach a force to strike the Richmond and Danville road, by a rapid march, at the nearest point, tearing up the track at every practicable point between there and Burkeville.

"From Sutherlands I shall move the main body of my command by the Great road (breaking the railroad at every convenient point) directly to Burkeville, which, if we succeed in capturing, will afford us the opportunity of prosecuting our work with great advantage. As soon as I have made dispositions for communicating with Hunter and done all the damage possible, I shall move with all possible rapidity for Danville and Grenboro'.

"Circumstances must, however, is a great degree control our movements after leaving Burkeville.

"If Sheridan will look after Hampton, I apprehend no difficulty, and hope to be able to do the enemy great damage. The ammunition issued to my command is very defective. The implements for destroying roads have not yet arrived, but I learn from General Ingalls that they will certainly be here early to-morrow.

"[Signed] J. H. WILSON,

"Brigadier-General Commanding."

The moment I received orders from General Meade to go to the relief of Wilson, I hastened with Torbert and Gregg by way of Prince George Court House and Lee's Mills to Ream's Station. Here I found the Sixth Corps, which Meade had pushed out on his left flank immediately on hearing of Wilson's mishap, but I was too late to render any material assistance, Wilson having already disappeared, followed by the enemy. However, I at once sent out parties to gather information, and soon learned that Wilson had got safe across the Nottoway at Peter's bridge and was making for the army by way of Blunt's bridge, on the Blackwater.

The benefits derived from this expedition, in the destruction of the Southside and Danville railroads, were considered by General Grant as equivalent for the losses sustained in Wilson's defeat, for the wrecking of the railroads and cars was most complete, occasioning at this, time serious embarrassment to the Confederate Government; but I doubt if all this compensated for the artillery and prisoners that fell into the hands of the enemy in the swamps of Hatcher's Run and Rowanty Creek. Wilson's retreat from the perilous situation at Ream's station was a most creditable performance—in the face of two brigades of infantry and three divisions of cavalry—and in the conduct of the whole expedition the only criticism that can hold against him is that he placed too much reliance on meeting our infantry at Ream's station, seeing that uncontrollable circumstances might, and did, prevent its being there. He ought to have marched on the 28th by Jarrett's Station to Peter's bridge, on the Nottoway, and Blunts bridge on the Blackwater, to the rear of the Army of the Potomac.

When the safety of Wilson's command was assured, I was ordered back to Light House Point, where I had gone into camp after crossing the James River to rest and recruit my command, now very much reduced in numbers by reason of casualties to both horses and men. It had been marching and fighting for fifty consecutive days, and the fatiguing service had told so fearfully on my animals that the number of dismounted men in the corps was very large. With the exception of about four hundred horses that I received at the White House, no animals were furnished to supply the deficiencies which had arisen from the wearing marches of the past two months until I got to this camp at Light House Point; here my needs were so obvious that they could no longer be neglected.

I remained at Light House Point from the 2d to the 26th of July, recuperating the cavalry, the intensely warm weather necessitating almost an entire suspension of hostilities on the part of the Army of the Potomac. Meanwhile fifteen hundred horses were sent me here, and these, with the four hundred already mentioned, were all that my troops received while I held the personal command of the Cavalry Corps, from April 6 to August 1, 1864. This was not near enough to mount the whole command, so I disposed the men who could not be supplied in a dismounted camp.

By the 26th of July our strength was pretty well restored, and as General Grant was now contemplating offensive operations for the purpose of keeping Lee's army occupied around Richmond, and also of carrying Petersburg by assault if possible, I was directed to move to the north side of the James River in conjunction with General Hancock's corps, and, if opportunity offered, to make a second expedition against the Virginia Central railroad, and again destroy the bridges on the North Anna, the Little and the South Anna rivers.

I started out on the afternoon of the 26th and crossed the Appomattox at Broadway landing. At Deep Bottom I was joined by Kautz's small division from the Army of the James, and here massed the whole command, to allow Hancock's corps to take the lead, it crossing to the north bank of the James River by the bridge below the mouth of Bailey's Creek. I moved late in the afternoon, so as not to come within the enemy's view before dark, and after night-fall Hancock's corps passed me and began crossing the pontoon-bridge about 2 o'clock in the morning.

By daylight Hancock was across, the cavalry following. Soon a portion of his corps attacked the enemy's works on the east side of Bailey's Creek, and, aided by the cavalry moving on its right, captured four pieces of artillery. This opened the way for Hancock to push out his whole corps, and as he advanced by a wheel, with his left as a pivot, the cavalry joined in the movement, pressing forward on the New Market and Central or Charles City roads.

We did not go far before we found the enemy's infantry posted across these two roads behind a strong line of intrenchments on the west bank of Bailey's Creek. His videttes in front of Ruffin's house on the New Market road were soon driven in on their main line, and the high ground before the house was immediately occupied by Torbert and Gregg, supported by Kautz's division. By the time the cavalry line was formed the Confederate General Kershaw, with his own division of infantry and those of Wilcox and Heath, advanced to attack us. Directing the most of his troops against the cavalry, which was still mounted, Kershaw drove it back some distance over the high ground. When it reached the eastern face of the ridge, however, it was quickly dismounted, and the men directed to lie down in line of battle about fifteen yards from the crest, and here the onset of the enemy was awaited. When Kershaw's men reached the crest such a severe fire was opened on them, and at such close quarters, that they could not withstand it, and gave way in disorder. They were followed across the plain by the cavalry, and lost about two hundred and fifty prisoners and two battle-flags. The counter attack against the infantry by Torbert and Gregg re-established our line and gave us the victory of Darbytown, but it also demonstrated the fact that General Lee had anticipated the movement around his left flank by transferring to the north side of the James a large portion of his infantry and W. H. F. Lee's division of cavalry.

This development rendered useless any further effort on Hancock's part or mine to carry out the plan of the expedition, for General Grant did not intend Hancock to assault the enemy's works unless there should be found in them but a very thin line of infantry which could be surprised. In such event, Hancock was to operate so that the cavalry might turn the Confederates on the Central or Charles City road, but the continually increasing force of the enemy showed this to be impracticable. The long front presented by Hancock's corps and the cavalry deceived General Lee, and he undoubtedly thought that nearly all of Grant's army had been moved to the north side of the James River; and to meet the danger he transferred the most of his own strength to the same side to confront his adversary, thinning the lines around Petersburg to reinforce those opposing us on the Central and New Market roads. This was what Grant hoped Lee would do in case the operations of Hancock and myself became impracticable, for Grant had an alternative plan for carrying Petersburg by assault in conjunction with the explosion of a mine that had been driven under the enemy's works from the front of Burnside's corps.

Now that there was no longer a chance for the cavalry to turn the enemy's left, our attention was directed to keeping up the deception of Lee, and on the afternoon of the 28th Hancock's corps withdrew to a line nearer the head of the bridge, the cavalry drawing back to a position on his right. From now on, all sorts of devices and stratagems were practiced—anything that would tend to make the Confederates believe we were being reinforced, while Hancock was preparing for a rapid return to Petersburg at the proper time. In order to delude the enemy still more after night-fall of the 28th I sent one of my divisions to the south side of the James, first covering the bridgeway with refuse hay to keep the tram of the horses from being heard. After daylight the next morning, I marched this division back again on foot, in full view of the enemy, to create the impression of a continuous movement large bodies of infantry to the north side, while the same time Kautz was made to skirmish with the enemy on our extreme right. These various artifices had the effect intended, for by the evening of the 29th Lee had transferred all his infantry to the north bank of the James, except three divisions, and all his cavalry save one.

The morning of the 30th had been fixed upon to explode the mine and assault the enemy's works, so after dark on the evening of the 29th Hancock hastily but quietly withdrew his corps to the south side to take part in the engagement which was to succeed the explosion, and I was directed to follow Hancock. This left me on the north side of the river confronting two-thirds of Lee's army in a perilous position, where I could easily be driven into Curl's Neck and my whole command annihilated. The situation, therefore, was not a pleasant one to contemplate, but it could not be avoided. Luckily the enemy did not see fit to attack, and my anxiety was greatly relieved by getting the whole command safely across the bridge shortly after daylight, having drawn in the different brigades successively from my right. By 10 o'clock on the morning of the 30th my leading division was well over toward the left of our army in front of Petersburg, marching with the purpose to get around the enemy's right flank during the operations that were to succeed the mine explosion, but when I reached General Meade's headquarters I found that lamentable failure had attended the assault made when the enemy's works were blown up in the morning. Blunder after blunder had rendered the assault abortive, and all the opportunities opened by our expedition to the north side were irretrievably lost, so General Meade at once arrested the movement of the cavalry.

In the expedition to Deep Bottom I was under the command of Major-General Hancock, who, by seniority, was to control my corps as well as his own until the way was opened for me to get out on the Virginia Central railroad. If this opportunity was gained, I was to cut loose and damage Lee's communications with the Shenandoah Valley in such manner as best suited the conditions, but my return was not to be jeopardized nor long delayed. This necessitated that Hancock's line should extend to Bottom's bridge on the Chickahominy. The enemy's early discovery of the movement and his concentration of troops on the north side prevented Hancock from accomplishing the programme laid out for him. Its impracticability was demonstrated early on the 27th, and Hancock's soldierly instincts told him this the moment he unexpectedly discovered Kershaw blocking the New Market and Charles City roads. To Hancock the temptation to assault Kershaw's position was strong indeed, but if he carried it there would still remain the dubious problem of holding the line necessary for my safe return, so with rare judgment he desisted zealously turning to the alternative proposition—the assault on Petersburg—for more significant results. This was the only occasion during the war in which I was associated with Hancock in campaign. Up till then we had seldom met, and that was the first opportunity I had to observe his quick apprehension, his physical courage, and the soldierly personality which had long before established his high reputation.

On the 1st of August, two days after the mine explosion, I was. relieved from the personal command of the Cavalry Corps, and ordered to the Shenandoah Valley, where at a later date Torbert's and Wilson's divisions joined me. Practically, after I went to the valley, my command of the Cavalry Corps became supervisory merely. During the period of my immediate control of the corps, I tried to carry into effect, as far as possible, the views I had advanced before and during the opening of the Wilderness campaign, i.e., "that our cavalry ought to fight the enemy's cavalry, and our infantry the enemy's infantry"; for there was great danger of breaking the spirit of the corps if it was to be pitted against the enemy's compact masses of foot-troops posted behind intrenchments, and unless there was some adequate tactical or strategical advantage to be gained, such a use of it would not be justified. Immediately succeeding the battles of the Wilderness, opportunity offered to put this plan into execution to some extent, and from that time forward—from the battle of Yellow Tavern—our success was almost continuous, resulting finally, before the close of the war, in the nearly total annihilation of the enemy's cavalry.

The constant activity of the corps from May 5 till August 1 gave little opportunity for the various division and brigade commanders to record its work in detail; so there exists but meagre accounts of the numerous skirmishes and graver conflicts in which, in addition to the fights mentioned in this narrative, it engaged. A detailed history of its performances is not within the province of a work of this nature; but in review, it can be said, without trespassing on the reader's time, that the Cavalry Corps led the advance of the Army of the Potomac into the Wilderness in the memorable campaign of 1864; that on the expedition by way of Richmond to Haxall's it marked out the army's line of march to the North Anna; that it again led the advance to the Tolopotomy, and also to Cold Harbor, holding that important strategic point at great hazard; and that by the Trevillian expedition it drew away the enemy's cavalry from the south side of the Chickahominy, and thereby assisted General Grant materially in successfully marching to the James River and Petersburg. Subsequently, Wilson made his march to Staunton bridge, destroying railroads and supplies of inestimable value, and though this was neutralized by his disaster near Ream's Station, the temporary set-back there to one division was soon redeemed by victory over the Confederate infantry at the battle of Darbytown.

In the campaign we were almost always on the march, night and day, often unable to care properly for our wounded, and obliged to bury our dead where they fell; and innumerable combats attest the part the cavalry played in Grant's march from the Rapidan to Petersburg. In nearly all of these our casualties were heavy, particularly so when, as was often the case, we had to engage the Confederate infantry; but the enemy returned such a full equivalent in dead and wounded in every instance, that finally his mounted power, which from the beginning of the war had been nurtured with a wise appreciation of its value, was utterly broken.

CHAPTER XXIII.
GENERAL HUNTER'S SUCCESSFUL MARCH AND SUBSEQUENT RETREAT—GENERAL JUBAL A. EARLY THREATENS WASHINGTON—CHAMBERSBURG, PA., BURNED— SELECTED TO OPERATE AGAINST GENERAL EARLY—THE SHENANDOAH VALLEY— THE CONFEDERATE ARMY.

When the attempt to take Petersburg in conjunction with the mine explosion resulted in such a dismal failure, all the operations contemplated in connection with that project came to a standstill, and there was every prospect that the intensely hot and sultry weather would prevent further activity in the Army of the Potomac till a more propitious season. Just now, however, the conditions existing in the Shenandoah Valley and along the upper Potomac demanded the special attention of General Grant, for, notwithstanding the successful march that Major-General David Hunter had made toward Lynchburg early in the summer, what he had first gained was subsequently lost by strategical mistakes, that culminated in disaster during the retreat he was obliged to make from the vicinity of Lynchburg to the Kanawha Valley. This route of march uncovered the lower portion of the Valley of the Shenandoah, and with the exception of a small force of Union troops under General Franz Sigel posted aft Martinsburg for the purpose of covering the Baltimore and Ohio railroad, there was nothing at hand to defend the lower valley.

The different bodies of Confederates which compelled Hunter's retreat were under command of General Jubal A. Early, who had been sent to Lynchburg with Ewell's corps after the defeat of the Confederate General

W. C. Jones near Staunton on the 5th of June, to take command of the Valley District. When Early had forced Hunter into the Kanawha region far enough to feel assured that Lynchburg could not again be threatened from that direction, he united to his own corps General John C. Breckenridge's infantry division and the cavalry of Generals J. H. Vaughn, John McCausland. B. T. Johnson, and J. D. Imboden, which heretofore had been operating in southwest and western Virginia under General Robert Ransom, Jr., and with the column thus formed, was ready to turn his attention to the lower Shenandoah Valley. At Early's suggestion General Lee authorized him to move north at an opportune moment, cross the upper Potomac into Maryland and threaten Washington. Indeed, General Lee had foreshadowed such a course when Early started toward Lynchburg for the purpose of relieving the pressure in front of Petersburg, but was in some doubt as to the practicability of the movement later, till persuaded to it by the representations of Early after that general had driven Hunter beyond the mountains and found little or nothing opposing except the small force of Sigel, which he thought he could readily overcome by celerity of movement.

By rapid marching Early reached Winchester on the 2d of July, and on the 4th occupied Martinsburg, driving General Sigel out of that place the same day that Hunter's troops, after their fatiguing retreat through the mountains, reached Charlestown, West Virginia. Early was thus enabled to cross the Potomac without difficulty, when, moving around Harper's Ferry, through the gaps of the South Mountain, he found his path unobstructed till he reached the Monocacy, where Ricketts's division of the Sixth Corps, and some raw troops that had been collected by General Lew Wallace, met and held the Confederates till the other reinforcements that had been ordered to the capital from Petersburg could be brought up. Wallace contested the line of the Monocacy with obstinacy, but had to retire finally toward Baltimore. The road was then open to Washington, and Early marched to the outskirts and began against the capital the demonstrations which were designed to divert the Army of the Potomac from its main purpose in front of Petersburg.

Early's audacity in thus threatening Washington had caused some concern to the officials in the city, but as the movement was looked upon by General Grant as a mere foray which could have no decisive issue, the Administration was not much disturbed till the Confederates came in close proximity. Then was repeated the alarm and consternation of two years before, fears for the safety of the capital being magnified by the confusion and discord existing among the different generals in Washington and Baltimore; and the imaginary dangers vanished only with the appearance of General Wright, who, with the Sixth Corps and one division of the Nineteenth Corps, pushed out to attack Early as soon as he could get his arriving troops in hand, but under circumstances that precluded celerity of movement; and as a consequence the Confederates escaped with little injury, retiring across the Potomac to Leesburg, unharassed save by some Union cavalry that had been sent out into Loudoun County by Hunter, who in the meantime had arrived at Harper's Ferry by the Baltimore and Ohio railroad. From Leesburg Early retired through Winchester toward Strasburg, but when the head of his column reached this place he found that he was being followed by General Crook with the combined troops of Hunter and Sigel only, Wright having returned to Washington under orders to rejoin Meade at Petersburg. This reduction of the pursuing force tempting Early to resume the offensive, he attacked Crook at Kernstown, and succeeded in administering such a check as to necessitate this general's retreat to Martinsburg, and finally to Harper's Ferry. Crook's withdrawal restored to Early the line of the upper Potomac, so, recrossing this stream, he advanced again into Maryland, and sending McCausland on to Chambersburg, Pennsylvania, laid that town in ashes, leaving three thousand non-combatants without shelter or food.

When Early fell back from the vicinity of Washington toward Strasburg, General Grant believed that he would rejoin Lee, but later manoeuvres of the enemy indicated that Early had given up this idea, if he ever entertained it, and intended to remain in the valley, since it would furnish Lee and himself with subsistence, and also afford renewed opportunities for threatening Washington. Indeed, the possession of the Valley of the Shenandoah at this time was of vast importance to Lee's army, and on every hand there were indications that the Confederate Government wished to hold it at least until after the crops could be gathered in to their depots at Lynchburg and Richmond. Its retention, besides being of great advantage in the matter of supplies, would also be a menace to the North difficult for General Grant to explain, and thereby add an element of considerable benefit to the Confederate cause; so when Early's troops again appeared at Martinsburg it was necessary for General Grant to confront them with a force strong enough to put an end to incursions north of the Potomac, which hitherto had always led to National discomfiture at some critical juncture, by turning our army in eastern Virginia from its chief purpose—the destruction of Lee and the capture of the Confederate capital.

This second irruption of Early, and his ruthless destruction of Chambersburg led to many recommendations on the part of General Grant looking to a speedy elimination of the confusion then existing among the Union forces along the upper Potomac, but for a time the authorities at Washington would approve none of his propositions. The President and Secretary Stanton seemed unwilling to adopt his suggestions, and one measure which he deemed very important—the consolidation into a single command of the four geographical districts into which, to relieve political pressure no doubt, the territory had been divided—met with serious opposition. Despite Grant's representations, he could not prevail on the Administration to approve this measure, but finally the manoeuvres of Early and the raid to Chambersburg compelled a partial compliance, though Grant had somewhat circumvented the difficulty already by deciding to appoint a commander for the forces in the field that were to operate against Early.

On the 31st of July General Grant selected me as this commander, and in obedience to his telegraphic summons I repaired to his headquarters at City Point. In the interview that followed, he detailed to me the situation of affairs on the upper Potomac, telling me that I was to command in the field the troops that were to operate against Early, but that General Hunter, who was at the head of the geographical department, would be continued in his position for the reason that the Administration was reluctant to reconstruct or consolidate the different districts. After informing me that one division of the Cavalry Corps would be sent to my new command, he went on to say that he wanted me to push the enemy as soon as this division arrived, and if Early retired up the Shenandoah Valley I was to pursue, but if he crossed the Potomac I was to put myself south of him and try to compass his destruction. The interview having ended, I returned to Hancock Station to prepare for my departure, and on the evening of August 1 I was relieved from immediate duty with the Army of the Potomac, but not from command of the cavalry as a corps organization.

I arrived at Washington on the 4th of August, and the next day received instructions from General Halleck to report to General Grant at Monocacy Junction, whither he had gone direct from City Point, in consequence of a characteristic despatch from the President indicating his disgust with the confusion, disorder, and helplessness prevailing along the upper Potomac, and intimating that Grant's presence there was necessary.

In company with the Secretary of War I called on the President before leaving Washington, and during a short conversation Mr. Lincoln candidly told me that Mr. Stanton had objected to my assignment to General Hunter's command, because he thought me too young, and that he himself had concurred with the Secretary; but now, since General Grant had "ploughed round" the difficulties of the situation by picking me out to command the "boys in the field," he felt satisfied with what had been done, and "hoped for the best." Mr. Stanton remained silent during these remarks, never once indicating whether he, too, had become reconciled to my selection or not; and although, after we left the White House, he conversed with me freely in regard to the campaign I was expected to make, seeking to impress on me the necessity for success from the political as well as from the military point of view, yet he utterly ignored the fact that he had taken any part in disapproving the recommendation of the general-in-chief.

August 6, I reported to General Grant at the Monocacy, and he there turned over to me the following instructions, which he had previously prepared for General Hunter in the expectation that general would continue to command the department:

"HEADQUARTERS IN THE FIELD,
"Monocacy Bridge, Md., Aug. 5, 1864.

"GENERAL: Concentrate all your available force without delay in the vicinity of Harper's Ferry, leaving only such railroad guards and garrisons for public property as may be necessary.

"Use in this concentration the railroad, if by so doing time can be saved. From Harper's Ferry, if it is found that the enemy has moved north of the Potomac in large force, push north, following and attacking him wherever found; following him, if driven south of the Potomac, as long as it is safe to do so. If it is ascertained that the enemy has but a small force north of the Potomac, then push south the main force, detaching, under a competent commander, a sufficient force to look after the raiders and drive them to their homes. In detaching such a force, the brigade of cavalry now en route from Washington via Rockville may be taken into account.

"There are now on the way to join you three other brigades of the best of cavalry, numbering at least five thousand men and horses. These will be instructed, in the absence of further orders, to join you by the south side of the Potomac. One brigade will probably start to-morrow.

"In pushing up the Shenandoah Valley, as it is expected you will have to go first or last, it is desirable that nothing should be left to invite the enemy to return. Take all provisions, forage, and stock wanted for the use of your command. Such as cannot be consumed, destroy. It is not desirable that the buildings should be destroyed—they should, rather, be protected; but the people should be informed that so long as an army can subsist among them recurrences of these raids must be expected, and we are determined to stop them at all hazards.

"Bear in mind, the object is to drive the enemy south; and to do this you want to keep him always in sight. Be guided in your course by the course he takes.

"Make your own arrangements for supplies of all kinds, giving regular vouchers for such as may be taken from loyal citizens in the country through which you march.

"Very respectfully,

"U. S. GRANT, Lieut.-General."

"Major-General D. HUNTER,
"Commanding Department of West Virginia."

When I had read the letter addressed to Hunter, General Grant said I would be expected to report directly to him, as Hunter had asked that day to be wholly relieved, not from any chagrin at my assignment to the control of the active forces of his command, but because he thought that his fitness for the position he was filling was distrusted by General Halleck, and he had no wish to cause embarrassment by remaining where he could but remove me one degree from the headquarters of the army. The next day Hunter's unselfish request was complied with, and an order was issued by the President, consolidating the Middle Department, the Department of Washington, the Department of the Susquehanna, and the Department of West Virginia.

Under this order these four geographical districts constituted the Middle Military Division, and I was temporarily assigned to command it. Hunter's men had been bivouacking for some days past in the vicinity of

Monocacy Junction and Frederick, but before General Grant's instructions were written out, Hunter had conformed to them by directing the concentration at Halltown, about four miles in front of Harper's Ferry, of all his force available for field service. Therefore the different bodies of troops, with the exception of Averell's cavalry, which had followed McCausland toward Moorefield after the burning of Chambersburg, were all in motion toward Halltown on August 6.

Affairs at Monocacy kept me but an hour or two, and these disposed of, I continued on to Harper's Ferry by the special train which had brought me from Washington, that point being intended as my headquarters while making preparations to advance. The enemy was occupying Martinsburg, Williamsport, and Shepherdstown at the time; sending occasional raiding parties into Maryland as far as Hagerstown. The concentration of my troops at Halltown being an indication to Early that we intended to renew the offensive, however, he immediately began counter preparations by drawing in all his detached columns from the north side of the Potomac, abandoning a contemplated raid into Maryland, which his success against Crook at Kernstown had prompted him to project, and otherwise disposing himself for defense.

At Harper's Ferry I made my headquarters in the second story of a small and very dilapidated hotel, and as soon as settled sent for Lieutenant John R. Meigs, the chief engineer officer of the command, to study with him the maps of my geographical division. It always came rather easy to me to learn the geography of a new section, and its important topographical features as well; therefore I found that, with the aid of Meigs, who was most intelligent in his profession, the region in which I was to operate would soon be well fixed in my mind. Meigs was familiar with every important road and stream, and with all points worthy of note west of the Blue Ridge, and was particularly well equipped with knowledge regarding the Shenandoah Valley, even down to the farmhouses. He imparted with great readiness what he knew of this, clearly pointing out its configuration and indicating the strongest points for Confederate defense, at the same time illustrating scientifically and forcibly the peculiar disadvantages under which the Union army had hitherto labored.

The section that received my closest attention has its northern limit along the Potomac between McCoy's ferry at the eastern base of the North Mountain, and Harper's Ferry at the western base of the Blue Ridge. The southern limit is south of Staunton, on the divide which separates the waters flowing into the Potomac from those that run to the James. The western boundary is the eastern slope of the Alleghany Mountains, the eastern, the Blue Ridge; these two distinct mountain ranges trending about southwest inclose a stretch of quite open, undulating country varying in width from the northern to the southern extremity, and dotted at frequent intervals with patches of heavy woods: At Martinsburg the valley is about sixty miles broad, and on an east and west line drawn through Winchester about forty-five, while at Strasburg it narrows down to about twenty-five. Just southeast of Strasburg, which is nearly midway between the eastern and western walls of the valley, rises an abrupt range of mountains called Massanutten, consisting of several ridges which extend southward between the North and South Forks of the Shenandoah River until, losing their identity, they merge into lower but broken ground between New Market and Harrisonburg. The Massanutten ranges, with their spurs and hills, divide the Shenandoah Valley into two valleys, the one next the Blue Ridge being called the Luray, while that next the North Mountain retains the name of Shenandoah.

A broad macadamized road, leading south from Williamsport, Maryland, to Lexington, Virginia, was built at an early day to connect the interior of the latter State with the Chesapeake and Ohio canal, and along this road are situated the principal towns and villages of the Shenandoah Valley, with lateral lines of communication extending to the mountain ranges on the east and west. The roads running toward the Blue Ridge are nearly all macadamized, and the principal ones lead to the railroad system of eastern Virginia through Snicker's, Ashby's Manassas, Chester, Thornton's Swift Run, Brown's and Rock-fish gaps, tending to an ultimate centre at Richmond. These gaps are low and easy, offering little obstruction to the march of an army coming from eastern Virginia, and thus the Union troops operating west of the Blue Ridge were always subjected to the perils of a flank attack; for the Confederates could readily be brought by rail to Gordonsville and Charlottesville, from which points they could move with such celerity through the Blue Ridge that, on more than one occasion, the Shenandoah Valley had been the theatre of Confederate success, due greatly to the advantage of possessing these interior lines.

Nature had been very kind to the valley, making it rich and productive to an exceptional degree, and though for three years contending armies had been marching up and down it, the fertile soil still yielded ample subsistence for Early's men, with a large surplus for the army of Lee. The ground had long been well cleared of timber, and the rolling surface presented so few obstacles to the movement of armies that they could march over the country in any direction almost as well as on the roads, the creeks and rivers being everywhere fordable, with little or no difficulty beyond that of leveling the approaches.

I had opposing me an army largely composed of troops that had operated in this region hitherto under "Stonewall" Jackson with marked success, inflicting defeat on the Union forces almost every time the two armies had come in contact. These men were now commanded by a veteran officer of the Confederacy-General Jubal A. Early—whose past services had so signalized his ability that General Lee specially selected him to take charge of the Valley District, and, notwithstanding the misfortunes that befell him later, clung to him till the end, of the war. The Confederate army at this date was about twenty thousand strong, and consisted of Early's own corps, with Generals Rodes, Ramseur, and Gordon commanding its divisions; the infantry of Breckenridge from southwestern Virginia; three battalions of artillery; and the cavalry brigades of Vaughn, Johnson, McCausland, and Imboden. This cavalry was a short time afterward organized into a division under the command of General Lomax.

After discovering that my troops were massing in front of Harper's Ferry, Early lost not a moment in concentrating his in the vicinity of Martinsburg, in positions from which he could continue to obstruct the Baltimore and Ohio railroad, and yet be enabled to retire up the valley under conditions of safety when I should begin an offensive campaign.

When I took command of the Army of the Shenandoah its infantry force comprised the Sixth Corps, one division of the Nineteenth Corps, and two divisions from West Virginia. The Sixth Corps was commanded by Major-General Horatio G. Wright; its three divisions by Brigadier-Generals David A. Russell, Geo. W. Getty, and James B. Ricketts. The single division of the Nineteenth Corps had for its immediate chief Brigadier-General William Dwight, the corps being commanded by Brigadier-General Wm. H. Emory. The troops from West Virginia were under Brigadier-General George Crook, with Colonels Joseph Thoburn and Isaac H. Duval as division commanders, and though in all not more than one fair-sized division, they had been designated, on account of the department they belonged to, the Army of West Virginia. General Torbert's division, then arriving from the Cavalry Corps of the Army of the Potomac, represented the mounted arm of the service, and in the expectation that Averell would soon join me with his troopers, I assigned General Torbert as chief of cavalry, and General Wesley Merritt succeeded to the command of Torbert's division.

General Wright, the commander of the Sixth Corps, was an officer of high standing in the Corps of Engineers, and had seen much active service during the preceding three years. He commanded the Department of the Ohio throughout the very trying period of the summer and fall of 1862, and while in that position he, with other prominent officers, recommended my appointment as a brigadier-general. In 1863 he rendered valuable service at the battle of Gettysburg, following which he was assigned to the Sixth Corps, and commanded it at the capture of the Confederate works at Rappahannock Station and in the operations at Mine Run. He ranked me as a major-general of volunteers by nearly a year in date of commission, but my assignment by the President to the command of the army in the valley met with Wright's approbation, and, so far as I have ever known, he never questioned the propriety of the President's action. The Sixth Corps division commanders, Getty, Russell, and Ricketts, were all educated soldiers, whose records, beginning with the Mexican War, had already been illustrated in the war of the rebellion by distinguished service in the Army of the Potomac.

General Emory was a veteran, having graduated at the Military Academy in 1831, the year I was born. In early life he had seen much service in the Artillery, the Topographical Engineers, and the Cavalry, and in the war of the rebellion had exhibited the most soldierly characteristics at Port Hudson and on the Red River campaign. At this time he had but one division of the Nineteenth Corps present, which division was well commanded by General Dwight, a volunteer officer who had risen to the grade of brigadier-general through constant hard work. Crook was a classmate of mine—at least, we entered the Military Academy the same year, though he graduated a year ahead of me. We had known each other as boys before we entered the army, and later as men, and I placed implicit faith in his experience and qualifications as a general.

The transfer of Torbert to the position of chief of cavalry left Merritt, as I have already said, in command of the First Cavalry Division. He had been tried in the place before, and from the day he was selected as one of a number of young men to be appointed general officers, with the object of giving life to the Cavalry Corps, he filled the measure of expectation. Custer was one of these young men too, and though as yet commanding a brigade under Merritt, his gallant fight at Trevillian Station, as well as a dozen others during the summer, indicated that he would be equal to the work that was to fall to him when in a few weeks he should succeed Wilson. But to go on down the scale of rank, describing the officers who commanded in the Army of the Shenandoah, would carry me beyond all limit, so I refrain from the digression with regret that I cannot pay to each his well-earned tribute.

The force that I could take with me into the field at this time numbered about 26,000 men. Within the limits of the geographical division there was a much greater number of troops than this. Baltimore, Washington, Harper's Ferry, Hagerstown, Frederick, Cumberland, and a score of other points; besides the strong detachments that it took to keep the Baltimore and Ohio railroad open through the mountains of West Virginia, and escorts for my trains, absorbed so many men that the column which could be made available for field operations was small when compared with the showing on paper. Indeed, it was much less than it ought to have been, but for me, in the face of the opposition made by different interests involved, to detach troops from any of the points to which they had been distributed before I took charge was next to impossible.

In a few days after my arrival preparations were completed, and I was ready to make the first move for the possession of the Shenandoah Valley. For the next five weeks the operations on my part consisted almost wholly of offensive and defensive manoeuvring for certain advantages, the enemy confining himself meanwhile to measures intended to counteract my designs. Upon the advent of Torbert, Early immediately grew suspicious, and fell back twelve miles south of Martinsburg, to Bunker Hill and vicinity, where his right flank would be less exposed, but from which position he could continue to maintain the break in the Baltimore and Ohio railroad, and push reconnoitring parties through Smithfield to Charlestown. These reconnoitring parties exhibited considerable boldness at times, but since they had no purpose in view save to discover whether or not we were moving, I did not contest any ground with them except about our outposts. Indeed, I desired that Early might remain at some point well to the north till I was fully prepared to throw my army on his right and rear and force a battle, and hence I abstained from disturbing him by premature activity, for I thought that if I could beat him at Winchester, or north of it, there would be far greater chances of weighty results. I therefore determined to bring my troops, if it were at all possible to do so, into such a position near that town as to oblige Early to fight. The sequel proved, however, that he was accurately informed of all my movements. To anticipate them, therefore, he began his retreat up the valley the day that I moved out from Halltown, and consequently was able to place himself south of Winchester before I could get there.

CHAPTER XXIV.
MOVING ON GENERAL EARLY—GENERAL GRANT'S LETTER OF INSTRUCTIONS— DESTROYING THE RESOURCES OF THE VALLEY—REASON FOR THE DESTRUCTION— WITHDRAWAL TO HALLTOWN—ALARM IN THE NORTH OVER THE RETROGRADE MOVEMENT—RENEWING THE ADVANCE UP THE VALLEY—GENERAL ANDERSON'S ATTEMPT TO RETURN TO PETERSBURG—STRENGTH OF THE ARMIES.

For a clear understanding of the operations which preceded the victories that resulted in almost annihilating General Early's army in the Shenandoah Valley, it is necessary to describe in considerable detail the events that took place prior to the 19th of September. My army marched from Harper's Ferry on the 10th of August, 1864, General Torbert with Merritt's division of cavalry moving in advance through Berryville, going into position near White Post. The Sixth Corps, under General Wright, moved by way of Charlestown and Summit Point to Clifton; General Emory, with Dwight's division of the Nineteenth Corps, marched along the Berryville pike through Berryville to the left of the position of the Sixth Corps at Clifton; General Crook's command, moving on the Kabletown road, passed through Kabletown to the vicinity of Berryville, and went into position on the left of Dwight's division, while Colonel Lowell, with a detached force of two small regiments of cavalry, marched to Summit Point; so that on the night of August 10 my infantry occupied a line stretching from Clifton to Berryville, with Merritt's cavalry at White Post and Lowell's at Summit Point. The enemy, as stated before, moved at the same time from Bunker Hill and vicinity, and stretched his line from where the Winchester and Potomac railroad crosses Opequon Creek to the point at which the Berryville and Winchester pike crosses the same stream, thus occupying the west bank to cover Winchester.

On the morning of the 11th the Sixth Corps was ordered to move across the country toward the junction of the Berryville-Winchester pike and the Opequon, and to take the crossing and hold it, Dwight's division being directed to move through Berryville on the White Post road for a mile, then file to the right by heads of regiments at deploying distances, and carry the crossing of Opequon Creek at a ford about three-fourths of a mile from the left of the Sixth Corps, while Crook was instructed to move out on the White Post road, a mile and a half beyond Berryville, then head to the right and secure the ford about a mile to the left of Dwight; Torbert's orders were to push Merritt's division up the Millwood pike toward Winchester, attack any force he might run against, and ascertain the movements of the Confederate army; and lastly, Lowell received instructions to close in from Summit Point on the right of the Sixth Corps.

My object in securing the fords was to further my march on Winchester from the southeast, since, from all the information gathered during the 10th, I still thought Early could be brought to a stand at that point; but in this I was mistaken, as Torbert's reconnoissance proved, for on the morning of the 11th, when Merritt had driven the Confederate cavalry, then covering the Millwood pike west of the Opequon, off toward Kernstown, he found that their infantry and artillery were retreating south, up the Valley pike.

As soon as this information was obtained Torbert moved quickly through the toll-gate on the Front Royal and Winchester road to Newtown, to strike the enemy's flank and harass him in his retreat, Lowell following up through Winchester, on the Valley pike; Crook was turned to the left and ordered to Stony Point, while Emory and Wright, marching to the left also, were directed to take post on the night of the 11th between the Millwood and Front Royal roads, within supporting distance of Crook. Merritt meeting some of the enemy's cavalry at the tollgate, drove it in the direction of Newtown till it got inside the line of Gordon's division of infantry, which had been thrown out and posted behind barricades to cover the flank of the main force in its retreat. A portion of Merritt's cavalry attacked this infantry and drove in its skirmish-line, and though not able to dislodge Gordon, Merritt held the ground gained till night-fall, when the Confederate infantry moved off under cover of darkness to Hupp's

Hill, between Strasburg and Cedar Creek

The next morning Crook marched from Stony Point to Cedar Creek, Emory followed with Dwight, and the cavalry moved to the same point by way of Newtown and the Valley pike, the Sixth Corps following the cavalry. That night Crook was in position at Cedar Creek, on the left of the Valley pike, Emory on the right of the pike, the Sixth Corps on the right of Emory, and the cavalry on the flanks. In the afternoon a heavy skirmish-line had been thrown forward to the heights on the south side of Cedar Creek, and a brisk affair with the enemy's pickets took place, the Confederates occupying with their main force the heights north of Strasburg. On the morning of the 13th my cavalry went out to reconnoitre toward Strasburg, on the middle road, about two and a half miles west of the Valley pike, and discovered that Early's infantry was at Fisher's Hill, where he had thrown up behind Tumbling Run earthworks extending clear across the narrow valley between the Massanutten and North mountains. On the left of these works he had Vaughan's, McCausland's, and Johnson's brigades of cavalry under General Lomax, who at this time relieved General Ramseur from the command of the Confederate mounted forces.

Within the past day or two I had received information that a column of the enemy was moving up from Culpeper Court House and approaching Front Royal through Chester Gap, and although the intelligence was unconfirmed, it caused me much solicitude; for there was strong probability that such a movement would be made, and any considerable force advancing through Front Royal toward Winchester could fall upon my rear and destroy my communication with Harper's Ferry, or, moving along the base of Massanutten Mountain, could attack my flank in conjunction with the force at Fisher's Hill without a possibility of my preventing it.

Neither Wilson's cavalry nor Grower's infantry had yet joined me, and the necessities, already explained, which obliged me to hold with string garrisons Winchester and other points heretofore mentioned. had so depleted my line of battle strength that I knew the enemy would outnumber me when Anderson's corps should arrive in the valley. I deemed it advisable, therefore, to act with extreme caution, so, with the exception of a cavalry reconnoissance on the 13th, I remained on the defensive, quietly awaiting developments. In the evening of that day the enemy's skirmishers withdrew to Tumbling Run, his main force remaining inactive behind the intrenchments at Fisher's Hill waiting for the arrival of Anderson.

The rumors in regard to the force advancing from Culpeper kept increasing every hour, so on the morning of the 14th I concluded to send a brigade of cavalry to Front Royal to ascertain definitely what was up. At the same time I crossed the Sixth Corps to the south side of Cedar Creek, and occupied the heights near Strasburg. That day I received from the hands of Colonel Chipman, of the Adjutant-General's Department, the following despatch, to deliver which he had ridden in great haste from Washington through Snicker's Gap, escorted by a regiment of cavalry:

"CITY POINT, August 12, 1864—9 A. M.
"MAJOR-GENERAL HALLECK
"Inform General Sheridan that it is now certain two (2) divisions of infantry have gone to Early, and some cavalry and twenty (20) pieces of artillery. This movement commenced last Saturday night. He must be cautious, and act now on the defensive until movements here force them to detach to send this way. Early's force, with this increase, cannot exceed forty thousand men, but this is too much for General Sheridan to attack. Send General Sheridan the remaining brigade of the Nineteenth Corps.

"I have ordered to Washington all the one-hundred-day men. Their time will soon be out, but for the present they will do to serve in the defenses.

"U. S. GRANT, Lieutenant-General."

The despatch explained the movement from Culpeper, and on the morning of the 15th Merritt's two remaining brigades were sent to Front Royal to oppose Anderson, and the Sixth Corps withdrawn to the north side of Cedar Creek, where it would be in a position enabling me either to confront Anderson or to act defensively, as desired by General Grant.

To meet the requirements of his instructions I examined the map of the valley for a defensive line—a position where a smaller number of troops could hold a larger number—for this information led me to suppose that Early's force would greatly exceed mine when Anderson's two divisions of infantry and Fitzhugh Lee's cavalry had joined him. I could see but one such position, and that was at Halltown, in front of Harper's Ferry. Subsequent experience convinced me that there was no other really defensive line in the Shenandoah Valley, for at almost any other point the open country and its peculiar topography invites rather than forbids flanking operations.

This retrograde movement would also enable me to strengthen my command by Grower's division of the Nineteenth Corps and Wilson's cavalry, both of which divisions were marching from Washington by way of Snicker's Gap.

After fully considering the matter, I determined to move back to Halltown, carrying out, as I retired, my instructions to destroy all the forage and subsistence the country afforded. So Emory was ordered to retire to Winchester on the night of the 15th, and Wright and Crook to follow through Winchester to Clifton the next night.

For the cavalry, in this move to the rear, I gave the following instructions:

" ... In pushing up the Shenandoah Valley, as it is expected you will have to go first or last, it is desirable that nothing should be left to invite the enemy to return. Take all provisions, forage, and stock wanted for the use of your command. Such as cannot be consumed, destroy. It is not desirable that buildings should be destroyed—they should, rather, be protected; but the people should be informed that so long as an army can subsist among them, recurrences of these raids must be expected, and we are determined to stop them at all hazards ... " [Grant's letter of instructions.]

"HEADQUARTERS MIDDLE MILITARY DIVISION,
"Cedar Creek, Va., August 16, 1864.

"GENERAL: In compliance with instructions of the Lieutenant-General commanding, you will make the necessary arrangements and give the necessary orders for the destruction of the wheat and hay south of a line from Millwood to Winchester and Petticoat Gap. You will seize all mules, horses, and cattle that may be useful to our army. Loyal citizens can bring in their claims against the Government for this necessary destruction. No houses will be burned, and officers in charge of this delicate but necessary duty must inform the people that the object is to make this valley untenable for the raiding parties of the rebel army.

"Very respectfully,
"P. H. SHERIDAN,
"Major-General Commanding.

"BRIGADIER-GENERAL A. T. A. TORBERT,
"Chief of Cavalry, Middle Military Division."

During his visit to General Hunter at the Monocacy, General Grant had not only decided to retain in the Shenandoah Valley a large force sufficient to defeat Early's army or drive it back to Lee, but he had furthermore determined to make that sections by the destruction of its supplies, untenable for continued occupancy by the Confederates. This would cut off one of Lee's main-stays in the way of subsistence, and at the same time diminish the number of recruits and conscripts he received; the valley district while under his control not only supplying Lee with an abundance of food, but also furnishing him many men for his regular and irregular forces. Grant's instructions to destroy the valley began with the letter of August 5 to Hunter, which was turned over to me, and this was followed at intervals by more specific directions, all showing the earnestness of his purpose.

"CITY POINT, Va., Aug. 16—3:30 P. M., 1864.
"MAJOR-GENERAL SHERIDAN, Winchester, Va.:

"If you can possibly spare a division of cavalry, send them through Loudoun County to destroy and carry off the crops, animals, negroes, and all men under fifty years of age capable of bearing arms. In this way you will get many of Mosby's men. All male citizens under fifty can fairly be held as prisoners of war, not as citizen prisoners. If not already soldiers, they will be made so the moment the rebel army gets hold of them.
"U. S. GRANT, Lieutenant-General."

"HEADQUARTERS ARMIES OF THE UNITED STATES,
"CITY POINT, Aug. 21, 1864.
"MAJOR-GENERAL SHERIDAN, Charlestown, Va.:

"In stripping Loudoun County of supplies, etc., impress from all loyal persons so that they may receive pay for what is taken from them. I am informed by the Assistant Secretary of War that Loudoun County has a large population of Quakers, who are all favorably disposed to the Union. These people may be exempted from arrest.
"U. S. GRANT, Lieutenant-General."

"HEADQUARTERS ARMIES OF THE UNITED STATES
"CITY POINT, Va., Aug. 26, 2:30 P. M. 1864.
"MAJOR-GENERAL SHERIDAN, Halltown, Va.:

"Telegraphed you that I had good reason for believing that Fitz Lee had been ordered back here. I now think it likely that all troops will be ordered back from the valley except what they believe to be the minimum number to detain you. My reason for supposing this is based upon the fact that yielding up the Weldon road seems to be a blow to the enemy he cannot stand. I think I do not overstate the loss of the enemy in the last two weeks at 10,000 killed and wounded. We have lost heavily, mostly in captured when the enemy gained temporary advantages. Watch closely, and if you find this theory correct, push with all vigor. Give the enemy no rest, and if it is possible to follow to the Virginia Central road, follow that far. Do all he damage to railroads and crops you can. off stock of all descriptions and negroes, so as to prevent further planting. If the war is to last another year we want the Shenandoah Valley to remain a barren waste.

"U. S. GRANT, Lieutenant-General.

"HEADQUARTERS ARMIES OF THE UNITED STATES,
"CITY POINT, Va., Sept. 4,—10 A. M.—1864.
"MAJOR-GENERAL SHERIDAN, Charlestown, Va.:

"In cleaning out the arms-bearing community of Loudoun County and the subsistence for armies, exercise your own judgment as to who should be exempt from arrest, and as to who should receive pay for their stock, grain, etc. It is our interest that that county should not be capable of subsisting a hostile army, and at the same time we want to inflict as little hardship upon Union men as possible.

"U. S. GRANT, Lieutenant-General."

"CITY POINT, Va., Nov. 9, 1864.
"MAJOR-GENERAL SHERIDAN, Cedar Creek, Va.:

"Do you not think it advisable to notify all citizens living east of the Blue Ridge to move out north of the Potomac all their stock, grain, and provisions of every description? There is no doubt about the necessity of clearing out that country so that it will not support Mosby's gang. And the question is whether it is not better that the people should save what they can. So long as the war lasts they must be prevented from raising another crop, both there and as high up the valley as we can control.

"U. S. GRANT, Lieutenant-General."

He had rightly concluded that it was time to bring the war home to a people engaged in raising crops from a prolific soil to feed the country's enemies, and devoting to the Confederacy its best youth. I endorsed the programme in all its parts, for the stores of meat and grain that the valley provided, and the men it furnished for Lee's depleted regiments, were the strongest auxiliaries he possessed in the whole insurgent section. In war a territory like this is a factor of great importance, and whichever adversary controls it permanently reaps all the advantages of its prosperity. Hence, as I have said, I endorsed Grant's programme, for I do not hold war to mean simply that lines of men shall engage each other in battle, and material interests be ignored. This is but a duel, in which one combatant seeks the other's life; war means much more, and is far worse than this. Those who rest at home in peace and plenty see but little of the horrors attending such a duel, and even grow indifferent to them as the struggle goes on, contenting themselves with encouraging all who are able-bodied to enlist in the cause, to fill up the shattered ranks as death thins them. It is another matter, however, when deprivation and suffering are brought to their own doors. Then the case appears much graver, for the loss of property weighs heavy with the most of mankind; heavier often, than the sacrifices made on the field of battle. Death is popularly considered the maximum of punishment in war, but it is not; reduction to poverty brings prayers for peace more surely and more quickly than does the destruction of human life, as the selfishness of man has demonstrated in more than one great conflict.

In the afternoon of the 16th I started back to Winchester, whence I could better supervise our regressive march. As I was passing through Newtown, I heard cannonading from the direction of Front Royal, and on reaching Winchester, Merritt's couriers brought me word that he had been attacked at the crossing of the Shenandoah by Kershaw's division of Anderson's corps and two brigades of Fitzhugh Lee's cavalry, but that the attack had been handsomely repulsed, with a capture of two battle-flags and three hundred prisoners. This was an absolute confirmation of the despatch from Grant; and I was now more than satisfied with the wisdom of my withdrawal.

At daylight of the 17th Emory moved from Winchester to Berryville, and the same morning Crook and Wright reached Winchester, having started from Cedar Creek the day before. From Winchester, Crook and Wright resumed their march toward Clifton, Wright, who had the rear guard, getting that day as far as the Berryville crossing of the Opequon, where he was ordered to remain, while Crook went ahead till he reached the vicinity of Berryville. On the afternoon of the 17th Lowell with his two regiments of troopers came into Winchester, where he was joined by Wilson's mounted division, which had come by a rapid march from Snicker's ferry. In the mean time Merritt, after his handsome engagement with Kershaw near Front Royal, had been ordered back to the neighborhood of White Post, so that my cavalry outposts now extended from this last point around to the west of Winchester.

During all these operations the enemy had a signal-station on Three Top Mountain, almost overhanging Strasburg, from which every movement made by our troops could be plainly seen; therefore, early on the morning of the 17th he became aware of the fact that we were retiring down the valley, and at once made after us, and about sundown drove Torbert out of Winchester, he having been left there-with Wilson and Lowell, and the Jersey brigade of the Sixth Corps, to develop the character of the enemy's pursuit. After a severe skirmish Wilson and Lowell fell back to Summit Point, and the Jersey brigade joined its corps at the crossing of the Opequon. This affair demonstrated that Early's whole army had followed us from Fisher's Hill, in concert with Anderson and Fitzhugh Lee from Front Royal, and the two columns joined near Winchester the morning of the 18th.

That day I moved the Sixth Corps by way of Clifton to Flowing Spring, two and a half miles west of Charlestown, on the Smithfield pike; and Emory, with Dwight's and Grower's divisions (Grower's having joined that morning from Washington), to a position about the same distance south of Charlestown, on the Berryville pike. Following these movements, Merritt fell back to Berryville, covering the Berryville pike crossing of the Opequon, and Wilson was stationed at Summit Point, whence he held a line along the Opequon as far north as the bridge at Smithfield. Crook continued to hold on near Clifton until the next day, and was then moved into place on the left of Emory.

This line was practically maintained till the 21st, when the enemy, throwing a heavy force across the Opequon by the bridge at Smithfield, drove in my cavalry pickets to Summit Point, and followed up with a rapid advance against the position of the Sixth Corps near Flowing Spring. A sharp and obstinate skirmish with a heavy picket-line of the Sixth Corps grew out of this manoeuvre, and resulted very much in our favor, but the quick withdrawal of the Confederates left no opportunity for a general engagement. It seems that General Early thought I had taken position near Summit Point, and that by moving rapidly around through Smithfield he could fall upon my rear in concert with an attack in front by Anderson, but the warm reception given him disclosed his error, for he soon discovered that my line lay in front of Charlestown instead of where he supposed.

In the manoeuvre Merritt had been attacked in front of Berryville and Wilson at Summit Point, the former by cavalry and the latter by Anderson's infantry. The exposed positions of Merritt and Wilson necessitated their withdrawal if I was to continue to act on the defensive; so, after the army had moved back to Halltown the preceding night, without loss or inconvenience, I called them in and posted them on the right of the infantry.

My retrograde move from Strasburg to Halltown caused considerable alarm in the North, as the public was ignorant of the reasons for it; and in the excited state of mind then prevailing, it was generally expected that the reinforced Confederate army would again cross the Potomac, ravage Maryland and Pennsylvania, and possibly capture Washington. Mutterings of dissatisfaction reached me from many sources, and loud calls were made for my removal, but I felt confident that my course would be justified when the true situation was understood, for I knew that I was complying with my instructions. Therefore I paid small heed to the adverse criticisms pouring down from the North almost every day, being fully convinced that the best course was to bide my time, and wait till I could get the enemy into a position from which he could not escape without such serious misfortune as to have some bearing on the general result of the war. Indeed, at this time I was hoping that my adversary would renew the boldness he had exhibited the early part of the month, and strike for the north side of the Potomac, and wrote to General Grant on the 20th of August that I had purposely left everything in that direction open to the enemy.

On the 22d the Confederates moved to Charlestown and pushed well up to my position at Halltown. Here for the next three days they skirmished with my videttes and infantry pickets, Emory and Cook receiving the main attention; but finding that they could make no impression, and judging it to be an auspicious time to intensify the scare in the North, on the 25th of August Early despatched Fitzhugh Lee's cavalry to Williamsport, and moved all the rest of his army but Anderson's infantry and McCausland's cavalry to Kerneysville. This same day there was sharp picket firing along the whole front of my infantry line, arising, as afterward ascertained, from a heavy demonstration by Anderson.

During this firing I sent Torbert, with Merritt's and Wilson's divisions, to Kerrteysville, whence he was to proceed toward Leetown and learn what had become of Fitz. Lee.

About a mile from Leetown Torbert met a small force of Confederate cavalry, and soon after encountering it, stumbled on Breckenridge's corps of infantry on the march, apparently heading for Shepherdstown. The surprise was mutual, for Torbert expected to meet only the enemy's cavalry, while the Confederate infantry column was anticipating an unobstructed march to the Potomac. Torbert attacked with such vigor as at first to double up the head of Breckenridge's corps and throw it into confusion, but when the Confederates realized that they were confronted only by cavalry, Early brought up the whole of the four infantry divisions engaged in his manoeuvre, and in a sharp attack pushed Torbert rapidly back.

All the advantages which Torbert had gained by surprising the enemy were nullified by this counter-attack, and he was obliged to withdraw Wilson's division toward my right, to the neighborhood of Duffield's Station, Merritt drawing back to the same point by way of the Shepherdstown ford. Custer's brigade becoming isolated after the fight while assisting the rear guard, was also obliged to retire, which it did to Shepherdstown and there halted, picketing the river to Antietam ford.

When Torbert reported to me the nature of his encounter, and that a part of Early's infantry was marching to the north, while Fitzhugh Lee's cavalry had gone toward Martinsburg, I thought that the Confederate general meditated crossing his cavalry into Maryland, so I sent Wilson by way of Harper's Ferry to watch his movements from Boonesboro', and at the same time directed Averell, who had reported from West Virginia some days before, to take post at Williamsport and hold the crossing there until he was driven away. I also thought it possible that Early might cross the Potomac with his whole army, but the doubts of a movement like this outweighed the probabilities favoring it. Nevertheless, to meet such a contingency I arranged to throw my army on his rear should the occasion arise, and deeming my position at Halltown the most advantageous in which to await developments, my infantry was retained there.

If General Early had ever intended to cross the Potomac, Torbert's discovery of his manoeuvre put an end to his scheme of invasion, for he well knew that and success he might derive from such a course would depend on his moving with celerity, and keeping me in ignorance of his march till it should be well under way; so he settled all the present uncertainties by retiring with all his troops about Kerneysville to his old position at Bunker Hill behind the Opequon, and on the night of the 26th silently withdrew Anderson and McCausland from my front at Halltown to Stephenson's depot.

By the 27th all of Early's infantry was in position at Brucetown and Bunker Hill, his cavalry holding the outposts of Leetown and Smithfield, and on that day Merritt's division attacked the enemy's horse at Leetown, and pressed it back through Smithfield to the west side of the Opequon. This reconnoissance determined definitely that Early had abandoned the projected movement into Maryland, if he ever seriously contemplated it; and I marched my infantry out from Halltown to the front of Charlestown, with the intention of occupying a line between Clifton and Berryville the moment matters should so shape themselves that I could do so with advantage. The night of the 28th Wilson joined me near Charlestown from his points of observation in Maryland, and the next day Averell crossed the Potomac at Williamsport and advanced to Martinsburg.

Merritt's possession of Smithfield bridge made Early somewhat uneasy, since it afforded opportunity for interposing a column between his right and left flanks, so he concluded to retake the crossing, and, to this end, on the 29th advanced two divisions of infantry. A severe fight followed, and Merritt was forced to retire, being driven through the village toward Charlestown with considerable loss. As Merritt was nearing my infantry line, I ordered Ricketts's division of the Sixth Corps to his relief, and this in a few minutes turned the tide, the Smithfield crossing of the Opequon being regained, and afterward held by Lowell's brigade, supported by Ricketts. The next morning I moved Torbert, with Wilson and Merritt, to Berryville, and succeeding their occupation of that point there occurred along my whole line a lull, which lasted until the 3d of September, being undisturbed except by a combat near Bunker Hill between Averell's cavalry and a part of McCausland's, supported by Rodes's division of infantry, in which affair the Confederates were defeated with the loss of about fifty prisoners and considerable property in the shape of wagons and beef-cattle.

Meanwhile Torbert's movement to Berryville had alarmed Early, and as a counter move on the 2d of September he marched with the bulk of his army to Summit Point, but while reconnoitring in that region on the 3d he learned of the havoc that Averell was creating in his rear, and this compelled him to recross to the west side of the Opequon and mass his troops in the vicinity of Stephenson's depot, whence he could extend down to Bunker Hill, continue to threaten the Baltimore and Ohio railroad, and at the same time cover Winchester.

The same day I was moving my infantry to take up the Clifton-Berryville line, and that afternoon Wright went into position at Clifton, Crook occupied Berryville, and Emory's corps came in between them, forming almost a continuous line. Torbert had moved to White Post meanwhile, with directions to reconnoitre as far south as the Front Royal Pike.

My infantry had just got fairly into this position about an hour before sunset, when along Crook's front a combat took place that at the time caused me to believe it was Early's purpose to throw a column between Crook and Torbert, with the intention of isolating the latter; but the fight really arose from the attempt of General Anderson to return to Petersburg with Kershaw's division in response to loud calls from General Lee. Anderson started south on the 3d of September, and possibly this explains Early's reconnoissance that day to Summit Point as a covering movement, but his rapid withdrawal left him in ignorance of my advance, and Anderson marched on heedlessly toward Berryville, expecting to cross the Blue Ridge through Ashby's Gap. At Berryville however, he blundered into Crook's lines about sunset, and a bitter little fight ensued, in which the Confederates got so much the worst of it that they withdrew toward Winchester. When General Early received word of this encounter he hurried to Anderson's assistance with three divisions, but soon perceiving what was hitherto unknown to him, that my whole army was on a new line, he decided, after some slight skirmishing, that Anderson must remain at Winchester until a favorable opportunity offered for him to rejoin Lee by another route.

Succeeding the discomfiture of Anderson, some minor operations took place on the part of, Averell on the right and McIntosh's brigade of Wilson's division on the left, but from that time until the 19th of September no engagement of much importance occurred. The line from Clifton to Berryville was occupied by the Sixth Corps and Grower's and Dwight's divisions of the Nineteenth, Crook being transferred to Summit Point, whence I could use him to protect my right flank and my communication with Harper's Ferry, while the cavalry threatened the enemy's right flank and line of retreat up the valley.

The difference of strength between the two armies at this date was considerably in my favor, but the conditions attending my situation in a hostile region necessitated so much detached service to protect trains, and to secure Maryland and Pennsylvania from raids, that my excess in numbers was almost canceled by these incidental demands that could not be avoided, and although I knew that I was strong, yet, in consequence of the injunctions of General Grant, I deemed it necessary to be very cautious; and the fact that the Presidential election was impending made me doubly so, the authorities at Washington having impressed upon me that the defeat of my army might be followed by the overthrow of the party in power, which event, it was believed, would at least retard the progress of the war, if, indeed, it did not lead to the complete abandonment of all coercive measures. Under circumstances such as these I could not afford to risk a disaster, to say nothing of the intense disinclination every soldier has for such results; so, notwithstanding my superior strength, I determined to take all the time necessary to equip myself with the fullest information, and then seize an opportunity under such conditions that I could not well fail of success.

VOLUME 2

CHAPTER I.

ORGANIZING SCOUTS—MISS REBECCA WRIGHT—IMPORTANT INFORMATION—DECIDE TO MOVE ON NEWTOWN—MEETING GENERAL GRANT—ORGANIZATION OF THE UNION ARMY—OPENING OF THE BATTLE OF THE OPEQUON—DEATH OF GENERAL RUSSELL—A TURNING MOVEMENT—A SUCCESSFUL CAVALRY CHARGE—VICTORY—THREE LOYAL GIRLS—APPOINTED A BRIGADIER-GENERAL IN THE REGULAR ARMY—REMARKS ON THE BATTLE.

While occupying the ground between Clifton and Berryville, referred to in the last chapter of the preceding volume, I felt the need of an efficient body of scouts to collect information regarding the enemy, for the defective intelligence-establishment with which I started out from Harper's Ferry early in August had not proved satisfactory. I therefore began to organize my scouts on a system which I hoped would give better results than had the method hitherto pursued in the department, which was to employ on this service doubtful citizens and Confederate deserters. If these should turn out untrustworthy, the mischief they might do us gave me grave apprehension, and I finally concluded that those of our own soldiers who should volunteer for the delicate and hazardous duty would be the most valuable material, and decided that they should have a battalion organization and be commanded by an officer, Major H. K. Young, of the First Rhode Island Infantry. These men were disguised in Confederate uniforms whenever necessary, were paid from the Secret-Service Fund in proportion to the value of the intelligence they furnished, which often stood us in good stead in checking the forays of Gilmore, Mosby, and other irregulars. Beneficial results came from the plan in many other ways too, and particularly so when in a few days two of my scouts put me in the way of getting news conveyed from Winchester. They had learned that just outside of my lines, near Millwood, there was living an old colored man, who had a permit from the Confederate commander to go into Winchester and return three times a week, for the purpose of selling vegetables to the inhabitants. The scouts had sounded this man, and, finding him both loyal and shrewd, suggested that he might be made useful to us within the enemy's lines; and the proposal struck me as feasible, provided there could be found in Winchester some reliable person who would be willing to co-operate and correspond with me. I asked General Crook, who was acquainted with many of the Union people of Winchester, if he knew of such a person, and he recommended a Miss Rebecca Wright, a young lady whom he had met there before the battle of Kernstown, who, he said, was a member of the Society of Friends and the teacher of a small private school. He knew she was faithful and loyal to the Government, and thought she might be willing to render us assistance, but he could not be certain of this, for on account of her well known loyalty she was under constant surveillance. I hesitated at first, but finally deciding to try it, despatched the two scouts to the old negro's cabin, and they brought him to my headquarters late that night. I was soon convinced of the negro's fidelity, and asking him if he was acquainted with Miss Rebecca Wright, of Winchester, he replied that he knew her well. There upon I told him what I wished to do, and after a little persuasion he agreed to carry a letter to her on his next marketing trip. My message was prepared by writing it on tissue paper, which was then compressed into a small pellet, and protected by wrapping it in tin-foil so that it could be safely carried in the man's mouth. The probability, of his being searched when he came to the Confederate picket-line was not remote, and in such event he was to swallow the pellet. The letter appealed to Miss Wright's loyalty and patriotism, and requested her to furnish me with information regarding the strength and condition of Early's army. The night before the negro started one of the scouts placed the odd-looking communication in his hands, with renewed injunctions as to secrecy and promptitude. Early the next morning it was delivered to Miss Wright, with an intimation that a letter of importance was enclosed in the tin-foil, the negro telling her at the same time that she might expect him to call for a message in reply before his return home. At first Miss Wright began to open the pellet nervously, but when told to be careful, and to preserve the foil as a wrapping for her answer, she proceeded slowly and carefully, and when the note appeared intact the messenger retired, remarking again that in the evening he would come for an answer.

On reading my communication Miss Wright was much startled by the perils it involved, and hesitatingly consulted her mother, but her devoted loyalty soon silenced every other consideration, and the brave girl resolved to comply with my request, notwithstanding it might jeopardize her life. The evening before a convalescent Confederate officer had visited her mother's house, and in conversation about the war had disclosed the fact that Kershaw's division of infantry and Cutshaw's battalion of artillery had started to rejoin General Lee. At the time Miss Wright heard this she attached little if any importance to it, but now she perceived the value of the intelligence, and, as her first venture, determined to send it to me at once, which she did with a promise that in the future she would with great pleasure continue to transmit information by the negro messenger.

"SEPTEMBER 15, 1864.

"I learn from Major-General Crook that you are a loyal lady, and still love the old flag. Can you inform me of the position of Early's forces, the number of divisions in his army, and the strength of any or all of them, and his probable or reported intentions? Have any more troops arrived from Richmond, or are any more coming, or reported to be coming?

"You can trust the bearer."

"I am, very respectfully, your most obedient servant,

"P. H. SHERIDAN, Major-General Commanding."

"SEPTEMBER 16, 1864.

"I have no communication whatever with the rebels, but will tell you what I know. The division of General Kershaw, and Cutshaw's artillery, twelve guns and men, General Anderson commanding, have been sent away, and no more are expected, as they cannot be spared from Richmond. I do not know how the troops are situated, but the force is much smaller than represented. I will take pleasure hereafter in learning all I can of their strength and position, and the bearer may call again.

"Very respectfully yours,

" ....

Miss Wright's answer proved of more value to me than she anticipated, for it not only quieted the conflicting reports concerning Anderson's corps, but was most important in showing positively that Kershaw was gone, and this circumstance led, three days later, to the battle of the Opequon, or Winchester as it has been unofficially called. Word to the effect that some of Early's troops were under orders to return to Petersburg, and would start back at the first favorable opportunity, had been communicated to me already from many sources, but we had not been able to ascertain the date for their departure. Now that they had actually started, I decided to wait before offering battle until Kershaw had gone so far as to preclude his return, feeling confident that my prudence would be justified by the improved chances of victory; and then, besides, Mr. Stanton kept reminding me that positive success was necessary to counteract the political dissatisfaction existing in some of the Northern States. This course was advised and approved by General Grant, but even with his powerful backing it was difficult to resist the persistent pressure of those whose judgment, warped by their interests in the Baltimore and Ohio railroad, was often confused and misled by stories of scouts (sent out from Washington), averring that Kershaw and Fitzhugh Lee had returned to Petersburg, Breckenridge to southwestern Virginia, and at one time even maintaining that Early's whole army was east of the Blue Ridge, and its commander himself at Gordonsville.

During the inactivity prevailing in my army for the ten days preceding Miss Wright's communication the infantry was quiet, with the exception of Getty's division, which made a reconnoissance to the Opequon, and developed a heavy force of the enemy at Edwards's Corners. The cavalry, however, was employed a good deal in this interval skirmishing heavily at times to maintain a space about six miles in width between the hostile lines, for I wished to control this ground so that when I was released from the instructions of August 12, I could move my men into position for attack without the knowledge of Early. The most noteworthy of these mounted encounters was that of McIntosh's brigade, which captured the Eighth South Carolina at Abraham's Creek September 13.

It was the evening of the 16th of September that I received from Miss Wright the positive information that Kershaw was in march toward Front Royal on his way by Chester Gap to Richmond. Concluding that this was my opportunity, I at once resolved to throw my whole force into Newtown the next day, but a despatch from General Grant directing me to meet him at Charlestown, whither he was coming to consult with me, caused me to defer action until after I should see him. In our resulting interview at Charlestown, I went over the situation very thoroughly, and pointed out with so much confidence the chances of a complete victory should I throw my army across the Valley pike near Newtown that he fell in with the plan at once, authorized me to resume the offensive, and to attack Early as soon as I deemed it most propitious to do so; and although before leaving City Point he had outlined certain operations for my army, yet he neither discussed nor disclosed his plans, my knowledge of the situation striking him as being so much more accurate than his own.

[Extract from Grant's Memoirs," page 328.]
" . . . Before starting I had drawn up a plan of campaign for Sheridan, which I had brought with me; but seeing that he was so clear and so positive in his views, and so confident of success, I said nothing about this, and did not take it out of my pocket . . . "

The interview over, I returned to my army to arrange for its movement toward Newtown, but while busy with these preparations, a report came to me from General Averell which showed that Early was moving with two divisions of infantry toward Martinsburg. This considerably altered the state of affairs, and I now decided to change my plan and attack at once the two divisions remaining about Winchester and Stephenson's depot, and later, the two sent to Martinsburg; the disjointed state of the enemy giving me an opportunity to take him in detail, unless the Martinsburg column should be returned by forced marches.

While General Early was in the telegraph office at Martinsburg on the morning of the 18th, he learned of Grant's visit to me; and anticipating activity by reason of this circumstance, he promptly proceeded to withdraw so as to get the two divisions within supporting distance of Ramseur's, which lay across the Berryville pike about two miles east of Winchester, between Abraham's Creek and Red Bud Run, so by the night of the 18th Wharton's division, under Breckenridge, was at Stephenson's depot, Rodes near there, and Gordon's at Bunker Hill. At daylight of the 19th these positions of the Confederate infantry still obtained, with the cavalry of Lomax, Jackson, and Johnson on the right of Ramseur, while to the left and rear of the enemy's general line was Fitzhugh Lee, covering from Stephenson's depot west across the Valley pike to Applepie Ridge.

My army moved at 3 o'clock that morning. The plan was for Torbert to advance with Merritt's division of cavalry from Summit Point, carry the crossings of the Opequon at Stevens's and Lock's fords, and form a junction near Stephenson's depot, with Averell, who was to move south from Darksville by the Valley pike. Meanwhile, Wilson was to strike up the Berryville pike, carry the Berryville crossing of the Opequon, charge through the gorge or canyon on the road west of the stream, and occupy the open ground at the head of this defile. Wilson's attack was to be supported by the Sixth and Nineteenth corps, which were ordered to the Berryville crossing, and as the cavalry gained the open ground beyond the gorge, the two infantry corps, under command of General Wright, were expected to press on after and occupy Wilson's ground, who was then to shift to the south bank of Abraham's Creek and cover my left; Crook's two divisions, having to march from Summit Point, were to follow the Sixth and Nineteenth corps to the Opcquon, and should they arrive before the action began, they were to be held in reserve till the proper moment came, and then, as a turning-column, be thrown over toward the Valley pike, south of Winchester.

McIntosh's brigade of Wilson's division drove the enemy's pickets away from the Berryville crossing at dawn, and Wilson following rapidly through the gorge with the rest of the division, debouched from its western extremity with such suddenness as to capture a small earthwork in front of General Ramseur's main line; and not-withstanding the Confederate infantry, on recovering from its astonishment, tried hard to dislodge them, Wilson's troopers obstinately held the work till the Sixth Corps came up. I followed Wilson to select the ground on which to form the infantry. The Sixth Corps began to arrive about 8 o'clock, and taking up the line Wilson had been holding, just beyond the head of the narrow ravine, the cavalry was transferred to the south side of Abraham's Creek.

The Confederate line lay along some elevated ground about two miles east of Winchester, and extended from Abraham's Creek north across the Berryville pike, the left being hidden in the heavy timber on Red Bud Run. Between this line and mine, especially on my right, clumps of woods and patches of underbrush occurred here and there, but the undulating ground consisted mainly of open fields, many of which were covered with standing corn that had already ripened.

Much time was lost in getting all of the Sixth and Nineteenth corps through the narrow defile, Grover's division being greatly delayed there by a train of ammunition wagons, and it was not until late in the forenoon that the troops intended for the attack could be got into line ready to advance. General Early was not slow to avail himself of the advantages thus offered him, and my chances of striking him in detail were growing less every moment, for Gordon and Rodes were hurrying their divisions from Stephenson's depot—across-country on a line that would place Gordon in the woods south of Red Bud Run, and bring Rodes into the interval between Gordon and Ramseur.

When the two corps had all got through the canyon they were formed with Getty's division of the Sixth to the left of the Berryville pike, Rickett's division to the right of the pike, and Russell's division in reserve in rear of the other two. Grover's division of the Nineteenth Corps came next on the right of Rickett's, with Dwight to its rear in reserve, while Crook was to begin massing near the Opequon crossing about the time Wright and Emory were ready to attack.

Just before noon the line of Getty, Ricketts, and Grover moved forward, and as we advanced, the Confederates, covered by some heavy woods on their right, slight underbrush and corn-fields along their Centre, and a large body of timber on their left along the Red Bud, opened fire from their whole front. We gained considerable ground at first, especially on our left but the desperate resistance which the right met with demonstrated that the time we had unavoidably lost in the morning had been of incalculable value to Early, for it was evident that he had been enabled already to so far concentrate his troops as to have the different divisions of his army in a connected line of battle, in good shape to resist.

Getty and Ricketts made some progress toward Winchester in connection with Wilson's cavalry, which was beyond the Senseny road on Getty's left, and as they were pressing back Ramseur's infantry and Lomax's cavalry Grover attacked from the right with decided effect. Grover in a few minutes broke up Evans's brigade of Gordon's division, but his pursuit of Evans destroyed the continuity of my general line, and increased an interval that had already been made by the deflection of Ricketts to the 1eft, in obedience to instructions that had been given him to guide his division on the Berryville pike. As the line pressed forward, Ricketts observed this widening interval and endeavored to fill it with the small brigade of Colonel Keifer, but at this juncture both Gordon and Rodes struck the weak spot where the right of the Sixth Corps and the left of the Nineteenth should have been in conjunction, and succeeded in checking my advance by driving back a part of Ricketts's division, and the most of Grover's. As these troops were retiring I ordered Russell's reserve division to be put into action, and just as the flank of the enemy's troops in pursuit of Grover was presented, Upton's brigade, led in person by both Russell and Upton, struck it in a charge so vigorous as to drive the Confederates back in turn to their original ground.

The success of Russell enabled me to re-establish the right of my line some little distance in advance of the position from which it started in the morning, and behind Russell's division (now commanded by Upton) the broken regiments of Ricketts's division were rallied. Dwight's division was then brought up on the right, and Grover's men formed behind it.

The charge of Russell was most opportune, but it cost many men in killed and wounded. Among the former was the courageous Russell himself; killed by a piece of shell that passed through his heart, although he had previously been struck by a bullet in the left breast, which wound, from its nature, must have proved mortal, yet of which he had not spoken. Russell's death oppressed us all with sadness, and me particularly. In the early days of my army life he was my captain and friend, and I was deeply indebted to him, not only for sound advice and good example, but for the inestimable service he had just performed, and sealed with his life, so it may be inferred how keenly I felt his loss.

As my lines were being rearranged, it was suggested to me to put Crook into the battle, but so strongly had I set my heart on using him to take possession of the Valley pike and cut off the enemy, that I resisted this advice, hoping that the necessity for putting him in would be obviated by the attack near Stephenson's depot that Torbert's cavalry was to make, and from which I was momentarily expecting to hear. No news of Torbert's progress came, however, so, yielding at last, I directed Crook to take post on the right of the Nineteenth Corps and, when the action was renewed, to push his command forward as a turning-column in conjunction with Emory. After some delay in the annoying defile, Crook got his men up, and posting Colonel Thoburn's division on the prolongation of the Nineteenth Corps, he formed Colonel Duval's division to the right of Thoburn. Here I joined Crook, informing him that I had just got word that Torbert was driving the enemy in confusion along the Martinsburg pike toward Winchester; at the same time I directed him to attack the moment all of Duval's men were in line. Wright was instructed to advance in concert with Crook, by swinging Emory and the right of the Sixth Corps to the left together in a half-wheel. Then leaving Crook, I rode along the Sixth and Nineteenth corps, the open ground over which they were passing affording a rare opportunity to witness the precision with which the attack was taken up from right to left. Crook's success began the moment he started to turn the enemy's left; and assured by the fact that Torbert had stampeded the Confederate cavalry and thrown Breckenridge's infantry into such disorder that it could do little to prevent the envelopment of Gordon's left, Crook pressed forward without even a halt.

Both Emory and Wright took up the fight as ordered, and as they did so I sent word to Wilson, in the hope that he could partly perform the work originally laid out for Crook, to push along the Senseny road and, if possible, gain the valley pike south of Winchester. I then returned toward my right flank, and as I reached the Nineteenth Corps the enemy was contesting the ground in its front with great obstinacy; but Emory's dogged persistence was at length rewarded with success, just as Crook's command emerged from the morass of Red Bud Run, and swept around Gordon, toward the right of Breckenridge, who, with two of Wharton's brigades, was holding a line at right angles with the Valley pike for the protection of the Confederate rear. Early had ordered these two brigades back from Stephenson's depot in the morning, purposing to protect with them his right flank and line of retreat, but while they were en route to this end, he was obliged to recall them to his left to meet Crook's attack.

To confront Torbert, Patton's brigade of infantry and some of Fitzhugh Lee's cavalry had been left back by Breckenridge, but, with Averell on the west side of the Valley pike and Merritt on the east, Torbert began to drive this opposing force toward Winchester the moment he struck it near Stephenson's depot, keeping it on the go till it reached the position held by Breckenridge, where it endeavored to make a stand.

The ground which Breckenridge was holding was open, and offered an opportunity such as seldom had been presented during the war for a mounted attack, and Torbert was not slow to take advantage of it. The instant Merritt's division could be formed for the charge, it went at Breckenridge's infantry and Fitzhugh Lee's cavalry with such momentum as to break the Confederate left, just as Averell was passing around it. Merritt's brigades, led by Custer, Lowell, and Devin, met from the start with pronounced success, and with sabre or pistol in hand literally rode down a battery of five guns and took about 1,200 prisoners. Almost simultaneously with this cavalry charge, Crook struck Breckenridge's right and Gordon's left, forcing these divisions to give way, and as they retired, Wright, in a vigorous attack, quickly broke Rodes up and pressed Ramseur so hard that the whole Confederate army fell back, contracting its lines within some breastworks which had been thrown up at a former period of the war, immediately in front of Winchester.

Here Early tried hard to stem the tide, but soon Torbert's cavalry began passing around his left flank, and as Crook, Emory, and Wright attacked in front, panic took possession of the enemy, his troops, now fugitives and stragglers, seeking escape into and through Winchester.

When this second break occurred, the Sixth and Nineteenth corps were moved over toward the Millwood pike to help Wilson on the left, but the day was so far spent that they could render him no assistance, and Ramseur's division, which had maintained some organization, was in such tolerable shape as to check him. Meanwhile Torbert passed around to the west of Winchester to join Wilson, but was unable to do so till after dark. Crook's command pursued the enemy through the town to Mill Greek, I going along.

Just after entering the town, Crook and I met, in the main street, three young girls, who gave us the most hearty reception. One of these young women was a Miss Griffith, the other two Miss Jennie and Miss Susie Meredith. During the day they had been watching the battle from the roof of the Meredith residence, with tears and lamentations, they said, in the morning when misfortune appeared to have overtaken the Union troops, but with unbounded exultation when, later, the, tide set in against the Confederates. Our presence was, to them, an assurance of victory, and their delight being irrepressible, they indulged in the most unguarded manifestations and expressions. When cautioned by Crook, who knew them well, and reminded that the valley had hitherto been a race-course—one day in the possession of friends, and the next of enemies—and warned of the dangers they were incurring by such demonstrations, they assured him that they had no further fears of that kind now, adding that Early's army was so demoralized by the defeat it had just sustained that it would never be in condition to enter Winchester again. As soon as we had succeeded in calming the excited girls a little I expressed a desire to find some place where I could write a telegram to General Grant informing him of the result of the battle, and General Crook conducted me to the home of Miss Wright, where I met for the first time the woman who had contributed so much to our success, and on a desk in her school-room wrote the despatch announcing that we had sent Early's army whirling up the valley.

My losses in the battle of the Opequon were heavy, amounting to about 4,500 killed, wounded, and missing. Among the killed was General Russell, commanding a division, and the wounded included Generals Upton, McIntosh and Chapman, and Colonels Duval and Sharpe. The Confederate loss in killed, wounded, and prisoners about equaled mine, General Rodes being of the killed, while Generals Fitzhugh Lee and York were severely wounded.

We captured five pieces of artillery and nine battle-flags. The restoration of the lower valley—from the Potomac to Strasburg—to the control of the Union forces caused great rejoicing in the North, and relieved the Administration from further solicitude for the safety of the Maryland and Pennsylvania borders. The President's appreciation of the victory was expressed in a despatch so like Mr. Lincoln that I give a facsimile of it to the reader:

[In the handwriting of President Lincoln]
"EXECUTIVE DEPARTMENT
"WASHINGTON, Sep. 20, 1864
"MAJOR-GENERAL SHERMAN
"WINCHESTER, VA.

"Have just heard of your great victory. God bless you all, officers and men. Strongly inclined to come up and see you.

"A. LINCOLN."

This he supplemented by promoting me to the grade of brigadier-general in the regular army, and assigning me to the permanent command of the Middle Military Department, and following that came warm congratulations from Mr. Stanton and from Generals Grant, Sherman, and Meade.

The battle was not fought out on the plan in accordance with which marching orders were issued to my troops, for I then hoped to take Early in detail, and with Crook's force cut off his retreat. I adhered to this purpose during the early part of the contest, but was obliged to abandon the idea because of unavoidable delays by which I was prevented from getting the Sixth and Nineteenth corps through the narrow defile and into position early enough to destroy Ramseur while still isolated. So much delay had not been anticipated, and this loss of time was taken advantage of by the enemy to recall the troops diverted to Bunker Hill and Martinsburg on the 17th, thus enabling him to bring them all to the support of Ramseur before I could strike with effect. My idea was to attack Ramseur and Wharton, successively, at a very early hour and before they could get succor, but I was not in condition to do it till nearly noon, by which time Gordon and Rodes had been enabled to get upon the ground at a point from which, as I advanced, they enfiladed my right flank, and gave it such a repulse that to re-form this part of my line I was obliged to recall the left from some of the ground it had gained. It was during this reorganization of my lines that I changed my plan as to Crook, and moved him from my left to my right. This I did with great reluctance, for I hoped to destroy Early's army entirely if Crook continued on his original line of march toward the Valley pike, south of Winchester; and although the ultimate results did, in a measure vindicate the change, yet I have always thought that by adhering to the original plan we might have captured the bulk of Early's army.

CHAPTER 11.

PURSUING EARLY—A SECRET MARCH—FISHER'S HILL—A GREAT SUCCESS—REMOVAL OF AVERELL—THE RETREAT—CAPTURING AN OLD COMRADE—THE MURDER OF LIEUTENANT MEIGS.

The night of the 19th of September I gave orders for following Early up the valley next morning—the pursuit to begin at daybreak—and in obedience to these directions Torbert moved Averell out on the Back road leading to Cedar Creek, and Merritt up the Valley pike toward Strasburg, while Wilson was directed on Front Royal by way of Stevensburg. Merritt's division was followed by the infantry, Emory's and Wright's columns marching abreast in the open country to the right and left of the pike, and Crook's immediately behind them. The enemy having kept up his retreat at night, presented no opposition whatever until the cavalry discovered him posted at Fisher's Hill, on the first defensive line where he could hope to make any serious resistance. No effort was made to dislodge him, and later in the day, after Wright and Emory came up, Torbert shifted Merritt over toward the Back road till he rejoined Averell. As Merritt moved to the right, the Sixth and Nineteenth corps crossed Cedar Creek and took up the ground the cavalry was vacating, Wright posting his own corps to the west of the Valley pike overlooking Strasburg, and Emory's on his left so as to extend almost to the road leading from Strasburg to Front Royal. Crook, as he came up the same evening, went into position in some heavy timber on the north bank of Cedar Creek.

A reconnoissance made pending these movements convinced me that the enemy's position at Fisher's Hill was so strong that a direct assault would entail unnecessary destruction of life, and, besides, be of doubtful result. At the point where Early's troops were in position, between the Massanutten range and Little North Mountain, the valley is only about three and a half miles wide. All along the precipitous bluff which overhangs Tumbling Run on the south side, a heavy line of earthworks had been constructed when Early retreated to this point in August, and these were now being strengthened so as to make them almost impregnable; in fact, so secure did Early consider himself that, for convenience, his ammunition chests were taken from the caissons and placed behind the breastworks. Wharton, now in command of Breckenridge's division—its late commander having gone to southwest Virginia—held the right of this line, with Gordon next him; Pegram, commanding Ramseur's old division, joined Gordon. Ramseur with Rodes's division, was on Pegram's left, while Lomax's cavalry, now serving as foot-troops, extended the line to the Back road. Fitzhugh Lee being wounded, his cavalry, under General Wickham, was sent to Milford to prevent Fisher's Hill from being turned through the Luray Valley.

In consequence of the enemy's being so well protected from a direct assault, I resolved on the night of the 20th to use again a turning-column against his left, as had been done on the 19th at the Opequon. To this end I resolved to move Crook, unperceived if possible, over to the eastern face of Little North Mountain, whence he could strike the left and rear of the Confederate line, and as he broke it up, I could support him by a left half-wheel of my whole line of battle. The execution of this plan would require perfect secrecy, however, for the enemy from his signal-station on Three Top could plainly see every movement of our troops in daylight. Hence, to escape such observation, I marched Crook during the night of the 20th into some heavy timber north of Cedar Creek, where he lay concealed all day the 21st. This same day Wright and Emory were moved up closer to the Confederate works, and the Sixth Corps, after a severe fight, in which Ricketts's and Getty were engaged, took up some high ground on the right of the Manassas Gap railroad in plain view of the Confederate works, and confronting a commanding point where much of Early's artillery was massed. Soon after General Wright had established this line I rode with him along it to the westward, and finding that the enemy was still holding an elevated position further to our right, on the north side of Tumbling Run, I directed this also to be occupied. Wright soon carried the point, which gave us an unobstructed view of the enemy's works and offered good ground for our artillery. It also enabled me to move the whole of the Sixth Corps to the front till its line was within about seven hundred yards of the enemy's works; the Nineteenth Corps, on the morning of the 22d, covering the ground vacated by the Sixth by moving to the front and extending to the right, but still keeping its reserves on the railroad.

In the darkness of the night of the 91st, Crook was brought across Cedar Creek and hidden in a clump of timber behind Hupp's Hill till daylight of the 22d, when, under cover of the intervening woods and ravines, he was marched beyond the right of the Sixth Corps and again concealed not far from the Back road. After Crook had got into this last position, Ricketts's division was pushed out until it confronted the left of the enemy's infantry, the rest of the Sixth Corps extending from Ricketts's left to the Manassas Gap railroad, while the Nineteenth Corps filled in the space between the left of the Sixth and the North Fork of the Shenandoah.

When Ricketts moved out on this new line, in conjunction with Averell's cavalry on his right, the enemy surmising, from information secured from his signal-station, no doubt, that my attack was to be made from Ricketts's front, prepared for it there, but no such intention ever existed. Ricketts was pushed forward only that he might readily join Crook's turning-column as it swung into the enemy's rear. To ensure success, all that I needed now was enough daylight to complete my arrangements, the secrecy of movement imposed by the situation consuming many valuable hours.

While Ricketts was occupying the enemy's attention, Crook, again moving unobserved into the dense timber on the eastern face of Little North Mountain, conducted his command south in two parallel columns until he gained the rear of the enemy's works, when, marching his divisions by the left flank, he led them in an easterly direction down the mountain-side. As he emerged from the timber near the base of the mountain, the Confederates discovered him, of course, and opened with their batteries, but it was too late—they having few troops at hand to confront the turning-column. Loudly cheering, Crook's men quickly crossed the broken stretch in rear of the enemy's left, producing confusion and consternation at every step.

About a mile from the mountain's base Crook's left was joined by Ricketts, who in proper time had begun to swing his division into the action, and the two commands moved along in rear of the works so rapidly that, with but slight resistance, the Confederates abandoned the guns massed near the centre. The swinging movement of Ricketts was taken up successively from right to left throughout my line, and in a few minutes the enemy was thoroughly routed, the action, though brief, being none the less decisive. Lomax's dismounted cavalry gave way first, but was shortly followed by all the Confederate infantry in an indescribable panic, precipitated doubtless by fears of being caught and captured in the pocket formed by Tumbling Run and the North Fork of the Shenandoah River. The stampede was complete, the enemy leaving the field without semblance of organization, abandoning nearly all his artillery and such other property as was in the works, and the rout extending through the fields and over the roads toward Woodstock, Wright and Emory in hot pursuit.

Midway between Fisher's Hill and Woodstock there is some high ground, where at night-fall a small squad endeavored to stay us with two pieces of artillery, but this attempt at resistance proved fruitless, and, notwithstanding the darkness, the guns were soon captured. The chase was then taken up by Devin's brigade as soon as it could be passed to the front, and continued till after daylight the next morning, but the delays incident to a night pursuit made it impossible for Devin to do more than pick up stragglers.

Our success was very great, yet I had anticipated results still more pregnant. Indeed, I had high hopes of capturing almost the whole of Early's army before it reached New Market, and with this object in view, during the manoeuvres of the 21st I had sent Torbert up the Luray Valley with Wilson's division and two of Merritt's brigades, in the expectation that he would drive Wickham out of the Luray Pass by Early's right, and by crossing the Massanutten Mountain near New Market, gain his rear. Torbert started in good season, and after some slight skirmishing at Gooney Run, got as far as Milford, but failed to dislodge Wickham. In fact, he made little or no attempt to force Wickham from his position, and with only a feeble effort withdrew. I heard nothing at all from Torbert during the 22d, and supposing that everything was progressing favorably, I was astonished and chagrined on the morning of the 23d, at Woodstock, to receive the intelligence that he had fallen back to Front Royal and Buckton ford. My disappointment was extreme, but there was now no help for the situation save to renew and emphasize Torbert's orders, and this was done at once, notwithstanding that I thought, the delay, had so much diminished the chances of his getting in the rear of Early as to make such a result a very remote possibility, unless, indeed, far greater zeal was displayed than had been in the first attempt to penetrate the Luray Valley.

The battle of Fisher's Hill was, in a measure, a part of the battle of the Opequon; that is to say, it was an incident of the pursuit resulting from that action. In many ways, however, it was much more satisfactory, and particularly so because the plan arranged on the evening of the 20th was carried out to the very letter by Generals Wright, Crook, and Emory, not only in all their preliminary manoeuvres, but also during the fight itself. The only drawback was with the cavalry, and to this day I have been unable to account satisfactorily for Torbert's failure. No doubt, Wickham's position near Milford was a strong one, but Torbert ought to have made a fight. Had he been defeated in this, his withdrawal then to await the result at Fisher's Hill would have been justified, but it does not appear that he made any serious effort of all to dislodge the Confederate cavalry: his impotent attempt not only chagrined me very much, but occasioned much unfavorable comment throughout the army.

We reached Woodstock early on the morning of the 23d, and halted there some little time to let the troops recover their organization, which had been broken in the night march they had just made. When the commands had closed up we pushed on toward Edinburg, in the hope of making more captures at Narrow Passage Creek; but the Confederates, too fleet for us, got away; so General Wright halted the infantry not far from Edinburg, till rations could be brought the men. Meanwhile I, having remained at Woodstock, sent Dedin's brigade to press the enemy under every favorable opportunity, and if possible prevent him from halting long enough to reorganize. Notwithstanding Devin's efforts the Confederates managed to assemble a considerable force to resist him, and being too weak for the rearguard, he awaited the arrival of Averell, who, I had informed him, would be hurried to the front with all possible despatch, for I thought that Averell must be close at hand. It turned out, however, that he was not near by at all, and, moreover, that without good reason he had refrained from taking any part whatever in pursuing the enemy in the flight from Fisher's Hill; and in fact had gone into camp and left to the infantry the work of pursuit.

It was nearly noon when Averell came up, and a great deal of precious time had been lost. We had some hot words, but hoping that he would retrieve the mistake of the night before, I directed him to proceed to the front at once, and in conjunction with Devin close with the enemy. He reached Devin's command about 3 o'clock in the afternoon, just as this officer was pushing the Confederates so energetically that they were abandoning Mount Jackson, yet Averell utterly failed to accomplish anything. Indeed, his indifferent attack was not at all worthy the excellent soldiers he commanded, and when I learned that it was his intention to withdraw from the enemy's front, and this, too, on the indefinite report of a signal-officer that a "brigade or division" of Confederates was turning his right flank, and that he had not seriously attempted to verify the information, I sent him this order:

"HEADQUARTERS MIDDLE MILITARY DIVISION,
"Woodstock, Va., Sept. 23, 1864
"BREVET MAJOR-GENERAL AVERELL

"Your report and report of signal-officer received. I do not want you to let the enemy bluff you or your command, and I want you to distinctly understand this note. I do not advise rashness, but I do desire resolution and actual fighting, with necessary casualties, before you retire. There must now be no backing or filling by you without a superior force of the enemy actually engaging you.

"P. H. SHERIDAN,
"Major-General Commanding.'

Some little time after this note went to Averell, word was brought me that he had already carried out the programme indicated when forwarding the report of the expected turning of his right, and that he had actually withdrawn and gone into camp near Hawkinsburg. I then decided to relieve him from the command of his division, which I did, ordering him to Wheeling, Colonel William H. Powell being assigned to succeed him.

The removal of Averell was but the culmination of a series of events extending back to the time I assumed command of the Middle Military Division. At the outset, General Grant, fearing discord on account of Averell's ranking Torbert, authorized me to relieve the former officer, but I hoped that if any trouble of this sort arose, it could be allayed, or at least repressed, during the campaign against Early, since the different commands would often have to act separately. After that, the dispersion of my army by the return of the Sixth Corps and Torbert's cavalry to the Army of the Potomac would take place, I thought, and this would restore matters to their normal condition; but Averell's dissatisfaction began to show itself immediately after his arrival at Martinsburg, on the 14th of August, and, except when he was conducting some independent expedition, had been manifested on all occasions since. I therefore thought that the interest of the service would be subserved by removing one whose growing indifference might render the best-laid plans inoperative.

"HEADQUARTERS MIDDLE MILITARY DIVISION.
"HARRISONBURG, VA., SEPT. 25, 1864 11:30 P. M.
"LIEUT-GENERAL GRANT, Comd'g, City Point, Va.

"I have relieved Averell from his command. Instead of following the enemy when he was broken at Fisher's Hill (so there was not a cavalry organization left), he went into camp and let me pursue the enemy for a distance of fifteen miles, with infantry, during the night.

"P. H. SHERIDAN, Major-General."

The failure of Averell to press the enemy the evening of the 23d gave Early time to collect his scattered forces and take up a position on the east side of the North Fork of the Shenandoah, his left resting on the west side of that stream at Rude's Hill, a commanding point about two miles south of Mt. Jackson. Along this line he had constructed some slight works during the night, and at daylight on the 24th, I moved the Sixth and Nineteenth corps through Mt. Jackson to attack him, sending Powell's division to pass around his left flank, toward Timberville, and Devin's brigade across the North Fork, to move along the base of Peaked Ridge and attack his right. The country was entirely open, and none of these manoeuvres could be executed without being observed, so as soon as my advance began, the enemy rapidly retreated in line of battle up the valley through New Market, closely followed by Wright and Emory, their artillery on the pike and their columns on its right and left. Both sides moved with celerity, the Confederates stimulated by the desire to escape, and our men animated by the prospect of wholly destroying Early's army. The stern-chase continued for about thirteen miles, our infantry often coming within range, yet whenever we began to deploy, the Confederates increased the distance between us by resorting to a double quick, evading battle with admirable tact. While all this was going on, the open country permitted us a rare and brilliant sight, the bright sun gleaming from the arms and trappings of the thousands of pursuers and pursued.

Near New Market, as a last effort to hold the enemy, I pushed Devin's cavalry—comprising about five hundred men—with two guns right up on Early's lines, in the hope that the tempting opportunity given him to capture the guns would stay his retreat long enough to let my infantry deploy within range, but he refused the bait, and after momentarily checking Devin he continued on with little loss and in pretty good order.

All hope of Torbert's appearing in rear of the Confederates vanished as they passed beyond New Market. Some six miles south of this place Early left the Valley Pike and took the road to Keezletown, a move due in a measure to Powell's march by way of Timberville toward Lacy's Springs, but mainly caused by the fact that the Keezletown road ran immediately along the base of Peaked Mountain—a rugged ridge affording protection to Early's right flank—and led in a direction facilitating his junction with Kershaw, who had been ordered back to him from Culpeper the day after the battle of the Opequon. The chase was kept up on the Keezeltown road till darkness overtook us, when my weary troops were permitted to go into camp; and as soon as the enemy discovered by our fires that the pursuit had stopped, he also bivouacked some five miles farther south toward Port Republic.

The next morning Early was joined by Lomax's cavalry from Harrisonburg, Wickham's and Payne's brigades of cavalry also uniting with him from the Luray Valley. His whole army then fell back to the mouth of Brown's Gap to await Kershaw's division and Cutshaw's artillery, now on their return.

By the morning of the 25th the main body of the enemy had disappeared entirely from my front, and the capture of some small, squads of Confederates in the neighboring hills furnished us the only incidents of the day. Among the prisoners was a tall and fine looking officer, much worn with hunger and fatigue. The moment I saw him I recognized him as a former comrade, George W. Carr, with whom I had served in Washington Territory. He was in those days a lieutenant in the Ninth Infantry, and was one of the officers who superintended the execution of the nine Indians at the Cascades of the Columbia in 1856. Carr was very much emaciated, and greatly discouraged by the turn events had recently taken. For old acquaintance sake I gave him plenty to eat, and kept him in comfort at my headquarters until the next batch of prisoners was sent to the rear, when he went with them. He had resigned from the regular army at the commencement of hostilities, and, full of high anticipation, cast his lot with the Confederacy, but when he fell into our hands, his bright dreams having been dispelled by the harsh realities of war, he appeared to think that for him there was no future.

Picking up prisoners here and there, my troops resumed their march directly south on the Valley pike, and when the Sixth and Nineteenth corps reached Harrisonburg, they went into camp, Powell in the meanwhile pushing on to Mt. Crawford, and Crook taking up a position in our rear at the junction of the Keezletown road and the Valley pike. Late in the afternoon Torbert's cavalry came in from New Market arriving at that place many hours later than it had been expected.

The succeeding day I sent Merritt to Port Republic to occupy the enemy's attention, while Torbert, with Wilson's division and the regular brigade, was ordered to Staunton, whence he was to proceed to Waynesboro' and blow up the railroad bridge. Having done this, Torbert, as he returned, was to drive off whatever cattle he could find, destroy all forage and breadstuffs, and burn the mills. He took possession of Waynesboro' in due time, but had succeeded in only partially demolishing the railroad bridge when, attacked by Pegram's division of infantry and Wickham's cavalry, he was compelled to fall back to Staunton. From the latter place he retired to Bridgewater, and Spring Hill, on the way, however, fully executing his instructions regarding the destruction of supplies.

While Torbert was on this expedition, Merritt had occupied Port Republic, but he happened to get there the very day that Kershaw's division was marching from Swift Run Gap to join Early. By accident Kershaw ran into Merritt shortly after the latter had gained the village. Kershaw's four infantry brigades attacked at once, and Merrit, forced out of Port Republic, fell back toward Cross Keys; and in anticipation that the Confederates could be coaxed to that point, I ordered the infantry there, but Torbert's attack at Waynesboro' had alarmed Early, and in consequence he drew all his forces in toward Rock-fish Gap. This enabled me to re-establish Merritt at Port Republic, send the Sixth and Nineteenth corps to the neighborhood of Mt. Crawford to await the return of Torbert, and to post Crook at Harrisonburg; these dispositions practically obtained till the 6th of October, I holding a line across the valley from Port Republic along North River by Mt. Crawford to the Back road near the mouth of Briery Branch Gap.

It was during this period, about dusk on the evening of October 3, that between Harrisonburg and Dayton my engineer officer, Lieutenant John R. Meigs, was murdered within my lines. He had gone out with two topographical assistants to plot the country, and late in the evening, while riding along the public road on his return to camp, he overtook three men dressed in our uniform. From their dress, and also because the party was immediately behind our lines and within a mile and a half of my headquarters, Meigs and his assistants naturally thought that they were joining friends, and wholly unsuspicious of anything to the contrary, rode on with the three men some little distance; but their perfidy was abruptly discovered by their suddenly turning upon Meigs with a call for his surrender. It has been claimed that, refusing to submit, he fired on the treacherous party, but the statement is not true, for one of the topographers escaped—the other was captured—and reported a few minutes later at my headquarters that Meigs was killed without resistance of any kind whatever, and without even the chance to give himself up. This man was so cool, and related all the circumstances of the occurrence with such exactness, as to prove the truthfulness of his statement. The fact that the murder had been committed inside our lines was evidence that the perpetrators of the crime, having their homes in the vicinity, had been clandestinely visiting them, and been secretly harbored by some of the neighboring residents. Determining to teach a lesson to these abettors of the foul deed—a lesson they would never forget—I ordered all the houses within an area of five miles to be burned. General Custer, who had succeeded to the command of the Third Cavalry division (General Wilson having been detailed as chief of cavalry to Sherman's army), was charged with this duty, and the next morning proceeded to put the order into execution. The prescribed area included the little village of Dayton, but when a few houses in the immediate neighborhood of the scene of the murder had been burned, Custer was directed to cease his desolating work, but to fetch away all the able-bodied males as prisoners.

CHAPTER III.

REASONS FOR NOT PURSUING EARLY THROUGH THE BLUE RIDGE—GENERAL TORBERT DETAILED TO GIVE GENERAL ROSSER A "DRUBBING"—GENERAL ROSSER ROUTED— TELEGRAPHED TO MEET STANTON—LONGSTREET'S MESSAGE—RETURN TO WINCHESTER—THE RIDE TO CEDAR CREEK—THE RETREATING ARMY—RALLYING THE TROOPS—REFORMING THE LINE—COMMENCING THE ATTACK—DEFEAT OF THE CONFEDERATES—APPOINTED A MAJOR-GENERAL IN THE REGULAR ARMY—RESULTS OF THE BATTLE.

While we lay in camp at Harrisonburg it became necessary to decide whether or not I would advance to Brown's Gap, and, after driving the enemy from there, follow him through the Blue Ridge into eastern Virginia. Indeed, this question began to cause me solicitude as soon as I knew Early had escaped me at New Market, for I felt certain that I should be urged to pursue the Confederates toward Charlottesville and Gordonsville, and be expected to operate on that line against Richmond. For many reasons I was much opposed to such a plan, but mainly because its execution would involve the opening of the Orange and Alexandria railroad. To protect this road against the raids of the numerous guerrilla bands that infested the region through which it passed, and to keep it in operation, would require a large force of infantry, and would also greatly reduce my cavalry; besides, I should be obliged to leave a force in the valley strong enough to give security to the line of the upper Potomac and the Baltimore and Ohio railroad, and this alone would probably take the whole of Crook's command, leaving me a wholly inadequate number of fighting men to prosecute a campaign against the city of Richmond. Then, too, I was in doubt whether the besiegers could hold the entire army at Petersburg; and in case they could not, a number of troops sufficient to crush me might be detached by Lee, moved rapidly by rail, and, after overwhelming me, be quickly returned to confront General Meade. I was satisfied, moreover, that my transportation could not supply me further than Harrisonburg, and if in penetrating the Blue Ridge I met with protracted resistance, a lack of supplies might compel me to abandon the attempt at a most inopportune time.

I therefore advised that the Valley campaign be terminated north of Staunton, and I be permitted to return, carrying out on the way my original instructions for desolating the Shenandoah country so as to make it untenable for permanent occupation by the Confederates. I proposed to detach the bulk of my army when this work of destruction was completed, and send it by way of the Baltimore and Ohio railroad through Washington to the Petersburg line, believing that I could move it more rapidly by that route than by any other. I was confident that if a movement of this character could be made with celerity it would culminate in the capture of Richmond and possibly of General Lee's army, and I was in hopes that General Grant would take the same view of the matter; but just at this time he was so pressed by the Government and by public-opinion at the North, that he advocated the wholly different conception of driving Early into eastern Virginia, and adhered to this plan with some tenacity. Considerable correspondence regarding the subject took place between us, throughout which I stoutly maintained that we should not risk, by what I held to be a false move, all that my army had gained. I being on the ground, General Grant left to me the final decision of the question, and I solved the first step by determining to withdraw down the valley at least as far as Strasburg, which movement was begun on the 6th of October.

The cavalry as it retired was stretched across the country from the Blue Ridge to the eastern slope of the Alleghanies, with orders to drive off all stock and destroy all supplies as it moved northward. The infantry preceded the cavalry, passing down the Valley pike, and as we marched along the many columns of smoke from burning stacks, and mills filled with grain, indicated that the adjacent country was fast losing the features which hitherto had made it a great magazine of stores for the Confederate armies.

During the 6th and 7th of October, the enemy's horse followed us up, though at a respectful distance. This cavalry was now under command of General T. W. Rosser, who on October 5 had joined Early with an additional brigade from Richmond. As we proceeded the Confederates gained confidence, probably on account of the reputation with which its new commander had been heralded, and on the third day's march had the temerity to annoy my rear guard considerably. Tired of these annoyances, I concluded to open the enemy's eyes in earnest, so that night I told Torbert I expected him either to give Rosser a drubbing next morning or get whipped himself, and that the infantry would be halted until the affair was over; I also informed him that I proposed to ride out to Round Top Mountain to see the fight. When I decided to have Rosser chastised, Merritt was encamped at the foot of Round Top, an elevation just north of Tom's Brook, and Custer some six miles farther north and west, near Tumbling Run. In the night Custer was ordered to retrace his steps before daylight by the Back road, which is parallel to and about three miles from the Valley pike, and attack the enemy at Tom's Brook crossing, while Merritt's instructions were to assail him on the Valley pike in concert with Custer. About 7 in the morning, Custer's division encountered Rosser himself with three brigades, and while the stirring sounds of the resulting artillery duel were reverberating through the valley Merritt moved briskly to the front and fell upon Generals Lomax and Johnson on the Valley pike. Merritt, by extending his right, quickly established connection with Custer, and the two divisions moved forward together under Torbert's direction, with a determination to inflict on the enemy the sharp and summary punishment his rashness had invited.

The engagement soon became general across the valley, both sides fighting mainly mounted. For about two hours the contending lines struggled with each other along Tom's Brook, the charges and counter charges at many points being plainly visible from the summit of Round Top, where I had my headquarters for the time.

The open country permitting a sabre fight, both sides seemed bent on using that arm. In the centre the Confederates maintained their position with much stubbornness, and for a time seemed to have recovered their former spirit, but at last they began to give way on both flanks, and as these receded, Merritt and Custer went at the wavering ranks in a charge along the whole front. The result was a general smash-up of the entire Confederate line, the retreat quickly degenerating into a rout the like of which was never before seen. For twenty-six miles this wild stampede kept up, with our troopers close at the enemy's heels; and the ludicrous incidents of the chase never ceased to be amusing topics around the camp-fires of Merritt and Custer. In the fight and pursuit Torbert took eleven pieces of artillery, with their caissons, all the wagons and ambulances the enemy had on the ground, and three hundred prisoners. Some of Rosser's troopers fled to the mountains by way of Columbia Furnace, and some up the Valley pike and into the Massamitten Range, apparently not discovering that the chase had been discontinued till south of Mount Jackson they rallied on Early's infantry.

After this catastrophe, Early reported to General Lee that his cavalry was so badly demoralized that it should be dismounted; and the citizens of the valley, intensely disgusted with the boasting and swaggering that had characterized the arrival of the "Laurel Brigade" in that section, baptized the action (known to us as Tom's Brook) the "Woodstock Races," and never tired of poking fun at General Rosser about his precipitate and inglorious flight. (When Rosser arrived from Richmond with his brigade he was proclaimed as the savior of the Valley, and his men came all bedecked with laurel branches.)

On the 10th my army, resuming its retrograde movement, crossed to the north side of Cedar Creek. The work of repairing the Manassas Gap branch of the Orange and Alexandria railroad had been begun some days before, out from Washington, and, anticipating that it would be in readiness to transport troops by the time they could reach Piedmont, I directed the Sixth Corps to continue its march toward Front Royal, expecting to return to the Army of the Potomac by that line. By the 12th, however, my views regarding the reconstruction of this railroad began to prevail, and the work on it was discontinued. The Sixth Corps, therefore, abandoned that route, and moved toward Ashby's Gap with the purpose of marching direct to Washington, but on the 13th I recalled it to Cedar Creek, in consequence of the arrival of the enemy's infantry at Fisher's Hill, and the receipt, the night before, of the following despatch, which again opened the question of an advance on Gordonsville and Charlottesville:

(Cipher.)
"WASHINGTON, October 12, 1864, 12 M.
"MAJOR-GENERAL SHERIDAN:

"Lieutenant-General Grant wishes a position taken far enough south to serve as a base for further operations upon Gordonsville and Charlottesville. It must be strongly fortified and provisioned. Some point in the vicinity of Manassas Gap would seem best suited for all purposes. Colonel Alexander, of the Engineers, will be sent to consult with you as soon as you connect with General Augur.

"H. W. HALLECK, Major-General."

As it was well known in Washington that the views expressed in the above despatch were counter to my convictions, I was the next day required by the following telegram from Secretary Stanton to repair to that city:

"WASHINGTON, October 13, 1864.
"MAJOR-GENERAL SHERIDAN (through General Augur)
"If you can come here, a consultation on several points is extremely desirable. I propose to visit General Grant, and would like to see you first.
"EDWIN M. STANTON,
"Secretary of War."

I got all ready to comply with the terms of Secretary Stanton's despatch, but in the meantime the enemy appeared in my front in force, with infantry and cavalry, and attacked Colonel Thoburn, who had been pushed out toward Strasburg from Crook's command, and also Custer's division of cavalry on the Back road. As afterward appeared, this attack was made in the belief that all of my troops but Crook's had gone to Petersburg. From this demonstration there ensued near Hupp's Hill a bitter skirmish between Kershaw and Thoburn, and the latter was finally compelled to withdraw to the north bank of Cedar Creek. Custer gained better results, however, on the Back road, with his usual dash driving the enemy's cavalry away from his front, Merritt's division then joining him and remaining on the right.

The day's events pointing to a probability that the enemy intended to resume the offensive, to anticipate such a contingency I ordered the Sixth Corps to return from its march toward Ashby's Gap. It reached me by noon of the 14th, and went into position to the right and rear of the Nineteenth Corps, which held a line along the north bank of Cedar Creek, west of the Valley pike. Crook was posted on the left of the Nineteenth Corps and east of the Valley pike, with Thoburn's division advanced to a round hill, which commanded the junction of Cedar Creek and the Shenandoah River, while Torbert retained both Merritt and Custer on the right of the

Sixth Corps, and at the same time covered with Powell the roads toward Front Royal. My head-quarters were at the Belle Grove House, which was to the west of the pike and in rear of the Nineteenth Corps. It was my intention to attack the enemy as soon as the Sixth Corps reached me, but General Early having learned from his demonstration that I had not detached as largely as his previous information had led him to believe, on the night of the 13th withdrew to Fisher's Hill; so, concluding that he could not do us serious hurt from there, I changed my mind as to attacking, deciding to defer such action till I could get to Washington, and come to some definite understanding about my future operations.

To carry out this idea, on the evening of the 15th I ordered all of the cavalry under General Torbert to accompany me to Front Royal, again intending to push it thence through Chester Gap to the Virginia Central railroad at Charlottesville, to destroy the bridge over the Rivanna River, while I passed through Manassas Gap to Rectortown, and thence by rail to Washington. On my arrival with the cavalry near Front Royal on the 16th, I halted at the house of Mrs. Richards, on the north bank of the river, and there received the following despatch and inclosure from General Wright, who had been left in command at Cedar Creek:

"HEADQUARTERS MIDDLE MILITARY Division,
"October 16, 1864.
"GENERAL:
"I enclose you despatch which explains itself. If the enemy should be strongly reenforced in cavalry, he might, by turning our right, give us a great deal of trouble. I shall hold on here until the enemy's movements are developed, and shall only fear an attack on my right, which I shall make every preparation for guarding against and resisting.
"Very respectfully, your obedient servant,
"H. G. WRIGHT, Major-General Commanding.

"MAJOR-GENERAL P. H. SHERIDAN,
"Commanding Middle Military Division."

[INCLOSURE.] "To LIEUTENANT-GENERAL EARLY:
"Be ready to move as soon as my forces join you, and we will crush Sheridan.
"LONGSTREET, Lieutenant-General."

The message from Longstreet had been taken down as it was being flagged from the Confederate signal-station on Three Top Mountain, and afterward translated by our signal officers, who knew the Confederate signal code. I first thought it a ruse, and hardly worth attention, but on reflection deemed it best to be on the safe side, so I abandoned the cavalry raid toward Charlottesville, in order to give General Wright the, entire strength of the army, for it did not seem wise to reduce his numbers while reinforcement for the enemy might be near, and especially when such pregnant messages were reaching Early from one of the ablest of the Confederate generals. Therefore I sent the following note to General Wright:

"HEADQUARTERS MIDDLE MILITARY DIVISION,
"Front Royal, October 16, 1864.

"GENERAL: The cavalry is all ordered back to you; make your position strong. If Longstreet's despatch is true, he is under the impression that we have largely detached. I will go over to Augur, and may get additional news. Close in Colonel Powell, who will be at this point. If the enemy should make an advance, I know you will defeat him. Look well to your ground and be well prepared. Get up everything that can be spared. I will bring up all I can, and will be up on Tuesday, if not sooner.

"P. H. SHERIDAN, Major-General.

"MAJOR-GENERAL H. G. WRIGHT,
"Commanding Sixth Army Corps."

At 5 o'clock on the evening of the 16th I telegraphed General Halleck from Rectortown, giving him the information which had come to me from Wright, asking if anything corroborative of it had been received from General Grant, and also saying that I would like to see Halleck; the telegram ending with the question: "Is it best for me to go to see you?" Next morning I sent back to Wright all the cavalry except one regiment, which escorted me through Manassas Gap to the terminus of the railroad from Washington. I had with me Lieutenant-Colonel James W. Forsyth, chief-of-staff, and three of my aides, Major George A. Forsyth, Captain Joseph O'Keefe, and Captain Michael V. Sheridan. I rode my black horse, Rienzi, and the others their own respective mounts.

Before leaving Cedar Creek I had fixed the route of my return to be by rail from Washington to Martinsburg, and thence by horseback to Winchester and Cedar Creek, and had ordered three hundred cavalry to Martinsburg to escort me from that point to the front. At Rectortown I met General Augur, who had brought a force out from Washington to reconstruct and protect the line of railroad, and through him received the following reply from General Halleck:

"HEADQUARTERS ARMIES OF THE UNITED STATES,
"WASHINGTON, D.C., October 16 1864
"To MAJOR-GENERAL SHERIDAN,
"Rectortown, Va.

General Grant says that Longstreet brought with him no troops from Richmond, but I have very little confidence in the information collected at his headquarters. If you can leave your command with safety, come to Washington, as I wish to give you the views of the authorities here.
"H. W. HALLECK, Major-General, Chief-of-Staff."

In consequence of the Longstreet despatch, I felt a concern about my absence which I could hardly repress, but after duly considering what Halleck said, and believing that Longstreet could not unite with Early before I got back, and that even if he did Wright would be able to cope with them both, I and my staff, with our horses, took the cars for Washington, where we arrived on the morning of the 17th at about 8 o'clock. I proceeded at an early hour to the War Department, and as soon as I met Secretary Stanton, asked him for a special train to be ready at 12 o'clock to take me to Martinsburg, saying that in view of existing conditions I must get back to my army as quickly as possible. He at once gave the order for the train, and then the Secretary, Halleck, and I proceeded to hold a consultation in regard to my operating east of the Blue Ridge. The upshot was that my views against such a plan were practically agreed to, and two engineer officers were designated to return with me for the purpose of reporting on a defensive line in the valley that could be held while the bulk of my troops were being detached to Petersburg. Colonel Alexander and Colonel Thom both of the Engineer Corps, reported to accompany me, and at 12 o'clock we took the train.

We arrived about dark at Martinsburg, and there found the escort of three hundred men which I had ordered before leaving Cedar Creek. We spent that night at Martinsburg, and early next morning mounted and started up the Valley pike for Winchester, leaving Captain Sheridan behind to conduct to the army the Commissioners whom the State of New York had sent down to receive the vote of her troops in the coming Presidential election. Colonel Alexander was a man of enormous weight, and Colonel Thom correspondingly light, and as both were unaccustomed to riding we had to go slowly, losing so much time, in fact, that we did not reach Winchester till between 3 and 4 o'clock in the afternoon, though the distance is but twenty-eight miles. As soon as we arrived at Colonel Edwards's headquarters in the town, where I intended stopping for the night, I sent a courier to the front to bring me a report of the condition of affairs, and then took Colonel Alexander out on the heights about Winchester, in order that he might overlook the country, and make up his mind as to the utility of fortifying there. By the time we had completed our survey it was dark, and just as we reached Colonel Edwards's house on our return a courier came in from Cedar Creek bringing word that everything was all right, that the enemy was quiet at Fisher's Hill, and that a brigade of Grover's division was to make a reconnoissance in the morning, the 19th, so about 10 o'clock I went to bed greatly relieved, and expecting to rejoin my headquarters at my leisure next day.

Toward 6 o'clock the morning of the 19th, the officer on picket duty at Winchester came to my room, I being yet in bed, and reported artillery firing from the direction of Cedar Creek. I asked him if the firing was continuous or only desultory, to which he replied that it was not a sustained fire, but rather irregular and fitful. I remarked: "It's all right; Grover has gone out this morning to make a reconnoissance, and he is merely feeling the enemy." I tried to go to sleep again, but grew so restless that I could not, and soon got up and dressed myself. A little later the picket officer came back and reported that the firing, which could be distinctly heard from his line on the heights outside of Winchester, was still going on. I asked him if it sounded like a battle, and as he again said that it did not, I still inferred that the cannonading was caused by Grover's division banging away at the enemy simply to find out what he was up to. However, I went down-stairs and requested that breakfast be hurried up, and at the same time ordered the horses to be saddled and in readiness, for I concluded to go to the front before any further examinations were made in regard to the defensive line.

We mounted our horses between half-past 8 and 9, and as we were proceeding up the street which leads directly through Winchester, from the Logan residence, where Edwards was quartered, to the Valley pike, I noticed that there were many women at the windows and doors of the houses, who kept shaking their skirts at us and who were otherwise markedly insolent in their demeanor, but supposing this conduct to be instigated by their well-known and perhaps natural prejudices, I ascribed to it no unusual significance. On reaching the edge of the town I halted a moment, and there heard quite distinctly the sound of artillery firing in an unceasing roar. Concluding from this that a battle was in progress, I now felt confident that the women along the street had received intelligence from the battle, field by the "grape-vine telegraph," and were in raptures over some good news, while I as yet was utterly ignorant of the actual situation. Moving on, I put my head down toward the pommel of my saddle and listened intently, trying to locate and interpret the sound, continuing in this position till we had crossed Mill Creek, about half a mile from Winchester. The result of my efforts in the interval was the conviction that the travel of the sound was increasing too rapidly to be accounted for by my own rate of motion, and that therefore my army must be falling back.

At Mill Creek my escort fell in behind, and we were going ahead at a regular pace, when, just as we made the crest of the rise beyond the stream, there burst upon our view the appalling spectacle of a panic-stricken army—hundreds of slightly wounded men, throngs of others unhurt but utterly demoralized, and baggage-wagons by the score, all pressing to the rear in hopeless confusion, telling only too plainly that a disaster had occurred at the front. On accosting some of the fugitives, they assured me that the army was broken up, in full retreat, and that all was lost; all this with a manner true to that peculiar indifference that takes possession of panic-stricken men. I was greatly disturbed by the, sight, but at once sent word to Colonel Edwards commanding the brigade in Winchester, to stretch his troops across the valley, near Mill Creek, and stop all fugitives, directing also that the transportation be passed through and parked on the north side of the town.

As I continued at a walk a few hundred yards farther, thinking all the time of Longstreet's telegram to Early, "Be ready when I join you, and we will crush Sheridan," I was fixing in my mind what I should do. My first thought was too stop the army in the suburbs of Winchester as it came back, form a new line, and fight there; but as the situation was more maturely considered a better conception prevailed. I was sure the troops had confidence in me, for heretofore we had been successful; and as at other times they had seen me present at the slightest sign of trouble or distress, I felt that I ought to try now to restore their broken ranks, or, failing in that, to share their fate because of what they had done hitherto.

About this time Colonel Wood, my chief commissary, arrived from the front and gave me fuller intelligence, reporting that everything was gone, my headquarters captured, and the troops dispersed. When I heard this I took two of my aides-de-camp, Major. George A. Forsyth and Captain Joseph O'Keefe, and with twenty men from the escort started for the front, at the same time directing Colonel James W. Forsyth and Colonels Alexander and Thom to remain behind and do what they could to stop the runaways.

For a short distance I traveled on the road, but soon found it so blocked with wagons and wounded men that my progress was impeded, and I was forced to take to the adjoining fields to make haste. When most of the wagons and wounded were past I returned to the road, which was thickly lined with unhurt men, who, having got far enough to the rear to be out of danger, had halted, without any organization, and begun cooking coffee, but when they saw me they abandoned their coffee, threw up their hats, shouldered their muskets, and as I passed along turned to follow with enthusiasm and cheers. To acknowledge this exhibition of feeling I took off my hat, and with Forsyth and O'Keefe rode some distance in advance of my escort, while every mounted officer who saw me galloped out on either side of the pike to tell the men at a distance that I had come back. In this way the news was spread to the stragglers off the road, when they, too, turned their faces to the front and marched toward the enemy, changing in a moment from the depths of depression, to the extreme of enthusiasm. I already knew that even in the ordinary condition of mind enthusiasm is a potent element with soldiers, but what I saw that day convinced me that if it can be excited from a state of despondency its power is almost irresistible. I said nothing except to remark as I rode among those on the road: "If I had been, with you this morning this disaster would not have happened. We must face the other way; we will go back and recover our camp."

My first halt was made just north of Newtown, where I met a chaplain digging his heels into the sides of his jaded horse, and making for the rear with all possible speed. I drew up for an instant, and inquired of him how matters were going at the front. He replied, "Everything is lost; but all will be right when you get there"; yet notwithstanding this expression of confidence in me, the parson at once resumed his breathless pace to the rear. At Newtown I was obliged to make a circuit to the left, to get round the village. I could not pass through it, the streets were so crowded, but meeting on this detour Major McKinley, of Crook's staff, he spread the news of my return through the motley throng there.

When nearing the Valley pike, just south of Newtown I saw about three-fourths of a mile west of the pike a body of troops, which proved to be Ricketts's and Wheaton's divisions of the Sixth Corps, and then learned that the Nineteenth Corps had halted a little to the right and rear of these; but I did not stop, desiring to get to the extreme front. Continuing on parallel with the pike, about midway between Newtown and Middletown I crossed to the west of it, and a little later came up in rear of Getty's division of the Sixth Corps. When I arrived, this division and the cavalry were the only troops in the presence of and resisting the enemy; they were apparently acting as a rear-guard at a point about three miles north of the line we held at Cedar Creek when the battle began. General Torbert was the first officer to meet me, saying as he rode up, "My God! I am glad you've come." Getty's division, when I found it, was about a mile north of Middletown, posted on the reverse slope of some slightly rising ground, holding a barricade made with fence-rails, and skirmishing slightly with the enemy's pickets. Jumping my horse over the line of rails, I rode to the crest of the elevation, and there taking off my hat, the men rose up from behind their barricade with cheers of recognition. An officer of the Vermont brigade, Colonel A. S. Tracy, rode out to the front, and joining me, informed me that General Louis A. Grant was in command there, the regular division commander, General Getty, having taken charge of the Sixth Corps in place of Ricketts, wounded early in the action, while temporarily commanding the corps. I then turned back to the rear of Getty's division, and as I came behind it, a line of regimental flags rose up out of the ground, as it seemed, to welcome me. They were mostly the colors of Crook's troops, who had been stampeded and scattered in the surprise of the morning. The color-bearers, having withstood the panic, had formed behind the troops of Getty. The line with the colors was largely composed of officers, among whom I recognized Colonel R. B. Hayes, since president of the United States, one of the brigade commanders. At the close of this incident I crossed the little narrow valley, or depression, in rear of Getty's line, and dismounting on the opposite crest, established that point as my headquarters. In a few minutes some of my staff joined me, and the first directions I gave were to have the Nineteenth Corps and the two divisions of Wright's corps brought to the front, so they could be formed on Getty's division, prolonged to the right; for I had already decided to attack the enemy from that line as soon as I could get matters in shape to take the offensive. Crook met me at this time, and strongly favored my idea of attacking, but said, however, that most of his troops were gone. General Wright came up a little later, when I saw that he was wounded, a ball having grazed the point of his chin so as to draw the blood plentifully.

Wright gave me a hurried account of the day's events, and when told that we would fight the enemy on the line which Getty and the cavalry were holding, and that he must go himself and send all his staff to bring up the troops, he zealously fell in with the scheme; and it was then that the Nineteenth Corps and two divisions of the Sixth were ordered to the front from where they had been halted to the right and rear of Getty.

After this conversation I rode to the east of the Valley pike and to the left of Getty's division, to a point from which I could obtain a good view of the front, in the mean time sending Major Forsyth to communicate with Colonel Lowell (who occupied a position close in toward the suburbs of Middletown and directly in front of Getty's left) to learn whether he could hold on there. Lowell replied that he could. I then ordered Custer's division back to the right flank, and returning to the place where my headquarters had been established I met near them Ricketts's division under General Keifer and General Frank Wheaton's division, both marching to the front. When the men of these divisions saw me they began cheering and took up the double quick to the front, while I turned back toward Getty's line to point out where these returning troops should be placed. Having done this, I ordered General Wright to resume command of the Sixth Corps, and Getty, who was temporarily in charge of it, to take command of his own division. A little later the Nineteenth Corps came up and was posted between the right of the Sixth Corps and Middle Marsh Brook.

All this had consumed a great deal of time, and I concluded to visit again the point to the east of the Valley pike, from where I had first observed the enemy, to see what he was doing. Arrived there, I could plainly see him getting ready for attack, and Major Forsyth now suggested that it would be well to ride along the line of battle before the enemy assailed us, for although the troops had learned of my return, but few of them had seen me. Following his suggestion I started in behind the men, but when a few paces had been taken I crossed to the front and, hat in hand, passed along the entire length of the infantry line; and it is from this circumstance that many of the officers and men who then received me with such heartiness have since supposed that that was my first appearance on the field. But at least two hours had elapsed since I reached the ground, for it was after mid-day, when this incident of riding down the front took place, and I arrived not later, certainly, than half-past 10 o'clock.

After re-arranging the line and preparing to attack I returned again to observe the Confederates, who shortly began to advance on us. The attacking columns did not cover my entire front, and it appeared that their onset would be mainly directed against the Nineteenth Corps, so, fearing that they might be too strong for Emory on account of his depleted condition (many of his men not having had time to get up from the rear), and Getty's division being free from assault I transferred a part of it from the extreme left to the support of the Nineteenth Corps. The assault was quickly repulsed by Emory, however, and as the enemy fell back Getty's troops were returned to their original place. This repulse of the Confederates made me feel pretty safe from further offensive operations on their part, and I now decided to suspend the fighting till my thin ranks were further strengthened by the men who were continually coming up from the rear, and particularly till Crook's troops could be assembled on the extreme left.

In consequence of the despatch already mentioned, "Be ready when I join you, and we will crush Sheridan," since learned to have been fictitious, I had been supposing all day that Longstreet's troops were present, but as no definite intelligence on this point had been gathered, I concluded, in the lull that now occurred, to ascertain something positive regarding Longstreet; and Merritt having been transferred to our left in the morning, I directed him to attack an exposed battery then at the edge of Middletown, and capture some prisoners. Merritt soon did this work effectually, concealing his intention till his troops got close in to the enemy, and then by a quick dash gobbling up a number of Confederates. When the prisoners were brought in, I learned from them that the only troops of Longstreet's in the fight were of Kershaw's division, which had rejoined Early at Brown's Gap in the latter part of September, and that the rest of Longstreet's corps was not on the field. The receipt of this information entirely cleared the way for me to take the offensive, but on the heels of it came information that Longstreet was marching by the Front Royal pike to strike my rear at Winchester, driving Powell's cavalry in as he advanced. This renewed my uneasiness, and caused me to delay the general attack till after assurances came from Powell denying utterly the reports as to Longstreet, and confirming the statements of the prisoners.

Between half-past and 4 o'clock, I was ready to assail, and decided to do so by advancing my infantry line in a swinging movement, so as to gain the Valley pike with my right between Middletown and the Belle Grove House; and when the order was passed along, the men pushed steadily forward with enthusiasm and confidence. General Early's troops extended some little distance beyond our right, and when my flank neared the overlapping enemy, he turned on it, with the effect of causing a momentary confusion, but General McMillan quickly realizing the danger, broke the Confederates at the reentering angle by a counter charge with his brigade, doing his work so well that the enemy's flanking troops were cut off from their main body and left to shift for themselves. Custer, who was just then moving in from the west side of Middle Marsh Brook, followed McMillan's timely blow with a charge of cavalry, but before starting out on it, and while his men were forming, riding at full speed himself, to throw his arms around my neck. By the time he had disengaged himself from this embrace, the troops broken by McMillan had gained some little distance to their rear, but Custer's troopers sweeping across the Middletown meadows and down toward Cedar Creek, took many of them prisoners before they could reach the stream—so I forgave his delay.

My whole line as far as the eye could see was now driving everything before it, from behind trees, stone walls, and all such sheltering obstacles, so I rode toward the left to ascertain how matters were getting on there. As I passed along behind the advancing troops, first General Grover, and then Colonel Mackenzie, rode up to welcome me. Both were severely wounded, and I told them to leave the field, but they implored permission to remain till success was certain. When I reached the Valley pike Crook had reorganized his men, and as I desired that they should take part in the fight, for they were the very same troops that had turned Early's flank at Winchester and at Fisher's Hill, I ordered them to be pushed forward; and the alacrity and celerity with which they moved on Middletown demonstrated that their ill-fortune of the morning had not sprung from lack of valor.

Meanwhile Lowell's brigade of cavalry, which, it will be remembered, had been holding on, dismounted, just north of Middletown ever since the time I arrived from Winchester, fell to the rear for the purpose of getting their led horses. A momentary panic was created in the nearest brigade of infantry by this withdrawal of Lowell, but as soon as his men were mounted they charged the enemy clear up to the stone walls in the edge of Middletown; at sight of this the infantry brigade renewed its attack, and the enemy's right gave way. The accomplished Lowell received his death-wound in this courageous charge.

All our troops were now moving on the retreating Confederates, and as I rode to the front Colonel Gibbs, who succeeded Lowell, made ready for another mounted charge, but I checked him from pressing the enemy's right, in the hope that the swinging attack from my right would throw most of the Confederates to the east of the Valley pike, and hence off their line of retreat through Strasburg to Fisher's Hill. The eagerness of the men soon frustrated this anticipation, however, the left insisting on keeping pace with the centre and right, and all pushing ahead till we regained our old camps at Cedar Creek. Beyond Cedar Creek, at Strasburg, the pike makes a sharp turn to the west toward Fisher's Hill, and here Merritt uniting with Custer, they together fell on the flank of the retreating columns, taking many prisoners, wagons, and guns, among the prisoners being Major-General Ramseur, who, mortally wounded, died the next day.

When the news of the victory was received, General Grant directed a salute of one hundred shotted guns to be fired into Petersburg, and the President at once thanked the army in an autograph letter. A few weeks after, he promoted me, and I received notice of this in a special letter from the Secretary of War, saying:

> "—that for the personal gallantry, military skill, and just confidence in the courage and patriotism of your troops, displayed by you on the 19th day of October at Cedar Run, whereby, under the blessing of Providence, your routed army was reorganized, a great National disaster averted, and a brilliant victory achieved over the rebels for the third time in pitched battle within thirty days, Philip H. Sheridan is appointed a major-general in the United States Army."

The direct result of the battle was the recapture of all the artillery, transportation, and camp equipage we had lost, and in addition twenty-four pieces of the enemy's artillery, twelve hundred prisoners, and a number of battle-flags. But more still flowed from this victory, succeeding as it did the disaster of the morning, for the reoccupation of our old camps at once re-established a morale which for some hours had been greatly endangered by ill-fortune.

It was not till after the battle that I learned fully what had taken place before my arrival, and then found that the enemy, having gathered all the strength he could through the return of convalescents and other absentees, had moved quietly from Fisher's Hill, in the night of the 18th and early on the morning of the 19th, to surprise my army, which, it should be remembered, was posted on the north bank of Cedar Creek, Crook holding on the left of the Valley pike, with Thoburn's division advanced toward the creek on Duval's (under Colonel Rutherford B. Hayes) and Kitching's provisional divisions to the north and rear of Thoburn. The Nineteenth Corps was on the right of Crook, extending in a semi-circular line from the pike nearly to Meadow Brook, while the Sixth Corps lay to the west of the brook in readiness to be used as a movable column. Merritt's division was to the right and rear of the Sixth Corps, and about a mile and a half west of Merrit was Custer covering the fords of Cedar Creek as far west as the Middle road.

General Early's plan was for one column under General Gordon, consisting of three divisions of infantry (Gordon's, Ramseur's, and Pegram's), and Payne's brigade of cavalry to cross the Shenandoah River directly east of the Confederate works at Fisher's Hill, march around the northerly face of the Massanutten Mountain, and again cross the Shenandoah at Bowman's and McInturff's fords. Payne's task was to capture me at the Belle Grove House. General Early himself, with Kershaw's and Wharton's divisions, was to move through Strasburg, Kershaw, accompanied by Early, to cross Cedar Creek at Roberts's ford and connect with Gordon, while Wharton was to continue on the Valley pike to Hupp's Hill and join the left of Kershaw, when the crossing of the Valley pike over Cedar Creek became free.

Lomax's cavalry, then in the Luray Valley, was ordered to join the right of Gordon on the field of battle, while Rosser was to carry the crossing of Cedar Creek on the Back road and attack Custer. Early's conceptions were carried through in the darkness with little accident or delay, Kershaw opening the fight by a furious attack on Thoburn's division, while at dawn and in a dense fog Gordon struck Crook's extreme left, surprising his pickets, and bursting into his camp with such suddenness as to stampede Crook's men. Gordon directing his march on my headquarters (the Belle

Grove House), successfully turned our position as he gained the Valley pike, and General Wright was thus forced to order the withdrawal of the Nineteenth Corps from its post at the Cedar Creek crossing, and this enabled Wharton to get over the stream there unmolested and join Kershaw early in the action.

After Crook's troops had been driven from their camps, General Wright endeavored to form a line with the Sixth Corps to hold the Valley pike to the left of the Nineteenth, but failing in this he ordered the withdrawal of the latter corps, Ricketts, temporarily commanding the Sixth Corps, checking Gordon till Emory had retired. As already stated, Wharton was thus permitted to cross Cedar Creek on the pike, and now that Early had a continuous line, he pressed his advantage so vigorously that the whole Union army was soon driven from its camps in more or less disorder; and though much disjointed resistance was displayed, it may be said that no systematic stand was made until Getty's division, aided by Torbert's cavalry, which Wright had ordered to the left early in the action, took up the ground where, on arriving from Winchester, I found them.

When I left my command on the 16th, little did I anticipate that anything like this would happen. Indeed, I felt satisfied that Early was, of himself, too weak to take the offensive, and although I doubted the Longstreet despatch, yet I was confident that, even should it prove true, I could get back before the junction could be made, and at the worst I felt certain that my army was equal to confronting the forces of Longstreet and Early combined. Still, the surprise of the morning might have befallen me as well as the general on whom it did descend, and though it is possible that this could have been precluded had Powell's cavalry been closed in, as suggested in my despatch from Front Royal, yet the enemy's desperation might have prompted some other clever and ingenious scheme for relieving his fallen fortunes in the Shenandoah Valley.

CHAPTER IV.
GENERAL EARLY REORGANIZES HIS FORCES—MOSBY THE GUERRILLA—GENERAL MERRITT SENT TO OPERATE AGAINST MOSBY—ROSSER AGAIN ACTIVE—GENERAL CUSTER SURPRISED—COLONEL YOUNG SENT TO CAPTURE GILMORE THE GUERRILLA—COLONEL YOUNG'S SUCCESS—CAPTURE OF GENERAL KELLY AND GENERAL CROOK—SPIES—WAS WILKES BOOTH A SPY?—DRIVING THE CONFEDERATES OUT OF THE VALLEY—THE BATTLE OF WAYNESBORO'—MARCHING TO JOIN THE ARMY OF THE POTOMAC.

Early's broken army practically made no halt in its retreat after the battle of Cedar-Creek until it reached New Market, though at Fisher's Hill was left a small rear-guard of cavalry, which hastily decamped, however, when charged by Gibbs's brigade on the morning of the 20th. Between the date of his signal defeat and the 11th of November, the enemy's scattered forces had sufficiently reorganized to permit his again making a reconnoissance in the valley as far north as Cedar Creek, my army having meanwhile withdrawn to Kernstown, where it had been finally decided that a defensive line should be held to enable me to detach troops to General Grant, and where, by reconstructing the Winchester and Potomac railroad from Stephenson's depot to Harper's Ferry, my command might be more readily, supplied. Early's reconnoissance north of Cedar Creek ended in a rapid withdrawal of his infantry after feeling my front, and with the usual ill-fortune to his cavalry; Merritt and Custer driving Rosser and Lomax with ease across Cedar Creek on the Middle and Back roads, while Powell's cavalry struck McCausland near Stony Point, and after capturing two pieces of artillery and about three hundred officers and men chased him into the Luray Valley.

Early got back to New Market on the 14th of November, and, from lack of subsistence, being unable to continue demonstrations to prevent my reinforcement of General Grant, began himself to detach to General Lee by returning Kershaw's division to Petersburg, as was definitely ascertained by Torbert in a reconnoissance to Mount Jackson. At this time General Grant wished me to send him the Sixth Corps, and it was got ready for the purpose, but when I informed him that Torbert's reconnoissance had developed the fact that Early still retained four divisions of infantry and one of cavalry, it was decided, on my suggestion, to let the Sixth Corps remain till the season should be a little further advanced, when the inclemency of the weather would preclude infantry campaigning. These conditions came about early in December, and by the middle of the month the whole of the Sixth Corps was at Petersburg; simultaneously with its transfer to that line Early sending his Second Corps to Lee.

During the entire campaign I had been annoyed by guerrilla bands under such partisan chiefs as Mosby, White, Gilmore, McNeil, and others, and this had considerably depleted my line-of-battle strength, necessitating as it did large, escorts for my supply-trains. The most redoubtable of these leaders was Mosby, whose force was made up from the country around Upperville, east of the Blue Ridge, to which section he always fled for a hiding-place when he scented danger. I had not directed any special operations against these partisans while the campaign was active, but as Mosby's men had lately killed, within my lines, my chief quartermaster, Colonel Tolles, and Medical Inspector Ohlenchlager, I concluded to devote particular attention to these "irregulars" during the lull that now occurred; so on the 28th of November, I directed General Merritt to march to the Loudoun Valley and operate against Mosby, taking care to clear the country of forage and subsistence, so as to prevent the guerrillas from being harbored there in the future their destruction or capture being well-nigh impossible, on account of their intimate knowledge of the mountain region. Merritt carried out his instructions with his usual sagacity and thoroughness, sweeping widely over each side of his general line of march with flankers, who burned the grain and brought in large herds of cattle, hogs and sheep, which were issued to the troops.

While Merritt was engaged in this service the Baltimore and Ohio railroad once more received the attention of the enemy; Rosser, with two brigades of cavalry, crossing the Great North Mountain, capturing the post of New Creek, with about five hundred prisoners and seven guns, destroying all the supplies of the garrison, and breaking up the railroad track. This slight success of the Confederates in West Virginia, and the intelligence that they were contemplating further raids in that section, led me to send, Crook there with one division, his other troops going to City Point; and, I hoped that all the threatened places would thus be sufficiently protected, but negligence at Beverly resulted in the capture of that station by Rosser on the 11th of January.

In the meanwhile, Early established himself with Wharton's division at Staunton in winter quarters, posting his cavalry in that neighborhood also, except a detachment at New Market, and another small one at the signalstation on Three Top Mountain. The winter was a most severe one, snow falling frequently to the depth of several inches, and the mercury often sinking below zero. The rigor of the season was very much against the success of any mounted operations, but General Grant being very desirous to have the railroads broken up about Gordonsville and Charlottesville, on the 19th of December I started the cavalry out for that purpose, Torbert, with Merritt and Powell, marching through Chester Gap, while Custer moved toward Staunton to make a demonstration in Torbert's favor, hoping to hold the enemy's troops in the valley. Unfortunately, Custer did not accomplish all that was expected of him, and being surprised by Rosser and Payne near Lacy's Springs before reveille, had to abandon his bivouac and retreat down the valley, with the loss of a number of prisoners, a few horses, and a good many horse equipments, for, because of the suddenness of Rosser's attack, many of the men had no time to saddle up. As soon as Custer's retreat was assured, Wharton's division of infantry was sent to Charlottesville to check Torbert, but this had already been done by Lomax, with the assistance of infantry sent up from Richmond. Indeed, from the very beginning of the movement the Confederates had been closely observing the columns of Torbert and Custer, and in consequence of the knowledge thus derived, Early had marched Lomax to Gordonsville in anticipation of an attack there, at the same time sending Rosser down the valley to meet Custer. Torbert in the performance of his task captured two pieces of artillery from Johnson's and McCausland's brigades, at Liberty Mills on the Rapidan River, but in the main the purpose of the raid utterly failed, so by the 27th of December he returned, many, of his men badly frost-bitten from the extreme cold which had prevailed.

This expedition practically closed all operations for the season, and the cavalry was put into winter cantonment near Winchester. The distribution of my infantry to Petersburg and West Virginia left with me in the beginning of the new year, as already stated, but the one small division of the Nineteenth Corps. On account of this diminution of force, it became necessary for me to keep thoroughly posted in regard to the enemy, and I now realized more than I had done hitherto how efficient my scouts had become since under the control of Colonel Young; for not only did they bring me almost every day intelligence from within Early's lines, but they also operated efficiently against the guerrillas infesting West Virginia.

Harry Gilmore, of Maryland, was the most noted of these since the death of McNeil, and as the scouts had reported him in Harrisonburg the latter part of January, I directed two of the most trustworthy to be sent to watch his movements and ascertain his purposes. In a few days these spies returned with the intelligence that Gilmore was on his way to Moorefield, the centre of a very disloyal section in West Virginia, about ninety miles southwest of Winchester, where, under the guise of a camp-meeting, a gathering was to take place, at which he expected to enlist a number of men, be joined by a party of about twenty recruits coming from Maryland, and then begin depredations along the Baltimore and Ohio railroad. Believing that Gilmore might be captured, I directed Young to undertake the task, and as a preliminary step he sent to Moorefield two of his men who early in the war had "refugeed" from that section and enlisted in one of the Union regiments from West Virginia. In about a week these men came back and reported that Gilmore was living at a house between three and four miles from Moorefield, and gave full particulars as to his coming and going, the number of men he had about there and where they rendezvoused.

With this knowledge at hand I directed Young to take twenty of his best men and leave that night for Moorefield, dressed in Confederate uniforms, telling him that I would have about three hundred cavalry follow in his wake when he had got about fifteen miles start, and instructing him to pass his party off as a body of recruits for Gilmore coming from Maryland and pursued by the Yankee cavalry. I knew this would allay suspicion and provide him help on the road; and, indeed, as Colonel Whittaker, who alone knew the secret, followed after the fleeing "Marylanders," he found that their advent had caused so little remark that the trail would have been lost had he not already known their destination. Young met with a hearty, welcome wherever he halted on the way, and as he passed through the town of Moorefield learned with satisfaction that Gilmore still made his headquarters at the house where the report of the two scouts had located him a few days before. Reaching the designated place about 12 o'clock on the night of the 5th of February, Young, under the representation that he had come directly from Maryland and was being pursued by the Union cavalry, gained immediate access to Gilmore's room. He found the bold guerrilla snugly tucked in bed, with two pistols lying on a chair near by. He was sleeping so soundly that to arouse him Young had to give him a violent shake. As he awoke and asked who was disturbing his slumbers, Young, pointing at him a cocked six-shooter, ordered him to dress without delay, and in answer to his inquiry, informed him that he was a prisoner to one of Sheridan's staff. Meanwhile Gilmore's men had learned of his trouble, but the early appearance of Colonel Whittaker caused them to disperse; thus the last link between Maryland and the Confederacy was carried a prisoner to Winchester, whence he was sent to Fort Warren.

The capture of Gilmore caused the disbandment of the party he had organized at the "camp-meeting," most of the men he had recruited returning to their homes discouraged, though some few joined the bands of Woodson and young Jesse McNeil, which, led by the latter, dashed into Cumberland, Maryland, at 3 O'clock on the morning of the 21st of February and made a reprisal by carrying off General Crook and General Kelly, and doing their work so silently and quickly that they escaped without being noticed, and were some distance on their way before the colored watchman at the hotel where Crook was quartered could compose himself enough to give the alarm. A troop of cavalry gave hot chase from Cumberland, striving to intercept the party at Moorefield and other points, but all efforts were fruitless, the prisoners soon being beyond reach.

Although I had adopted the general rule of employing only soldiers as scouts, there was an occasional exception to it. I cannot say that these exceptions proved wholly that an ironclad observance of the rule would have been best, but I am sure of it in one instance. A man named Lomas, who claimed to be a Marylander, offered me his services as a spy, and coming highly recommended from Mr. Stanton, who had made use of him in that capacity, I employed him. He made many pretensions, often appearing over anxious to impart information seemingly intended to impress me with his importance, and yet was more than ordinarily intelligent, but in spite of that my confidence in him was by no means unlimited. I often found what he reported to me as taking place within the Confederate lines corroborated by Young's men, but generally there were discrepancies in his tales, which led me to suspect that he was employed by the enemy as well as by me. I felt, however, that with good watching he could do me little harm, and if my suspicions were incorrect he might be very useful, so I held on to him.

Early in February Lomas was very solicitous for me to employ a man who, he said, had been with Mosby, but on account of some quarrel in the irregular camp had abandoned that leader. Thinking that with two of them I might destroy the railroad bridges east of Lynchburg, I concluded, after the Mosby man had been brought to my headquarters by Lomas about 12 o'clock one night, to give him employment, at the same time informing Colonel Young that I suspected their fidelity, however, and that he must test it by shadowing their every movement. When Lomas's companion entered my room he was completely disguised, but on discarding the various contrivances by which his identity was concealed he proved to be a rather slender, dark-complexioned, handsome young man, of easy address and captivating manners. He gave his name as Renfrew, answered all my questions satisfactorily, and went into details about Mosby and his men which showed an intimacy with them at some time. I explained to the two men the work I had laid out for them, and stated the sum of money I would give to have it done, but stipulated that in case of failure there would be no compensation whatever beyond the few dollars necessary for their expenses. They readily assented, and it was arranged that they should start the following night. Meanwhile Young had selected his men to shadow them, and in two days reported my spies as being concealed at Strasburg, where they remained, without making the slightest effort to continue on their mission, and were busy, no doubt, communicating with the enemy, though I was not able to fasten this on them. On the 16th of February they returned to Winchester, and reported their failure, telling so many lies about their hazardous adventure as to remove all remaining doubt as to their double-dealing. Unquestionably they were spies from the enemy, and hence liable to the usual penalties of such service; but it struck me that through them, I might deceive Early as to the time of opening the spring campaign, I having already received from General Grant an intimation of what was expected of me. I therefore retained the men without even a suggestion of my knowledge of their true character, Young meanwhile keeping close watch over all their doings.

Toward the last of February General Early had at Staunton two brigades of infantry under Wharton. All the rest of the infantry except Echol's brigade, which was in southwestern Virginia, had been sent to Petersburg during the winter, and Fitz. Lee's two brigades of cavalry also. Rosser's men were mostly at their homes, where, on account of a lack of subsistence and forage in the valley, they had been permitted to go, subject to call. Lomax's cavalry was at Millboro', west of Staunton, where supplies were obtainable. It was my aim to get well on the road before Early could collect these scattered forces, and as many of the officers had been in the habit of amusing themselves fox-hunting during the latter part of the winter, I decided to use the hunt as an expedient for stealing a march on the enemy, and had it given out officially that a grand fox-chase would take place on the 29th of February. Knowing that Lomas, and Renfrew would spread the announcement South, they were permitted to see several red foxes that had been secured, as well as a large pack of hounds which Colonel Young had collected for the sport, and were then started on a second expedition to burn the bridges. Of course, they were shadowed as usual, and two days later, after they had communicated with friends from their hiding-place, in Newtown, they were arrested. On the way north to Fort Warren they escaped from their guards when passing through Baltimore, and I never heard of them again, though I learned that, after the assassination of, Mr. Lincoln, Secretary Stanton strongly suspected his friend Lomas of being associated with the conspirators, and it then occurred to me that the good-looking Renfrew may have been Wilkes Booth, for he certainly bore a strong resemblance to Booth's pictures.

On the 27th of February my cavalry entered upon the campaign which cleared the Shenandoah Valley of every remnant of organized Confederates. General Torbert being absent on leave at this time, I did not recall him, but appointed General Merritt Chief of Cavalry. for Torbert had disappointed me on two important occasions—in the Luray Valley during the battle of Fisher's Hill, and on the recent Gordonsville expedition—and I mistrusted his ability to conduct any operations requiring much self-reliance. The column was composed of Custer's and Devin's divisions of cavalry, and two sections of artillery, comprising in all about 10,000 officers and men. On wheels we had, to accompany this column, eight ambulances, sixteen ammunition wagons, a pontoon train for eight canvas boats, and a small supply-train, with fifteen days' rations of coffee, sugar, and salt, it being intended to depend on the country for the meat and bread ration, the men carrying in their haversacks nearly enough to subsist them till out of the exhausted valley.

Grant's orders were for me to destroy the Virginia Central railroad and the James River canal, capture Lynchburg if practicable, and then join General Sherman in North Carolina wherever he might be found, or return to Winchester, but as to joining Sherman I was to be governed by the state of affairs after the projected capture of Lynchburg. The weather was cold, the valley and surrounding mountains being still covered with snow; but this was fast disappearing, however, under the heavy rain that was coming down as the column moved along up the Valley pike at a steady gait that took us to Woodstock the first day. The second day we crossed the North Fork of the Shenandoah on our pontoon-bridge, and by night-fall reached Lacy's Springs, having seen nothing of the enemy as yet but a few partisans who hung on our flanks in the afternoon.

March 1 we encountered General Rosser at Mt. Crawford, he having been able to call together only some five or six hundred of his troops, our unsuspected march becoming known to Early only the day before. Rosser attempted to delay us here, trying to burn the bridges over the Middle Fork of the Shenandoah, but two regiments from Colonel Capehart's brigade swam the stream and drove Rosser to Kline's Mills, taking thirty prisoners and twenty ambulances and wagons.

Meanwhile General Early was busy at Staunton, but not knowing my objective point, he had ordered the return of Echol's brigade from southwestern Virginia for the protection of Lynchburg, directed Lomax's cavalry to concentrate at Pond Gap for the purpose of harassing me if I moved toward Lynchburg, and at the same time marched Wharton's two brigades of infantry, Nelson's artillery, and Rosser's cavalry to Waynesboro', whither he went also to remain till the object of my movement was ascertained.

I entered Staunton the morning of March 2, and finding that Early had gone to Waynesboro' with his infantry and Rosser, the question at once arose whether I should continue my march to Lynchburg direct, leaving my adversary in my rear, or turn east and open the way through Rockfish Gap to the Virginia Central railroad and James River canal. I felt confident of the success of the latter plan, for I knew that Early numbered there not more than two thousand men; so, influenced by this, and somewhat also by the fact that Early had left word in Staunton that he would fight at Waynesboro', I directed Merritt to move toward that place with Custer, to be closely followed by Devin, who was to detach one brigade to destroy supplies at Swoope's'depot. The by-roads were miry beyond description, rain having fallen almost incessantly since we left Winchester, but notwithstanding the down-pour the column pushed on, men and horses growing almost unrecognizable from the mud covering them from head to foot.

General Early was true to the promise made his friends in Staunton, for when Custer neared Waynesboro' he found, occupying a line of breastworks on a ridge west of the town, two brigades of infantry, with eleven pieces of artillery and Rosser's cavalry. Custer, when developing the position of the Confederates, discovered that their left was somewhat exposed instead of resting on South River; he therefore made his dispositions for attack, sending around that flank the dismounted regiments from Pennington's brigade, while he himself, with two brigades, partly mounted and partly dismounted, assaulted along the whole line of breastworks. Pennington's flanking movement stampeded the enemy in short order, thus enabling Custer to carry the front with little resistance, and as he did so the Eighth New York and First Connecticut, in a charge in column, broke through the opening made by Custer, and continued on through the town of Waynesboro', never stopping till they crossed South River. There, finding themselves immediately in the enemy's rear, they promptly formed as foragers and held the east bank of the stream till all the Confederates surrendered except Rosser, who succeeded in making his way back to the valley, and Generals Early, Wharton, Long, and Lilley, who, with fifteen or twenty men, escaped across the Blue Ridge. I followed up the victory immediately by despatching Capehart through Rock-fish Gap, with orders to encamp on the east side of the Blue Ridge. By reason of this move all the enemy's stores and transportation fell into our hands, while we captured on the field seventeen battle flags, sixteen hundred officers and men, and eleven pieces of artillery. This decisive victory closed hostilities in the Shenandoah Valley. The prisoners and artillery were sent back to Winchester next morning, under a guard of 1,500 men, commanded by Colonel J. H. Thompson, of the First New Hampshire.

The night of March 2 Custer camped at Brookfield, Devin remaining at Waynesboro'. The former started for Charlottesville the next morning early, followed by Devin with but two brigades, Gibbs having been left behind to blow up the iron railroad bridge across South River. Because of the incessant rains and spring thaws the roads were very soft, and the columns cut them up terribly, the mud being thrown by the sets of fours across the road in ridges as much as two feet high, making it most difficult to get our wagons along, and distressingly wearing on the animals toward the middle and rear of the columns. Consequently I concluded to rest at Charlottesville for a couple of days and recuperate a little, intending at the same time to destroy, with small parties, the railroad from that point toward Lynchburg. Custer reached Charlottesville the 3d, in the afternoon, and was met at the outskirts by a deputation of its citizens, headed by the mayor, who surrendered the town with medieval ceremony, formally handing over the keys of the public buildings and of the University of Virginia. But this little scene did not delay Custer long enough to prevent his capturing, just beyond the village, a small body of cavalry and three pieces of artillery. Gibbs's brigade, which was bringing up my mud-impeded train, did not arrive until the 5th of March. In the mean time Young's scouts had brought word that the garrison of Lynchburg was being increased and the fortifications strengthened, so that its capture would be improbable. I decided, however, to move toward the place as far as Amherst Court House, which is sixteen miles short of the town, so Devin, under Merritt's supervision, marched along the James River, destroying the canal, while Custer pushed ahead on the railroad and broke it up. The two columns were to join at New Market, whence I intended to cross the James River at some point east of Lynchburg, if practicable, so as to make my way to Appomattox Court House, and destroy the Southside railroad as far east as Farmville. Owing to its swollen condition the river was unfordable but knowing that there was a covered bridge at Duguidsville, I hoped to secure it by a dash, and cross there, but the enemy, anticipating this, had filled the bridge with inflammable material, and just as our troops got within striking distance it burst into flames. The bridge at Hardwicksville also having been burned by the enemy, there was now no means of crossing except by pontoons. but, unfortunately, I had only eight of these, and they could not be made to span the swollen river.

Being thus unable to cross until the river should fall, and knowing that it was impracticable to join General Sherman, and useless to adhere to my alternative instructions to return to Winchester, I now decided to destroy still more thoroughly the James River canal and the Virginia Central railroad and then join General Grant in front of Petersburg. I was master of the whole country north of the James as far down as Goochland; hence the destruction of these arteries of supply could be easily compassed, and feeling that the war was nearing its end, I desired my cavalry to be in at the death.

On March 9 the main column started eastward down the James River, destroying locks, dams, and boats, having been preceded by Colonel Fitzhugh's brigade of Devin's division in a forced march to Goochland and Beaver Dam Creek, with orders to destroy everything below Columbia. I made Columbia on the 10th, and from there sent a communication to General Grant reporting what had occurred, informing him of my condition and intention, asking him to send forage and rations to meet me at the White House, and also a pontoon-bridge to carry me over the Pamunkey, for in view of the fact that hitherto it had been impracticable to hold Lee in the trenches around Petersburg, I regarded as too hazardous a march down the south bank of the Pamunkey, where the enemy, by sending troops out from Richmond, might fall upon my flank and rear. It was of the utmost importance that General Grant should receive these despatches without chance of failure, in order that I might, depend absolutely on securing supplies at the White House; therefore I sent the message in duplicate, one copy overland direct to City Point by two scouts, Campbell and Rowan, and the other by Fannin and Moore, who were to go down the James River in a small boat to Richmond, join the troops in the trenches in front of Petersburg, and, deserting to the Union lines, deliver their tidings into General Grant's hands. Each set of messengers got through, but the copy confided to Campbell and Rowan was first at Grant's headquarters.

I halted for one day at Columbia to let my trains catch up, for it was still raining and the mud greatly delayed the teams, fatiguing and wearying the mules so much that I believe we should have been forced to abandon most of the wagons except for the invaluable help given by some two thousand negroes who had attached themselves to the column: they literally lifted the wagons out of the mud. From Columbia Merritt, with Devin's division, marched to Louisa Court House and destroyed the Virginia Central to Frederick's Hall. Meanwhile Custer was performing similar work from Frederick's Hall to Beaver Dam Station, and also pursued for a time General Early, who, it was learned from despatches captured in the telegraph office at Frederick's Hall, was in the neighborhood with a couple of hundred men. Custer captured some of these men and two of Early's staff-officers, but the commander of the Valley

District, accompanied by a single orderly, escaped across the South Anna and next day made his way to Richmond, the last man of the Confederate army that had so long contended with us in the Shenandoah Valley.

At Frederick's Hall, Young's scouts brought me word from Richmond that General Longstreet was assembling a force there to prevent my junction with Grant, and that Pickett's division, which had been sent toward Lynchburg to oppose my march, and Fitzhugh Lee's cavalry, were moving east on the Southside railroad, with the object of circumventing me. Reasoning that Longstreet could interpose effectually only by getting to the White House ahead of me, I pushed one column under Custer across the South Anna, by way of Ground Squirrel bridge, to Ashland, where it united with Merritt, who had meanwhile marched through Hanover Junction. Our appearance at Ashland drew the Confederates out in that direction, as was hoped, so, leaving Colonel Pennington's brigade there to amuse them, the united command retraced its route to Mount Carmel church to cross the North Anna. After dark Pennington came away, and all the troops reached the church by midnight of the 15th.

Resuming the march at an early hour next morning, we took the road by way of King William Court House to the White House, where, arriving on the 18th, we found, greatly to our relief, the supplies which I had requested to be sent there. In the meanwhile the enemy had marched to Hanover Court House, but being unable either to cross the Pamunkey there or forestall me at the White House on the south side of the river, he withdrew to Richmond without further effort to impede my column.

The hardships of this march far exceeded those of any previous campaigns by the cavalry. Almost incessant rains had drenched us for sixteen days and nights, and the swollen streams and well-nigh bottomless roads east of Staunton presented grave difficulties on every hand, but surmounting them all, we destroyed the enemy's means of subsistence, in quantities beyond computation, and permanently crippled the Virginia Central railroad, as well as the James River canal, and as each day brought us nearer the Army of the Potomac, all were filled with the comforting reflection that our work in the Shenandoah Valley had been thoroughly done, and every one was buoyed up by the cheering thought that we should soon take part in the final struggle of the war.

CHAPTER V.

TRANSFERRED TO PETERSBURG—GENERAL RAWLINS CORDIAL WELCOME—GENERAL GRANT'S ORDERS AND PLANS—A TRIP WITH MR. LINCOLN AND GENERAL GRANT— MEETING GENERAL SHERMAN—OPPOSED TO JOINING THE ARMY OF THE TENNESSEE —OPENING OF THE APPOMATTOX CAMPAIGN—GENERAL GRANT AND GENERAL RAWLINS.

The transfer of my command from the Shenandoah Valley to the field of operations in front of Petersburg was not anticipated by General Grant; indeed, the despatch brought from Columbia by my scouts, asking that supplies be sent me at the White House, was the first word that reached him concerning the move. In view of my message the general-in-chief decided to wait my arrival before beginning spring operations with the investing troops south of the James River, for he felt the importance of having my cavalry at hand in a campaign which he was convinced would wind up the war. We remained a few days at the White House resting and refitting the cavalry, a large amount of shoeing being necessary; but nothing like enough horses were at hand to replace those that had died or been disabled on the mud march from Staunton to the Pamunkey River, so a good many of the men were still without mounts, and all such were sent by boat to the dismounted camp near City Point. When all was ready the column set out for Hancock Station, a point on the military railroad in front of Petersburg, and arriving there on the 27th of March, was in orders reunited with its comrades of the Second Division, who had been serving with the Army of the Potomac since we parted from them the previous August. General Crook, who had been exchanged within a few days, was now in command of this Second Division. The reunited corps was to enter upon the campaign as a separate army, I reporting directly to General Grant; the intention being thus to reward me for foregoing, of my own choice, my position as a department commander by joining the armies at Petersburg.

Taking the road across the Peninsula, I started from the White House with Merritt's column on the 25th of March and encamped that night at Harrison's Landing. Very early next morning, in conformity with a request from General Grant, I left by boat for City Point, Merritt meanwhile conducting the column across the James River to the point of rendezvous, The trip to City Point did not take long, and on arrival at army headquarters the first person I met was General John A. Rawlins, General Grant's chief-of-staff. Rawlins was a man of strong likes and dislikes, and positive always both in speech and action, exhibiting marked feelings when greeting any one, and on this occasion met me with much warmth. His demonstrations of welcome over, we held a few minutes' conversation about the coming campaign, he taking strong ground against a part of the plan of operations adopted, namely, that which contemplated my joining General Sherman's army. His language was unequivocal and vehement, and when he was through talking, he conducted me to General Grant's quarters, but he himself did not enter.

General Grant was never impulsive, and always met his officers in an unceremonious way, with a quiet "How are you" soon putting one at his ease, since the pleasant tone in which he spoke gave assurance of welcome, although his manner was otherwise impassive. When the ordinary greeting was over, he usually waited for his visitor to open the conversation, so on this occasion I began by giving him the details of my march from Winchester, my reasons for not joining Sherman, as contemplated in my instructions, and the motives which had influenced me to march to the White House. The other provision of my orders on setting out from Winchester—the alternative return to that place—was not touched upon, for the wisdom of having ignored that was fully apparent. Commenting on this recital of my doings, the General referred only to the tortuous course of my march from Waynesboro' down, our sore trials, and the valuable services of the scouts who had brought him tidings of me, closing with the remark that it was, rare a department commander voluntarily deprived himself of independence, and added that I should not suffer for it. Then turning to the business for which he had called me to

City Point, he outlined what he expected me to do; saying that I was to cut loose from the Army of the Potomac by passing its left flank to the southward along the line of the Danville railroad, and after crossing the Roanoke River, join General Sherman. While speaking, he handed me a copy of a general letter of instructions that had been drawn up for the army on the 24th. The letter contained these words concerning the movements of my command:

"The cavalry under General Sheridan, joined by the division now under General Davies, will move at the same time (29th inst.) by the Weldon road and the Jerusalem plank-road, turning west from the latter before crossing the Nottoway, and west with the whole column before reaching Stony Creek. General Sheridan will then move independently under other instructions which will be given him. All dismounted cavalry belonging to the Army of the Potomac, and the dismounted cavalry from the Middle Military Division not required for guarding property belonging to their arm of the service, will report to Brigadier-General Benham to be added to the defenses of City Point."

When I had gone over the entire letter I showed plainly that I was dissatisfied with it, for, coupled with what the General had outlined orally, which I supposed was the "other instructions," I believed it foreshadowed my junction with General Sherman. Rawlins thought so too, as his vigorous language had left no room to doubt, so I immediately began to offer my objections to the programme. These were, that it would be bad policy to send me down to the Carolinas with a part of the Army of the Potomac, to come back to crush Lee after the destruction of General Johnston's army; such a course would give rise to the charge that his own forces around Petersburg were not equal to the task, and would seriously affect public opinion in the North; that in fact my cavalry belonged to the Army of the Potomac, which army was able unaided to destroy Lee, and I could not but oppose any dispersion of its strength.

All this was said in a somewhat emphatic manner, and when I had finished he quietly told me that the portion of my instructions from which I so strongly dissented was intended as a "blind" to cover any check the army in its general move, to the left might meet with, and prevent that element in the North which held that the war could be ended only through negotiation, from charging defeat. The fact that my cavalry was not to ultimately join Sherman was a great relief to me, and after expressing the utmost confidence in the plans unfolded for closing the war by directing every effort to the annihilation of Lee's army, I left him to go to General Ingalls's quarters. On the way I again met Rawlins, who, when I told him that General Grant had intimated his intention to modify the written plan of operations so far as regarded the cavalry, manifested the greatest satisfaction, and I judged from this that the new view of the matter had not previously been communicated to the chief-of-staff, though he must have been acquainted of course with the programme made out on the 24th of March.

Toward noon General Grant sent for me to accompany him up the river. When I joined the General he informed me that the President was on board the boat—the steamer Mary Martin. For some days Mr. Lincoln had been at City Point, established on the steamer River Queen, having come down from Washington to be nearer his generals, no doubt, and also to be conveniently situated for the reception of tidings from the front when operations began, for he could not endure the delays in getting news to Washington. This trip up the James had been projected by General Meade, but on account of demands at the front he could not go, so the President, General Grant, and I composed the party. We steamed up to where my cavalry was crossing on the pontoon-bridge below the mouth of the Dutch Gap canal, and for a little while watched the column as it was passing over the river, the bright sunshine presaging good weather, but only to delude, as was proved by the torrents of rain brought by the succeeding days of March. On the trip the President was not very cheerful. In fact, he was dejected, giving no indication of his usual means of diversion, by which (his quaint stories) I had often heard he could find relief from his cares. He spoke to me of the impending operations and asked many questions, laying stress upon the one, "What would be the result when the army moved out to the left, if the enemy should come down and capture City Point?" the question being prompted, doubtless, by the bold assault on our lines and capture of Fort Steadman two days before by General Gordon. I answered that I did not think it at all probable that General Lee would undertake such a desperate measure to relieve the strait he was in; that General Hartranft's successful check to Gordon had ended, I thought, attacks of such a character; and in any event General Grant would give Lee all he could attend to on the left. Mr. Lincoln said nothing about my proposed route of march, and I doubt if he knew of my instructions, or was in possession at most of more than a very general outline of the plan of campaign. It was late when the Mary Martin returned to City Point, and I spent the night there with General Ingalls.

The morning of the 27th I went out to Hancock Station to look after my troops and prepare for moving two days later. In the afternoon I received a telegram from General Grant, saying: "General Sherman will be here this evening to spend a few hours. I should like to have you come down." Sherman's coming was a surprise—at least to me it was— this despatch being my first intimation of his expected arrival. Well knowing the zeal and emphasis with which General Sherman would present his views, there again came into my mind many misgivings with reference to the movement of the cavalry, and I made haste to start for Grant's headquarters. I got off a little after 7 o'clock, taking the rickety military railroad, the rails of which were laid on the natural surface of the ground, with grading only here and there at points of absolute necessity, and had not gone far when the locomotive jumped the track. This delayed my arrival at City Point till near midnight, but on repairing to the little cabin that sheltered the general-in-chief, I found him and Sherman still up talking over the problem whose solution was near at hand. As already stated, thoughts as to the tenor of my instructions became uppermost the moment I received the telegram in the afternoon, and they continued to engross and disturb me all the way down the railroad, for I feared that the telegram foreshadowed, under the propositions Sherman would present, a more specific compliance with the written instructions than General Grant had orally assured me would be exacted.

My entrance into the shanty suspended the conversation for a moment only, and then General Sherman, without prelude, rehearsed his plans for moving his army, pointing out with every detail how he would come up through the Carolinas to join the troops besieging Petersburg and Richmond, and intimating that my cavalry, after striking the Southside and Danville railroads, could join him with ease. I made no comments on the projects for moving, his own troops, but as soon as opportunity offered, dissented emphatically from the proposition to have me join the Army of the Tennessee, repeating in substance what I had previously expressed to General Grant.

My uneasiness made me somewhat too earnest, I fear, but General Grant soon mollified me, and smoothed matters over by practically repeating what he had told me in regard to this point at the close of our interview the day before, so I pursued the subject no further. In a little while the conference ended, and I again sought lodging at the hospitable quarters of

Ingalls.

Very early the next morning, while I was still in bed, General Sherman came to me and renewed the subject of my joining him, but when he saw that I was unalterably opposed to it the conversation turned into other channels, and after we had chatted awhile he withdrew, and later in the day went up the river with the President, General Grant, and Admiral Porter, I returning to my command at Hancock Station, where my presence was needed to put my troops in march next day.

During the entire winter General Grant's lines fronting Petersburg had extended south of the Appomattox River, practically from that stream around to where the Vaughn road crosses Hatcher's Run, and this was nearly the situation when the cavalry concentrated at Hancock Station, General Weitzel holding the line north of the Appomattox, fronting Richmond and Bermuda Hundred.

The instructions of the 24th of March contemplated that the campaign should begin with the movement of Warren's corps (the Fifth) at 3 o'clock on the morning of the 29th, and Humphreys's (the Second) at 6; the rest of the infantry holding on in the trenches. The cavalry was to move in conjunction with Warren and Humphreys, and make its way out beyond our left as these corps opened the road.

The night of the 28th I received the following additional instructions, the general tenor of which again disturbed me, for although I had been assured that I was not to join General Sherman, it will be seen that the supplemental directions distinctly present that alternative, and I therefore feared that during the trip up the James River on the morning of the 28th General Grant had returned to his original views:

"HEADQUARTERS ARMIES OF THE UNITED STATES,
"City Point, Va., March 28, 1865.
"MAJOR-GENERAL P. H. SHERIDAN:

"The Fifth Army Corps will move by the Vaughn road at 3 A.M. tomorrow morning. The Second moves at about 9 A.M., having but about three miles to march to reach the point designated for it to take on the right of the Fifth Corps, after the latter reaches Dinwiddie Court House.

"Move your cavalry at as early an hour as you can, and without being confined to any particular road or roads. You may go out by the nearest roads in rear of the Fifth Corps, pass by its left, and passing near to or through Dinwiddie, reach the right and rear of the enemy as soon as you can. It is not the intention to attack the enemy in his intrenched position, but to force him out if possible. Should he come out and attack us, or get himself where he can be attacked, move in with your entire force in your own way, and with the full reliance that the army will engage or follow the enemy, as circumstances will dictate. I shall be on the field, and will probably be able to communicate with you; should I not do so, and you find that the enemy keeps within his main intrenched line, you may cut loose and push for the Danville road. If you find it practicable I would like you to cross the Southside road, between Petersburg and Burkeville, and destroy it to some extent. I would not advise much detention, however, until you reach the Danville road, which I would like you to strike as near to the Appomattox as possible; make your destruction of that road as complete as possible; you can then pass on to the Southside road, west of Burkeville, and destroy that in like manner.

"After having accomplished the destruction of the two railroads, which are now the only avenues of supply to Lee's army, you may return to this army, selecting your road farther south, or you may go on into North Carolina and join General Sherman. Should you select the latter course, get the information to me as early as possible, so that I may send orders to meet you at Goldsboro'.

"U. S. GRANT, Lieut.-General."

These instructions did not alter my line of march for the morrow, and I trusted matters would so come about as not to require compliance with those portions relative to the railroads and to joining Sherman; so early on the 29th I moved my cavalry out toward Ream's Station on the Weldon road, Devin commanding the First Division, with Colonels Gibbs, Stagg, and Fitzhugh in charge of the brigades; the Third Division under Custer, Colonels Wells, Capehart and Pennington being the brigade commanders. These two divisions united were commanded by Merritt, as they had been since leaving Winchester. Crook headed the Second Division, his brigades being under General Davies and Colonels John I. Gregg and Smith.

Our general direction was westward, over such routes as could be found, provided they did not embarrass the march of the infantry. The roads, from the winter's frosts and rains, were in a frightful state, and when it was sought to avoid a spot which the head of the column had proved almost bottomless, the bogs and quicksands of the adjoining fields demonstrated that to make a detour was to go from bad to worse. In the face of these discouragements we floundered on, however, crossing on the way a series of small streams swollen to their banks. Crook and Devin reached the county-seat of Dinwiddie about 5 o'clock in the evening, having encountered only a small picket, that at once gave way to our advance. Merritt left Custer at Malon's crossing of Rowanty Creek to care for the trains containing our subsistence and the reserve ammunition, these being stuck in the mire at, intervals all the way back to the Jerusalem plank-road; and to make any headway at all with the trains, Custer's men often had to unload the wagons and lift them out of the boggy places.

Crook and Devin camped near Dinwiddie Court House in such manner as to cover the Vaughn, Flatfoot, Boydton, and Five Forks roads; for, as these all intersected at Dinwiddie, they offered a chance for the enemy's approach toward the rear of the Fifth Corps, as Warren extended to the left across the Boydton road. Any of these routes leading to the south or west might also be the one on which, in conformity with one part of my instructions, I was expected to get out toward the Danville and Southside railroads, and the Five Forks road would lead directly to General Lee's right flank, in case opportunity was found to comply with the other part. The place was, therefore, of great strategic value, and getting it without cost repaid us for floundering through the mud.

Dinwiddie Court House, though a most important point in the campaign, was far from attractive in feature, being made up of a half-dozen unsightly houses, a ramshackle tavern propped up on two sides with pine poles, and the weatherbeaten building that gave official name to the cross-roads. We had no tents—there were none in the command—so I took possession of the tavern for shelter for myself and staff, and just as we had finished looking over its primitive interior a rain storm set in.

The wagon containing my mess equipment was back somewhere on the road, hopelessly stuck in the mud, and hence we had nothing to eat except some coffee which two young women living at the tavern kindly made for us; a small quantity of the berry being furnished from the haversacks of my escort. By the time we got the coffee, rain was falling in sheets, and the evening bade fair to be a most dismal one; but songs and choruses set up by some of my staff—the two young women playing accompaniments on a battered piano—relieved the situation and enlivened us a little. However, the dreary night brought me one great comfort; for General Grant, who that day had moved out to Gravelly Run, sent me instructions to abandon all idea of the contemplated raid, and directed me to act in concert with the infantry under his immediate command, to turn, if possible, the right flank of Lee's army. The despatch made my mind easy with respect to the objectionable feature of my original instructions, and of course relieved me also from the anxiety growing out of the letter received at Hancock Station the night of the 28th; so, notwithstanding the suspicions excited by some of my staff concerning the Virginia feather-bed that had been assigned me, I turned in at a late hour and slept most soundly.

The night of the 29th the left of General Grant's infantry—Warren's corps—rested on the Boydton road, not far from its intersection with the Quaker road. Humphreys's corps was next to Warren; then came Ord, next Wright, and then Parke, with his right resting on the Appomattox. The moving of Warren and Humphreys to the left during the day was early discovered by General Lee. He met it by extending the right of his infantry on the White Oak road, while drawing in the cavalry of W. H. F. Lee and Rosser along the south bank of Stony Creek to cover a crossroads called Five Forks, to anticipate me there; for assuming that my command was moving in conjunction with the infantry, with the ultimate purpose of striking the Southside railroad, Lee made no effort to hold Dinwiddie, which he might have done with his cavalry, and in this he made a fatal mistake. The cavalry of Fitz. Lee was ordered at this same time from Sunderland depot to Five Forks, and its chief placed in command of all the mounted troops of General Lee's army.

At daylight on the 30th I proceeded to make dispositions under the new conditions imposed by my modified instructions, and directed Merritt to push Devin out as far as the White Oak road to make a reconnoissance to Five Forks, Crook being instructed to send Davies's brigade to support Devin. Crook was to hold, with Gregg's brigade, the Stony Creek crossing of the Boydton plank road, retaining Smith's near Dinwiddie, for use in any direction required. On the 29th W. H. F. Lee conformed the march of his cavalry with that of ours, but my holding Stony Creek in this way forced him to make a detour west of Chambering's Run, in order to get in communication with his friends at Five Forks.

The rain that had been falling all night gave no sign of stopping, but kept pouring down all day long, and the swamps and quicksands mired the horses, whether they marched in the roads or across the adjacent fields. Undismayed, nevertheless, each column set out for its appointed duty, but shortly after the troops began to move I received from General Grant this despatch, which put a new phase on matters:

"HEADQUARTERS ARMIES OF THE UNITED STATES,
"GRAVELLY RUN, March 30, 1865.
"MAJOR-GENERAL SHERIDAN:

"The heavy rain of to-day will make it impossible for us to do much until it dries up a little, or we get roads around our rear repaired. You may, therefore, leave what cavalry you deem necessary to protect the left, and hold such positions as you deem necessary for that purpose, and send the remainder back to Humphrey's Station where they can get hay and grain. Fifty wagons loaded with forage will be sent to you in the morning. Send an officer back to direct the wagons back to where you want them. Report to me the cavalry you will leave back, and the position you will occupy. Could not your cavalry go back by the way of Stony Creek depot and destroy or capture the store of supplies there?

"U. S. GRANT, Lieut.-General."

When I had read and pondered this, I determined to ride over to General Grant's headquarters on Gravelly Run, and get a clear idea of what it was proposed to do, for it seemed to me that a suspension of operations would be a serious mistake. Mounting a powerful gray pacing horse called Breckenridge (from its capture from one of Breckenridge's staff-officers at Missionary Ridge), and that I knew would carry me through the mud, I set out accompanied by my Assistant Adjutant-General, Colonel Frederick C. Newhall, and an escort of about ten or fifteen men. At first we rode north up the Boydton plank-road, and coming upon our infantry pickets from a direction where the enemy was expected to appear, they began to fire upon us, but seeing from our actions that we were friends, they ceased, and permitted us to pass the outposts. We then struggled on in a northeasterly direction across-country, till we struck the Vaughn road. This carried us to army headquarters, which were established south of Gravelly Run in an old cornfield. I rode to within a few yards of the front of General Grant's tent, my horse plunging at every step almost to his knees in the mud, and dismounted near a camp-fire, apparently a general one, for all the staff-officers were standing around it on boards and rails placed here and there to keep them from sinking into the mire.

Going directly to General Grant's tent, I found him and Rawlins talking over the question of suspending operations till the weather should improve. No orders about the matter had been issued yet, except the despatch to me, and Rawlins, being strongly opposed to the proposition, was frankly expostulating with General Grant, who, after greeting me, remarked, in his quiet way: "Well, Rawlins, I think you had better take command." Seeing that there was a difference up between Rawlins and his chief, I made the excuse of being wet and cold, and went outside to the fire. Here General Ingalls met me and took me to his tent, where I was much more comfortable than when standing outside, and where a few minutes later we were joined by General Grant. Ingalls then retired, and General Grant began talking of our fearful plight, resulting from the rains and mud, and saying that because of this it seemed necessary to suspend operations. I at once begged him not to do so, telling him that my cavalry was already on the move in spite of the difficulties, and that although a suspension of operations would not be fatal, yet it would give rise to the very charge of disaster to which he had referred at City Point, and, moreover, that we would surely be ridiculed, just as General Burnside's army was after the mud march of 1863. His better judgment was against suspending operations, but the proposition had been suggested by all sorts of complaints as to the impossibility of moving the trains and the like, so it needed little argument to convince him, and without further discussion he said, in that manner which with him meant a firmness of purpose that could not be changed by further complainings, "We will go on." I then told him that I believed I could break in the enemy's right if he would let me have the Sixth Corps; but saying that the condition of the roads would prevent the movement of infantry, he replied that I would have to seize Five Forks with the cavalry alone.

On my way back to Dinwiddie I stopped at the headquarters of General Warren, but the General being asleep, I went to the tent of one of his staff-officers. Colonel William T. Gentry, an old personal friend with whom I had served in Oregon. In a few minutes Warren came in and we had a short conversation, he speaking rather despondently of the outlook, being influenced no doubt by the depressing weather.

From Warren's headquarters I returned, by the Boydton road to Dinwiddie Court House, fording Gravelly Run with ease. When I got as far as the Dabney road I sent Colonel Newhall out on it toward Five Forks, with orders for Merritt to develop the enemy's position and strength, and then rode on to Dinwiddie to endeavor to get all my other troops up. Merritt was halted at the intersection of the Five Forks and Gravelly Church roads when Newhall delivered the orders, and in compliance moving out Gibbs's brigade promptly, sharp skirmishing was brought on, Gibbs driving the Confederates to Five Forks, where he found them behind a line of breastworks running along the White Oak road. The reconnoissance demonstrating the intention of the enemy to hold this point, Gibbs was withdrawn.

That evening, at 7 o'clock, I reported the position of the Confederate cavalry, and stated that it had been reinforced by Pickett's division of infantry. On receipt of this despatch, General Grant offered me the Fifth Corps, but I declined to take it, and again asked for the Sixth, saying that with it I believed I could turn the enemy (Pickett's) left, or break through his lines. The morning of the 31st General Grant replied that the Sixth Corps could not be taken from its position in the line, and offered me the Second; but in the mean time circumstances had changed, and no corps was ordered.

CHAPTER VI.

BATTLE OF DINWIDDIE COURT HOUSE—PICKETT REPULSED—REINFORCED BY THE FIFTH CORPS—BATTLE OF FIVE FORKS—TURNING THE CONFEDERATE LEFT—AN UNQUALIFIED SUCCESS—RELIEVING GENERAL WARREN—THE WARREN COURT OF INQUIRY—GENERAL SHERMAN'S OPINION.

The night of March 30 Merritt, with Devin's division and Davies's brigade, was camped on the Five Forks road about two miles in front of Dinwiddie, near J. Boisseau's. Crook, with Smith and Gregg's brigades, continued to cover Stony Creek, and Custer was still back at Rowanty Creek, trying to get the trains up. This force had been counted while crossing the creek on the 29th, the three divisions numbering 9,000 enlisted men, Crook having 3,300, and Custer and Devin 5,700.

During the 30th, the enemy had been concentrating his cavalry, and by evening General W. H. F. Lee and General Rosser had joined Fitzhugh Lee near Five Forks. To this force was added, about dark, five brigades of infantry—three from Pickett's division, and two from Johnson's—all under command of Pickett. The infantry came by the White Oak road from the right of General Lee's intrenchments, and their arrival became positively known to me about dark, the confirmatory intelligence being brought in then by some of Young's scouts who had been inside the Confederate lines.

On the 31st, the rain having ceased, directions were given at an early hour to both Merritt and Crook to make reconnoissances preparatory to securing Five Forks, and about 9 o'clock Merritt started for the crossroads, Davies's brigade supporting him. His march was necessarily slow because of the mud, and the enemy's pickets resisted with obstinacy also, but the coveted crossroads fell to Merritt without much trouble, as the bulk of the enemy was just then bent on other things. At the same hour that Merritt started, Crook moved Smith's brigade out northwest from Dinwiddie to Fitzgerald's crossing of Chamberlain's Creek, to cover Merritt's left, supporting Smith by placing Gregg to his right and rear. The occupation of this ford was timely, for Pickett, now in command of both the cavalry and infantry, was already marching to get in Merritt's rear by crossing Chamberlain's Creek.

To hold on to Fitzgerald's ford Smith had to make a sharp fight, but Mumford's cavalry attacking Devin, the enemy's infantry succeeded in getting over Chamberlain's Creek at a point higher up than Fitzgerald's ford, and assailing Davies, forced him back in a northeasterly direction toward the Dinwiddie and Five Forks road in company with Devin. The retreat of Davies permitted Pickett to pass between Crook and Merritt, which he promptly did, effectually separating them and cutting off both Davies and Devin from the road to Dinwiddie, so that to get to that point they had to retreat across the country to B. Boisseau's and then down the Boydton road.

Gibbs's brigade had been in reserve near the intersection of the Five Forks and Dabney roads, and directing Merritt to hold on there, I ordered Gregg's brigade to be mounted and brought to Merritt's aid, for if Pickett continued in pursuit north of the Five Forks road he would expose his right and rear, and I determined to attack him, in such case, from Gibbs's position. Gregg arrived in good season, and as soon as his men were dismounted on Gibbs's left, Merritt assailed fiercely, compelling Pickett to halt and face a new foe, thus interrupting an advance that would finally have carried Pickett into the rear of Warren's corps.

It was now about 4 o'clock in the afternoon and we were in a critical situation, but having ordered Merritt to bring Devin and Davies to Dinwiddie by the Boydton road, staff-officers were sent to hurry Custer to the same point, for with its several diverging roads the Court House was of vital importance, and I determined to stay there at all hazards. At the same time orders were sent to Smith's brigade, which, by the advance of Pickett past its right flank and the pressure of W. H. F. Lee on its front, had been compelled to give up Fitzgerald's crossing, to fall back toward Dinwiddie but to contest every inch of ground so as to gain time.

When halted by the attack of Gregg and Gibbs, Pickett, desisting from his pursuit of Devin, as already stated, turned his undivided attention to this unexpected force, and with his preponderating infantry pressed it back on the Five Forks road toward Dinwiddle, though our men, fighting dismounted behind barricades at different points, displayed such obstinacy as to make Pickett's progress slow, and thus give me time to look out a line for defending the Court House. I selected a place about three-fourths of a mile northwest of the crossroads, and Custer coming up quickly with Capehart's brigade, took position on the left of the road to Five Forks in some open ground along the crest of a gentle ridge. Custer got Capehart into place just in time to lend a hand to Smith, who, severely pressed, came back on us here from his retreat along Chamberlain's "bed"—the vernacular for a woody swamp such as that through which Smith retired. A little later the brigades of Gregg and Gibbs, falling to the rear slowly and steadily, took up in the woods a line which covered the Boydton Road some distance to the right of Capehart, the intervening gap to be filled with Pennington's brigade. By this time our horse-artillery, which for two days had been stuck in the mud, was all up, and every gun was posted in this line.

It was now near sunset, and the enemy's cavalry thinking the day was theirs, made a dash at Smith, but just as the assailants appeared in the open fields, Capehart's men opened so suddenly on their left flank as to cause it to recoil in astonishment, which permitted Smith to connect his brigade with Custer unmolested. We were now in good shape behind the familiar barricades, and having a continuous line, excepting only the gap to be filled with Pennington, that covered Dinwiddle and the Boydton Road. My left rested in the woods about half a mile west of the Court House, and the barricades extended from this flank in a semicircle through the open fields in a northeasterly direction, to a piece-of thick timber on the right, near the Boydton Road.

A little before the sun went down the Confederate infantry was formed for the attack, and, fortunately for us, Pennington's brigade came up and filled the space to which it was assigned between Capehart and Gibbs, just as Pickett moved out across the cleared fields in front of Custer, in deep lines that plainly told how greatly we were outnumbered.

Accompanied by Generals Merritt and Custer and my staff, I now rode along the barricades to encourage the men. Our enthusiastic reception showed that they were determined to stay. The cavalcade drew the enemy's fire, which emptied several of the saddles—among others Mr.

Theodore Wilson, correspondent of the New York Herald, being wounded. In reply our horse-artillery opened on the advancing Confederates, but the men behind the barricades lay still till Pickett's troops were within short range. Then they opened, Custer's repeating rifles pouring out such a shower of lead that nothing could stand up against it. The repulse was very quick, and as the gray lines retired to the woods from which but a few minutes before they had so confidently advanced, all danger of their taking Dinwiddie or marching to the left and rear of our infantry line was over, at least for the night. The enemy being thus checked, I sent a staff-officer—Captain Sheridan—to General Grant to report what had taken place during the afternoon, and to say that I proposed to stay at Dinwiddie, but if ultimately compelled to abandon the place, I would do so by retiring on the Vaughn road toward Hatcher's Run, for I then thought the attack might be renewed next morning. Devin and Davies joined me about dark, and my troops being now well in hand, I sent a second staff-officer—Colonel John Kellogg—to explain my situation more fully, and to assure General Grant that I would hold on at Dinwiddie till forced to let go.

By following me to Dinwiddie the enemy's infantry had completely isolated itself, and hence there was now offered the Union troops a rare opportunity. Lee was outside of his works, just as we desired, and the general-in-chief realized this the moment he received the first report of my situation; General Meade appreciated it too from the information he got from Captain Sheridan, en route to army headquarters with the first tidings, and sent this telegram to General Grant:

"HEADQUARTERS OF THE ARMY OF THE POTOMAC,
"March 31, 1865. 9:45 p.m.
"LIEUTENANT-GENERAL GRANT:

"Would it not be well for Warren to go down with his whole corps and smash up the force in front of Sheridan? Humphreys can hold the line to the Boydton plank-road, and the refusal along with it. Bartlett's brigade is now on the road from G. Boisseau's, running north, where it crosses Gravelly Run, he having gone down the White Oak road. Warren could go at once that way, and take the force threatening Sheridan in rear at Dinwiddie, and move on the enemy's rear with the other two.

"G. G. MEADE, Major-General."

An hour later General Grant replied in these words:

"HEADQUARTERS ARMIES OF THE UNITED STATES,
"DABNEY'S MILLS, March 311, 1865. 10:15 P. M.
"MAJOR-GENERAL MEADE,
"Commanding Army of the Potomac.

Let Warren move in the way you propose, and urge him not to stop for anything. Let Griffin (Griffin had been ordered by Warren to the Boydton road to protect his rear) go on as he was first directed.

"U. S. GRANT, Lieutenant-General."

These two despatches were the initiatory steps in sending the Fifth Corps, under Major-General G. K. Warren, to report to me, and when I received word of its coming and also that Genera Mackenzie's cavalry from the Army of the James was likewise to be added to my command, and that discretionary authority was given me to use all my forces against Pickett, I resolved to destroy him, if it was within the bounds of possibility, before he could rejoin Lee.

In a despatch, dated 10:05 p.m., telling me of the coming of Warren and Mackenzie, General Grant also said that the Fifth Corps should reach me by 12 o'clock that night, but at that hour not only had none of the corps arrived, but no report from it, so believing that if it came all the way down to Dinwiddie the next morning, our opportunity would be gone, I concluded that it would be best to order Warren to move in on the enemy's rear while the cavalry attacked in front, and, therefore, at 3 o'clock in the morning of April 1 sent this despatch to General Warren:

"CAVALRY HEADQUARTERS, DINWIDDIE C. H.,
"April 1, 1865—3. A.M.
"MAJOR-GENERAL WARREN,
"Commanding Fifth Army Corps.

"I am holding in front of Dinwiddie Court House, on the road leading to Five Forks, for three-quarters of a mile with General Custer's division. The enemy are in his immediate front, lying so as to cover the road just this side of A. Adams's house, which leads across Chamberlain's bed, or run. I understand you have a division at J.[G] Boisseau's; if so, you are in rear of the enemy's line and almost on his flank. I will hold on here. Possibly they may attack Custer at daylight; if so, attack instantly and in full force.

Attack at daylight anyhow, and I will make an effort to get the road this side of Adams's house, and if I do, you can capture the whole of them. Any force moving down the road I am holding, or on the White Oak road, will be in the enemy's rear, and in all probability get any force that may escape you by a flank movement. Do not fear my leaving here. If the enemy remains, I shall fight at daylight.

"P. H. SHERIDAN, Major-General."

With daylight came a slight fog, but it lifted almost immediately, and Merritt moved Custer and Devin forward. As these divisions advanced the enemy's infantry fell back on the Five Forks road, Devin pressing him along the road, while Custer extended on the left over toward Chamberlain's Run, Crook being held in watch along Stony Creek, meanwhile, to be utilized as circumstances might require when Warren attacked.

The order of General Meade to Warren the night of March 31—a copy being sent me also—was positive in its directions, but as midnight came without a sign of or word from the Fifth Corps, notwithstanding that was the hour fixed for its arrival, I nevertheless assumed that there were good reasons for its non-appearance, but never once doubted that measures would be taken to comply with my despatch of 3 A. M. and therefore hoped that, as Pickett was falling back slowly toward Five Forks, Griffin's and Crawford's divisions would come in on the Confederate left and rear by the Crump road near J.[G] Boisseau's house.

But they did not reach there till after the enemy had got by. As a matter of fact, when Pickett was passing the all-important point Warren's men were just breaking from the bivouac in which their chief had placed them the night before, and the head of Griffin's division did not get to Boisseau's till after my cavalry, which meanwhile had been joined by Ayres's division of the Fifth Corps by way of the Boydton and Dabney roads. By reason of the delay in moving Griffin and Crawford, the enemy having escaped, I massed the Fifth Corps at J.[G] Boisseau's so that the men could be rested, and directed it to remain there; General Warren himself had not then come up. General Mackenzie, who had reported just after daybreak, was ordered at first to stay at Dinwiddie Court House, but later was brought along the Five Forks road to Dr. Smith's, and Crook's division was directed to continue watching the crossings of Stony Creek and Chamberlain's Run.

That we had accomplished nothing but to oblige our foe to retreat was to me bitterly disappointing, but still feeling sure that he would not give up the Five Forks crossroads without a fight, I pressed him back there with Merritt's cavalry, Custer advancing on the Scott road, while Devin drove the rearguard along that leading from J.[G] Boisseau's to Five Forks.

By 2 o'clock in the afternoon Merritt had forced the enemy inside his intrenchments, which began with a short return about three-quarters of a mile east of the Forks and ran along the south side of the White Oak road to a point about a mile west of the Forks. From the left of the return over toward Hatcher's Run was posted Mumford's cavalry, dismounted. In the return itself was Wallace's brigade, and next on its right came Ransom's, then Stewart's, then Terry's, then Corse's. On the right of Corse was W. H. F. Lee's division of cavalry. Ten pieces of artillery also were in this line, three on the right of the works, three near the centre at the crossroads, and four on the left, in the return. Rosser's cavalry was guarding the Confederate trains north of Hatcher's Run beyond the crossing of the Ford road.

I felt certain the enemy would fight at Five Forks—he had to—so, while we were getting up to his intrenchments, I decided on my plan of battle. This was to attack his whole front with Merritt's two cavalry divisions, make a feint of turning his right flank, and with the Fifth Corps assail his left. As the Fifth Corps moved into action, its right flank was to be covered by Mackenzie's cavalry, thus entirely cutting off Pickett's troops from communication with Lee's right flank, which rested near the Butler house at the junction of the Claiborne and White Oaks roads. In execution of this plan, Merritt worked his men close in toward the intrenchments, and while he was thus engaged, I ordered Warren to bring up the Fifth Corps, sending the order by my engineer officer, Captain Gillespie, who had reconnoitred the ground in the neighborhood of Gravelly Run Church, where the infantry was to form for attack.

Gillespie delivered the order about 1 o'clock, and when the corps was put in motion, General Warren joined me at the front. Before he came, I had received, through Colonel Babcock, authority from General Grant to relieve him, but I did not wish to do it, particularly on the eve of battle; so, saying nothing at all about the message brought me, I entered at once on the plan for defeating Pickett, telling Warren how the enemy was posted, explaining with considerable detail, and concluding by stating that I wished his troops to be formed on the Gravelly Church road, near its junction with the White Oak road, with two divisions to the front, aligned obliquely to the White Oak road, and one in reserve, opposite the centre of these two.

General Warren seemed to understand me clearly, and then left to join his command, while I turned my attention to the cavalry, instructing Merritt to begin by making demonstrations as though to turn the enemy's right, and to assault the front of the works with his dismounted cavalry as soon as Warren became engaged. Afterward I rode around to Gravelly Run Church, and found the head of Warren's column just appearing, while he was sitting under a tree making a rough sketch of the ground. I was disappointed that more of the corps was not already up, and as the precious minutes went by without any apparent effort to hurry the troops on to the field, this disappointment grew into disgust. At last I expressed to Warren my fears that the cavalry might expend all their ammunition before the attack could be made, that the sun would go down before the battle could be begun, or that troops from Lee's right, which, be it remembered, was less than three miles away from my right, might, by striking my rear, or even by threatening it, prevent the attack on Pickett.

Warren did not seem to me to be at all solicitous; his manner exhibited decided apathy, and he remarked with indifference that "Bobby Lee was always getting people into trouble." With unconcern such as this, it is no wonder that fully three hours' time was consumed in marching his corps from J.[G] Boisseau's to Gravelly Run Church, though the distance was but two miles. However, when my patience was almost worn out, Warren reported his troops ready, Ayres's division being formed on the west side of the Gravelly Church road, Crawford's on the east side, and Griffin in reserve behind the right of Crawford, a little different from my instructions. The corps had no artillery present, its batteries, on account of the mud, being still north of Gravelly Run. Meanwhile Merritt had been busy working his men close up to the intrenchments from the angle of the return west, along the White Oak road.

About 4 o'clock Warren began the attack. He was to assault the left flank of the Confederate infantry at a point where I knew Pickett's intrenchments were refused, almost at right angles with the White Oak road. I did not know exactly how far toward Hatcher's Run this part of the works extended, for here the videttes of Mumford's cavalry were covering, but I did know where the refusal began. This return, then, was the point I wished to assail, believing that if the assault was made with spirit, the line could be turned. I therefore intended that Ayres and Crawford should attack the refused trenches squarely, and when these two divisions and Merritt's cavalry became hotly engaged, Griffin's division was to pass around the left of the Confederate line; and I personally instructed Griffin how I wished him to go in, telling him also that as he advanced, his right flank would be taken care of by Mackenzie, who was to be pushed over toward the Ford road and Hatcher's Run.

The front of the corps was oblique to the White Oak road; and on getting there, it was to swing round to the left till perpendicular to the road, keeping closed to the left. Ayres did his part well, and to the letter, bringing his division square up to the front of the return near the angle; but Crawford did not wheel to the left, as was intended. On the contrary, on receiving fire from Mumford's cavalry, Crawford swerved to the right and moved north from the return, thus isolating his division from Ayres; and Griffin, uncertain of the enemy's position, naturally followed Crawford.

The deflection of this division on a line of march which finally brought it out on the Ford road near C. Young's house, frustrated the purpose I had in mind when ordering the attack, and caused a gap between Ayres and Crawford, of which the enemy quickly took advantage, and succeeded in throwing a part of Ayres's division into confusion. At this juncture I sent word to General Warren to have Crawford recalled; for the direction he was following was not only a mistaken one, but, in case the assault at the return failed, he ran great risk of capture. Warren could not be found, so I then sent for Griffin—first by Colonel Newhall, and then by Colonel Sherman—to come to the aid of Ayres, who was now contending alone with that part of the enemy's infantry at the return. By this time Griffin had observed and appreciated Crawford's mistake, however, and when the staff-officers reached him, was already faced to the left; so, marching across Crawford's rear, he quickly joined Ayres, who meanwhile had rallied his troops and carried the return.

When Ayres's division went over the flank of the enemy's works, Devin's division of cavalry, which had been assaulting the front, went over in company with it; and hardly halting to reform, the intermingling infantry and dismounted cavalry swept down inside the intrenchments, pushing to and beyond Five Forks, capturing thousands of prisoners. The only stand the enemy tried to make was when he attempted to form near the Ford road. Griffin pressed him so hard there, however, that he had to give way in short order, and many of his men, with three pieces of artillery, fell into the hands of Crawford while on his circuitous march.

The right of Custer's division gained a foothold on the enemy's works simultaneously with Devin's, but on the extreme left Custer had a very severe combat with W. H. F. Lee's cavalry, as well as with Corse's and Terry's infantry. Attacking Terry and Corse with Pennington's brigade dismounted, he assailed Lee's cavalry with his other two brigades mounted, but Lee held on so obstinately that Custer gained but little ground till our troops, advancing behind the works, drove Corse and Terry out. Then Lee made no further stand except at the west side of the Gillian field, where, assisted by Corse's brigade, he endeavored to cover the retreat, but just before dark Custer, in concert with some Fifth Corps regiments under Colonel Richardson, drove the last of the enemy westward on the White Oak road.

Our success was unqualified; we had overthrown Pickett, taken six guns, thirteen battle-flags, and nearly six thousand prisoners. When the battle was practically over, I turned to consider my position with reference to the main Confederate army. My troops, though victorious, were isolated from the Army of the Potomac, for on the 31st of March the extreme left of that army had been thrown back nearly to the Boydton plank-road, and hence there was nothing to prevent the enemy's issuing from his trenches at the intersection of the White Oak and Claiborne roads and marching directly on my rear. I surmised that he might do this that night or early next morning. It was therefore necessary to protect myself in this critical situation, and General Warren having sorely disappointed me, both in the moving of his corps and in its management during the battle, I felt that he was not the man to rely upon under such circumstances, and deeming that it was to the best interest of the service as well as but just to myself, I relieved him, ordering him to report to General Grant.

I then put Griffin in command of the Fifth Corps, and directed him to withdraw from the pursuit as quickly as he could after following the enemy a short distance, and form in line of battle near Gravelly Run Church, at right angles with the White Oak road, with Ayres and Crawford facing toward the enemy at the junction of the White Oak and Claiborne roads, leaving Bartlett, now commanding Griffin's division, near the Ford road. Mackenzie also was left on the Ford road at the crossing of Hatcher's Run, Merritt going into camp on the Widow Gillian's plantation. As I had been obliged to keep Crook's division along Stony Creek throughout the day, it had taken no active part in the battle.

Years after the war, in 1879, a Court of Inquiry was given General

Warren in relation to his conduct on the day of the battle. He assumed that the delay in not granting his request for an inquiry, which was first made at the close of the war, was due to opposition on my part. In this he was in error; I never opposed the ordering of the Court, but when it was finally decided to convene it I naturally asked to be represented by counsel, for the authorization of the Inquiry was so peculiarly phrased that it made me practically a respondent.

"NEW YORK CITY, May 3, 1880
"MAJOR-GENERAL W. S. HANCOCK, U. S. A.
"President Court of Inquiry, Governor's Island.

"Sir: Since my arrival in this city, under a subpoena to appear and testify before the Court of which you are president, I have been indirectly and unofficially informed that the Court some time ago forwarded an invitation to me (which has not been received) to appear personally or by counsel, in order to aid it in obtaining a knowledge as to the facts concerning the movements terminating in the battle of 'Five Forks,' with reference to the direct subjects of its inquiry. Any invitation of this character I should always and do consider it incumbent on me to accede to, and do everything in my power in furtherance of the specific purposes for which courts of inquiry are by law instituted.

"The order convening the Court (a copy of which was not received by me at my division headquarters until two days after the time appointed for the Court to assemble) contemplates an inquiry based on the application of Lieutenant Colonel G. K. Warren, Corps of Engineers, as to his conduct while major-general commanding the Fifth Army Corps, under my command, in reference to accusations or imputations assumed in the order to have been made against him, and I understand through the daily press that my official report of the battle of Five Forks has been submitted by him as a basis of inquiry.

"If it is proposed to inquire, either directly or indirectly, as to any action of mine so far as the commanding general Fifth Army Corps was concerned, or my motives for such action, I desire to be specifically informed wherein such action or transaction is alleged to contain an accusation or imputation to become a subject of inquiry, so that, knowing what issues are raised, I may intelligently aid the Court in arriving at the facts.

"It is a long time since the battle of Five Forks was fought, and during the time that has elapsed the official reports of that battle have been received and acknowledged by the Government; but now, when the memory of events has in many instances grown dim, and three of the principal actors on that field are dead—Generals Griffin, Custer, and Devin, whose testimony would have been valuable—an investigation is ordered which might perhaps do injustice unless the facts pertinent to the issues are fully developed.

"My duties are such that it will not be convenient for me to be present continuously during the sessions of the Court. In order, however, that everything may be laid before it in my power pertinent to such specific issues as are legally raised, I beg leave to introduce Major Asa Bird Gardner as my counsel.

"Very respectfully,

"P. H. SHERIDAN, Lieut.-General."

Briefly stated, in my report of the battle of Five Forks there were four imputations concerning General Warren. The first implied that Warren failed to reach me on the 1st of April, when I had reason to expect him; the second, that the tactical handling of his corps was unskillful; the third, that he did not exert himself to get his corps up to Gravelly Run Church; and the fourth, that when portions of his line gave way he did not exert himself to restore confidence to his troops. The Court found against him on the first and second counts, and for him on the third and fourth. This finding was unsatisfactory to General Warren, for he hoped to obtain such an unequivocal recognition of his services as to cast discredit on my motives for relieving him. These were prompted by the conditions alone—by the conduct of General Warren as described, and my consequent lack of confidence in him.

It will be remembered that in my conversation with General Grant on the 30th, relative to the suspension of operations because of the mud, I asked him to let me have the Sixth Corps to help me in breaking in on the enemy's right, but that it could not be sent me; it will be recalled also that the Fifth Corps was afterward tendered and declined. From these facts it has been alleged that I was prejudiced against General Warren, but this is not true. As we had never been thrown much together I knew but little of him. I had no personal objection to him, and certainly could have none to his corps. I was expected to do an extremely dangerous piece of work, and knowing the Sixth Corps well—my cavalry having campaigned with it so successfully in the Shenandoah Valley, I naturally preferred it, and declined the Fifth for no other reason. But the Sixth could not be given, and the turn of events finally brought me the Fifth after my cavalry, under the most trying difficulties, had drawn the enemy from his works, and into such a position as to permit the realization of General Grant's hope to break up with my force Lee's right flank. Pickett's isolation offered an opportunity which we could not afford to neglect, and the destruction of his command would fill the measure of General Grant's expectations as well as meet my own desires. The occasion was not an ordinary one, and as I thought that Warren had not risen to its demand in the battle, I deemed it injudicious and unsafe under the critical conditions existing to retain him longer. That I was justified in this is plain to all who are disposed to be fair-minded, so with the following extract from General Sherman's review of the proceedings of the Warren Court, and with which I am convinced the judgment of history will accord, I leave the subject:

" . . . It would be an unsafe and dangerous rule to hold the commander of an army in battle to a technical adherence to any rule of conduct for managing his command. He is responsible for results, and holds the lives and reputations of every officer and soldier under his orders as subordinate to the great end—victory. The most important events are usually compressed into an hour, a minute, and he cannot stop to analyze his reasons. He must act on the impulse, the conviction, of the instant, and should be sustained in his conclusions, if not manifestly unjust. The power to command men, and give vehement impulse to their joint action, is something which cannot be defined by words, but it is plain and manifest in battles, and whoever commands an army in chief must choose his subordinates by reason of qualities which can alone be tested in actual conflict.

"No one has questioned the patriotism, integrity, and great intelligence of General Warren. These are attested by a long record of most excellent service, but in the clash of arms at and near Five Forks, March 31 and April 1, 1865, his personal activity fell short of the standard fixed by General Sheridan, on whom alone rested the great responsibility for that and succeeding days.

"My conclusion is that General Sheridan was perfectly justified in his action in this case, and he must be fully and entirely sustained if the United States expects great victories by her arms in the future."

CHAPTER VII.
RESULT OF THE BATTLE OF FIVE FORKS—RETREAT OF LEE—AN INTERCEPTED DESPATCH—AT AMELIA COURT HOUSE—BATTLE OF SAILOR'S CREEK—THE CONFEDERATES' STUBBORN RESISTANCE—A COMPLETE VICTORY—IMPORTANCE OF THE BATTLE.

When the news of the battle at Five Forks reached General Grant, he realized that the decisive character of our victory would necessitate the immediate abandonment of Richmond and Petersburg by the enemy; and fearing that Lee would escape without further injury, he issued orders, the propriety of which must be settled by history, to assault next morning the whole intrenched line. But Lee could not retreat at once. He had not anticipated disaster at Five Forks, and hence was unprepared to withdraw on the moment; and the necessity of getting off his trains and munitions of war, as well as being obliged to cover the flight of the Confederate Government, compelled him to hold on to Richmond and Petersburg till the afternoon of the 2d, though before that Parke, Ord, and Wright had carried his outer intrenchments at several points, thus materially shortening the line of investment.

The night of the 1st of April, General Humphreys's corps—the Second—had extended its left toward the White Oak road, and early next morning, under instructions from General Grant, Miles's division of that corps reported to me, and supporting him with Ayres's and Crawford's divisions of the Fifth Corps, I then directed him to advance toward Petersburg and attack the enemy's works at the intersection of the Claiborne and White Oak roads.

Such of the enemy as were still in the works Miles easily forced across Hatcher's Run, in the direction of Sutherland's depot, but the Confederates promptly took up a position north of the little stream, and Miles being anxious to attack, I gave him leave, but just at this time General Humphreys came up with a request to me from General Meade to return Miles. On this request I relinquished command of the division, when, supported by the Fifth Corps it could have broken in the enemy's right at a vital point; and I have always since regretted that I did so, for the message Humphreys conveyed was without authority from General Grant, by whom Miles had been sent to me, but thinking good feeling a desideratum just then, and wishing to avoid wrangles, I faced the Fifth Corps about and marched it down to Five Forks, and out the Ford road to the crossing of Hatcher's Run. After we had gone, General Grant, intending this quarter of the field to be under my control, ordered Humphreys with his other two divisions to move to the right, in toward Petersburg. This left Miles entirely unsupported, and his gallant attack made soon after was unsuccessful at first, but about 3 o'clock in the afternoon he carried the point which covered the retreat from Petersburg and Richmond.

Merritt had been sent westward, meanwhile, in the direction of Ford's Station, to break the enemy's horse which had been collecting to the north of Hatcher's Run. Meeting, with but little opposition, Merritt drove this cavalry force in a northerly direction toward Scott's Corners, while the Fifth Corps was pushed toward Sutherland's depot, in the hope of coming in on the rear of the force that was confronting Miles when I left him. Crawford and Merritt engaged the enemy lightly just before night, but his main column, retreating along the river road south of the Appomattox, had got across Namozine Creek, and the darkness prevented our doing more than to pick up some stragglers. The next morning the pursuit was resumed, the cavalry again in advance, the Fifth Corps keeping up with it all the while, and as we pressed our adversaries hundreds and hundreds of prisoners, armed and unarmed, fell into our hands, together with many wagons and five pieces of artillery. At Deep Creek the rearguard turned on us, and a severe skirmish took place. Merritt, finding the enemy very strong, was directed to await the arrival of Crook and for the rear division of the Fifth Corps; but by the time they reached the creek, darkness had again come to protect the Confederates, and we had to be content with meagre results at that point.

From the beginning it was apparent that Lee, in his retreat, was making for Amelia Court House, where his columns north and south of the Appomattox River could join, and where, no doubt, he expected to meet supplies, so Crook was ordered to march early on April 4 to strike the Danville railroad, between Jettersville and Burkeville, and then move south along the railroad toward Jettersville, Merritt to move toward Amelia Court House, and the Fifth Corps to Jettersville itself.

The Fifth Corps got to Jettersville about 5 in the afternoon, and I immediately intrenched it across the Burkeville road with the determination to stay there till the main army could come up, for I hoped we could force Lee to surrender at Amelia Court House, since a firm hold on Jettersville would cut him off from his line of retreat toward Burkeville.

Accompanied only by my escort—the First United States Cavalry, about two hundred strong—I reached Jettersville some little time before the Fifth Corps, and having nothing else at hand I at once deployed this handful of men to cover the crossroads till the arrival of the corps. Just as the troopers were deploying, a man on a mule, heading for Burkeville, rode into my pickets. He was arrested, of course, and being searched there was found in his boots this telegram in duplicate, signed by Lee's Commissary General.

"The army is at Amelia Court House, short of provisions. Send 300,000 rations quickly to Burkeville Junction." One copy was addressed to the supply department at Danville, and the other to that at Lynchburg. I surmised that the telegraph lines north of Burkeville had been broken by Crook after the despatches were written, which would account for their being transmitted by messenger. There was thus revealed not only the important fact that Lee was concentrating at Amelia Court House, but also a trustworthy basis for estimating his troops, so I sent word to Crook to strike up the railroad toward me, and to Merritt—who, as I have said, had followed on the heels of the enemy—to leave Mackenzie there and himself close in on Jettersville. Staff-officers were also despatched to hurry up Griffin with the Fifth Corps, and his tired men redoubled their strides.

My troops too were hard up for rations, for in the pursuit we could not wait for our trains, so I concluded to secure if possible these provisions intended for Lee. To this end I directed Young to send four of his best scouts to Burkeville Junction. There they were to separate, two taking the railroad toward Lynchburg and two toward Danville, and as soon as a telegraph station was reached the telegram was to be transmitted as it had been written and the provisions thus hurried forward.

Although the Fifth Corps arrived at Jettersville the evening of April 4, as did also Crook's and Merritt's cavalry, yet none of the army of the Potomac came up till about 3 o'clock the afternoon of the 5th, the Second Corps, followed by the Sixth, joining us then. General Meade arrived at Jettersville an hour earlier, but being ill, requested me to put his troops in position. The Fifth Corps being already intrenched across the Amelia Court House road facing north, I placed the Sixth on its right and the Second on its left as they reached the ground.

As the enemy had been feeling us ever since morning—to learn what he was up to I directed Crook to send Davies's brigade on a reconnoissance to Paine's crossroads. Davies soon found out that Lee was trying to escape by that flank, for at the crossroads he found the Confederate trains and artillery moving rapidly westward. Having driven away the escort, Davies succeeded in burning nearly two hundred wagons, and brought off five pieces of artillery. Among these wagons were some belonging to General, Lee's and to General Fitzhugh Lee's headquarters. This work through, Davies withdrew and rejoined Crook, who, with Smith and Gregg, was established near Flat Creek.

It being plain that Lee would attempt to escape as soon as his trains were out of the way, I was most anxious to attack him when the Second Corps began to arrive, for I felt certain that unless we did so he would succeed in passing by our left flank, and would thus again make our pursuit a stern-chase; but General Meade, whose plan of attack was to advance his right flank on Amelia Court House, objected to assailing before all his troops were up.

I then sent despatches to General Grant, explaining what Davies had done, and telling him that the Second Corps was arriving, and that I wished he himself was present. I assured him of my confidence in our capturing Lee if we properly exerted ourselves, and informed him, finally, that I would put all my cavalry, except Mackenzie, on my left, and that, with such a disposition of my forces, I could see no escape for Lee. I also inclosed him this letter, which had just been captured:

"AMELIA C. H., April 5, 1865.
"DEAR MAMMA:
"Our army is ruined, I fear. We are all safe as yet. Shyron left us sick. John Taylor is well—saw him yesterday. We are in line of battle this morning. General Robert Lee is in the field near us. My trust is still in the

justice of our cause, and that of God. General Hill is killed. I saw Murray a few minutes since. Bernard, Terry said, was taken prisoner, but may yet get out. I send this by a negro I see passing up the railroad to Mechlenburg. Love to all.

"Your devoted son,

"Wm. B. TAYLOR, Colonel."

General Grant, who on the 5th was accompanying General Ord's column toward Burkeville Junction, did not receive this intelligence till nearly nightfall, when within about ten miles of the Junction. He set out for Jettersville immediately, but did not reach us till near midnight, too late of course to do anything that night. Taking me with him, we went over to see Meade, whom he then directed to advance early in the morning on Amelia Court House. In this interview Grant also stated that the orders Meade had already issued would permit Lee's escape, and therefore must be changed, for it was not the aim only to follow the enemy, but to get ahead of him, remarking during the conversation that, "he had no doubt Lee was moving right then." On this same occasion Meade expressed a desire to have in the proposed attack all the troops of the Army of the Potomac under his own command, and asked for the return of the Fifth Corps. I made no objections, and it was ordered to report, to him.

When, on the morning of the 6th, Meade advanced toward Amelia Court House, he found, as predicted, that Lee was gone. It turned out that the retreat began the evening of the 5th and continued all night. Satisfied that this would be the case, I did not permit the cavalry to participate in Meade's useless advance, but shifted it out toward the left to the road running from Deatonsville to Rice's station, Crook leading and Merritt close up. Before long the enemy's trains were discovered on this road, but Crook could make but little impression on them, they were so strongly guarded; so, leaving Stagg's brigade and Miller's battery about three miles southwest of Deatonsville—where the road forks, with a branch leading north toward the Appomattox—to harass the retreating column and find a vulnerable point, I again shifted the rest of the cavalry toward the left, across-country, but still keeping parallel to the enemy's line of march.

Just after crossing Sailor's Creek, a favorable opportunity offering, both Merritt and Crook attacked vigorously, gained the Rice's Station road, destroyed several hundred wagons, made many prisoners, and captured sixteen pieces of artillery. This was important, but more valuable still was the fact that we were astride the enemy's line of retreat, and had cut off from joining Longstreet, waiting at Rice's Station, a corps of Confederate infantry under General Ewell, composed of Anderson's, Kershaw's, and Custis Lee's divisions. Stagg's brigade and Miller's battery, which, as I have said, had been left at the forks of the Deatonsville road, had meanwhile broken in between the rear of Ewell's column and the head of Gordon's, forcing Gordon to abandon his march for Rice's Station, and to take the right-hand road at the forks, on which he was pursued by General Humphreys.

The complete isolation of Ewell from Longstreet in his front and Gordon in his rear led to the battle of Sailor's Creek, one of the severest conflicts of the war, for the enemy fought with desperation to escape capture, and we, bent on his destruction, were no less eager and determined. The capture of Ewell, with six of his generals and most of his troops, crowned our success, but the fight was so overshadowed by the stirring events of the surrender three days later, that the battle has never been accorded the prominence it deserves.

The small creek from which the field takes its name flows in a northwesterly direction across the road leading from Deatonsville to Rice's Station. By shifting to the left, Merritt gained the Rice's Station road west of the creek, making havoc of the wagon-trains, while Crook struck them further on and planted himself square across the road. This blocked Ewell, who, advancing Anderson to some high ground west of the creek, posted him behind barricades, with the intention of making a hard fight there, while the main body should escape through the woods in a westerly direction to roads that led to Farmville. This was prevented, however, by Crook forming his division, two brigades dismounted and one mounted, and at once assaulting all along Anderson's front and overlapping his right, while Merritt fiercely attacked to the right of Crook. The enemy being thus held, enabled the Sixth Corps—which in the meantime I had sent for—to come upon the ground, and Ewell, still contending with the cavalry, found himself suddenly beset by this new danger from his rear. To, meet it, he placed Kershaw to the right and Custis Lee to the left of the Rice's Station road, facing them north toward and some little distance from Sailor's Creek, supporting Kershaw with Commander Tucker's Marine brigade. Ewell's skirmishers held the line of Sailor's Creek, which runs through a gentle valley, the north slope of which was cleared ground.

By General Grant's directions the Sixth Corps had been following my route of march since the discovery, about 9 o'clock in the morning, that Lee had decamped from Amelia Court House. Grant had promptly informed me of this in a note, saying, "The Sixth Corps will go in with a vim any place you may dictate," so when I sent word to Wright of the enemy's isolation, and asked him to hurry on with all speed, his gallant corps came as fast as legs could carry them, he sending to me successively Major McClellan and Colonel Franklin, of his staff, to report his approach.

I was well advised as to the position of the enemy through information brought me by an intelligent young soldier, William A. Richardson, Company "A," Second Ohio, who, in one of the cavalry charges on Anderson, had cleared the barricades and made his way back to my front through Ewell's line. Richardson had told me just how the main body of the enemy was posted, so as Seymour's division arrived I directed General Wright to put it on the right of the road, while Wheaton's men, coming up all hot and out of breath, promptly formed on Seymour's left. Both divisions thus aligned faced southwest toward Sailor's Creek, and the artillery of the corps being massed to the left and front of the Hibbon house, without waiting for Getty's division—for I feared that if we delayed longer the enemy might effect his escape toward Farmville—the general attack was begun. Seymour and Wheaton, moving forward together, assailed the enemy's front and left, and Stagg's brigade, too, which in the mean time had been placed between Wheaton's left and Devin's right, went at him along with them, Merritt and Crook resuming the fight from their positions in front of Anderson. The enemy, seeing little chance of escape, fought like a tiger at bay, but both Seymour and Wheaton pressed him vigorously, gaining ground at all points except just to the right of the road, where Seymour's left was checked. Here the Confederates burst back on us in a counter-charge, surging down almost to the creek, but the artillery, supported by Getty, who in the mean time had come on the ground, opened on them so terribly that this audacious and furious onset was completely broken, though the gallant fellows fell back to their original line doggedly, and not until after they had almost gained the creek. Ewell was now hemmed in on every side, and all those under his immediate command were captured. Merritt and Crook had also broken up Anderson by this time, but he himself, and about two thousand disorganized men escaped by making their way through the woods toward the Appomattox River before they could be entirely enveloped. Night had fallen when the fight was entirely over, but Devin was pushed on in pursuit for about two miles, part of the Sixth Corps following to clinch a victory which not only led to the annihilation of one corps of Lee's retreating army, but obliged Longstreet to move up to Farmville, so as to take a road north of the Appomattox River toward Lynchburg instead of continuing toward Danville.

At the close of the battle I sent one of my staff—Colonel Redwood Price—to General Grant to report what had been done; that we had taken six generals and from nine to ten thousand prisoners. On his way Price stopped at the headquarters of General Meade, where he learned that not the slightest intelligence of the occurrence on my line had been received, for I not being under Meade's command, he had paid no attention to my movements. Price gave the story of the battle, and General Meade, realizing its importance, sent directions immediately to General Wright to make his report of the engagement to the headquarters of the Army of the Potomac, assuming that Wright was operating independently of me in the face of Grant's despatch Of 2 o'clock, which said that Wright was following the cavalry and would "go in with a vim" wherever I dictated. Wright could not do else than comply with Meade's orders in the case, and I, being then in ignorance of Meade's reasons for the assumption, could say nothing. But General Grant plainly intending, and even directing, that the corps should be under my command, remedied this phase of the matter, when informed of what had taken place, by requiring Wright to send a report of the battle through me. What he then did, and what his intentions and orders were, are further confirmed by a reference to the episode in his "Memoirs," where he gives his reasons for ordering the Sixth Corps to abandon the move on Amelia Court House and pass to the left of the army. On the same page he also says, referring to the 6th of April: "The Sixth Corps now remained with the cavalry under Sheridan's direct command until after the surrender." He unquestionably intended all of this, but his purpose was partly frustrated by General Meade's action next morning in assuming direction of the movements of the corps; and before General Grant became aware of the actual conditions the surrender was at hand.

CHAPTER VIII.
LINCOLN'S LACONIC DESPATCH—CAPTURING LEE'S SUPPLIES—DELIGHTED ENGINEERS—THE CONFEDERATES' LAST EFFORT—A FLAG OF TRUCE—GENERAL GEARY'S "LAST DITCH" ABSURDITY—MEETING OF GRANT AND LEE—THE SURRENDER—ESTIMATE OF GENERAL GRANT.

The first report of the battle of Sailor's Creek that General Grant received was, as already stated, an oral message carried by Colonel Price, of my staff. Near midnight I sent a despatch giving the names of the generals captured. These were Ewell, Kershaw, Barton, Corse, Dubose, and Custis Lee. In the same despatch I wrote: "If the thing is pressed, I think that Lee will surrender." When Mr. Lincoln, at City Point, received this word from General Grant, who was transmitting every item of news to the President, he telegraphed Grant the laconic message: "Let the thing be pressed." The morning of the 7th we moved out at a very early hour, Crook's division marching toward Farmville in direct pursuit, while Merritt and Mackenzie were ordered to Prince Edward's Court House to anticipate any effort Lee might make to escape through that place toward Danville since it had been discovered that Longstreet had slipped away already from the front of General Ord's troops at Rice's Station. Crook overtook the main body of the Confederates at Farmville, and promptly attacked their trains on the north side of the Appomattox with Gregg's brigade, which was fiercely turned upon and forced to re-cross the river with the loss of a number of prisoner's, among them Gregg himself. When Crook sent word of this fight, it was clear that Lee had abandoned all effort to escape to the southwest by way of Danville. Lynchburg was undoubtedly his objective point now; so, resolving to throw my cavalry again across his path, and hold him till the infantry could overtake him, I directed everything on Appomattox depot, recalling Crook the night of the 7th to Prospect Station, while Merritt camped at Buffalo Creek, and Mackenzie made a reconnoissance along the Lynchburg railroad.

At break of day, April 8, Merritt and Mackenzie united with Crook at Prospect Station, and the cavalry all moved then toward Appomattox depot. Hardly had it started when one of the scouts—Sergeant White—informed me that there were four trains of cars at the depot loaded with supplies for Lee's army; these had been sent from Lynchburg, in compliance with the telegram of Lee's commissary-general, which message, it will be remembered, was captured and transmitted to Lynchburg by two of Young's scouts on the 4th. Sergeant White, who had been on the lookout for the trains ever since sending the despatch, found them several miles west of Appomattox depot feeling their way along, in ignorance of Lee's exact position. As he had the original despatch with him, and took pains to dwell upon the pitiable condition of Lee's army, he had little difficulty in persuading the men in charge of the trains to bring them east of Appomattox Station, but fearing that the true state of affairs would be learned before long, and the trains be returned to Lynchburg, he was painfully anxious to have them cut off by breaking the track west of the station.

The intelligence as to the trains was immediately despatched to Crook, and I pushed on to join him with Merritt's command. Custer having the advance, moved rapidly, and on nearing the station detailed two regiments to make a detour southward to strike the railroad some distance beyond and break the track. These regiments set off at a gallop, and in short order broke up the railroad enough to prevent the escape of the trains, Custer meanwhile taking possession of the station, but none too soon, for almost at the moment he did so the advance-guard of Lee's army appeared, bent on securing the trains. Without halting to look after the cars further, Custer attacked this advance-guard and had a spirited fight, in which he drove the Confederates away from the station, captured twenty-five pieces of artillery, a hospital train, and a large park of wagons, which, in the hope that they would reach Lynchburg next day, were being pushed ahead of Lee's main body.

Devin coming up a little before dusk, was put in on the right of Custer, and one of Crook's brigades was sent to our left and the other two held in reserve. I then forced the enemy back on the Appomattox road to the vicinity of the Court House, and that the Confederates might have no rest, gave orders to continue the skirmishing throughout the night. Meanwhile the captured trains had been taken charge of by locomotive engineers, soldiers of the command, who were delighted evidently to get back at their old calling. They amused themselves by running the trains to and fro, creating much confusion, and keeping up such an unearthly screeching with the whistles that I was on the point of ordering the cars burned. They finally wearied of their fun, however, and ran the trains off to the east toward General Ord's column.

The night of the 8th I made my headquarters at a little frame house just south of the station. I did not sleep at all, nor did anybody else, the entire command being up all night long; indeed, there had been little rest in the, cavalry for the past eight days. The necessity of getting Ord's column up was so obvious now that staff-officer after staff-officer was sent to him and to General Grant requesting that the infantry be pushed on, for if it could get to the front, all knew that the rebellion would be ended on the morrow. Merritt, Crook, Custer, and Devin were present at frequent intervals during the night, and everybody was overjoyed at the prospect that our weary work was about to end so happily. Before sun-up General Ord arrived, and informed me of the approach of his column, it having been marching the whole night. As he ranked me, of course I could give him no orders, so after a hasty consultation as to where his troops should be placed we separated, I riding to the front to overlook my line near Appomattox Court House, while he went back to urge along his weary troops.

The night before General Lee had held a council with his principal generals, when it was arranged that in the morning General Gordon should undertake to break through my cavalry, and when I neared my troops this movement was beginning, a heavy line of infantry bearing down on us from the direction of the village. In front of Crook and Mackenzie firing had already begun, so riding to a slight elevation where a good view of the Confederates could be had, I there came to the conclusion that it would be unwise to offer more resistance than that necessary to give Ord time to form, so I directed Merritt to fall back, and in retiring to shift Devin and Custer to the right so as to make room for Ord, now in the woods to my rear. Crook, who with his own and Mackenzie's divisions was on my extreme left covering some by-roads, was ordered to hold his ground as long as practicable without sacrificing his men, and, if forced to retire, to contest with obstinacy the enemy's advance.

As already stated, I could not direct General Ord's course, he being my senior, but hastily galloping back to where he was, at the edge of the timber, I explained to him what was taking place at the front. Merritt's withdrawal inspired the Confederates, who forthwith began to press Crook, their line of battle advancing with confidence till it reached the crest whence I had reconnoitred them. From this ground they could see Ord's men emerging from the woods, and the hopelessness of a further attack being plain, the gray lines instinctively halted, and then began to retire toward a ridge immediately fronting Appomattox Court House, while Ord, joined on his right by the Fifth Corps, advanced on them over the ground that Merritt had abandoned.

I now directed my steps toward Merritt, who, having mounted his troopers, had moved them off to the right, and by the time I reached his headquarters flag he was ready for work, so a move on the enemy's left was ordered, and every guidon was bent to the front. As the cavalry marched along parallel with the Confederate line, and in toward its left, a heavy fire of artillery opened on us, but this could not check us at such a time, and we soon reached some high ground about half a mile from the Court House, and from here I could see in the low valley beyond the village the bivouac undoubtedly of Lee's army. The troops did not seem to be disposed in battle order, but on the other side of the bivouac was a line of battle—a heavy rear-guard—confronting, presumably, General Meade.

I decided to attack at once, and formations were ordered at a trot for a charge by Custer's and Devin's divisions down the slope leading to the camps. Custer was soon ready, but Devin's division being in rear its formation took longer, since he had to shift further to the right; Devin's preparations were, therefore, but partially completed when an aide-decamp galloped up to with the word from Custer, "Lee has surrendered; do not charge; the white flag is up." The enemy perceiving that Custer was forming for attack, had sent the flag out to his front and stopped the charge just in time. I at once sent word of the truce to General Ord, and hearing nothing more from Custer himself, I supposed that he had gone down to the Court House to join a mounted group of Confederates that I could see near there, so I, too, went toward them, galloping down a narrow ridge, staff and orderlies following; but we had not got half way to the Court House when, from a skirt of timber to our right, not more than three hundred yards distant, a musketry fire was opened on us. This halted us, when, waving my hat, I called out to the firing party that we were under a truce, and they were violating it. This did not stop them, however, so we hastily took shelter in a ravine so situated as to throw a ridge between us and the danger.

We traveled in safety down this depression to its mouth, and thence by a gentle ascent approached the Court House. I was in advance, followed by a sergeant carrying my battleflag. When I got within about a hundred and fifty yards of the enemy's line, which was immediately in front of the Court House, some of the Confederates leveled their pieces at us, and I again halted. Their officers kept their men from firing, however, but meanwhile a single-handed contest had begun behind me, for on looking back I heard a Confederate soldier demanding my battle-flag from the color-bearer, thinking, no doubt, that we were coming in as prisoners. The sergeant had drawn his sabre and was about to cut the man down, but at a word from me he desisted and carried the flag back to my staff, his assailant quickly realizing that the boot was on the other leg.

These incidents determined me to remain where I was till the return of a staff-officer whom I had sent over to demand an explanation from the group of Confederates for which I had been heading. He came back in a few minutes with apologies for what had occurred, and informed me that General Gordon and General Wilcox were the superior officers in the group. As they wished me to join them I rode up with my staff, but we had hardly met when in front of Merritt firing began. At the sound I turned to General Gordon, who seemed embarrassed by the occurrence, and remarked: "General, your men fired on me as I was coming over here, and undoubtedly they are treating Merritt and Custer the same way. We might as well let them fight it out." He replied, "There must be some mistake." I then asked, "Why not send a staff-officer and have your people cease firing; they are violating the flag." He answered, "I have no staff-officer to send." Whereupon I said that I would let him have one of mine, and calling for Lieutenant Vanderbilt Allen, I directed him to carry General Gordon's orders to General Geary, commanding a small brigade of South Carolina cavalry, to discontinue firing. Allen dashed off with the message and soon delivered it, but was made a prisoner, Geary saying, "I do not care for white flags: South Carolinians never surrender . . . " By this time Merritt's patience being exhausted, he ordered an attack, and this in short order put an end to General Geary's "last ditch" absurdity, and extricated Allen from his predicament.

When quiet was restored Gordon remarked: "General Lee asks for a suspension of hostilities pending the negotiations which he is having with General Grant." I rejoined: "I have been constantly informed of the progress of the negotiations, and think it singular that while such discussions are going on, General Lee should have continued his march and attempted to break through my lines this morning. I will entertain no terms except that General Lee shall surrender to General Grant on his arrival here. If these terms are not accepted we will renew hostilities." Gordon replied: "General Lee's army is exhausted. There is no doubt of his surrender to General Grant."

It was then that General Ord joined us, and after shaking hands all around, I related the situation to him, and Gordon went away agreeing to meet us again in half an hour. When the time was up he came back accompanied by General Longstreet, who brought with him a despatch, the duplicate of one that had been sent General Grant through General Meade's lines back on the road over which Lee had been retreating.

General Longstreet renewed the assurances that already had been given by Gordon, and I sent Colonel Newhall with the despatch to find General Grant and bring him to the front. When Newhall started, everything on our side of the Appomattox Court House was quiet, for inevitable surrender was at hand, but Longstreet feared that Meade, in ignorance of the new conditions on my front might attack the Confederate rearguard. To prevent this I offered to send Colonel J. W. Forsyth through the enemy's lines to let Meade know of my agreement, for he too was suspicious that by a renewed correspondence Lee was endeavoring to gain time for escape. My offer being accepted, Forsyth set out accompanied by Colonel Fairfax, of Longstreet's staff, and had no difficulty in accomplishing his mission.

About five or six miles from Appomattox, on the road toward Prospect Station near its intersection with the Walker's Church road, my adjutant-general, Colonel Newhall, met General Grant, he having started from north of the Appomattox River for my front the morning of April 9, in consequence of the following despatches which had been sent him the night before, after we had captured Appomattox Station and established a line intercepting Lee:

"CAVALRY HEADQUARTERS, April 8, 1865—9:20 P. M.
"LIEUTENANT-GENERAL U. S. GRANT,
"Commanding Armies of the U. S.

"General: I marched early this morning from Buffalo Creek and Prospect Station on Appomattox Station, where my scouts had reported trains of cars with supplies for Lee's army. A short time before dark General Custer, who had the advance, made a dash at the station, capturing four trains of supplies with locomotives. One of the trains was burned and the others were run back toward Farmville for security. Custer then pushed on toward Appomattox Court House, driving the enemy—who kept up a heavy fire of artillery—charging them repeatedly and capturing, as far as reported, twenty-five pieces of artillery and a number of prisoners and wagons. The First Cavalry Division supported him on the right. A reconnoissance sent across the Appomattox reports the enemy moving on the Cumberland road to Appomattox Station, where they expect to get supplies. Custer is still pushing on. If General Gibbon and the Fifth Corps can get up to-night, we will perhaps finish the job in the morning. I do not think Lee means to surrender until compelled to do so.

"P. H. SHERIDAN, Major-General."

"HEADQUARTERS CAVALRY, April 8, 1865—9:40 p.m.
"LIEUTENANT-GENERAL U. S. GRANT.
"Commanding Armies U. S.

"GENERAL: Since writing the accompanying despatch, General Custer reports that his command has captured in all thirty-five pieces of artillery, one thousand prisoners—including one general officer—and from one hundred and fifty to two hundred wagons.

"P. H. SHERIDAN, Major-General."

In attempting to conduct the lieutenant-general and staff back by a short route, Newhall lost his bearings for a time, inclining in toward the enemy's lines too far, but regained the proper direction without serious loss of time. General Grant arrived about 1 o'clock in the afternoon, Ord and I, dismounted, meeting him at the edge of the town, or crossroads, for it was little more. He remaining mounted, spoke first to me, saying simply,

"How are you, Sheridan?" I assured him with thanks that I was "first-rate," when, pointing toward the village, he asked, "Is General Lee up there?" and I replied: "There is his army down in that valley, and he himself is over in that house (designating McLean's house) waiting to surrender to you." The General then said, "Come, let us go over," this last remark being addressed to both Ord and me. We two then mounted and joined him, while our staff-officers followed, intermingling with those of the general-in-chief as the cavalcade took its way to McLean's house near by, and where General Lee had arrived some time before, in consequence of a message from General Grant consenting to the interview asked for by Lee through Meade's front that morning—the consent having been carried by Colonel Babcock.

When I entered McLean's house General Lee was standing, as was also his military secretary, Colonel Marshall, his only staff-officer present. General Lee was dressed in a new uniform and wore a handsome sword. His tall, commanding form thus set off contrasted strongly with the short figure of General Grant, clothed as he was in a soiled suit, without sword or other insignia of his position except a pair of dingy shoulder-straps. After being presented, Ord and I, and nearly all of General Grant's staff, withdrew to await the agreement as to terms, and in a little while Colonel Babcock came to the door and said, "The surrender had been made; you can come in again."

When we re-entered General Grant was writing; and General Lee, having in his hand two despatches, which I that morning requested might be returned, as I had no copies of them, addressed me with the remark: "I am sorry. It is probable that my cavalry at that point of the line did not fully understand the agreement." These despatches had been sent in the forenoon, after the fighting had been stopped, notifying General Lee that some of his cavalry in front of Crook was violating the suspension of hostilities by withdrawing. About 3 o'clock in the afternoon the terms of surrender were written out and accepted, and General Lee left the house, as he departed cordially shaking hands with General Grant. A moment later he mounted his chunky gray horse, and lifting his hat as he passed out of the yard, rode off toward his army, his arrival there being announced to us by cheering, which, as it progressed, varying in loudness, told he was riding through the bivouac of the Army of Northern Virginia.

The surrender of General Lee practically ended the war of the rebellion. For four years his army had been the main-stay of the Confederacy; and the marked ability with which he directed its operations is evidenced both by his frequent successes and the length of time he kept up the contest. Indeed, it may be said that till General Grant was matched against him, he never met an opponent he did not vanquish, for while it is true that defeat was inflicted on the Confederates at Antietam and Gettysburg, yet the fruits of these victories were not gathered, for after each of these battles Lee was left unmolested till he had a chance to recuperate.

The assignment of General Grant to the command of the Union armies in the winter of 1863-64 gave presage of success from the start, for his eminent abilities had already been proved, and besides, he was a tower of strength to the Government, because he had the confidence of the people. They knew that henceforth systematic direction would be given to our armies in every section of the vast territory over which active operations were being prosecuted, and further, that this coherence, this harmony of plan, was the one thing needed to end the war, for in the three preceding years there had been illustrated most lamentable effects of the absence of system. From the moment he set our armies in motion simultaneously, in the spring of 1864, it could be seen that we should be victorious ultimately, for though on different lines we were checked now and then, yet we were harassing the Confederacy at so many vital points that plainly it must yield to our blows. Against Lee's army, the forefront of the Confederacy, Grant pitted himself; and it may be said that the Confederate commander was now, for the first time, overmatched, for against all his devices—the products of a mind fertile in defense—General Grant brought to bear not only the wealth of expedient which had hitherto distinguished him, but also an imperturbable tenacity, particularly in the Wilderness and on the march to the James, without which the almost insurmountable obstacles of that campaign could not have been overcome. During it and in the siege of Petersburg he met with many disappointments—on several occasions the shortcomings of generals, when at the point of success, leading to wretched failures. But so far as he was concerned, the only apparent effect of these discomfitures was to make him all the more determined to discharge successfully the stupendous trust committed to his care, and to bring into play the manifold resources of his well ordered military mind. He guided every subordinate then, and in the last days of the rebellion, with a fund of common sense and superiority of intellect, which have left an impress so distinct as to exhibit his great personality. When his military history is analyzed after the lapse of years, it will show, even more clearly than now, that during these as well as in his previous campaigns he was the steadfast Centre about and on which everything else turned.

CHAPTER IX.
ORDERED TO GREENSBORO', N. C.—MARCH TO THE DAN RIVER—ASSIGNED TO THE COMMAND WEST OF THE MISSISSIPPI—LEAVING WASHINGTON—FLIGHT OF GENERAL EARLY—MAXIMILIAN—MAKING DEMONSTRATIONS ON THE UPPER RIO GRANDE—CONFEDERATES JOIN MAXIMILIAN—THE FRENCH INVASION OF MEXICO AND ITS RELATIONS TO THE REBELLION—ASSISTING THE LIBERALS— RESTORATION OF THE REPUBLIC.

The surrender at Appomattox put a stop to all military operations on the part of General Grant's forces, and the morning of April 10 my cavalry began its march to Petersburg, the men anticipating that they would soon be mustered out and returned to their homes. At Nottoway Court House I heard of the assassination of the President. The first news came to us the night after the dastardly deed, the telegraph operator having taken it from the wires while in transmission to General Meade. The despatch ran that Mr. Lincoln had been, shot at 10 o'clock that morning at Willard's Hotel, but as I could conceive of nothing to take the President there I set the story down as a canard, and went to bed without giving it further thought. Next morning, however, an official telegram confirmed the fact of the assassination, though eliminating the distorted circumstances that had been communicated the night before.

When we reached Petersburg my column was halted, and instructions given me to march the cavalry and the Sixth Corps to Greensboro', North Carolina, for the purpose of aiding General Sherman (the surrender of General Johnston having not yet been effected), so I made the necessary preparations and moved on the 24th of April, arriving at South Boston, on the Dan River, the 28th, the Sixth Corps having reached Danville meanwhile. At South Boston I received a despatch from General Halleck, who immediately after Lee's surrender had been assigned to command at Richmond, informing me that General Johnston had been brought to terms. The necessity for going farther south being thus obviated we retraced our steps to Petersburg, from which place I proceeded by steamer to Washington, leaving, the cavalry to be marched thither by easy stages.

The day after my arrival in Washington an important order was sent me, accompanied by the following letter of instructions, transferring me to a new field of operations:

"HEADQUARTERS ARMIES OF THE UNITED STATES.
"Washington, D. C., May 17, 1865.

"GENERAL: Under the orders relieving you from the command of the Middle Military Division and assigning you to command west of the Mississippi, you will proceed without delay to the West to arrange all preliminaries for your new field of duties.

"Your duty is to restore Texas, and that part of Louisiana held by the enemy, to the Union in the shortest practicable time, in a way most effectual for securing permanent peace.

"To do this, you will be given all the troops that can be spared by Major-General Canby, probably twenty-five thousand men of all arms; the troops with Major-General J. J. Reynolds, in Arkansas, say twelve thousand, Reynolds to command; the Fourth Army Corps, now at Nashville, Tennessee, awaiting orders; and the Twenty-Fifth Army Corps, now at City Point, Virginia, ready to embark.

"I do not wish to trammel you with instructions; I will state, however, that if Smith holds out, without even an ostensible government to receive orders from or to report to, he and his men are not entitled to the considerations due to an acknowledged belligerent. Theirs are the conditions of outlaws, making war against the only Government having an existence over the territory where war is now being waged.

"You may notify the rebel commander west of the Mississippi—holding intercourse with him in person, or through such officers of the rank of major-general as you may select—that he will be allowed to surrender all his forces on the same terms as were accorded to Lee and Johnston. If he accedes, proceed to garrison the Red River as high up as Shreveport, the seaboard at Galveston, Malagorda Bay, Corpus Christi, and mouth of the Rio Grande.

"Place a strong force on the Rio Grande, holding it at least to a point opposite Camargo, and above that if supplies can be procured.

"In case of an active campaign (a hostile one) I think a heavy force should be put on the Rio Grande as a first preliminary. Troops for this might be started at once. The Twenty-Fifth Corps is now available, and to it should be added a force of white troops, say those now under Major-General Steele.

"To be clear on this last point, I think the Rio Grande should be strongly held, whether the forces in Texas surrender or not, and that no time should be lost in getting troops there. If war is to be made, they will be in the right place; if Kirby Smith surrenders, they will be on the line which is to be strongly garrisoned.

"Should any force be necessary other than those designated, they can be had by calling for them on Army Headquarters.

"U. S. GRANT,
"Lieutenant-General.

"To MAJOR-GENERAL P. H. SHERIDAN,
"United States Army."

On receipt of these instructions I called at once on General Grant, to see if they were to be considered so pressing as to preclude my remaining in Washington till after the Grand Review, which was fixed for the 23d and 24th of May, for naturally I had a strong desire to head my command on that great occasion. But the General told me that it was absolutely necessary to go at once to force the surrender of the Confederates under Kirby Smith. He also told me that the States lately in rebellion would be embraced in two or three military departments, the commanders of which would control civil affairs until Congress took action about restoring them to the Union, since that course would not only be economical and simple, but would give the Southern people confidence, and encourage them to go to work, instead of distracting them with politics.

At this same interview he informed me that there was an additional motive in sending me to the new command, a motive not explained by the instructions themselves, and went on to say that, as a matter of fact, he looked upon the invasion of Mexico by Maximilian as a part of the rebellion itself, because of the encouragement that invasion had received from the Confederacy, and that our success in putting down secession would never be complete till the French and Austrian invaders were compelled to quit the territory of our sister republic. With regard to this matter, though, he said it would be necessary for me to act with great circumspection, since the Secretary of State, Mr. Seward, was much opposed to the use of our troops along the border in any active way that would be likely to involve us in a war with European powers.

Under the circumstances, my disappointment at not being permitted to participate in the review had to be submitted to, and I left Washington without an opportunity of seeing again in a body the men who, while under my command, had gone through so many trials and unremittingly pursued and, assailed the enemy, from the beginning of the campaign of 1864 till the white flag came into their hands at Appomattox Court House.

I went first to St. Louis, and there took the steamboat for New Orleans, and when near the mouth of the Red River received word from General Canby that Kirby Smith had surrendered under terms similar to those accorded Lee and Johnston. But the surrender was not carried out in good faith, particularly by the Texas troops, though this I did not learn till some little time afterward when I was informed that they had marched off to the interior of the State in several organized bodies, carrying with them their camp equipage, arms, ammunition, and even some artillery, with the ultimate purpose of going to Mexico. In consequence of this, and also because of the desire of the Government to make a strong showing of force in Texas, I decided to traverse the State with two columns of cavalry, directing one to San Antonio under Merritt, the other to Houston under Custer. Both commands were to start from the Red River—Shreveport and Alexandria—being the respective initial points—and in organizing the columns, to the mounted force already on the Red River were added several regiments of cavalry from the east bank of the, Mississippi, and in a singular way one of these fell upon the trail of my old antagonist, General Early. While crossing the river somewhere below Vicksburg some of the men noticed a suspicious looking party being ferried over in a rowboat, behind which two horses were swimming in tow. Chase was given, and the horses, being abandoned by the party, fell into the hands of our troopers, who, however, failed to capture or identify the people in the boat. As subsequently ascertained, the men were companions of Early, who was already across the Mississippi, hidden in the woods, on his way with two or three of these followers to join the Confederates in Texas, not having heard of Kirby Smith's surrender. A week or two later I received a letter from Early describing the affair, and the capture of the horses, for which he claimed pay, on the ground that they were private property, because he had taken them in battle. The letter also said that any further pursuit of Early would be useless, as he "expected to be on the deep blue sea" by the time his communication reached me. The unfortunate man was fleeing from imaginary dangers, however, for striking his trail was purely accidental, and no effort whatever was being made to arrest him personally. Had this been especially desired it might have been accomplished very readily just after Lee's surrender, for it was an open secret that Early was then not far away, pretty badly disabled with rheumatism.

By the time the two columns were ready to set out for San Antonio and Houston, General Frank Herron,—with one division of the Thirteenth Corps, occupied Galveston, and another division under General Fred Steele had gone to Brazos Santiago, to hold Brownsville and the line of the Rio Grande, the object being to prevent, as far as possible, the escaping Confederates from joining Maximilian. With this purpose in view, and not forgetting Grant's conviction that the French invasion of Mexico was linked with the rebellion, I asked for an increase of force to send troops into Texas in fact, to concentrate at available points in the State an army strong enough to move against the invaders of Mexico if occasion demanded. The Fourth and Twenty-fifth army corps being ordered to report to me, accordingly, I sent the Fourth Corps to Victoria and San Antonio, and the bulk of the Twenty-fifth to Brownsville. Then came the feeding and caring for all these troops—a difficult matter—for those at Victoria and San Antonio had to be provisioned overland from Indianola across the "hog-wallow prairie," while the supplies for the forces at Brownsville and along the Rio Grande must come by way of Brazos Santiago, from which point I was obliged to construct, with the labor of the men, a railroad to Clarksville, a distance of about eighteen miles.

The latter part of June I repaired to Brownsville myself to impress the Imperialists, as much as possible, with the idea that we intended hostilities, and took along my chief of scouts—Major Young—and four of his most trusty men, whom I had had sent from Washington. From Brownsville I despatched all these men to important points in northern Mexico, to glean information regarding the movements of the Imperial forces, and also to gather intelligence about the ex-Confederates who had crossed the Rio Grande. On information furnished by these scouts, I caused General Steele to make demonstrations all along the lower Rio Grande, and at the same time demanded the return of certain munitions of war that had been turned over by ex-Confederates to the Imperial General (Mejia) commanding at Matamoras. These demands, backed up as they were by such a formidable show of force created much agitation and demoralization among the Imperial troops, and measures looking to the abandonment of northern Mexico were forthwith adopted by those in authority—a policy that would have resulted in the speedy evacuation of the entire country by Maximilian, had not our Government weakened; contenting itself with a few pieces of the contraband artillery varnished over with the Imperial apologies. A golden opportunity was lost, for we had ample excuse for crossing the boundary, but Mr. Seward being, as I have already stated, unalterably opposed to any act likely to involve us in war, insisted on his course of negotiation with Napoleon.

As the summer wore away, Maximilian, under Mr. Seward's policy, gained in strength till finally all the accessible sections of Mexico were in his possession, and the Republic under President Juarez almost succumbed. Growing impatient at this, in the latter part of September I decided to try again what virtue there might be in a hostile demonstration, and selected the upper Rio Grande for the scene of my attempt. Merritt's cavalry and the Fourth Corps still being at San Antonio, I went to that place and reviewed these troops, and having prepared them with some ostentation for a campaign, of course it was bruited about that we were going to invade Mexico. Then, escorted by a regiment of horse I proceeded hastily to Fort Duncan, on the Rio Grande just opposite the Mexican town of Piedras Negras. Here I opened communication with President Juarez, through one of his staff, taking care not to do this in the dark, and the news, spreading like wildfire, the greatest significance was ascribed to my action, it being reported most positively and with many specific details that I was only awaiting the arrival of the troops, then under marching orders at San Antonio, to cross the Rio Grande in behalf of the Liberal cause.

Ample corroboration of the reports then circulated was found in my inquiries regarding the quantity of forage we could depend upon getting in Mexico, our arrangements for its purchase, and my sending a pontoon train to Brownsville, together with which was cited the renewed activity of the troops along the lower Rio Grande. These reports and demonstrations resulted in alarming the Imperialists so much that they withdrew the French and Austrian soldiers from Matamoras, and practically abandoned the whole of northern Mexico as far down as Monterey, with the exception of Matamoras, where General Mejia continued to hang on with a garrison of renegade Mexicans.

The abandonment of so much territory in northern Mexico encouraged General Escobedo and other Liberal leaders to such a degree that they collected a considerable army of their followers at Comargo, Mier, and other points. At the same time that unknown quantity, Cortinas, suspended his free-booting for the nonce, and stoutly harassing Matamoras, succeeded in keeping its Imperial garrison within the fortifications. Thus countenanced and stimulated, and largely supplied with arms and ammunition, which we left at convenient places on our side of the river to fall into their hands, the Liberals, under General Escobedo—a man of much force of character—were enabled in northern Mexico to place the affairs of the Republic on a substantial basis.

But in the midst of what bade fair to cause a final withdrawal of the foreigners, we were again checked by our Government, as a result of representations of the French Minister at Washington. In October, he wrote to Mr. Seward that the United States troops on the Rio Grande were acting "in exact opposition to the repeated assurances Your Excellency has given me concerning the desire of the Cabinet at Washington to preserve the most strict neutrality in the events now taking place in Mexico," and followed this statement with an emphatic protest against our course. Without any investigation whatever by our State Department, this letter of the French Minister was transmitted to me, accompanied by directions to preserve a strict neutrality; so, of course, we were again debarred from anything like active sympathy.

After this, it required the patience of Job to abide the slow and poky methods of our State Department, and, in truth, it was often very difficult to restrain officers and men from crossing the Rio Grande with hostile purpose. Within the knowledge of my troops, there had gone on formerly the transfer of organized bodies of ex-Confederates to Mexico, in aid of the Imperialists, and at this period it was known that there was in preparation an immigration scheme having in view the colonizing, at Cordova and one or two other places, of all the discontented elements of the defunct Confederacy—Generals Price, Magruder, Maury, and other high personages being promoters of the enterprise, which Maximilian took to readily. He saw in it the possibilities of a staunch support to his throne, and therefore not only sanctioned the project, but encouraged it with large grants of land, inspirited the promoters with titles of nobility, and, in addition, instituted a system of peonage, expecting that the silver hook thus baited would be largely swallowed by the Southern people.

The announcement of the scheme was followed by the appointment of commissioners in each of the Southern States to send out emigrants; but before any were deluded into starting, I made to General Grant a report of what was going on, with the recommendation that measures be taken, through our State Department, looking to the suppression of the colony; but, as usual, nothing could be effected through that channel; so, as an alternative, I published, in April, 1866, by authority of General Grant, an order prohibiting the embarkation from ports in Louisiana and Texas, for ports in Mexico, of any person without a permit from my headquarters. This dampened the ardor of everybody in the Gulf States who had planned to go to Mexico; and although the projectors of the Cordova Colonization Scheme—the name by which it was known—secured a few innocents from other districts, yet this set-back led ultimately to failure.

Among the Liberal leaders along the Rio Grande during this period there sprang up many factional differences from various causes, some personal, others political, and some, I regret to say, from downright moral obliquity—as, for example, those between Cortinas and Canales—who, though generally hostile to the Imperialists, were freebooters enough to take a shy at each other frequently, and now and then even to join forces against Escobedo, unless we prevented them by coaxing or threats. A general who could unite these several factions was therefore greatly needed, and on my return to New Orleans I so telegraphed General Grant, and he, thinking General Caravajal (then in Washington seeking aid for the Republic) would answer the purpose, persuaded him to report to me in New Orleans. Caravajal promptly appeared, but he did not impress me very favorably. He was old and cranky, yet, as he seemed anxious to do his best, I sent him over to Brownsville, with credentials, authorizing him to cross into Mexico, and followed him myself by the next boat. When I arrived in Brownsville, matters in Matamoras had already reached a crisis. General Mejia, feeling keenly the moral support we were giving the Liberals, and hard pressed by the harassing attacks of Cortinas and Canales, had abandoned the place, and Caravajal, because of his credentials from our side, was in command, much to the dissatisfaction of both those chiefs whose differences it was intended he should reconcile.

The, day after I got to Brownsville I visited Matamoras, and had a long interview with Caravajal. The outcome of this meeting was, on my part, a stronger conviction than ever that he was unsuitable, and I feared that either Canales or Cortinas would get possession of the city. Caravajal made too many professions of what he would do—in short, bragged too much—but as there was no help for the situation, I made the best of it by trying to smooth down the ruffled feathers of Canales and Cortinas. In my interview with Caravajal I recommended Major Young as a confidential man, whom he could rely upon as a "go-between" for communicating with our people at Brownsville, and whom he could trust to keep him informed of the affairs of his own country as well.

A day or two afterward I recrossed the Gulf to New Orleans, and then, being called from my headquarters to the interior of Texas, a fortnight passed before I heard anything from Brownsville. In the meanwhile Major Young had come to New Orleans, and organized there a band of men to act as a body-guard for Caravajal, the old wretch having induced him to accept the proposition by representing that it had my concurrence. I at once condemned the whole business, but Young, having been furnished with seven thousand dollars to recruit the men and buy their arms, had already secured both, and was so deeply involved in the transaction, he said, that he could not withdraw without dishonor, and with tears in his eyes he besought me to help him. He told me he had entered upon the adventure in the firm belief that I would countenance it; that the men and their equipment were on his hands; that he must make good his word at all hazards; and that while I need not approve, yet I must go far enough to consent to the departure of the men, and to loan him the money necessary to provision his party and hire a schooner to carry them to Brazos. It was hard in deed to resist the appeals of this man, who had served me so long and so well, and the result of his pleading was that I gave him permission to sail, and also loaned him the sum asked for; but I have never ceased to regret my consent, for misfortune fell upon the enterprise almost from its inception.

By the time the party got across the Gulf and over to Brownsville, Caravajal had been deposed by Canales, and the latter would not accept their services. This left Young with about fifty men to whom he was accountable, and as he had no money to procure them subsistence, they were in a bad fix. The only thing left to do was to tender their services to General Escobedo, and with this in view the party set out to reach the General's camp, marching up the Rio Grande on the American side, intending to cross near Ringgold Barracks. In advance of them, however, had spread far and wide the tidings of who they were, what they proposed to do, and where they were going, and before they could cross into Mexico they were attacked by a party of ex-Confederates and renegade Mexican rancheros. Being on American soil, Young forbade his men to return the fire, and bent all his efforts to getting them over the river; but in this attempt they were broken up, and became completely demoralized. A number of the men were drowned while swimming the river, Young himself was shot and killed, a few were captured, and those who escaped—about twenty in all—finally joined Escobedo, but in such a plight as to be of little use. With this distressing affair came to an end pretty much all open participation of American sympathizers with the Liberal cause, but the moral support afforded by the presence of our forces continued, and this was frequently supplemented with material aid in the shape of munitions of war, which we liberally supplied, though constrained to do so by the most secret methods.

The term of office of Juarez as President of the Mexican Republic expired in December, 1865, but to meet existing exigencies he had continued himself in office by proclamation, a course rendered necessary by the fact that no elections could be held on account of the Imperial occupation of most of the country. The official who, by the Mexican Constitution, is designated for the succession in such an emergency, is the President of the Supreme Court, and the person then eligible under this provision was General Ortega, but in the interest of the Imperialists he had absented himself from Mexico, hence the patriotic course of Juarez in continuing himself at the head of affairs was a necessity of the situation. This action of the President gave the Imperialists little concern at first, but with the revival of the Liberal cause they availed themselves of every means to divide its supporters, and Ortega, who had been lying low in the United States, now came forward to claim the Presidency. Though ridiculously late for such a step, his first act was to issue a manifesto protesting against the assumption of the executive authority by Juarez. The protest had little effect, however, and his next proceeding was to come to New Orleans, get into correspondence with other disaffected Mexicans, and thus perfect his plans. When he thought his intrigue ripe enough for action, he sailed for Brazos, intending to cross the Rio Grande and assert his claims with arms. While he was scheming in New Orleans, however, I had learned what he was up to, and in advance of his departure had sent instructions to have him arrested on American soil. Colonel Sedgwick, commanding at Brownsville, was now temporary master of Matamoras also, by reason of having stationed some American troops there for the protection of neutral merchants, so when Ortega appeared at Brazos, Sedgwick quietly arrested him and held him till the city of Matamoras was turned over to General Escobedo, the authorized representative of Juarez; then Escobedo took charge, of Ortega, and with ease prevented his further machinations.

During the winter and spring of 1866 we continued covertly supplying arms and ammunition to the Liberals—sending as many as 30,000 muskets from Baton Rouge Arsenal alone—and by mid-summer Juarez, having organized a pretty good sized army, was in possession of the whole line of the Rio Grande, and, in fact, of nearly the whole of Mexico down to San Louis Potosi. Then thick and fast came rumors pointing to the tottering condition of Maximilian's Empire—first, that Orizaba and Vera Cruz were being fortified; then, that the French were to be withdrawn; and later came the intelligence that the Empress Carlotta had gone home to beg assistance from Napoleon, the author of all of her husband's troubles. But the situation forced Napoleon to turn a deaf ear to Carlotta's prayers. The brokenhearted woman besought him on her knees, but his fear of losing an army made all pleadings vain. In fact, as I ascertained by the following cablegram which came into my hands, Napoleon's instructions for the French evacuation were in Mexico at the very time of this pathetic scene between him and Carlotta. The despatch was in cipher when I received it, but was translated by the telegraph operator at my headquarters, who long before had mastered the key of the French cipher:

"PARIS, January 10, 1867. FRENCH CONSUL, New Orleans, La.

"To GENERAL CASTELNAU, at Mexico.

"Received your despatch of the 9th December. Do not compel the Emperor to abdicate, but do not delay the departure of the troops; bring back all those who will not remain there. Most of the fleet has left.

"NAPOLEON."

This meant the immediate withdrawal of the French. The rest of the story—which has necessarily been but in outline—is soon told. Maximilian, though deserted, determined to hold out to the last, and with the aid of disloyal Mexicans stuck to his cause till the spring. When taken prisoner at Queretaro, he was tried and executed under circumstances that are well known. From promptings of humanity Secretary Seward tried hard to save the Imperial prisoner, but without success. The Secretary's plea for mercy was sent through me at New Orleans, and to make speed I hired a steamer to proceed with it across the Gulf to Tampico. The document was carried by Sergeant White, one of my scouts, who crossed the country from Tampico, and delivered it to Escobedo at Queretaro; but Mr. Seward's representations were without avail—refused probably because little mercy had been shown certain Liberal leaders unfortunate enough to fall into Maximilian's hands during the prosperous days of his Empire.

At the close of our war there was little hope for the Republic of Mexico. Indeed, till our troops were concentrated on the Rio Grande there was none. Our appearance in such force along the border permitted the Liberal leaders, refugees from their homes, to establish rendezvous whence they could promulgate their plans in safety, while the countenance thus given the cause, when hope was well-nigh gone, incited the Mexican people to renewed resistance. Beginning again with very scant means, for they had lost about all, the Liberals saw their cause, under the influence of such significant and powerful backing, progress and steadily grow so strong that within two years Imperialism had received its death-blow. I doubt very much whether such, results could have been achieved without the presence of an American army on the Rio Grande, which, be it remembered, was sent there because, in General Grant's words, the French invasion of Mexico was so closely related to the rebellion as to be essentially a part of it.

CHAPTER X.

A. J. HAMILTON APPOINTED PROVISIONAL GOVERNOR OF TEXAS—ASSEMBLES A CONSTITUTIONAL CONVENTION—THE TEXANS DISSATISFIED—LAWLESSNESS— OPPRESSIVE LEGISLATION—EX-CONFEDERATES CONTROLLING LOUISIANA—A CONSTITUTIONAL CONVENTION—THE MEETING SUPPRESSED—A BLOODY RIOT—MY REPORTS OF THE MASSACRE—PORTIONS SUPPRESSED BY PRESIDENT JOHNSON— SUSTAINED BY A CONGRESSIONAL COMMITTEE—THE RECONSTRUCTION LAWS.

Although in 1865-66 much of my attention was directed to international matters along the Rio Grande, the civil affairs of Texas and Louisiana required a certain amount of military supervision also in the absence of regularly established civil authority. At the time of Kirby Smith's surrender the National Government had formulated no plan with regard to these or the other States lately in rebellion, though a provisional Government had been set up in Louisiana as early as 1864. In consequence of this lack of system, Governor Pendleton Murray, of Texas, who was elected under Confederate rule, continued to discharge the duties of Governor till President Johnson, on June 17, in harmony with his amnesty proclamation of May 29, 1865, appointed A. J. Hamilton provisional Governor. Hamilton was empowered by the President to call a Constitutional convention, the delegates to which were to be elected, under certain prescribed qualifications, for the purpose of organizing the political affairs of the State, the Governor to be guided by instructions similar to those given the provisional Governor of North Carolina (W. W.

Holden), when appointed in May.

The convening of this body gave rise to much dissatisfaction among the people of Texas. They had assumed that affairs were to go on as of old, and that the reintegration of the State was to take place under the administration of Governor Murray, who, meanwhile, had taken it upon himself, together with the Legislature, to authorize the election of delegates to a State Convention, without restriction as to who should be entitled to vote. Thus encouraged, the element but lately in armed rebellion was now fully bent on restoring the State to the Union without any intervention whatever of the Federal Government; but the advent of Hamilton put an end to such illusions, since his proclamation promptly disfranchised the element in question, whose consequent disappointment and chagrin were so great as to render this factor of the community almost uncontrollable. The provisional Governor at once rescinded the edict of Governor Murray, prohibited the assembling of his convention, and shortly after called, one himself, the delegates to which were to b chosen by voters who could take the amnesty-oath. The proclamation convening this assemblage also announced the policy that would be pursued in governing the State until its affairs were satisfactorily reorganized, defined in brief the course to be followed by the Judiciary, and provided for the appointment, by the Governor, of county officials to succeed those known to be disloyal. As this action of Hamilton's disfranchised all who could not take the amnesty oath, and of course deprived them of the offices, it met at once with pronounced and serious opposition, and he quickly realized that he had on his hands an arduous task to protect the colored people, particularly as in the transition state of society just after the close of the war there prevailed much lawlessness, which vented itself chiefly on the freedmen. It was greatly feared that political rights were to be given those so recently in servitude, and as it was generally believed that such enfranchisement would precipitate a race war unless the freedmen were overawed and kept in a state of subjection, acts of intimidation were soon reported from all parts of the State.

Hamilton, an able, determined, and fearless man, tried hard to curb this terrorism, but public opinion being strong against him, he could accomplish little without military aid. As department commander, I was required, whenever called upon, to assist his government, and as these requisitions for help became necessarily very frequent, the result was that shortly after he assumed his duties, detachments of troops were stationed in nearly every county of the State. By such disposition of my forces fairly good order was maintained under the administration of Hamilton, and all went well till the inauguration of J. W. Throckmorton, who, elected Governor in pursuance of an authorization granted by the convention which Hamilton had called together, assumed the duties of the office August 9, 1866.

One of Governor Throckmorton's first acts was to ask the withdrawal or non-interference of the military. This was not all granted, but under his ingenious persuasion President Johnson, on the 13th of August, 1866, directed that the new State officials be entrusted with the unhampered control of civil affairs, and this was more than enough to revive the bulldozing methods that had characterized the beginning of Hamilton's administration. Oppressive legislation in the shape of certain apprentice and vagrant laws quickly followed, developing a policy of gross injustice toward the colored people on the part of the courts, and a reign of lawlessness and disorder ensued which, throughout the remote districts of the State at least, continued till Congress, by what are known as the Reconstruction Acts, took into its own hands the rehabilitation of the seceded States.

In the State of Louisiana a provisional government, chosen by the loyal element, had been put in operation, as already mentioned, as early as 1864. This was effected under encouragement given by President Lincoln, through the medium of a Constitutional convention, which met at New Orleans in April, 1864, and adjourned in July. The constitution then agreed upon was submitted to the people, and in September, 1864, was ratified by a vote of the few loyal residents of the State.

The government provided under this constitution being looked upon as provisional merely, was never recognized by Congress, and in 1865 the returned Confederates, restored to citizenship by the President's amnesty proclamation, soon got control of almost all the State. The Legislature was in their hands, as well as most of the State and municipal offices; so, when the President, on the 20th of August, 1866, by proclamation, extended his previous instructions regarding civil affairs in Texas so as to have them apply to all the seceded States, there at once began in Louisiana a system of discriminative legislation directed against the freedmen, that led to flagrant wrongs in the enforcement of labor contracts, and in the remote parishes to numbers of outrages and murders.

To remedy this deplorable condition of things, it was proposed, by those who had established the government of 1864, to remodel the constitution of the State; and they sought to do this by reassembling the convention, that body before its adjournment having provided for reconvening under certain conditions, in obedience to the call of its president. Therefore, early in the summer of 1866, many members of this convention met in conference at New Orleans, and decided that a necessity existed for reconvening the delegates, and a proclamation was issued accordingly by B. K. Howell, President-pro-tempore.

Mayor John T. Monroe and the other officials of New Orleans looked upon this proposed action as revolutionary, and by the time the convention assembled (July 30), such bitterness of feeling prevailed that efforts were made by the mayor and city police to suppress the meeting. A bloody riot followed, resulting, in the killing and wounding of about a hundred and sixty persons.

I happened to be absent from the city at the time, returning from Texas, where I had been called by affairs on the Rio Grande. On my way up from the mouth of the Mississippi I was met on the night of July 30 by one of my staff, who reported what had occurred, giving the details of the massacre—no milder term is fitting—and informing me that, to prevent further slaughter, General Baird, the senior military officer present, had assumed control of the municipal government. On reaching the city I made an investigation, and that night sent the following report of the affair:

"HEADQUARTERS MILITARY DIVISION OF THE GULF, "NEW ORLEANS, LA., Aug. 1, 1866.
 "GENERAL U. S. GRANT:

"You are doubtless aware of the serious riot which occurred in this city on the 30th. A political body, styling themselves the Convention of 1864, met on the 30th, for, as it is alleged, the purpose of remodeling the present constitution of the State. The leaders were political agitators and revolutionary men, and the action of the convention was liable to produce breaches of the public peace. I had made up my mind to arrest the head men, if the proceedings of the convention were calculated to disturb the tranquility of the Department; but I had no cause for action until they committed the overt act. In the meantime official duty called me to Texas, and the mayor of the city, during my absence suppressed the convention by the use of the police force, and in so doing attacked the members of the convention, and a party of two hundred negroes, with fire-arms, clubs, and knives, in a manner so unnecessary and atrocious as to compel me to say that it was murder. About forty whites and blacks were thus killed, and about one hundred and sixty wounded. Everything is now quiet, but I deem it best to maintain a military supremacy in the city for a few days, until the affair is fully investigated. I believe the sentiment of the general community is great regret at this unnecessary cruelty, and that the police could have made any arrest they saw fit without sacrificing lives.

"P. H. SHERIDAN,

"Major-General Commanding."

On receiving the telegram, General Grant immediately submitted it to the President. Much clamor being made at the North for the publication of the despatch, Mr. Johnson pretended to give it to the newspapers. It appeared in the issues of August 4, but with this paragraph omitted, viz.:

"I had made up my mind to arrest the head men, if the proceedings of the convention were calculated to disturb the tranquility of the Department, but I had no cause for action until they committed the overt act. In the mean time official duty called me to Texas, and the mayor of the city, during my absence, suppressed the convention by the use of the police force, and in so doing attacked the members of the convention, and a party of two hundred negroes, with fire-arms, clubs, and knives, in a manner so unnecessary and atrocious as to compel me to say it was murder."

Against this garbling of my report—done by the President's own order—I strongly demurred; and this emphatic protest marks the beginning of Mr. Johnson's well-known personal hostility toward me. In the mean time I received (on August 3) the following despatch from General Grant approving my course:

"HEADQUARTERS ARMIES OF THE UNITED STATES,
"WAR DEPT., WASHINGTON, D. C.,
"August 3, 1866—5 p.m.
"MAJOR-GENERAL P. H. SHERIDAN,
"Commanding Mil. Div. of the Gulf,
"New Orleans, La.
"Continue to enforce martial law, so far as may be necessary to preserve the

peace; and do not allow any of the civil authorities to act, if you deem such action dangerous to the public safety. Lose no time in investigating and reporting the causes that led to the riot, and the facts which occurred.

"U. S. GRANT,

"Lieutenant-General."

In obedience to the President's directions, My report of August 1 was followed by another, more in detail, which I give in full, since it tells the whole story of the riot:

"HEADQUARTERS MILITARY DIVISION OF THE GULF,
"NEW ORLEANS, LA., August 6, 1866.
"His EXCELLENCY ANDREW JOHNSON,
"President United States

"I have the honor to make the following reply to your despatch of August 4. A very large number of colored people marched in procession on Friday night, July twenty-seven (27), and were addressed from the steps of the City Hall by Dr. Dostie, ex-Governor Hahn, and others. The speech of Dostie was intemperate in language and sentiment. The speeches of the others, so far as I can learn, were characterized by moderation. I have not given you the words of Dostie's speech, as the version published was denied; but from what I have learned of the man, I believe they were intemperate.

"The convention assembled at twelve (12) M. on the thirtieth (30), the timid members absenting themselves because the tone of the general public was ominous of trouble. I think there were about twenty-six (26) members present. In front of the Mechanics Institute, where the meeting was held, there were assembled some colored men, women, and children, perhaps eighteen (18) or twenty (20), and in the Institute a number of colored men, probably one hundred and fifty (150). Among those outside and inside there might have been a pistol in the possession of every tenth (10) man.

"About one (1) p. m. a procession of say from sixty (60) to one hundred and thirty (130) colored men marched up Burgundy Street and across Canal Street toward the convention, carrying an American flag. These men had about one pistol to every ten men, and canes and clubs in addition. While crossing Canal Street a row occurred. There were many spectators on the street, and their manner and tone toward the procession unfriendly. A shot was fired, by whom I am not able to state, but believe it to have been by a policeman, or some colored man in the procession. This led to other shots and a rush after the procession. On arrival at the front of the Institute there was some throwing of brickbats by both sides. The police, who had been held well in hand, were vigorously marched to the scene of disorder. The procession entered the Institute with the flag, about six (6) or eight (8) remaining outside. A row occurred between a policeman and one of these colored men, and a shot was again fired by one of the parties, which led to an indiscriminate fire on the building through the windows by the policemen. This had been going on for a short time, when a white flag was displayed from the windows of the Institute, whereupon the firing ceased, and the police rushed into the building.

"From the testimony of wounded men, and others who were inside the building, the policemen opened an indiscriminate fire upon the audience until they had emptied their revolvers, when they retired, and those inside barricaded the doors. The door was broken in, and the firing again commenced, when many of the colored and white people either escaped throughout the door or were passed out by the policemen inside; but as they came out the policemen who formed the circle nearest the building fired upon them, and they were again fired upon by the citizens that formed the outer circle. Many of those wounded and taken prisoners, and others who were prisoners and not wounded, were fired upon by their captors and by citizens. The wounded were stabbed while lying on the ground, and their heads beaten with brickbats. In the yard of the building, whither some of the colored men had escaped and partially secreted themselves, they were fired upon and killed or wounded by policemen. Some were killed and wounded several squares from the scene. Members of the convention were wounded by the police while in their hands as prisoners, some of them mortally.

"The immediate cause of this terrible affair was the assemblage of this Convention; the remote cause was the bitter and antagonistic feeling which has been growing in this community since the advent of the present Mayor, who, in the organization of his police force, selected many desperate men, and some of them known murderers. People of clear views were overawed by want of confidence in the Mayor, and fear of the thugs, many of which he had selected for his police force. I have frequently been spoken to by prominent citizens on this subject, and have heard them express fear, and want of confidence in Mayor Monroe. Ever since the intimation of this last convention movement I must condemn the course of several of the city papers for supporting, by their articles, the bitter feeling of bad men. As to the merciless manner in which the convention was broken up, I feel obliged to confess strong repugnance.

"It is useless to disguise the hostility that exists on the part of a great many here toward Northern men, and this unfortunate affair has so precipitated matters that there is now a test of what shall be the status of Northern men—whether they can live here without being in constant dread or not, whether they can be protected in life and property, and have justice in the courts. If this matter is permitted to pass over without a thorough and determined prosecution of those engaged in it, we may look out for frequent scenes of the same kind, not only here, but in other places. No steps have as yet been taken by the civil authorities to arrest citizens who were engaged in this massacre, or policemen who perpetrated such cruelties. The members of the convention have been indicted by the grand jury, and many of them arrested and held to bail. As to whether the civil authorities can mete out ample justice to the guilty parties on both sides, I must say it is my opinion, unequivocally, that they cannot. Judge Abell, whose course I have closely watched for nearly a year, I now consider one of the most dangerous men that we have here to the peace and quiet of the city. The leading men of the convention—King, Cutler, Hahn, and others—have been political agitators, and are bad men. I regret to say that the course of Governor Wells has been vacillating, and that during the late trouble he has shown very little of the man.

"P. H. SHERIDAN,

"Major-General Commanding."

Subsequently a military commission investigated the subject of the riot, taking a great deal of testimony. The commission substantially confirmed the conclusions given in my despatches, and still later there was an investigation by a select committee of the House of Representatives, of which the Honorables Samuel Shellabarger, of Ohio, H. L. Elliot, of Massachusetts, and B. M. Boyer, of Pennsylvania, were the members. The majority report of the committee also corroborated, in all essentials, my reports of the distressing occurrence. The committee likewise called attention to a violent speech made by Mr. Johnson at St. Louis in September, 1866, charging the origin of the riot to Congress, and went on to say of the speech that "it was an unwarranted and unjust expression of hostile feeling, without pretext or foundation in fact." A list of the killed and wounded was embraced in the committee's report, and among other conclusions reached were the following: "That the meeting of July 30 was a meeting of quiet citizens, who came together without arms and with intent peaceably to discuss questions of public concern . . . There has been no occasion during our National history when a riot has occurred so destitute of justifiable cause, resulting in a massacre so inhuman and fiend-like, as that which took place at New Orleans on the 30th of July last. This riotous attack upon the convention, with its terrible results of massacre and murder, was not an accident. It was the determined purpose of the mayor of the city of New Orleans to break up this convention by armed force."

The statement is also made, that, "He [the President] knew that 'rebels' and 'thugs' and disloyal men had controlled the election of Mayor Monroe, and that such men composed chiefly his police force."

The committee held that no legal government existed in Louisiana, and recommended the temporary establishment of a provisional government therein; the report concluding that "in the meantime the safety of all Union men within the State demands that such government be formed for their protection, for the well being of the nation and the permanent peace of the Republic."

The New Orleans riot agitated the whole country, and the official and other reports served to intensify and concentrate the opposition to President Johnson's policy of reconstruction, a policy resting exclusively on and inspired solely by the executive authority—for it was made plain, by his language and his acts, that he was seeking to rehabilitate the seceded States under conditions differing not a whit from those existing before the rebellion; that is to say, without the slightest constitutional provision regarding the status of the emancipated slaves, and with no assurances of protection for men who had remained loyal in the war.

In December, 1866, Congress took hold of the subject with such vigor as to promise relief from all these perplexing disorders, and, after much investigation and a great deal of debate, there resulted the so-called "Reconstruction Laws," which, for a clear understanding of the powers conferred on the military commanders, I deem best to append in full:

> AN ACT to provide for the more efficient government of the rebel States.
> WHEREAS, no legal State governments or adequate protection for life or

property now exist in the rebel States of Virginia, North Carolina, South Carolina, Georgia, Mississippi, Alabama, Louisiana, Florida, Texas, and Arkansas; and whereas, it is necessary that peace and good order should be enforced in said States until loyal and republican State governments can be legally established; therefore,

BE IT ENACTED by the Senate and House of Representatives of the United States of America in Congress assembled, That said rebel States shall be divided into military districts and made subject to the military authority of the United States as hereinafter prescribed; and for that purpose Virginia shall constitute the first district; North Carolina and South Carolina, the second district; Georgia, Alabama, and Florida, the third district; Mississippi and Arkansas, the fourth district; and Louisiana and Texas, the fifth district.

SEC. 2. And be it further enacted, That it shall be the duty of the President to assign to the command of each of said districts an officer of the army not below the rank of brigadier-general, and to detail a sufficient military force to enable such officer to perform his duties and enforce his authority within the district to which he is assigned.

SEC. 3. And be it further enacted, That it shall be the duty of each officer assigned as aforesaid to protect all persons in their rights of person and property, to suppress insurrection, disorder, and violence, and to punish, or cause to be punished, all disturbers of the public peace and criminals, and to this end he may allow local civil tribunals to take jurisdiction of and to try offenders, or, when in his judgment it may be necessary for the trial of offenders, he shall have power to organize military commissions or tribunals for that purpose, and all interference, under cover of State authority, with the exercise of military authority under this act, shall be null and void.

SEC. 4. And be it further enacted, That all persons put under military arrest by virtue of this act shall be tried without unnecessary delay, and no cruel or unjust punishment shall be inflicted; and no sentence of any military commission or tribunal hereby authorized affecting the life or liberty of any person, shall be executed until it is approved by the officer in command of the district; and the laws and regulations for the government of the army shall not be affected by this act except in so far as they conflict with its provisions: Provided, That no sentence of death, under the provisions of this act, shall be carried into effect without the approval of the President.

SEC. 5. And be it further enacted, That when the people of any one of said rebel States shall have formed a constitution of government in conformity with the Constitution of the United States in all respects, framed by a convention of delegates elected by the male citizens of said State twenty-one years old and upward, of whatever race, color, or previous condition, who have been resident in said State for one year previous to the day of such election, except such as may be disfranchised for participation in the rebellion, or for felony at common law; and when such constitution shall provide that the elective franchise shall be enjoyed by all such persons as have the qualifications herein stated for electors of delegates; and when such constitution shall be ratified by a majority of the persons voting on the question of ratification who are qualified as electors for delegates, and when such constitution shall have been submitted to Congress for examination and approval, and Congress shall have approved the same; and when said State, by a vote of its legislature elected under said constitution, shall have adopted the amendment to the Constitution of the United States proposed by the Thirty-ninth Congress, and known as article fourteen; and when said article shall have become a part of the Constitution of the United States, said State shall be declared entitled to representation in Congress, and senators and representatives shall be admitted therefrom on their taking the oath prescribed by law; and then and thereafter the preceding sections of this act shall be inoperative in said State: Provided, That no person excluded from the privilege of holding office by said proposed amendment to the Constitution of the United States shall be eligible to election as a member of the convention to frame a constitution for any of said rebel States, nor shall any such person vote for members of such convention.

SEC. 6. And be it further enacted, That until the people of said rebel States shall be by law admitted to representation in the Congress of the United States, any civil government which may exist therein shall be deemed provisional only, and in all respects subject to the paramount authority of the United States at any time to abolish, modify, control, or supersede the same; and in all elections to any office under such provisional governments all persons shall be entitled to vote, and none others, who are entitled to vote under the fifth section of this act; and no person shall be eligible to any office under any such provisional governments who would be disqualified from holding office under the provisions of the third article of said constitutional amendment.

SCHUYLER COLFAX, Speaker of the House of Representatives.

LAFAYETTE S. FOSTER, President of the Senate pro tempore.

AN ACT supplementary to an act entitled "An act to provide for the more efficient government of the rebel States," passed March second, eighteen hundred and sixty-seven, and to facilitate restoration.

Be it enacted by the Senate and House of Representatives of the United States of America in Congress assembled, That before the first day of September, eighteen hundred and sixty-seven, the commanding general in each district defined by an act entitled "An act to provide for the more efficient government of the rebel States," passed March second, eighteen hundred and sixty-seven, shall cause a registration to be made of the male citizens of the United States, twenty-one years of age and upwards, resident in each county or parish in the State or States included in his district, which registration shall include only those persons who are qualified to vote for delegates by the act aforesaid, and who shall have taken and subscribed the following oath or affirmation: "I,———, do solemnly swear (or affirm), in the presence of the Almighty God, that I am a citizen of the State of ————; that I have resided in said State for——months next preceding this day, and now reside in the county of ————, or the parish of ————, in said State, (as the case may be); that I am twenty-one years old; that I have not been disfranchised for participation in any rebellion or civil war against the United States, nor for felony committed against the laws of any State or of the United States; that I have never been a member of any State Legislature, nor held any executive or judicial office in any State, and afterwards engaged in insurrection or rebellion against the United States, or given aid or comfort to the enemies thereof; that I have never taken an oath as a member of Congress of the United States, or as an officer of the United States, or as a member of any State Legislature, or as an executive or judicial officer of any State, to support the constitution of the United States, and afterwards engaged in insurrection or rebellion against the United States or given aid or comfort to the enemies thereof; that I will faithfully support the Constitution and obey the laws of the United States, and will, to the best of my ability, encourage others so to do: so help me God."; which oath or affirmation may be administered by any registering officer.

SEC. 2. And be it further enacted, That after the completion of the registration hereby provided for in any State, at such time and places therein as the commanding general shall appoint and direct, of which at least thirty days' public notice shall be given, an election shall be held of delegates to a convention for the purpose of establishing a constitution and civil government for such State loyal to the Union, said convention in each State, except Virginia, to consist of the same number of members as the most numerous branch of the State Legislature of such State in the year eighteen hundred and sixty, to be apportioned among the several districts, counties, or parishes of such State by the commanding general, giving each representation in the ratio of voters registered as aforesaid as nearly as may be. The convention in Virginia shall consist of the same number of members as represented the territory now constituting Virginia in the most numerous branch of the Legislature of said State in the year eighteen hundred and sixty, to be apportioned as aforesaid.

SEC. 3. And be it further enacted, That at said election the registered voters of each State shall vote for or against a convention to form a constitution therefor under this act. Those voting in favor of such a convention shall have written or printed on the ballots by which they vote for delegates, as aforesaid, the words "For a convention," and those voting against such a convention shall have written or printed on such ballot the words "Against a convention." The persons appointed to superintend said election, and to make return of the votes given thereat, as herein provided, shall count and make return of the votes given for and against a convention; and the commanding general to whom the same shall have been returned shall ascertain and declare the total vote in each State for and against a convention. If a majority of the votes given on that question shall be for a convention, then such convention shall be held as hereinafter provided; but if a majority of said votes shall, be against a convention, then no such convention shall be held under this act: Provided, That such convention shall not be held unless a majority of all such registered voters shall have voted on the question of holding such convention.

SEC. 4. And be it further enacted, That the commanding general of each district shall appoint as many boards of registration as may be necessary, consisting of three loyal officers or persons, to make and complete the registration, superintend the election, and make return to him of the votes, list of voters, and of the persons elected as delegates by a plurality of the votes cast at said election; and upon receiving said returns he shall open the same, ascertain the persons elected as delegates, according to the returns of the officers who conducted said election, and make proclamation thereof; and if a majority of the votes given on that question shall be for a convention, the commanding general, within sixty days from the date of election, shall notify the delegates to assemble in convention, at a time and place to be mentioned in the notification, and said convention, when organized, shall proceed to frame a constitution and civil government according to the provisions of this act, and the act to which it is supplementary; and when the same shall have been so framed, said constitution shall be submitted by the convention for ratification to the persons registered under the provisions of this act at an election to be conducted by the officers or persons appointed or to be appointed by the commanding general, as hereinbefore provided, and to be held after the expiration of thirty days from the date of notice thereof, to be given by said convention; and the returns thereof shall be made to the commanding general of the district.

SEC. 5. And be it further enacted, That if, according to said returns, the constitution shall be ratified by a majority of the votes of the registered electors qualified as herein specified, cast at said election, at least one-half of all the registered voters voting upon the question of such ratification, the president of the convention shall transmit a copy of the same, duly certified, to the President of the United States, who shall forthwith transmit the same to Congress, if then in session, and if not in session, then immediately upon its next assembling; and if it shall moreover appear to Congress that the election was one at which all the registered and qualified electors in the State had an opportunity to vote freely, and without restraint, fear, or the influence of fraud, and if the Congress shall be satisfied that such constitution meets the approval of a majority of all the qualified electors in the State, and if the said constitution shall be declared by Congress to be in conformity with the provisions of the act to which this is supplementary, and the other provisions of said act shall have been complied with, and the said constitution shall be approved by Congress, the State shall be declared entitled to representation, and senators and representatives shall be admitted therefrom as therein provided.

SEC. 6. And be it further enacted, That all elections in the States mentioned in the said "Act to provide for the more efficient government of the rebel States" shall, during the operation of said act, be by ballot; and all officers making the said registration of voters and conducting said elections, shall, before entering upon the discharge of their duties, take and subscribe the oath prescribed by the act approved July second, eighteen hundred and sixty-two, entitled "An act to prescribe an oath of office": Provided, That if any person shall knowingly and falsely take and subscribe any oath in this act prescribed, such person so offending and being thereof duly convicted, shall be subject to the pains, penalties, and disabilities which by law are provided for the punishment of the crime of wilful and corrupt perjury.

SEC. 7. And be if further enacted, That all expenses incurred by the several commanding generals, or by virtue of any orders issued, or appointments made, by them, under or by virtue of this act, shall be paid out of any moneys in the treasury not otherwise appropriated.

SEC. 8. And be it further enacted, That the convention for each State shall prescribe the fees, salary, and compensation to be paid to all delegates and other officers and agents herein authorized or necessary to carry into effect the purposes of this act not herein otherwise provided for, and shall provide for the levy and collection of such taxes on the property in such State as may be necessary to pay the same.

SEC. 9. And be it further enacted, That the word "article," in the sixth section of the act to which this is supplementary, shall be construed to mean, "section."

SCHUYLER COLFAX, Speaker of the House of Representatives.

B. F. WADE, President of the Senate pro tempore.

CHAPTER XI.

PASSAGE OF THE RECONSTRUCTION ACT OVER THE PRESIDENT'S VETO—PLACED IN COMMAND OF THE FIFTH MILITARY DISTRICT—REMOVING OFFICERS—MY REASONS FOR SUCH ACTION—AFFAIRS IN LOUISIANA AND TEXAS—REMOVAL OF GOVERNOR WELLS—REVISION OF THE JURY LISTS—RELIEVED FROM THE COMMAND OF THE FIFTH MILITARY DISTRICT.

The first of the Reconstruction laws was passed March 2, 1867, and though vetoed by the President, such was the unanimity of loyal sentiment and the urgency demanding the measure, that the bill became a law over the veto the day the President returned it to Congress. March the 11th this law was published in General Orders No. 10, from the Headquarters of the Army, the same order assigning certain officers to take charge of the five military districts into which the States lately in rebellion were subdivided, I being announced as the commander of the Fifth Military District, which embraced Louisiana and Texas, a territory that had formed the main portion of my command since the close of the war.

Between the date of the Act and that of my assignment, the Louisiana Legislature, then in special session, had rejected a proposed repeal of an Act it had previously passed providing for an election of certain municipal officers in New Orleans. This election was set for March 11, but the mayor and the chief of police, together with General Mower, commanding the troops in the city, having expressed to me personally their fears that the public peace would be disturbed by the election, I, in this emergency, though not yet assigned to the district, assuming the authority which the

Act conferred on district commanders, declared that the election should not take place; that no polls should be opened on the day fixed; and that the whole matter would stand postponed till the district commander should be appointed, or special instructions be had. This, my first official act under the Reconstruction laws, was rendered necessary by the course of a body of obstructionists, who had already begun to give unequivocal indications of their intention to ignore the laws of Congress.

A copy of the order embodying the Reconstruction law, together with my assignment, having reached me a few days after, I regularly assumed control of the Fifth Military District on March 19, by an order wherein I declared the State and municipal governments of the district to be provisional only, and, under the provisions of the sixth section of the Act, subject to be controlled, modified, superseded, or abolished. I also announced that no removals from office would be made unless the incumbents failed to carry out the provisions of the law or impeded reorganization, or unless willful delays should necessitate a change, and added: "Pending the reorganization, it is, desirable and intended to create as little disturbance in the machinery of the various branches of the provisional governments as possible, consistent with the law of Congress and its successful execution, but this condition is dependent upon the disposition shown by the people, and upon the length of time required for reorganization."

Under these limitations Louisiana and Texas retained their former designations as military districts, the officers in command exercising their military powers as heretofore. In addition, these officers were to carry out in their respective commands all provisions of the law except those specially requiring the action of the district commander, and in cases of removals from and appointment to office.

In the course of legislation the first Reconstruction act, as I have heretofore noted, had been vetoed. On the very day of the veto, however, despite the President's adverse action, it passed each House of Congress by such an overwhelming majority as not only to give it the effect of law, but to prove clearly that the plan of reconstruction presented was, beyond question, the policy endorsed by the people of the country. It was, therefore, my determination to see to the law's zealous execution in my district, though I felt certain that the President would endeavor to embarrass me by every means in his power, not only on account of his pronounced personal hostility, but also because of his determination not to execute but to obstruct the measures enacted by Congress.

Having come to this conclusion, I laid down, as a rule for my guidance, the principle of non-interference with the provisional State governments, and though many appeals were made to have me rescind rulings of the courts, or interpose to forestall some presupposed action to be taken by them, my invariable reply was that I would not take cognizance of such matters, except in cases of absolute necessity. The same policy was announced also in reference to municipal affairs throughout the district, so long as the action of the local officers did not conflict with the law.

In a very short time, however, I was obliged to interfere in municipal matters in New Orleans, for it had become clearly apparent that several of the officials were, both by acts of omission and commission, ignoring the law, so on the 27th of March I removed from office the Mayor, John T. Monroe; the Judge of the First District Court, E. Abell; and the Attorney-General of the State, Andrew S. Herron; at the same time appointing to the respective offices thus vacated Edward Heath, W. W. Howe, and B. L. Lynch. The officials thus removed had taken upon themselves from the start to pronounce the Reconstruction acts unconstitutional, and to advise such a course of obstruction that I found it necessary at an early date to replace them by men in sympathy with the law, in order to make plain my determination to have its provisions enforced. The President at once made inquiry, through General Grant, for the cause of the removal, and I replied:

"HEADQUARTERS FIFTH MILITARY DISTRICT,
"New Orleans, La., April 19, 1867.

"GENERAL: On the 27th day of March last I removed from office Judge E. Abell, of the Criminal Court of New Orleans; Andrew S. Herron, Attorney-General of the State of Louisiana; and John T. Monroe, Mayor of the City of New Orleans. These removals were made under the powers granted me in what is usually termed the 'military bill,' passed March 2, 1867, by the Congress of the United States.

"I did not deem it necessary to give any reason for the removal of these men, especially after the investigations made by the military board on the massacre Of July 30, 1866, and the report of the congressional committee on the same massacre; but as some inquiry has been made for the cause of removal, I would respectfully state as follows:

"The court over which judge Abell presided is the only criminal court in the city of New Orleans, and for a period of at least nine months previous to the riot of July 30 he had been educating a large portion of the community to the perpetration of this outrage, by almost promising no prosecution in his court against the offenders, in case such an event occurred. The records of his court will show that he fulfilled his promise, as not one of the guilty has been prosecuted.

"In reference to Andrew J. Herron, Attorney-General of the State of Louisiana, I considered it his duty to indict these men before this criminal court. This he failed to do, but went so far as to attempt to impose on the good sense of the whole nation by indicting the victims of the riot instead of the rioters; in other words, making the innocent guilty and the guilty innocent. He was therefore, in my belief, an able coadjutor with judge Abell in bringing on the massacre of July 30.

"Mayor Monroe controlled the element engaged in this riot, and when backed by an attorney-general who would not prosecute the guilty, and a judge who advised the grand jury to find the innocent guilty and let the murderers go free, felt secure in engaging his police force in the riot and massacre.

"With these three men exercising a large influence over the worst elements of the population of this city, giving to those elements an immunity for riot and bloodshed, the general-in-chief will see how insecurely I felt in letting them occupy their respective positions in the troubles which might occur in registration and voting in the reorganization of this State.

"I am, General, very respectfully, your obedient servant,

"P. H. SHERIDAN,

"Major-General U. S. A.

"GENERAL U. S. GRANT,

"Commanding Armies of the United States, "Washington, D. C."

To General Grant my reasons were satisfactory, but not so to the President, who took no steps, however, to rescind my action, for he knew that the removals were commended by well-nigh the entire community in the city, for it will be understood that Mr. Johnson was, through his friends and adherents in Louisiana and Texas, kept constantly advised of every step taken by me. Many of these persons were active and open opponents of mine, while others were spies, doing their work so secretly and quickly that sometimes Mr. Johnson knew of my official acts before I could report them to General Grant.

The supplemental Reconstruction act which defined the method of reconstruction became a law despite the President's veto on March 23. This was a curative act, authorizing elections and prescribing methods of registration. When it reached me officially I began measures for carrying out its provisions, and on the 28th of March issued an order to the effect that no elections for the State, parish, or municipal officers would be held in Louisiana until the provisions of the laws of Congress entitled "An act to provide for the more efficient government of the rebel States," and of the act supplemental thereto, should have been complied with. I also announced that until elections were held in accordance with these acts, the law of the Legislature of the State providing for the holding over of those persons whose terms of office otherwise would have expired, would govern in all cases excepting only those special ones in which I myself might take action. There was one parish, Livingston, which this order did no reach in time to prevent the election previously ordered there, and which therefore took place, but by a supplemental order this election was declare null and void.

In April I began the work of administering the Supplemental Law, which, under certain condition of eligibility, required a registration of the voter of the State, for the purpose of electing delegate to a Constitutional convention. It therefore became necessary to appoint Boards of Registration throughout the election districts, and on April 10 the boards for the Parish of Orleans were given out, those for the other parishes being appointed ten days later. Before announcing these boards, I had asked to be advised definitely as to what persons were disfranchised by the law, and was directed by General Grant to act upon my own interpretation of it, pending an opinion expected shortly from the Attorney-General—Mr. Henry Stanbery—so, for the guidance of the boards, I gave the following instructions:

"HEADQUARTERS FIFTH MILITARY DISTRICT.
"New Orleans, La., April 10, 1867.
"Special Orders, No. 15.
"....In obedience to the directions contained in the first section of the Law of Congress entitled "An Act supplemental to an Act entitled 'An Act

to provide for the more efficient government of the rebel States'" the registration of the legal voters, according to that law in the Parish of Orleans, will be commenced on the 15th instant, and must be completed by the 15th of May.

"The four municipal districts of the City of New Orleans and the Parish of Orleans, right bank (Algiers), will each constitute a Registration district. Election precincts will remain as at present constituted.

"....Each member of the Board of Registers, before commencing his duties, will file in the office of the Assistant-Inspector-General at these headquarters, the oath required in the sixth section of the Act referred to, and be governed in the execution of his duty by the provisions of the first section of that Act, faithfully administering the oath therein prescribed to each person registered.

"Boards of Registers will immediately select suitable offices within their respective districts, having reference to convenience and facility of registration, and will enter upon their duties on the day designated. Each Board will be entitled to two clerks. Office-hours for registration will be from 8 o'clock till 12 A. M., and from 4 till 7 P. M.

"When elections are ordered, the Board of Registers for each district will designate the number of polls and the places where they shall be opened in the election precincts within its district, appoint the commissioners and other officers necessary for properly conducting the elections, and will superintend the same.

"They will also receive from the commissioners of elections of the different precincts the result of the vote, consolidate the same, and forward it to the commanding general.

"Registers and all officers connected with elections will be held to a rigid accountability and will be subject to trial by military commission for fraud, or unlawful or improper conduct in the performance of their duties. Their rate of compensation and manner of payment will be in accordance with the provisions of sections six and seven of the supplemental act.

"....Every male citizen of the United States, twenty-one years old and upward, of whatever race, color, or previous condition, who has been resident in the State of Louisiana for one year and Parish of Orleans for three months previous to the date at which he presents himself for registration, and who has not been disfranchised by act of Congress or for felony at common law, shall, after having taken and subscribed the oath prescribed in the first section of the act herein referred to, be entitled to be, and shall be, registered as a legal voter in the Parish of Orleans and State of Louisiana.

"Pending the decision of the Attorney-General of the United States on the question as to who are disfranchised by law, registers will give the most rigid interpretation to the law, and exclude from registration every person about whose right to vote there may be a doubt. Any person so excluded who may, under the decision of the Attorney-General, be entitled to vote, shall be permitted to register after that decision is received, due notice of which will be given.

"By command of Major-General P. H. SHERIDAN,
"GEO. L. HARTSUFF,
"Assistant Adjutant-General."

The parish Boards of Registration were composed of three members each. Ability to take what was known as the "ironclad oath" was the qualification exacted of the members, and they were prohibited from becoming candidates for office. In the execution of their duties they were to be governed by the provisions of the supplemental act. It was also made one of their functions to designate the number and location of the polling-places in the several districts, to appoint commissioners for receiving the votes and in general to attend to such other matters as were necessary, in order properly to conduct the voting, and afterward to receive from the commissioners the result of the vote and forward it to my headquarters. These registers, and all other officers having to do with elections, were to be held to a rigid accountability, and be subject to trial by military commission for fraud or unlawful or improper conduct in the performance of their duties; and in order to be certain that the Registration Boards performed their work faithfully and intelligently, officers of the army were appointed as supervisors. To this end the parishes were grouped together conveniently in temporary districts, each officer having from three to five parishes to supervise. The programme thus mapped out for carrying out the law in Louisiana was likewise adhered to in Texas, and indeed was followed as a model in some of the other military districts.

Although Military Commissions were fully authorized by the Reconstruction acts, yet I did not favor their use in governing the district, and probably would never have convened one had these acts been observed in good faith. I much preferred that the civil courts, and the State and municipal authorities already in existence, should perform their functions without military control or interference, but occasionally, because the civil authorities neglected their duty, I was obliged to resort to this means to ensure the punishment Of offenders. At this time the condition of the negroes in Texas and Louisiana was lamentable, though, in fact, not worse than that of the few white loyalists who had been true to the Union during the war. These last were singled out as special objects of attack, and were, therefore, obliged at all times to be on the alert for the protection of their lives and property. This was the natural outcome of Mr. Johnson's defiance of Congress, coupled with the sudden conversion to his cause of persons in the North—who but a short time before had been his bitterest enemies; for all this had aroused among the disaffected element new hopes of power and place, hopes of being at once put in political control again, with a resumption of their functions in State and National matters without any preliminary authorization by Congress. In fact, it was not only hoped, but expected, that things were presently to go on just as if there had been no war.

In the State of Texas there were in 1865 about 200,000 of the colored race—roughly, a third of the entire population—while in Louisiana there were not less than 350,000, or more than one-half of all the people in the State. Until the enactment of the Reconstruction laws these negroes were without rights, and though they had been liberated by the war, Mr. Johnson's policy now proposed that they should have no political status at all, and consequently be at the mercy of a people who, recently their masters, now seemed to look upon them as the authors of all the misfortunes that had come upon the land. Under these circumstances the blacks naturally turned for protection to those who had been the means of their liberation, and it would have been little less than inhuman to deny them sympathy. Their freedom had been given them, and it was the plain duty of those in authority to make it secure, and screen them from the bitter political resentment that beset them, and to see that they had a fair chance in the battle of life. Therefore, when outrages and murders grew frequent, and the aid of the military power was an absolute necessity for the protection of life, I employed it unhesitatingly— the guilty parties being brought to trial before military commissions—and for a time, at least, there occurred a halt in the march of terrorism inaugurated by the people whom Mr. Johnson had deluded.

The first, Military Commission was convened to try the case of John W. Walker, charged with shooting a negro in the parish of St. John. The proper civil authorities had made no effort to arrest Walker, and even connived at his escape, so I had him taken into custody in New Orleans, and ordered him tried, the commission finding him guilty, and sentencing him to confinement in the penitentiary for six months. This shooting was the third occurrence of the kind that had taken place in St. John's parish, a negro being wounded in each case, and it was plain that the intention was to institute there a practice of intimidation which should be effective to subject the freedmen to the will of their late masters, whether in making labor contracts, or in case these newly enfranchised negroes should evince a disposition to avail themselves of the privilege to vote.

The trial and conviction of Walker, and of one or two others for similiar outrages, soon put a stop to every kind of "bull-dozing" in the country parishes; but about this time I discovered that many members of the police force in New Orleans were covertly intimidating the freedmen there, and preventing their appearance at the registration offices, using milder methods than had obtained in the country, it is true, but none the less effective.

Early in 1866 the Legislature had passed an act which created for the police of New Orleans a residence qualification, the object of which was to discharge and exclude from the force ex-Union soldiers. This of course would make room for the appointment of ex-Confederates, and Mayor Monroe had not been slow in enforcing the provisions of the law. It was, in fact, a result of this enactment that the police was so reorganized as to become the willing and efficient tool which it proved to be in the riot of 1866; and having still the same personnel, it was now in shape to prevent registration by threats, unwarranted arrests, and by various other influences, all operating to keep the timid blacks away from the registration places.

That the police were taking a hand in this practice of repression, I first discovered by the conduct of the assistant to the chief of the body, and at once removed the offender, but finding this ineffectual I annulled that part of the State law fixing the five years' residence restriction, and restored the two years' qualification, thus enabling Mayor Heath, who by my appointment had succeeded Monroe, to organize the force anew, and take about one-half of its members from ex-Union soldiers who when discharged had settled in New Orleans. This action put an end to intimidation in the parish of Orleans; and now were put in operation in all sections the processes provided by the supplemental Reconstruction law for the summoning of a convention to form a Constitution preparatory to the readmission of the State, and I was full of hope that there would now be much less difficulty in administering the trust imposed by Congress.

During the two years previous great damage had been done the agricultural interests of Louisiana by the overflow of the Mississippi, the levees being so badly broken as to require extensive repairs, and the Legislature of 1866 had appropriated for the purpose $4,000,000, to be raised by an issue of bonds. This money was to be disbursed by a Board of Levee Commissioners then in existence, but the term of service of these commissioners, and the law creating the board, would expire in the spring of 1867. In order to overcome this difficulty the Legislature passed a bill continuing the commissioners in office but as the act was passed inside of ten days before the adjournment of the Legislature, Governor Wells pocketed the bill, and it failed to become a law. The Governor then appointed a board of his own, without any warrant of law whatever. The old commissioners refused to recognize this new board, and of course a conflict of authority ensued, which, it was clear, would lead to vicious results if allowed to continue; so, as the people of the State had no confidence in either of the boards, I decided to end the contention summarily by appointing an entirely new commission, which would disburse the money honestly, and further the real purpose for which it had been appropriated. When I took this course the legislative board acquiesced, but Governor Wells immediately requested the President to revoke my order, which, however, was not done, but meanwhile the Secretary of War directed me to suspend all proceedings in the matter, and make a report of the facts. I complied in the following telegram:

"HEADQUARTERS FIFTH MILITARY DISTRICT,
"NEW ORLEANS, La., June 3, 1867.

"SIR: I have the honor to acknowledge the receipt of your telegram of this date in reference to the Levee Commissioners in this State.

"The following were my reasons for abolishing the two former boards, although I intended that my order should be sufficiently explanatory:

"Previous to the adjournment of the Legislature last winter it passed an act continuing the old Levee board in office, so that the four millions of dollars ($4,000,000) in bonds appropriated by the Legislature might be disbursed by a board of rebellious antecedents.

"After its adjournment the Governor of the State appointed a board of his own, in violation of this act, and made the acknowledgment to me in person that his object was to disburse the money in the interest of his own party by securing for it the vote of the employees at the time of election.

"The board continued in office by the Legislature refused to turn over to the Governor's board, and each side appealed to me to sustain it, which I would not do. The question must then have gone to the courts, which, according to the Governor's judgment when he was appealing to me to be sustained, would require one year for decision. Meantime the State was overflowed, the Levee boards tied up by political chicanery, and nothing done to relieve the poor people, now fed by the charity of the Government and charitable associations of the North.

"To obviate this trouble, and to secure to the overflowed districts of the State the immediate relief which the honest disbursement of the four millions ($4,000,000) would give, my order dissolving both boards was issued.

"I say now, unequivocally, that Governor Wells is a political trickster and a dishonest man. I have seen him myself, when I first came to this command, turn out all the Union men who had supported the Government, and put in their stead rebel soldiers who had not yet doffed their gray uniform. I have seen him again, during the July riot of 1866, skulk away where I could not find him to give him a guard, instead of coming out as a manly representative of the State and joining those who were preserving the peace. I have watched him since, and his conduct has been as sinuous as the mark left in the dust by the movement of a snake.

"I say again that he is dishonest, and that dishonesty is more than must be expected of me.

"P. H. SHERIDAN,
"Major-General, U. S. A.

"Hon. E. M. STANTON,
"Secretary of War, Washington, D. C."

The same day that I sent my report to the Secretary of War I removed from office Governor Wells himself, being determined to bear no longer with the many obstructions he had placed in the way of reorganizing the civil affairs of the State. I was also satisfied that he was unfit to retain the place, since he was availing himself of every opportunity to work political ends beneficial to himself. In this instance Wells protested to me against his removal, and also appealed to the President for an opinion of the Attorney-General as to my power in the case; and doubtless he would have succeeded in retaining his office, but for the fact that the President had been informed by General James B. Steadman and others placed to watch me that Wells was wholly unworthy.

"NEW ORLEANS, June 19, 1867.
"ANDREW JOHNSON, President United States,
"Washington City:

"Lewis D. Campbell leaves New Orleans for home this evening. Want of respect for Governor Wells personally, alone represses the expression of indignation felt by all honest and sensible men at the unwarranted usurpation of General Sheridan in removing the civil officers of Louisiana. It is believed here that you will reinstate Wells. He is a bad man, and has no influence.

"I believe Sheridan made the removals to embarrass you, believing the feeling at the North would sustain him. My conviction is that on account of the bad character of Wells and Monroe, you ought not to reinstate any who have been removed, because you cannot reinstate any without reinstating all, but you ought to prohibit the exercise of this power in the future.

"Respectfully yours,
"JAMES B. STEADMAN."

I appointed Mr. Thomas J. Durant as Wells's successor, but he declining, I then appointed Mr. Benjamin F. Flanders, who, after I had sent a staff-officer to forcibly eject Wells in case of necessity, took possession of the Governor's office. Wells having vacated, Governor Flanders began immediately the exercise of his duties in sympathy with the views of Congress, and I then notified General Grant that I thought he need have no further apprehension about the condition of affairs in Louisiana, as my appointee was a man of such integrity and ability that I already felt relieved of half my labor. I also stated in the same despatch that nothing would answer in Louisiana but a bold and firm course, and that in taking such a one I felt that I was strongly supported; a statement that was then correct, for up to this period the better classes were disposed to accept the

Congressional plan of reconstruction.

During the controversy over the Levee Commissioners, and the correspondence regarding the removal of Governor Wells, registration had gone on under the rules laid down for the boards. The date set for closing the books was the 3oth of June, but in the parish of Orleans the time was extended till the 15th of July. This the President considered too short a period, and therefore directed the registry lists not to be closed before the 1st of August, unless there was some good reason to the contrary. This was plainly designed to keep the books open in order that under the Attorney-General's interpretation of the Reconstruction laws, published June 20, many persons who had been excluded by the registration boards could yet be registered, so I decided to close the registration, unless required by the President unconditionally, and in specific orders, to extend the time. My motives were manifold, but the main reasons were that as two and a half months had been given already, the number of persons who, under the law, were qualified for registry was about exhausted; and because of the expense I did not feel warranted in keeping up the boards longer, as I said, "to suit new issues coming in at the eleventh hour," which would but open a "broad macadamized road for perjury and fraud."

When I thus stated what I intended to do, the opinion of the Attorney-General had not yet been received. When it did reach me it was merely in the form of a circular signed by Adjutant-General Townsend, and had no force of law. It was not even sent as an order, nor was it accompanied by any instructions, or by anything except the statement that it was transmitted to the 11 respective military commanders for their information, in order that there might be uniformity in the execution of the Reconstruction acts. To adopt Mr. Stanbery's interpretation of the law and reopen registration accordingly, would defeat the purpose of Congress, as well as add to my perplexities. Such a course would also require that the officers appointed by me for the performance of specified duties, under laws which I was empowered to interpret and enforce, should receive their guidance and instructions from an unauthorized source, so on communicating with General Grant as to how I should act, he directed me to enforce my own construction of the military bill until ordered to do otherwise.

Therefore the registration continued as I had originally directed, and nothing having been definitely settled at Washington in relation to my extending the time, on the 10th of July I ordered all the registration boards to select, immediately, suitable persons to act as commissioners of election, and at the same time specified the number of each set of commissioners, designated the polling-places, gave notice that two days would be allowed for voting, and followed this with an order discontinuing registration the 31st of July, and then another appointing the 27th and 28th of September as the time for the election of delegates to the State convention.

In accomplishing the registration there had been little opposition from the mass of the people, but the press of New Orleans, and the office-holders and office-seekers in the State generally, antagonized the work bitterly and violently, particularly after the promulgation of the opinion of the Attorney-General. These agitators condemned everybody and everything connected with the Congressional plan of reconstruction; and the pernicious influence thus exerted was manifested in various ways, but most notably in the selection of persons to compose the jury lists in the country parishes it also tempted certain municipal officers in New Orleans to perform illegal acts that would seriously have affected the credit of the city had matters not been promptly corrected by the summary removal from office of the comptroller and the treasurer, who had already issued a quarter of a million dollars in illegal certificates. On learning of this unwarranted and unlawful proceeding, Mayor Heath demanded an investigation by the Common Council, but this body, taking its cue from the evident intention of the President to render abortive the Reconstruction acts, refused the mayor's demand. Then he tried to have the treasurer and comptroller restrained by injunction, but the city attorney, under the same inspiration as the council, declined to sue out a writ, and the attorney being supported in this course by nearly all the other officials, the mayor was left helpless in his endeavors to preserve the city's credit. Under such circumstances he took the only step left him—recourse to the military commander; and after looking into the matter carefully I decided, in the early part of August, to give the mayor officials who would not refuse to make an investigation of the illegal issue of certificates, and to this end I removed the treasurer, surveyor, comptroller, city attorney, and twenty-two of the aldermen; these officials, and all of their assistants, having reduced the financial credit of New Orleans to a disordered condition, and also having made efforts—and being then engaged in such—to hamper the execution of the Reconstruction laws.

This action settled matters in the city, but subsequently I had to remove some officials in the parishes—among them a justice of the peace and a sheriff in the parish of Rapides; the justice for refusing to permit negro witnesses to testify in a certain murder case, and for allowing the murderer, who had foully killed a colored man, to walk out of his court on bail in the insignificant sum of five hundred dollars; and the sheriff, for conniving at the escape from jail of another alleged murderer. Finding, however, even after these removals, that in the country districts murderers and other criminals went unpunished, provided the offenses were against negroes merely (since the jurors were selected exclusively from the whites, and often embraced those excluded from the exercise of the election franchise) I, having full authority under the Reconstruction laws, directed such a revision of the jury lists as would reject from them every man not eligible for registration as a voter. This order was issued August 24, and on its promulgation the President relieved me from duty and assigned General Hancock as my successor.

"HEADQUARTERS FIFTH MILITARY DISTRICT,
"NEW ORLEANS, LA., August 24, 1867.
"SPECIAL ORDERS, No. 125.

"The registration of voters of the State of Louisiana, according to the law of Congress, being complete, it is hereby ordered that no person who is not registered in accordance with said law shall be considered as, a duly qualified voter of the State of Louisiana. All persons duly registered as above, and no others, are consequently eligible, under the laws of the State of Louisiana, to serve as jurors in any of the courts of the State.

"The necessary revision of the jury lists will immediately be made by the proper officers.

"All the laws of the State respecting exemptions, etc., from jury duty will remain in force.

"By command of Major-General P. H. SHERIDAN.
"GEO. L. HARTNUFF, Asst. Adj't-General."

Pending the arrival of General Hancock, I turned over the command of the district September 1 to General Charles Griffin; but he dying of yellow fever, General J. A. Mower succeeded him, and retained command till November 29, on which date General Hancock assumed control. Immediately after Hancock took charge, he revoked my order of August

24 providing for a revision of the jury lists; and, in short, President Johnson's policy now became supreme, till Hancock himself was relieved in March, 1868.

My official connection with the reconstruction of Louisiana and Texas practically closed with this order concerning the jury lists. In my judgment this had become a necessity, for the disaffected element, sustained as it was by the open sympathy of the President, had grown so determined in its opposition to the execution of the Reconstruction acts that I resolved to remove from place and power all obstacles; for the summer's experience had convinced me that in no other way could the law be faithfully administered.

The President had long been dissatisfied with my course; indeed, he had harbored personal enmity against me ever since he perceived that he could not bend me to an acceptance of the false position in which he had tried to place me by garbling my report of the riot of 1866. When Mr. Johnson decided to remove me, General Grant protested in these terms, but to no purpose:

"HEADQUARTERS ARMIES OF THE UNITED STATES,
"WASHINGTON, D. C., August 17, 1867

"SIR: I am in receipt of your order of this date directing the assignment of General G. H. Thomas to the command of the Fifth Military District, General Sheridan to the Department of the Missouri, and General Hancock to the Department of the Cumberland; also your note of this date (enclosing these instructions), saying: 'Before you issue instructions to carry into effect the enclosed order, I would be pleased to hear any suggestions you may deem necessary respecting the assignments to which the order refers.'

"I am pleased to avail myself of this invitation to urge—earnestly urge—urge in the name of a patriotic people, who have sacrificed hundreds of thousands of loyal lives and thousands of millions of treasure to preserve the integrity and union of this country—that this order be not insisted on. It is unmistakably the expressed wish of the country that General Sheridan should not be removed from his present command.

"This is a republic where the will of the people is the law of the land. I beg that their voice may be heard.

"General Sheridan has performed his civil duties faithfully and intelligently. His removal will only be regarded as an effort to defeat the laws of Congress. It will be interpreted by the unreconstructed element in the South—those who did all they could to break up this Government by arms, and now wish to be the only element consulted as to the method of restoring order—as a triumph. It will embolden them to renewed opposition to the will of the loyal masses, believing that they have the Executive with them.

"The services of General Thomas in battling for the Union entitle him to some consideration. He has repeatedly entered his protest against being assigned to either of the five military districts, and especially to being assigned to relieve General Sheridan.

"There are military reasons, pecuniary reasons, and above all, patriotic reasons, why this should not be insisted upon.

"I beg to refer to a letter marked 'private,' which I wrote to the President when first consulted on the subject of the change in the War Department. It bears upon the subject of this removal, and I had hoped would have prevented it.

"I have the honor to be, with great respect, your obedient servant,
"U. S. GRANT,
"General U. S. A., Secretary of War ad interim.

"His Excellency A. JOHNSON,
"President of the United States."

I was ordered to command the Department of the Missouri (General Hancock, as already noted, finally becoming my successor in the Fifth Military District), and left New Orleans on the 5th of September. I was not loath to go. The kind of duty I had been performing in Louisiana and Texas was very trying under the most favorable circumstances, but all the more so in my case, since I had to contend against the obstructions which the President placed in the way from persistent opposition to the acts of Congress as well as from antipathy to me—which obstructions he interposed with all the boldness and aggressiveness of his peculiar nature.

On more than one occasion while I was exercising this command, impurity of motive was imputed to me, but it has never been truthfully shown (nor can it ever be) that political or corrupt influences of any kind controlled me in any instance. I simply tried to carry out, without fear or favor, the Reconstruction acts as they came to me. They were intended to disfranchise certain persons, and to enfranchise certain others, and, till decided otherwise, were the laws of the land; and it was my duty to execute them faithfully, without regard, on the one hand, for those upon whom it was thought they bore so heavily, nor, on the other, for this or that political party, and certainly without deference to those persons sent to Louisiana to influence my conduct of affairs.

Some of these missionaries were high officials, both military and civil, and I recall among others a visit made me in 1866 by a distinguished friend of the President, Mr. Thomas A. Hendricks. The purpose of his coming was to convey to me assurances of the very high esteem in which I was held by the President, and to explain personally Mr. Johnson's plan of reconstruction, its flawless constitutionality, and so on. But being on the ground, I had before me the exhibition of its practical working, saw the oppression and excesses growing out of it, and in the face of these experiences even Mr. Hendricks's persuasive eloquence was powerless to convince me of its beneficence. Later General Lovell H. Rousseau came down on a like mission, but was no more successful than Mr. Hendricks.

During the whole period that I commanded in Louisiana and Texas my position was a most unenviable one. The service was unusual, and the nature of it scarcely to be understood by those not entirely familiar with the conditions existing immediately after the war. In administering the affairs of those States, I never acted except by authority, and always from conscientious motives. I tried to guard the rights of everybody in accordance with the law. In this I was supported by General Grant and opposed by President Johnson. The former had at heart, above every other consideration, the good of his country, and always sustained me with approval and kind suggestions. The course pursued by the President was exactly the opposite, and seems to prove that in the whole matter of reconstruction he was governed less by patriotic motives than by personal ambitions. Add to this his natural obstinacy of character and personal enmity toward me, and no surprise should be occasioned when I say that I heartily welcomed the order that lifted from me my unsought burden.

CHAPTER XII.
AT FORT LEAVENWORTH—THE TREATY OF MEDICINE LODGE—GOING TO FORT DODGE—DISCONTENTED INDIANS—INDIAN OUTRAGES—A DELEGATION OF CHIEFS—TERRIBLE INDIAN RAID—DEATH OF COMSTOCK—VAST HERDS OF BUFFALO—PRE PARING FOR A WINTER CAMPAIGN—MEETING "BUFFALO BILL"—HE UNDERTAKES A DANGEROUS TASK—FORSYTH'S GALLANT FIGHT—RESCUED.

The headquarters of the military department to which I was assigned when relieved from duty at New Orleans was at Fort Leavenworth, Kansas, and on the 5th of September I started for that post. In due time I reached St. Louis, and stopped there a day to accept an ovation tendered in approval of the course I had pursued in the Fifth Military District—a public demonstration apparently of the most sincere and hearty character.

From St. Louis to Leavenworth took but one night, and the next day I technically complied with my orders far enough to permit General Hancock to leave the department, so that he might go immediately to New Orleans if he so desired, but on account of the yellow fever epidemic then prevailing, he did not reach the city till late in November.

My new command was one of the four military departments that composed the geographical division then commanded by Lieutenant-General Sherman. This division had been formed in 1866, with a view to controlling the Indians west of the Missouri River, they having become very restless and troublesome because of the building of the Pacific railroads through their hunting-grounds, and the encroachments of pioneers, who began settling in middle and western Kansas and eastern

Colorado immediately after the war.

My department embraced the States of Missouri and Kansas, the Indian Territory, and New Mexico. Part of this section of country—western Kansas particularly—had been frequently disturbed and harassed during two or three years past, the savages every now and then massacring an isolated family, boldly attacking the surveying and construction parties of the Kansas-Pacific railroad, sweeping down on emigrant trains, plundering and burning stage-stations and the like along the Smoky Hill route to Denver and the Arkansas route to New Mexico.

However, when I relieved Hancock, the department was comparatively quiet. Though some military operations had been conducted against the hostile tribes in the early part of the previous summer, all active work was now suspended in the attempt to conclude a permanent peace with the Cheyennes, Arapahoes, Kiowas, and Comanches, in compliance with the act of Congress creating what was known as the Indian Peace Commission of 1867.

Under these circumstances there was little necessity for my remaining at Leavenworth, and as I was much run down in health from the Louisiana climate, in which I had been obliged to live continuously for three summers (one of which brought epidemic cholera, and another a scourge of yellow fever), I took a leave of absence for a few months, leaving Colonel A. J. Smith, of the Seventh Cavalry, temporarily in charge of my command.

On this account I did not actually go on duty in the department of the Missouri till March, 1868. On getting back I learned that the negotiations of the Peace Commissioners held at Medicine Lodge, about seventy miles south of Fort Larned had resulted in a treaty with the Cheyennes, Arapahoes, Kiowas, and Comanches, by which agreement it was supposed all troubles had been settled. The compact, as concluded, contained numerous provisions, the most important to us being one which practically relinquished the country between the Arkansas and Platte rivers for white settlement; another permitted the peaceable construction of the Pacific railroads through the same region; and a third requiring the tribes signing the treaty to retire to reservations allotted them in the Indian Territory. Although the chiefs and head-men were well-nigh unanimous in ratifying these concessions, it was discovered in the spring of 1868 that many of the young men were bitterly opposed to what had been done, and claimed that most of the signatures had been obtained by misrepresentation and through proffers of certain annuities, and promises of arms and ammunition to be issued in the spring of 1868. This grumbling was very general in extent, and during the winter found outlet in occasional marauding, so, fearing a renewal of the pillaging and plundering at an early day, to prepare myself for the work evidently ahead the first thing I did on assuming permanent command was to make a trip to Fort Larned and Fort Dodge, near which places the bulk of the Indians had congregated on Pawnee and Walnut creeks. I wanted to get near enough to the camps to find out for myself the actual state of feeling among the savages, and also to familiarize myself with the characteristics of the Plains Indians, for my previous experience had been mainly with mountain tribes on the Pacific coast. Fort Larned I found too near the camps for my purpose, its proximity too readily inviting unnecessary "talks," so I remained here but a day or two, and then went on to Dodge, which, though considerably farther away from the camps, was yet close enough to enable us to obtain easily information of all that was going on.

It took but a few days at Dodge to discover that great discontent existed about the Medicine Lodge concessions, to see that the young men were chafing and turbulent, and that it would require much tact and good management on the part of the Indian Bureau to persuade the four tribes to go quietly to their reservations, under an agreement which, when entered into, many of them protested had not been fully understood.

A few hours after my arrival a delegation of prominent chiefs called on me and proposed a council, where they might discuss their grievances, and thus bring to the notice of the Government the alleged wrongs done them; but this I refused, because Congress had delegated to the Peace Commission the whole matter of treating with them, and a council might lead only to additional complications. My refusal left them without hope of securing better terms, or of even delaying matters longer; so henceforth they were more than ever reckless and defiant. Denunciations of the treaty became outspoken, and as the young braves grew more and more insolent every day, it amounted to conviction that, unless by some means the irritation was allayed, hostilities would surely be upon us when the buffalo returned to their summer feeding-grounds between the Arkansas and the Platte.

The principal sufferers in this event would be the settlers in middle and western Kansas, who, entirely ignorant of the dangers hanging over them, were laboring to build up homes in a new country. Hence the maintenance of peace was much to be desired, if it could be secured without too great concessions, and although I would not meet the different tribes in a formal council, yet, to ward off from settlers as much as possible the horrors of savage warfare, I showed, by resorting to persuasive methods, my willingness to temporize a good deal. An abundant supply of rations is usually effective to keep matters quiet in such cases, so I fed them pretty freely, and also endeavored to control them through certain men who, I found, because of former associations, had their confidence. These men, employed as scouts, or interpreters, were Mr. William Comstock, Mr. Abner S. Grover, and Mr. Richard Parr. They had lived on the Plains for many years with different tribes of Indians, had trapped and hunted with them, and knew all the principal chiefs and headmen. Through such influences, I thought I saw good chances of preserving peace, and of inducing the discontented to go quietly to their reservations in the Indian Territory as soon as General Hazen, the representative of the Peace Commissioners, was ready to conduct them there from Fort Larned.

Before returning to Leavenworth I put my mediators (as I may call them) under charge of an officer of the army, Lieutenant F. W. Beecher, a very intelligent man, and directed him to send them out to visit among the different tribes, in order to explain what was intended by the treaty of Medicine Lodge, and to make every effort possible to avert hostilities. Under these instructions Comstock and Grover made it their business to go about among the Cheyennes—the most warlike tribe of all—then camping about the headwaters of Pawnee and Walnut creeks, and also to the north and west of Fort Wallace, while Parr spent his time principally with the Kiowas and Comanches.

From the different posts—Wallace, Dodge, and Larned Lieutenant Beecher kept up communication with all three scouts, and through him I heard from them at least once a week. Every now and then some trouble along the railroad or stage routes would be satisfactorily adjusted and quiet restored, and matters seemed to be going on very well, the warm weather bringing the grass and buffalo in plenty, and still no outbreak, nor any act of downright hostility. So I began to hope that we should succeed in averting trouble till the favorite war season of the Indians was over, but the early days of August rudely ended our fancied tranquility.

In July the encampments about Fort Dodge began to break up, each band or tribe moving off to some new location north of the Arkansas, instead of toward its proper reservation to the south of that river. Then I learned presently that a party of Cheyennes had made a raid on the Kaws—a band of friendly Indians living near Council Grove—and stolen their horses, and also robbed the houses of several white people near Council Grove. This raid was the beginning of the Indian war of 1868. Immediately following it, the Comanches and Kiowas came to Fort Larned to receive their annuities, expecting to get also the arms and ammunition promised them at Medicine Lodge, but the raid to Council Grove having been reported to the Indian Department, the issue of arms was suspended till reparation was made. This action of the Department greatly incensed the savages, and the agent's offer of the annuities without guns and pistols was insolently refused, the Indians sulking back to their camps, the young men giving themselves up to war-dances, and to powwows with "medicine-men," till all hope of control was gone.

Brevet Brigadier-General Alfred Sully, an officer of long experience in Indian matters, who at this time was in command of the District of the Arkansas, which embraced Forts Larned and Dodge, having notified me of these occurrences at Larned, and expressed the opinion that the Indians were bent on mischief, I directed him there immediately to act against them. After he reached Larned, the chances for peace appeared more favorable. The Indians came to see him, and protested that it was only a few bad young men who had been depredating, and that all would be well and the young men held in check if the agent would but issue the arms and ammunition. Believing their promises, Sully thought that the delivery of the arms would solve all the difficulties, so on his advice the agent turned them over along with the annuities, the Indians this time condescendingly accepting.

This issue of arms and ammunition was a fatal mistake; Indian diplomacy had overreached Sully's experience, and even while the delivery was in progress a party of warriors had already begun a raid of murder and rapine, which for acts of devilish cruelty perhaps has no parallel in savage warfare. The party consisted of about two hundred Cheyennes and a few Arapahoes, with twenty Sioux who had been visiting their friends, the Cheyennes. As near as could be ascertained, they organized and left their camps along Pawnee Creek about the 3d of August. Traveling northeast, they skirted around Fort Harker, and made their first appearance among the settlers in the Saline Valley, about thirty miles north of that post. Professing friendship and asking food at the farm-houses, they saw the unsuspecting occupants comply by giving all they could spare from their scanty stores. Knowing the Indian's inordinate fondness for coffee, particularly when well sweetened, they even served him this luxury freely. With this the demons began their devilish work. Pretending to be indignant because it was served them in tin cups, they threw the hot contents into the women's faces, and then, first making prisoners of the men, they, one after another, ravished the women till the victims became insensible. For some inexplicable reason the two farmers were neither killed nor carried off, so after the red fiends had gone, the unfortunate women were brought in to Fort Harker, their arrival being the first intimation to the military that hostilities had actually begun.

Leaving the Saline, this war-party crossed over to the valley of the Solomon, a more thickly settled region, and where the people were in better circumstances, their farms having been started two or three years before. Unaware of the hostile character of the raiders, the people here received them in the friendliest way, providing food, and even giving them ammunition, little dreaming of what was impending. These kindnesses were requited with murder and pillage, and worse, for all the women who fell into their hands were subjected to horrors indescribable by words. Here also the first murders were committed, thirteen men and two women being killed. Then, after burning five houses and stealing all the horses they could find, they turned back toward the Saline, carrying away as prisoners two little girls named Bell, who have never been heard of since.

It was probably the intention to finish, as they marched back to the south, the devilish work begun on the Saline, but before they reached that valley on the return, the victims left there originally had fled to Fort Harker, as already explained, and Captain Benteen was now nearing the little settlement with a troop of cavalry, which he had hurriedly marched from Fort Zarah. The savages were attacking the house of a Mr. Schermerhorn, where a few of the settlers had collected for defense, when Benteen approached. Hearing the firing, the troopers rode toward the sound at a gallop, but when they appeared in view, coming over the hills, the Indians fled in all directions, escaping punishment through their usual tactics of scattering over the Plains, so as to leave no distinctive trail.

When this frightful raid was taking place, Lieutenant Beecher, with his three scouts—Comstock, Grover, and Parr—was on Walnut Creek. Indefinite rumors about troubles on the Saline and Solomon reaching him, he immediately sent Comstock and Grover over to the headwaters of the Solomon, to the camp of a band of Cheyennes, whose chief was called "Turkey Leg," to see if any of the raiders belonged there; to learn the facts, and make explanations, if it was found that the white people had been at fault. For years this chief had been a special friend of Comstock and Grover. They had trapped, hunted, and lived with his band, and from this intimacy they felt confident of being able to get "Turkey Leg" to quiet his people, if any of them were engaged in the raid; and, at all events, they expected, through him and his band, to influence the rest of the Cheyennes. From the moment they arrived in the Indian village, however, the two scouts met with a very cold reception. Neither friendly pipe nor food was offered them, and before they could recover from their chilling reception, they were peremptorily ordered out of the village, with the intimation that when the Cheyennes were on the war-path the presence of whites was intolerable. The scouts were prompt to leave, of course, and for a few miles were accompanied by an escort of seven young men, who said they were sent with them to protect the two from harm. As the party rode along over the prairie, such a depth of attachment was professed for Comstock and Grover that, notwithstanding all the experience of their past lives, they were thoroughly deceived, and in the midst of a friendly conversation some of the young warriors fell suddenly to the rear and treacherously fired on them.

At the volley Comstock fell from his horse instantly killed. Grover, badly wounded in the shoulder, also fell to the ground near Comstock Seeing his comrade was dead, Grover made use of his friend's body to protect himself, lying close behind it. Then took place a remarkable contest, Grover, alone and severely wounded, obstinately fighting the seven Indians, and holding them at bay for the rest of the day. Being an expert shot, and having a long-range repeating rifle, he "stood off" the savages till dark. Then cautiously crawling away on his belly to a deep ravine, he lay close, suffering terribly from his wound, till the following night, when, setting out for Fort Wallace, he arrived there the succeeding day, almost crazed from pain and exhaustion.

Simultaneously with the fiendish atrocities committed on the Saline and Solomon rivers and the attack on Comstock and Grover, the pillaging and murdering began on the Smoky Hill stage-route, along the upper

Arkansas River and on the headwaters of the Cimarron. That along the Smoky Hill and north of it was the exclusive work of, the Cheyennes, a part of the Arapahoes, and the few Sioux allies heretofore mentioned, while the raiding on the Arkansas and Cimarron was done principally by the Kiowas under their chief, Satanta, aided by some of the Comanches. The young men of these tribes set out on their bloody work just after the annuities and guns were issued at Larned, and as soon as they were well on the road the rest of the Comanches and Kiowas escaped from the post and fled south of the Arkansas. They were at once pursued by General Sully with a small force, but by the time he reached the Cimarron the war-party had finished its raid on the upper Arkansas, and so many Indians combined against Sully that he was compelled to withdraw to Fort Dodge, which he reached not without considerable difficulty, and after three severe fights.

These, and many minor raids which followed, made it plain that a general outbreak was upon us. The only remedy, therefore, was to subjugate the savages immediately engaged in the forays by forcing the several tribes to settle down on the reservations set apart by the treaty of Medicine Lodge. The principal mischief-makers were the Cheyennes. Next in deviltry were the Kiowas, and then the Arapahoes and Comanches. Some few of these last two tribes continued friendly, or at least took no active part in the raiding, but nearly all the young men of both were the constant allies of the Cheyennes and Kiowas. All four tribes together could put on the war-path a formidable force of about 6,000 warriors. The subjugation of this number of savages would be no easy task, so to give the matter my undivided attention I transferred my headquarters from Leavenworth to Fort Hays, a military post near which the prosperous town of Hays City now stands.

Fort Hays was just beyond the line of the most advanced settlements, and was then the terminus of the Kansas-Pacific railroad. For this reason it could be made a depot of supplies, and was a good point from which to supervise matters in the section of country to be operated in, which district is a part of the Great American Plains, extending south from the Platte River in Nebraska to the Red River in the Indian Territory, and westward from the line of frontier settlements to the foothills of the Rocky Mountains, a vast region embracing an area of about 150,000 square miles. With the exception of a half-dozen military posts and a few stations on the two overland emigrant routes—the Smoky Hill to Denver, and the Arkansas to New Mexico—this country was an unsettled waste known only to the Indians and a few trappers. There were neither roads nor well-marked trails, and the only timber to be found—which generally grew only along the streams—was so scraggy and worthless as hardly to deserve the name. Nor was water by any means plentiful, even though the section is traversed by important streams, the Republican, the Smoky Hill, the Arkansas, the Cimarron, and the Canadian all flowing eastwardly, as do also their tributaries in the main. These feeders are sometimes long and crooked, but as a general thing the volume of water is insignificant except after rain-falls. Then, because of unimpeded drainage, the little streams fill up rapidly with torrents of water, which quickly flows off or sinks into the sand, leaving only an occasional pool without visible inlet or outlet.

At the period of which I write, in 1868, the Plains were covered with vast herds of buffalo—the number has been estimated at 3,000,000 head—and with such means of subsistence as this everywhere at hand, the 6,000 hostiles were wholly unhampered by any problem of food-supply. The savages were rich too according to Indian standards, many a lodge owning from twenty to a hundred ponies; and consciousness of wealth and power, aided by former temporizing, had made them not only confident but defiant. Realizing that their thorough subjugation would be a difficult task, I made up my mind to confine operations during the grazing and hunting season to protecting the people of the new settlements and on the overland routes, and then, when winter came, to fall upon the savages relentlessly, for in that season their ponies would be thin, and weak from lack of food, and in the cold and snow, without strong ponies to transport their villages and plunder, their movements would be so much impeded that the troops could overtake them.

At the outbreak of hostilities I had in all, east of New Mexico, a force of regulars numbering about 2,600 men—1,200 mounted and 1,400 foot troops. The cavalry was composed of the Seventh and Tenth regiments; the infantry, of the Third and Fifth regiments and four companies of the Thirty-Eighth. With these few troops all the posts along the Smoky Hill and Arkansas had to be garrisoned, emigrant trains escorted, and the settlements and routes of travel and the construction parties on the Kansas-Pacific railway protected. Then, too, this same force had to furnish for the field small movable columns, that were always on the go, so it will be rightly inferred that every available man was kept busy from the middle of August till November; especially as during this period the hostiles attacked over forty widely dispersed places, in nearly all cases stealing horses, burning houses, and killing settlers. It was of course impossible to foresee where these descents would be made, but as soon as an attack was heard of assistance was always promptly rendered, and every now and then we succeeded in killing a few savages. As a general thing, though, the raiders escaped before relief arrived, and when they had a few miles the start, all efforts to catch them were futile. I therefore discouraged long pursuits, and, in fact, did not approve of making any at all unless the chances of obtaining paying results were very evident, otherwise the troops would be worn out by the time the hard work of the winter was demanded from them.

To get ready for a winter campaign of six months gave us much to do. The thing most needed was more men, so I asked for additional cavalry, and all that could be spared—even troops of the Fifth Cavalry—was sent to me. Believing this reinforcement insufficient, to supplement it I applied for a regiment of Kansas volunteers, which request being granted, the organization of the regiment was immediately begun at Topeka. It was necessary also to provide a large amount of transportation and accumulate quantities of stores, since the campaign probably would not end till spring. Another important matter was to secure competent guides for the different columns of troops, for, as I have said, the section of country to be operated in was comparatively unknown.

In those days the railroad town of Hays City was filled with so called "Indian scouts," whose common boast was of having slain scores of redskins, but the real scout—that is, a 'guide and trailer knowing the habits of the Indians—was very scarce, and it was hard to find anybody familiar with the country south of the Arkansas, where the campaign was to be made. Still, about Hays City and the various military posts there was some good material to select from, and we managed to employ several men, who, from their experience on the Plains in various capacities, or from natural instinct and aptitude, soon became excellent guides and courageous and valuable scouts, some of them, indeed, gaining much distinction. Mr. William F. Cody ("Buffalo Bill"), whose renown has since become world-wide, was one of the men thus selected. He received his sobriquet from his marked success in killing buffaloes for a contractor, to supply fresh meat to the construction parties, on the Kansas-Pacific railway. He had given up this business, however, and was now in the employ of the quartermaster's department of the army, and was first brought to my notice by distinguishing himself in bringing me an important despatch from Fort Larned to Fort Hays, a distance of sixty-five miles, through a section infested with Indians. The despatch informed me that the Indians near Larned were preparing to decamp, and this intelligence required that certain orders should be carried to Fort Dodge, ninety-five miles south of Hays. This too being a particularly dangerous route—several couriers having been killed on it—it was impossible to get one of the various "Petes," "Jacks," or "Jims" hanging around Hays City to take my communication. Cody learning of the strait I was in, manfully came to the rescue, and proposed to make the trip to Dodge, though he had just finished his long and perilous ride from Larned. I gratefully accepted his offer, and after four or five hours' rest he mounted a fresh horse and hastened on his journey, halting but once to rest on the way, and then only for an hour, the stop being made at Coon Creek, where he got another mount from a troop of cavalry. At Dodge he took six hours' sleep, and then continued on to his own post—Fort Larned— with more despatches. After resting twelve hours at Larned, he was again in the saddle with tidings for me at Fort Hays, General Hazen sending him, this time, with word that the villages had fled to the south of the Arkansas. Thus, in all, Cody rode about 350 miles in less than sixty hours, and such an exhibition of endurance and courage was more than enough to convince me that his services would be extremely valuable in the campaign, so I retained him at Fort Hays till the battalion of the Fifth Cavalry arrived, and then made him chief of scouts for that regiment.

The information brought me by Cody on his second trip from Larned indicated where the villages would be found in the winter, and I decided to move on them about the 1st of November. Only the women and children and the decrepit old men were with the villages, however enough, presumably, to look after the plunder most of the warriors remaining north of the Arkansas to continue their marauding. Many severe fights occurred between our troops and these marauders, and in these affairs, before November 1 over a hundred Indians were killed, yet from the ease with which the escaping savages would disappear only to fall upon remote settlements with pillage and murder, the results were by no means satisfactory. One of the most noteworthy of these preliminary affairs was the gallant fight made on the Republican River the 17th of September by my Aide, Colonel George A. Forsyth, and party, against about seven hundred Cheyennes and Sioux. Forsyth, with Lieutenant Beecher, and Doctor J. H. Mooers as surgeon, was in charge of a company of citizen scouts, mostly expert rifle-shots, but embracing also a few Indian fighters, among these Grover and Parr. The company was organized the latter part of August for immediate work in defense of the settlements, and also for future use in the Indian Territory when the campaign should open there. About the time the company had reached its complement—it was limited to forty-seven men and three officers—a small band of hostiles began depredations near Sheridan City, one of the towns that grew up over-night on the Kansas-Pacific railway. Forsyth pursued this party, but failing to overtake it, made his way into Fort Wallace for rations, intending to return from there to Fort Hays. Before he started back, however, another band of Indians appeared near the post and stole some horses from the stage company. This unexpected raid made Forsyth hot to go for the marauders, and he telegraphed me for permission, which I as promptly gave him. He left the post on the 10th of September, the command consisting of himself, Lieutenant Beecher, Acting Assistant Surgeon Mooers, and the full strength, forty-seven men, with a few pack mules carrying about ten days' rations.

He headed north toward the Republican River. For the first two days the trail was indistinct and hard to follow. During the next three it continued to grow much larger, indicating plainly that the number of Indians ahead was rapidly increasing. Of course this sign meant a fight as soon as a large enough force was mustered, but as this was what Forsyth was after, he pushed ahead with confidence and alacrity. The night of the 16th of September he encamped on the Arickaree branch of the Republican, not far from the forks of the river, with the expectation of resuming the march as usual next day, for the indications were that the main body of the savages must be still a long way off, though in the preceding twenty-four hours an occasional Indian had been seen.

But the enemy was much nearer than was thought, for at daybreak on the morning of the 17th he made known his immediate presence by a sudden dash at Forsyth's horses, a few of which were stampeded and captured before the scouts could reach them. This dash was made by a small party only to get the horses, so those engaged in it were soon driven off, but a few minutes later hundreds of savages—it was afterward learned that seven hundred warriors took part in the fight—hitherto invisible, showed themselves on the hills overlooking the camp and so menacingly as to convince Forsyth that his defense must be one of desperation. The only place at hand that gave any hope of successful resistance was a small island in the Arickaree, the channel on one side being about a foot deep while on the other it was completely dry; so to this position a hurried retreat was made. All the men and the remaining animals reached the island in safety, but on account of the heavy fire poured in from the neighboring hills the packs containing the rations and medicines had to be abandoned.

On seeing Forsyth's hasty move, the Indians, thinking they had him, prepared to overwhelm the scouts by swooping down on one side of the island with about five hundred mounted warriors, while about two hundred, covered by the tall grass in the river-bottom attacked the other side, dismounted. But the brave little band sadly disappointed them. When the charge came it was met with such a deadly fire that a large number of the fiends were killed, some of them even after gaining the bank of the island. This check had the effect of making the savages more wary, but they were still bold enough to make two more assaults before mid-day. Each of these ending like the first, the Indians thereafter contented themselves with shooting all the horses, which had been tied up to some scraggy little cottonwood-trees, and then proceeded to lay siege to the party.

The first man struck was Forsyth himself. He was hit three times in all—twice in one leg, both serious wounds, and once on the head, a slight abrasion of the scalp. A moment later Beecher was killed and Doctor Mooers mortally wounded: and in addition to these misfortunes the scouts kept getting hit, till several were killed, and the whole number of casualties had reached twenty-one in a company of forty-seven. Yet with all this, and despite the seeming hopelessness of the situation, the survivors kept up their pluck undiminished, and during a lull succeeding the third repulse dug into the loose soil till the entire party was pretty well protected by rifle-pits. Thus covered they stood off the Indians for the next three days, although of course their condition became deplorable from lack of food, while those who were hurt suffered indescribable agony, since no means were at hand for dressing their wounds.

By the third day the Indians, seeming to despair of destroying the beleaguered party before succor might arrive, began to draw off, and on the fourth wholly disappeared. The men were by this time nearly famished for food. Even now there was nothing to be had except horse-meat from the carcasses of the animals killed the first day, and this, though decidedly unpalatable, not to say disgusting, had to be put up with, and so on such unwholesome stuff they managed to live for four days longer, at the end of which time they were rescued by a column of troops under Colonel Bankhead, which had hastened from Fort Wallace in response to calls for help, carried there by two brave fellows—Stilwell and Truedell—who, volunteering to go for relief, had slipped through the Indians, and struck out for that post in the night after the first day's fight.

CHAPTER XIII.

FITTING OUT THE WINTER EXPEDITION—ACCOMPANYING THE MAIN FORCE—THE OTHER COLUMNS—STRUCK BY A BLIZZARD—CUSTER'S FIGHT ON THE WASHITA— DEFEAT AND DEATH OF BLACK KETTLE—MASSACRE OF ELLIOTT'S PARTY—RELIEF OF COLONEL CRAWFORD.

The end of October saw completed the most of my arrangements for the winter campaign, though the difficulties and hardships to be encountered had led several experienced officers of the army, and some frontiersmen like Mr. James Bridger, the famous scout and, guide of earlier days, to discourage the project. Bridger even went so far as to come out from St. Louis to dissuade me, but I reasoned that as the soldier was much better fed and clothed than the Indian, I had one great advantage, and that, in short, a successful campaign could be made if the operations of the different columns were energetically conducted. To see to this I decided to go in person with the main column, which was to push down into the western part of the Indian Territory, having for its initial objective the villages which, at the beginning of hostilities, had fled toward the head-waters of the Red River, and those also that had gone to the same remote region after decamping from the neighborhood of Larned at the time that General Hazen sent Buffalo Bill to me with the news

The column which was expected to do the main work was to be composed of the Nineteenth Kansas Volunteer Cavalry, commanded by Colonel Crawford; eleven troops of the Seventh United States Cavalry, under General Custer, and a battalion of five companies of infantry under Brevet Major John H. Page. To facilitate matters, General Sully, the district commander, was ordered to rendezvous these troops and establish a supply depot about a hundred miles south of Fort Dodge, as from such a point operations could be more readily conducted. He selected for the depot a most suitable place at the confluence of Beaver and Wolf creeks, and on his arrival there with Custer's and Page's commands, named the place Camp Supply.

In conjunction with the main column, two others also were to penetrate the Indian Territory. One of these, which was to march east from New Mexico by way of Fort Bascom was to be composed of six troops of the Third Cavalry and two companies of infantry, the whole under Colonel A. W. Evans. The other, consisting of seven troops of the Fifth Cavalry, and commanded by Brevet Brigadier-General Eugene A. Carr, was to march southeast from Fort Lyon; the intention being that Evans and Carr should destroy or drive in toward old Fort Cobb any straggling bands that might be prowling through the country west of my own line of march; Carr, as he advanced, to be joined by Brevet Brigadier-General W. H. Penrose, with five troops of cavalry already in the field southeast of Lyon. The Fort Bascom column, after establishing a depot of supplies at Monument Creek, was to work down the main Canadian, and remain out as long as it could feed itself from New Mexico; Carr, having united with Penrose on the North Canadian, was to operate toward the Antelope Hills and headwaters of the Red River; while I, with the main column was to move southward to strike the Indians along the Washita, or still farther. south on branches of the Red River.

It was no small nor easy task to outfit all these troops by the time cold weather set in, and provide for them during the winter, but by the 1st of November I had enough supplies accumulated at Forts Dodge and Lyon for my own and Carr's columns, and in addition directed subsistence and forage for three months to be sent to Fort Gibson for final delivery at Fort Arbuckle, as I expected to feed the command from this place when we arrived in the neighborhood of old Fort Cobb, but through some mismanagement few of these stores got further than Gibson before winter came on.

November 1, all being ready, Colonel Grawford was furnished with competent guides, and, after sending two troops to Fort Dodge to act as my escort, with the rest of his regiment he started from Topeka November 5, under orders to march straight for the rendezvous at the junction of Beaver and Wolf creeks. He was expected to reach his destination about the 20th, and there unite with the Seventh Cavalry and the battalion of infantry, which in the mean time were on the march from Dodge. A few days later Carr and Evans began their march also, and everything being now in motion, I decided to go to Camp Supply to give the campaign my personal attention, determined to prove that operations could be successfully conducted in spite of winter, and bent on showing the Indians that they were not secure from punishment because of inclement weather—an ally on which they had hitherto relied with much assurance.

We started from Fort Hays on the 15th of November, and the first night out a blizzard struck us and carried away our tents; and as the gale was so violent that they could not be put up again, the rain and snow drenched us to the skin. Shivering from wet and cold, I took refuge under a wagon, and there spent such a miserable night that, when at last morning came, the gloomy predictions of old man Bridger and others rose up before me with greatly increased force. As we took the road the sleet and snow were still falling, but we labored on to Dodge that day in spite of the fact that many of the mules played out on the way. We stayed only one night at Dodge, and then on the 17th, escorted by a troop of cavalry and Forsyth's scouts, now under the command of Lieutenant Lewis Pepoon, crossed the Arkansas and camped the night of the 18th at Bluff Creek, where the two troops of the Nineteenth Kansas, previously detailed as my escort, were awaiting our coming. As we were approaching this camp some suspicious looking objects were seen moving off at a long distance to the east of us, but as the scouts confidently pronounced them buffalo, we were unaware of their true character till next morning, when we became satisfied that what we had seen were Indians, for immediately after crossing Beaver Creek we struck a trail, leading to the northeast, of a war party that evidently came up from the head-waters of the Washita River.

The evening of November 21we arrived at the Camp Supply depot, having traveled all day in another snowstorm that did not end till twenty-four hours later. General Sully, with Custer's regiment and the infantry battalion, had reached the place several days before, but the Kansas regiment had not yet put in an appearance. All hands were hard at work trying to shelter the stores and troops, but from the trail seen that morning, believing that an opportunity offered to strike an effective blow, I directed Custer to call in his working parties and prepare to move immediately, without waiting for Crawford's regiment, unaccountably absent. Custer was ready to start by the 23d, and he was then instructed to march north to where the trail had been seen near Beaver Creek and follow it on the back track, for, being convinced that the war party had come from the Washita, I felt certain that this plan would lead directly to the villages.

The difficulties attending a winter campaign were exhibited now with their full force, as the march had to be conducted through a snow-storm that hid surrounding objects, and so covered the country as to alter the appearance of the prominent features, making the task of the guides doubly troublesome; but in spite of these obstacles fifteen miles had been traversed when Custer encamped for the night. The next day the storm had ceased, and the weather was clear and cold. The heavy fall of snow had of course obliterated the trail in the bottoms, and everywhere on the level; but, thanks to the wind, that had swept comparatively bare the rough places and high ground, the general direction could be traced without much trouble. The day's march, which was through a country abounding with buffalo, was unattended by any special incident at first, but during the afternoon, after getting the column across the Canadian River—an operation which, on account of the wagons, consumed considerable time—Custer's scouts (friendly Osages) brought back word that, some miles ahead, they had struck fresh signs, a trail coming into the old one from the north, which, in their opinion, indicated that the war party was returning to the villages.

On the receipt of this news, Custer, leaving a guard with the wagons, hastily assembled the rest of his men and pushing on rapidly, overtook the scouts and a detailed party from his regiment which had accompanied them, all halted on the new trail awaiting his arrival. A personal examination satisfied Custer that the surmises of his scouts were correct; and also that the fresh trail in the deep snow could at night be followed with ease. After a short halt for supper and rest the pursuit was resumed, the Osage scouts in advance, and although the hostile Indians were presumed to be yet some distance off, every precaution was taken to prevent detection and to enable our troops to strike them unawares. The fresh trail, which it was afterward ascertained had been made by raiders from Black Kettle's village of Cheyennes, and by some Arapahoes, led into the valley of the Washita, and growing fresher as the night wore on, finally brought the Osages upon a campfire, still smoldering, which, it was concluded, had been built by the Indian boys acting as herders of the ponies during the previous day. It was evident, then, that the village could be but a few miles off; hence the pursuit was continued with redoubled caution until, a few hours before dawn of the 27th, as the leading scouts peered over a rise on the line of march, they discovered a large body of animals in the valley below.

As soon as they reported this discovery, Custer determined to acquaint himself with the situation by making a reconnoissance in person, accompanied by his principal officers. So, sending back word to halt the cavalry, he directed the officers to ride forward with him; then dismounting, the entire party crept cautiously to a high point which overlooked the valley, and from where, by the bright moon then shining, they saw just how the village was situated. Its position was such as to admit of easy approach from all sides. So, to preclude an escape of the Indians, Custer decided to attack at daybreak, and from four different directions.

The plan having been fully explained to the officers, the remaining hours of the night were employed in making the necessary dispositions. Two of the detachments left promptly, since they had to make a circuitous march of several miles to Teach the points designated for their attack; the third started a little later; and then the fourth and last, under Custer himself, also moved into position. As the first light grew visible in the east, each column moved closer in to the village, and then, all dispositions having been made according to the prearranged plan, from their appointed places the entire force to the opening notes of "Garry Owen," played by the regimental band as the signal for the attack—dashed at a gallop into the village. The sleeping and unsuspecting savages were completely surprised by the onset; yet after the first confusion, during which the impulse to escape principally actuated them, they seized their weapons, and from behind logs and trees, or plunging into the stream and using its steep bank as a breastwork, they poured upon their assailants a heavy fire, and kept on fighting with every exhibition of desperation. In such a combat mounted men were useless, so Custer directed his troopers to fight on, foot, and the Indians were successively driven from one point of vantage to another, until, finally, by 9 o'clock the entire camp was in his possession and the victory complete. Black Kettle and over one hundred of his warriors were killed, and about fifty women and children captured; but most of the noncombatants, as well as a few warriors and boys, escaped in the confusion of the fight. Making their way down the river, these fugitives alarmed the rest of the Cheyennes and Arapahoes, and also the Kiowas and Comanches, whose villages were in close proximity—the nearest not more than two miles off.

Then of course all the warriors of these tribes rallied to attack Custer, who meantime was engaged burning Black Kettle's camp and collecting his herds of ponies. But these new foes were rather wary and circumspect, though they already had partial revenge in an unlooked for way by cutting off Major Elliott and fifteen men, who had gone off in pursuit of a batch of young warriors when the fight was going on at the village. In fact, the Indians had killed Elliott's whole party, though neither the fate of the poor fellows, nor how they happened to be caught, was known till long afterward. It was then ascertained that the detachment pursued a course due south, nearly at right angles to the Washita River, and after galloping a couple of miles over the hills, crossing a small branch of the Washita on the way, they captured some of the fugitives. In bringing the prisoners back, Elliott was in turn attacked on the open prairie by a large number of savages from farther down the Washita, who by this time were swarming to the aid of Black Kettle's village. The little band fought its way gallantly to within rifle-range of the small creek referred to, but could get no farther, for the Indians had taken up a position in the bed of the stream, and from under cover of its banks Elliott and all his remaining men were quickly killed. No relief was sent them, for Custer, not having seen Elliott set out, knew nothing of the direction taken, and, besides, was busy burning the villages and securing the ponies, and deeply concerned, too, with defending himself from the new dangers menacing him. Elliott and his brave little party were thus left to meet their fate alone.

While Custer was burning the lodges and plunder and securing the ponies, the Indians from the villages down the Washita were gathering constantly around him till by mid-day they had collected in thousands, and then came a new problem as to what should be done. If he attacked the other villages, there was great danger of his being overwhelmed, and should he start back to Camp Supply by daylight, he would run the risk of losing his prisoners and the ponies, so, thinking the matter over, he decided to shoot all the ponies, and keep skirmishing with the savages till nightfall, and then, under cover of the darkness, return to Camp Supply; a programme that was carried out successfully, but Custer's course received some severe criticism because no effort was made to discover what had become of Elliott.

Custer had, in all, two officers and nineteen men killed, and two officers and eleven men wounded. The blow struck was a most effective one, and, fortunately, fell on one of the most villanous of the hostile bands that, without any provocation whatever, had perpetrated the massacres on the Saline and Solomon, committing atrocities too repulsive for recital, and whose hands were still red from their bloody work on the recent raid. Black Kettle, the chief, was an old man, and did not himself go with the raiders to the Saline and Solomon, and on this account his fate was regretted by some. But it was old age only that kept him back, for before the demons set out from Walnut Creek he had freely encouraged them by "making medicine," and by other devilish incantations that are gone through with at war and scalp dances.

When the horrible work was over he undertook to shield himself by professions of friendship, but being put to the test by my offering to feed and care for all of his band who would come in to Fort Dodge and remain there peaceably, he defiantly refused. The consequence of this refusal was a merited punishment, only too long delayed.

I received the first news of Custer's fight on the Washita on the morning of November 29. It was brought to me by one of his white scouts, "California Joe," a noted character, who had been experiencing the ups and downs of pioneer life ever since crossing the Plains in 1849. Joe was an invaluable guide and Indian fighter whenever the clause of the statute prohibiting liquors in the Indian country happened to be in full force. At the time in question the restriction was by no means a dead letter, and Joe came through in thirty-six hours, though obliged to keep in hiding during daylight of the 28th. The tidings brought were joyfully received by everybody at Camp Supply, and they were particularly agreeable to me, for, besides being greatly worried about the safety of the command in the extreme cold and deep snows, I knew that the immediate effect a victory would be to demoralize the rest of the hostiles, which of course would greatly facilitate and expedite our ultimate success. Toward evening the day after Joe arrived the head of Custer's column made its appearance on the distant hills, the friendly Osage scouts and the Indian prisoners in advance. As they drew near, the scouts began a wild and picturesque performance in celebration of the victory, yelling, firing their guns, throwing themselves on the necks and sides of their horses to exhibit their skill in riding, and going through all sorts of barbaric evolutions and gyrations, which were continued till night, when the rejoicings were ended with the hideous scalp dance.

The disappearance of Major Elliott and his party was the only damper upon our pleasure, and the only drawback to the very successful expedition. There was no definite information as to the detachment, and Custer was able to report nothing more than that he had not seen Elliott since just before the fight began. His theory was, however, that Elliott and his men had strayed off on account of having no guide, and would ultimately come in all right to Camp Supply or make their way back to Fort Dodge; a very unsatisfactory view of the matter, but as no one knew the direction Elliott had taken, it was useless to speculate on other suppositions, and altogether too late to make any search for him. I was now anxious to follow up Custer's stroke by an immediate move to the south with the entire column, but the Kansas regiment had not yet arrived. At first its nonappearance did not worry me much, for I attributed the delay to the bad weather, and supposed Colonel Crawford had wisely laid up during the worst storms. Further, waiting, however, would give the Indians a chance to recover from the recent dispiriting defeat, so I sent out scouting parties to look Crawford up and hurry him along. After a great deal of searching, a small detachment of the regiment was found about fifty miles below us on the North Canadian, seeking our camp. This detachment was in a pretty bad plight, and when brought in, the officer in charge reported that the regiment, by not following the advice of the guide sent to conduct it to Camp Supply, had lost its way. Instead of relying on the guides, Crawford had undertaken to strike through the canyons of the Cimarron by what appeared to him a more direct route, and in the deep gorges, filled as they were with snow, he had been floundering about for days without being able to extricate his command. Then, too, the men were out of rations, though they had been able to obtain enough buffalo meat to keep from starving. As for the horses, since they could get no grass, about seven hundred of them had already perished from starvation and exposure. Provisions and guides were immediately sent out to the regiment, but before the relief could reach Crawford his remaining horses were pretty much all gone, though the men were brought in without loss of life. Thus, the regiment being dismounted by this misfortune at the threshold of the campaign, an important factor of my cavalry was lost to me, though as foot-troops the Kansas volunteers continued to render very valuable services till mustered out the next spring.

CHAPTER XIV.

A WINTER EXPEDITION—HERDS OF BUFFALO—WOLVES—BLIZZARDS—A TERRIBLE NIGHT—FINDING THE BODIES OF ELLIOTT'S PARTY—THE ABANDONED INDIAN CAMPS—PUSHING DOWN THE WASHITA—THE CAPTURED CHIEFS—EVANS'S SUCCESSFUL FIGHT—ESTABLISHING FORT SILL—"CALIFORNIA JOE"—DUPLICITY OF THE CHEYENNES—ORDERED TO REPAIR TO WASHINGTON.

A few days were necessarily lost setting up and refitting the Kansas regiment after its rude experience in the Cimarron canyons. This through with, the expedition, supplied with thirty days' rations, moved out to the south on the 7th of December, under my personal command. We headed for the Witchita Mountains, toward which rough region all the villages along the Washita River had fled after Custer's fight with Black Kettle. My line of march was by way of Custer's battle-field, and thence down the Washita, and if the Indians could not sooner be brought to terms, I intended to follow them into the Witchita Mountains from near old Fort Cobb. The snow was still deep everywhere, and when we started the thermometer was below zero, but the sky being clear and the day very bright, the command was in excellent spirits. The column was made up of ten companies of the Kansas regiment, dismounted; eleven companies of the Seventh Cavalry, Pepoon's scouts, and the Osage scouts. In addition to Pepoon's men and the Osages, there was also "California Joe," and one or two other frontiersmen besides, to act as guides and interpreters. Of all these the principal one, the one who best knew the country, was Ben Clark, a young man who had lived with the Cheyennes during much of his boyhood, and who not only had a pretty good knowledge of the country, but also spoke fluently the Cheyenne and Arapahoe dialects, and was an adept in the sign language.

The first day we made only about ten miles, which carried us to the south bank of Wolf Creek. A considerable part of the day was devoted to straightening out matters in the command, and allowing time for equalizing the wagon loads, which as a general thing, on a first day's march, are unfairly distributed. And then there was an abundance of fire-wood at Wolf Creek; indeed, here and on Hackberry Creek—where I intended to make my next camp—was the only timber north of the Canadian River; and to select the halting places near a plentiful supply of wood was almost indispensable, for as the men were provided with only shelter-tents, good fires were needed in order to keep warm.

The second day, after marching for hours through vast herds of buffalo, we made Hackberry Creek; but not, however, without several stampedes in the wagon-train, the buffalo frightening the mules so that it became necessary to throw out flankers to shoot the leading bulls and thus turn off the herds. In the wake of every drove invariably followed a band of wolves. This animal is a great coward usually, but hunger had made these so ravenous that they would come boldly up to the column, and as quick as a buffalo was killed, or even disabled, they would fall upon the carcass and eagerly devour it. Antelope also were very numerous, and as they were quite tame— being seldom chased—and naturally very inquisitive, it was not an unfrequent thing to see one of the graceful little creatures run in among the men and be made a prisoner. Such abundance of game relieved the monotony of the march to Hackberry Creek, but still, both men and animals were considerably exhausted by their long tramp, for we made over thirty miles that day.

We camped in excellent shape on the creek and it was well we did, for a "Norther," or "blizzard," as storms on the Plains are now termed struck us in the night. During the continuance of these blizzards, which is usually about three days, the cold wind sweeps over the Plains with great force, and, in the latitude of the Indian Territory, is weighted with great quantities of sleet and snow, through which it is often impossible to travel; indeed, these "Northers" have many times proved fatal to the unprotected frontiersman. With our numbers the chance of any one's being lost, and perishing alone (one of the most common dangers in a blizzard), was avoided; but under any circumstances such a storm could but occasion intense suffering to all exposed to it, hence it would have been well to remain in camp till the gale was over, but the time could not be spared. We therefore resumed the march at an early hour next morning, with the expectation of making the south bank of the main Canathan and there passing the night, as Clark assured me that timber was plentiful on that side of the river. The storm greatly impeded us, however, many of the mules growing discouraged, and some giving out entirely, so we could not get to Clark's "good camp," for with ten hours of utmost effort only about half a day's distance could be covered, when at last, finding the struggle useless, we were forced to halt for the night in a bleak bottom on the north bank of the river. But no one could sleep, for the wind swept over us with unobstructed fury, and the only fuel to be had was a few green bushes. As night fell a decided change of temperature added much to our misery, the mercury, which had risen when the "Norther" began, again falling to zero. It can be easily imagined that under such circumstances the condition of the men was one of extreme discomfort; in truth, they had to tramp up and down the camp all night long to keep from freezing. Anything was a relief to this state of things, so at the first streak of day we quit the dreadful place and took up the march.

A seemingly good point for crossing the Canadian was found a couple of miles down the stream, where we hoped to get our train over on the ice, but an experiment proving that it was not strong enough, a ford had to be made, which was done by marching some of the cavalry through the river, which was about half a mile wide, to break up the large floes when they had been cut loose with axes. After much hard work a passage-way was thus opened, and by noon the command was crossed to the south bank, and after thawing out and drying our clothes before big fires, we headed for a point on the Washita, where Clark said there was plenty of wood, and good water too, to make us comfortable till the blizzard had blown over.

We reached the valley of the Washita a little before dark, and camped some five or six miles above the scene of Custer's fight, where I concluded to remain at least a day, to rest the command and give it a chance to refit. In the mean time I visited the battle field in company with Custer and several other officers, to see if there was a possibility of discovering any traces of Elliott's party. On arriving at the site of the village, and learning from Custer what dispositions had been made in approaching for the attack, the squadron of the escort was deployed and pushed across the river at the point where Elliott had crossed. Moving directly to the south, we had not gone far before we struck his trail, and soon the whole story was made plain by our finding, on an open level space about two miles from the destroyed village, the dead and frozen bodies of the entire party. The poor fellows were all lying within a circle not more than fifteen or twenty paces in diameter, and the little piles of empty cartridge shells near each body showed plainly that every man had made a brave fight. None were scalped, but most of them were otherwise horribly mutilated, which fiendish work is usually done by the squaws. All had been stripped of their clothing, but their comrades in the escort were able to identify the bodies, which being done, we gave them decent burial. Their fate was one that has overtaken many of our gallant army in their efforts to protect the frontiersmen's homes and families from savages who give no quarter, though they have often received it, and where the possibility of defeat in action carries with it the certainty of death and often of preceding torture.

From the meadow where Elliott was found we rode to the Washita, and then down the river through the sites of the abandoned villages, that had been strung along almost continuously for about twelve miles in the timber skirting the stream. On every hand appeared ample evidence that the Indians had intended to spend the winter here, for the ground was littered with jerked meat, bales of buffalo robes, cooking utensils, and all sorts of plunder usually accumulated in a permanent Indian camp. There were, also, lying dead near the villages hundreds of ponies, that had been shot to keep them from falling into our hands, the scant grazing and extreme cold having made them too weak to be driven along in the flight. The wholesale slaughter of these ponies was a most cheering indication that our campaign would be ultimately successful, and we all prayed for at least a couple of months more of cold weather and plenty of snow.

At the Kiowa village we found the body of a white woman—a Mrs. Blynn—and also that of her child. These captives had been taken by the Kiowas near Fort Lyon the previous summer, and kept close prisoners until the stampede began, the poor woman being reserved to gratify the brutal lust of the chief, Satanta; then, however, Indian vengeance demanded the murder of the poor creatures, and after braining the little child against a tree, the mother was shot through the forehead, the weapon, which no doubt brought her welcome release, having been fired so close that the powder had horribly disfigured her face. The two bodies were wrapped in blankets and taken to camp, and afterward carried along in our march, till finally they were decently interred at Fort Arbuckle..

At an early hour on December 12 the command pulled out from its cosy camp and pushed down the valley of the Washita, following immediately on the Indian trail which led in the direction of Fort Cobb, but before going far it was found that the many deep ravines and canyons on this trail would delay our train very much, so we moved out of the valley and took the level prairie on the divide. Here the traveling was good, and a rapid gait was kept up till mid-day, when, another storm of sleet and snow coming on, it became extremely difficult for the guides to make out the proper course; and fearing that we might get lost or caught on the open plain without wood or water—as we had been on the Canadian—I turned the command back to the valley, resolved to try no more shortcuts involving the risk of a disaster to the expedition. But to get back was no slight task, for a dense fog just now enveloped us, obscuring all landmarks. However, we were headed right when the fog set in, and we had the good luck to reach the valley before night-fall, though there was a great deal of floundering about, and also much disputing among the guides as to where the river would be found Fortunately we struck the stream right at a large grove of timber, and established ourselves, admirably. By dark the ground was covered with twelve or fifteen inches of fresh snow, and as usual the temperature rose very sensibly while the storm was on, but after night-fall the snow ceased and the skies cleared up. Daylight having brought zero weather again, our start on the morning of the 17th was painful work, many of the men freezing their fingers while handling the horse equipments, harness, and tents. However, we got off in fairly good season, and kept to the trail along the Washita notwithstanding the frequent digging and bridging necessary to get the wagons over ravines.

Continuing on this line for three days, we at length came to a point on the Washita where all signs indicated that we were nearing some of the villages. Wishing to strike them as soon as possible, we made a very early start next morning, the 17th. A march of four or five miles brought us to a difficult ravine, and while we were making preparations to get over, word was brought that several Indians had appeared in our front bearing a white flag and making signs that they had a communication to deliver. We signaled back that they would be received, when one of the party came forward alone and delivered a letter, which proved to be from General Hazen, at Fort Cobb. The letter showed that Hazen was carrying on negotiations with the Indians, and stated that all the tribes between Fort

Cobb and my column were friendly, but the intimation was given that the Cheyennes and Arapahoes were still hostile, having moved off southward toward, the Red River. It was added that Satanta and Lone Wolf—the chiefs of the Kiowas—would give information of the whereabouts of the hostiles; and such a communication coming direct from the representative of the Indian Department, practically took the Kiowas—the village at hand was of that tribe—under its protection, and also the Comanches, who were nearer in to Cobb. Of course, under such circumstances I was compelled to give up the intended attack, though I afterward regretted that I had paid any heed to the message, because Satanta and Lone Wolf proved, by trickery and double dealing, that they had deceived Hazen into writing the letter.

When I informed the Klowas that I would respect Hazen's letter provided they all came into Fort Cobb and gave themselves up, the two chiefs promised submission, and, as an evidence of good faith, proposed to accompany the column to Fort Cobb with a large body of warriors, while their villages moved to the same point by easy stages, along the opposite bank of the river—claiming this to be necessary from the poor condition of the ponies. I had some misgivings as to the sincerity of Satanta and Lone Wolf, but as I wanted to get the Kiowas where their surrender would be complete, so that the Cheyennes and Arapahoes could then be pursued, I agreed to the proposition, and the column moved on. All went well that day, but the next it was noticed that the warriors were diminishing, and an investigation showed that a number of them had gone off on various pretexts—the main one being to help along the women and children with the villages. With this I suspected that they were playing me false, and my suspicions grew into certainty when Satanta himself tried to make his escape by slipping beyond the flank of the column and putting spurs to his pony. Fortunately, several officers saw him, and quickly giving chase, overhauled him within a few hundred yards. I then arrested both him and Lone Wolf and held them as hostages—a measure that had the effect of bringing back many of the warriors already beyond our reach.

When we arrived at Fort Cobb we found some of the Comanches already there, and soon after the rest. of them, excepting one band, came in to the post. The Kiowas, however, were not on hand, and there were no signs to indicate their coming. At the end of two days it was plain enough that they were acting in bad faith, and would continue to unless strong pressure was brought to bear. Indeed, they had already started for the

Witchita Mountains, so I put on the screws at once by issuing an order to hang Satanta and Lone Wolf, if their people did not surrender at Fort Cobb within forty-eight hours. The two chiefs promised prompt compliance, but begged for more time, seeking to explain the non-arrival of the women and children through the weak condition of the ponies; but I was tired of their duplicity, and insisted on my ultimatum.

The order for the execution brought quick fruit. Runners were sent out with messages, by the two prisoners, appealing to their people to save the lives of their chiefs, and the result was that the whole tribe came in to the post within the specified time. The two manacled wretches thus saved their necks; but it is to be regretted that the execution did not come off; for some years afterward their devilish propensities led them into Texas, where both engaged in the most horrible butcheries.

The Kiowas were now in our hands, and all the Comanches too, except one small band, which, after the Custer fight, had fled toward the headwaters of the Red River. This party was made up of a lot of very bad Indians—outlaws from the main tribe—and we did not hope to subdue them except by a fight, and of this they got their fill; for Evans, moving from Monument Creek toward the western base of the Witchita Mountains on Christmas Day, had the good fortune to strike their village. In the snow and cold his approach was wholly unexpected, and he was thus enabled to deal the band a blow that practically annihilated it. Twenty-five warriors were killed outright, most of the women and children captured, and all the property was destroyed. Only a few of the party escaped, and some of these made their way in to Fort Cobb, to join the rest of their tribe in confinement; while others, later in the season, surrendered at Fort Bascom.

This sudden appearance of Evans in the Red River region also alarmed the Cheyennes and Arapahoes, and their thoughts now began to turn to submission. Food was growing scarce with them, too, as there was but little game to be found either in the Witchita Mountains or on the edge of the Staked Plains, and the march of Carr's column from Antelope Hills precluded their returning to where the buffalo ranged. Then, too, many of their ponies were dead or dying, most of their tepees and robes had been abandoned, and the women and children, having been kept constantly on the move in the winter's storms, were complaining bitterly of their sufferings.

In view of this state of things they intimated, through their Comanche-Apache friends at Fort Cobb, that they would like to make terms. On receiving their messages I entered into negotiations with Little Robe, chief of the Cheyennes, and Yellow Bear, chief of the Arapahoes, and despatched envoys to have both tribes understand clearly that they must recognize their subjugation by surrendering at once, and permanently settling on their reservations in the spring. Of course the usual delays of Indian diplomacy ensued, and it was some weeks before I heard the result.

Then one of my messengers returned with word that Little Robe and Yellow Bear were on their way to see me. They arrived a few days later, and, promptly acceding to the terms, promised to bring their people in, but as many of them would have to come on foot on account of the condition of the ponies, more time was solicited. Convinced of the sincerity of their professions I gave them a reasonable extension, and eventually Yellow Bear made good his word, but Little Robe, in spite of earnest and repeated efforts, was unable to deliver his people till further operations were begun against them.

While these negotiations were in progress I came to the conclusion that a permanent military post ought to be established well down on the Kiowa and Comanche reservation, in order to keep an eye on these tribes in the future, Fort Cobb, being an unsuitable location, because too far to the north to protect the Texas frontier, and too far away from where it was intended to permanently place the Indians. With this purpose in view I had the country thoroughly explored, and afterward a place was fixed upon not far from the base of the Witchita Mountains, and near the confluence of Medicine Bluff and Cash creeks, where building stone and timber could be obtained in plenty, and to this point I decided to move. The place was named Camp Sill—now Fort Sill—in honor of my classmate, General Sill, killed at Stone River; and to make sure of the surrendered Indians, I required them all, Kiowas, Comanches, and Comanche-Apaches, to accompany us to the new post, so they could be kept under military control till they were settled.

During the march to the new camp the weather was not so cold as that experienced in coming down from Camp Supply; still, rains were frequent, and each was invariably followed by a depression of temperature and high winds, very destructive to our animals, much weakened by lack of food. The men fared pretty well, however, for on the rough march along the Washita, and during our stay at Fort Cobb, they had learned to protect themselves materially from the cold. For this they had contrived many devices, the favorite means being dugouts—that is, pits dug in the ground, and roofed over, with shelter-tents, and having at one end a fire-place and chimney ingeniously constructed with sod. In these they lived very snugly— four men in each—and would often amuse themselves by poking their heads out and barking at the occupants of adjacent huts in imitation of the prairie-dog, whose comfortable nests had probably suggested the idea of dugouts. The men were much better off, in fact, than many of the officers, for the high winds frequently made havoc with our wall-tents. The horses and mules suffered most of all. They could not be sheltered, and having neither grain nor grass, the poor beasts were in no condition to stand the chilling blasts. Still, by cutting down cottonwood-trees, and letting the animals browse on the small soft branches, we managed to keep them up till, finally even this wretched food beginning to grow scarce, I had all except a few of the strongest sent to Fort Arbuckle, near which place we had been able, fortunately, to purchase some fields of corn from the half-civilized Chickasaws and Choctaws.

Through mismanagement, as previously noted, the greater part of the supplies which I had ordered hauled to Arbuckle the preceding fall had not got farther on the way than Fort Gibson, which post was about four hundred miles off, and the road abominable, particularly east of Arbuckle, where it ran through a low region called "boggy bottom." All along this route were abandoned wagons, left sticking in the mud, and hence the transportation was growing so short that I began to fear trouble in getting subsistence up for the men. Still, it would not do to withdraw, so I made a trip to Arbuckle chiefly for the purpose of reorganizing the transportation, but also with a view to opening a new route to that post, the road to lie on high ground, so as to avoid the creeks and mud that had been giving us so much trouble. If such a road could be made, I hoped to get up enough rations and grain from the cornfields purchased to send out a formidable expedition against the Cheyennes, so I set out for Arbuckle accompanied by my quartermaster, Colonel A. J. McGonigle. "California Joe" also went along to guide us through the scrub-oaks covering the ridge, but even the most thorough exploration failed to discover any route more practicable than that already in use, indeed, the high ground was, if anything, worse than the bottom land, our horses in the springy places and quicksands often miring to their knees. The ground was so soft and wet, in fact, that we had to make most of the way on foot, so by the time we reached Arbuckle I was glad to abandon the new road project.

Finding near Arbuckle more fields of corn than those already purchased, I had them bought also, and ordered more of the horses back there to be fed. I next directed every available mule to be put to hauling rations, having discovered that the full capacity of the transportation had not yet been brought into play in forwarding stores from Gibson, and with this regulation of the supply question I was ready to return immediately to Camp Sill. But my departure was delayed by California Joe, who, notwithstanding the prohibitory laws of the Territory, in some unaccountable way had got gloriously tipsy, which caused a loss of time that disgusted me greatly; but as we could not well do without Joe, I put off starting till the next day, by which time it was thought he would sober up. But I might just as well have gone at first, for at the end of the twenty-four hours the incorrigible old rascal was still dead drunk. How he had managed to get the grog to keep up his spree was a mystery which we could not solve, though we had had him closely watched, so I cut the matter short by packing him into my ambulance and carrying him off to Camp Sill.

By the time I got back to Sill, the Arapahoes were all in at the post, or near at hand. The promised surrender of the Cheyennes was still uncertain of fulfillment, however, and although Little Robe and his family had remained with us in evidence of good faith, the messages he sent to his followers brought no assurance of the tribe's coming in—the runners invariably returning with requests for more time, and bringing the same old excuse of inability to move because the ponies were so badly off. But more time was just what I was determined not to grant, for I felt sure that if a surrender was not forced before the spring grass came, the ponies would regain their strength, and then it would be doubtful if the Cheyennes came in at all.

To put an end to these delays, Custer proposed to go out and see the Cheyennes himself, taking with him for escort only such number of men as could be fairly well mounted from the few horses not sent back to Arbuckle. At first I was inclined to disapprove Custer's proposition, but he urged it so strongly that I finally consented, though with some misgivings, for I feared that so small a party might tempt the Cheyennes to forget their pacific professions and seek to avenge the destruction of Black Kettle's band. However, after obtaining my approval, Custer, with characteristic energy, made his preparations, and started with three or four officers and forty picked men, taking along as negotiators Yellow Bear and Little Robe, who were also to conduct him to the head-waters of the

Red River, where it was supposed the Cheyennes would be found. His progress was reported by couriers every few days, and by the time he got to the Witchita foot-hills he had grown so sanguine that he sent California Joe back to me with word that he was certain of success. Such hopeful anticipation relieved me greatly, of course, but just about the time I expected to hear that his mission had been achieved I was astonished by the party's return. Inquiring as to the trouble, I learned that out toward the Staked Plains every sign of the Cheyennes had disappeared. Surprised and disappointed at this, and discouraged by the loneliness of his situation—for in the whole region not a trace of animal life was visible, Custer gave up the search, and none too soon, I am inclined to believe, to save his small party from perishing.

This failure put a stop to all expeditions till the latter part of February, by which time I had managed to lay in enough rations to feed the command for about thirty days; and the horses back at Arbuckle having picked up sufficiently for field service they were ordered to Sill, and this time I decided to send Custer out with his own and the Kansas regiment, with directions to insist on the immediate surrender of the Cheyennes, or give them a sound thrashing. He was ordered to get everything ready by March 1, and then move to the mouth of Salt Creek, on the North Fork of the Red River, at which place I proposed to establish a new depot for feeding the command. Trains could reach this point from Camp Supply more readily than from Arbuckle, and wishing to arrange this part of the programme in person, I decided to return at once to Supply, and afterward rejoin Custer at Salt Creek, on what, I felt sure, was to be the final expedition of the campaign. I made the three hundred and sixty miles from Sill to Supply in seven days, but much to my surprise there found a despatch from General Grant directing me to repair immediately to Washington. These orders precluded, of course, my rejoining the command; but at the appointed time it set out on the march, and within three weeks brought the campaign to a successful close.

In this last expedition, for the first few days Custer's route was by the same trail he had taken in January—that is to say, along the southern base of the Witchita Mountains—but this time there was more to encourage him than before, for, on getting a couple of marches beyond old Camp Radziminski, on all sides were fresh evidences of Indians, and every effort was bent to strike them.

From day to day the signs grew hotter, and toward the latter part of

March the game was found. The Indians being in a very forlorn condition, Custer might have destroyed most of the tribe, and certainly all their villages, but in order to save two white women whom, it was discovered, they held as captives, he contented himself with the renewal of the Cheyennes' agreement to come in to Camp Supply. In due time the entire tribe fulfilled its promise except one small band under "Tall Bull," but this party received a good drubbing from General Carr on the Republican early in May. After this fight all the Indians of the southern Plains settled down on their reservations, and I doubt whether the peace would ever again have been broken had they not in after years been driven to hostilities by most unjust treatment.

It was the 2d of March that I received at Camp Supply Grant's despatch directing me to report immediately in Washington. It had been my intention, as I have said, to join Custer on the North Fork of the Red River, but this new order required me to recast my plans, so, after arranging to keep the expedition supplied till the end of the campaign, I started for Washington, accompanied by three of my staff—Colonels McGonigle and Crosby, and Surgeon Asch, and Mr. Deb. Randolph Keim, a representative of the press, who went through the whole campaign, and in 1870 published a graphic history of it. The day we left Supply we, had another dose of sleet and snow, but nevertheless we made good time, and by night-fall reached Bluff Creek. In twenty-four hours more we made Fort Dodge, and on the 6th of March arrived at Fort Hays. Just south of the Smoky Hill River, a little before we got to the post, a courier heading for Fort Dodge passed us at a rapid gait. Suspecting that he had despatches for me, I directed my outrider to overtake him and find out. The courier soon turned back, and riding up to my ambulance handed me a telegram notifying me that General Grant, on the day of his inauguration, March 4, 1869, had appointed me Lieutenant-General of the Army. When I reported in Washington, the President desired me to return to New Orleans and resume command of the Fifth Military District, but this was not at all to my liking, so I begged off, and was assigned to take charge of the Division of the Missouri, succeeding General Sherman, who had just been ordered to assume command of the Army.

CHAPTER XV.

INSPECTING MILITARY POSTS IN UTAH AND MONTANA—DESIRE TO WITNESS THE FRANCO-GERMAN WAR—ON A SAND-BAR IN THE MISSOURI—A BEAR HUNT—AN INDIAN SCARE—MYRIADS OF MOSQUITOES—PERMISSION GIVEN TO VISIT EUROPE—CALLING ON PRESIDENT GRANT—SAILING FOR LIVERPOOL—ARRIVAL IN BERLIN.

After I had for a year been commanding the Division of the Missouri, which embraced the entire Rocky Mountain region, I found it necessary to make an inspection of the military posts in northern Utah and Montana, in order by personal observation to inform myself of their location and needs, and at the same time become acquainted with the salient geographical and topographical features of that section of my division. Therefore in May, 1870, I started west by the Union-Pacific railroad, and on arriving at Corinne Station, the next beyond Ogden, took passage by stage-coach for Helena, the capital of Montana Territory. Helena is nearly five hundred miles north of Corinne, and under ordinary conditions the journey was, in those days, a most tiresome one. As the stage kept jogging on day and night, there was little chance for sleep, and there being with me a sufficient number of staff-officers to justify the proceeding, we chartered the "outfit," stipulating that we were to stop over one night on the road to get some rest. This rendered the journey more tolerable, and we arrived at Helena without extraordinary fatigue.

Before I left Chicago the newspapers were filled with rumors of impending war between Germany and France. I was anxious to observe the conflict, if it was to occur, but reports made one day concerning the beginning of hostilities would be contradicted the next, and it was not till I reached Helena that the despatches lost their doubtful character, and later became of so positive a nature as to make it certain that the two nations would fight. I therefore decided to cut short my tour of inspection, so that I could go abroad to witness the war, if the President would approve. This resolution limited my stay in Helena to a couple of days, which were devoted to arranging for an exploration of what are now known as the Upper and the Lower Geyser Basins of the Yellowstone Park. While journeying between Corinne and Helena I had gained some vague knowledge of these geysers from an old mountaineer named Atkinson, but his information was very indefinite, mostly second-hand; and there was such general uncertainty as to the character of this wonderland that I authorized an escort of soldiers to go that season from Fort Ellis with a small party, to make such superficial explorations as to justify my sending an engineer officer with a well-equipped expedition there next summer to scientifically examine and report upon the strange country. When the arrangements for this preliminary expedition were completed I started for Fort Benton, the head of navigation on the Missouri River, on the way passing through Fort Shaw, on Sun River. I expected to take at Benton a steamboat to Fort Stevenson, a military post which had been established about eighty miles south of Fort Buford, near a settlement of friendly Mandan and Arickaree Indians, to protect them from the hostile Sioux. From there I was to make my way overland, first to Fort Totten near Devil's lake in Dakota, and thence by way of Fort Abercrombie to Saint Cloud, Minnesota, the terminus of the railroad.

Luckily I met with no delay in getting a boat at Benton, and though the water was extremely low, we steamed down the channel of the Missouri with but slight detention till we got within fifty miles of Fort Buford. Here we struck on a sandbar with such force of steam and current as to land us almost out of the water from stem to midships. This bad luck was tantalizing, for to land on a bar when your boat is under full headway down-stream in the Missouri River is no trifling matter, especially if you want to make time, for the rapid and turbid stream quickly depositing sand under the hull, makes it commonly a task of several days to get your boat off again. As from our mishap the loss of much time was inevitable, I sent a messenger to Fort Buford for a small escort, and for horses to take my party in to the post. Colonel Morrow, the commandant, came himself to meet us, bringing a strong party of soldiers and some friendly Indian scouts, because, he said, there were then in the region around Buford so many treacherous band of Sioux as to make things exceedingly unsafe.

Desiring to reach the post without spending more than one night on the way, we abandoned our steamer that evening, and set off at an early hour the next morning. We made camp at the end of the day's march within ten miles of Buford, and arrived at the post without having had any incident of moment, unless we may dignify as one a battle with three grizzly bears, discovered by our friendly Indians the morning of our second day's journey. While eating our breakfast—a rather slim one, by the way—spread on a piece of canvas, the Indians, whose bivouac was some distance off, began shouting excitedly, "Bear! bear!" and started us all up in time to see, out on the plain some hundreds of yards away, an enormous grizzly and two almost full-grown cubs. Chances like this for a bear hunt seldom offered, so there was hurried mounting—the horses being already saddled—and a quick advance made on the game from many directions, Lieutenant Townsend, of the escort, and five or six of the Indians going with me. Alarmed by the commotion, bruin and her cubs turned about, and with an awkward yet rapid gait headed for a deep ravine, in which there was brushwood shelter.

My party rode directly across the prairie and struck the trail not far behind the game. Then for a mile or more the chase was kept up, but with such poor shooting because of the "buck fever" which had seized most of us, that we failed to bring down any of the grizzlies, though the cubs grew so tired that the mother was often obliged to halt for their defense, meanwhile urging them on before her. When the ravine was gained she hid the cubs away in the thick brushwood, and then coming out where we could plainly see her, stood on the defense just within the edge of the thicket, beyond the range of our rifles though, unless we went down into the canyon, which we would have to do on foot, since the precipitous wall precluded going on horseback. For an adventure like this I confess I had little inclination, and on holding a council of war, I found that the Indians had still less, but Lieutenant Townsend, who was a fine shot, and had refrained from firing hitherto in the hope that I might bag the game, relieved the embarrassing situation and saved the credit of the party by going down alone to attack the enemy. Meanwhile I magnanimously held his horse, and the Sioux braves did a deal of shouting, which they seemed to think of great assistance.

Townsend, having descended to the bottom of the ravine, approached within range, when the old bear struck out, dashing into and out of the bushes so rapidly, however, that he could not get fair aim at her, but the startled cubs running into full view, he killed one at the first shot and at the second wounded the other. This terribly enraged the mother, and she now came boldly out to fight, exposing herself in the open ground so much as to permit a shot, that brought her down too, with a broken shoulder. Then the Indians and I, growing very brave, scrambled down to—take part in the fight. It was left for me to despatch the wounded cub and mother, and having recovered possession of my nerves, I did the work effectively, and we carried off with us the skins of the three animals as trophies of the hunt and evidence of our prowess.

As good luck would have it, when we reached Buford we found a steamboat there unloading stores, and learned that it would be ready to start down the river the next day. Embarking on her, we got to Stevenson in a few hours, and finding at the post camp equipage that had been made ready for our use in crossing overland to Fort Totten, we set out the following forenoon, taking with us a small escort of infantry, transported in two light wagons, a couple of Mandans and the post interpreter going along as mounted guides.

To reach water we had to march the first day to a small lake forty miles off, and the oppressive heat, together with the long distance traveled, used up one of the teams so much that, when about to start out the second morning, we found the animals unable to go on with any prospect of finishing the trip, so I ordered them to be rested forty-eight hours longer, and then taken back to Stevenson. This diminished the escort by one-half, yet by keeping the Indians and interpreter on the lookout, and seeing that our ambulance was kept closed up on the wagon carrying the rest of the detachment, we could, I thought, stand off any ordinary party of hostile Indians.

About noon I observed that the scouts in advance had left the trail and begun to reconnoitre a low ridge to their right, the sequel of which was that in a few minutes they returned to the wagons on a dead run and reported Sioux just ahead. Looking in the direction indicated, I could dimly see five or six horsemen riding in a circle, as Indians do when giving warning to their camp, but as our halt disclosed that we were aware of their proximity, they darted back again behind the crest of the ridge. Anticipating from this move an immediate attack, we hastily prepared for it by unhooking the mules from the wagon and ambulance, so that we could use the vehicles as a barricade. This done, I told the interpreter to take the Mandan scouts and go over toward the ridge and reconnoitre again. As the scouts neared the crest two of them dismounted, and, crawling slowly on their bellies to the summit, took a hasty look and returned at once to their horses, coming back with word that in the valley beyond was a camp of at least a hundred Sioux lodges, and that the Indians were hurriedly getting ready to attack us. The news was anything but cheering, for with a village of that size the warriors would number two or three hundred, and could assail us from every side.

Still, nothing could be done, but stand and take what was to come, for there was no chance of escape—it being supreme folly to undertake in wagons a race with Indians to Fort Stevenson, sixty miles away. To make the best of the situation, we unloaded the baggage, distributing and adjusting the trunks, rolls of bedding, crackerboxes, and everything else that would stop a bullet, in such manner as to form a square barricade, two sides of which were the wagons, with the mules haltered to the wheels. Every man then supplied himself with all the ammunition he could carry, and the Mandan scouts setting up the depressing wail of the Indian death-song, we all awaited the attack with the courage of despair.

But no attack came; and time slipping by, and we still unmolested, the interpreter and scouts were sent out to make another reconnoissance. Going through just such precautions as before in approaching the ridge, their slow progress kept us in painful suspense; but when they got to the crest the strain on our nerves was relieved by seeing them first stand up boldly at full height, and then descend beyond. Quickly returning, they brought welcome word that the whole thing was a mistake, and no Sioux were there at all. What had been taken for a hundred Indian lodges turned out to be the camp of a Government train on its way to Fort Stevenson, and the officer in charge seeing the scouts before they discovered him, and believing them to be Sioux, had sent out to bring his herds in. It would be hard to exaggerate the relief that this discovery gave us, and we all breathed much easier. The scare was a bad one, and I have no hesitation in saying that, had we been mounted, it is more than likely that, instead of showing fight, we would have taken up a lively pace for Fort Stevenson.

After reciprocal explanations with the officer in charge of the train, the march was resumed, and at the close of that day we camped near a small lake about twenty miles from Fort Totten. From Totten we journeyed on to Fort Abercrombie. The country between the two posts is low and flat, and I verily believe was then the favorite abiding-place of the mosquito, no matter where he most loves to dwell now; for myriads of the pests rose up out of the tall rank grass—more than I ever saw before or since—and viciously attacked both men and animals. We ourselves were somewhat protected by gloves and head-nets, provided us before leaving Totten, but notwithstanding these our sufferings were well-nigh intolerable; the annoyance that the poor mules experienced must, therefore, have been extreme; indeed, they were so terribly stung that the blood fairly trickled down their sides. Unluckily, we had to camp for one night in this region; but we partly evaded the ravenous things by banking up our tent walls with earth, and then, before turning in, sweeping and smoking out such as had got inside. Yet with all this there seemed hundreds left to sing and sting throughout the night. The mules being without protection, we tried hard to save them from the vicious insects by creating a dense smoke from a circle of smothered fires, within which chain the grateful brutes gladly stood; but this relief was only partial, so the moment there was light enough to enable us to hook up we pulled out for Abercrombie in hot haste.

From Abercrombie we drove on to Saint Cloud, the terminus of the railroad, where, considerably the worse for our hurried trip and truly wretched experience with the mosquitoes, we boarded the welcome cars. Two days later we arrived in Chicago, and having meanwhile received word from General Sherman that there would be no objection to my going to Europe, I began making arrangements to leave, securing passage by the steamship Scotia.

President Grant invited me to come to see him at Long Branch before I should sail, and during my brief visit there he asked which army I wished to accompany, the German or the French. I told him the German, for the reason that I thought more could be seen with the successful side, and that the indications pointed to the defeat of the French. My choice evidently pleased him greatly, as he had the utmost contempt for Louis Napoleon, and had always denounced him as a usurper and a charlatan. Before we separated, the President gave me the following letter to the representatives of our Government abroad, and with it I not only had no trouble in obtaining permission to go with the Germans, but was specially favored by being invited to accompany the headquarters of the King of Prussia:

"LONG BRANCH, N. J., July 25, 1870.

"Lieutenant-General P. H. Sheridan, of the United State Army, is authorized to visit Europe, to return at his own pleasure, unless otherwise ordered. He is commended to the good offices of all representatives of this Government whom he may meet abroad.

"To citizens and representatives of other Governments I introduce General Sheridan as one of the most skillful, brave and deserving soldiers developed by the great struggle through which the United States Government has just passed. Attention paid him will be duly appreciated by the country he has served so faithfully and efficiently.

"U. S. GRANT."

Word of my intended trip was cabled to Europe in the ordinary press despatches, and our Minister to France, Mr. Elihu B. Washburn, being an intimate friend of mine, and thinking that I might wish to attach myself to the French army, did me the favor to take preliminary steps for securing the necessary authority. He went so far as to broach the subject to the French Minister of War, but in view of the informality of the request, and an unmistakable unwillingness to grant it being manifested, Mr. Washburn pursued the matter no further. I did not learn of this kindly interest in my behalf till after the capitulation of Paris, when Mr. Washburn told me what he had done of his own motion. Of course I thanked him gratefully, but even had he succeeded in getting the permission he sought I should not have accompanied the French army.

I sailed from New York July 27, one of my aides-de-camp, General James W. Forsyth, going with me. We reached Liverpool August 6, and the next day visited the American Legation in London, where we saw all the officials except our Minister, Mr. Motley, who, being absent, was represented by Mr. Moran, the Secretary of the Legation. We left London August 9 for Brussels, where we were kindly cared for by the American Minister, Mr. Russell Jones who the same evening saw us off for Germany. Because of the war we secured transportation only as far as Vera, and here we received information that the Prussian Minister of War had telegraphed to the Military Inspector of Railroads to take charge of us on our arrival a Cologne, and send us down to the headquarter of the Prussian army, but the Inspector, for some unexplained reason, instead of doing this, sent us on to Berlin. Here our Minister, Mr. George Bancroft, met us with a telegram from the German Chancellor, Count Bismarck, saying we were expected to come direct to the King's headquarters and we learned also that a despatch had been sent to the Prussian Minister at Brussels directing him to forward us from Cologne to the army, instead of allowing us to go on to Berlin, but that we had reached and quit Brussels without the Minister's knowledge.

CHAPTER XVI.

LEAVING FOR THE SEAT OF WAR—MEETING WITH PRINCE BISMARCK—HIS INTEREST IN PUBLIC OPINION IN AMERICA—HIS INCLINATIONS IN EARLY LIFE—PRESENTED TO THE KING—THE BATTLE OF GRAVELOTTE—THE GERMAN PLAN—ITS FINAL SUCCESS—SENDING NEWS OF THE VICTORY—MISTAKEN FOR A FRENCHMAN.

Shortly after we arrived in Berlin the Queen sent a messenger offering us an opportunity to pay our respects, and fixed an hour for the visit, which was to take place the next day; but as the tenor of the despatch Mr. Bancroft had received from Count Bismarck indicated that some important event which it was desired I should witness was about to happen at the theatre of war, our Minister got us excused from our visit of ceremony, and we started for the headquarters of the German army that evening—our stay in the Prussian capital having been somewhat less than a day.

Our train was a very long one, of over eighty cars, and though drawn by three locomotives, its progress to Cologne was very slow and the journey most tedious. From Cologne we continued on by rail up the valley of the Rhine to Bingebruck, near Bingen, and thence across through Saarbrucken to Remilly, where we left the railway and rode in a hay-wagon to Pont-a-Mousson, arriving there August 17, late in the afternoon. This little city had been ceded to France at the Peace of Westphalia, and although originally German, the people had become, in the lapse of so many years, intensely French in sentiment. The town was so full of officers and men belonging to the German army that it was difficult to get lodgings, but after some delay we found quite comfortable quarters at one of the small hotels, and presently, after we had succeeded in getting a slender meal, I sent my card to Count von Bismarck, the Chancellor of the North German Confederation, who soon responded by appointing an hour—about 9 o'clock the same evening—for an interview.

When the Count received me he was clothed in the undress uniform of the Cuirassier regiment, of which he was the colonel. During the interview which ensued, he exhibited at times deep anxiety regarding the conflict now imminent, for it was the night before the battle of Gravelotte, but his conversation was mostly devoted to the state of public sentiment in America, about which he seemed much concerned, inquiring repeatedly as to which side—France or Prussia—was charged with bringing on the war. Expressing a desire to witness the battle which was expected to occur the next day, and remarking that I had not had sufficient time to provide the necessary transportation, he told me to be ready at 4 o'clock in the morning, and he would take me out in his own carriage and present me to the King—adding that he would ask one of his own staff-officers, who he knew had one or two extra horses, to lend me one. As I did not know just what my status would be, and having explained to the President before leaving America that I wished to accompany the German army unofficially, I hardly knew whether to appear in uniform or not, so I spoke of this matter too, and the Count, after some reflection, thought it best for me to wear my undress uniform, minus the sword, however, because I was a non combatant.

At 4 o'clock the next morning, the 18th, I repaired to the Chancellor's quarters. The carriage was at the door, also the saddle-horse, but as no spare mount could be procured for General Forsyth, he had to seek other means to reach the battle-field. The carriage was an open one with two double seats, and in front a single one for a messenger; it had also a hand-brake attached.

Count Bismarck and I occupied the rear seat, and Count Bismarck-Bohlen—the nephew and aide-decamp to the Chancellor—and Doctor Busch were seated facing us. The conveyance was strong, serviceable, and comfortable, but not specially prepossessing, and hitched to it were four stout horses—logy, ungainly animals, whose clumsy harness indicated that the whole equipment was meant for heavy work. Two postilions in uniform, in high military saddles on the nigh horse of each span, completed the establishment.

All being ready, we took one of the roads from Pont-a-Mousson to Rezonville, which is on the direct road from Metz to Chalons, and near the central point of the field where, on the 16th of August, the battle of

Mars-la-Tour had been fought. It was by this road that the Pomeranians, numbering about 30,000 men, had been ordered to march to Gravelotte, and after proceeding a short distance we overtook the column. As this contingent came from Count Bismarck's own section of Germany, there greeted us as we passed along, first in the dim light of the morning, and later in the glow of the rising sun, continuous and most enthusiastic cheering for the German Chancellor.

On the way Count Bismarck again recurred to the state of public opinion in America with reference to the war. He also talked much about our form of government, and said that in early life his tendencies were all toward republicanism, but that family influence had overcome his preferences, and intimated that, after adopting a political career, he found that Germany was not sufficiently advanced for republicanism. He said, further, that he had been reluctant to enter upon this public career, that he had always longed to be a soldier, but that here again family opposition had turned him from the field of his choice into the sphere of diplomacy.

Not far from Mars-la-Tour we alighted, and in a little while an aide-de-camp was introduced, who informed me that he was there to conduct and present me to his Majesty, the King of Prussia. As we were walking along together, I inquired whether at the meeting I should remove my cap, and he said no; that in an out-of-door presentation it was not etiquette to uncover if in uniform. We were soon in presence of the King, where—under the shade of a clump of second-growth poplar-trees, with which nearly all the farms in the north of France are here and there dotted—the presentation was made in the simplest and most agreeable manner.

His Majesty, taking my hand in both of his, gave me a thorough welcome, expressing, like Count Bismarck, though through an interpreter, much interest as to the sentiment in my own country about the war. At this time William the First of Prussia was seventy-three years of age, and, dressed in the uniform of the Guards, he seemed to be the very ideal soldier, and graced with most gentle and courteous manners. The conversation, which was brief, as neither of us spoke the other's native tongue, concluded by his Majesty's requesting me in the most cordial way to accompany his headquarters during the campaign. Thanking him for his kindness, I rejoined Count Bismarck's party, and our horses having arrived meantime, we mounted and moved off to the position selected for the King to witness the opening of the battle.

This place was on some high ground overlooking the villages of Rezonville and Gravelotte, about the centre of the battlefield of Mars-la-Tour, and from it most of the country to the east toward Metz could also be seen. The point chosen was an excellent one for the purpose, though in one respect disagreeable, since the dead bodies of many of the poor fellows killed there two days before were yet unburied. In a little while the King's escort began to remove these dead, however, bearing them away on stretchers improvised with their rifles, and the spot thus cleared was much more acceptable. Then, when such unexploded shells as were lying around loose had been cautiously carried away, the King, his brother, Prince Frederick Charles Alexander, the chief-of-staff, General von Moltke, the Minister of War, General von Roon, and Count von Bismarck assembled on the highest point, and I being asked to join the group, was there presented to General von Moltke. He spoke our language fluently, and Bismarck having left the party for a time to go to a neighboring house to see his son, who had been wounded at Mars-la-Tour, and about whom he was naturally very anxious, General von Moltke entertained me by explaining the positions of the different corps, the nature and object of their movements then taking place, and so on.

Before us, and covering Metz, lay the French army, posted on the crest of a ridge extending north, and about its centre curving slightly westward toward the German forces. The left of the French position was but a short distance from the Moselle, and this part of the line was separated from the Germans by a ravine, the slopes, fairly well wooded, rising quite sharply; farther north, near the centre, this depression disappeared, merged in the general swell of the ground, and thence on toward the right the ground over which an approach to the French line must be made was essentially a natural open glacis, that could be thoroughly swept by the fire of the defenders.

The line extended some seven or eight miles. To attack this position, formidable everywhere, except perhaps on the right flank, the Germans were bringing up the combined forces of the First and Second armies, troops that within the past fortnight had already successfully met the French in three pitched battles. On the right was the First Army, under command of General Von Steinmetz, the victors, August 6, of Spicheren, near Saar, and, eight days later, of Colombey, to the east of Metz; while the centre and left were composed of the several corps of the Second Army, commanded by Prince Frederick Charles of Prussia, a part of whose troops had just been engaged in the sanguinary battle of Mars-la-Tour, by which Bazaine was cut off from the Verdun road, and forced back toward Metz.

At first the German plan was simply to threaten with their right, while the corps of the Second Army advanced toward the north, to prevent the French, of whose intentions there was much doubt, from escaping toward Chalons; then, as the purposes of the French might be, developed, these corps were to change direction toward the enemy successively, and seek to turn his right flank. But the location of this vital turning-point was very uncertain, and until it was ascertained and carried, late in the afternoon, the action raged with more or less intensity along the entire line.

But as it is not my purpose to describe in detail the battle of Gravelotte, nor any other, I will speak of some of its incidents merely. About noon, after many preliminary skirmishes, the action was begun according to the plan I have already outlined, the Germans advancing their left while holding on strongly with their right, and it was this wing (the First Army) that came under my observation from the place where the King's headquarters were located. From here we could see, as I have said, the village of Gravelotte. Before it lay the German troops, concealed to some extent, especially to the left, by clumps of timber here and there. Immediately in front of us, however, the ground was open, and the day being clear and sunny, with a fresh breeze blowing (else the smoke from a battle between four hundred thousand men would have obstructed the view altogether), the spectacle presented was of unsurpassed magnificence and sublimity. The German artillery opened the battle, and while the air was filled with shot and shell from hundreds of guns along their entire line, the German centre and left, in rather open order, moved out to the attack, and as they went forward the reserves, in close column, took up positions within supporting distances, yet far enough back to be out of range.

The French artillery and mitrailleuses responded vigorously to the Krupps, and with deadly effect, but as far as we could see the German left continued its advance, and staff-officers came up frequently to report that all was going on well at points hidden from our view These reports were always made to the King first, and whenever anybody arrived with tidings of the fight we clustered around to hear the news, General Von Moltke unfolding a map meanwhile, and explaining the situation. This done, the chief of the staff, while awaiting the next report, would either return to a seat that had been made for him with some knapsacks, or would occupy the time walking about, kicking clods of dirt or small stones here and there, his hands clasped behind his back, his face pale and thoughtful. He was then nearly seventy years old, but because of his emaciated figure, the deep wrinkles in his face, and the crow's-feet about his eyes, he looked even older, his appearance being suggestive of the practice of church asceticisms rather than of his well-known ardent devotion to the military profession.

By the middle of the afternoon the steady progress of the German left and centre had driven the French from their more advanced positions from behind stone walls and hedges, through valleys and hamlets, in the direction of Metz, but as yet the German right had accomplished little except to get possession of the village of Gravelotte, forcing the French across the deep ravine I have mentioned, which runs north and south a little distance east of the town.

But it was now time for the German right to move in earnest to carry the Rozerieulles ridge, on which crest the French had evidently decided to make an obstinate fight to cover their withdrawal to Metz. As the Germans moved to the attack here, the French fire became heavy and destructive, so much so, indeed, as to cause General Von Steinmetz to order some cavalry belonging to the right wing to make a charge. Crossing the ravine before described, this body of horse swept up the slope beyond, the front ranks urged forward by the momentum from behind. The French were posted along a sunken road, behind stone walls and houses, and as the German cavalry neared these obstructions it received a dreadful fire without the least chance of returning it, though still pushed on till the front ranks were crowded into the deep cut of the road. Here the slaughter was terrible, for the horsemen could make no further headway; and because of the blockade behind, of dead and wounded men and animals, an orderly retreat was impossible, and disaster inevitable.

About the time the charge was ordered, the phase of the battle was such that the King concluded to move his headquarters into the village of Gravelotte; and just after getting there, we first learned fully of the disastrous result of the charge which had been entered upon with such spirit; and so much indignation was expressed against Steinmetz, who, it was claimed, had made an unnecessary sacrifice of his cavalry, that I thought he would be relieved on the spot; though this was not done.

Followed by a large staff, General Steinmetz appeared in the village presently, and approached the King. When near, he bowed with great respect, and I then saw that he was a very old man though his soldierly figure, bronzed face, and shortcropped hair gave some evidence of vigor still. When the King spoke to him I was not close enough to learn what was said; but his Majesty's manner was expressive of kindly feeling, and the fact that in a few moments the veteran general returned to the command of his troops, indicated that, for the present at least, his fault had been overlooked.

The King then moved out of the village, and just a little to the east and north of it the headquarters were located on high, open ground, whence we could observe the right of the German infantry advancing up the eastern face of the ravine. The advance, though slow and irregular, resulted in gradually gaining ground, the French resisting stoutly with a stubborn musketry fire all along the slopes. Their artillery was silent, however; and from this fact the German artillery officers grew jubilant, confidently asserting that their Krupp guns had dismounted the French batteries and knocked their mitrailleuses to pieces. I did not indulge in this confidence, however; for, with the excellent field-glass I had, I could distinctly see long columns of French troops moving to their right, for the apparent purpose of making a vigorous fight on that flank; and I thought it more than likely that their artillery would be heard from before the Germans could gain the coveted ridge.

The Germans labored up the glacis slowly at the most exposed places; now crawling on their bellies, now creeping on hands and knees, but, in the main, moving with erect and steady bearing. As they approached within short range, they suddenly found that the French artillery and mitrallleuses had by no means been silenced—about two hundred pieces opening on them with fearful effect, while at the same time the whole crest blazed with a deadly fire from the Chassepot rifles. Resistance like this was so unexpected by the Germans that it dismayed them; and first wavering a moment, then becoming panic-stricken, they broke and fled, infantry, cavalry, and artillery coming down the slope without any pretence of formation, the French hotly following and pouring in a heavy and constant fire as the fugitives fled back across the ravine toward Gravelotte. With this the battle on the right had now assumed a most serious aspect, and the indications were that the French would attack the heights of Gravelotte; but the Pomeranian corps coming on the field at this crisis, was led into action by Von Moltke himself, and shortly after the day was decided in favor of the Germans.

When the French guns opened fire, it was discovered that the King's position was within easy range, many of the shells falling near enough to make the place extremely uncomfortable; so it was suggested that he go to a less exposed point. At first he refused to listen to this wise counsel, but yielded finally—leaving the ground with reluctance, however—and went back toward Rezonville. I waited for Count Bismarck, who did not go immediately with the King, but remained at Gravelotte, looking after some of the escort who had been wounded. When he had arranged for their care, we set out to rejoin the King, and before going far, overtook his Majesty, who had stopped on the Chalons road, and was surrounded by a throng of fugitives, whom he was berating in German so energetic as to remind me forcibly of the "Dutch" swearing that I used to hear in my boyhood in Ohio. The dressing down finished to his satisfaction, the King resumed his course toward Rézonville, halting, however, to rebuke in the same emphatic style every group of runaways he overtook.

Passing through Rezonville, we halted just beyond the village; there a fire was built, and the King, his brother, Prince Frederick Charles, and Von Roon were provided with rather uncomfortable seats about it, made by resting the ends of a short ladder on a couple of boxes. With much anxiety and not a little depression of spirits news from the battle-field was now awaited, but the suspense did not last long, for presently came the cheering intelligence that the French were retiring, being forced back by the Pomeranian corps, and some of the lately broken right wing organizations, that had been rallied on the heights of Gravelotte. The lost ground being thus regained, and the French having been beaten on their right, it was not long before word came that Bazaine's army was falling back to Metz, leaving the entire battle-field in possession of the Germans.

During the excitement of the day I had not much felt the want of either food or water, but now that all was over I was nearly exhausted, having had neither since early morning. Indeed, all of the party were in like straits; the immense armies had not only eaten up nearly everything in the country, but had drunk all the wells dry, too, and there seemed no relief for us till, luckily, a squad of soldiers came along the road with a small cask of wine in a cart. One of the staff-officers instantly appropriated the keg, and proceeded to share his prize most generously. Never had I tasted anything so refreshing and delicious, but as the wine was the ordinary sour stuff drunk by the peasantry of northern France, my appreciation must be ascribed to my famished condition rather than to any virtues of the beverage itself.

After I had thus quenched my thirst the King's, brother called me aside, and drawing from his coat-tail pocket a piece of stale black bread, divided it with me, and while munching on this the Prince began talking of his son—General Prince Frederick Charles, popularly called the Red Prince—who was in command of the Second Army in this battle—the German left wing. In recounting his son's professional career the old man's face was aglow with enthusiasm, and not without good cause, for in the war between Prussia and Austria in 1866, as well as in the present campaign, the Red Prince had displayed the highest order of military genius.

The headquarters now became the scene of much bustle, despatches announcing the victory being sent in all directions. The first one transmitted was to the Queen, the King directing Count Bismarck to prepare it for his signature; then followed others of a more official character, and while these matters were being attended to I thought I would ride into the village to find, if possible, some water for my horse. Just as I entered the chief street, however, I was suddenly halted by a squad of soldiers, who, taking me for a French officer (my coat and forage cap resembling those of the French), leveled their pieces at me. They were greatly excited, so much so, indeed, that I thought my hour had come, for they could not understand English, and I could not speak German, and dare not utter explanations in French. Fortunately a few disconnected German words came to me in the emergency. With these I managed to delay my execution, and one of the party ventured to come up to examine the "suspect" more closely. The first thing he did was to take off my cap, and looking it over carefully, his eyes rested on the three stars above the visor, and, pointing to them, he emphatically pronounced me French. Then of course they all became excited again, more so than before, even, for they thought I was trying to practice a ruse, and I question whether I should have lived to recount the adventure had not an officer belonging to the King's headquarters been passing by just then, when, hearing the threatenings and imprecations, he rode up to learn the cause of the hubbub, and immediately recognized and released me. When he told my wrathy captors who I was, they were much mortified of course, and made the most profuse apologies, promising that no such mistake should occur again, and so on; but not feeling wholly reassured, for my uniform was still liable to mislead, I was careful to return to headquarters in company with my deliverer. There I related what had occurred, and after a good laugh all round, the King provided me with a pass which he said would preclude any such mishap in the future, and would also permit me to go wherever I pleased—a favor rarely bestowed.

CHAPTER XVII

SEARCHING FOR QUARTERS—HUNTING UP PROVISIONS—A SLENDER BREAKFAST— GOING OVER THE BATTLEFIELD—THE GERMAN ARTILLERY—A GROUP OF WOUNDED—DINING WITH THE KING—ON THE MARCH—THE BAVARIANS—KIRSCHWASSER— URGING ON THE TROOPS.

While I was absent, as related in the preceding chapter, it had been decided that the King's quarters should be established for the night in the village of Rezonville; and as it would be very difficult, at such a late hour, to billet the whole party regularly, Count Bismarck and I went off to look for shelter for ourselves. Remembering that I had seen, when seeking to water my horse, a partly burned barn with some fresh-looking hay in it, I suggested that we lodge there. He too thought it would answer our purpose, but on reaching it we found the unburned part of the barn filled with wounded, and this necessitating a further search we continued on through the village in quest of some house not yet converted into a hospital. Such, however, seemed impossible to come upon, so at last the Count fixed on one whose upper floor, we learned, was unoccupied, though the lower one was covered with wounded.

Mounting a creaky ladder—there was no stairway—to the upper story, we found a good-sized room with three large beds, one of which the Chancellor assigned to the Duke of Mecklenburg and aide, and another to Count Bismarck-Bohlen and me, reserving the remaining one for himself. Each bed, as is common in Germany and northern France, was provided with a feather tick, but the night being warm, these spreads were thrown off, and discovering that they would make a comfortable shakedown on the floor, I slept there leaving Bismarck-Bohlen unembarrassed by companionship—at least of a human kind.

At daylight I awoke, and seeing that Count Bismarck was already dressed and about to go down the ladder, I felt obliged to follow his example, so I too turned out, and shortly descended to the ground—floor, the only delays of the toilet being those incident to dressing, for there were no conveniences for morning ablutions. Just outside the door I met the Count, who, proudly exhibiting a couple of eggs he had bought from the woman of the house, invited me to breakfast with him, provided we could beg some coffee from the king's escort. Putting the eggs under my charge, with many injunctions as to their safe-keeping, he went off to forage for the coffee, and presently returned, having been moderately successful. One egg apiece was hardly enough, however, to appease the craving of two strong men ravenous from long fasting. Indeed, it seemed only to whet the appetite, and we both set out on an eager expedition for more food. Before going far I had the good luck to meet a sutler's wagon, and though its stock was about all sold, there were still left four large bologna sausages, which I promptly purchased—paying a round sum for them too—and hastening back found the Count already returned, though without bringing anything at all to eat; but he had secured a couple of bottles of brandy, and with a little of this—it was excellent, too—and the sausages, the slim ration of eggs and coffee was amply reinforced.

Breakfast over, the Chancellor invited me to accompany him in a ride to the battle-field, and I gladly accepted, as I very much desired to pass over the ground in front of Gravelotte, particularly so to see whether the Krupp guns had really done the execution that was claimed for them by the German artillery officers. Going directly through the village of Gravelotte, following the causeway over which the German cavalry had passed to make its courageous but futile charge, we soon reached the ground where the fighting had been the most severe. Here the field was literally covered with evidences of the terrible strife, the dead and wounded strewn thick on every side.

In the sunken road the carnage had been awful; men and horses having been slaughtered there by hundreds, helpless before the murderous fire delivered from behind a high stone wall impracticable to mounted troops. The sight was sickening to an extreme, and we were not slow to direct our course elsewhere, going up the glacis toward the French line, the open ground over which we crossed being covered with thousands of helmets, that had been thrown off by the Germans during the fight and were still dotting the field, though details of soldiers from the organizations which had been engaged here were about to begin to gather up their abandoned headgear.

When we got inside the French works, I was astonished to observe how little harm had been done the defenses by the German artillery, for although I had not that serene faith in the effectiveness of their guns held by German artillerists generally, yet I thought their terrific cannonade must have left marked results. All I could perceive, however, was a disabled gun, a broken mitrailleuse, and two badly damaged caissons.

Everything else, except a little ammunition in the trenches, had been carried away, and it was plain to see, from the good shape in which the French left wing had retired to Metz, that its retreat had been predetermined by the disasters to the right wing.

By this hour the German cavalry having been thrown out to the front well over toward Metz, we, following it to get a look at the city, rode to a neighboring summit, supposing it would be a safe point of observation; but we shortly realized the contrary, for scarcely had we reached the crest when some of the French pickets, lying concealed about six hundred yards off, opened fire, making it so very hot for us that, hugging the necks of our horses, we incontinently fled. Observing what had taken place, a troop of German cavalry charged the French outpost and drove it far enough away to make safe our return, and we resumed possession of the point, but only to discover that the country to the east was so broken and hilly that no satisfactory view of Metz could be had.

Returning to Gravelotte, we next visited that part of the battlefield to the northeast of the village, and before long Count Bismarck discovered in a remote place about twenty men dreadfully wounded. These poor fellows had had no attention whatever, having been overlooked by the hospital corps, and their condition was most pitiful. Yet there was one very handsome man in the group—a captain of artillery—who, though shot through the right breast, was talkative and cheerful, and felt sure of getting well. Pointing, however, to a comrade lying near, also shot in the breast, he significantly shook his head; it was easy to see on this man's face the signs—of fast approaching death.

An orderly was at once despatched for a surgeon, Bismarck and I doing what we could meanwhile to alleviate the intense sufferings of the maimed men, bringing them water and administering a little brandy, for the Count still had with him some of the morning's supply. When the surgeons came, we transferred the wounded to their care, and making our way to Rezonville, there took the Count's carriage to rejoin the King's headquarters, which in the mean time had been moved to Pont-a-Mousson. Our route led through the village of Gorze, and here we found the streets so obstructed with wagons that I feared it would take us the rest of the day to get through, for the teamsters would not pay the slightest heed to the cries of our postilions. The Count was equal to the emergency, however, for, taking a pistol from behind his cushion, and bidding me keep my seat, he jumped out and quickly began to clear the street effectively, ordering wagons to the right and left. Marching in front of the carriage and making way for us till we were well through the blockade, he then resumed his seat, remarking, "This is not a very dignified business for the Chancellor of the German Confederation, but it's the only way to get through."

At Pont-a-Mousson I was rejoined by my aide, General Forsyth, and for the next two days our attention was almost wholly devoted to securing means of transportation. This was most difficult to obtain, but as I did not wish to impose on the kindness of the Chancellor longer, we persevered till, finally, with the help of Count Bismarck-Bohlen, we managed to get tolerably well equipped with a saddle-horse apiece, and a two-horse carriage. Here also, on the afternoon of August 21, I had the pleasure of dining with the King. The dinner was a simple one, consisting of soup, a joint, and two or three vegetables; the wines vin ordinaire and Burgundy. There were a good many persons of high rank present, none of whom spoke English, however, except Bismarck, who sat next the King and acted as interpreter when his Majesty conversed with me. Little was said of the events taking place around us, but the King made many inquiries concerning the war of the rebellion, particularly with reference to Grant's campaign at Vicksburg; suggested, perhaps, by the fact that there, and in the recent movements of the German army, had been applied many similar principles of military science.

The French army under Marshal Bazaine having retired into the fortifications of Metz, that stronghold was speedily invested by Prince Frederick Charles. Meantime the Third Army, under the Crown Prince of Prussia—which, after having fought and won the battle of Worth, had been observing the army of Marshal MacMahon during and after the battle of Gravelotte—was moving toward Paris by way of Nancy, in conjunction with an army called the Fourth, which had been organized from the troops previously engaged around Metz, and on the 22d was directed toward Bar-le-Duc under the command of the Crown Prince of Saxony. In consequence of these operations the King decided to move to Commercy, which place we reached by carriage, traveling on a broad macadamized road lined on both sides with poplar-trees, and our course leading through a most beautiful country thickly dotted with prosperous-looking villages.

On reaching Commercy, Forsyth and I found that quarters had been already selected for us, and our names written on the door with chalk the quartermaster charged with the billeting of the officers at headquarters having started out in advance to perform this duty and make all needful preparations for the King before he arrived, which course was usually pursued thereafter, whenever the royal headquarters took up a new location.

Forsyth and I were lodged with the notary of the village, who over and over again referred to his good fortune in not having to entertain any of the Germans. He treated us most hospitably, and next morning, on departing, we offered compensation by tendering a sum—about what our bill would have been at a good hotel—to be used for the "benefit of the wounded or the Church." Under this stipulation the notary accepted, and we followed that plan of paying for food and lodging afterward, whenever quartered in private houses.

The next day I set out in advance of the headquarters, and reached Bar-le-Duc about noon, passing on the way the Bavarian contingent of the Crown Prince's army. These Bavarians were trim-looking soldiers, dressed in neat uniforms of light blue; they looked healthy and strong, but seemed of shorter stature than the North Germans I had seen in the armies of Prince Frederick Charles and General von Steinmetz. When, later in the day the King arrived, a guard for him was detailed from this Bavarian contingent; a stroke of policy no doubt, for the South Germans were so prejudiced against their brothers of the North that no opportunity to smooth them down was permitted to go unimproved.

Bar-le-Duc, which had then a population of about 15,000, is one of the prettiest towns I saw in France, its quaint and ancient buildings and beautiful boulevards charming the eye as well as exciting deep interest. The King and his immediate suite were quartered on one of the best boulevards in a large building—the Bank of France—the balcony of which offered a fine opportunity to observe a part of the army of the Crown

Prince the next day on its march toward Vitry. This was the first time his Majesty had had a chance to see any of these troops—as hitherto he had accompanied either the army of Prince Frederick Charles, or that of General Steinmetz—and the cheers with which he was greeted by the Bavarians left no room for doubting their loyalty to the Confederation, notwithstanding ancient jealousies.

While the troops were passing, Count Bismarck had the kindness to point out to me the different organizations, giving scraps of their history, and also speaking concerning the qualifications of the different generals commanding them. When the review was over we went to the Count's house, and there, for the first time in my life, I tasted kirschwasser, a very strong liquor distilled from cherries. Not knowing anything about the stuff, I had to depend on Bismarck's recommendation, and he proclaiming it fine, I took quite a generous drink, which nearly strangled me and brought on a violent fit of coughing. The Chancellor said, however, that this was in no way due to the liquor, but to my own inexperience, and I was bound to believe the distinguished statesman, for he proved his words by swallowing a goodly dose with an undisturbed and even beaming countenance, demonstrating his assertion so forcibly that I forthwith set out with Bismarck-Bohlen to lay in a supply for myself.

I spent the night in a handsome house, the property of an exceptionally kind and polite gentleman bearing the indisputably German name of Lager, but who was nevertheless French from head to foot, if intense hatred of the Prussians be a sign of Gallic nationality. At daybreak on the 26th word came for us to be ready to move by the Chalons road at 7 o'clock, but before we got off, the order was suspended till 2 in the afternoon. In the interval General von Moltke arrived and held a long conference with the King, and when we did pull out we traveled the remainder of the afternoon in company with a part of the Crown Prince's army, which after this conference inaugurated the series of movements from Bar-le-Duc northward, that finally compelled the surrender at Sedan. This sudden change of direction I did not at first understand, but soon learned that it was because of the movements of Marshal MacMahon, who, having united the French army beaten at Worth with three fresh corps at Chalons, was marching to relieve Metz in obedience to orders from the Minister of War at Paris.

As we passed along the column, we noticed that the Crown Prince's troops were doing their best, the officers urging the men to their utmost exertions, persuading weary laggards and driving up stragglers. As a general thing, however, they marched in good shape, notwithstanding the rapid gait and the trying heat, for at the outset of the campaign the Prince had divested them of all impedimenta except essentials, and they were therefore in excellent trim for a forced march.

The King traveled further than usual that day—to Clermont—so we did not get shelter till late, and even then not without some confusion, for the quartermaster having set out toward Chalons before the change of programme was ordered, was not at hand to provide for us. I had extreme good luck, though, in being quartered with a certain apothecary, who, having lived for a time in the United States, claimed it as a privilege even to lodge me, and certainly made me his debtor for the most generous hospitality. It was not so with some of the others, however; and Count Bismarck was particularly unfortunate, being billeted in a very small and uncomfortable house, where, visiting him to learn more fully what was going on, I found him, wrapped in a shabby old dressing-gown, hard at work. He was established in a very small room, whose only furnishings consisted of a table—at which he was writing—a couple of rough chairs, and the universal feather-bed, this time made on the floor in one corner of the room. On my remarking upon the limited character of his quarters, the Count replied, with great good-humor, that they were all right, and that he should get along well enough. Even the tramp of his clerks in the attic, and the clanking of his orderlies' sabres below, did not disturb him much; he said, in fact, that he would have no grievance at all were it not for a guard of Bavarian soldiers stationed about the house for his safety, he presumed the sentinels from which insisted on protecting and saluting the Chancellor of the North German Confederation in and out of season, a proceeding that led to embarrassment sometimes, as he was much troubled with a severe dysentery. Notwithstanding his trials, however, and in the midst of the correspondence on which he was so intently engaged, he graciously took time to explain that the sudden movement northward from Bar-le-Duc was, as I have previously recounted, the result of information that Marshal MacMahon was endeavoring to relieve Metz by marching along the Belgian frontier; "a blundering manoeuvre," remarked the Chancellor, "which cannot be accounted for, unless it has been brought about by the political situation of the French."

CHAPTER XVIII.

AFTER MACMAHON—THE BATTLE AT BEAUMONT—THE FRENCH SURPRISED—THE MARCHING OF THE GERMAN SOLDIERS—THE BATTLE OF SEDAN—GALLANT CAVALRY CHARGES—DEFEAT OF THE FRENCH—THE SURRENDER OF NAPOLEON—BISMARCK AND THE KING—DECORATING THE SOLDIERS.

All night long the forced march of the army went on through Clermont, and when I turned out, just after daylight, the columns were still pressing forward, the men looking tired and much bedraggled, as indeed they had reason to be, for from recent rains the roads were very sloppy. Notwithstanding this, however, the troops were pushed ahead with all possible vigor to intercept MacMahon and force a battle before he could withdraw from his faulty movement, for which it has since been ascertained he was not at all responsible. Indeed, those at the royal headquarters seemed to think of nothing else than to strike MacMahon, for, feeling pretty confident that Metz could not be relieved, they manifested not the slightest anxiety on that score.

By 8 o'clock, the skies having cleared, the headquarters set out for Grand Pre', which place we reached early in the afternoon, and that evening I again had the pleasure of dining with the King. The conversation at table was almost wholly devoted to the situation, of course, everybody expressing surprise at the manoeuvre of the French at this time, their march along the Belgian frontier being credited entirely to Napoleon. Up to bed-time there was still much uncertainty as to the exact positions of the French, but next morning intelligence being received which denoted the probability of a battle, we drove about ten miles, to Buzancy, and there mounting our horses, rode to the front.

The French were posted not far from Buzancy in a strong position, their right resting near Stonne and the left extending over into the woods beyond Beaumont. About 10 o'clock the Crown Prince of Saxony advanced against this line, and while a part of his army turned the French right, compelling it to fall back rapidly, the German centre and right attacked with great vigor and much skill, surprising one of the divisions of General De Failly's corps while the men were in the act of cooking their breakfast.

The French fled precipitately, leaving behind their tents and other camp equipage, and on inspecting the ground which they had abandoned so hastily, I noticed on all sides ample evidence that not even the most ordinary precautions had been taken to secure the division from surprise, The artillery horses had not been harnessed, and many of them had been shot down at the picketrope where they had been haltered the night before, while numbers of men were lying dead with loaves of bread or other food instead of their muskets in their hands.

Some three thousand prisoners and nearly all the artillery and mitrailleuses of the division—were captured, while the fugitives were pursued till they found shelter behind—Douay's corps and the rest of De Failly's beyond Beaumont. The same afternoon there were several other severe combats along the Meuse, but I had no chance of witnessing any of them, and just before night-fall I started back to Buzancy, to which place the King's headquarters had been brought during the day.

The morning of the 31st the King moved to Vendresse. First sending our carriage back to Grand Pre' for our trunks, Forsyth and I mounted our horses and rode to the battle-field accompanied by an English nobleman, the Duke of Manchester. The part of the field we traversed was still thickly strewn with the dead of both armies, though all the wounded had been collected in the hospitals. In the village of Beaumont, we stopped to take a look at several thousand French prisoners, whose worn clothing and evident dejection told that they had been doing a deal of severe marching under great discouragements.

The King reached the village shortly after, and we all continued on to Chemery, just beyond where his Majesty alighted from his carriage to observe his son's troops file past as they came in from the direction of Stonne. This delay caused us to be as late as 9 o'clock before we got shelter that night, but as it afforded me the best opportunity I had yet had for seeing the German soldiers on the march, I did not begrudge the time. They moved in a somewhat open and irregular column of fours, the intervals between files being especially intended to give room for a peculiar swinging gait, with which the men seemed to urge themselves over the ground with ease and rapidity. There was little or no straggling, and being strong, lusty young fellows, and lightly equipped—they carried only needle-guns, ammunition, a very small knapsack, a water-bottle, and a haversack-they strode by with an elastic step, covering at least three miles an hour.

It having been definitely ascertained that the demoralized French were retiring to Sedan, on the evening of August 31 the German army began the work of hemming them in there, so disposing the different corps as to cover the ground from Donchery around by Raucourt to Carignan. The next morning this line was to be drawn in closer on Sedan; and the Crown Prince of Saxony was therefore ordered to take up a position to the north of Bazeilles, beyond the right bank of the Meuse, while the Crown Prince of Prussia was to cross his right wing over the Meuse at Remilly, to move on Bazeilles, his centre meantime marching against a number of little hamlets still held by the French between there and Donchery. At this last-mentioned place strong reserves were to be held, and from it the Eleventh Corps, followed by the Fifth and a division of cavalry, was to march on St. Menges.

Forsyth and I started early next morning, September 1, and in a thick fog-which, however, subsequently gave place to bright sunshine—we drove to the village of Chevenges, where, mounting our horses, we rode in a northeasterly direction to the heights of Frenois and Wadelincourt, bordering the river Meuse on the left bank, where from the crest we had a good view of the town of Sedan with its circling fortifications, which, though extensive, were not so formidable as those around Metz. The King and his staff were already established on these heights, and at a point so well chosen that his Majesty could observe the movements of both armies immediately east and south of Sedan, and also to the northwest toward Floing and the Belgian frontier.

The battle was begun to the east and northeast of Sedan as early as half-past 4 o'clock by the German right wing—the fighting being desultory—and near the same hour the Bavarians attacked Bazeilles. This village, some two miles southeast of Sedan, being of importance, was defended with great obstinacy, the French contesting from street to street and house to house the attack of the Bavarians till near 10 o'clock, when, almost every building being knocked to pieces, they were compelled to relinquish the place. The possession of this village gave the Germans to the east of Sedan a continuous line, extending from the Meuse northward through La Moncelle and Daigny to Givonne, and almost to the Belgian frontier.

While the German centre and right were thus engaged, the left had moved in accordance with the prescribed plan. Indeed, some of these troops had crossed the Meuse the night before, and now, at a little after 6 o'clock, their advance could be seen just north of the village of Floing. Thus far these columns, under the immediate eye of the Crown Prince of Prussia, had met with no opposition to their march, and as soon as they got to the high ground above the village they began extending to the east, to connect with the Army of the Meuse. This juncture was effected at Illy without difficulty, and the French army was now completely encompassed.

After a severe fight, the Crown Prince drove the French through Floing, and as the ground between this village and Sedan is an undulating open plain, everywhere visible, there was then offered a rare opportunity for seeing the final conflict preceding the surrender. Presently up out of the little valley where Floing is located came the Germans, deploying just on the rim of the plateau a very heavy skirmish-line, supported by a line of battle at close distance. When these skirmishers appeared, the French infantry had withdrawn within its intrenched lines, but a strong body of their cavalry, already formed in a depression to the right of the Floing road, now rode at the Germans in gallant style, going clear through the dispersed skirmishers to the main line of battle. Here the slaughter of the French was awful, for in addition to the deadly volleys from the solid battalions of their enemies, the skirmishers, who had rallied in knots at advantageous places, were now delivering a severe and effective fire. The gallant horsemen, therefore, had to retire precipitately, but re-forming in the depression, they again undertook the hopeless task of breaking the German infantry, making in all four successive charges. Their ardor and pluck were of no avail, however, for the Germans, growing stronger every minute by the accession of troops from Floing, met the fourth attack in such large force that, even before coming in contact with their adversaries, the French broke and retreated to the protection of the intrenchments, where, from the beginning of the combat, had been lying plenty of idle infantry, some of which at least, it seemed plain to me, ought to have been thrown into the fight. This action was the last one of consequence around Sedan, for, though with the contraction of the German lines their batteries kept cannonading more or less, and the rattle of musketry continued to be heard here and there, yet the hard fighting of the day practically ended on the plateau of Floing.

By 3 o'clock, the French being in a desperate and hopeless situation, the King ordered the firing to be stopped, and at once despatched one of his staff—Colonel von Bronsart—with a demand for a surrender. Just as this officer was starting off, I remarked to Bismarck that Napoleon himself would likely be one of the prizes, but the Count, incredulous, replied, "Oh no; the old fox is too cunning to be caught in such a trap; he has doubtless slipped off to Paris"—a belief which I found to prevail pretty generally about headquarters.

In the lull that succeeded, the King invited many of those about him to luncheon, a caterer having provided from some source or other a substantial meal of good bread, chops and peas, with a bountiful supply of red and sherry wines. Among those present were Prince Carl, Bismarck, Von Moltke, Von Roon, the Duke of Weimar, the Duke of Coburg, the Grand-Duke of Mecklenburg, Count Hatzfeldt, Colonel Walker, of the English army, General Forsyth, and I. The King was agreeable and gracious at all times, but on this occasion he was particularly so, being naturally in a happy frame of mind because this day the war had reached a crisis which presaged for the near future the complete vanquishment of the French.

Between 4 and 5 o'clock Colonel von Bronsart returned from his mission to Sedan, bringing word to the King that the commanding officer there General Wimpffen, wished to know, in order that the further effusion of blood might be spared, upon what terms he might surrender. The Colonel brought the intelligence also that the French Emperor was in the town. Soon after Von Bronsart's arrival a French officer approached from Sedan, preceded by a white flag and two German officers. Coming up the road till within a few hundred yards of us, they halted; then one of the Germans rode forward to say that the French officer was Napoleon's adjutant, bearing an autograph letter from the Emperor to the King of Prussia. At this the King, followed by Bismarck, Von Moltke, and Von Roon, walked out to the front a little distance and halted, his Majesty still in advance, the rest of us meanwhile forming in a line some twenty paces to the rear of the group. The envoy then approached, at first on horseback, but when within about a hundred yards he dismounted, and uncovering, came the remaining distance on foot, bearing high up in his right hand the despatch from Napoleon. The bearer proved to be General Reille, and as he handed the Emperor's letter to the King, his Majesty saluted him with the utmost formality and precision. Napoleon's letter was the since famous one, running so characteristically, thus: "Not having been able to die in the midst of my troops, there is nothing left me but to place my sword in your Majesty's hands." The reading finished, the King returned to his former post, and after a conference with Bismarck, Von Moltke, and Von Roon, dictated an answer accepting Napoleon's surrender, and requesting him to designate an officer with power to treat for the capitulation of the army, himself naming Von Moltke to represent the Germans. The King then started for Vendresse, to pass the night. It was after 7 o'clock now, and hence too late to arrange anything more where we were, so further negotiations were deferred till later in the evening; and I, wishing to be conveniently near Bismarck, resolved to take up quarters in Donchery. On our way thither we were met by the Count's nephew, who assuring us that it would be impossible to find shelter there in the village, as all the houses were filled with wounded, Forsyth and I decided to continue on to Chevenge. On the other hand, Bismarck-Bohlen bore with him one great comfort—some excellent brandy. Offering the flask to his uncle, he said: "You've had a hard day of it; won't you refresh yourself?" The Chancellor, without wasting time to answer, raised the bottle to his lips, exclaiming: "Here's to the unification of Germany!" which sentiment the gurgling of an astonishingly long drink seemed to emphasize. The Count then handed the bottle back to his nephew, who, shaking it, ejaculated, "Why, we can't pledge you in return—there is nothing left!" to which came the waggish response, "I beg pardon; it was so dark I couldn't see"; nevertheless there was a little remaining, as I myself can aver.

Having left our carriage at Chevenge, Forsyth and I stopped there to get it, but a long search proving fruitless, we took lodging in the village at the house of the cure, resolved to continue the hunt in the morning. But then we had no better success, so concluding that our vehicle had been pressed into the hospital service, we at an early hour on the 2d of September resumed the search, continuing on down the road in the direction of Sedan. Near the gate of the city we came on the German picket-line, and one of the Officers, recognizing our uniforms—he having served in the war of the rebellion—stepped forward and addressed me in good English. We naturally fell into conversation, and in the midst of it there came out through the gate an open carriage, or landau, containing two men, one of whom, in the uniform of a general and smoking a cigarette, we recognized, when the conveyance drew near, as the Emperor Louis Napoleon. The landau went on toward Donchery at a leisurely pace, and we, inferring that there was something more important at hand just then than the recovery of our trap, followed at a respectful distance. Not quite a mile from Donchery is a cluster of three or four cottages, and at the first of these the landau stopped to await, as we afterward ascertained, Count Bismarck, with whom the diplomatic negotiations were to be settled. Some minutes elapsed before he came, Napoleon remaining seated in his carriage meantime, still smoking, and accepting with nonchalance the staring of a group of German soldiers near by, who were gazing on their fallen foe with curious and eager interest.

Presently a clattering of hoofs was heard, and looking toward the sound, I perceived the Chancellor cantering down the road. When abreast of the carriage he dismounted, and walking up to it, saluted the Emperor in a quick, brusque way that seemed to startle him. After a word or two, the party moved perhaps a hundred yards further on, where they stopped opposite the weaver's cottage so famous from that day. This little house is on the east side of the Donchery road, near its junction with that to Frenois, and stands about twenty paces back from the highway. In front is a stone wall covered with creeping vines, and from a gate in this wall runs to the front door a path, at this time bordered on both sides with potato vines.

The Emperor having alighted at the gate, he and Bismarck walked together along the narrow path and entered the cottage. Reappearing in about a quarter of an hour, they came out and seated themselves in the open air, the weaver having brought a couple of chairs. Here they engaged in an animated conversation, if much gesticulation is any indication. The talk lasted fully an hour, Bismarck seeming to do most of it, but at last he arose, saluted the Emperor, and strode down the path toward his horse. Seeing me standing near the gate, he joined me for a moment, and asked if I had noticed how the Emperor started when they first met, and I telling him that I had, he added, "Well, it must have been due to my manners, not my words, for these we're, 'I salute your Majesty just as I would my King.'" Then the Chancellor continued to chat a few minutes longer, assuring me that nothing further was to be done there, and that we had better go to the Chateau Bellevue, where, he said, the formal surrender was to take place. With this he rode off toward Vendresse to communicate with his sovereign, and Forsyth and I made ready to go to the Chateau Bellevue.

Before we set out, however, a number of officers of the King's suite arrived at the weaver's cottage, and from them I gathered that there were differences at the royal headquarters as to whether peace should be made then at Sedan, or the war continued till the French capital was taken. I further heard that the military advisers of the King strongly advocated an immediate move on Paris, while the Chancellor thought it best to make peace now, holding Alsace and Lorraine, and compelling the payment of an enormous levy of money; and these rumors were most likely correct, for I had often heard Bismarck say that France being the richest country in Europe, nothing could keep her quiet but effectually to empty her pockets; and besides this, he impressed me as holding that it would be better policy to preserve the Empire.

On our way to the chateau we fell in with a number of artillery officers bringing up their guns hurriedly to post them closer in to the beleaguered town on a specially advantageous ridge. Inquiring the cause of this move, we learned that General Wimpffen had not yet agreed to the terms of surrender; that it was thought he would not, and that they wanted to be prepared for any such contingency. And they were preparing with a vengeance too, for I counted seventy-two Krupp guns in one continuous line trained on the Chateau Bellevue and Sedan.

Napoleon went directly from the weaver's to the Chateau Bellevue, and about 10 o'clock the King of Prussia arrived from Frenois, accompanied by a few of his own suite and the Crown Prince with several members of his staff; and Von Moltke and Wimpffen having settled their points of difference before the two monarchs met, within the next half-hour the articles of capitulation were formally signed.

On the completion of the surrender—the occasion being justly considered a great one—the Crown Prince proceeded to distribute among the officers congregated in the chateau grounds 'the order of the Iron Cross'—a generous supply of these decorations being carried in a basket by one of his orderlies, following him about as he walked along. Meantime the King, leaving Napoleon in the chateau to ruminate on the fickleness of fortune, drove off to see his own victorious soldiers, who greeted him with huzzas that rent the air, and must have added to the pangs of the captive Emperor.

CHAPTER XIX.

RIDING OVER THE BATTLEFIELD—DESTRUCTION OF BAZEILLES—MISTAKES OF THE FRENCH—MARSHAL BAZAINE ON TO PARIS—A WEEK IN MEAUX—RHEIMS—ON THE PICKETLINE-UNDER FIRE—A SURRENDER—AT VERSAILLES—GENERAL BURNSIDE AND MR. FORBES IN PARIS.

The Crown Prince having got to the bottom of his medal basket—that is to say, having finished his liberal distribution of decorations to his officers—Forsyth and I rode off by way of Wadelincourt to Bazeilles to see what had taken place on that part of the field, and the sight that met our eyes as we entered the village was truly dreadful to look upon. Most of the houses had been knocked down or burned the day before, but such as had been left standing were now in flames, the torch having been applied because, as it was claimed, Frenchmen concealed in them had fired on the wounded. The streets were still encumbered with both German and French dead, and it was evident that of those killed in the houses the bodies had not been removed, for the air was loaded with odors of burning flesh. From Bazeille we rode on toward the north about two miles, along where the fight had been largely an artillery duel, to learn what we could of the effectiveness of the Krupp gun. Counting all the French dead we came across killed by artillery, they figured up about three hundred—a ridiculously small number; in fact, not much more than one dead man for each Krupp gun on that part of the line. Although the number of dead was in utter disproportion to the terrific six-hour cannonade, yet small as it was the torn and mangled bodies made such a horrible sight that we turned back toward Bazeilles without having gone further than Givonne.

At Bazeilles we met the King, accompanied by Bismarck and several of the staff. They too had been riding over the field, the King making this a practice, to see that the wounded were not neglected. As I drew up by the party, Bismarck accosted me with, "Well, General, aren't you hungry? This is just the place to whet one's appetite—these burning Frenchmen—Ugh!" and shrugging his shoulders in evident disgust, he turned away to join his Majesty in further explorations, Forsyth and I continuing on to Chevenges. Here we got the first inkling of what had become of our carriage since leaving it two days before: it had been pressed into service to carry wounded officers from the field during the battle, but afterward released, and was now safe at the house in Vendresse where we had been quartered the night of the 31st, so, on hearing this, we settled to go there again to lodge, but our good friend, the cure', insisting that we should stay with him, we remained in Chevenges till next morning.

On September 3 the King removed from Vendresse to Rethel, where he remained two days; in the mean while the Germans, 240,000 strong, beginning their direct march to Paris. The French had little with which to oppose this enormous force, not more, perhaps, than 50,000 regular troops; the rest of their splendid army had been lost or captured in battle, or was cooped up in the fortifications of Metz, Strasburg, and other places, in consequence of blunders without parallel in history, for which Napoleon and the Regency in Paris must be held accountable. The first of these gross faults was the fight at Worth, where MacMahon, before his army was mobilized, accepted battle with the Crown Prince, pitting 50,000 men against 175,000; the next was Bazaine's fixing upon Metz as his base, and stupidly putting himself in position to be driven back to it, when there was no possible obstacle to his joining forces with MacMahon at Chalons; while the third and greatest blunder of all was MacMahon's move to relieve Metz, trying to slip 140,000 men along the Belgian frontier. Indeed, it is exasperating and sickening to think of all this; to think that Bazaine carried into Metz—a place that should have been held, if at all, with not over 25,000 men—an army of 180,000, because it contained, the excuse was, "an accumulation of stores." With all the resources of rich France to draw upon, I cannot conceive that this excuse was sincere; on the contrary, I think that the movement of Bazaine must have been inspired by Napoleon with a view to the maintenance of his dynasty rather than for the good of France.

As previously stated, Bismarck did not approve of the German army's moving on Paris after the battle of Sedan. Indeed, I think he foresaw and dreaded the establishment of a Republic, his idea being that if peace was made then, the Empire could be continued in the person of the Prince Imperial who, coming to the throne under German influences, would be pliable in his hands. These views found frequent expression in private, and in public too; I myself particularly remember the Chancellor's speaking thus most unguardedly at a dinner in Rheims. But he could not prevent the march to Paris; it was impossible to stop the Germans, flushed with success. "On to Paris" was written by the soldiers on every door, and every fence-board along the route to the capital, and the thought of a triumphant march down the Champs Elysees was uppermost with every German, from the highest to the lowest grade.

The 5th of September we set out for Rheims. There it was said the Germans would meet with strong resistance, for the French intended to die to the last man before giving up that city. But this proved all fudge, as is usual with these "last ditch" promises, the garrison decamping immediately at the approach of a few Uhlans. So far as I could learn, but a single casualty happened; this occurred to an Uhlan, wounded by a shot which it was reported was fired from a house after the town was taken; so, to punish this breach of faith, a levy of several hundred bottles of champagne was made, and the wine divided about headquarters, being the only seizure made in the city, I believe, for though Rheims, the centre of the champagne district, had its cellars well stocked, yet most of them being owned by German firms, they received every protection.

The land about Rheims is of a white, chalky character, and very poor, but having been terraced and enriched with fertilizers, it produces the champagne grape in such abundance that the region, once considered valueless, and named by the peasantry the "land of the louse," now supports a dense population. We remained in Rheims eight days, and through the politeness of the American Consul—Mr. Adolph Gill—had the pleasure of seeing all the famous wine cellars, and inspecting the processes followed in champagne making, from the step of pressing the juice from the grape to that which shows the wine ready for the market. Mr. Gill also took us to see everything else of special interest about the city, and there being much to look at— fine old churches, ancient fortifications, a Roman gateway, etc.—the days slipped by very quickly, though the incessant rains somewhat interfered with our enjoyment.

For three or four days all sorts of rumors were rife as to what was doing in Paris, but nothing definite was learned till about the 9th; then Count Bismarck informed me that the Regency had been overthrown on the 4th, and that the Empress Eugenie had escaped to Belgium. The King of Prussia offered her an asylum with the Emperor at Wilhelmshohe, "where she ought to go," said the Chancellor, "for her proper place is with her husband," but he feared she would not. On the same occasion he also told me that Jules Favre—the head of the Provisional Government—had sent him the suggestion that, the Empire being gone, peace should be made and the Germans withdrawn, but that he (Bismarck) was now compelled to recognize the impossibility of doing this till Paris was taken, for although immediately after the surrender of Sedan he desired peace, the past few days had made it plain that the troops would not be satisfied with anything short of Paris, no matter what form of Government the French should ultimately adopt.

The German army having met with no resistance whatever in its march on Paris, its advance approached the capital rapidly, and by the 14th of September the royal headquarters moved by a fine macadamized road to the Chateau Thierry, and on the 5th reached Meaux, about twenty-eight miles from Paris, where we remained four days awaiting the reconstruction of some railroad and canal bridges. The town of Meaux has a busy population of about 10,000 souls, in peaceable times principally occupied in manufacturing flour for the Paris market, having a fine waterpower for the many mills. These were kept going day and night to supply the German army; and it was strange to see with what zeal Frenchmen toiled to fill the stomachs of their inveterate enemies, and with what alacrity the mayor and other officials filled requisitions for wine, cheese, suits of livery, riding-whips, and even squab pigeons.

During our stay at Meaux the British Minister Lord Lyons, endeavored to bring about a cessation of hostilities, to this end sending his secretary out from Paris with a letter to Count Bismarck, offering to serve as mediator. The Chancellor would not agree to this, however, for he conjectured that the action of the British Minister had been inspired by Jules Favre, who, he thought, was trying to draw the Germans into negotiations through the medium of a third party only for purposes of delay. So the next morning Lord Lyons's secretary, Mr. Edward Malet, returned to Paris empty-handed, except that he bore a communication positively declining mediation; which message, however, led no doubt to an interview between Bismarck and Favre a couple of days later.

The forenoon of September 19 the King removed to the Chateau Ferrieres—a castle belonging to the Rothschild family, where Napoleon had spent many happy days in the time of his prosperity. His Majesty took up his quarters here at the suggestion of the owner, we were told, so that by the presence of the King the magnificent chateau and its treasures of art would be unquestionably protected from all acts of vandalism.

All of the people at headquarters except the King's immediate suite were assigned quarters at Lagny; and while Forsyth and I, accompanied by Sir Henry Havelock, of the British army, were driving thither, we passed on the road the representative of the National Defense Government, Jules Favre, in a carriage heading toward Meaux. Preceded by a flag of truce and accompanied by a single, companion, be was searching for Count Bismarck, in conformity, doubtless, with the message the Chancellor had sent to Paris on the 17th by the British secretary. A half-mile further on we met Bismarck. He too was traveling toward Meaux, not in the best of humor either, it appeared, for having missed finding the French envoy at the rendezvous where they had agreed to meet, he stopped long enough to say that the "air was full of lies, and that there were many persons with the army bent on business that did not concern them."

The armies of the two Crown Princes were now at the outskirts of Paris. They had come from Sedan mainly by two routes—the Crown Prince of Saxony marching by the northern line, through Laon and Soissons, and the Crown Prince of Prussia by the southern line, keeping his right wing on the north bank of the Marne, while his left and centre approached the French capital by roads between that river and the Seine.

The march of these armies had been unobstructed by any resistance worth mentioning, and as the routes of both columns lay through a region teeming with everything necessary for their support, and rich even in luxuries, it struck me that such campaigning was more a vast picnic than like actual war. The country supplied at all points bread, meat, and wine in abundance, and the neat villages, never more than a mile or two apart, always furnished shelter; hence the enormous trains required to feed and provide camp equipage for an army operating in a sparsely settled country were dispensed with; in truth, about the only impedimenta of the Germans was their wagons carrying ammunition, pontoon-boats, and the field-telegraph.

On the morning of the 20th I started out accompanied by Forsyth and

Sir Henry Havelock, and took the road through Boissy St. George, Boissy St. Martins and Noisy Le Grand to Brie. Almost every foot of the way was strewn with fragments of glass from wine bottles, emptied and then broken by the troops. There was, indeed, so much of this that I refrain from making any estimate of the number of bottles, lest I be thought to exaggerate, but the road was literally paved with glass, and the amount of wine consumed (none was wasted) must have been enormous, far more, even, than I had seen evidence of at any time before. There were two almost continuous lines of broken bottles along the roadsides all the way down from Sedan; but that exhibit was small compared with what we saw about Brie.

At Brie we were taken charge of by the German commandant of the place. He entertained us most hospitably for an hour or so, and then, accompanied by a lieutenant, who was to be our guide, I set out ahead of my companions to gain a point on the picket-line where I expected to get a good look at the French, for their rifle-pits were but a few hundred yards off across the Marne, their main line being just behind the rifle-pits. As the lieutenant and I rode through the village, some soldiers warned us that the adventure would be dangerous, but that we could probably get to the desired place unhurt if we avoided the French fire by forcing our horses to a run in crossing some open streets where we would be exposed. On getting to the first street my guide galloped ahead to show the way, and as the French were not on the lookout for anything of the kind at these dangerous points, only a few stray shots were drawn by the lieutenant, but when I followed, they were fully up to what was going on, and let fly a volley every time they saw me in the open. Fortunately, however, in their excitement they overshot, but when I drew rein alongside of my guide under protection of the bluff where the German picket was posted, my hair was all on end, and I was about as badly scared as ever I had been in my life. As soon as I could recover myself I thought of Havelock and Forsyth, with the hope that they would not follow; nor did they, for having witnessed my experience, they wisely concluded that, after all, they did not care so much to see the French rifle-pits.

When I had climbed to the top of the bluff I was much disappointed, for I could see but little—only the advanced rifle-pits across the river, and Fort Nogent beyond them, not enough, certainly, to repay a non-combatant for taking the risk of being killed. The next question was to return, and deciding to take no more such chances as those we had run in coming out, I said we would wait till dark, but this proved unnecessary, for to my utter astonishment my guide informed me that there was a perfectly safe route by which we might go back. I asked why we had not taken it in coming, and he replied that he had thought it "too long and circuitous." To this I could say nothing, but I concluded that that was not quite the correct reason; the truth is that early that morning the young fellow had been helping to empty some of the many wine bottles I saw around Brie, and consequently had a little more "Dutch courage"—was a little more rash—than would have been the case under other conditions.

I rode back to Brie by the "long and circuitous" route, and inquiring there for my companions, found Havelock waiting to conduct me to the village of Villiers, whither, he said, Forsyth had been called to make some explanation about his passport, which did not appear to be in satisfactory shape. Accordingly we started for Villiers, and Havelock, being well mounted on an English "hunter," and wishing to give me an exhibition of the animal's training and power, led the way across ditches and fences, but my horse, never having followed "the hounds," was unsafe to experiment with, so, after trying a low fence or two, I decided to leave my friend alone in his diversion, and a few moments later, seeing both horse and rider go down before a ditch and high stone wall, I was convinced that my resolution was a discreet one. After this mishap, which luckily resulted in no harm, I hoped Sir Henry would give up the amusement, but by failure becoming only the more determined, in a second effort he cleared the wall handsomely and rode across-country to the villages. Following the road till it passed under a railway bridge, I there thought I saw a chance to gain Villiers by a short-cut, and changing my course accordingly, I struck into a large vineyard to the left, and proceeding a few hundred yards through the vines, came suddenly upon a German picket-post. The guard immediately leveled their rifles at me, when, remembering my Rezonville experience of being taken for a French officer because of my uniform, I hastily flung myself from the saddle in token of surrender. The action being rightly interpreted, the men held their fire, and as my next thought was the King's pass I reached under my coat-skirt for the document, but this motion being taken as a grab for my pistol, the whole lot of them—some ten in number—again aimed at me, and with such loud demands for surrender that I threw up my hands and ran into their ranks. The officer of the guard then coming up, examined my credentials, and seeing that they were signed by the King of Prussia, released me and directed the recovery of my horse, which was soon caught, and I was then conducted to the quarters of the commandant, where I found Forsyth with his pass properly vised, entirely ignorant of my troubles, and contentedly regaling himself on cheese and beer. Havelock having got to the village ahead of me, thanks to his cross-country ride, was there too, sipping beer with Forsyth; nor was I slow to follow their example, for the ride of the day, though rather barren in other results, at any rate had given me a ravenous appetite.

Late that evening, the 20th, we resumed our old quarters at Lagny, and early next day I made a visit to the royal headquarters at Ferrires, where I observed great rejoicing going on, the occasion for it being an important victory gained near Mendon, a French corps of about 30,000 men under General Ducrot having been beaten by the Fifth Prussian and Second Bavarian corps. Ducrot had been stubbornly holding ground near Mendon for two or three days, much to the embarrassment of the Germans too, since he kept them from closing a gap in their line to the southwest of Paris; but in the recent fight he had been driven from the field with such heavy loss as to render impossible his maintaining the gap longer. The Crown Prince of Prussia was thus enabled to extend his left, without danger, as far as Bougival, north of Versailles, and eventually met the right of the Crown Prince of Saxony, already at Denil, north of St. Denis. The unbroken circle of investment around Paris being well-nigh assured, news of its complete accomplishment was momentarily expected; therefore everybody was jubilant on account of the breaking up of Ducrot, but more particularly because word had been received the same morning that a correspondence had begun between Bazaine and Prince Frederick Charles, looking to the capitulation of Metz, for the surrender of that place would permit the Second Army to join in the siege of Paris.

Learning all this, and seeing that the investment was about completed, I decided to take up my quarters at Versailles, and started for that place on the 22d, halting at Noisy le Grand to take luncheon with some artillery officers, whose acquaintance we had made the day of the surrender at Sedan. During the meal I noticed two American flags flying on a couple of houses near by. Inquiring the significance of this, I was told that the flags had been put up to protect the buildings—the owners, two American citizens, having in a bad fright abandoned their property, and, instead of remaining outside, gone into Paris,—"very foolishly," said our hospitable friends, "for here they could have obtained food in plenty, and been perfectly secure from molestation."

We arrived at Versailles about 7 o'clock that evening and settled ourselves in the Hotel Reservoir, happy to find there two or three American families, with whom, of course, we quickly made acquaintance. This American circle was enlarged a few days later by the arrival of General Wm. B. Hazen, of our army, General Ambrose E. Burnside, and Mr. Paul Forbes. Burnside and Forbes were hot to see, from the French side, something of the war, and being almost beside themselves to get into Paris, a permit was granted them by Count Bismarck, and they set out by way of Sevres, Forsyth and I accompanying them as far as the Palace of St. Cloud, which we, proposed to see, though there were strict orders against its being visited generally. After much trouble we managed, through the "open sesame" of the King's pass, to gain access to the palace; but to our great disappointment we found that all the pictures had been cut from the frames and carried off to Paris, except one portrait, that of Queen Victoria, against whom the French were much incensed. All other works of art had been removed, too—a most fortunate circumstance, for the palace being directly on the German line, was raked by the guns from the fortress of Mont Valerien, and in a few days burned to the ground.

In less than a week Burnside and Forbes returned from Paris. They told us their experience had been interesting, but were very reticent as to particulars, and though we tried hard to find out what they had seen or done, we could get nothing from them beyond the general statement that they had had a good time, and that General Trochu had been considerate enough to postpone a sortie, in order to let them return; but this we did not quite swallow. After a day or two they went into Paris again, and I then began to suspect that they were essaying the role of mediators, and that Count Bismarck was feeding their vanity with permits, and receiving his equivalent by learning the state of affairs within the beleaguered city.

From about the 1st of October on, the Germans were engaged in making their enveloping lines impenetrable, bringing up their reserves, siege guns, and the like, the French meanwhile continuing to drill and discipline the National Guard and relieving the monotony occasionally by a more or less spirited, but invariably abortive, sortie. The most notable of these was that made by General Vinoy against the heights of Clamart, the result being a disastrous repulse by the besiegers. After this, matters settled down to an almost uninterrupted quietude, only a skirmish here and there; and it being plain that the Germans did not intend to assault the capital, but would accomplish its capture by starvation, I concluded to find out from Count Bismarck about when the end was expected, with the purpose of spending the interim in a little tour through some portions of Europe undisturbed by war, returning in season for the capitulation. Count Bismarck having kindly advised me as to the possible date,

Forsyth and I, on the 14th of October, left Versailles, going first direct to the Chateau Ferrieres to pay our respects to the King, which we did, and again took luncheon with him. From the chateau we drove to Meaux, and there spent the night; resuming our journey next morning, we passed through Epernay, Rheims, and Rethel to Sedan, where we tarried a day, and finally, on October 18, reached Brussels.

CHAPTER XX.
BRUSSELS—DECIDING TO VISIT EASTERN EUROPE—AUSTRIA—DOWN THE DANUBE—IN CONSTANTINOPLE—THE LADIES OF THE HAREM—THE SULTAN—TURKISH SOLDIERS—A BANQUET—A VISIT IN ATHENS—KING GEORGE OF GREECE—VICTOR EMMANUEL—"BEDEVILED WITH CARES OF STATE"—DEER SHOOTING—A MILITARY DINNER—RETURN TO VERSAILLES—GERMANS ENTERING PARIS—CRITICISM ON THE FRANCO-PRUSSIAN WAR—CONCLUSION.

On reaching Brussels, one of the first things to do was to pay my respects to the King of Belgium, which I did, accompanied by our Minister, Mr. Russell Jones. Later I dined with the King and Queen, meeting at the dinner many notable people, among them the Count and Countess of Flanders. A day or two in Brussels sufficed to mature our plans for spending the time up to the approximate date of our return to Paris; and deciding to visit eastern Europe, we made Vienna our first objective, going there by way of Dresden.

At Vienna our Minister, Mr. John Jay, took charge of us—Forsyth was still with me—and the few days' sojourn was full of interest. The Emperor being absent from the capital, we missed seeing him; but the Prime Minister, Count von Beust, was very polite to us, and at his house we had the pleasure of meeting at dinner Count Andrassy, the Prime Minister of Hungary.

From Vienna we went to Buda-Pesth, the Hungarian capital; and thence, in a small, crowded, and uncomfortable steamboat, down the Danube to Rustchuck, whence we visited Bucharest—all who travel in eastern Europe do so—and then directing our course southward, we went first to Varna, and from that city by steamer through the Black Sea to Constantinople.

We reached the Turkish capital at the time of Ramadan, the period of the year (about a month) during which the Mohammedans are commanded by the Koran to keep a rigorous fast every day from sunrise till sunset. All the followers of the Prophet were therefore busy with their devotions—holding a revival, as it were; hence there was no chance whatever to be presented to the Sultan, Abdul Aziz, it being forbidden during the penitential season for him to receive unbelievers, or in fact any one except the officials of his household. However, the Grand Vizier brought me many messages of welcome, and arranged that I should be permitted to see and salute his Serene Highness on the Esplanade as he rode by on horseback to the mosque.

So, the second day after arrival, the Grand Vizier drove me in a barouche to the Esplanade, where we took station about midway of its length an hour or so before the Sultan was to appear. Shortly after we reached the Esplanade, carriages occupied by the women of the Sultan's harem began to appear, coming out from the palace grounds and driving up and down the roadway. Only a few of the women were closely veiled, a majority of them wearing an apology for veiling, merely a strip of white lace covering the forehead down to the eyebrows. Some were yellow, and some white-types of the Mongolian and Caucasian races. Now and then a pretty face was seen, rarely a beautiful one. Many were plump, even to corpulence, and these were the closest veiled, being considered the greatest beauties I presume, since with the Turk obesity is the chief element of comeliness. As the carriages passed along in review, every now and then an occupant, unable or unwilling to repress her natural promptings, would indulge in a mild flirtation, making overtures by casting demure side-glances, throwing us coquettish kisses, or waving strings of amber beads with significant gestures, seeming to say: "Why don't you follow?" But this we could not do if we would, for the Esplanade throughout its entire length was lined with soldiers, put there especially to guard the harem first, and later, the Sultan on his pilgrimage to the mosque.

But as it was now time for His Serene Highness to make his appearance the carriages containing his wives drove off into the palace grounds, which were inclosed by a high wall, leaving the Esplanade wholly unencumbered except by the soldiers. Down between the two ranks, which were formed facing each other, came the Sultan on a white steed—a beautiful Arabian—and having at his side his son, a boy about ten or twelve years old, who was riding a pony, a diminutive copy of his father's mount, the two attended by a numerous body-guard, dressed in gorgeous Oriental uniforms. As the procession passed our carriage, I, as pre-arranged, stood up and took off my hat, His Serene Highness promptly acknowledging the salute by raising his hand to the forehead. This was all I saw of him, yet I received every kindness at his hands, being permitted to see many of his troops, to inspect all the ordnance, equipment, and other military establishments about Constantinople, and to meet numbers of the high functionaries of the Empire.

Among other compliments tendered through his direction, and which I gladly accepted, was a review of all the troops then in Stamboul—about 6,000—comprising infantry, cavalry, and artillery.

They were as fine looking a body of soldiers as I ever saw—well armed and well clothed, the men all large and of sturdy appearance.

After the review we attended a grand military dinner given by the Grand Vizier. At the hour set for this banquet we presented ourselves at the palace of the Grand Vizier, and being ushered into a large drawing-room, found already assembled there the guests invited to meet us. Some few spoke French, and with these we managed to exchange an occasional remark; but as the greater number stood about in silence, the affair, thus far, was undeniably a little stiff. Just before the dinner was announced, all the Turkish officers went into an adjoining room, and turning their faces to the east, prostrated themselves to the floor in prayer. Then we were all conducted to a large salon, where each being provided with a silver ewer and basin, a little ball of highly perfumed soap and a napkin, set out on small tables, each guest washed his hands. Adjacent to this salon was the dining-room, or, rather, the banqueting room, a very large and artistically frescoed hall, in the centre of which stood a crescent-shaped table, lighted with beautiful silver candelabra, and tastefully decorated with flowers and fruits. The viands were all excellent; cooked, evidently, by a French chef, and full justice was done the dishes, especially by the Turks, who, of course, had been fasting all day.

At the close of the banquet, which consisted of not less than fifteen courses, we withdrew to a smoking-room, where the coffee was served and cigarettes and chibouks offered us—the latter a pipe having a long flexible stem with an amber mouthpiece. I chose the chibouk, and as the stem of mine was studded with precious stones of enormous value, I thought I should enjoy it the more; but the tobacco being highly flavored with some sort of herbs, my smoke fell far short of my anticipations. The coffee was delicious, however, and I found this to be the case wherever I went in Constantinople, whether in making calls or at dinner, the custom of offering coffee and tobacco on these occasions being universal.

The temptations to linger at Constantinople were many indeed, not the least being the delightful climate; and as time pressed, we set out with much regret on the return journey, stopping a few days at Athens, whence we made several short excursions into the interior. King George and Queen Olga made our stay in Athens one of extreme interest and exceeding pleasure. Throwing aside all ceremony, they breakfasted and dined us informally, gave us a fine ball, and in addition to these hospitalities showed us much personal attention, his Majesty even calling upon me, and the Queen sending her children to see us at our hotel.

Of course we visited all that remained of the city's ancient civilization—the Acropolis, temples, baths, towers, and the like; nor did we omit to view the spot where St. Paul once instructed the Athenians in lessons of Christianity. We traveled some little through the country districts outside of Athens, and I noticed that the peasantry, in point of picturesqueness of dress and color of complexion, were not unlike the gypsies we see at times in America. They had also much of the same shrewdness, and, as far as I could learn, were generally wholly uneducated, ignorant, indeed, except as to one subject—politics—which I was told came to them intuitively, they taking to it, and a scramble for office, as naturally as a duck to water. In fact, this common faculty for politics seems a connecting link between the ancient and modern Greek.

Leaving Athens with the pleasantest recollections, we sailed for Messina, Sicily, and from there went to Naples, where we found many old friends; among them Mr. Buchanan Read, the artist and poet, and Miss Brewster, as well as a score or more of others of our countrymen, then or since distinguished, in art and letters at home and abroad. We remained some days in Naples, and during the time went to Pompeii to witness a special excavation among the ruins of the buried city, which search was instituted on account of our visit. A number of ancient household articles were dug up, and one, a terra cotta lamp bearing upon its crown in bas-relief the legend of "Leda and the Swan," was presented to me as a souvenir of the occasion, though it is usual for the Government to place in its museums everything of such value that is unearthed.

From Naples to Rome by rail was our next journey. In the Eternal City we saw picture-galleries, churches, and ruins in plenty, but all these have been so well described by hundreds of other travelers that I shall not linger even to name them. While at Rome we also witnessed an overflow of the Tiber, that caused great suffering and destroyed much property. The next stage of our tour took us to Venice, then to Florence—the capital of Italy—for although the troops of the King of Italy had taken possession of Rome the preceding September, the Government itself had not yet removed thither.

At Florence, our Minister, Mr. Marsh, though suffering with a lame foot, took me in charge, and in due course of time I was presented to King Victor-Emmanuel. His Majesty received me informally at his palace in a small, stuffy room—his office, no doubt—and an untidy one it was too. He wore a loose blouse and very baggy trousers; a comfortable suit, certainly, but not at all conducing to an ideal kingliness of appearance.

His Majesty's hobby was hunting, and no sooner had I made my bow than he began a conversation on that subject, thrusting his hands nearly up to the elbows into the pockets of his trousers. He desired to learn about the large game of America, particularly the buffalo, and when I spoke of the herds of thousands and thousands I had seen on the plains of western Kansas, he interrupted me to bemoan the fate which kept him from visiting America to hunt, even going so far as to say that "he didn't wish to be King of Italy, anyhow, but would much prefer to pass his days hunting than be bedeviled with the cares of state." On one of his estates, near Pisa, he had several large herds of deer, many wild boars, and a great deal of other game. Of this preserve he was very proud, and before we separated invited me to go down there to shoot deer, adding that he would be there himself if he could, but feared that a trip which he had to take to Milan would interfere, though he wished me to go in any event.

I gladly accepted the invitation, and in two or three days was notified when I would be expected at the estate. At the designated time I was escorted to Pisa by an aide-de-camp, and from there we drove the few miles to the King's chateau, where we fortified ourselves for the work in hand by an elaborate and toothsome breakfast of about ten courses. Then in a carriage we set out for the King's stand in the hunting-grounds, accompanied by a crowd of mounted game-keepers, who with great difficulty controlled the pack of sixty or seventy hounds, the dogs and keepers together almost driving me to distraction with their yelping and yelling. On reaching the stand, I was posted within about twenty' yards of a long, high picket-fence, facing the fence and covered by two trees very close together. It was from behind these that the King usually shot, and as I was provided with a double-barreled shot-gun, I thought I could do well, especially since close in rear of me stood two game-keepers to load and hand me a second gun when the first was emptied.

Meantime the huntsmen and the hounds had made a circuit of the park to drive up the game. The yelps of the hounds drawing near, I cautiously looked in the direction of the sound, and the next moment saw a herd of deer close in to the fence, and coming down at full speed. Without a miss, I shot the four leading ones as they tried to run the gauntlet, for in passing between the stand and the fence, the innocent creatures were not more than ten to fifteen paces from me. At the fourth I stopped, but the game-keepers insisted on more butchery, saying, "No one but the King ever did the like" (I guess no one else had ever had the chance), so, thus urged, I continued firing till I had slaughtered eleven with eleven shots—an easy task with a shot-gun and buckshot cartridges.

The "hunt" being ended—for with this I had had enough, and no one else was permitted to do any shooting—the aide-decamp directed the game to be sent to me in Florence, and we started for the chateau. On the way back I saw a wild boar the first and only one I ever saw— my attention being drawn to him by cries from some of the game-keepers. There was much commotion, the men pointing out the game and shouting excitedly, "See the wild boar!" otherwise I should not have known what was up, but now, looking in the indicated direction, I saw scudding over the plain what appeared to me to be nothing but a halfgrown black pig, or shoat. He was not in much of a hurry either, and gave no evidence of ferocity, yet it is said that this insignificant looking animal is dangerous when hunted with the spear —the customary way. After an early dinner at the chateau we returned to Florence, and my venison next day arriving, it was distributed among my American friends in the city.

Shortly after the hunt the King returned from Milan, and then honored me with a military dinner, his Majesty and all the guests, numbering eighty, appearing in full uniform. The banqueting hall was lighted with hundreds of wax candles, there was a profusion of beautiful flowers, and to me the scene altogether was one of unusual magnificence. The table service was entirely of gold—the celebrated set of the house of Savoy—and behind the chair of each guest stood a servant in powdered wig and gorgeous livery of red plush. I sat at the right of the King, who—his hands resting on his sword, the hilt of which glittered with jewels—sat through the hour and a half at table without once tasting food or drink, for it was his rule to eat but two meals in twenty-four hours—breakfast at noon, and dinner at midnight. The King remained silent most of the time, but when he did speak, no matter on what subject, he inevitably drifted back to hunting. He never once referred to the Franco-Prussian war, nor to the political situation in his own country, then passing through a crisis. In taking leave of his Majesty I thanked him with deep gratitude for honoring me so highly, and his response was that if ever he came to America to hunt buffalo, he should demand my assistance.

From Florence I went to Milan and Geneva, then to Nice, Marseilles, and Bordeaux. Assembled at Bordeaux was a convention which had been called together by the government of the National Defense for the purpose of confirming or rejecting the terms of an armistice of twenty-one days, arranged between Jules Favre and Count Bismarck in negotiations begun at Versailles the latter part of January. The convention was a large body, chosen from all parts of France, and was unquestionably the most noisy, unruly and unreasonable set of beings that I ever saw in a legislative assembly. The frequent efforts of Thiers, Jules Favre, and other leading men to restrain the more impetuous were of little avail. When at the sittings a delegate arose to speak on some question, he was often violently pulled to his seat and then surrounded by a mob of his colleagues, who would throw off their coats and gesticulate wildly, as though about to fight.

But the bitter pill of defeat had to be swallowed in some way, so the convention delegated M. Thiers to represent the executive power of the country, with authority to construct a ministry three commissioners were appointed by the Executive, to enter into further negotiations with Count Bismarck at Versailles and arrange a peace, the terms of which, however, were to be submitted to the convention for final action. Though there had been so much discussion, it took but a few days to draw up and sign a treaty at Versailles, the principal negotiators being Thiers and Jules Favre for France, and Bismarck on the part of the Germans. The terms agreed upon provided for the occupation of Paris till ratification should be had by the convention at Bordeaux; learning of which stipulation from our

Minister, Mr. Washburn, I hurried off to Paris to see the conquerors make their triumphal entry.

In the city the excitement was at fever heat, of course; the entire population protesting with one voice that they would never, never look upon the hated Germans marching through their beloved city. No! when the day arrived they would hide themselves in their houses, or shut their eyes to such a hateful sight. But by the 1st of March a change had come over the fickle Parisians, for at an early hour the sidewalks were jammed with people, and the windows and doors of the houses filled with men, women, and children eager to get a look at the conquerors. Only a few came in the morning, however—an advance-guard of perhaps a thousand cavalry and infantry. The main column marched from the Arc-de-Triomphe toward the middle of the afternoon. In its composition it represented United Germany—Saxons, Bavarians, and the Royal Guard of Prussia—and, to the strains of martial music, moving down the Champ Elysees to the Place de la Concorde, was distributed thence over certain sections of the city agreed upon beforehand. Nothing that could be called a disturbance took place during the march; and though there was a hiss now and then and murmurings of discontent, yet the most noteworthy mutterings were directed against the defunct Empire. Indeed, I found everywhere that the national misfortunes were laid at Napoleon's door—he, by this time, having become a scapegoat for every blunder of the war.

The Emperor William (he had been proclaimed German Emperor at Versailles the 18th of January) did not accompany his troops into Paris, though he reviewed them at Long Champs before they started. After the occupation of the city he still remained at Versailles, and as soon as circumstances would permit, I repaired to the Imperial headquarters to pay my respects to his Majesty under his new title and dignities, and to say good-bye.

Besides the Emperor, the only persons I me at Versailles were General von Moltke and Bismarck. His Majesty was in a very agreeable frame of mind, and as bluff and hearty as usual. His increased rank and power had effected no noticeable change of any kind in him, and by his genial and cordial ways he made me think that my presence with the German army had contributed to his pleasure. Whether this was really so or not, I shall always believe it true, for his kind words and sincere manner could leave no other conclusion.

General von Moltke was, as usual, quiet and reserved, betraying not the slightest consciousness of his great ability, nor the least indication of pride on account of his mighty work. I say this advisedly, for it is an undoubted fact that it was. his marvelous mind that perfected the military system by which 800,000 men were mobilized with unparalleled celerity and moved with such certainty of combination that, in a campaign of seven months, the military power of France was destroyed and her vast resources sorely crippled.

I said good-bye to Count Bismarck, also, for at that busy time the chances of seeing him again were very remote. The great Chancellor manifested more joy over the success of the Germans than did anyone else at the Imperial headquarters. Along with his towering strength of mind and body, his character partook of much of the enthusiasm and impulsiveness commonly restricted to younger men, and now in his frank, free way be plainly showed his light-heartedness and gratification at success. That which for years his genius had been planning and striving for—permanent unification of the German States, had been accomplished by the war. It had welded them together in a compact Empire which no power in Europe could disrupt, and as such a union was the aim of Bismarck's life, he surely had a right to feel jubilant.

Thanks to the courtesies extended me, I had been able to observe the principal battles, and study many of the minor details of a war between two of the greatest military nations of the world, and to examine critically the methods followed abroad for subsisting, equipping, and manoeuvring vast bodies of men during a stupendous, campaign. Of course I found a great deal to interest and instruct me, yet nowadays war is pretty much the same everywhere, and this one offered no marked exception to my previous experiences. The methods pursued on the march were the same as we would employ, with one most important exception. Owing to the density of population throughout France it was always practicable for the Germans to quarter their troops in villages, requiring the inhabitants to subsist both officers and men. Hence there was no necessity for camp and garrison equipage, nor enormous provision trains, and the armies were unencumbered by these impedimenta, indispensable when operating in a poor and sparsely settled country. As I have said before, the only trains were those for ammunition, pontoon-boats, and the field telegraph, and all these were managed by special corps. If transportation was needed for other purposes, it was obtained by requisition from the invaded country, just as food and forage were secured. Great celerity of combination was therefore possible, the columns moving in compact order, and as all the roads were broad and macadamized, there was little or nothing to delay or obstruct the march of the Germans, except when their enemy offered resistance, but even this was generally slight and not very frequent, for the French were discouraged by disaster from the very outset of the campaign

The earlier advantages gained by the Germans may be ascribed to the strikingly prompt mobilization of their armies, one of the most noticeable features of their perfect military system, devised by almost autocratic power; their later successes were greatly aided by the blunders of the French, whose stupendous errors materially shortened the war, though even if prolonged it could, in my opinion, have had ultimately no other termination.

As I have previously stated, the first of these blunders was the acceptance of battle by MacMahon at Worth; the second in attaching too much importance to the fortified position of Metz, resulting in three battles Colombey, Mars-la-Tour, and Gravelotte—all of which were lost; and the third, the absurd movement of MacMahon along the Belgian frontier to relieve Metz, the responsibility for which, I am glad to say, does not belong to him.

With the hemming in of Bazaine at Metz and the capture of MacMahon's army at Sedan the crisis of the war was passed, and the Germans practically the victors. The taking of Paris was but a sentiment—the money levy could have been made and the Rhine provinces held without molesting that city, and only the political influences consequent upon the changes in the French Government caused peace to be deferred.

I did not have much opportunity to observe the German cavalry, either on the march or in battle. The only time I saw any of it engaged was in the unfortunate charge at Gravelotte. That proved its mettle good and discipline fair, but answered no other purpose. Such of it as was not attached to the infantry was organized in divisions, and operated in accordance with the old idea of covering the front and flanks of the army, a duty which it thoroughly performed. But thus directed it was in no sense an independent corps, and hence cannot be, said to have accomplished anything in the campaign, or have had a weight or influence at all proportionate to its strength. The method of its employment seemed to me a mistake, for, being numerically superior to the French cavalry, had it been massed and manoeuvred independently of the infantry, it could easily have broken up the French communications, and done much other work of weighty influence in the prosecution of the war.

The infantry was as fine as I ever saw, the men young and hardy in appearance, and marching always with an elastic stride. The infantry regiment, however, I thought too large—too many men for a colonel to command unless he has the staff of a general—but this objection may be counterbalanced by the advantages resulting from associating together thus intimately the men from the same district, or county as we would call it; the celerity of mobilization, and, in truth, the very foundation of the German system, being based on this local or territorial scheme of recruiting.

There was no delay when the call sounded for the march; all turned out promptly, and while on the road there was very little straggling, only the sick falling out. But on such fine, smooth roads, and with success animating the men from the day they struck the first blow, it could hardly be expected that the columns would not keep well closed up. Then, too, it must be borne in mind that, as already stated, 'campaigning' in France—that is, the marching, camping, and subsisting of an army—is an easy matter, very unlike anything we, had during the war of the rebellion. To repeat: the country is rich, beautiful, and densely populated, subsistence abundant, and the roads—all macadamized highways; thus the conditions; are altogether different from those existing with us. I think that under the same circumstances our troops would have done as well as the Germans, marched as admirably, made combinations as quickly and accurately, and fought with as much success. I can but leave to conjecture how. the Germans would have got along on bottomless roads—often none at all—through the swamps and quicksands of northern Virginia, from, the Wilderness to Petersburg, and from Chattanooga to Atlanta and the sea.

Following the operations of the German armies from the battle of Gravelotte to the siege of Paris, I may, in conclusion, say that I saw no new military principles developed, whether of strategy or grand tactics, the movements of the different armies and corps being dictated and governed by the same general laws that have so long obtained, simplicity of combination and manoeuvre, and the concentration of a numerically superior force at the vital point.

After my brief trip to Versailles, I remained in Paris till the latter part of March. In company with Mr. Washburn, I visited the fortifications for the defense of the city, and found them to be exceptionally heavy; so strong, indeed, that it would have been very hard to carry the place by a general assault. The Germans, knowing the character of the works, had refrained from the sacrifice of life that such an attempt must entail, though they well knew that many of the forts were manned by unseasoned soldiers. With only a combat here and there, to tighten their lines or repulse a sortie, they wisely preferred to wait till starvation should do the work with little loss and absolute certainty.

The Germans were withdrawn from Paris on the 3d of March, and no sooner were they gone than factional quarrels, which had been going on at intervals ever since the flight of the Empress and the fall of her regency on the 4th of September, were renewed with revolutionary methods that eventually brought about the Commune. Having witnessed one or two of these outbreaks, and concluding that while such turbulence reigned in the city it would be of little profit for me to tarry there, I decided to devote the rest of the time I could be away from home to travel in England, Ireland, and Scotland. My journeys through those countries were full of pleasure and instruction, but as nothing I saw or did was markedly different from what has been so often described by others, I will save the reader this part of my experience. I returned to America in the fall, having been absent a little more than a year, and although I saw much abroad of absorbing interest, both professional and general, yet I came back to my native land with even a greater love for her, and with increased admiration for her institutions.

www.ingramcontent.com/pod-product-compliance
Lightning Source LLC
Chambersburg PA
CBHW031305150426
43191CB00005B/83